KIRBY SMITH'S CONFEDERACY

Kirby Smith's Confederacy

THE TRANS-MISSISSIPPI SOUTH, 1863–1865

by Robert L. Kerby

Columbia University Press
NEW YORK AND LONDON 1972

FOR MY SONS, BOBBY AND JAMIE,
that they may know peace

AND FOR THE FATHER OF MY CHURCH,
PATRIARCH MAXIMOS V HAKIM,
an Apostle of peace

PREFACE 🌿

Despite the vast number of books already written about the American Civil War, the bibliography on the war still includes some significant omissions. In particular, until the present there has been no comprehensive analytical account of the military and domestic affairs of the Confederacy's Trans-Mississippi Department during the period between the capitulation of Vicksburg and the conclusion of hostilities. Following Vicksburg's fall, the states and territories of the Southwest were separated from the remainder of the Confederacy by the Federals' Mississippi River blockade, and were forced, for the most part, to fend for themselves through the last two years of the conflict. While the Trans-Mississippi Department's fate was bound to that of the Cis-Mississippi South, and although the Department's doom was sealed on the battlefields of the East, nonetheless the story of the Trans-Mississippi's struggle adds some new dimensions to the history of the Confederate States, and serves to illumine and complement the familiar history of wartime Dixie.

This work attempts to tie together the mass of available data concerning "Kirby Smith's Confederacy" into a coherent synthetic narrative. The concept of this book first occurred to me fifteen years ago, while I was writing a modest little campaign account of Civil War operations in New Mexico Territory. Sporadic reading into the topic was begun during my service as a Regular Air Force officer, but serious research was undertaken only after my return to academic life at Columbia University. It is impossible to acknowledge each debt accumulated during the whole of this period, or to express my gratitude for every contribution made by others toward the completion of this work. And yet, in token recognition of the debts which I owe, some mention of the institutions and persons without whose help this book could not have been written is both necessary and fitting.

First of all, the staffs of several archives and libraries have made my exploratory expeditions both fruitful and pleasant. They include archivists and librarians at: The Arkansas Historical Commission, Little Rock; Columbia University, New York City; Kansas Historical Society, Topeka; Library of Congress, Washington, D.C.; Lincoln Township Public Library, Stevensville, Michigan; Louisiana State University, Baton Rouge; National Archives, Washington, D.C.; New-York Historical Society, New York City; New York Public Library, New York City; State Historical Society of Missouri, Columbia, Missouri; Texas State Archives, Austin; University of North Carolina, Chapel Hill; University of Notre Dame, South Bend, Indiana; and the University of Texas, Austin.

The typists who cooperated on the initial drafts include Sandra Appel, Ann Kamisha, Elaine Schwartz, and Carol Zane. Carol Zane produced the final manuscript.

Individuals whose many special favors deserve particular mention include Jennifer Corbett, Marian Jude Byrne, Mary Ann Bergfeld, Jane Campion, Patricia Considine, Constance Anne Carroll, Mary Fritz, Helen Rose Fuchs, Faith Huppler, Joyce Hassett, Therese Klein, Martha Leyden, Patricia McCarney, Mary Lue Meyer, Anne Therese Mistretta, Rosemary Ryan, Therese Sherlock, Maxim Chaloub, John Considine, Elie Denissoff, Paul Donlan, Daniel Dougherty, George Flahiff, Albert Gorayeb, Armand Jacopin, Lawrence Kenney, Paul LeBlanc, Nicholas Locascio, Solomon Makoul, John Malecki, John Malkowski, Lucien Malouf, John Mescall, Paul Meier, Donald Panella, Orest Ranum, John Remaklus, James Shenton, Bernard Tallerico, Joseph Tawil, Jacob Willebrands, Leo and Jean Burke, Joseph and Mary Curley, Joseph and Jean Ann Geis, Michael and Cecelia Kerin, John and Frances Naughton, John and Barbara Leonard, Philip Corbett, James and Suzanne Corbett, Sarah Kerby, William Bernhardt, Mary Ann Gamrat, Amy Hackett, and Donald Horrigan. Particular thanks are due to Professor Eric McKitrick, without whose advice and insight this book would still be a gleam in a graduate student's eye. And, finally, I owe far more than I can ever acknowledge to the constancy, encouragement, and faith of my wife, Mary.

Robert L. Kerby

Columbia University, New York City
January 27, 1972
Feast of St. John Chrysostom

CONTENTS 🌿

MAPS

KIRBY SMITH'S CONFEDERACY

CHAPTER ONE

THE TRANS-MISSISSIPPI
SOUTH, 1861–1863

On June 4, 1863, three months after assuming command of the Trans-Mississippi Department of the Confederate States Army, Lieutenant General Edmund Kirby Smith grumbled to an old comrade, General Joseph E. Johnston, that "I would willingly be back under your command at any personal sacrifice. I have a herculanian task before me on this side of the Miss—no army—no means—an empire in extent, no system, no order, all to be done from the beginning. I have entered my duties with misgivings, but believe the resources are here, and only require developing, to make the Dept self sustaining." Seven months later he was still complaining about his "vast empire, the weight of whose government both civil & military is thrown on my shoulders—without means, without troops, with resources undeveloped." As he told Senator R. W. Johnson of Arkansas, "The commander of this department has no bed of roses, nor is it a field in which laurels are to be gained or reputation made." The western Confederacy had been "left to struggle against immense odds, as best we may, with feeble resources at our command." He assured the Senator that "I do not shrink from the task, neither do I despair," but he added, "I feel the only recompense the commander of this department can ever reasonably expect will be the consciousness of having discharged his duty with purity and rectitude of purpose."

Theoretically, the Trans-Mississippi Department covered almost

600,000 square miles, extending from the Mississippi River to the southeastern border of California, and from Keokuk, Iowa, to the mouth of the Rio Grande. The Department embraced Missouri, Arkansas, Texas, the western four-fifths of Louisiana, the Indian Territory (Oklahoma), and the ephemeral Confederate Territory of Arizona (roughly the southern two-fifths of the modern states of New Mexico and Arizona). For purposes of administration and operational control, the Department was divided into three military districts, the Districts of Arkansas, West Louisiana, and Texas. From headquarters in Little Rock, Lieutenant General Theophilus Holmes commanded the army of the District of Arkansas, including regular and irregular troops deployed in Missouri and in "the Nations" of Indian Territory. The District of West Louisiana was under the control of a native son, Major General Richard Taylor, who maintained his headquarters at Alexandria. And from Houston Major General John Magruder directed affairs in the District of Texas, New Mexico, and Arizona.[1]

According to the census of 1860, Missouri, Arkansas, Texas, and the trans-Mississippi parishes of Louisiana contained a settled population somewhat in excess of 2,639,150 persons. Of these, about 1,971,450 were white, 600 were civilized Indians, 9,000 were "free persons of color," and 658,000 were slaves. Missouri's 1,063,500 whites outnumbered those of the other three states combined, but Missouri had fewer Negroes—3,572 free and 114,900 enslaved—than either Texas or West Louisiana. Texas was inhabited by 421,234 whites, 403 civilized Indians, 355 free Negroes, and 182,566 slaves. Western Louisiana, which covered four-fifths of the state's area, was occupied by less than three-fifths of its people, because of the concentration of 23 percent of Louisiana's inhabitants in the cis-Mississippi metropolis of New Orleans. The thirty-one complete parishes and the parts of six additional parishes located west of the Mississippi contained about 163,000 whites, 150 civilized Indians, 5,000 freedmen, and 245,000 slaves. West Louisiana was the only portion of the trans-Mississippi Southwest in which slaves outnumbered citizens. Arkansas was the home of 324,-143 whites, 48 civilized Indians, 144 free Negroes, and 115,115 bondsmen.

In 1860, the United States Territory of New Mexico covered the area now organized into the states of New Mexico and Arizona, plus

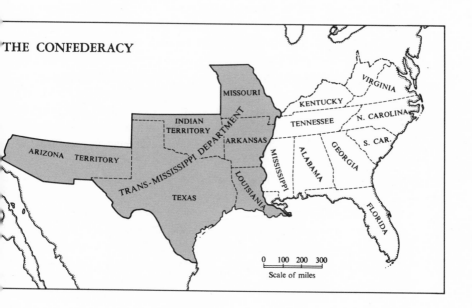

THE CONFEDERACY

MISSOURI

INDIAN
TERRITORY

ARKANSAS

VIRGINIA

KENTUCKY

TENNESSEE

N. CAROLINA

S. CAR.

ARIZONA   TERRITORY

TRANS-MISSISSIPPI DEPARTMENT

MISSISSIPPI

ALABAMA

GEORGIA

LOUISIANA

TEXAS

FLORIDA

0   100   200   300

Scale of miles

the southern tip of Nevada. New Mexico Territory claimed 93,516 settlers and an estimated 55,000 nomadic or savage Indians. The settlers
included 82,924 whites, 10,452 civilized Indians, 55 "breeds," and 85
Negroes; none of the Negroes were enslaved. Roughly one-third of the
settlers, about 31,000 in all, occupied the barren counties below 34 de-
grees North latitude, the region soon to be claimed by the Confederate
States.

The Five Civilized Nations of Indian Territory contained 58,311
free Indians, whites, and Negroes, and 7,369 Negro slaves. Perhaps another 30,000 to 40,000 semicivilized and nomadic "blanket" Indians
used the Leased Lands west of the Chickasaw Nation and the Public
Land Strip of the Territorial panhandle as campsites and hunting
grounds.

Allowing for the inevitable errors in census returns, for the fact
that some Texas frontier counties failed to submit reports, for the indefinite character of returns from Indian Territory, and for the fact that
parish or county lines in West Louisiana and New Mexico Territory did
not always coincide with the boundaries of the Confederacy's Trans-
Mississippi Department, the prewar population of Kirby Smith's empire
approximated 2,860,000. Of these, at least 2,061,500 were white men,
61,500 were civilized Indians or half-breeds, 9,200 were free Negroes,
666,000 were slaves, and some 60,000 were resident or transient tribes-
men. The military population, composed of free white males in the
states and in New Mexico Territory and of free Indians and whites in
Indian Territory, consisted of 450,000 men between the ages of eighteen and forty-five. Slightly more than half of these potential soldiers
were Missourians.

The country was overwhelmingly rural. New Orleans, with its
168,675 inhabitants, and St. Louis, with its 160,773, were the only ma-
ture cities in the entire area. Besides St. Louis, Missouri claimed twenty-
five towns containing more than 3,000 persons apiece, a total which
none of the other states or territories could even approach. The West
Louisiana sugar country boasted two towns, Donaldsonville and St.
Landry, occupied by more than 10,000 inhabitants each, but they stand
out as the only examples of towns this size below the Missouri border.
San Antonio, the crossroads of the Southwest, was the home of 8,235
souls; Galveston, the major port west of New Orleans, had 7,307 inhab-

itants; Houston, the hub of the Texas railroad system, had 4,845. Little Rock had 3,727 people; Austin, 3,494; Brownsville, 2,734; Mesilla (Confederate Arizona, a short distance above El Paso), 2,420; Camden (Arkansas), 2,219; and Shreveport, 2,190. Two towns in Arkansas, four in West Louisiana, and fourteen in Texas were occupied by 1,000 to 2,000 people apiece. Opelousas, which served as Louisiana's Confederate capital in late 1862, had only 786 inhabitants in 1860. Washington, the capital of Confederate Arkansas after September, 1863, and Marshall, Texas, the residence of the Confederate governor of Missouri after 1861, were both so small that the 1860 census did not take notice of them.

Compared to New York or Pennsylvania, each of which possessed more than 22,000 manufacturing establishments and employed more than 220,000 industrial workers, the Industrial Revolution had barely dawned in the trans-Mississippi Southwest. There were 3,157 factories, mills, and shops in Missouri providing work for 19,681 people; but the state had, in addition to its farm and plantation slaves, 124,989 farmers, 39,396 farm laborers, 256 overseers, and 237 planters. The entire state of Louisiana contained 1,744 industrial works employing 8,789 laborers, but 14,996 white Louisianians were independent farmers, 5,483 were free farm laborers, 6,473 were planters, and 2,989 were overseers. Texas possessed 983 industrial establishments; Arkansas, 518; and New Mexico Territory, 82. On the average, each of these firms employed only four people. In comparison, Texas claimed 51,569 free farmers, 6,537 farm laborers, 1,254 overseers, and 265 planters; Arkansas had 48,475 farmers, 8,350 farm laborers, 1,071 overseers, and 438 planters; and New Mexico Territory included 5,922 farmers, 8,360 laborers or peons, and 21 overseers. The capital absorbed by industry constituted 4 percent of Missouri's total investment in property, 1 percent in Louisiana, less than 1 percent in Texas, and less than one-half of 1 percent in Arkansas.

With very few exceptions, the industrial establishments in the trans-Mississippi West were too small to fabricate heavy machinery. Although Texas had four little steam machinery plants, and 78 Missourians were employed making steamboat boilers, not one factory in the entire area could produce and assemble the components of a complete railroad locomotive. For the most part, the region's factories and mills served the needs of agriculture. The 983 firms of Texas, for instance, included 192 sawmills, 182 flour mills, 62 wagon makers, 48 saddleries, 46 manufacturers of farm tools and implements, 37 tanners, 23 commercial cotton gins, 22 breweries and distilleries, and four wholesale bakeries. The vast majority of the Southwest's 8,000 blacksmiths were occupied repairing and renovating farm equipment, and even the five piano tuners in Louisiana, the two perfume manufacturers in Missouri, and the single oculist in Arkansas probably catered to fair numbers of farm and plantation folk.[2]

Except in Missouri, the Gulf and Delta parishes of Louisiana, the hill country, and on the frontier, cotton was king in the rural Southwest. Cotton's domain included the west bank of the Mississippi, the alluvial valleys of the Arkansas, Ouachita, and Red river systems, the East Texas lowlands between the Sabine and the Neches rivers, and the coastal plain drained by the Brazos, Colorado, and Guadalupe river networks. The exploding cotton kingdom of Texas might have stretched all the way from the Sabine to the Guadalupe, since the land was rich enough to yield from one to three bales per acre, but because Trinity River was usually too shallow to float a cotton merchant's steamboat, little cotton was cultivated between the Neches and the Brazos. The ordinary overland freight charge of twenty cents per ton-mile generally made it impractical to ship 400-pound bales produced any distance from a navigable river.

In this cotton kingdom were concentrated most of the Southwest's great plantations, some of them covering more than 5,000 acres. And here the majority of the region's slaves endured the endless routine of planting and harvesting, a routine which consumed nine months of every year. In four West Louisiana cotton parishes, strung along the Mississippi between the mouths of the Arkansas and the Red, slaves outnumbered whites by six to one. In 1860, before the war encouraged some planters to convert to cereal and vegetable crops, Louisiana produced 777,738 bales of cotton and ranked third, after Mississippi and Alabama, among the cotton states of the Union. Texas ranked fifth and produced 431,463 bales, while Arkansas ranked sixth with its 367,393 bales. Missouri cultivated 41,188 bales, and a few hundred bales were even produced by the Indian Nations and in New Mexico Territory.

The Evangeline country of southern Louisiana, interlaced by lakes,

TRANS-MISSISSIPPI DEPARTMENT

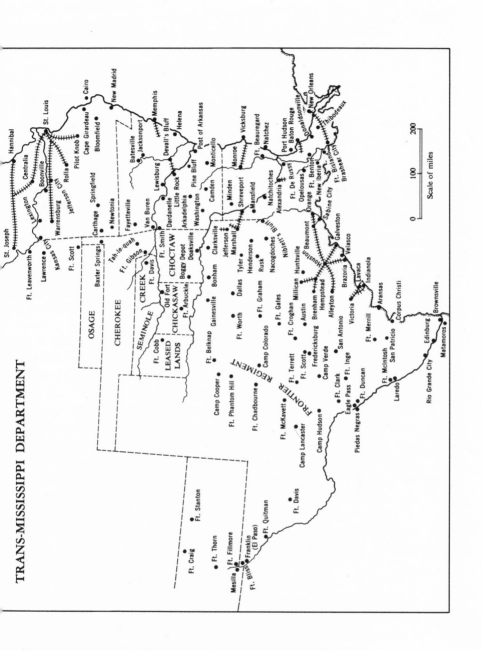

Scale of miles

0   100   200

streams, and swamps, and drained by such bayous as the Lafourche, the Atchafalaya, and the serene and beautiful Teche, was dominated by more than 1,200 opulent estates given over to the cultivation of cane sugar. Along the Gulf Coast, where the land was even too marshy to support the production of sugar, a belt of prosperous rice plantations flourished. In 1860, southern Louisiana produced 221,726 hogsheads of cane sugar, 13,439,772 pounds of molasses, and 6,331,257 pounds of rice. In contrast to Louisiana's large and relatively underpopulated western parishes, where there were almost as many whites as Negroes, the sugar and rice parishes contained two or three slaves for each white inhabitant. And in contrast to the cotton country above Opelousas, where most of the citizens were of Anglo-Saxon stock, the majority of the common whites in the sugar country were Louisiana Creoles. These people were less inclined to be rigid about the shibboleths of Southern culture than their English-speaking neighbors, since they quietly permitted almost 1,000 free Negroes—one-fifth of all the freedmen in West Louisiana—to live and prosper in the Creole stronghold of St. Landry Parish. A few of these freedmen were substantial and respected slave-owning planters. But if the Creoles were lax about enforcing Southern mores, they were also careless about the niceties of law and order. Before the war St. Landry and the neighboring parishes were considered hotbeds of bushwhacking and banditry, a reputation which the war did nothing to improve. After fifteen mellowing years had passed, General Taylor could maintain that he did not "recall so fair, so bountiful, and so happy a land" as Creole Louisiana, but one of his soldiers serving in the area insisted that it was "a low, marshy, sickly, poor country, not fit for anything but alligators, frogs, and tadpoles. I would not give two bits for the whole country." [3]

Missouri was the garden of the trans-Mississippi South. This single state produced more tobacco, wool, flax, hemp, wheat, rye, Indian corn, oats, and buckwheat, and supported far more mines and miles of railroad track, than the rest of the Southwest put together. Missouri also raised more horses and swine than either Texas or Arkansas, while only Texas cattle and Louisiana mules outnumbered Missouri livestock. Because Missouri made no serious attempt to compete in the cultivation of cotton or sugar, the state's slave population was relatively small, and consequently its total investment in property was somewhat less than

Louisiana's. But in almost everything else, from industrial, extractive, and agricultural productivity to population and urbanization, Missouri had no peer west of the Mississippi. Missouri's society was sufficiently prosperous to support such ornaments of affluence as 271 musicians, four sculptors, two taxidermists, and 82 "professors."

Throughout the Civil War, Confederate authorities persisted in the delusion that the bulk of Missouri's people yearned for liberation by the rebel army. Before the war, years of preliminary skirmishing between proslavery Missouri bushwhackers and free-state Kansas jayhawkers had convinced most Southerners that Missouri would cast her lot with the South. Once secession became a fact, enough Missourians adhered to the Confederacy to give some substance to the Southerners' dreams. But no matter how often the gray cavalry raided the state, no matter how many rebel irregulars and recruiting teams scoured the countryside behind Union lines, no matter how badly the Northern occupation forces treated Missouri's people, and no matter what the Missouri exiles sitting in the Richmond Congress said, Missouri refused to side with her Southern sisters.

When the secession of the Lower South forced Missourians to choose sides, the people of the state, in convention assembled, firmly declined to secede. By 1861, Missouri's future lay with the North. Missouri needed markets for her cereal grains, and those markets existed in the Northeast. The state's extensive railroad network, with its focus at St. Louis, tied Missouri to the Ohio Valley and to the Old Northwest. Missouri's dream, to become the terminal of the first transcontinental railroad, was predicated upon cooperation with Kansas. The execrable roads through the hills of northern Arkansas discouraged communication with the region due south. Finally, Missouri was boxed on three sides by free states, and her northern and western marches were not protected by natural barriers. Like Maryland, therefore, Missouri was exceptionally vulnerable to invasion from the North, and even the state's slaveowners appreciated that the inevitable consequence of a Yankee invasion would be the confiscation of their slaves. The slave-owning conservatives of Missouri had been fighting for the status quo for decades, and in 1861 the defense of the status quo, reinforced by a dose of self-interest, induced most of them to appeal for the neutrality of Missouri and the reconciliation of the Union. Under the leadership of Sterling Price, they negotiated a nonaggression pact with the state's Unionist faction. But this agreement lasted only long enough for Nathaniel Lyon to raise an army of Unionist Missourians and chase the secessionists out of the capitol. Missouri then professed her unqualified loyalty to the Union, and sealed this profession in blood by sending more of her sons to the Federal armies than did two-thirds of the other Union states. When Missouri's boys were called to the colors, 40,000 donned Confederate gray and 109,000 put on Union blue.[4]

A modest simulacrum of Missouri's prosperous breadbasket was located on the well-watered, well-timbered, relatively fertile land of interior East Texas, between and beyond the two great cotton fields of the Texas coastal plain. In this region, some cotton was grown for export, but most of the land was sown in grain and vegetables; and here the majority of cultivators were free men. This area of diversified farming spilled across the Red River into the eastern third of Indian Territory, and included not only much of the land occupied by the Five Civilized Nations but also a few patches in the far western parishes and counties of Louisiana and Arkansas. To the west and northwest, this region was bounded by prairies, and to the northeast by the mountains of western Arkansas. Across these mountains, Missouri's own granary spread into the north-central counties of Arkansas, counties which led that state in the production of foodstuffs. A significant amount of grain—especially Indian corn—was grown even in the cotton country and the sugar parishes of the trans-Mississippi Southwest. In ordinary times, the settled flatlands between San Antonio and Hannibal produced enough grain and truck crops to be self-sufficient.

West of a line drawn through Del Rio, San Antonio, Austin, and Dallas, the Texas coastal plain abruptly rises toward the rough, broken, and barren terrain of the Balcones Escarpment. North of Dallas, the effects of erosion gradually transform this escarpment into rolling prairies, which stretch through central Oklahoma and on into Kansas. Small fragments of prairie intermingle with the farmland of the Red, Sabine, and Arkansas river valleys and straggle eastward toward the Mississippi. Above the Davis Mountains of West Texas, and beyond the Oklahoma prairie, the Llano Estacado or High Plain of the Texas and Oklahoma panhandles marks the beginning of the "Great American Desert."

The High Plain, the prairies, the hill country of West Texas, and the dusty scrub range south of San Antonio lacked the timber and rainfall which farmers of the 1860s considered essential for successful homesteading. Consequently this vast territory was abandoned to herds of cattle, sheep, and buffalo, and to the nomadic tribes of Plains Indians. The Texas cattle kingdom was concentrated in the wedge between the Nueces River and Brownsville, an area which, by 1860, contained very few people and too many cows. Starting after the Mexican War with a few wild Spanish bulls and some American milch cows, a handful of cattlemen had covered this region with more than 3,700,000 tough Texas longhorns, enough meat on the hoof to feed half of the Union. But these herds were virtually worthless, since no way had yet been found to convey the beeves to distant consumers. The cows just dropped more and more calves, and Texas beef prices dropped with them. Before the Civil War, occasional pioneering overland drives delivered a few thousand head to Monterrey, New Orleans, Shreveport, the mining camps in New Mexico and Colorado, and the California gold fields, but not until the war was over did Texas cowboys blaze the great cattle trails to the railheads at Abilene and Dodge City.

During the decade of the 1850s, the South Texas ranch land was also the scene of a spectacular sheep boom. By 1859 almost 800,000 sheep had been imported into or bred in the area, and it seemed that sheep would soon become as important an asset—or as great a liability —as the state's longhorn cattle. But the severe winter of 1859–60 decimated the Texas sheep flocks and discouraged further development of the sheep industry. By 1860 New Mexico Territory, with its 830,000 sheep, had 80,000 more than Texas and was well on its way to becoming the sheep capital of the Southwest.

In addition to its stocks of cattle and sheep, the Southwest possessed an animal population quite sufficient to meet the demands of war. In 1860, 5,542,000 swine, 917,000 horses—two for every man of military age in the area—503,000 oxen, and 305,000 mules and asses were on hand, ready to supply meat, mounts, and draft animals to the army and people of the Trans-Mississippi Confederacy.

When the Civil War erupted, the Southwest's ephemeral "line" of frontier settlements meandered northward from the Big Bend country of Texas, along the eastern fringes of the Texas and Indian Territory panhandles, and on into southeastern Kansas. Nearly all of the settlements in Texas and Indian Territory, with the single exception of the village of Franklin (El Paso), were well east of the 100th meridian of longitude. Of the 152 counties then organized in Texas, 149 lay east of this line, while three abnormally large and abnormally vacant counties— Kinney, Presidio, and El Paso—hugged the Rio Grande in the state's southwestern corner. North of these three counties, and west of a tier of homesteads strung between Maverick County in the Big Bend country and Hardeman County on the Red River, there were neither settlements nor civil governments. The High Plains of the Texas and Indian Territory panhandles were consigned to the "blanket" Indians (chiefly Comanches and Kiowas) and to the buffalo. The hazy borderland along the "edge" of civilization was protected by a score of small stockade forts, scattered from Fort Duncan in Maverick County to Fort Cobb on the western frontier of the Chickasaw Nation. Beyond this line of military demarcation a few additional installations, including Forts Quitman, Davis, Bliss, and Fillmore, protected the two wagon roads connecting San Antonio with Franklin and Mesilla. In New Mexico Territory, other forts paralleled the overland mail routes running from Mesilla northward to Santa Fe and westward to Tucson and Fort Yuma.[5]

⚓ II   Although the Confederate Trans-Mississippi Department claimed dominion over the entire area between Hannibal and Fort Yuma, by the beginning of 1863 political and military reverses had severely reduced the extent of the Department's actual authority. In 1861 and 1862 the war west of the Mississippi had gone poorly for the Confederacy. By the time General Kirby Smith arrived in the region, the Confederate "Territory of Arizona" had been lost to the enemy; the Confederate state of Missouri consisted of an exiled civil government, an exiled army, some refugees, some guerrillas, and a star on the rebel flag; most of the Cherokee Nation and most of Arkansas above the Arkansas River were no-man's-lands; Confederate West Louisiana was little more than a single crowded river valley; and only Texas, less the Llano Estacado (one-third of the state) and a substantial chunk around Franklin, bore much resemblance to a viable social organism.

    By September, 1862, the Confederate Territory of Arizona was nothing but a dim memory. In the spring of 1861, popular conventions in Mesilla and Tucson had effected the secession of lower New Mexico Territory, and by February, 1862, the Confederate government had organized a civil administration for the region. A month later, Brigadier General Henry H. Sibley's Texas cavalry brigade had marched into the Union segment of New Mexico and had occupied Santa Fe. But then Union columns from New Mexico, Colorado, and California had converged upon the isolated rebel brigade and had sent it reeling back down the Rio Grande Valley. Pressed on all sides and in danger of annihilation, Sibley's troopers had fled from the Territory. A small crowd of secessionist politicians, refugees, and Arizona recruits had trailed along behind. When Kirby Smith reached Shreveport, the United States flag had been flying over Mesilla, Franklin, and Forts Fillmore, Bliss, Davis, and Quitman for more than six months, and Federal cavalry patrols ranged freely through the Davis Mountains of western Texas. The Confederate government continued to entertain all sorts of schemes for the reconquest of Arizona; a Territorial Delegate continued to sit in the Richmond Congress; a few battalions of Confederate Arizona Volunteers continued to serve until the bitter end; and occasional rebel scouting parties even managed to poke into the Territory—but otherwise Confederate Arizona had ceased to be. Its governor, Colonel John R. Baylor, occupied himself for the next three years by performing the duties of an army officer and a Texas Congressman, while its people were left to the mercies of the Apaches, the Comanches, the Navahos, and an exceptionally vicious gang of imported Yankee carpetbaggers.[6]

Because it would have been impossible to subsist a Union army advancing eastward from Mesilla, the United States made no attempt to mount an invasion of the settled portion of Texas from the Federal base in New Mexico. The wilderness of the Davis Mountains and the Panhandle hunting grounds of the Plains Indians remained an impenetrable buffer separating the Union troops in New Mexico from the Confederates in Texas. Yet until the end of the war, the Confederates were obliged to maintain a significant military force on the Texas frontier, to defend western Texas not only from the Federals but also from a far more terrible enemy, the warrior tribes of the High Plains.

Ever since 1856, hostile Indian war parties had been harassing homesteads along the fringe of Texas settlement. Most of the raiders were Comanches, but several bands of Apaches, Kiowas, Lipans, and Kickapoos shared in the harvest of scalps. By 1858, fifty ranches in Webb County were abandoned, and there was only one white family left in Montague County. Within the next two years the United States Cavalry managed to contain most of the Indians and to restore a measure of tranquillity to the frontier, but one immediate consequence of the secession of Texas was the demobilization of this cavalry screen and the exposure of the settlers to renewed attack. The Texas secession convention arranged for the one-year enlistment of a state regiment to guard the frontier, and soon afterwards Colonel Henry E. McCulloch's First Regiment, Texas Mounted Rifles, occupied the line of abandoned forts along the eastern edge of the Panhandle. The First Regiment provided some security, but not nearly enough. In November, 1861, Governor Francis R. Lubbock announced a new epidemic of violence in the border country, and, because of the impending termination of the enlistments of McCulloch's troops, requested the state legislature to grant authority for the enrollment of another, stronger frontier defense force. In December the legislators complied, providing for the enlistment of a "Frontier Regiment"; in January, 1862, Colonel James M. Norris took charge of this command; and by the end of April the outfit mustered 1,089 officers and men and 1,347 horses. The Frontier Regiment's nine companies were dispersed among eighteen posts spread from Gainesville on the Red River to old Fort Duncan on the Rio Grande; daily reconnaissance patrols, shuttling between these installations, gave warning whenever signs were discovered indicating the presence of marauders.

Adapting quickly to Colonel Norris' passive defense system, the Indians soon learned to hide their tracks and to circumvent the patrols. Filtering between the Frontier Regiment's forts and slipping into the settlements, the savages continued to lay waste whole counties. By the summer of 1862 panicky pioneers were fleeing Gillespie County in droves, and Clay County was fast becoming a depopulated desert.

The Frontier Regiment's difficulties were complicated by its anomalous legal status. Technically, it was neither an organization of the Confederate States Army nor a unit of the Texas State Militia, but rather a Texas volunteer army. By state law, the regiment's men were entitled to the same pay and subsistence as Confederate soldiers, but Texas was reluctant to dip into its own treasury to fund and supply the command. Arguing that the Frontier Regiment was defending the western extremities of the entire Confederacy, Governor Lubbock and the Texas legislature felt that the cost of maintaining the unit should be borne by the general government. Early in 1862, Texas offered the regiment to the War Department, with the proviso that, once mustered into Confederate service, it should never be transferred away from the state's Indian border. The Confederate Congress was amenable to such an arrangement, but President Jefferson Davis refused to accept the command unless he was also given full control over its disposition. For the next two years, Richmond and Austin bickered about the outfit, while its orphan troopers stayed alive by hunting buffalo.

Because of the Frontier Regiment's poor performance Colonel Norris became a political liability. In January, 1863, he was induced to resign in favor of Colonel J. E. McCord. McCord abandoned Norris' passive tactics and committed his squadrons to extensive search-and-destroy operations on the Plains, maneuvers which met with considerable success. During the first half of 1863, more engagements were fought, more braves were killed, and more horses were captured than during the entire year of 1862. In some areas, particularly in the vicinity of the Red River, the Indian menace was virtually eliminated. After a bitter struggle with "the red Devils" to determine "who should hold possession of Montague County [,] the citizens, or the savages, we the citizens have succeeded," exulted a correspondent of the Clarksville *Standard*. "Quietude is now restored." But the "red Devils" were by no means pacified, for although Montague County seemed secure, Cooke, Gillespie, Kerr, and Bandera counties continued to report barbarities.[7]

At the same time that the Texas secession convention organized Henry McCulloch's First Regiment for the Indian frontier, it authorized Colonel John S. Ford to raise a Second Regiment, Texas Mounted Rifles, for service along the Rio Grande. Since the end of the Mexican War, the Texas side of the Rio Grande Valley had been a happy hunting ground for Mexican bandit chiefs. The most illustrious was Juan N. Cortina, an accomplished cattle rustler, mail robber, and murderer, who looked upon every visit to his mother's Cameron County ranch as another opportunity for a raid. Neither the domestic political turmoil in Mexico, nor the intervention of the French in Mexican affairs, nor the confusion created by the outbreak of the American Civil War did much to help the situation. After the South seceded, the ranks of the Mexican outlaw gangs were swelled by refugees from Texas, many of whom considered banditry preferable to conscription into the Confederate army. In 1862 local Confederate authorities attempted to suppress the turmoil by proclaiming martial law in three border counties, but this had little effect. By 1863 some of the bandit companies were so large and so audacious that they did not hesitate to attack Confederate army wagon convoys proceeding to frontier military installations under armed guard.

Besides mounting an ineffectual patrol of the river border, Colonel Ford, in early 1862, attempted to retaliate against the Mexicans by permitting an outlaw named Jose-Maria Carvajal to use Brownsville as his base for filibustering raids into Tamaulipas State. Ford's enterprise angered Santiago Vidaurri, the governor of Nuevo León and Coahuila states and tempororily the self-proclaimed potentate of all of northeastern Mexico. Vidaurri responded by raising tariff duties along the border and by dispatching a lengthy protest to Richmond. Richmond, considering Vidaurri's friendship and Mexican trade to be more valuable than the peace of the border, reprimanded Ford and ordered him to desist from aiding and abetting Carvajal.

In the months that followed, Ford's state troops were replaced by Confederate units, northern Mexico experienced a few changes of government, and a prominent Texas Unionist, Judge Edmund J. Davis, was commissioned by the United States to raise the First Regiment Texas Volunteer Cavalry, United States Army. Davis proceeded to Matamoros, the large Mexican border town across the Rio Grande from Brownsville, and began recruiting Texas Unionists, Confederate army deserters, and Mexican freebooters for his Federal regiment. His activities were no secret; on December 5, 1862, the *Houston Tri-Weekly Telegraph* gave a full description of Davis' motley command, and prayed God to "grant that their carcasses may all enrich the soil their lives have cursed!" Prompted by the United States consul at Matamoros, and with the tacit support of General Traconis (Vidaurri's current successor as Strong Man of Tamaulipas), Colonel Davis staged a murderous raid into Texas early in 1863. In reply, Colonel James Duff's Confederate Regiment of Texas Partisan Rangers ignored diplomatic niceties, swept across the border, and attacked Davis' camp. According to the Brownsville *Flag,* Davis' "renegades soon found that fighting was not their

game, and they commenced a lively skedaddle over the sand hills."
Davis himself did not run fast enough; he was captured and spirited
back to Texas. But he was rescued from hanging through the interces-
sion of the governor of Tamaulipas, who by now was General Lopez.
Incensed by Colonel Duff's disregard for Mexican sovereignty, Lopez
induced General Hamilton P. Bee, commanding the Western Subdistrict
of the District of Texas, to order Davis' repatriation to Mexican soil.
Bee's compliance with Lopez' demand secured a measure of amity along
the Rio Grande border, but since Lopez was unable to dissuade Mexican bandits from sacking Texas homesteads the relations between the
Confederates and the Mexicans, in the early spring of 1863, were still
less than cordial.[8]

The Texas coastline, running northeastward from the mouth of the
Rio Grande to the mouth of the Sabine, is a 700-mile stretch of
beaches, dunes, sandbars, offshore islands, inlets, bays, shallows,
sounds, and river deltas. In 1861 this shore was virtually undefended,
and nothing short of a miracle could have enabled the Confederates to
make the entire Texas coast impervious to amphibious assault. Yet in
August, 1861, Commander W. W. Hunter of the Confederate States
Navy set out to try. Given responsibility for the shore defense of Texas,
Hunter devised ambitious plans for the construction of forts and water
batteries, and recommended the concentration of strong garrisons at
such vital locations as Sabine Pass (covering the port of Sabine City and
railheads at Orange and Beaumont), Galveston Island (protecting Galveston Port, the mouth of the Trinity River, canal connections with the
Brazos River, the Buffalo Bayou approach to Houston, Houston's railroad network, and a fairly sophisticated local road system), Pass Cav-
allo (controlling the principal ship channel into Matagorda Bay, the
ports and railheads at Indianola and Lavaca, and several roads to Austin and San Antonio), and Port Aransas (guarding Corpus Christi and
the Goliad road to San Antonio). But Hunter's plans overreached the
Confederacy's resources. By the end of 1861, Galveston's chief defenses
consisted of a few "batteries" of dummy Quaker guns—logs painted to
look like cannon—and a battalion of city militia, and the other places
were no more secure. In 1862, military reverses in Tennessee and Arkansas forced the transfer eastward of many of the Confederate army
units in Texas, which left most of the Texas coast guarded by squads of

county constables. A few cotton steamers were converted into gunboats, and some efforts were made to block ship channels and mine coastal bridges, but these were all desperation measures. When Brigadier General Paul O. Hebert, then commanding the District of Texas, removed his headquarters from Galveston to the relative safety of Houston, and when Governor Lubbock issued a proclamation ordering all citizens living on the Gulf coastal islands to move themselves and their property to the security of the mainland, it became obvious that the coast of Texas was indefensible.

Galveston, situated on a sea island and boasting the best harbor and port facilities in Texas, was the most tempting prize on the Texas coast; and so Galveston was the first major beachhead the Federals tried to take. Early in October, 1862, the city was summoned to capitulate. The Confederates responded by evacuating all able-bodied men and all of the machinery from the town, leaving it in the possession of 350 old men, a company of firemen, a volunteer relief committee, and some 2,000 women and children. On the morning of October 9 four Federal blockaders approached the city's waterfront, dropped anchor, and landed five hundred men, who took the town without firing a shot. Very "few people witnessed the praceedings [*sic*] of the fleet, and the few present looked on sad and gloomy," reported a correspondent to the *San Antonio Herald.* "Galveston is very quiet and very dull." [9]

Galveston did not remain quiet and dull for long. Governor Lubbock sealed off all approaches to the island, ordered the local militia to cooperate with Confederate authorities, and, at General Hebert's request, prepared to draft 5,000 militia from all corners of the state. The day after Galveston fell, Major General Magruder, then in Virginia, was assigned to command the District of Texas. In the last two days of December, shortly after reaching Houston, Magruder issued secret orders directing Sibley's old New Mexico brigade, the newly enrolled Texas militia, and the few Confederate units available in the immediate neighborhood to assemble on the mainland opposite Galveston Island. He also ordered two river steamers recently converted into gunboats, the *Neptune* and *Bayou City,* to support the land forces. Then, in the small hours of the new year, the Confederate ships, manned by sharpshooters from the Twenty-sixth Texas Cavalry, suddenly appeared before Galveston. Simultaneously, Magruder's troops rushed the railroad causeway linking Galveston to the mainland. The ensuing battle was brisk but brief. The Confederate "navy" lost the *Neptune,* but the men of the *Bayou City* managed to disable, board, and capture the formidable Federal steam gunboat *Harriet Lane,* five guns. Fire from both land and water, plus some poor navigation by the Federal pilots, also cost the Union navy the vessels *Westfield,* a six-gun brig, the *Saxon,* a transport, and two coal scows. Meanwhile, Magruder's little army swallowed up three companies of the Forty-second Massachusetts Infantry, the only Federals in Galveston. As soon as the town was secure, Magruder began to mount cannon along the waterfront. The remainder of the Federal fleet took one glance at the guns' black muzzles and steamed for open sea. General Magruder immediately announced that the blockade of Galveston was raised, which the Union navy promptly denied. To make their point, the Federals doubled the number of blockade vessels standing off the Galveston bar. But the Confederate commander of the Galveston garrison, Colonel X. B. DeBray, was once again securely ensconced in the palace of the city's Catholic bishop, and DeBray and his successor, Colonel Ashbel Smith, would continue to enjoy the bishop's hospitality until the end of the war.

A similar victory occurred almost simultaneously farther up the coast, at the mouth of the Sabine River. On September 25, 1862, a Federal expeditionary force took the fort at Sabine Pass, demolished a railroad bridge over Taylor's Bayou, captured eight unwary blockade runners which anchored in the harbor before discovering who held it, introduced an epidemic of smallpox to the neighborhood, and burned down most of Sabine City. A month later, a battalion of the Twenty-first Texas Infantry surprised and disabled one of the Union vessels in the harbor, the steamboat *Dan.* Convinced that a rebel army was descending on them, the Federals withdrew to the security of their anchored ships. Then, at 6:30 A.M., January 21, 1863, two Confederate cotton-clad gunboats, the *Josiah A. Bell* and *Uncle Ben,* chugged down the Sabine and engaged the two Union blockaders on station, the *Velocity* and *Morning Light.* Both blockaders were captured, 139 prisoners were taken, and the Confederate flag was again hoisted over the rubble of Sabine City. General Magruder proclaimed the end of another blockade, the Federals again denied it, and five Union blockaders arrived to emphasize the denial. Nevertheless, Sabine Pass was once again a relatively safe haven for blockade runners; during the remainder of 1863, half a dozen little merchantmen slipped into the port each week.

Having swept the Federals from the Texas shore, Magruder and Lubbock did their best to prevent another "landing of the Abolition Hordes, upon our coast." Three thousand slaves were hired or impressed into service, and work was begun on coastal defenses. Ship channels were obstructed with piles and mines; guns were mounted on sea islands and sandspits; fortifications were thrown up around the major ports. By April, 1863, Union officers felt that any attempt to take Galveston with gunboats alone would be suicidal, while any attempt to storm Galveston Island would necessitate the commitment of at least 5,000 troops. Now and then the blockade fleet shelled the city of Galveston, but until September, 1863, when the Federals again attacked Sabine City, the only Union troops on the Texas shore were the occasional scouts who leaked across the Sabine River from Louisiana.[10]

≈ III   The Louisiana coastline was full of bluecoats. In February, 1862, Admiral Farragut's armada had appeared at the mouth of the Mississippi. In April, New Orleans had fallen to Farragut's fleet and General Benjamin Butler's Federal army. In May, Baton Rouge had been occupied by 4,500 Union troops. And in June President Abraham Lincoln had appointed George F. Shepley military governor of Louisiana. Louisiana's rebel governor, Thomas Overton Moore, had been forced to flee, with his family and his legislature, to the Creole village of Opelousas; from there, he bombarded Jefferson Davis with appeals for aid. Not only were the people demoralized by the disasters they had suffered, he said, but the survival of Louisiana, and of the whole western Confederacy, depended upon prompt and vigorous action by the general government. Of first importance was the need to keep open lines of communication across the Mississippi. With one Union army in Memphis and another in Baton Rouge, only the 150-mile segment of the Mississippi between the fortresses at Vicksburg and Port Hudson remained under Confederate control. Should these two forts fall, the Mississippi would be lost, the trans-Mississippi Confederacy would be isolated, and enemy forces would have access, by way of the Red River Valley, to the interior of West Louisiana and East Texas.

Moore wanted troops and a good general to command them. Richmond supplied the general, Richard Taylor, but failed to forward any troops. Arriving at Opelousas in August, 1862, Taylor passed two days in consultation with Moore, and then inspected the dispositions of the Confederate forces deployed between Alexandria on the Red River and Berwick's Bay on the Gulf. What he saw appalled him: there were no dispositions and virtually no forces in the southern half of West Louisiana. By calling up militia units from as far away as Natchitoches, Governor Moore had managed to gather a few companies of cavalry (armed with fowling pieces, if armed at all), and Major Edward Waller's troopers of the Second Texas Cavalry had just straggled over from New Mexico (with worthless flintlock muskets slung across their saddles), but otherwise all the country below the Red River had been stripped of men to reenforce the armies in Mississippi and Arkansas. "Such was the military destitution" of Louisiana, reminisced Taylor, "that a regiment of [Union] cavalry could have ridden over the State" unopposed.

Even the terrain conspired against Taylor. "To defend the lower part of the district against an enemy supreme on the water," he explained to General John C. Pemberton, "is simply an impossibility. The country is penetrated in every direction by large, deep bayous and lakes, the defense of which would require a large army." [11] Almost any creek big enough to float a cockboat could be navigated by shallow-draft, paddle-wheel tinclads, while the Lafourche, the Atchafalaya, the Teche, and half a dozen other major rivers were sufficiently broad and deep at most seasons of the year to carry the Union navy's ironclads into the heart of every sugar parish. Since most of these bayous intersected or were interconnected by steamboat and irrigation canals, scarcely an acre of ground southeast of New Iberia was beyond the range of naval guns. Adequate defense of this area would have required the erection of countless forts, an enterprise beyond reason. Taylor could only dredge up a few scuttled cannon from the bottom of Berwick's and Barataria bays and mount them in two primitive earthworks, Fort Bisland on the lower Teche and Fort Benton on the Atchafalaya. These "forts" were two-gun water batteries, manned by fifty to a hundred men each; they might delay a single tinclad, but they could not withstand concerted attacks by land and naval forces.

Until October, the Federals refrained from testing Taylor's defenses. After scattering a few garrison companies along the 88-mile railroad running westward from New Orleans toward Brashear City, General Butler was distracted by Confederate General John C. Breckinridge, who, with 3,000 East Louisiana troops, besieged and recaptured Baton Rouge. While Butler was still off balance, Major Waller's Texas battalion raided a small Union supply depot on the Brashear railroad, plundering enough Enfields to arm itself decently.

Meanwhile, General Taylor journeyed over the countryside in an old army ambulance, gathering troops wherever he could. By the beginning of October his forces south of the Red River included, in addition to Waller's cavalry and some state militia, two skeleton Louisiana infantry regiments (the Consolidated Eighteenth and the Crescent), Major F. H. Clark's small infantry battalion, three field batteries, and a gunboat, the *J. A. Cotton.* Taylor also enlisted a general officer, Alfred Mouton, under whom he brigaded his 1,000 infantry. These organizations, plus the Twenty-eighth Louisiana Infantry and a detachment of the First Texas Heavy Artillery posted in the Red and Ouachita valleys, mustered 4,697 effectives.

Toward the end of October, 1862, Butler ordered Godfrey Weitzel's brigade, 4,000 strong, to seize Donaldsonville, march down the Lafourche, and slash its way "through Western Louisiana, for the purpose of dispersing the forces assembled there under General Richard Taylor." At the same time two Union infantry regiments were directed to proceed along the railroad from New Orleans to Brashear City, while a fleet of armed steamers was sent toward Berwick's Bay and Grand Lake to interdict the Confederate line of retreat to Opelousas. Butler even dreamed that Weitzel might "be able to move upon Texas." When Weitzel arrived on the Lafourche and began pillaging his way toward Thibodeaux, the local parish seat, Taylor was off visiting Vicksburg, trying to extort some troops from General Pemberton's army. Mouton collected 500 infantry and a battery, positioned them eight miles above Thibodeaux at Labadieville, and waited for Weitzel. In a hectic, stubborn fight, which cost Mouton half of his men and all of his ammunition, the rebels managed to repulse each element of the Union force in detail. However, rumors of the presence of a Federal fleet in the vicinity of Berwick's Bay then obliged Mouton to beat a hasty retreat westward, in order to escape encirclement. While the *Cotton* held the Union gunboats south of Brashear City, Mouton's battalion crossed the Atchafalaya and went into camp on the lower Teche. This retreat resulted in the loss of the Lafourche country, but at least Mouton salvaged his command and succeeded in covering the approaches to New Iberia and Opelousas. He also organized camps of instruction for conscripts at New Iberia and Monroe, and began filling the thin ranks of his regiments with green draftees.[12]

The Confederacy's early resort to conscription says much about the South's inclination and capacity to fight a long war, and General Taylor's early disillusionment over the "notorious" fact that "a large number" of West Louisiana citizens were dodging the Conscript Bureau's agents tells quite as much about his District's morale in the autumn of 1862. One did not have to look far for evidence of public despondency. Draft evasion was already so endemic that Governor Moore found it necessary to call upon the entire Louisiana militia to help round up the recusants, while General Taylor informed the Secretary of War that it was often necessary to dispatch Confederate cavalry to drag recruits to induction centers. Louisiana's demoralization even infected Texas, for so many Louisiana draftees experienced "a sudden anxiety for Texas air" that General Magruder urged Governor Lubbock to hunt them down with the Texas militia. Yet somehow, Taylor's recruiting produced 8,200 West Louisiana conscripts before the end of 1862, though neither Taylor nor anyone else had much faith in their eagerness to fight. On October 22, 1862, seven runaway draftees were paraded before the army, lined up, and shot.[13]

Draft dodging and desertion were not the only indices of West Louisiana's demoralization. On December 1, 1862, Governor Moore warned President Davis that unless the Louisiana regiments serving in other theaters were immediately returned home "to prevent the utter ruin of this State," the citizens of Louisiana might well demand the state's secession from the Confederacy. Officers assigned to the District complained bitterly of West Louisiana's destitution and defenseless condition, while many frightened planters began sending their slaves to Texas, or even to the imagined security of the Federal lines. This exodus of slaves from the Gulf and Mississippi River parishes left millions of dollars' worth of sugar cane and cotton untended. When, in December, the Louisiana legislature convened in extra session at Opelousas, it acknowledged the state's distress by postponing until 1864 the collection of state taxes, and by resorting almost exclusively to inflated bond and currency issues to raise revenue. This legislature also bore witness to Confederate Louisiana's desperation by giving blanket authorization for the impressment of slaves and other property needed for defense, by urging citizens' committees along the upper Red to fortify the river valley, by passing a stringent and highly unpopular militia law embracing all white males between the ages of seventeen and fifty, and by providing for the enlistment of a 20,000-man Louisiana State Army. Perhaps the clearest sign of the legislature's apprehension was the enactment of a law designating Shreveport, in the far northwestern corner of the state, as Louisiana's wartime capital. Governor Moore followed the legislature and state supreme court to Shreveport, while General Taylor moved his headquarters northward to Alexandria.[14]

Meanwhile, down in Union Louisiana, preparations were under way for the obliteration of the rebel remnant of the state. On December 14, 1862, a division of Federal reinforcements arrived at New Orleans. Three days later, General Nathaniel P. Banks assumed command of the Department of the Gulf. On the 16th Banks ordered Cuvier Grover's fresh division, 12,000 strong, to take and hold Baton Rouge. At dawn the following day, after scaring away the 500 rebels posted in the town, Grover's troops marched into it, looked on while the State capitol burned down, and raised the Union flag over the debris. While Grover consolidated his position and threw reconnaisance patrols toward Port Hudson, Banks (complaining to his wife that most of Butler's henchmen had spent their time "stealing other peoples' property") cleaned out Butler's friends, brought their flourishing private trade with the rebels under a measure of government control, and reintroduced discipline to the demoralized regiments inherited from Butler. He also established programs for the employment and control of "contraband" Negroes, organized a provisional civil court for Federal Louisiana, arranged for the state to be represented in the Lower House of the United States 37th Congress, and, in a sharp reversal of Butler's repressive policies, did his best to pacify and conciliate the citizens under his authority. By January, Banks was ready to mount an offensive against Taylor's little army, which was still camped along the lower reaches of the bayous Teche and Atchafalaya.

Banks's immediate objective was the Confederate water battery on the Atchafalaya, Fort Benton. If this were taken, Union vessels staging from Brashear City could navigate, via Grand Lake and the Atchafalaya, all the way to the mouth of the Red River. From there, they could proceed toward Alexandria, or cooperate with Federal forces attempting to invest Vicksburg, or approach the Confederate stronghold at Port Hudson from the rear. Even if a flotilla merely held station at the mouth of the Red, it would interfere with the rebels' control of their segment of the Mississippi, and would interdict waterborne communication between the Mississippi and the Red.

Banks proposed to envelop Fort Benton in a pincer: from the east, William Emory's division was to push overland from Baton Rouge, through Plaquemine, and on to Fort Benton, while from the south Weitzel's augmented brigade and a four-gunboat fleet were to move from Brashear City, through Grand Lake, and up the Atchafalaya to the fort. But Weitzel and Banks were both apprehensive about the threat posed by Mouton's force. If Weitzel moved northward, his communications with the Gulf and New Orleans would be exposed; Mouton, who now commanded some 1,300 men and the steamer *Cotton,* might rush Brashear City and leave Weitzel stranded in the midst of rebel country. Before striking toward Fort Benton, therefore, Weitzel had first to protect his left flank by eliminating Mouton. Consequently, on January 14, 1863, Weitzel began marching up the Teche, hoping to draw Mouton into battle. With him, he brought seven infantry regiments, three field batteries, two companies of cavalry, and four decrepit tinclads. A short distance below Fort Bisland, this array ran into Mouton's command, consisting of two small regiments and one battalion of infantry, ten guns, and one riverboat. Mouton wisely declined to give battle. Instead, he fired all the baled cotton within reach of the bluecoats, deployed snipers to harass the Federal infantry, blockaded the Teche by scuttling the *Cotton* in the middle of the bayou, and retired to the safety of Fort Bisland. Since the *Cotton*'s hulk prevented the Union tinclads from approaching the fort, Weitzel, who was not inclined to storm the rebel earthwork without the help of his naval cannon, turned around and marched back to Brashear City. He contributed little else to the campaign.

Almost a month later, Emory's division made a sortie from Plaquemine toward Fort Benton, but because the country between the Mississippi and the Atchafalaya was flooded (Fort Benton itself was almost submerged!) Emory used up his troops moving aimlessly from one soggy hillside to another. He eventually concluded that infantry could do little in the swamp west of Plaquemine, and so withdrew to the Mississippi, having accomplished nothing. In the spring, Taylor gathered more troops (including 1,300 badly armed veterans of Sibley's Texas cavalry brigade and William Vincent's Second Louisiana Cavalry), built his strength to more than 9,000, and waited to see what Banks would do next.[15]

At the beginning of 1863, Banks's troops were not by any means the only Federals in West Louisiana, although they were the only ones in the state paying much attention to Taylor's forces. In the flat, waterlogged country north of the Red River, between Bayou Maçon (an eastern tributary of the Ouachita) and the Mississippi, 40,000 men belonging to Ulysses S. Grant's XIII and XV Army Corps were camped along the west bank of the Mississippi, in the vicinity of Milliken's Bend. Grant was beginning another one of his protracted investments of Vicksburg. Having failed in his most recent attempt to descend upon the stronghold from the north, and unable to find good campsites between the Mississippi and the Yazoo, Grant had crossed John McClernand's and William T. Sherman's troops to the undefended Louisiana side of the Mississippi. There they caught catfish, complained about short rations and rain, tore up half of the railroad between the river and Monroe, and captured a Confederate division at Fort Hindman (Arkansas Post) while waiting for Grant to decide upon his next move.

Since another frontal assault against Vicksburg seemed futile, Grant eventually decided to move his army and fleet south of the fortress, turn it, and take it from the rear. To do this, he had to find a way for his gunboats and transports to circumnavigate the rebel stronghold beyond the range of General Pemberton's guns. Vicksburg was then situated on a high bluff overlooking and commanding the eastern extremity of a hairpin turn on the Mississippi. If Grant tried to pass his vessels below the fort by way of the river, they would come under fire the whole length of the turn. Rather than expose his fleet to this punishment, Grant thought it better to slip his ships past the fortress through waterways in West Louisiana.

To accomplish this design, Grant proposed two schemes, both of which sounded good but neither of which worked. The first was to cut a canal through the base of the peninsula directly opposite Vicksburg. By using such a canal, vessels above the fort could pass below it without running the gantlet along the hairpin curve. In February, 1863, Grant imported a cargo of picks and shovels and issued them to Sherman's men. They dug for a month before the Mississippi breached the dam protecting the work, swamped the unfinished ditch, and forced them to flee for their lives.

Grant's second scheme was no more successful. He noticed that Lake Providence, a short distance below the Arkansas border and an even shorter distance west of the Mississippi, drained into Tensas and Maçon bayous. The Tensas and the Maçon flowed into the Ouachita, and the Ouachita into the lower Red. Grant understood the strategic value of the lower Red as well as Banks did: if a fleet departing Lake Providence could steam to the mouth of the Red, it could then double up the Mississippi and approach Vicksburg in reverse. In order to place a fleet on Lake Providence he would have to cut a canal between the Lake and the Mississippi. A ship channel below the Lake would also have to be discovered, explored, and possibly dredged, but at the time these inconveniences did not seem insurmountable. To test Grant's theory, his weary soldiers spent ten days dragging a riverboat over the 8,000 yards of marshy ground separating the Mississippi and Lake Providence; through February and early March the boat puffed around the Lake and poked into numerous overgrown streams, searching for an inland channel big enough to accept her. But she found none. In late March, about the same time Sherman's canal was inundated, the steamboat's fruitless adventure was also terminated, leaving 40,000 frustrated bluecoats immobilized in the neighborhood of Milliken's Bend.

A notable thing about Grant's perambulations through West Louisiana was the total lack of Confederate resistance. For all practical purposes, General Taylor had simply abandoned Carroll and Madison parishes to the Federals. As far as President Lincoln was concerned, the Confederates had also lost Plaquemines, Jefferson, St. Charles, St. John the Baptist, St. James, Ascension, Assumption, Lafourche, Terrebonne, St. Mary, and St. Martin parishes in the trans-Mississippi Delta country, for these were among the districts excepted from the provisions of his Emancipation Proclamation. However, there was nowhere a sharp "front" dividing the two Louisianas. There was, instead, a vacuous belt of disputed territory sandwiched between the Union and Confederate portions of the state, a belt in which the countryside was controlled by the nearest roving cavalry patrol. Even Lincoln's official claims were misleading. The most important town in "Union" St. Martin Parish was New Iberia, where Taylor had half his army and a conscript camp, while Federal authority was more than apparent in the portions of the unreconstructed parishes of Iberville and East Baton Rouge occupied by Emory's and Grover's 15,000 troops.

An episode far more ominous for the future of Confederate Louisiana than either Banks's or Grant's invasions occurred just before Kirby Smith arrived in the state. On the night of February 10, 1863, the Union tinclad *Queen of the West,* escorted by the cottonclad *De Soto* and a coal scow, ran the Vicksburg batteries and steamed unopposed into the Confederate Mississippi. On the 11th the *Queen* and her consorts drifted downriver, and during the following two days they cautiously probed the lower Red. On the 14th the little fleet came within range of the Confederate guns at Fort De Russy. The *Queen* was holed, beached, and abandoned; the *De Soto* and the coal scow were forced to retire. Then, while the Confederates raised and repaired the *Queen,* a tiny rebel cottonclad, the *Frank Webb,* pursued the *De Soto* into the Mississippi. There, the *Webb* unexpectedly encountered the formidable Federal ironclad *Indianola,* which had since slipped by the Vicksburg guns. As the *Indianola*'s black hull loomed out of the morning fog, the *Webb* hastily came about and churned back to Fort De Russy, bearing the news that a Yankee monster was loose on Confederate water.

General Taylor ordered the *Webb* and the still unseaworthy *Queen,* the only rebel "men-of-war" on the Red River, to return to the Mississippi and dispose of the *Indianola.* About 9:40 P.M., February 24, the *Indianola* was found resting at anchor close by the west bank of the river opposite Joseph Davis' plantation. Her lights were out, her boilers were cool, her gun-ports were shut, and she swung lazily at her mooring, her head quartering away from the current. Without giving the Federal sailors a chance to get up steam or to lay a broadside, the *Queen* drove into the ironclad's flank. Both rebel steamers then repeatedly rammed the *Indianola*. Forty-five minutes after the fight began the Federal ironclad struck her colors and settled slowly to the bottom.

The *Indianola* affair advertised the vulnerability of Confederate communications across the Mississippi, for while she dominated the water between Vicksburg and Port Hudson traffic across the river virtually ceased. One of the travelers inconvenienced by her presence was the new commander of the Trans-Mississippi Department, General Kirby Smith, who was forced to wait at Mobile until the river was cleared. And the *Indianola* was but an omen of what was to come, for within weeks after her destruction other Federal vessels ran the batteries at both ends of the Confederate Mississippi, and began denying rebel steamers the right to use the river. By the beginning of May, Union warships and troop transports enjoyed free passage on the segment of the Mississippi between Vicksburg and Port Hudson, and one gunboat had even dared to steam up the Red as far as Fort De Russy. As General Taylor affirmed, well before Vicksburg and Port Hudson fell to the enemy "the navigation of the great river was permanently lost to us." [16]

⚜ IV   Immediately after the *Indianola* was put out of action, General Kirby Smith, with his family and his staff, proceeded from Mobile to Port Hudson and took a riverboat to Alexandria. Smith assumed command of the Department and then journeyed overland to Little Rock, in order to inspect conditions along his northern front. For months prior to his arrival, rumors had been floating out of Arkansas telling of universal disorder, confusion, and demoralization throughout General Thomas Hindman's district. It was said that more than half of Hindman's army had recently deserted, that Arkansas citizens were disaffected and threatened by famine, and that large bands of lawless desperadoes were swarming over the countryside, plundering what little the people possessed. Hindman was reputed to be an odious despot, while his superior, Theophilus Holmes (who maintained Department headquarters at Little Rock), was considered an ineffectual fool. That there was some truth to these allegations soon became evident, for as Smith and his staff passed along the road from Camden to Little Rock Smith's

chief of staff, General William Boggs, noticed "many" dejected deserters strolling along the roadside. Their desertion, Boggs commented,
"was entirely too systematic."

Smith reached Little Rock on March 17. "General Holmes was
glad to see me," he informed his wife two days later. Holmes was "delighted at the idea of being relieved. . . . He says he gives up the
charge of the 'elephant' to us with great satisfaction." In a report to
President Davis, Smith acknowledged that there was "no general system, no common head," no order, no sense of purpose, and a very inadequate Confederate military force in the District. He rejected appeals
from Holmes, Governor Thomas Reynolds of Missouri, and "the citizens" of Little Rock "to establish my head q^{rs} at this point," and instead decided to settle further south, in the town of Shreveport. Though
he apologized to his wife for the fact that Shreveport was "a miserable
place with a miserable population," he explained that it was "best situated geographically for Dept H^d Q^{rs}." Evidently, he did not care to
rule his empire from a city threatened by the enemy. For by the beginning of 1863 Little Rock was loosely enveloped on three sides by
Union armies, and little was left of the District of Arkansas except for
the region below the White and Arkansas rivers.[17]

The Federals had overrun the state of Missouri even before the
Confederates attached it to their Trans-Mississippi Department. During
the first summer of the war, after Nathaniel Lyon's Unionists drove
Governor Claiborne Jackson and his secessionist legislators from Jefferson City, a popular convention installed Hamilton R. Gamble and a
pro-Union legislature in the Missouri statehouse. Jackson fled southward to the little town of Neosho, convened a rump legislature, and
proclaimed Missouri's independence from the United States. Meanwhile, Sterling Price collected an army—5,000 Missouri militia, N. B.
Pearce's 2,500 Arkansas militia, and 3,200 Confederate allies under
General Benjamin McCulloch—and prepared to liberate the state. On
August 10, 1861, the rebels fell upon Lyon's troops at Wilson's Creek,
killed Lyon, and routed his army. Leaving behind the Arkansas and
Confederate regiments, Price then drove northward along the Kansas
border, gathering Missouri recruits as he marched. After capturing Lexington, he established winter quarters at Springfield and settled down to
wait for the spring thaw. But early one morning in February, 1862,

scouts brought word that a huge Federal column was descending upon Price's position. Hastily breaking camp, the Missouri rebels retreated all the way to the Boston Mountains of Arkansas, barely a jump ahead of General Samuel R. Curtis' pursuing bluecoats. Once in Arkansas, Price's 5,700 Missouri militia were reinforced by 8,400 Confederates under Ben McCulloch, 1,000 troops from the Indian Nations under Albert Pike, and several hundred Arkansas mountaineers. The new commander of the new Confederate Trans-Mississippi Department, General Earl Van Dorn, took over-all command of the rebel gathering, and offered battle to Curtis. The stubborn, vicious three-day battle of Pea Ridge determined once and for all the fate of Missouri. Ben McCulloch was killed, Pike's Indian warriors withdrew from the fight, Curtis' Federals held their ground, and Van Dorn was forced to retire to Van Buren. His withdrawal exposed the Ozark region and most of northwestern Arkansas to occupation by the Union army. Rebel troopers might raid Missouri during the remaining three years of the war, but never again would they winter in the state.

As Price retreated to the Boston Mountains, Governor Jackson abandoned Neosho and went in search of another capital. Upon his sudden death, his lieutenant governor, Thomas C. Reynolds, inherited Jackson's office. By the time Kirby Smith crossed the Mississippi, Reynolds was governing the Confederate State of Missouri from the village of Marshall, Texas. Since the Confederate legislature of Missouri never again convened, since the Missouri state courts were all taken over by Unionist sympathizers, and since President Davis never bothered to staff the state's district courts, Reynolds and the Missouri contingent in the Richmond Congress constituted the entire Confederate civil government for the state. After April, 1862, when Price's troops were mustered into the Confederate army and Price himself was awarded a Confederate major general's commission, Missouri's exiled governor could not even claim authority over an embodied militia.

Shortly after the battle of Pea Ridge, Van Dorn, Price, and 22,000 trans-Mississippi troops were transferred east of the Great River, a maneuver which practically stripped Arkansas of defenders. General John S. Roane, left in nominal command of the state, had at his disposal only about 1,000 Confederate and Arkansas soldiers, a third of whom were unarmed. The governor of Arkansas, Henry Rector, and the Arkansas delegation at Richmond complained loudly, threatening everything from mass desertion of the Arkansas regiments serving outside the state to the outright secession of Arkansas from the Confederacy. In reply, President Davis dispatched a general across the Mississippi with orders to raise an army. The general was Thomas Hindman. Using his authority under the volunteer enlistment, partisan ranger, and conscription acts, and stretching his authority beyond the limits of the current habeas corpus acts, Hindman divided his area of responsibility into enrollment districts, assigned recruiting and conscript officers to each of the districts, expedited the officers' work by imposing martial law upon the entire state of Arkansas, imported troops from Texas to bolster Arkansas morale, commissioned guerrillas to harry the Federals' communications, encouraged the local manufacture of war matériel, and bravely announced that he himself had come to Arkansas "to drive out the enemy or to perish in the attempt." [18]

Hindman's methods were sometimes crude—his cavalry carted thousands of skulking conscripts to induction centers at Pine Bluff and Little Rock, his staff kidnapped five Texas regiments en route to Beauregard's army, and his firing squads shot scores of deserters—but by the end of July, 1862, Arkansas had yielded a crop of 18,000 soldiers and 7,000 more unorganized draftees. Hindman's propaganda was even more prolific than his recruiting, for the Federal General Curtis, still in northwestern Arkansas, was firmly convinced that Hindman commanded at least double that number of men. Fearing that Hindman would soon pounce on his army, Curtis decided to effect a junction with some other Union force. The nearest significant Union forces were at the opposite end of Arkansas: recent victories at Island No. 10, New Madrid, and Shiloh had given the Federals control of the Mississippi all the way down to Vicksburg, and the wide-open river towns like Memphis and Helena were now swarming with boys in blue. A small Federal flotilla, consisting of two ironclads and three transports, had even entered the lower White River, and was on station about halfway between Helena and Little Rock. Curtis decided to march across Arkansas and to link up with the Navy. His anabasis took his ten thousand men from Elkhorn (Pea Ridge) to Yellville, and then down the east bank of the upper White through Batesville, Jacksonport, Augusta, and Clarendon; at times his pickets were within thirty-five miles of Little Rock. His army, destitute of supplies and subsisting on spartan rations by the time it reached Batesville, suffered far more from exposure and hunger than it did from Hindman's forces. Five thousand Confederate conscripts, commanded by a politician named Albert Rust and armed with squirrel guns and pikes, did catch sight of Curtis' column in the vicinity of Clarendon, but they offered no real obstacle to Curtis' progress.

Curtis' plan would have worked perfectly if the Federal flotills had been where he expected it to be. But shortly before Curtis reached Clarendon, one of the White River ironclads, the *Mound City,* had been put out of action by a rebel water battery at Devall's Bluff, and the other, the *St. Louis,* had been forced to retire for repairs. The *St. Louis* did not return to Clarendon until several hours after Curtis passed by. Thinking they had been abandoned by the Navy, Curtis' footsore troops struck overland for Helena, which they reached on July 13—emaciated, exhausted, and delighted to be alive.

If nothing else, Curtis' adventure exhibited the fact that Confederate authority in northern Arkansas was a sham. A small, isolated Union army spent three months hiking through the region, encountering very little opposition, burning thousands of bales of cotton, enlisting whole regiments of Union Arkansas volunteers, and liberating an untold number of slaves. Even the Arkansas legislature was impressed by Curtis' performance; as his troops approached Little Rock the legislators packed their archives and prepared to evacuate the city. General Hindman suppressed his own embarrassment by blaming the whole sorry debacle upon the unfortunate General Rust.

As a reward for his achievement, Curtis was promoted to the command of the Federal Department of Missouri, which then included Arkansas, Kansas, and Indian Territory. General Frederick Steele took charge of the fagged troops at Helena and spent the next year rebuilding his force, laying waste the country between Helena and Pine Bluff, and trying to find some way to care for the thousands of refugee Negroes who came looking for the Jubilee in the squalid contraband camps around Helena. In January, 1863, McClernand's corps and Porter's fleet gobbled up 5,000 rebels trapped at Arkansas Post, thus opening the lower Arkansas River to navigation by Union gunboats, but except for this affair there were no additional major operations in eastern Arkansas until the following summer.[19]

Western Arkansas was another matter. Curtis' departure from Elkhorn left a vacuum above Van Buren, a vacuum which both sides tried
to fill. Upon assuming command of the Trans-Mississippi Department,
General Holmes placed Hindman in immediate charge of the northwestern frontier of Arkansas. Hindman was ordered to raise another army
and to cover the approaches to Fayetteville, Van Buren, and Fort
Smith. Hindman arrived at Fort Smith on August 24, 1862, and by employing his usual recruiting techniques he soon collected more than
10,000 men. Holmes designated Hindman's force as the "First Corps,
Army of the Trans-Mississippi Department." Hindman's cavalry, concentrated near Newtonia, Missouri, was composed of some 3,500 Indian and mixblood warriors under Pike's successor, Colonel Douglas
Cooper, and 2,000 Missouri volunteers belonging to a horse brigade recently recruited behind enemy lines by Colonel Joseph O. Shelby. The
remainder of Hindman's First Corps, commanded by General James
Rains and consisting of dismounted cavalry and infantry, was deployed
along the northwestern border of Arkansas, above Elkhorn and Fayetteville.

On September 10, 1862, Hindman was recalled to Little Rock to
confer with General Holmes. The First Corps was temporarily placed in
General Rains's charge, and Rains was given strict orders not to engage
the enemy. But while Hindman was absent, Curtis gathered 11,000
troops from western Missouri and Kansas, placed them under General
John Schofield, and directed Schofield to reoccupy northwestern Arkansas. Schofield's "Army of the Frontier" suddenly descended on Newtonia, routed Cooper's braves, pushed aside Shelby's cavalry, and, after
a lightning march southward, shattered Rains's main line. By the middle
of October, when Hindman returned to Fort Smith and cashiered Rains,
the Confederates had again lost everything north of the Arkansas River.
Schofield, believing the campaign to be at an end, posted General James
G. Blunt's division of Kansas Federals at Fayetteville to guard the
passes through the Boston Mountains, and retired with the remainder of
his force to winter quarters in Missouri.

Hindman, however, was still determined to liberate northwestern
Arkansas, so determined that he was prepared to defy both General
Holmes and President Davis. Because of Van Dorn's disastrous defeat
at Corinth, in October, 1862, there came from Richmond another req-

uisition for 10,000 Trans-Mississippi troops to be transferred to the East. Holmes dutifully advised Hindman to terminate his operations and to bring his First Corps to Little Rock. Hindman protested that to obey this order would mean the abandonment of western Arkansas and Indian Territory; he flatly refused to comply. Instead, without further ado, he ordered General John S. Marmaduke to take Shelby's Missouri and Charles A. Carroll's Arkansas cavalry brigades northward, and to drive Blunt from the state. Marmaduke skirmished his way through the Boston Mountains, fought a sharp engagement with Blunt at Cane Hill on November 28, and was driven back to Van Buren.

This reverse made Hindman even more determined to expel the invader. Gathering together his entire command, including a few companies of guerrilla bushwhackers, Hindman again marched northward, confident that his 11,500 men and 22 guns were at least a match for Blunt's 7,000 bluecoats. Blunt thought so too. He urged General Frederick J. Herron, in camp at Wilson's Creek, to forward every available man. Without bothering to consult his superiors, Herron collected 6,000 men and 30 guns from the winter camps in southwestern Missouri, and marched them 150 miles in four days. By December 7, when Hindman ran into Blunt's Kansans and a rabble of "Arkansaw Feds" above Cane Hill, Herron's first detachments were already on the field. The result was the nightmare battle of Prairie Grove. Some of Herron's soldiers dropped dead from exhaustion before rebel bullets could find them; a regiment of Arkansas Confederates went over to the enemy; a Union battery mowed down a Union skirmish line; a herd of Hindman's Arkansas conscripts, refusing to fight the National flag, charged and died with empty muskets in their hands. After nightfall, when the firing ceased, hundreds of hogs rooted about the battlefield, feasting on warm meat.

Hindman lost the battle. For the third time in as many months, his First Corps evacuated northwestern Arkansas and retired to the Arkansas River. But this time, the Federals pursued the dispirited rebels, took Fort Smith and Van Buren, and drove the remains of the Confederate army on toward Little Rock. Except for Marmaduke's cavalry division, which preserved its organization as it withdrew in fairly respectable order down the Arkansas to Lewisburg, Hindman's First Corps simply evaporated. In an exultant report to General Curtis, Herron exclaimed that the rebels had abandoned 4,000 sick and wounded, had retreated in great confusion, and "are demoralized and broken up. . . . I think this section is rid of Hindman. . . . I also think Little Rock will be abandoned, and a new demonstration will cause them to abandon the whole line of the Arkansas River." Herron went on to say that the Prairie Grove campaign "has done more to demoralize the [Confederate] army, to create a distrust in the leaders, and to satisfy the people that we can accomplish what we undertake, than anything done in this quarter. They are ready and willing to give it up." [20]

But Hindman still had one ace to play. In a desperate effort to draw the Federals away from the Arkansas Valley, Hindman authorized Marmaduke to raid Missouri and strike the Union base at Springfield. Taking Shelby's and J. C. Porter's brigades, Emmett McDonald's battalion, and Joe Bledsoe's horse artillery—2,370 men, all Missourians— Marmaduke broke camp on December 31, cut loose from his own supply lines, and galloped off on the first great cavalry raid of the war west of the Mississippi. On January 8, after burning and pillaging their way through the Ozarks, the horse soldiers shot their way down the streets of Springfield, hoisted a rebel flag over a girls' finishing school, and shot their way out through the opposite side of town. They then rode for the Arkansas border, destroying bridges and razing blockhouses along the way. During the last days of the retreat a raging snowstorm caused acute suffering to the jaded command's men and horses, forcing Marmaduke to abandon his wagons and some of his wounded, but most of the troopers safely reached winter quarters at Batesville by the end of January. Once there, they killed their debilitated horses, amputated a few frostbitten feet, and looted most of the neighboring farms for mounts, forage, and food.

Marmaduke's raid accomplished its objective. Fearing interdiction of their communications, the Federals evacuated Fort Smith and Van Buren, left garrisons at Carrollton and Fayetteville, and withdrew most of their forces to the relative security of Missouri. Confederate troops slipped back into Van Buren and Fort Smith. Except for the squads of irregulars who emerged to terrorize the land, the countryside between the Arkansas River and the Missouri line was left virtually devoid of soldiers.

The disintegration of Confederate authority in northwestern Arkansas demoralized the entire state. Once again the Little Rock legislature packed its archives. The Confederate voters of Arkansas routed Governor Rector by pouring an avalanche of ballots on Harris Flanagin, whose chief qualification for the office seems to have been his service as a soldier east of the Mississippi since the beginning of the year. President Davis finally saw fit to authorize the suspension of the writ of habeas corpus throughout the state. Holmes's headquarters, in hopes that some of Hindman's late troops might be induced to rally to the colors, offered a general amnesty to all deserters. Hindman himself was hastily transferred to Vicksburg. A thousand citizens of Fayetteville and its environs implored the Union military governor of Arkansas, Colonel John S. Phelps, to secure representation for the state in the United States Congress. Phelps began to swear units of the Arkansas militia into Federal service. And Holmes, who was still under orders to dispatch 10,000 troops to the eastern armies, answered a long, pleading letter from President Davis by arguing that the exportation of any soldiers from the district would cost the Confederacy the troops (who would not go), the state, and ultimately the entire Trans-Mississippi. Under the circumstances, Holmes politely but firmly declined to obey the President's command. Whether Richmond liked it or not, the Trans-Mississippi, by General Holmes's fiat, was no longer the eastern Confederacy's recruiting ground. During Kirby Smith's administration the general government would twice attempt to procure soldiers from the West, but Smith, like Holmes, would provide none.[21]

꙰ V   The epidemic of despair spreading along the Department's Arkansas River front was not confined to the region east of the Indian Territory line. On January 8, 1863, Colonel Cooper advised General Hindman that troopers of his Creek and Cherokee cavalry regiments were defecting to the enemy, and that Colonel David N. McIntosh, the commander of the First Creek, had been entertaining overtures made to him by William A. Phillips, colonel of the Third Indian Regiment (Union). Cooper insisted that "unless a large white force, well appointed and furnished for service, be sent into the Indian Territory soon, . . . upon the advent of the Federals next spring the people will be prepared to submit for the sake of saving land and property. There

is a strong undercurrent drifting them that way now." Cooper had reason to worry. Eleven days earlier, Colonel Phillips had informed General Blunt that he had "entered into negotiations with Colonel McIntosh, and am to meet him to-morrow. I expect to disarm or bring over
the whole Creek Nation. I sent messengers to the Choctaw Nation, and
[am] in hopes of opening the gates to Texas through friends." [22]

Despite the Civilized Tribes' commitment to a slave economy and
their treaties with the Confederacy, uncertainty concerning their allegiance was prevalent. Geography, domestic feuds, and the progress of
the white man's war, quite as much as any sentimental affinity for one
government or the other, determined the Indians' loyalties. The farther
a Nation's lands were from the Texas border, the less eager that Nation
was to terminate its relationships with the United States. The Choctaws
and the Chickasaws shared the Red River frontier of Texas; as soon as
Texas left the Union, these so-called Twin Tribes had aligned themselves with the South and had begun to enlist troops for service with the
rebel army. The Creeks, whose country lay farther north, had been
more cautious. Their lifeline was the Arkansas River, and not until Arkansas belatedly seceded did the Creeks' incumbent pro-Southern chiefs,
led by Dave and Chilly McIntosh, induce a majority of the Nation to
throw in with the Confederacy. Those who did so were mostly Christian
mixbloods. The pagan fullbloods, who had been at odds with the McIntosh faction for the past two generations, were less inclined to favor the
new alliance. They rallied to the ancient O-poeth-le-yo-ho-la, once Principal Chief of the Tribe and the man who, thirty years earlier, had murdered the McIntoshes' father. The remnants of the Seminole Nation,
now poor clients of the more affluent Creeks, split along the same lines:
John Jumper's half-breeds allied with the McIntosh Creeks, while Billy
Bowlegs' and Alligator's purebloods joined O-poeth-le-yo-ho-la's clans.

The richest, most powerful, and most populous Nation was the
Cherokee, a portion of whose country extended across the Kansas frontier. In 1861 the dominant "red" faction of the Cherokee Tribe, under
Principal Chief John Ross, was most reluctant to antagonize Kansas
jayhawkers by repudiating the Nation's treaties with Washington. Ross
issued a proclamation of strict neutrality, and then waited to see
whether the blue or the gray longknives would gain the upper hand. A
significant minority of mixblood Cherokees, led by Stand Watie, advo-

cated the immediate negotiation of an alliance with Richmond, but not until August, 1861—when the battle of Wilson's Creek gave the Confederates temporary control of southwestern Missouri—did Ross agree to treat with agents of the Confederate government. On August 21 he summoned his people, half-breeds and purebloods, to a great rally at Tah-le-quah, the Cherokee capital. The 4,000 who came elected commissioners to meet with the Confederacy's itinerant diplomat, Albert Pike, and voted to raise two cavalry regiments, one to be commanded by Watie and the other by John Drew, a member of the Ross faction.

Meanwhile, Albert Pike was driving about the Territory, negotiating treaties with both the civilized and the "blanket" tribes. On July 10, he signed his first agreement with the Creeks. During the next three months he concluded conventions with the Chickasaws, the Choctaws, the Seminoles, the eleven small "Reserve" tribes on the Ouachita Agency Leased Lands, four roving bands of Comanches, the Kansas Osages, the Quapaws, Senecas, and Shawnees, and finally, at Tah-la-quah on October 7, with the Cherokee Nation. The agreements between the Richmond government and the Five Civilized Tribes were, in most respects, treaties between sovereign equals, according to which the Tribes enjoyed the status of autonomous commonwealths in close alliance with the Confederacy. Until the end of the Civil War, the South was exceedingly careful to preserve this delicate relationship, avoiding any taint of interference in the several Nations' domestic political, judicial, or social affairs. The Osages, Shawnees, Senecas, and Quapaws became dependencies of the Confederate States, while the "blanket" Indians were simply given rations and trinkets in return for their promises to behave themselves. Pike's conventions were warmly applauded by the Indians' Southern neighbors, who found in them reason to hope that not too many Confederate hairlocks would be shorn during the war.

By the time the spring campaign season of 1862 arrived, the Five Nations had enlisted for Confederate service four regiments and two battalions of cavalry and a number of miscellaneous regular and irregular companies. One year later, an additional regiment was on the rolls. Except for a period during the summer of 1862, after the mass defection of more than 1,000 Cherokees and Creeks decimated its ranks, the Indian brigade's over-all strength fluctuated between 3,500 and 4,000 —though Pike once claimed to have 7,000 enrolled, and a later return showed an aggregate "present and absent" strength of over 9,000. Besides the soldiers of the Five Nations, the only other significant body of Indian troopers to go on the warpath in Confederate gray was Major Broken Arm's Osage Battalion.

The men of the Indian brigade suffered their full share of agony on the West's fields of battle. Most tragically, their first major campaign was directed against the fullblood Creeks and Seminoles who refused to acknowledge the Confederate alliance. As early as June, 1861, some of O-poeth-le-yo-ho-la's braves slipped through neutral Cherokee country and across the Kansas border, seeking aid from Jim Lane's jayhawkers and the bluecoat longknives at Fort Scott. In the fall, Ross's compact with the Confederacy interposed a hostile Nation between O-poeth-le-yo-ho-la and his Kansas friends, forcing the aged chief to choose between submission and escape. He chose escape. At his invitation some 3,500 of his followers, including more than 1,000 warriors, piled their belongings on wagons and carts, drove their cattle before them, and marched for the promised land of Kansas. But Colonel Cooper gathered 1,400 raw troopers from Forts Gibson and Davis and set out in pursuit. On November 19, Cooper intercepted O-poeth-le-yo-ho-la's column, but after a bitter skirmish was beaten off by the refugees' rear guard. Twice again, in December, the Confederate Indians tried to stop O-poeth-le-yo-ho-la, but on both occasions the fullblood braves managed to fight their way through the rebel force. Once the refugees were assisted, to some degree, by Drew's pureblood Cherokee regiment, which switched sides for the day. After O-poeth-le-yo-ho-la escaped into Kansas, and into a dismal purgatory of discrimination and injustice at the hands of his Unionist saviors, Cooper led his beaten warriors, including Drew's First Cherokees, back to winter quarters along the Arkansas River.

In the spring of 1862 the brigade followed Pike to Pea Ridge, where the soldiers of the First Cherokee Cavalry scalped a number of live Confederates. Defeated once more, and now all but abandoned by Van Dorn's eastbound army, the Indians hastily fell back to Forts Davis and Gibson and went on the defensive. They were none too soon. Up in Kansas, at Fort Scott, a veteran jayhawker named William Weer was organizing an expedition for an invasion of the Nations. By June, Weer commanded three regiments of white cavalry, two of white infantry, two batteries, and the First and Second Indian Home Guards (Union). The last two organizations, 1,500 strong, were composed of mounted refugees from the Nations; most of them were O-poeth-le-yo-ho-la's men. With this force, Weer pushed down the eastern edge of Indian Territory, soon capturing both Tah-le-quah and Principal Chief John Ross without firing a shot. A large number of fullblood Cherokees, including most of Drew's regiment, came over to the Federals. Drew's troopers were mustered into the Federal army, placed under the command of William Phillips, and redesignated as the Third Indian Home Guards (Union). Weer made a few token efforts to chase down the rest of the Confederate brigade, but because of his soldiers' ill discipline and his own affinity for drink, these came to nothing. Finally, his officers mutinied and marched his command back to Missouri.

The officers of the Confederate brigade were having problems of their own. On May 4, 1862, Pike accused Van Dorn of stealing his brigade's supplies; he also accused the Superintendent of Indian Affairs, Elias Rector, of incompetence. In reply, Rector accused Pike of embezzling $17,000 in gold consigned to the Osages. Rector resigned. Pike resigned. Hindman relieved Pike of command. Cooper applied both for command of the brigade and for the post of superintendent. Pike withdrew his resignation, continued to command the brigade, and accused Hindman and Henry McCulloch of stealing his brigade's supplies. Hindman's staff accused Pike of embezzling $125,000. Cooper advised the President that Pike was mad. On November 3, Hindman ordered a detachment of Jo Shelby's cavalry to arrest Pike and drag him back to Little Rock. But just as Shelby's troopers caught Pike, word came from Richmond that Pike's original resignation had been accepted. Pike was released from military custody and the imbroglio simmered down, despite the exhaustive epistles Pike began to write accusing one and all of perfidious treachery.

With Pike, Elias Rector, Drew, and Ross all out of the picture, a reorganization of the Indian subdistrict was an obvious necessity. The Confederate Cherokees elected Stand Watie Principal Chief, struck Drew's regiment from the rolls, and redesignated Watie's Second Cherokee Regiment as the First. Cooper was nominated to the command of the subdistrict and to the office of Superintendent of Indian Affairs. Assuming these posts, he designated Colonel Watie field commander of the Indian brigade. However, because of Cooper's drinking habits and a host of political enemies, the Senate denied him the superintendency and waited until February, 1864, to award him his brigadier's wreathed stars. Much to Cooper's chagrin, William Steele, a real brigadier with a real superintendent's commission, arrived at Fort Smith on January 8, 1863. Steele's advent reduced Cooper to the command of the brigade and Watie to the command of his regiment; but, in order to keep peace in his official household, Steele permitted Colonel Cooper to call himself a brigadier general.

During Cooper's brief incumbency as head of the subdistrict, the Indian brigade suffered another disaster at the battle of Newtonia, and was chased all the way to the Arkansas River line by William Phillips' Federal Indians. Phillips even managed to seize Forts Gibson and Davis and to open negotiations for the transfer of the First Creek Regiment to the Union army, but the sudden withdrawal of Herron and Blunt from northwestern Arkansas obliged him to fall back to Missouri. By the time Kirby Smith crossed the Mississippi, the Confederate Indian brigade was hopelessly scattered, a small Arkansas cavalry brigade was posted at Fort Smith to cover the approaches to the Territory, and General Steele was frantically trying to muster some troops to help protect settlements along the Red River frontier from raiding Comanche war parties.

"On my arrival at Fort Smith," Steele later reported, "the appearance of everything was of the most gloomy description." He found the Indian country's resources "utterly exhausted," the troops half-armed, half-dismounted, dressed in wretched rags, "undisciplined, ill-equipped, and demoralized," their officers "incompetent and negligent," the few existing quartermaster and commissary stores "stolen and scattered to all parts of the country," and the people "desponding, hopeless, and, with a few honorable exceptions, thoroughly demoralized." Very many of the Indian troopers were either away on furlough or absent without leave, but Cooper's staff was so inefficient that Steele was unable to extort a strength report from it. "Thus impressed," Steele concluded, "I ordered the main body of the troops in the Territory to encamp as near Red River as was convenient," not only to subsist and recruit the regiments from Texas, but to move them as far as possible from the Union army. To all intents and purposes, this concentration along the Red left most of the Indian Territory beyond the control of the Confederate States.[23]

Yet here and there a rebel flag still proclaimed a Confederate presence. Though the Cherokee and Seminole Nations were virtually abandoned, the line of forts along the Arkansas River—Forts Smith, Gibson, and Davis—and a single stockade in the Chickasaw Nation, Fort Arbuckle, marked a "front" of sorts extending across the middle of the Creek Nation and on into the Ouachita Reserve. The westernmost post on this line was Fort Cobb, located in the Leased Lands beyond the Chickasaw frontier and north of the Texas border. If there was ever an outpost at the edge of oblivion, that place was Fort Cobb. On May 13, 1863, the fort experienced one of its few visitations from the outside world when a reconnaissance patrol of the Texas Frontier Regiment, ranging across the Red River, encountered a scouting party from the fort.

After traveling some distance capt Loyd discovered four men on horse back and went to them finding them to be a white man & three cadow [Caddo] Indians which told us that they was soldiers & trying to protect their frontier people & also told us that their co was at Fort cob after dinner we then taken ten men from each company [twenty men] & set out for Ft cob to see what was going on there & when we arrived there we found capt George Washington & his men who was all perfectly friendly they was white men cadow Indians & comanchies so after talking with them some time we struck up camp for the night.

Fort Cobb was the knot in the noose around Kirby Smith's Confederacy. By the spring of 1863, the Trans-Mississippi Department's amorphous front line wandered from Cobb down the crooked row of Frontier Regiment stockades to Fort Duncan, on the Rio Grande. It then descended the river to its mouth, where it turned northward and ascended the Texas Gulf Coast as far as Sabine Pass. From there the front meandered inland, passing through General Taylor's forward positions at Forts Bisland, Benton, De Russy, and Beauregard. Crossing the Arkansas border well west of the Mississippi River, the line straggled northward through the "poor 'piney woods' country" near the village of Monticello Post Office, and on to the garrison town of Pine Bluff, the water battery on White River at Devall's Bluff, and Marmaduke's winter camps in the vicinity of Batesville. There the line curved sharply toward the southwest. Cutting between the Boston Mountains and Van Buren, it intersected the Arkansas River forts in Indian Territory before closing upon itself at Fort Cobb.[24]

None of the Trans-Mississippi Department's front was truly invulnerable. And although every overland stretch of the military frontier was susceptible to penetration, none was as weak, in proportion to the enemy force pressing against it, as the line from Pine Bluff to Fort Gibson. After the capitulation of Arkansas Post, the evaporation of Hindman's corps, and the near disintegration of the Indian brigade, it seemed that little but the prayers of the beleaguered Department's people kept the Union's western armies from sweeping through Arkansas and on to the Gulf.

꽃 VI   Little did, except for the rebel guerrillas in Missouri. Without much assistance, encouragement, or control from Confederate headquarters, innumerable gangs of bushwhacking irregulars preoccupied, and to some degree pinned down, most of General Curtis' 37,000 bluecoats. The partisans' motives were seldom noble, and their methods were rarely appealing, but they were among the most effective soldiers employed by the Confederate States. As General Hindman reported to the War Department, the gray ghosts of Missouri "rendered important services" to the regular Confederate forces by interdicting Federal communications, intercepting Yankee couriers, annihilating Union patrols, wrecking bridges, blockading passes, blocking roads, "destroying wagon trains and transports, tearing up railways, breaking telegraph lines, capturing towns, and thus compelling the enemy to keep there a large force that might have been employed elsewhere."

Yet even Hindman's summation of the guerrillas' achievements failed to give them due credit, for they deprived the Federals of much more than secure bases and reliable communications. They also deprived them of friends. The rebel irregulars waged war not only against faceless invaders but also against neighbors and relatives who might otherwise have assisted the Federals. The partisans acknowledged no distinction between hostile soldiers and lukewarm citizens. Anyone who did not cooperate with them was an enemy.

And enemies, whether soldiers or civilians, were given no quarter. A veteran captain of the Seventh Kansas Cavalry recalled that the guerrillas made no effort to observe "the common amenities of civilized war," and one of William Quantrill's own nightriders, "Captain" Kit Dalton, was quite prepared "to agree that guerrilla warfare claims no kinship to a pink tea." "It was a fight to the death," protested the Kansas captain. "It was our intention to fight to the death," replied the Missouri bushwhacker.[25]

The rebel irregular was customarily condemned, out of hand, as a pirate and an assassin. On March 13, 1862, Union headquarters at St. Louis published a general order advising citizens "that every man who enlists" in a partisan company "forfeits his life and becomes an outlaw. All persons are hereby warned that if they join any guerrilla band they will not if captured be treated as ordinary prisoners of war but will be hung as robbers and murderers." A month later, General James Totten, commanding at Jefferson City, ordered the prompt execution of captive irregulars "in order that these great, growing and terrible outrages of every sort may be put to an end and the outlaws infesting the district exterminated." Two months after Totten's directive appeared, General Blunt advised all officers in his District of Kansas that rebel partisans "shall not be treated as prisoners of war, but be summarily tried by drumhead court-martial, and if proved guilty, be executed (by hanging or shooting on the spot), as no punishment can be too prompt or severe for such unnatural enemies of the human race." And on March 30, 1863, General Curtis even deprived guerrillas of the slight comfort of drumhead court-martial, by telling his subordinates that there was no reason to accept a bushwhacker's offer of surrender. Curtis added that irregulars were to be liquidated immediately "if they are unfortunately taken alive." These orders, and others like them, were not idle threats. In October, 1862, General John McNeil, in charge of Missouri's Rolla District, hanged ten guerrillas in the Palmyra courthouse square.

Nevertheless, the Confederacy's shadow soldiers continued to break the rules of "civilized warfare." To them,

The purpose of war is to kill and the object of its votaries is to murder, sanctioned by Christian and pagan nations alike. . . . Civilized, barbarous, savage, guerilla, bushwhacking, jayhawking, and all methods of modern and ancient warfare have the same aim in view—death, devastation, pillage, and plunder. . . . leaden death from a high power rifle in the hands of a regular is just about as permanent as death from a blunderbuss in the hands of a jayhawker. The "regulars" who answer to taps and the reveille have no higher aim in view than to kill those who oppose them. . . . There is no more moral wrong in a small body of men seeking to take advantage of another small body than there is in a vast army seeking to out-manoeuver another army of equal importance. They are both after the enemy's throat.[26]

It would be misleading to attempt to describe guerrilla units as if they were elements of a regular army disciplined to wage conventional war. The guerrilla was disciplined, but disciplined to think for himself, to avoid the very appearance of organization, to seek safety in anonymity. The irregular operated in a theater nominally controlled by the enemy; he could never allow himself the luxury of acting like a soldier. To preserve his anonymity he continued to farm, or he pursued some other innocuous occupation—until a summons from his chief called him to war. Then he might absent himself for a night, a couple of days, perhaps a week; but he soon returned home, resumed his civilian identity, and, in order to stay alive, forgot where he had been.

The Missouri bushwhacker was an effective soldier precisely because he did not join an army, put on a uniform, and march bravely off to some far distant front. He fought a better war at home than he could under Holmes or Robert E. Lee. He knew his own country and his own people better than any outsider possibly could. The Union generals in St. Louis and Springfield, and the rebel brass down at Little Rock, had to plot their grand strategies with the help of piles of paper: regimental returns, reconnaissance reports, intelligence reports, quartermaster and commissary reports, ordnance reports, and, most especially, maps (not very good maps, at that). The local partisan needed no paper; he planned his operations by watching the current and depth of nearby streams, by knowing the condition of neighboring pastures, by feeling the mood of soldiers and civilians, by listening to whispers in the breeze. He was intimately aware of things which no map and no morning report could ever convey. Free of the debilitating inertia induced by complex organization, he could choose his own time and place to attack, and he could melt back into the populace before the nearest Union general could find the right map to design a response.

The reason General Curtis could not advance was the fact that he was surrounded. His flags flew over towns, forts, blockhouses, and camps all the way down to Fayetteville, but the farms, the pastures, the roads, the passes, the brush, the woods, the hills—these belonged to the guerrilla. Curtis did not enjoy the initiative; he was on the defensive. An ethereal host of silent spirits had his army under siege.

Ironically, considering the Federal high command's persistent attempts to stamp out guerrillas, the first irregulars to ravage Missouri were Unionist jayhawkers enlisted for border service by veteran Kansas redlegs. At the beginning of the Civil War, James Lane, Kansas' own "Grim Chieftain," raised a "ragged, half-armed, diseased, and mutinous rabble" to invade Missouri. From camps on the Kansas side of the line, camps that were "little better than vast pig-pens," Lane's "brigade" swept across the frontier to sack Osceola, loot Butler, raze Parkville, and otherwise disturb Missouri's peace. When Lane's victories won him the reward of a seat in the United States Senate, his boots were filled by Charles "Doc" Jennison, the fur-capped, poker-playing physician who happened to be colonel of the Seventh Kansas Cavalry. "Jennison's Jayhawkers," as the regiment was known, systematically decorated southwestern Missouri with hundreds of "Jennison's tombstones," the bleak, blackened chimneys which marked the remains of "rebel" homesteads. "The Missouri mothers hush their children to sleep by whispering the name of 'Doc Jennison,' " boasted the old Doc himself.

Some Union officers complained that Lane, Jennison, and their men "have so enraged the people of Missouri, that it is estimated that there is a majority of 80,000 against the government." Curtis' predecessor in command of the Department warned, "I will keep them out of Missouri or have them shot." But Curtis—the same Curtis who raised the black flag against Confederate guerrillas—was more understanding. He refrained from interfering with the jayhawkers' activities, saying that as far as Missouri's Southern sympathizers were concerned, "a reign of terror is the proper check to them. . . . We have got to fight fire with fire. . . . let terror reign among the rebels."

The jayhawkers' operations produced a like response from the other side. Though initially reluctant to encourage guerrilla warfare, by the end of 1861 various rebel generals and the Confederate War Department had extended a measure of quasi-official recognition to some irregular commands. The Richmond Congress endeavored, by means of the Partisan Ranger Act of April 21, 1862, to afford the more respectable guerrillas the protection of lawful commissions. But these concessions did nothing to legitimatize bushwhacking in the eyes of Union commanders, and the Confederate Ranger Act, which required irregulars to enroll and to observe at least some of the niceties of civilized war, may have actually reduced the effectiveness of the few guerrillas who bothered to obey it.

Some Confederate officials, like Secretary of War George Randolph, never could accustom themselves to the idea of employing irregulars. Randolph protested against the use of bushwhackers on the grounds that partisan bands "seriously impede recruiting for regiments of the line" by attracting volunteers who might otherwise enlist in the regular army. But he neglected to note that most Missourians did not have access to neighborhood Confederate recruiting stations, that before July, 1862, Jo Shelby, Quantrill, William Gregg, and other partisans succeeded in enlisting over twelve regiments and three battalions of "regular" Missouri Confederates behind the Union lines, that many bushwhackers had no desire to volunteer for service in Louisiana or Tennessee or Virginia, and that one guerrilla in Missouri may have been worth ten regulars in Arkansas. Secretary of War James A. Seddon, more in touch with reality, recommended on January 3, 1863, that the Ranger Act be revoked, and that guerrillas, unencumbered by the sanctions and disabilities of the law, be permitted to do as they pleased.[27]

Most irregulars did exactly that. Some, like "Major" Thomas Livingston, attempted to observe the amenities; he did not kill prisoners—but his prisoners killed him. Some, like Hinch West, did not make the same mistake, and survived. Some, like the "American Knights," the "Sons of Liberty," the "Knights of the Golden Circle," and the other proto-Klansmen of northeastern Missouri, spent a great deal of time organizing themselves, and little or no time damaging the enemy. Some were careless, like the certain "Colonel Porter" who appeared on the scene only long enough to be hanged at Palmyra. And some did damage, were not careless, and lived to ravage Missouri. There were, for instance, Bill Gregg, William Haller, and George Todd, Quantrill's trusty lieutenants. There was William Anderson, "Bloody Bill," border ruffian, cattle thief, murderer. There was the incomparable Merriwether

Jefferson Thompson, the "Missouri Swamp Fox," in his bobtail coat and feathered slouch hat, the terror of the Missouri "boot," sometime poet, sometime brigadier general of the Confederate States Army. And, brooding over them all, there hovered the dark, mysterious, enigmatic shadow of William Clarke Quantrill, the archetype of the species guerrilla, a man who knew how to hate. The mutual escalation of retaliatory terror, which characterized the war in the border-country bush, was to achieve its apotheosis in August, 1863, with Quantrill's sack of Lawrence, Kansas.

The sum effect of the guerrilla war waged in Missouri can never be measured. Not only was this warfare too ephemeral to be gauged by the standards ordinarily employed to determine military success or failure, but in addition it left such legacies of bitterness, lawlessness, and social disintegration that no mere objective evaluation, confined to the statistics of the war years alone, seems adequate to calculate its impact. Some things can, in theory, be measured: the guerrillas collected so much raw intelligence, recruited so many troops, forced the enemy to fight on the defensive, destroyed so much Federal property and communications, killed so many Union soldiers. But these incidentals cannot afford a total comprehension of Missouri's crucifixion. For beyond these, the guerrillas encouraged an unknown proportion of Missouri's populace to persevere, despite all obstacles—and even despite the despair of final defeat—in intense loyalty to the lost Confederate cause. One senses that certain large areas of Missouri, the northeast, the southeast, and the southwestern border, remained more thoroughly Confederate in sympathy than equivalent areas in the Trans-Mississippi Confederate States further south.

The Union state of Missouri was governed by both its nominal authorities and its home-grown vigilantes more like an occupied province than a free commonwealth. The Federal army, suspicious and afraid, reacted to the rebel irregulars' violence with severe, indiscriminate repression, treating every citizen as if he were a covert bushwhacker, and regulating civilian conduct down to the most minute detail. Oaths of loyalty and allegiance were so often demanded that it was said that "a person could hardly go through his ordinary day's work without having taken an oath once or twice." Those citizens who were genuinely loyal to the Union, or those who reacted to guerrilla outrages with belated protestations of loyalty, were inclined, from excited convictions or from a sense of self-preservation, to advertise their sentiments in ways quite as vicious as those of the irregulars. Shortly before the Lawrence massacre, a newspaper correspondent from the sophisticated East managed to describe Missouri's agony in a few terse sentences: "Bushwhacking still continues as violently as ever. In some portions there appears to be a war of extermination going on. Union men have banded together and are hunting the bushwhackers to the death. . . . Secession sympathizers [are] expelled and their property destroyed."

In June, 1863, General Kirby Smith, a professional soldier trained in the tradition of "civilized" warfare, was not yet prepared to admit the utility of the more primitive style of war conducted within the limits of his new command. As he informed both General Holmes and Governor Reynolds, "The effects of the partisan and guerrilla warfare now waged in M° is only to entail new persecution & misery on our friends there without advancing the cause one jot or tittle." But Bloody Bill Anderson was a nonprofessional officer whose only concern was killing; he measured military progress simply by counting corpses. And, according to his standards, a beardless boy belonging to his band, Private Jesse James, was "the best fighter in the command." [28]

CHAPTER TWO 🌿

THE HOME FRONT
1861–1863

By the beginning of 1863, the soldiers and citizens of the western Confederacy could see little reason to hope for the ultimate vindication of the Southern cause. Their mood approached despair. "We are ashamed of the Trans-Mississippi department," admitted one Texas editor:

> In this department there is some error of management, which brings the most splendid preparations to the most lame and impotent conclusions. With an army of 50,000 men; and equip[p]ed by the government to the extent of our demands, we have abandoned the whole North West, lost the upper Arkansas River[,] had our steamers destroyed by a paltry band of cavalry; immense army stores lost; the whole of our Indian allies abandoned to the mercy or machinations of the enemy; and the army disgusted with itself. It is a true picture, and there is no use in concealing it. The enemy already knows more about our army than some of our own generals. . . . We only know there is miserable inefficiency somewhere, and we write this in the faint hope, that through some channel or other, the matter may be brought to the notice of the War Department.

Other newspapers were quite prepared to identify the man responsible: "The government, while intending doubtless to select the very best men, has gone on with as much regularity as going down a pair of steps, from bad to worst, until it has finally settled upon Gen. Holmes, who, if not speedily relieved, is not likely to have a successor." The papers were full of uninhibited excoriations of "Old Granny" Holmes, and demanded his immediate replacement by a competent departmental commander.[1]

Such demands were not new. Ever since the fall of New Orleans the West had been trying to induce Richmond to dispatch someone other than a military castoff to take charge of the Trans-Mississippi. During the first week of May, 1862, both Governor Moore of Louisiana and Guy M. Bryan, aide and confidant of Governor Lubbock of Texas, had warned the general government that military reverses in Missouri and Arkansas and along the Mississippi necessitated the appointment of a western generalissimo possessing both plenary powers and talent. In July, 1862, the four Trans-Mississippi governors, Lubbock, Moore, Rector of Arkansas, and Jackson of Missouri, jointly advised President Davis that because of the probable interdiction of communications across the Mississippi the western Confederacy required the services of an exceptionally capable and versatile commanding general—a man able to rally public opinion, supervise the administration of a detached fragment of the nation, and organize and lead independent strategic campaigns, as well as a man both able and empowered to employ the extraordinary authority which these endeavors would demand. But instead of responding to the spirit of these appeals, Richmond had first replaced Van Dorn with Hindman, and then Hindman with Holmes, going "on with as much regularity as going down a pair of steps, from bad to worst."

By the beginning of 1863, however, the fact that the Trans-Mississippi had no confidence in Hindman and even less in Holmes had finally begun to impress the War Department. Richmond's military bureaucracy, from Secretary Seddon on down, seemed suddenly to discover that the "lamentable record of bad management and of failures" across the Mississippi did indeed make urgent the assignment of a good general to command the Department, if what little remained of the western Confederacy was to be salvaged. As the head of the Ordnance Bureau confided to his diary, "It requires some energetic genius to restore affairs in that quarter."

The "energetic genius" selected for the task was Lieutenant General Kirby Smith, whose unbroken string of victories in Virginia, Tennessee, and Kentucky had made his name a household word on the far side of the Great River. Besides his good fortune on the battlefield,

Smith had other qualifications for the post: President Davis liked him; General Braxton Bragg, his immediate superior, did not; and the Arkansas delegation to the Confederate Congress had explicitly asked for him. Smith's appointment was a cause for rejoicing among most of the articulate spokesmen for the people of the West, although Smith's friends feared that he was being exiled to a thankless limbo and Smith himself was none too keen about the assignment. "I feel my responsibilities are great and that my troubles will soon commence," he told his wife. Yet "I shall be happy and cheerfully and manfully discharge my duty despite the abuse and fault finding which I . . . expect to attend my efforts." [2]

Arriving in West Louisiana on March 7, 1863, Smith made his discouraging inspection tour of the Arkansas front, returned to Alexandria for a brief visit with Taylor, and then, on April 24, settled his headquarters at Shreveport. Smith's advent produced few changes in the Department's order of battle. Magruder and Taylor remained in charge of their respective districts, and no significant alterations were made in the command structures of those districts. Holmes succeeded Hindman as commander of the District of Arkansas. John Walker, Steele, and Marmaduke retained command of their divisions, although Walker's fresh Texas division was soon to be reassigned to Louisiana. In exchange for Hindman, who was posted to Mississippi, Smith asked Pemberton to transfer Price to Arkansas. On April 1, Price assumed command of Hindman's old First Corps, now reduced in strength to an 8,500-man division.

Once he had time to review the miscellaneous (and often fragmentary) returns for the several Trans-Mississippi districts, Smith discovered that he commanded some 45,900 effective Confederate States troops of the line. More than half of these, 25,300, were deployed in the District of Arkansas; approximately 11,600 were stationed in the District of Texas; and about 9,000 were with Taylor in West Louisiana. In addition, the area under Smith's jurisdiction contained the 1,000-man Frontier Regiment of Texas, the beginnings of Governor Moore's "Army of Louisiana" (which never did get very far beyond the planning stage), an untold number of partisans and irregulars, the various state militias, and an assortment of home guard companies, city militia units, slave patrols, constables' posses, and self-appointed vigilante committees. Only the Frontier Regiment, the partisans, and the state militias made any real contribution to Smith's military strength, and the contribution made by the militias fell far short of expectations.

All of the Trans-Mississippi states boasted militia legislation, but the usefulness of the state militias was circumscribed by a number of factors. First, and most obviously, Union occupation of large areas of the Trans-Mississippi Department deprived Confederate authorities of the services of many militiamen. By 1863 the entire Missouri militia was under Federal command, and militia units in northern Arkansas and southern Louisiana seemed quite willing to respond to Union army musters. Second, the Arkansas militia law was a dead letter. Since the Arkansas legislature failed to revise its militia statute after 1861, the state's militia manpower pool was composed almost entirely of men subject to the Confederate draft. Third, the militiamen of Louisiana and Texas were mostly teenage boys and old men, or men engaged in such sensitive war-related occupations that their occasional service in the line may have done more to hinder the war effort than to help it. Their deployment, furthermore, was restricted both by their notorious lack of training and by the militia laws themselves, which generally provided that militiamen were not to be sent beyond the boundaries of their home states. And finally, a severe shortage of weapons made it impossible to use the manpower which was available. Texas, for example, could not arm and equip more than 5,000 state troops. Except for the Galveston campaign and for a brief period during the late winter and early spring of 1864, embodied militiamen did little to enhance the effective strength of the Department's regular armies.

The contribution made by the various home guard and vigilante units was even less significant, since, for the most part, the men who composed them had no wish to fight for anything more abstract than the interests of their own neighborhoods. Some of these outfits, like the city militias, the slave patrols, and the sheriffs' police, did free men for service at the front by enlisting draft exempts in their stead, and did enjoy the support of statute law and the encouragement of civil and military authorities. But others reduced the Department's capability to defend itself by diverting able-bodied manpower from the state and national armed forces. These organizations, whose allegiance was often dubious, seldom showed any desire to assist Confederate or militia recruiting officers, and existed without the approval of legitimate authority. They were free to function only because the authorities could think of no way to suppress them, or because the absence of real authority in certain districts seemed to necessitate tacit sufferance of them. Most of these extralegal organizations were concentrated in West Texas, where the pressures of frontier life combined with the threat of Indian massacres and the inevitable demoralization of war to produce an exceptionally rapid disintegration of the customary forms of social discipline.

Some self-appointed armed bands did profess nominal allegiance to the Confederate States. Along the Nueces River, for instance, two companies of deserters, vagabonds, local citizens, and adventurers, commanded by Captain James A. Ware and Major Matt Nolan, afforded the illusion of a Confederate presence and a genuine measure of police protection to a region otherwise ignored by army headquarters. On the other hand, some of these home guard units were composed of avowed Unionists, men willing to fight for their counties or towns but hardly prepared to sacrifice their lives for the Confederate States. Unionist sentiment was so strong in some Texas German communities that Governor Lubbock, early in 1863, was forced to offer them immunity from the draft and other concessions in order to keep them pacified. Finally, a few of these gangs were superpatriotic in the extreme. In November, 1862, a secret society called the "Minute Men" seized control of the wide-open garrison and depot town of San Antonio. According to "Captain" Asa Mitchell, the "holy" mission of his organization was to punish "evil doers, traitors, and all who transgress the law and the commandments." The Minute Men sometimes enforced the law and the commandments with unseemly zeal. Shortly after Mitchell's vigilantes started their crusade, one Bob Augustin, a draft dodger and a recent inmate of the Huntsville penitentiary, overturned a few chili stands in Alamo Plaza during a drunken binge. The sheriff arrested Augustin on charges of disorderly conduct, but Mitchell's band did not consider this sufficient to expiate Augustin's sin, so, one night, Augustin was spirited from the jailhouse and summarily hanged. "It made one's blood boil to think that these cowardly villains could . . . murder with impunity anyone against whom they had a spite," protested one of the Confederate troopers stationed in the vicinity. "They took no part in the war, and never one of them fired a shot for the country or its cause . . . but

[they] stayed at home and ruled . . . by their terrible secret power."

The congregation of national, state, local, and private armies existing within the limits of Kirby Smith's empire at the beginning of 1863 virtually exhausted the Department's military manpower resources. As General Smith advised President Davis, the "fighting population is with the armies east of the Mississippi. The male population remaining are old men, or have furnished substitutes, are lukewarm, or are wrapped up in speculations and money-making. It will be difficult to develop any force from such material." A Louisiana editor, protesting the insatiability of the Confederate and state draft laws, noted that the induction of men into the armies left "little behind besides the slave population and defenceless women and children." [3]

Any calculation of the Department's total manpower resources must take account of the labor provided by the region's Negro slaves. During the first two years of the war, the Confederacy was most reluctant to authorize the mass impressment of Negroes, but as the armies devoured regiment after regiment of whites various field commanders began "borrowing" slaves from neighboring plantations. Hired or impressed slaves released troops for line duty by performing construction and service tasks which the troops themselves would otherwise have to do. By the end of 1862 the Confederacy was fast running out of spare white men, and public opinion, excited by the increasing rigor of the draft laws and by the realization that the specter of defeat required extraordinary initiatives, began to demand the wholesale conscription of Negro laborers. As one Texas editor observed, "The idea that a white man can be taken away from his wife and children, and put into the field, not only to fight, but to do menial service, while a sleek negro cannot be reached, but stays at home in comfort, is monstrous." The editor urged Texas legislators to permit the army to impress slaves "to take the place of white men now kept out of the line of battle to do . . . occupations of drudgery."

Neither Texas nor Arkansas did enact such legislation, but local military commanders nevertheless continued to draft the thousands of Negroes needed to construct fortifications along the Arkansas River and the Texas Gulf Coast. Louisiana's peripatetic legislature, already in flight before the advancing enemy, may have been more fully aware of the Department's desperate condition; on December 29, 1862, it empowered parish police juries to conscript able-bodied male slaves to erect earthworks in the Red River Valley. Planters who were called upon to supply slaves to the army seldom met the requisitions with much enthusiasm, resorting to protests, petitions, and overt defiance to keep their Negroes at home, but after the beginning of 1863 the Department's military commanders seem to have had little trouble procuring the slaves they wanted.[4]

II Manpower is not the only resource required by an army. In order to maintain its ability to fight, an army needs weapons, ammunition, equipment, food, transportation, and communications. Moreover, in order to supply its army's needs a society must also produce provisions, manufactures, and services for its civilian labor force. The economic sophistication of the society, and the totality of the war in which it is engaged, determine the effectiveness with which it can employ the resources available. The less industrialized a nation is, and the more devastating the war to which it is committed, the greater will be the deprivation suffered by its people—the relative lack of industry prevents the efficient use of resources, and total war necessitates the profligate expenditure of those on hand. When a society can no longer endure suffering, its war effort collapses.

The Southern Confederacy was a vision shattered by the ugly realities of an immature economy and an unlimited conflict; in a very real sense, the Confederacy was an eighteenth-century country trying to support a nineteenth-century army in an effort to win the first twentieth-century war. Its ambition outstripped its capacities; engulfed in war, the South could neither sustain aggressive operations nor mount an inviolable defense. To fight as well and as long as it did, the Confederacy had to consume itself, to sacrifice its own people, its own wealth, and its own ideals in a desperate effort to propitiate the god of victories.

East of the Mississippi, the escalating ruthlessness of the war obscured the South's internal disintegration. The battle scars inflicted upon the Confederacy at such places as Shiloh Church and Antietam bled so profusely that few people had occasion to notice that the country's internal organs were also hemorrhaging. But in the Trans-Mississippi West, the South's surface wounds were less severe, and the symptoms of the country's interior corruption were consequently more apparent. When Kirby Smith took charge of his Department the signs of its decomposition were already evident, although it was destined to linger on for more than twenty-six months. By the beginning of 1863 the Confederate Southwest lacked not only surplus manpower but also many of the resources necessary to utilize what men it had, as well as the means with which to reinforce its population's sagging morale.

Evidence of the Trans-Mississippi Department's growing want and waning hope was abundant. Most obviously, every deserter who slipped away from his regiment, every conscript who dodged an enrolling officer, every militiaman who eluded a muster, and every civilian who harbored a recusant cast a silent vote against the prolongation of the war. By early 1863 such "votes" had so increased that both the Texas and the Arkansas legislatures found it expedient to enact draconic punitive laws for the prosecution of deserters and their accomplices.

A related indication of mounting dissatisfaction, and a mark of widening social division within the Confederacy, was the popular antipathy for many of the exemption provisions of the conscription acts, provisions which excluded from the draft the very people who appeared to have the most to gain from Southern independence. "The exemption of classes cannot continue," exclaimed one Texas newspaper. "All white men are recognized as equal under our Constitution, and must be by the spirit of the laws enacted under the Constitution." Arguing that poor men ought not to be called upon to fight a rich man's war, the paper called for "a little energetic legislation upon principles of political equality." Such protests were more than rhetorical. In the spring of 1863 a lively grassroots campaign advanced old Sam Houston as a candidate for the governorship of Texas, despite his refusal to swear allegiance to the Confederate States and his well-known distaste for "Jeffy Davis" and the rest of the secessionists in Richmond.

Soldiers were often as disaffected as the men who avoided service. Some simply stayed in camp to draw regular rations, while others preferred to raid and pillage the homesteads of friendly civilians. By 1863 many Arkansans thought of every member of any Texas or Missouri regiment as a bandit in uniform. Even in the secure area of East Texas the citizens "spoke with horror of the depredations committed in this part of the country by their own troops." In one of the bivouacs near

New Iberia an enterprising Louisiana infantry captain slept snugly between fine sheets of lace-fringed linen atop a majestic four-poster bed, which he had somehow expropriated from a lady's boudoir.

These exhibitions of ill discipline were too serious and too common to be written off as the high-jinks of adolescent soldier boys. They testified not only to the demoralization induced by conscription, incompetent commanders, and the habit of defeat, but also to the failure of the Trans-Mississippi Department's logistical arrangements to supply the commissary and quartermaster stores required to subsist the army. Official inspectors might report to the War Department that supplies were abundant in Kirby Smith's Confederacy, but the infantrymen in Arkansas who lived on blue beef, parched corn, and desiccated vegetables, or the cavalrymen in West Texas and the Nations who survived on a diet of buffalo meat, wild game, and prairie-dog steaks, enjoyed little of this alleged abundance. As one private soldier complained to his family, "Our rations are very scanty. The beeves that we eat here are so poor they can scarcely stand. It is an outrage that confederate soldiers should be compelled to live upon what we live on."

Nor was food the only necessity in short supply. In October, 1862, Shelby advised Marmaduke that his brigade included "a great many men without a blanket, overcoat, shoes, or socks. . . . We have never drawn any clothing, shoes, salt, or anything else. All we have in way of transportation is one wagon to the company, and they mostly two-horse wagons. We have but few cooking utensils, which we likewise have purchased with private means. We have a great many horses unserviceable, for the want of shoeing." As the "chill winter" of 1862–63 set in, newspaper columns were sprinkled with urgent appeals from various regiments for coats, trousers, footwear, hats, overcoats, and blankets. From Pine Buff, for instance, a trooper of the Thirty-first Texas Cavalry wrote to describe the "hard, heavy, severe suffering" of his comrades, and to ask whether "our kind friends, our countrymen, the good people of texas, [would] help aid and assist us with clothing for the winter? One pair of good yarn socks, may prevent a soldier's feet from being frozen. . . . How would your hearts rejoice to know that you had saved one poor soldier from the pangs of the crip[p]led." The Nineteenth Texas Cavalry even placed newspaper advertisements to solicit the donation of firearms!

These appeals usually produced some sympathetic response, but all too often the goods subscribed were inadequate to meet the soldiers' needs. Under the circumstances, the troops' frequent resort to illegal impressments and plunder was not surprising. Some even went so far as to loot government warehouses! Nor was it surprising that, when all else failed, disgusted soldiers preferred desertion to destitution. By the time winter gave way to spring, the columns of the newspapers contained scores of announcements offering the standard $30 reward for information leading to the arrest and confinement of prodigal enlistees. One advertisement in the May 13, 1863, issue of the *Dallas Herald* listed forty-three absentees from a single regiment; the June 3 edition of the same paper carried descriptions of forty-eight deserters from various organizations. The Clarksville *Standard* of May 9, 1863, carried a sad colonel's "Fair Notice" that "if the several members of Co. I 29th. Texas cavalry who are shamelessly absent from their company . . . do not *immediately* report for duty they will be severally described and advertised as deserters. . . . They sully the fair fame of the County of Bowie, from which, they come; for from the very outset it has been almost impossible to keep them in camp." [5]

The soldiers who quit often found conditions at home little better than those in the army. The February 4, 1863, edition of the *Washington Telegraph* contained two full columns of small print listing lots and farms in Lafayette County, Arkansas, which were offered at auction in default of taxes; the next four issues of the same paper consumed seven columns announcing sheriff's sales in Hempstead County. For those who escaped complete ruin, the ersatz quality of daily life testified to society's decay. Ladies made do with "Confederate dresses," the remains of their prewar wardrobes; table settings at the most fashionable homes were made of tin, not silver; rope halters had long since replaced leather bridles; the *Avoyelles Pelican,* a Louisiana newspaper, was printed on scraps of used wallpaper. And anyone who had reason to spend a dollar bill soon discovered that something was wrong. The 140-mile stagecoach journey from San Antonio to Alleyton (near Houston), which had cost $13 before the war, cost $40 in the early spring of 1863, and a pound of coffee in the San Antonio markets fetched $7 Confederate. Neither tins of coffee nor stagecoach rides were within the means of private soldiers, who earned only $11 each month; they, and their civilian kinfolk, had enough trouble finding the fifty cents needed to buy a pound of butter, or the forty cents for a dozen eggs.

The inflation of the currency was the best and most consistent index of the Trans-Mississippi Department's poverty and demoralization. The shortage of manufactures and agricultural produce (shortages induced by the lack of industry, the blockade, and the primitive domestic transportation systems), speculation, the multiplicity of note issues, the disappearance of specie, the increasing use of printing presses by both treasury officials and counterfeiters, and declining faith in the Confederate cause itself all contributed to the decline in value of the money in circulation. By the end of 1862 a Confederate dollar was worth no more than twenty-five cents in gold. A year later, the national currency was worth five cents on the dollar; by July, 1864, only three cents; and by December, 1864, two cents. The treasury warrants and state bills issued by Arkansas, Louisiana, and Texas lost value quite as rapidly as Confederate notes, while the private exchange instruments circulating in certain sections of the region—especially in Texas, where railroad corporations, merchants, and even a few barbers printed their own shinplasters—added immeasurably to the confusion.

By early 1863, no ordinary citizen could even be sure that the money in his pocket was genuine. In the vicinity of Brownsville, one counterfeiting ring passed $50,000 in bogus Confederate bills imported from New York; at Little Rock, another gang specialized in homemade $10 Arkansas treasury warrants; and even in Shreveport, three counterfeiters posing as army staff officers circulated $20,000 worth of bad Confederate fifties. The loss of faith in the currency was so severe that many people simply refused to accept paper money. A Shreveport newspaper declined to take anything but Confederate and Louisiana treasury notes in payment for subscriptions, and Governor Moore was impelled to order the Louisiana militia to arrest persons who would not honor the legal tender of the nation and the state.

Because inflation was an insidious foe, striking down prosperity in devious and unexpected ways, it would be misleading to present a single schedule of price fluctuations applicable to the entire Department. The prices of some goods (especially beef, dairy products, and the produce of local garden farms) remained fairly reasonable, while others shot up to great heights. But perhaps one of the most typical and most thoroughly documented inflationary spirals was that which engulfed the Southwestern Confederacy's newspaper industry after 1862. Before mid-1863, almost every respectable town in the region had its own newspaper, and subscription prices generally remained at prewar levels. Until November, 1862, the Arkansas *Washington Telegraph,* a weekly, asked $2.50 per year; until December, 1862, the *Shreveport Semi-Weekly News* sold for $4 a year; and until March, 1863, the *Houston Tri-Weekly Telegraph* held the line at $8. Then, during the last two months of 1862 and the first six of 1863, a whirlwind of rising costs and paper shortages gutted newspaper offices from Pine Bluff to Brownsville. The majority of the Department's papers suddenly disappeared, while those that survived did so only by doubling their rates. On March 20, 1863, E. H. Cushing, the editor of the *Houston Telegraph,* persuasively delineated the plight of his profession: "Before the war," he told his readers, "we bought paper at $3 per ream. The same paper is now held at $50 per ream." (On March 10, John Dickinson, publisher of the *Shreveport News,* had informed his customers that his newsprint cost more than thirteen cents a sheet, or $63 a ream!) "We then paid 40 cents per thousand, composition," Cushing continued. "We now pay $1. We then had rapid mails to bring intelligence, at little or no cost. We have had to establish expresses of our own now, at heavy cost. Our expenses last week for expressing and telegraphing alone were $250!" Apologizing for the escalation of the *Telegraph's* subscription price from $8 to $16, Cushing explained that "we yield to hard necessity." The *Shreveport News* had already raised its rates from $4 to $8 the previous December, and in August, 1863, it again raised its annual price to $12, or fifty cents a copy for a two-page paper. John Eakins' *Washington Telegraph* doubled its rate from $2.50 to $5 in November, 1862, and then held steady through 1863 by reducing the size of its issues. By the end of 1863 both the *Houston Telegraph* and the *Shreveport News* asked $20 for subscriptions; within the next three months the *Washington Telegraph* raised its rate from $5 to $20, and the *Shreveport News* from $20 to $30. By March, 1865, the Shreveport and Houston papers demanded payment in specie, but it was still possible to buy a subscription to the *Washington Telegraph* for $50 Confederate. Perhaps the only Trans-Mississippi newspaper to escape the slow strangulation of inflation was the Bellville, Texas, *Countryman,* which offered to barter a year's subscription for five bushels of corn.

At the turn of the year 1863, the legislatures of both Arkansas and Louisiana found it necessary to appropriate funds for the relief of indigent civilians—Louisiana appropriated $5,000,000, and Arkansas $1,200,000. Arkansas even instituted a grain dole to support refugees and the poverty-stricken families living on homesteads desolated by the armies. In Texas, where the enactment and administration of the poor laws was the responsibility of the country courts, a tangled jungle of local legislation was enacted to stay the progress of famine. A few boards of county commissioners issued bonds and authorized special taxes to provide welfare money, but the majority simply relegated relief to the supervision of amateur volunteer agencies. In February, 1863, a fund drive in Dallas yielded over $10,000 for the benefit of soldiers' wives and children, while each week the people of Houston donated almost $3,000 to the city's sick and poor. One remarkably generous farmer in Liberty County, Texas, was so touched by his neighbors' suffering that he gave them, free of charge, a thousand bushels of corn.

Yet none of these expedients prevented the Department's bankruptcy. On the contrary, relief legislation may have hastened the end by pouring a few more million dollars' worth of fragile state paper into the economy. The superabundance of dubious money encouraged the development of a large class of speculators, who exploited the unfortunate by manipulating the erratic relationship between the values of currency and goods. By the beginning of the third year of the war, speculation was beyond control. Despite the occasional (and illegal) efforts of the authorities to fix and hold prices, the prevalence of speculation gave eloquent witness to the disintegration of social coherence under the weight of imminent disaster. In April, 1863, a civilian visiting Fort Smith described that town in words which might have been applied to any market community in the Southwest. Fort Smith, he said, was "a filthy sink of corruption and iniquity, inhabited chiefly by a foul, speculating horde, our enemies at heart, who sell the comforts of life . . . at ten prices."

The inflationary fiscal policies of the Trans-Mississippi states were also to blame for much of this speculation. By the beginning of 1863, printing presses in Little Rock, the Red River Valley, and Austin were grinding out millions of dollars' worth of state treasury warrants and bonds; specie had disappeared; Arkansas and Louisiana had suspended

state taxation; Texas had refused to help Confederate agents collect
government levies; Texas and Arkansas had stayed the prosecution of
debtors. Only Texas made some slight effort to remain solvent. It raised
its property tax from 12.5 cents to 50 cents per $100 valuation, hiked
its poll tax from 50 cents to a dollar per year, multiplied its licensing
fees, and imposed an income tax of 25 cents on each $100 earned. Yet
Texas, which went into the war almost unencumbered by debt, came out
of it more than fifteen million dollars short.[6]

У III   During the first two years of the war, Confederate and state
authorities west of the Mississippi tried to encourage the development
of new industries, but their efforts met with relatively little success. The
scarcity of certain raw materials, the inefficiency with which others
were extracted and processed, the lack of investment capital, the primitive condition of the industrial base already in existence, the blockade,
the region's poor transportation facilities, and the army's consumption
of manpower all prevailed against an adequate wartime expansion of
manufacturing in the Confederate Southwest.

The Trans-Mississippi Department's abundant supplies of cotton,
wool, and cattle hides were not sufficient to guarantee the emergence of
adequate textile and leather industries. By early 1863, factories for the
production of clothing, blankets, shoes, and harness were still relatively
few. Since government encouragement seldom included subsidization,
most of the plants in operation were both privately owned and small. In
the rebel fragment of Arkansas, only John Matlock's cotton and woolen
mill at Murfreesboro was important enough to rate its own detachment
of military guards. Four other mills scattered between Van Buren and
Camden turned out limited quantities of rough cloth for neighborhood
military and civilian markets, but none of these had the capacity to produce surplus cloth for shipment to the District quartermaster's depot at
Little Rock. In fact, Merrill and McGill's woolen mill at Camden was
so unprofitable a venture that, in spite of the demand for textiles, it
ceased production during the latter half of the war. Had the Arkansas
textile industry been healthier, perhaps the legislature would not have
had to donate the statehouse carpets to the army for use as blankets.

The Arkansas leather industry consisted of a number of very small piecework tanneries clustered in the vicinity of Washington and Camden. These tanneries processed cattle hides procured from local stockmen or from the military commissariat, and then cobblers and saddlers —most of whom were soldiers detailed by the army—converted the leather into boots, shoes, cartridge boxes, and horse equipments. When the tanneries were unable to obtain cattle hides, the shoe- and harness-makers fashioned brogans and animal trappings from the skins of wild deer, squirrels, and raccoons.

Conditions were not much better in Texas. When that state joined the Confederacy, it had five privately owned cotton and woolen mills. During the next two years the legislature issued patents of incorporation to three additional textile firms. But these corporations needed more than legislative charters to weave cloth, and the usual scarcities of capital, machinery, and labor prevented them from achieving production. The Texas leather industry was made up of small tanneries scattered along old cattle trails between Houston and the Louisiana line. Perhaps the most productive tannery in the entire Department was Geiselman's, at Houston, which processed about three hundred hides per week. Geiselman's plant included shops for the manufacture of common varieties of harness-, sole-, and upper-shoe leather, a private wharf, and the only noteworthy glue factory in the Trans-Mississippi. Like leatherworkers in Arkansas, those in Texas often ran short of raw material; the Marshall *Texas Republican* of January 22, 1863, carried advertisements from four different firms soliciting hides to tan. And, like their Arkansas competitors, the Texan tanners were often forced to employ ersatz ingredients.

The capitulation of New Orleans cost Confederate Louisiana its only large clothing and textile mills and its only significant shoe factory, and virtually wiped out that state's immature textile and leather industries. General Taylor's District of West Louisiana contained no weaving or cloth fabrication plants, and its only tanneries were army establishments operated in conjunction with the military's meatpacking plant below Alexandria. The District needed leather so desperately that neither Governor Moore nor his legislature lodged any protest against Taylor's unauthorized investment of army funds, facilities, and manpower in the tanning, harness, and shoemaking trades.

West Louisiana was not the only place where the exigencies of war eroded the South's commitment to private enterprise. By November, 1862, the leading textile and leather factory in Arkansas was the Little Rock penitentiary, where the prisoners stitched together thousands of uniforms, boots, brogans, haversacks, harnesses, cartridge boxes, and tents. As many as five hundred of the Confederacy's drummer boys beat their calls on drumheads made by the inmates at Little Rock. A great deal of the raw cloth which Arkansas convicts turned into finished products was woven by prisoners of the Texas penitentiary at Huntsville, who worked off their time in the most elaborate complex of cotton and woolen mills constructed in the entire Department. In the year ending August 1, 1862, the mills of the Huntsville prison produced over one million yards of cloth, more than the rest of the Confederate Southwest's textile works put together. Yet, as Governor Lubbock complained, Huntsville's output was not sufficient to meet one-fifteenth of the requisitions submitted to himself and to the prison superintendent by military and civilian consumers. And instead of increasing production, Huntsville's shops manufactured progressively smaller amounts of cloth as time went on, as the state's inability to import replacement parts forced the retirement of dilapidated machinery.

By October, 1862, cloth allocation was occupying so much of Lubbock's time that he had little left to devote to other pressing problems. At this moment, General Holmes peremptorily demanded the authority to control the distribution of penitentiary cloth. After setting aside stocks of textiles for indigent Texas civilians, and after raising the price schedules for all cloth sold to the army, Lubbock and the Texas legislature awarded Holmes both the power he wanted and the accompanying headaches. The Huntsville penitentiary proceeded to earn 38 percent of Texas revenues during the remainder of the war, even though the state government was no longer obliged to attend to the day-by-day details of the wholesale textile business.

Once Taylor started manufacturing leather goods and Holmes nationalized a large portion of the cloth industry, official reluctance to acknowledge the fact that total war and free enterprise were incompatible diminished. Late in 1862 the Arkansas legislature offered outright bounties to anyone willing to try to manufacture salt, iron, or cotton-carding machines. Nobody seems to have protested in February, 1863, when purchasing agents for a new Confederate States Wool Agency began placing advertisements in the papers emphasizing the patriotic duty of every shepherd to give preferential treatment to military wool buyers; and by May the news that Confederate government tanneries and textile mills were being built near San Antonio was greeted with editorial praise.

This modest government intervention into the economy was hardly sufficient to create an industrial complex capable of satisfying the Southwest's demands for textile and leather goods. From first to last, home manufacture—highly inefficient but indispensable—remained the Trans-Mississippi Confederacy's primary source of clothing, shoes, and related items. Throughout the Department, thousands of women and young girls spun thread, wove cloth, knitted socks and scarves, fashioned hats, stitched shoes, hemmed blankets, rolled bandages, sewed together haversacks, and made cartridge boxes and harness straps. Some citizens even tanned their own leather, following instructions printed in the newspapers. Sometimes, when wagons were available, the ladies of a given district were able to resupply an entire company of neighborhood soldiers, but more often individual families were content to outfit themselves and their own military kin. On November 6, 1862, Thomas Farrow sent his absent son "1 cotton shirt, 2 pair socks, 2 pair linsay pants, 1 pair of Drawers, one Westcoat, 4 twists of tobacco, comfort." Eight days later another father mailed "2 pair pants 2 overshirts 2 pair drawers one pair shoes 4 pair socks" to his soldier son. Soldiers neglected by the folks back home were often obliged to beg clothing from their comrades. An infantryman informed his sister that a messmate named Grace "is all most naked his Breeches is in strings all he has got fit to ware is a over shirt Joe gave him a par of drars & shirt I gave him a par of breeches all I have except what I have on." [7]

The standards in uniform of most regiments fell short of the norms established by army regulations. Footwear, when available, ranged from low-quarter pumps and Indian moccasins to patent-leather riding boots; socks came in all colors; trousers were usually gray, blue, or plaid jeans; shirts were often gray cotton, but butternut brown, Union blue, and linen white were almost as common; vests, jackets, and greatcoats came in all sorts of single- and double-breasted designs, varied widely in color and pattern, and normally lacked the brass buttons and braid proper to military dress; and headgear included anything from beaver toppers and jet-black felts to Yankee forage caps and calico kerchiefs. In early 1863, most of the men of the Fourteenth Texas Cavalry Battalion were wearing plaid flannel shirts, wool trousers, short jack boots, enormous spurs, and black felt hats ornamented with the Lone Star of their state. Both the Second Texas Infantry and the Twenty-sixth Louisiana Infantry received—and wore—undyed white muslin coats. The Third Texas Infantry paraded in a promiscuous collection of blue and gray uniforms, French kepis, "wide-awake" hats, and Mexican sombreros. Captain Sam Richardson scowled his way through a photographer's sitting while wearing a high black cowboy hat, a ruffled gray shirt, yellow cavalry gantlets, a tooled leather belt with a big gilt buckle, a sheathed bowie knife, a carbine sling, two leopard-skin revolver holsters, and leopard-skin trousers with spangles down the seams.

Other infant industries attempted to satisfy other needs, but with few exceptions their productivity fell short of the Department's demands. One of the exceptions was the salt industry, which, despite primitive facilities and inefficiency, managed not only to produce enough salt for the Southwest but to export salt to the Cis-Mississippi Confederacy as long as communications across the River remained unimpaired.

Salt was more than a basic ingredient for a balanced diet. It was also indispensable for the curing and preservation of meats and other perishables, and for killing the taste of carelessly processed foods. During the winter of 1861–62, more than 30,000 beeves were salted and packed at the army slaughterhouse near Alexandria, a figure which represents no more than a fraction of the Department's total consumption of salted meat. The war increased the demand for salt, since thousands of dislocated soldiers and refugees were removed from their own farms and obliged to depend upon shipments of preserved commodities. Consequently, the state governments, the army, and numerous entrepreneurs made efforts to increase the output of known salines and to discover and develop new sources of salt.

The only known salt vein in rebel Arkansas was located along Saline Bayou, a short distance from Arkadelphia. Reports that wells dug in the vicinity sometimes struck saline water induced the Confederate army to detail to the area two officers, Captains J. M. King and M. S. Carpenter, with orders to erect and operate a saltworks. Employing military and slave labor, King and Carpenter sunk wells, built a network of aqueducts, and, using dismantled boilers removed from decrepit riverboats, constructed an evaporation plant. Before it shut down in the last days of the war, the Arkadelphia works processed hundreds of tons of salt for the army and for neighborhood civilian markets. In late 1862 the Arkansas legislature attempted to encourage further salt production by offering subsidies to firms willing to engage in it, but, except for the Ashley Salt Works established on Saline Bayou in 1864, no civilian companies seem to have entered the business.

At the beginning of the Civil War, two saltworks were operating in Texas: the Steens Saline in Smith County, and the Grand Saline in Van Zandt County. Undeveloped salines were known to exist elsewhere, including salt streams in the northwestern frontier counties, salt springs in Lampasas and Llano counties, the extensive dry salt lakes of the Panhandle, and the limitless waters of the Gulf. Because of the hostility of the Plains Indians the Panhandle salt flats were inaccessible, but Texan enterprise soon brought most of the other salines into production. The Grand Saline, with a daily output of 3,000 bushels (ten times the yield of any other Texas mine), remained the state's most important source, but by 1862 the new Brooks works were processing more salt than the older Steens firm. The state government operated a major saltworks in remote Shackleford County, in the Red River country; it was the chief source of supply for upper West Texas and the Confederate sliver of Indian Territory. A number of simple evaporation beds were diked off along the Gulf Coast, and a good many prospecters extracted salt from diggings sprinkled through the interior. The Texas legislature awarded liberal charters to salt manufacturing firms, regulated and policed the extraction and distribution of salt, and, in 1863, set aside $50,000 to subsidize the exploitation of salines for the benefit of the army. Wartime salt production figures are fragmentary, but it appears that Texas, unlike Arkansas, was more than able to satisfy its needs.

West Louisiana's salt resources were even more abundant than those of Texas. A number of private saltworks were clustered in the upper Red River Valley, in the parishes of Bienville, Bossier, and Winn, including the Drake Salt Works on Saline Bayou, King's and Rayburn's saltworks in Bienville Parish, and various salines spotted around the shores of Lake Bisteneau. By 1862 the Rayburn Works were processing 1,000 barrels a day, and more than 1,000 soldiers, civilians, and slaves were extracting over 6,000 barrels daily from the brine of Lake Bisteneau. Like the legislatures of Texas and Arkansas, that of Louisiana regulated salt extraction and willingly granted franchises to salt prospectors, but because of the wealth of the state's developed salines it saw no reason to subsidize new ventures.

On May 4, 1862, a laborer digging a well on Judge Daniel Avery's private island, south of New Iberia in Vermillion Bay, found a bed of pure rock salt forty feet thick and at least one hundred forty acres in extent. Richmond ordered General Taylor to occupy Avery's Island and go into the salt business. Within weeks, five hundred Negroes—guarded by two companies of infantry and a section of artillery—were producing over 1,300 bushels of crystal salt per day. For almost a year, the Avery mines supplied salt to Port Hudson and Vicksburg, and also to a new army meatpacking plant built by Taylor at New Iberia. But it was too good to last. On April 17, 1863, Federal troops from Brashear City overran the saltworks and demolished the installation. Since the subsequent Union conquest of the Mississippi cut off Avery's Island from its markets, Taylor's Confederates made no serious attempt to reoccupy the saline.[8]

Throughout the war, Nash's Iron Works, about twelve miles from Jefferson, Texas, was the only factory in the Confederate Southwest capable of mass-producing a respectable amount of good-quality pig iron. By 1863, most of Nash's output was shipped to Houston, Austin, Shreveport, and Camden, and four towns in which the Department's five large foundries were located. These foundries supplied processed bar and sheet iron to Confederate army arsenals at Little Rock, Camden, Arkadelphia, Shreveport, Marshall, Tyler, and San Antonio, to state arsenals at New Iberia and Austin, to the military shipyard at Shreveport, and to numerous private small-arms, ordnance, and machine shops scattered throughout the region. Yet neither Nash's plant nor the five foundries were able to satisfy more than a fraction of the Trans-Mississippi's need for iron. The arsenals and the other consumers depended, to a great degree, upon the output of local forges and smithies, which generally procured their raw material by scouring the countryside for scrap. Whenever an arsenal's iron stocks approached exhaustion, military authorities could usually be persuaded to impress a few old steamboat engines, to tear up a few miles of relatively idle railroad track, or to impound a consignment of iron goods en route to some unlucky civilian.

One victim of the iron shortage was the steam ram *Missouri,* the only ironclad warship which the rebels west of the Mississippi ever attempted to construct. When Kirby Smith arrived at Shreveport, the *Missouri*'s wooden skeleton was perched on the ways at the neighboring shipyard. Twenty-six months later, when the *Missouri* no longer had a flag to fight for, she was still nestled in her dry berth, still awaiting her armor.

As the wide dispersal of metalworking facilities suggests, the productivity of industry depended upon the availability of transportation. Pig iron from Jefferson had to be hauled to Camden, Shreveport, Austin, and Houston, and processed iron from the foundries had to be carted to arsenals and factories elsewhere. Since neither the Department's miserable railroads nor its shallow rivers were able to bear the bulk of this traffic (few of them interconnected, and most of them pointed in the wrong directions), ordinary wagons were needed to carry most of the loads overland. But by early 1863, only two factories—one attached to the Little Rock penitentiary, the other located in the military's industrial park at New Iberia—possessed the labor and equipment required to turn out a significant number of wagons. The Arkansas penitentiary manufactured two hundred fifty vehicles during 1862. A few private carriage- and wagon-makers contributed occasional wagons to the supply, but after 1861 the Department's chronic shortage of transportation induced the military authorities to resort to the wholesale purchase, hire, or impressment of privately owned farm and freight vehicles. Impressments were not legal until March, 1863, but by January of that year various generals, and even the Secretary of War, had already authorized Trans-Mississippi quartermasters to seize vehicles needed to transport army stores, industrial materials, and cotton. Quartermasters' advertisements, threatening to press wagons not offered for hire, frequently appeared in the newspapers. In the summer of 1863 the quartermaster at San Antonio, Major Simeon Hart, arranged the importation from New York, via Matamoros, of a boatload of mint-quality military wagons manufactured according to Union army specifications.

No industry entirely escaped the impact of the war. Most, like ironmongering and wagonmaking, experienced inadequate but modest expansion. By 1863, at least four large flour mills had been erected in the Confederate Southwest. Two brass foundries, at least one big corn mill, one medicinal drug laboratory, a soap and candle factory, a plant for the mass production of haversacks and knapsacks, and numerous other enterprises—all of which were owned by private individuals, but most of which depended upon labor provided by detailed conscripts and impressed slaves—had also been established. The distilling industry may have been the one to suffer serious adversity because of the war. By the spring of 1863, fears that grain crops would be insufficient to prevent famine caused both Arkansas and Louisiana to prohibit the distillation of alcoholic beverages. Texans were saved from the same fate by their state's exceptionally rich corn and wheat harvests of early 1863.

None of the Trans-Mississippi's experiments in industrialization relieved the population from dependence upon home manufactures and ersatz goods. Not even the salt mines were prolific enough to satisfy every need; homemade soap was usually as soft as putty, since few families could spare the salt required to harden the bars. Most of the seven-dollar tins of "coffee" sold in the markets contained mixtures of peanuts, sweet potatoes, green beans, rye, okra seeds, chickory, or corn meal—anything but coffee! "Tea" normally consisted of sassafras, sage, or orange leaves. Medicinal oils came from pressed seeds and roots; artificial "quinine" was compounded of an extract of willow bark and red pepper paste. Chinaware, ironware, toothbrushes, nails, ink, glass, sewing needles, hospital supplies, drugs, and opiates were exceedingly scarce; candles, soap, slouch hats, bedding, and fine yarns were almost entirely homemade. And paper was virtually unobtainable. In early 1863, when most of the Southwest's newspapers disappeared and the remainder began using cheap tissue sheets or reprocessed scraps, advertisements suddenly appeared in the surviving newspapers urging readers to maintain a "rag bag," in which to collect old rags for sale to itinerant agents of a new Texas state paper mill. However, the Texas paper factory did not begin production until the early months of 1865. In the meantime, the military cartridge works at New Iberia used wallpaper to wrap powder, buck, and ball, and soldiers near Little Rock were issued cartridge papers fashioned from the musty documents in the Arkansas statehouse archives.[9]

The Department's ordnance stores were far too small to arm every soldier for field service, and its firearm and equipment industries were never able to produce all of the guns and accouterments needed by the troops. During the first few months of the war the states issued stocks of militia or captured Federal weapons to enlistees, but by the autumn of 1861 the armories were almost bare. The governors of Texas and Louisiana both informed Richmond that they could no longer arm men mustered into the Confederate army, while all the western governors asked volunteers to bring their own firearms to induction centers. In the spring of 1862, the Confederate Congress enacted a law requiring every volunteer or conscript to arm himself before reporting to rendezvous. Enrolling officers were authorized to buy the firearms brought in or to contract to pay each soldier a dollar per month rent for the use of his gun; weapons bought by the army were to be stamped with Ordnance Bureau markings and converted, if possible, into standard .58 caliber percussion-lock rifles. But by 1862, hundreds of enlistees who owned no weapons or who preferred to leave theirs at home were crowding into the camps of instruction.

As early as the summer of 1861 at least one Ordnance Bureau agent, Ballard S. Dunn, was roaming the Trans-Mississippi countryside in search of guns to buy. By June, 1862, Dunn was in charge of a small brigade of government sleuths looking for purchasable firearms. Among Dunn's competitors were the states of Texas and Arkansas, whose military boards floated bond issues to finance the purchase or importation of firearms, and whose agents offered citizens more money for their weapons than the Ordnance Bureau was prepared to pay. His competitors also included army officers who openly advertised for weapons or who seized what they wanted. By the spring of 1862 even General Holmes was willing to authorize desperate regimental commanders to impress firearms possessed by civilians. Holmes, the army's purchasing agents, and the states also attempted to import weapons from the eastern Confederacy and from Mexico, but most of the shipments received were disappointingly small. When all else failed, soldiers near the front lines could always obtain Springfields from the Union army. Waller's battalion rearmed itself by raiding Banks's depot at Bayou des Allemands; Marmaduke's troopers salvaged four hundred rifles from the battlefield at Prairie Grove; and most of the irregulars operating in Missouri and northern Arkansas depended exclusively upon Federal quartermasters for their weapons and ammunition.

The Southwest's armament industry was little more than a gesture toward self-sufficiency. Ammunition seems to have been plentiful enough, despite the early loss of the lead mines of southern Missouri, but the materials, facilities, machine tools, and craftsmen required to mass-produce rifles or to manufacture cannon were lacking. The capitulation of New Orleans cost the western Confederacy two cannon foundries, two saber and bayonet factories, a large Enfield rifle plant, and the most extensive complex of ammunition laboratories and percussion cap shops in the entire Mississippi basin. The residue of the Trans-Mississippi's armament industry was unable to compensate for this single disaster.

Government arsenals for the repair and fitting of cannon were first established at Little Rock, Camden, Arkadelphia, and San Antonio. By mid-1863 the deteriorating military situation in Arkansas compelled the removal of many of the facilities operating there to Shreveport, Marshall, and Tyler. In time, some of these arsenals managed to fashion occasional cannon, but almost all of these locally manufactured guns were brass or bronze smooth-bores, far less accurate or reliable than the iron rifles turned out by eastern plants. The state arsenal at Austin and private forges at Houston and Lavaca also produced a few light field guns each, but the state shops at New Iberia and in the Little Rock penitentiary were only able to construct the gun carriages and limbers for tubes cast elsewhere.

Throughout the war, the deficiencies of industry obliged the Department to resort to other methods to equip its cannoneers with artillery. The Val Verde Battery boasted a matched set of Union army twelve-pounders appropriated from the enemy during the New Mexico expedition. The Texas military board conducted a prolonged search for the "Twin Sisters," two howitzers used during the Texas Revolution—only to find the antiquated pieces parked in Louisiana, too rusty and aged for service. Both the states' military boards and the Ordnance Bureau went to extraordinary lengths to import guns from abroad, funding purchases by selling cotton. And in late 1863 General Magruder, finding himself short of artillery for the defense of the Texas coastline, authorized the organization of the only rocket battery ever mustered into the Confederate army. Captain John S. Greer's Texas Rocket Battery was to be supplied with ammunition and launching gear made in a special workshop attached to a small government arsenal at Galveston, but during a preliminary test of the first missiles produced the weapons misfired, precipitating a stampede among the official observers. Following this fiasco the remaining stocks of rockets were dumped into Galveston Bay, and Greer's battery was refitted with cannon.

Rifles, carbines, and revolvers were produced by most of the arsenals, particularly the ones at San Antonio and Austin, but a fair proportion of the total output of small arms was contributed by private gunsmiths. The largest private rifle works in the Department was Yarbrough, Biscoe, and Short's factory at Tyler, which contracted—but failed—to supply the army with 5,000 .54 and .57 caliber Enfield-pattern weapons; in the autumn of 1863, after this plant had been in operation for a year and a half, it was purchased by the Ordnance Bureau and converted into a government repair arsenal. The most important pistol manufacturer appears to have been Tucker, Sherrod, and Co., whose shops were located at Lancaster, Texas; the company specialized in the manufacture of Colt-type .36 and .44 caliber revolvers for the cavalry. But the typical Trans-Mississippi gunshops were much smaller than either of these two firms. The revolver shops at Columbia and Marshall, Texas, turned out one or two dozen pistols per week. Whitescarver and Campbell, of Rusk County, Texas, made about four smooth-bore muskets per day. Barney Paynter and Jesse Overton, master gunsmiths working in Arkansas, patiently bored and fitted one or two fine rifles each week.

As late as the autumn of 1863, the combined output of all the small-arms manufacturers in Kirby Smith's Confederacy was still less than 800 weapons per month, far too few to go around. In November, 1862, after receiving a shipment of 3,000 rifles from the East, General Holmes reported that he needed 10,000 more to arm every soldier in his command. Twice within the next month Governor Lubbock complained that the Texas Confederate and state regiments were short 15,-000 muskets; in desperation, he offered to accept consignments of damaged or obsolete weapons discarded by troops east of the Mississippi, if nothing better could be supplied. And in May, 1863, General Magruder advised the Ordnance Bureau that the Trans-Mississippi army urgently required 40,000 new small arms. But until the end of the war, the Department's soldiers continued to march into battle armed with an assortment of mismatched Springfields, Enfields, Austrian and Belgian muskets, shotguns, fowling pieces, squirrel guns, Kentucky long rifles, flintlock muskets, six-shooters, five-shooters, pepperbox derringers, dueling pistols, carbines, pikes, cutlasses, swords, sabers, and bowie knives.

This diversity created a nightmare for ordnance officers who had to supply ammunition. Commanders in Arkansas solved the problem by issuing gunpowder, buckshot, lead bricks, and paper to their troops, with orders for the men to mould their own balls and roll their own cartridges. When lead ran short, the soldiers substituted fragments of ironware, smooth stones, and pebbles. But elsewhere ammunition was mass-produced; and even in rebel Arkansas hundreds of women and adolescents spent their evenings sitting around their firesides measuring powder and wrapping loads. The ingredients for gunpowder were collected by agents of the War Department's Nitre and Mining Bureau, who advertised for charcoal, sulphur, and saltpeter, and who sent wagons into the countryside to gather the supplies offered for sale. Forests yielded charcoal, and sulphur was abundant; only saltpeter was relatively difficult to obtain. The most prolific saltpeter beds were located in the mountains of Pike, Polk, and Montgomery counties, Arkansas, and in the extensive bat caves near Fredericksburg, Texas, but a considerable amount was also extracted from the earthen floors of old smokehouses.

Every Trans-Mississippi arsenal, with the exception of the one at Shreveport, included a gunpowder mill, and the state of Texas incorporated a private company devoted exclusively to the production of gun- and blasting-powders. These mills compounded more than enough powder to keep the region's cartridge and cap works well supplied. Cartridges were mass-produced at most of the Confederate arsenals (the shop at San Antonio turned out 100,000 to 120,000 each month), by the Louisiana arsenal at New Iberia, and by four state factories in Texas, located at Austin (which claimed two), Houston, and San Antonio. The state shops at Austin, operating in the old Land Office and Supreme Court buildings on Capitol Square, wrapped 14,000 rounds per day. For the most part, this delicate work was done by women and teenage children, some of whom were only twelve years old. Percussion cap laboratories were also attached to the arsenals, including the one at Shreveport, where copper for the caps was salvaged from the wreckage of abandoned or collapsed buildings. However, one of the most productive cap factories in the Department was located in Gillespie County, Texas, where two inventive German mechanics designed and operated a completely automated, if somewhat primitive, cap assembly line. Their homemade machinery stamped, loaded, and packed more than enough percussion caps to supply all of the troops stationed in Indian Territory and along the Texas frontier.[10]

If many of the Trans-Mississippi Department's attempts to industrialize were feeble, the region's agricultural abundance at least assured its people a measure of security from famine. The Department never suffered from a shortage of livestock. An army commissary inspector journeying through Louisiana and Texas in 1863 reported cattle droves being moved along the major roads and vast herds grazing on the prairies. There were so many cows in Texas that on February 25, 1863, the state legislature suspended the operation of the stray laws and tacitly authorized anyone to appropriate unfenced or unbranded cattle for his own use. Down along the Rio Grande the Thirty-second Texas Cavalry fed itself almost entirely on beeves cut out of roving herds, giving impressment vouchers for them only when (and if) ranchers pressed claims. Sheep, swine, and domestic fowl were abundant; horses and mules were also plentiful. According to legislation enacted by the Confederate Congress, officers, cavalry troopers, and artillerymen were expected to provide not only their own small arms but also their own mounts and caisson teams, receiving in return forty cents a day in lieu of forage for each animal and full compensation for those killed in action. Unlike troopers east of the Mississippi, who often found it impossible to obtain remounts, the "yellowlegs" west of the river generally experienced little difficulty in securing replacement animals. Only twice —once during the early months of 1863 and again during the closing months of the war—did the combination of severe weather, hard campaigning, and the lack of sufficient fodder deplete the army's equine ranks. The quartermasters relieved the first shortage; peace relieved the second.

The vicissitudes of war almost obliterated Louisiana's sugar plantations, but the Trans-Mississippi's cotton remained an important cash staple until the very end, while grain and truck farming flourished. In 1862 and again in 1863, the Confederate Congress, hoping to extort a recognition from the foreign nations which traditionally consumed Southern cotton, passed resolutions urging planters to refrain from cultivating cotton. Congress also enacted laws restricting the exportation of cotton and authorizing the summary destruction of all staples in danger of capture by the enemy's armed forces. The President, on April 4, 1863, issued a complementary proclamation calling upon planters to convert their land to the production of foodstuffs. Although these laws and exhortations generated marked results east of the Mississippi, beyond the Great River too many profitable temptations discouraged full cooperation with the appeals of the general government. Arkansas, which had little to lose in any case, obligingly crippled cotton cultivation by levying an astronomical $30 tax on every bale; but Louisiana and Texas, which enjoyed relatively free access to the open markets of northern Mexico, were the only two Confederate states which failed to legislate limitations on the production of the staple. When, in early 1863, public sentiment demanding the legal restriction of cotton yields in favor of grain crops forced the Texas Senate to debate the matter, the Senators, doubtless influenced as much by strong rhetoric from the cotton counties as by the military board's commitments to pay for imported war matériel with cotton, rejected the proposed legislation by a vote of eighteen to ten.

Despite the absence of regulatory legislation, many Texas and West Louisiana planters did grow grain instead of cotton. By April, 1863, two-thirds of the East Texas cotton fields were sown in Indian corn, wheat, and other provision crops. Numerous fields bore mixed crops, three rows of cotton alternating with two of corn or sugar. Because of mild temperatures and heavy rains during the preceding autumn and winter, the Southwest's rich soil brought forth bountiful yields of wheat, corn, oats, barley, and rye in the spring of 1863. Only the extreme scarcity of agricultural labor threatened to ruin the harvest. Virtually every able-bodied white man under the age of forty years was either in the army or avoiding the draft, leaving none but the elderly, the children, the women, and the slaves to bring in the crops. Yet manpower was found in time to save the yield. Negroes from the coastal cotton plantations, or from refugee coffles driven into the interior to escape emancipation, were hired and put to work by upland farmers; regiments of soldiers were detailed to assist in the harvest; the Texas district court sitting at Dallas adjourned until September, to permit its officers and veniremen to go into the fields. As a result, "the labor of the planter and of the farmer was crowned with an abundant yield, and their barns were filled with a rich harvest."

But omens for the future were discouraging; the spring harvest of 1863 was to be the Confederate Southwest's last rich one. Yields in the frontier counties of West Texas had been notably poorer than those to the east, as the first effects of a great drought had begun to wither grain and parch the land. The district around Brownsville had recorded no measurable rainfall since May, 1862. As the drought rolled eastward during the last two years of the war, it would compound the Trans-Mississippi's distress by consuming, as ravenously as any marauding army could, the one essential resource without which no society can endure, food.[11]

IV   Any survey of the Trans-Mississippi Department's economy brings to light certain anomalies, which cannot be explained by means of piecemeal descriptions of the several industries composing the region's economic base. The Department suffered gluts of cotton and wool, increased its facilities for the production of textiles, and experienced no significant immigration or population growth—and yet soldiers and citizens were dressed in rags. Hides were easy to obtain and process, and conscript shoemakers did their best to shoe every enlistee, yet barefoot soldiers left bloody footprints wherever they marched. Salt was exported, although there was not enough to harden homemade soap. Texas claimed the only unblockaded border in the entire Confederacy, and the state's stores of cotton were more than sufficient to pay for imported war matériel, and yet the army stationed in the Southwest was probably the most poorly armed of all the rebel commands. There were more than five beeves for every Texan, white or black, but troops and civilians in Arkansas and on the western frontiers were reduced to hunting or thievery in order to survive. Most grain crops were bountiful, but Arkansas had to dole out grain to its inhabitants.

The common factor underlying these discrepancies was the dire deficiency of the Southwest's transportation. Not only was industry impaired by the wide dispersal of facilities, but in addition the exchange and the distribution of available produce and manufactures were immeasurably complicated by the region's lack of efficient delivery systems. The domestic transportation and communication networks of Kirby Smith's empire were little better than those of Frederick Barbarossa's.

Neither the riverboats nor the railroads contributed a great deal to the area's economic coherence. With the exception of the major tributaries of the Mississippi—the White, the Arkansas, the Ouachita, the Red, and the sugar country bayous—the western rivers were not interconnected. The Calcasieu, the Sabine, the Trinity, the Brazos, the Colorado, the Guadalupe, the Nueces, and the Rio Grande all rose in the interior highlands and flowed independently to the Gulf, interrupting instead of expediting the normal flow of domestic traffic. Riverboats plying the waters of Texas, which descended from the northwest toward the southeast, navigated across instead of along the state's interior commercial routes, which linked the northeast with the southwest. Furthermore, unlike the Cis-Mississippi's deep and serene waterways, the streams of the Trans-Mississippi were generally narrow, rapid, and shoal, and navigable for any distance only during seasons of high water. Opelousas, nominally a steamboat town, was sometimes accessible only by flat-bottomed rowboats. Shreveport was allegedly the head of navigation on the Red, but after the passage of the spring floods the rapids at Alexandria were seldom much more than three feet deep. Trinity River sometimes ran dry. The Rio Grande might have been the "great river" of Texas, but deep-sea merchantmen were seldom inclined to plow thirty miles upstream to Matamoros; most stood safely off the river's mouth and transferred their cargoes to lighters. And, finally, the Department's rivers were exposed to interdiction by the enemy. By the spring of 1863 the Mississippi, the White, the Lafourche, and the Atchafalaya were already lost. The mouths of the Teche and the Arkansas were controlled by Union garrisons, and the upper Arkansas was practically defenseless. The lower Ouachita and the lower Red were vulnerable to Federal gunboats. The Calcasieu, the Sabine, and the Texas rivers—other than the international Rio Grande—were blockaded, and because of the indefensibility of the Texas coastline virtually every waterway in the state was in danger of penetration by Union expeditionary forces. The wonder is that the Department's river systems were able to contribute anything to the war effort.

The same can be said for the railroads. The portion of the Trans-Mississippi still in Confederate control at the beginning of 1863 contained fifteen railroads, one in Arkansas, four in West Louisiana, and ten in Texas. The region's most complex network of track was that which radiated from Houston, linking Houston to Galveston, Harrisburg, Columbia, Alleyton (a ramshackle shantytown which happened to be the railhead of the Buffalo Bayou, Brazos, and Colorado when the war terminated its construction), Brenham, Millican, Hempstead, Beaumont, and Orange, a village on Louisiana's southwestern border. The miniscule Eastern Texas Railroad, straggling a few miles northward from Sabine City, was aimed toward Beaumont and a junction with the Texas and New Orleans trunk line between Houston and Orange, but after hostilities broke out the garrison at Sabine Pass appropriated its track to brace the Pass's fortifications. The only railroad west of Houston's network was the San Antonio and Mexican Gulf, which consisted of a twenty-seven-mile main line from Port Lavaca to Victoria, and a short spur to Indianola. In 1863 and 1864 General Magruder mined its rails to harden the fortifications protecting Matagorda Bay. East of Houston, the Texas and New Orleans was supposed to merge at Orange with Louisiana's New Orleans, Opelousas, and Great Western, but by 1861 the latter company claimed only eighty-eight miles of track from Algiers (opposite New Orleans) to Brashear City, plus a finished roadbed between Brashear and New Iberia.

Besides the Opelousas line, three other railroads pushed into the Department from the west bank of the Mississippi. To some degree, at least, all three were unusable. The short Baton Rouge, Grosse Tete, and Opelousas railway, leading from a point opposite Baton Rouge some twenty miles into the West Louisiana swamps, was both worthless as a transportation link and overrun by Federals. The eastern third of the Vicksburg, Shreveport, and Texas, whose sixty miles of track extended from De Soto (opposite Vicksburg) to Monroe, had been washed out by the spring floods of 1862 and then torn up by Grant's army; the Confederates continued to employ the forty miles of rails remaining between Bayou Maçon and Monroe. The road was intended to proceed westward from Monroe, but during the war the proposed hundred-mile segment between that place and Shreveport remained unbuilt. The Memphis and Little Rock in Arkansas ran from Hopefield (opposite Memphis) to Madison, was interrupted by the absence of rails between Madison and Devall's Bluff, and then continued on into North Little Rock. The Federals used the eastern third of the line, the rebels the western third, and neither side attempted to lay track across the no-man's-land in between.

The remainder of the Trans-Mississippi's railroads were pathetic fragments going nowhere. The Alexandria and Cheneyville wandered from Alexandria about ten miles due south. The Memphis, El Paso, and Pacific in northeastern Texas consisted of five miles of track proceeding southwesterly from Swanson's Landing on the upper Red into Marshall, and a like amount of track aiming eastward from Marshall toward Shreveport. The two branches of this railroad may have employed different gauges. Under Kirby Smith's direction, efforts were made to extend the eastbound branch all the way into Shreveport, by tearing up and repositioning the rails belonging to a neighboring Southern Pacific spur. But before the gap between Marshall and Shreveport could be closed, the Southern Pacific ran out of iron. The loss of the Southern Pacific's services worked no great hardship upon the Department, since that road's track meandered only thirty-five miles northward from its terminal at Jefferson, and its rolling stock included but two boxcars, one flatcar, and no locomotives. As long as the railroad was kept in operation, its three-car train was powered by teams of six oxen: the animals pulled the cars up ascending grades, and coasted downhill riding aboard the flatcar.

The Memphis and El Paso, the Mississippi Valley spurs, and the three lines torn up by the iron-hungry army were not the only systems to suffer from the war. Even the six companies which operated trains over the 345 miles of track feeding into Houston—the only complex which counted for much—experienced serious difficulties. Not one paid a dividend during the duration, and as early as 1862 the short Washington County Railroad, between Hempstead and Brenham, was in the hands of receivers. Most of the traffic carried by the roads was military, but after 1863 the army, unable to pay even its own soldiers, ceased to honor vouchers presented by the railroads. The lack of operating capital, among other factors, made it impossible for the companies to keep their roads in repair. By 1863, because of heavy use and poor maintenance, the roadbeds were settling, the light rails were compressing and spreading, ties and joints were splitting, locomotives were rapidly deteriorating, and cars were falling apart. It was impossible for the Texas system to obtain engines, rails, and spare parts, all of which were essential to the efficient operation of the roads.

Even if it had been possible to hold the lines together, they were not capable of carrying a great deal of traffic. The roads were all single-tracked; altogether, they covered less distance than Missouri's system; they employed at least three and perhaps four different gauges; they were not interconnected (all cargoes passing through the Houston hub had to be transferred by wagon from one train to another); and virtually all of the locomotives were "American" 4-4-0 engines, able to pull no more than fifteen 20,000-pound boxcars at no more than twenty-five miles per hour. By April, 1863, the Trans-Mississippi's steam engines were too decrepit to meet even these undemanding design specifications. In order to mount one steep grade on the Buffalo Bayou, Brazos, and Colorado line, an engine drawing only two passenger cars was obliged to descend the facing hillside at full throttle, shoot across a rickety trestle bridge, and rocket up the forbidding incline itself, in hopes that the combination of steam power, momentum, and luck could overcome the slope.[12]

Because of the inadequacy of the Trans-Mississippi's steam transportation systems, most overland movement depended upon the region's mediocre network of unpaved roads. The roads of Arkansas, West Louisiana, and the northern Indian Territory were little more than supplementary tributaries designed to carry freight to and from convenient riverboat landings. All-weather turnpikes were rare even in the major river valleys, and nonexistent in the mountainous country of Arkansas, in West Louisiana's many marshy lowlands, and in the sparsely populated areas of southwestern Louisiana and the western Nations. Except for a complex of roads along the Shreveport-Marshall axis, there were no well-developed overland links binding together the road networks of the Mississippi Basin and East Texas. The East Texas web, including the important road junctions at Doaksville and Boggy Depot in the

Choctaw Nation, was the most coherent in the Department. Its focus was Houston, and it embraced the portion of the state bounded, roughly, by Corpus Christi, San Antonio, Austin, Dallas, Clarksville, and the Choctaw towns. But although the flat terrain and disoriented rivers of East Texas encouraged the construction of roads, the state's country court system of government, which relegated responsibility for the building and maintenance of roads to the county commissions, almost ensured that the roads built would be hardly better than cowpaths. Traffic always moved over them at a snail's pace. Although at least one express wagon train recorded an average speed of five miles per day, freighters usually expected any hundred-mile journey to consume thirty days. Passenger coaches operating on the best intercity routes occasionally careened along at ten miles per hour, but such speed was not the norm.

Beyond East Texas, roads were scarce. The old Butterfield Overland Mail Route constituted the primary link from East Texas to Franklin (El Paso) and the Far West, while below the Houston railroad complex only three major trails led all the way to the Rio Grande. The river crossings between Brownsville and Eagle Pass were connected by a transverse trail paralleling the northern bank of the Rio Grande, the Great River Road. Except for the Butterfield Route and segments of an old military road south of San Patricio, none of these frontier trails were well marked; teamsters simply drove their vehicles from one water hole to the next, without bothering to follow the ruts left by the wagons which went before them.

Although some light two- and four-wheel carts were used, most freight was carried in heavy wagons drawn by ten oxen or six mules. The largest road vehicles were huge sixteen- and twenty-four-oxen trucks introduced shortly before the war for the purpose of hauling baled cotton. The Union blockade effected a drastic reorientation of freight patterns by forcing the bulk of commercial traffic to be diverted toward the Rio Grande, over routes unprepared to accept it. By the middle of the war, there were "cotton roads in every direction" below Alleyton, Gonzales, and San Antonio.

In good weather, a cargo train staging from San Antonio could reach the Rio Grande in six to eight weeks, but several months were required for wagons to plod from interior terminals to the bordertown markets. In the desert country below the Nueces River, thirst, heat, dust, and often hunger caused much suffering among men and teams; the carcasses of hundreds of dead draft animals, grim reminders of the heavy toll taken by the climate and overwork, polluted the atmosphere near the major water holes. Even those trains which escaped the hazards of desert travel were not safe until they reached the security of their destinations. Bands of Indians and highwaymen often attempted to stampede mules corralled for the night, while along the Rio Grande wagons were in constant danger from raiding Mexican bandits and expatriate Texan Unionists.

Considering the difficulties faced by long-haul teamsters, they commanded exorbitant wages. In February, 1863, cotton speculators paid teamsters $9 per week plus ox feed, while army quartermasters were willing to offer $5 per week, rations, forage, and exemption from the draft. In May the army raised its own pay scale to $40 per month (Confederate), and ordered civilian shipping contractors to pay the army rate. Nonetheless, wagoneers were reluctant to sign on. The army had to detail conscripts to drive cargo trucks for a number of civilian commercial firms.

Stagecoach lines provided passenger service to most of the towns beyond the reach of steamboats or the Houston railroad net. Sawyer, Risher, and Hall, employing three hundred men and a hundred animals, operated fifteen lines in Texas alone. The routes crisscrossed in such a way that travelers could journey with reasonable speed through any of the more densely populated areas of the Department. About halfway through the war West Texas even experienced a mild stagecoach boom, as the growing importance of the Rio Grande trade necessitated the improvement of communications between East Texas and the border. During a single week in May, 1863, two new lines began service to Brownsville. But a man who really wanted to go somewhere with any haste still had to rely upon his own horse.

Among those who had to ride horseback were the army's staff couriers, upon whom the military communication and intelligence systems of the Department depended. In April, 1863, when Kirby Smith settled at Shreveport, no telegraph wires had yet been strung between that town and the district headquarters at Little Rock, Alexandria, and Houston. A courier dispatched from Shreveport could reach Alexan-

dria, the most proximate subordinate headquarters, in two or three days
—hence most of the mail addressed to Taylor probably went by steamboat. Little Rock and Houston were three or four days distant and inaccessible by riverboat; however, communications sent to Holmes or
Magruder could be carried part way by the few strands of electric wire
strung in the Arkansas Valley and East Texas. Smith immediately initiated construction of a telegraphic net and established courier relay stations along the major overland routes. In order to conserve manpower,
he authorized the enlistment of six companies of adolescent boys, aged
from thirteen to fifteen years, to serve as cavalry couriers. Although
work on the telegraph was pressed with vigor, it proved necessary to
keep these boys in the saddle until the end of the war.

  If Smith had trouble communicating with his generals, ordinary
citizens had even more when trying to communicate with each other or
with the boys at the front. Many old mail routes had been abandoned;
many others had been interdicted by enemy forces; those still in use
were often maddeningly roundabout; the mail seldom moved with expedition; and snow, sleet, hail, rain, dark of night, deserts, mountains, and
flooded rivers all conspired to frustrate the Post Office's best intentions.
Military organizations far from home ordinarily appointed civilians or
furloughed soldiers to collect and transmit their mail. Yet even these
couriers were stayed from their appointed rounds. In February, 1864, a
demoralized Texas Reb on duty in Louisiana complained to his wife:

> I have to begin with the same old tale—"The Last letter I have from you
> bears date Decr 13 & 14th [."] I was sadly disappointed on yesterday when
> the mail came and brought me no letter. . . . Your last letter was a good
> one but at the close you say "I hope I can do better when I get a letter to
> answer[."] I have sent you *five* letters since then. . . . Suppose you write
> me a letter anyhow, send it along whether it is a "good" one or not—.[13]

⚜ **V**   Most Trans-Mississippians still tried to observe the amenities
of civilized life. In June, 1862, D. E. Anderson, an itinerant school-
teacher, contracted to teach twenty weeks' worth of "Orthography,
Reading, Writing, Arithmetic, Geography, Grammar and Philosophy"
to twenty-five young scholars of Rusk County, Texas, at ten dollars a
head. In October, 1862, the Parsons Female College, twelve miles east

of Austin, advertised for a principal and a music teacher—"A gentleman whose wife teaches music will be preferred." Early in May, 1863, San Antonio's burgeoning plutocracy held a high-society supper party in the dining room of the fashionable Menager Hotel. A month later, the Presbyterian ladies of Clarksville entertained themselves with a dinner, a concert, and tableaux.[14] The August 21 issue of the *Houston Telegraph* announced that the Reverend D. Hutchison's Academy and the Catholic Young Ladies' Convent School would soon open their doors for the fall term, while five months' tuition at the Chappell Hill Female College would be $75 (Confederate), plus $75 for music lessons and $200 for board—all to be paid in advance. And the May 9 edition of the *San Antonio Herald* carried a reassuring description of the local Female College's annual examination day. The pupils "gave a concert and exhibition, consisting of music vocal and instrumental, dialogues and monologues. Specimens of paintings were also exhibited."

Yet no one could blot out the war. The alleys and lots of Houston, once a pretty town of brick and shingle, were crowded with the ugly shanties of ragged refugees. The poor were everywhere. The ladies of Dallas gave benefit suppers to aid them. The Clarksville *Standard* castigated farmers who were too selfish to donate surplus grain to them. Indian Territory and western Arkansas, where bread crops had been destroyed by the armies or left to rot, were populated with them. And the *Houston Telegraph* urged its subscribers to ostracize and blacklist wealthy planters who refused to aid them.

Like the poor, the death lists published in the papers and the proliferation of military hospitals were also grim reminders of war. The army's Medical Bureau maintained general hospitals at Little Rock, Shreveport, Galveston, and Houston, but by 1863 these institutions were far too inadequate to house all the men maimed in battle or ravaged by epidemics of smallpox and yellow fever. Louisiana was obliged to appropriate $100,000 to subsidize state hospitals at New Iberia, Natchitoches, and Monroe; a number of Texas counties converted hotels and inns into convalescent homes; and in Texas and Arkansas both the state governments and local military commanders tried to support extensive field hospitals. Citizens living within earshot of any of these facilities doubtless spent many a sleepless night listening to shrieking men.

The prisoner-of-war camps scattered about the "safe" areas of Texas were as dismal as the hospitals. Near Houston's railroad yards, four long rows of dingy cowsheds, guarded by trigger-happy militiamen, housed more than a thousand bluecoats. On the far West Texas frontier, near Camp Verde, six hundred emaciated and sun-baked captives squatted at the bottom of "prison gully," a muddy pit nestled in a box canyon. The most extensive military prison in the Department was Camp Ford, some four miles northeast of Tyler. In early 1863 the camp's facilities consisted of one guardhouse and a few bare sandhills watered by a single creek. Prisoners who wanted to shelter themselves from the bitter Texas winter winds had to dig their own "shebangs," foxholes or caves covered over with boards and split rails. In spite of the camp's lax security and the humane moderation of the prison commandant, Colonel R. T. P. Allen, few inmates attempted to escape, either because of apathy or because lone Yankees in the middle of East Texas had nowhere to go. Later on, as campaigns in Arkansas and West Louisiana brought in whole regiments of prisoners, ten acres were enclosed by an eighteen-foot-high log stockade and a thirty-foot-wide "dead line"; a more militant commandant and a pack of slavers' bloodhounds were assigned to the post; but nothing was done to provide the inmates with housing. By mid-1864, these ten desolate acres were populated by six thousand wretched souls.

Under the tensions and anxieties of wartime life, men were brutalized, and tempted to place their own interests before those of the community. Speculators were only the most ostentatious examples. One Shreveport editor devoted two lengthy and impassioned editorials to arguments in favor of exempting editors from the draft. The *Houston Telegraph,* railing against the way in which the conscript laws required common farmers to wage war for the benefit of exempted wealthy slaveowners, charged that the planters were selfishly "fattening on the blood and flesh of the brave soldiers who are fighting, bleeding, dying, to defend them and their property." Senator Williamson S. Oldham complained that innumerable army officers were expropriating impressed slaves assigned to labor gangs for use as personal body servants, without offering just compensation to their owners.[15]

Crime was rampant, especially in western Texas, "where it was the rule to take a man's life if only any kind of a pretext could be found for so doing. I never heard of anything like it, except perhaps in the French Revolution." Bandits took possession of the main highway between Fredericksburg and Austin, levied harsh tolls on everyone trying to use it, and killed those who declined to pay. Even in Houston, "the amount of burglary and thieving of late . . . calls loudly for something to be done. Thousands of dollars have been stolen. Dozens of houses have been entered. . . . More of this kind of thing has been done in the last month [May, 1862], than in two years before." By early 1864, lawlessness had engulfed so much of rebel Arkansas that the panicky legislature retaliated with a savage punitive code, extending the death penalty to every crime from murder, rape, horse- and Negro-stealing to the subornation to commit perjury, the forcing of a woman to marry, and the administration of aphrodisiacs with immoral intent.

Nor were the Arkansas legislators the only ones affected by the prevailing mood of rumor and hysteria. On March 5, 1863—at a time when there was not one Union squad under arms between the Sabine River and the Davis Mountains—the Texas legislature, trembling at the thought of slave insurrection, threatened any Federal officer who enlisted Negro troops in the state with fifteen years' confinement at Huntsville. Three months later, Louisiana condemned to death any ex-slave captured while bearing arms against the Confederacy. The Clarksville *Standard* had already warned its readers that "emissaries from Northern State prisons, are at large through the South. Every man who comes into our country, unless he can give satisfactory evidence of his good standing as a southern man, should be dealt with, without hesitation." Down in San Antonio, Asa Mitchell and his Minute Men took the *Standard* at its word and pressed their campaign to impose the law and the commandments upon persons tainted by un-Confederate activities. The trees around the Alamo Plaza were often weighed down by swinging corpses. A slave woman—a freight teamster!—who "doesn't like San Antonio at all" complained to a traveler that there was " 'too much hanging and murdering for me. . . .' She had seen a man hanged in the middle of the day, just in front of her door." [16]

Nothing exemplifies the populace's disaffection more eloquently than its hostile response to conscription. The principle of conscription was itself alien to the mind of the Southern yeoman, especially since the Confederacy's conscription laws seemed framed so as to make poor men fight a rich man's war. Moreover, the ways in which the laws were enforced did nothing to enhance their popularity. It was bad enough that militia and cavalry were used to hunt down recusants; what was worse was that recruiters and medical examiners treated cooperative enrollees like cattle. One irate citizen protested to the Secretary of War that "various commissions were given to Tom, Dick, and Harry" to raise troops. "Some were brainless upstarts and others notorious drunkards. . . . Have you all gone crazy about Richmond? . . . Above all things, have the moral courage to do your duty, and to get rid of incompetent, inefficient, and drunken officers and worthless surgeons, who in many instances are brutes and a disgrace to the Army." Congressman Malcolm D. Graham of Texas complained in particular about the arbitrary zeal of conscript officers, who refused to leave citizens in peace. He said that many of his constituents, "after being discharged on examination for *permanent* disability, to serve in the field, have again & again [been] required to enroll themselves, and [are] as often discharged." But neither voters nor politicians could reform the system. In June, 1864, a year and a half after Graham submitted his protest, a regimental surgeon serving near Alexandria complained to his wife:

The Conscript Board in Texas is doing things up in magnificent style—they are sending us men who are totally unfit for any kind of duty—Six have been rejected & sent back home from this Brigade in the last week—we discharged a man from this Regt. on the 26th of last *March* for Consumption —they conscripted him & sent him back to us—The [regimental medical] Board met at my tent this morning & we sent him back home again. If they would let the blind, the halt, the lame, the deaf & dumb stay at home & send those fat rascals around towns, who are eternally hunting up details they would do much better—[17]

Even conscripts healthy enough to shoulder muskets found their introductions to army life unpleasant. Arms, pay, tents, and uniforms were lacking. Officers competent to drill recruits were scarce. State commissaries were unable, and Confederate commissaries refused, to feed enlistees between the time they reported to camps of instruction and the time they were sworn into regiments, an interval which might consume weeks. Finally, to many conscripts it seemed foolish to march farmers away from home only to import other displaced farmers to defend the homesteads of the men marched away.

Once in the army, many conscripts did their best to get out. Some wrote to their congressmen. Others sued for writs of habeas corpus, arguing that the draft unconstitutionally denied their personal freedom. But because legal avenues of escape were usually obstructed, Private John Munn, Private Alexander Thomas, and thousands of others like them simply left the ranks. The epidemic of widespread desertion, which first infected the Trans-Mississippi army late in 1862, never abated. At times, the army and the militias made vigorous attempts to pursue and round up the deserters, but as often as not the armed deserters in a given district outnumbered the troops sent after them, and were able to drive away their pursuers. In Angelina County, Texas, an organized band of deserters ambushed and scattered a squadron of militia cavalry. Sixty deserters in Wood County, a hundred in Van Zandt County, and four hundred in Louisiana's Union Parish offered similar resistance to regular Confederate troopers. A large band of conscripts and fugitive slaves fortified and held the "Big Thicket" badlands near the San Jacinto River. Hundreds more hid away in the chaparral wilderness below the Nueces, waiting for opportunities to slip into Mexico. When, in the fall of 1863, the Frontier Regiment began to harass deserters who fled beyond the line of settlement, the fugitives responded by kidnapping squads of recruits en route to join the regiment. In October, 1863, General Henry W. Allen, soon to become rebel Louisiana's next governor, reported that the country below Alexandria was "full of deserters and runaway conscripts. . . . I am told they number 8,000—a terrible state of affairs." In northwestern Texas, some 1,400 recusants held off two small brigades of Confederate cavalry and a brigade of Texas militia. General Henry McCulloch was finally obliged to grant a general amnesty to absentees willing to live in peace and to enroll in home defense units. About 650 came out of hiding to take advantage of McCulloch's offer.[18]

Organized deserters were not the only insurrectionaries in the Trans-Mississippi states. In northwestern Arkansas, 130 members of a Unionist "Peace and Constitutional Society" were arrested by secessionist officials in December, 1861, but the society continued to flourish throughout the rebel portion of the state. In April, 1862, Governor Moore acknowledged that Unionist conspirators in Natchitoches and Sabine parishes were known to be plotting an uprising. Texans of Mexican extraction showed little love for the South; most of them did their best to evade military service, and not a few of them fled across the Rio Grande to enlist in companies of Unionist or bandit raiders. John Warren Hunter, himself a Texas Unionist, admitted the existence of numerous seditious cells in the populous Anglo-Saxon districts of East Texas. And during the latter half of 1862, the authorities in Texas twice found it necessary to put down armed rebellions.

The first of these uprisings involved some of the German-American inhabitants of Comal, Kendall, Gillespie, Kerr, Medina, and Bexar counties, between the towns of Fredericksburg (Gillespie) and San Antonio (Bexar). The Germans who had emigrated to this area were hostile to slavery and to disunion, and felt little affinity for the Confederate States. In 1861, determined to protect their interests and maintain their neutrality, a number of these citizens formed a "Union Loyal League," and announced their intention to avoid both sedition against Texas and commitment to the rebel war effort. But in the spring of 1862, conscript officers appeared in their communities and began drafting their youth into the army. On July 4, 1862, after protests and petitions failed to secure exemptions for the German boys, five hundred League members met on Bear Creek in Gillespie County, organized and armed three "militia" companies, and elected a "civil" executive and four military officers, three captains and "Major" Fritz Tegener. The avowed objective of the militia was to defend the German settlers from both marauding Indians and recruiting details.

General Hamilton Bee, commanding the Western Subdistrict of Texas, declared the six German counties to be in rebellion. He appointed Captain James Duff provost marshal for the region and dispatched him to Fredericksburg, with orders to put down the insurrection at all costs. Duff, himself a hard-bitten frontiersman, brought with him four companies of the tough Fourteenth Texas Cavalry Battalion, an outfit which never took prisoners.

As soon as Duff reached Fredericksburg, he imposed martial law and began to hang suspects rounded up by his troopers. Hundreds of Germans fled into the western wilderness, and some eighty militiamen, under Major Tegener, tried to escape to Mexico. On August 9, 1862, Tegener's men pitched camp on the west bank of the Nueces, about twenty miles from Fort Clark. At dawn on the 10th, ninety-four of

Duff's cavalrymen, commanded by Lieutenant C. D. McRae, stormed the German encampment, killed nineteen of the militiamen, wounded nine, and scattered the rest. The nine wounded Germans surrendered and were murdered; McRae reported "no prisoners." Six of the escapees were killed on October 18, as they attempted to cross the Rio Grande; eleven later joined the First Texas Cavalry (Union); and the remainder disappeared.

The Nueces massacre precipitated further disaffection among the German citizens of Texas. In the towns of the six rebellious counties Unionists paraded in the streets, sang Yankee battle songs, incited riots, and threatened revolution. In the neighboring counties of Fayette, Colorado, Washington, Austin, and Lavaca, the Germans held mass meetings, protested the enforcement of the conscription acts, and manhandled recruiters—the terrified enrolling officer for Austin County, A. J. Bell, informed his superiors that he was in dire need of a company of regulars to protect him for the citizenry.

In early 1863, both General Magruder and Governor Lubbock took steps to pacify the region. Magruder extended martial law into Fayette, Colorado, and Austin counties, and moved Sibley's brigade into the district. Sibley's troopers arrested a number of leading troublemakers, but were unable to quiet the disturbances. Lubbock was finally forced to excuse neutralist Germans from the draft and to permit them to form their own local home defense organizations. But until the end of the war, the Texas Germans continued to show hostility toward the Confederate States. Subsequent Federal attempts to occupy portions of the Texas coastline were partially encouraged by the expectations of Northern officials that, given a chance, the state's 20,000 German citizens would rally en masse to the Union flag.

The second Texas uprising, far less successful but far more bloody, occurred almost simultaneously in several northwestern Red River border counties. This area had been partially populated by displaced Northerners, who detested slavery and who cared little about states' rights. A secret organization, composed of more than 1,800 Unionists, neutralists, and skulkers, hatched a plot to raise an army, to seize Confederate stores, and to march to the Union lines in Kansas, cutting a trail of desolation through the Indian Nations. The conspiracy was first uncovered in Cooke County, when one of the participants revealed both the plan and the names of many of the men involved to the Confederate garrison commander at Gainesville. The names were made public, and an infuriated mob of rebel sympathizers lynched twenty-five of the suspects before the military and civil authorities bothered to arrest the others.

One hundred fifty Cooke County citizens were charged with treason and insurrection against the state, and were brought to trial before the county court. During the trial, several hundred spectators kept the courtroom in turmoil by shouting demands for a mass hanging. One of the jurors later acknowledged that the mob's shouts probably influenced the jury as much as the evidence did. Of the hundred fifty tried, the jury sent fifty-five to the gallows. Wise County executed five conspirators, and Grayson County's jurors condemned forty (Grayson's justices commuted thirty-nine of the sentences). In Denton County nobody was hanged, but an enraged "Secesh" invaded the county jail and shot one of the accused to death.[19]

Though many of the more formidable threats to the Trans-Mississippi's internal security had been suppressed by early 1863, an undercurrent of resentment, disaffection, and demoralization remained, eroding and dissipating the western Confederacy's will to fight. Between November, 1862, and February, 1864, all three Trans-Mississippi legislatures considered it necessary to enact stringent sanctions against those who gave aid or comfort to the enemy. A man who traveled through Texas during the latter half of 1863 reported that disloyalty was rife throughout the state, and that there were at least four or five thousand armed men hiding away in the "brush," hoping for the arrival of a Federal army of liberation. In October, 1863, General Allen of Louisiana informed the Secretary of War that "things over here look gloomy . . . and the people are desponding—very desponding." The conditions in the Nations, according to General Steele, were "so truly discouraging" that they "dispirit the troops and depress the minds of the people." A War Department inspector journeying through Arkansas and northern Louisiana advised Adjutant General Samuel Cooper that "the condition and temper of the people were very unsatisfactory. Great dissatisfaction prevailed in many sections, and generally among the mass our success [was] deemed almost a matter of indifference, and in many localities the advent of the enemy would be hailed as a relief." In July, 1863,

President Davis asked Kirby Smith whether there was any substance to the rumor that the Trans-Mississippi Department might secede from the Confederate States.

But the common folk were tired of fighting; they simply wanted the boys to come home. On February 27, 1863, Private Edwin Floyd's wife described the despair and sorrows of her neighbors in a letter to her soldier husband:

The case has been going very hard with Jimmy and Mrs Harrel since Frank went away and it will still be worse as he is dead. Sarah says she had rather have heard that the north had conquered us and that we had been compelled to surrender than to have heard of Franks death. Billy Howell is dead, and I hear today that Mose Ray and Jim Michael are dead. . . . Alick Pegnes is dead. . . . We have had no mails much since Christmas.

And two days later Mrs. Mary Maverick, who gave four sons to the rebel army, allowed her eldest to see the anguish in her own soul. "I have heard nothing from Sam. Oh how I hope this bloody war is over, and my darlings all coming home once more." [20]

CHAPTER THREE

THE LOSS OF THE
MISSISSIPPI VALLEY

By March, 1863, the forces in northern Arkansas were already engaged in heavy skirmishing, feeling out one another's dispositions. Marmaduke's scouts were ranging into Missouri, surveying the prospects for another cavalry raid; bluecoats from Helena and Milliken's Bend were nervously jabbing at the butternut pickets below Pine Bluff, trying to keep the Rebs off balance while Grant devised another way to steal a march toward Vicksburg; Porter's gunboats were massing for a rush into the Confederate Mississippi; the Federals in the Lafourche country were stripping the neighborhood of supplies, in anticipation of another offensive; and Banks, under vague instructions to cooperate with Grant, was wondering whether his orders were flexible enough to justify a thrust into the Red River Valley's rich land of cotton.

Except along the Arkansas front, where Holmes and Marmaduke still enjoyed a measure of initiative, the Trans-Mississippi rebels were on the defensive. Taylor, in particular, was too busy trying to materialize an army to indulge in dreams of conquest. With only 9,000 soldiers to garrison and defend his entire District, he could afford to concentrate no more than 4,000 on the lower Atchafalaya and Teche, hardly enough to contain a determined enemy force moving northward from Brashear City. Governor Moore attempted to reinforce Taylor by raising a few companies of local militia, while Lubbock and Magruder did their best to round up the many absentees from Taylor's army who had straggled over to East Texas, but these token efforts to fill Taylor's thin ranks produced very few additional fighting men. In late March, as the sharp intensification of Federal activity near Brashear City advertised Banks's decision to stage an offensive from that place, Taylor had no choice but to make do with the few troops at his disposal.

Realizing that Banks, like Weitzel before him, could not safely advance up the Atchafalaya without first occupying the lower Teche, Taylor gathered the bulk of his disposable force in the vicinity of Fort Bisland. Mouton's Louisiana infantry brigade and three field batteries were entrenched before the fort itself, adding their firepower to that of the fort's two heavy guns. Since the fort's left flank could be turned by an amphibious expedition operating on Grand Lake, Colonel James Reily's Fourth Texas Cavalry (Sibley's brigade), Colonel William Vincent's Second Louisiana Cavalry, and a section of artillery were posted behind and to the left of the main battle line, on the lakeshore at Hutchin's Point. The garrison manning the two heavy guns at Fort Benton was left in place and reinforced by the gunboat *Queen of the West,* which steamed down the Atchafalaya from the Red.

In late March General Banks made a small contribution to Taylor's defenses by sending the tinclad *Diana* poking up the Teche. Taylor's Texans seized the vessel before the Federals aboard could scuttle her; she was swung about and moored at the center of the Confederate line; and cannoneers were detailed to serve her three pieces, a thirty-pounder Parrott and two ten-pounder rifles. But the acquisition of the *Diana* gave Taylor no illusions about the impregnability of his position. Staff couriers were dispatched to New Iberia, with orders directing the immediate evacuation of machinery, army stores, and other military property from the town.

The *Diana* changed hands on March 28. During the next two weeks General Banks slowly completed the assembly of a field army of 16,000 men in the neighborhood of Brashear City. Finally, on April 12, 12,000 bluecoats, under the command of Generals Emory and Weitzel, crossed Berwick's Bay and slogged up the Teche's muddy banks toward the rebel stronghold at Fort Bisland. Well before nightfall the Federals had swept aside Taylor's vedettes, had planted artillery within range of the fort, and had opened a bombardment of the Confederate works. The shelling slackened at dusk, but was renewed with increasing vigor the following day. The *Diana* and a section of the Val Verde Battery were temporarily knocked out of action, and Mouton's Louisiana conscripts, thrown into disarray by the shot and shell pulverizing their breastworks, began breaking toward the rear.

At 4:30 P.M., April 13, Federal infantry attempted to storm the grayback line. A veteran rebel sergeant noted "the quick keen crack of our sharp-shooters[' and] then that of skirmishers['] rifles," as the Union foot soldiers, maneuvering behind a thin cavalry screen, came within small-arms range. A few moments later "the grave yard sound of the minnie bullets as they flew hissing over our head, re-assured us that they were coming. 'Here they come,' was shouted down our line as our skirmishers came running in and jumping over the works." As the bombardment lifted and the Union cavalry wheeled away, the Federal battle line emerged from the cover of an opposing wood and stepped off toward the waiting rebels. But the advance stalled on open ground, as Confederate fire chopped down whole platoons of men. The action, reduced to a fire fight, closed at dark, after the "Yankees had danced to our music for two and a half long hours, and finely [*sic*] were compelled to retreat without accomplishing any thing." The Texas sergeant, somewhat disappointed by the affair, complained that the Federals "didn't half try, as they did not come nigher than sixty yards of our works."

Taylor won the battle, but Banks won the day. Performing exactly as Taylor had anticipated, Banks had embarked an additional 4,000 troops aboard transports and had sent them into Grand Lake. Their commander, General Grover, had been ordered to occupy Fort Benton and to turn Taylor's left flank. On April 13 and 14 a small detachment of Grover's force, accompanied by a flotilla of tinclads, hammered Fort Benton to rubble, destroyed the *Queen of the West,* and opened navigation of the Atchafalaya to the Union fleet. Meanwhile, on the evening of the 13th, the bulk of Grover's division swarmed ashore at Hutchin's Point, shattered the two small regiments holding the beachhead, and drove the Confederates inland toward the village of Franklin.

At 9:00 P.M., April 13, Colonel Reily galloped down to Taylor's headquarters to warn him of the disaster. Taylor ordered Reily to hold Franklin at all costs, since the village sat astride the army's sole line of escape to New Iberia. Reily galloped back to Franklin, gathered the remnants of the Second Louisiana and Fourth Texas, threw up a triple line of earthworks, and dug in for a last-ditch stand.

While Reily held Grover away from Franklin, Taylor, under cover of the night and the rain, successfully disengaged Mouton's and Sibley's brigades, evacuated Fort Bisland, and pushed his wet and weary men toward New Iberia and safety. The initial portion of Taylor's retreat was shielded by the *Diana,* in what may well be a unique instance of a steamboat acting as an army's rear guard. Unfortunately the boat ran aground in the dark, and was recaptured by the pursuing Federals. Nevertheless, the *Diana* and Reily's command earned Taylor the time he needed to extract his army from Banks's trap. Taylor managed to carry off not only his soldiers but also his trains, his stores, and all but three of his cannon. Reily was killed, Vincent was wounded, and their commands were roughly handled; but because of their determination the point of Banks's battered columns did not reach Franklin until half an hour after the last retreating Johnny passed through.[1]

Above New Iberia the earth rises into a firm, flat, broad prairie, ground which offers a retreating army no good defensive positions. Taylor had no choice but to continue his withdrawal all the way to the lower Red River Valley, even though this meant the abandonment of the southern third of his district. The retreat was hard. Hunger, homesickness, the lack of forage for the army's animals, the demoralizing mood of defeat, the constant presence of Union cavalry hovering just beyond artillery range, the mounting casualty tolls produced by senseless little skirmishes at nameless little places, and the notorious ill discipline of both Mouton's conscripts and Sibley's frontier veterans all ate away at the army's strength. So many of Sibley's troopers straggled that Taylor, short-tempered enough under normal circumstances, "but noisy on retreats, with a tendency to cuss mules and wagons which stall in the road," ungracefully removed the equally irascible Sibley from command. "Big fish eat little fish," the Texas sergeant observed.

Colonel Thomas Green, the Texas brigade's ranking survivor, was selected as Sibley's successor. Yet not even Green, who was soon to prove himself an excellent field commander, was able to keep his boys from dropping away. When the army passed through Opelousas, Taylor, hoping to salvage whatever remained of the brigade, detached it from the main force and temporarily consigned it to the care of General

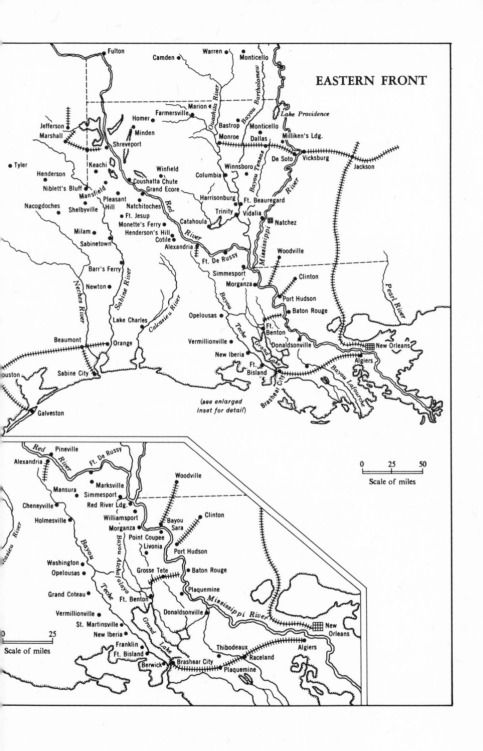

EASTERN FRONT

Fulton
Camden
Warren
Monticello

Marion
Farmersville
Homer
Bastrop
Monticello
Lake Providence

Jefferson
Marshall
Minden
Monroe
Dallas
Milliken's Ldg.

Shreveport

De Soto
Vicksburg

Tyler
Keachi
Winfield
Winnsboro
Jackson

Henderson
Columbia

Niblett's Bluff
Coushatta Chute
Grand Ecore

Mansfield
Pleasant
Hill
Natchitoches
Harrisonburg
Ft. Beauregard

Nacogdoches
Shelbyville
Ft. Jesup
Trinity
Vidalia

Milam
Monette's Ferry
Henderson's Hill
Catahoula
Natchez

Sabinetown
Cotile
Alexandria

Barr's Ferry
Ft. De Russy
Woodville

Newton
Simmesport
Morganza
Clinton

Lake Charles
Port Hudson

Beaumont
Opelousas
Baton Rouge

Orange
Vermillionville
Ft. Benton
Donaldsonville
New Orleans

New Iberia
Algiers

Sabine City
Ft. Bisland
Brashear City

Galveston
(see enlarged
inset for detail)

Houston

Red
Pineville

Alexandria
Ft. De Russy

Marksville
Woodville

Mansura
Simmesport

Cheneyville
Red River Ldg.

Holmesville
Williamsport
Bayou
Sara
Clinton

Morganza
Point Coupee
Livonia
Port Hudson

Washington
Grosse Tete
Baton Rouge

Opelousas

Grand Coteau
Ft. Benton
Plaquemine

Vermillionville
Donaldsonville

St. Martinsville

New Iberia
New
Orleans

Franklin
Thibodeaux
Algiers

Scale of miles
Ft. Bisland
Berwick
Brashear City
Raceland
Plaquemine

0   25   50
Scale of miles

0   25
Scale of miles

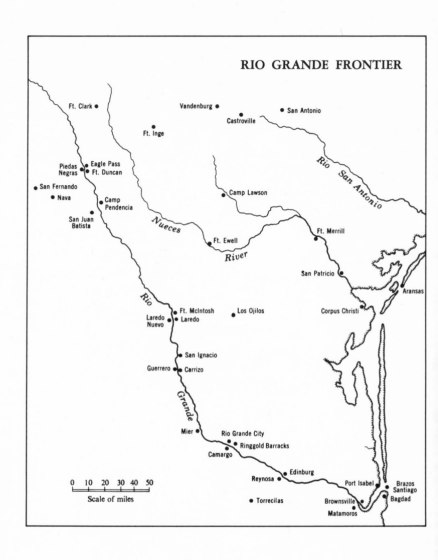

RIO GRANDE FRONTIER

Ft. Clark ●

Vandenburg ●

San Antonio ●

Castroville ●

Ft. Inge ●

Rio San Antonio

Piedras Negras ●
Eagle Pass ●
Ft. Duncan ●

San Fernando ●

Nava ●

Camp Pendencia ●

Camp Lawson ●

San Juan Batista ●

Nueces River

Ft. Ewell ●

Ft. Merrill ●

San Patricio ●

Aransas ●

Rio

Ft. McIntosh ●
Laredo Nuevo ●
Laredo ●

Los Ojilos ●

Corpus Christi ●

San Ignacio ●

Guerrero ● Carrizo ●

Grande

Mier ●

Rio Grande City ●
Ringgold Barracks ●

Camargo ●

Edinburg ●

Reynosa ●

Port Isabel ●

Brazos Santiago ●

Bagdad ●

Torrecilas ●

Brownsville ●

Matamoros ●

0 10 20 30 40 50
Scale of miles

NORTHERN FRONT

Wyandotte
Kansas City
Lexington
Westport
River
Independence
Glasgow
Big Blue River
Waverly
Little Blue
Lone Jack
Marshall
St. Charles
rence
Georgetown
Boonville
Mississippi
Warrensburg
Tipton
Missouri
River
St. Louis
Paola
Harrisonville
Sedalia
California
Franklin
Marais
des
Cygnes
Jefferson City
Linn
Mt. Sterling
Union
Clinton
Warsaw
St. Clair
Blooming
De Soto
Grove
River
Grand
Osage
River
Osage
Cuba
Mineral Point
Mine
Creek
Mound City
Gasconade River
Rolla
St. James
Caledonia
Little Osage R.
Osceola
Farmington
Marmiton
River
Ft.
Waynesville
Scott
Pilot Knob
Fredericktown
Ironton
Cape Girardeau
Arcadia
Dallas
Baxter
Springfield
Springs
Marshfield
Patterson
Greenville
Carthage
Bloomfield
Neosho
Mt. Vernon
Newtonia
West Plains
Poplar
Pineville
Alton
Bluff
Doniphan
Maysville
Elkhorn
Bentonville
Carrollton
River
Fayetteville
Yellville
Pilot Hill
Pocahontas
quah
Huntsville
White
Powhatan
Park Hill
Prairie Grove
Jasper
Mt. Olive
Cane Hill
Black
Greenville
Boonsborough
River
Batesville
Jacksonport
Clinton
Bolivar
Webber's Falls
Van Buren
Ozark
Bayou
Clarksville
Springfield
White
Cache
River
Ft. Smith
Arkansas
Dardanelle
Augusta
Hopefield
Danville
Lewisburg
Searcy
St. Francis
Greenwood
North
Devall's
Madison
Memphis
Perryville
Little Rock
Bluff
Waldron
Little Rock
Brownsville
Helena
Clarendon
Mount Ida
Benton
Mississippi
Hot Springs
Arkadelphia
Rockport
Pine Bluff
Post of
Murfreesborough
Antoine
Jenkins Ferry
Arkansas
Tulip
Saline
oaksville
Little
River
Marks
Mt. Elba
Washington
Princeton
Mill
Monticello
Napoleon
Columbus
Warren
Red
Laynesport
Camden
Ouachita River
River
Clarksville
Spring Hill
Gaines Landing

0 10 20 30 40 50

Scale of miles

EAST TEXAS AND ENVIRON

Ft. Cobb

North Arkansas River
Folk Town

Ft. Smith

Old Ft. Holmes Canadian River
Old Fort

Ft. Arbuckle Boggy Depot
Ft. Washita
Armstrong's Academy Doaksville
Ft. Towson

Red River

Gainesville Bonham Clarksville Laynesport Fulton
Paris De Kalb
Boston

Denton Tarrant Mt. Pleasant

Ft. Belknap

Jefferson

Ft. Worth Dallas Kaufman Swanson's Ldg. Shreveport
Gilmer Marshall
Jordan Saline
Kingsborough

Brazos River

Tyler Carthage Pulaski

Navarro Buffalo Henderson
Corsicana Niblett's Bluff Mansfield
Ft. Graham Logan's Ferry
Rusk Shelbyville
Palestine Douglas Hamilton Natchito
Springfield Nacogdoches
Ft. Gates San Augustine Sabinetown
Milam

Sabine River

Trinity

Leona Crokett
Franklin Alabama Zarala New
Cameron Cincinnati Woodville Jasper Colun
Ft. Croghan Nashville Livingston
Ft. Mason Booneville Huntsville Smithfield Salem Belgrade

Colorado River

Millican Anderson
Austin Washington Montgomery
Fredericksburg Brenham Hempstead Liberty Beaumont Orange
Bastrop Cypress City
Bellville San Houston Aurora
Camp Verde San Marcos La Grange Felipe Lynchb rg
New Braunfels Seguin Alleyton Pierce Jct. Harrisburg Chambersie Sabine City
Columbus Richmond
Castroville San Antonio de Bexar Rio Guadalupe Wharton Galveston
Vandenburg Columbia
Rio San Antonio Brazoria
Texana Quintana Velasco
Victoria 0 10 20 30 40 50
Lavaca
Camp Lawson Goliad Scale of miles
Indianola Port Austin

Mouton. Mouton and Green were instructed to take the brigade westward toward the Texas border, where horses could be foraged, men fed and rested, and stragglers rallied. Then, with the Louisiana infantry, Vincent's regiment of cavalry, the artillery and the train, Taylor continued northward. The retreat continued "full tilt" to Alexandria, which most of the army reached on April 24.[2]

Apparently Kirby Smith did not learn of Taylor's plight until April 14, the day on which both Forts Bisland and Benton fell; and on that date he heard only that Banks was concentrating some 15,000 men near Brashear City. But even this was enough to convince him that Taylor was in considerable danger. Simultaneously, word reached Smith that Grant's hibernating horde was finally coming to life, expanding its perimeter around Milliken's Bend and pressing tentacles westward toward Bayou Maçon and southward toward New Carthage. Smith jumped to the obvious but erroneous conclusion that the two Union armies were cooperating in a grand design to crush Taylor between them, to seize the lower Red, and then to overrun West Louisiana. On the 15th, Smith ordered Holmes to dispatch General John Walker's Texas Division from Pine Bluff to Monroe, whence it could be thrown against either Banks or Grant. On the 16th, he advised Magruder of Taylor's peril, and directed him to forward all available forces to Opelousas. On the 20th—the day on which the Federal flag was hoisted over Opelousas—Smith revoked his previous order to Magruder and advised him instead to collect troops at Niblett's Bluff on the Sabine, where they would be in position either to reinforce Taylor or to defend Texas. He also informed General William Scurry, commanding the Eastern Subdistrict of Texas, that an officer was en route to Texas with authority to apprehend the droves of deserters from Taylor's army who were stampeding across the Sabine; these men, too, were to be gathered at Niblett's Bluff. Smith even tried to wrest some reinforcements from Pemberton's garrisons at Vicksburg and Port Hudson, but Pemberton answered by asking Smith to reinforce him! Smith's old friend, General Joseph Johnston, also sent him a note expressing the hope that the Trans-Mississippi army might spare some men for Pemberton's command, "if your troops [are] not fully occupied west" of the River.

By April 20 Smith had learned of the loss of the sugar parishes and was aware of Taylor's pell-mell retreat. He had also received a dis-

patch announcing that five of Porter's gunboats had run past Vicksburg's batteries and were now at large in Confederate waters, able to
cooperate with either Grant or Banks. Smith advised Taylor that there
was little hope of defending the lower Red if Banks decided to press his
advantage. Walker's division was en route to Monroe, three small regiments of Texas cavalry (Colonel J. P. Major's "brigade," at most 650
men) had crossed the Sabine and were proceeding toward Alexandria,
and urgent appeals for assistance had been sent to Pemberton and the
War Department; but for the moment Taylor's inferior force could do
nothing but retreat.

On April 22, in a fit of despondency, Smith wrote his various subordinates that Pemberton had no troops to spare, that twelve ironclads
were at New Carthage preparing to steam into the Red, that Taylor's
retrograde march would carry him all the way to Shreveport, that
Walker should detour toward Shreveport, that the whole of Louisiana's
Red River Valley would probably be occupied by the enemy, that Department Headquarters would be located at Shreveport, and that
Holmes would have to make his own arrangements for the defense of
Arkansas since Smith's headquarters "will be too far away." The following day, Smith informed Adjutant General Cooper that he planned
to make a stand at Natchitoches, where he would "concentrate a force
of at least 10,000 men and take the offensive, with strong hopes of recovering the country when the waters fall." Where these men were to
come from he did not say; on the contrary, he told Cooper that "straggling and desertions have reduced General Taylor's command at least
one-third." (Taylor himself estimated that he had less than one thousand infantrymen left!)

On the 24th, Smith, who had come down to Alexandria to confer
with Taylor, was swept up in the "genuine stampede" of troops and refugees streaming through the town. Commandeering a riverboat, he hastily evacuated his staff to Shreveport, only to discover that his new capital was already infected with panic. Shreveport, once a "rather
decent-looking place" built to house some 3,000 souls, was now
swarming with civilian refugees, slave coffles, state legislators, surplus
colonels, and skulking privates. "We had the greatest difficulty in ob-
taining accommodations of any sort, so much so as to give the appearance of a desire to prevent headquarters being established there," remi-

nisced Smith's chief of staff. The contagion was even spreading to
Texas. In early May a stagecoach passenger traveling a short distance
west of the Sabine noted:

All the villages through which we passed were deserted except by women
and very old men. Their aspect was most melancholy. . . . We met several
planters on the road, who with their families and Negroes were taking refuge in Texas, after having abandoned their plantations in Louisiana on the
approach of Banks. One of them had as many as sixty slaves with him of all
ages and sizes.[3]

On the date Smith's staff fled Alexandria, Banks's advance guard
was only a day's march away. But then, much to everyone's surprise,
Banks interrupted his progress and bivouacked at Opelousas for the
next two weeks. His correspondence offers a bewildering kaleidoscope
of reasons for this delay: he feared his communications were exposed to
a flank attack by Green's cavalry; he was waiting for Porter's fleet to
open the mouth of the Red; he was trying to coordinate his movements
with Grant, who expected him to help with the investment of the Confederate citadels on the Mississippi (although, in fact, Grant exhibited
little interest in Banks's whereabouts before the second week in May);
he needed time to muster and equip 4,000 "contrabands" who took advantage of the proximity of Union recruiters to enlist in the Federal
army; he needed time to administer oaths of allegiance to 400 Confederate prisoners who volunteered to take them; he had to visit New Orleans to check on affairs elsewhere in his Department; his troops needed
a rest.

But whatever his other motives, Banks was also intrigued by the
abandoned piles of baled cotton scattered around Opelousas, cotton
begging to be confiscated. His entire wagon train was temporarily given
over to the task of collecting cotton. "Cotton is king," exclaimed one of
his soldiers, "for the army is doing nothing else but gathering cotton."
On May 4, Banks told Halleck: "I have deemed it expedient, in order
to prevent the reorganization of the rebel army and to deprive the rebel
Government of all possible means of support, to take possession of
mules, horses, cattle, and the staple products of the country—cotton,
sugar, and tobacco." Having thus intimated that he expected the rebels
to reoccupy the country, he proudly announced the positive achievements of his campaign: "In round numbers, I may say that 20,000

beeves, mules, and horses have been forwarded to Brashear City, with 5,000 bales of cotton and many hogsheads of sugar." Furthermore, this taste of the fruits of victory whetted Banks's appetite for more. He advised Halleck that "50,000 to 150,000 bales of cotton" could easily be impressed, "had we force enough to hold this country for any length of time."

Early the next morning, May 5, Banks received a dispatch from Admiral Porter informing him that Grant has crossed 36,000 of his troops to the east bank of the Mississippi at Grand Gulf, below Vicksburg, and "was driving the rebels before him. . . . Sherman will pass over into Mississippi in a day or two, and our effective force is or will be 50,000 men. The taking of Vicksburg is a mere matter of time." Since Grant no longer needed Porter's gunboats, Porter's nine men-of-war were steaming toward the mouth of the Red, ready to join forces with Banks. Banks promptly broke camp and resumed his march toward Alexandria. "I anticipate but little serious resistance to our advance," he assured Halleck. "Our naval force is sufficient to destroy that of the enemy, who, inferior in number and broken down in *morale,* will not, I think, attempt to make a stand against us."

As Banks expected, Taylor did not even try to contest possession of the lower Red. He had already dismantled Fort De Russy and had evacuated much of his supplies and machines from Alexandria. Then, as the Federals approached, Taylor ordered his troops and trains to march northward to Natchitoches. The retreat of his thousand infantrymen rapidly dissolved into "a regular race from the enemy."

Feet sore, dust intolerable. . . . Completely broken down. . . . When we halt, we squat ourselves down, no matter where—in the sand, in the mud, anywhere—and our only hope is that the halt will last fifteen minutes. At night you fall down too tired to be careful of selections, and go to sleep with one blanket, without taking off clothes, shoes or cap.

To complicate matters, the valley's roads were already "alive with Negroes, who are being 'run' into Texas out of Banks's way. We must have met hundreds of them, and many families of planters, who were much to be pitied, especially the ladies." But despite everything, the handful of soldiers who remained with their colors "nevertheless retain their spirits." [4]

On the evening of May 7, Porter's gunboats brushed aside two rebel cottonclads, the *Webb* and *Grand Duke,* and chugged upriver to Alexandria. Early the following day Banks's columns swung into the abandoned town, and Weitzel's brigade continued on toward Grand Ecore. On May 9, Kirby Smith warned Holmes that the Arkansas District's entire army might have to be pulled back to Shreveport, even if such a move meant abandonment of the whole Arkansas Valley. Two days later, he informed Taylor that swollen bayous and hard rains had bogged down Walker's division in the wilds of northern Louisiana, and that intelligence reports now indicated that Banks's force numbered 28,000. And on the 14th he told Magruder and Scurry that enemy occupation of the Red River Valley as far up as Jefferson, Texas, seemed inevitable—in fact, Banks probably intended to invade East Texas!

But once again, Banks's spastic campaign shuddered to a halt. On May 5 Banks had received a wire from Grant, asking his assistance east of the Mississippi. The telegram happened to be in a cipher for which Banks had no key, and some time passed before he was able to find a signal clerk who could read it. At first, Banks was reluctant to break off his own operation, but after reaching Alexandria he warmed to Grant's invitation. Perhaps the discovery that the Alexandria rapids were already too shallow to float Porter's ironclads helped him change his mind. Between May 8 and May 13, Banks and Grant worked out the details of a joint campaign against Vicksburg and Port Hudson. During this interlude Porter's gunboats steamed down to the Ouachita to shell Fort Beauregard—where they were beaten off by Colonel George W. Logan's two 24-pounders!—while Banks's soldiers piled three million dollars' worth of new loot into two thousand army wagons. What they could not carry away, they demolished. Finally, on the 14th, Banks moved. With his ranks swollen by Negro refugees and his trains bulging with cotton, he called in his pickets, formed his columns, threw out his flankers, and started marching his troops toward the Mississippi. Nine days later he was across the river; thirteen days later his men made their first assault upon the outer works at Port Hudson.

Taylor's infantry did not come about and advance southward from Natchitoches until May 20, and did not reoccupy Alexandria until the 24th. That same day, the 24th, Walker's division arrived on the upper Red and Major's cavalry brigade reached Alexandria, ten days too late to make any difference. Taylor, who came down to Alexandria by steamboat, detailed a force to garrison and rebuild Fort De Russy, and dispatched the rest of his available troops via Opelousas and New Iberia to Fort Bisland and the lower Teche. There they were joined by Mouton and Green's refreshed brigade. For all practical purposes, by the beginning of June the southern portion of the District of West Louisiana's front was disposed almost exactly as it had been on the evening of April 11, before Banks began to kick it to pieces.

The front was restabilized, but the land behind it had been reduced to a desert. Banks reported to Halleck that he had "destroyed the materials upon which an army could be organized or supported," and that it was now "impossible to . . . supply a large force from that country." A planter from Rapides Parish (Alexandria) told Governor Moore: "The country in many places below is *ruined*—fences were torn down and burnt—houses and provender destroyed, cattle turned into the fields [to trample and devour crops], and the negroes on many plantations driven off in a body. . . . every mule, horse and wagon was taken at the same time. . . . on the road to Simsport the destruction of property and crops was greater if possible." Governor Moore, writing to Governor Lubbock, described Banks's wholesale confiscation of vehicles, livestock, slaves, and cotton, and the utter desolation of the barren wasteland remaining. Even more appalling than the destruction of property, said Moore, was the mood of the people: loyal citizens were shocked by the ease with which the invaders had been permitted to lay waste their land, while the disloyal no longer bothered to conceal their true feelings about the Confederate States. The swamps were full of conscript deserters, and the "demoralization of the people at home . . . is very great." A Texan serving on Kirby Smith's staff informed Lubbock that he, too, was greatly alarmed over the "lukewarmness & disloyalty" shown by the people of West Louisiana; he feared that Louisiana's demoralization might soon contaminate East Texas. Kirby Smith himself was particularly upset by the large number of white civilians who had taken the Federal oath of allegiance during Banks's brief visit to the Red. He advised Taylor that these persons "must unhesitatingly be seized and sent beyond our lines. . . . Such . . . would be my Conduct towards any one who evidenced disloyalty during the temporary occupation of the country by the enemy." [5]

According to the peculiar usage of the time and place, "any one" did not include Negroes. For one thing, Negroes were property, not persons; for another, their disaffection was even more pronounced than that of the local whites; and for another, unlike disloyal whites who were satisfied with an oath, all too many slaves asked their Northern liberators for loaded muskets with which to shoot at their former masters. Now the very thought of an armed Negro terrified countless Southern whites; and so when Taylor's patrols began bringing in occasional Negro prisoners of war neither the rebel military nor the local civil authorities were inclined to show these "fugitives" any mercy. On June 13, 1863, Kirby Smith advised Taylor that no quarter should be extended to armed Negroes; whether they wore the Union uniform or not, they were to be treated not as enemy soldiers but rather as slave insurrectionaries, and should be hanged. However, in order to preclude retaliation upon Confederate prisoners of war by Union authorities, Smith recommended that Taylor turn over his captive Negroes to the state of Louisiana, for trial and punishment according to the provisions of the state's slave codes. (Seven days later Louisiana's legislature enacted a mandatory death penalty for any slave convicted of waging war, revolt, rebellion, or insurrection against the state or the Confederacy, and authorized any parish court to try and sentence any such Negro, whether he was the property of a local resident or not.) The result of Smith's proposition might well have been a bloody massacre, had not Richmond's War Department been sensible enough to modify his policy. On August 12, Secretary Seddon summed up the government's approach to the problem in a letter to Smith:

. . . a most marked distinction should be made in the treatment, when taken, of these negro troops and of the white men leading them. The latter had better be dealt with red-handed on the field or immediately thereafter. The former, to be considered rather as deluded victims of the hypocrisy and malignity of the enemy, should not be driven to desperation, but received readily to mercy, and encouraged to submit and return to their masters, with whom, after their brief experience of Yankee humanity and the perils of the military service, they will be more content than ever heretofore in the service and under the protection of their legitimate guardians.

Smith had little choice but to obey, but he suffered no illusions about the Negro soldier's eagerness to return to his master. The evidence accumulated in the region below Natchitoches demonstrated conclusively that Negro men left within reach of Federal enrollment officers too often preferred "Yankee humanity and the perils of the military service" to the quiet security of slavery. Consequently, in September, Smith advised his field commanders that since every exposed plantation was a Union recruiting ground, "Ablebodied male negroes . . . should be carried back [to 'safe' areas] in advance of our troops. . . . Every sound male black left for the enemy becomes a soldier, whom we have afterward to fight." Smith cautioned his officers that "great tact and judgement must be displayed" in the execution of this policy, "so as not to embitter the people against us—, they should be our instruments for carrying it out." But he need not have worried about the planters' reaction; if Banks's expedition had done nothing else, it had proven to West Louisiana's whites that their slaves were susceptible to the infection of freedom.[6]

꙰ II   The removal of Banks's and Grant's armies east of the Mississippi offered no respite to Kirby Smith's exhausted forces. Quite the contrary; the Union investments of Port Hudson and Vicksburg, which threatened to dismember the Confederacy and to isolate the Trans-Mississippi Department, necessitated the wholesale commitment of Western troops to operations in the Mississippi Valley. As Smith told Taylor, a cloud of urgent appeals for aid was descending upon Shreveport, and "public opinion would condemn us if we did not *try to do something*" to relieve the besieged rebel fortresses. Smith knew that he had "to do something," but he did not know what. Instead of concentrating his forces for a decisive thrust at one objective (even an objective as modest as that of covering an escape route for one of the surrounded garrisons), he expended his soldiers' energies in three separate maneuvers, none of which were coordinated with the others, none of which served to debilitate the enemy, and none of which did anything to prolong Confederate control of the Mississippi. Walker's division, augmented by some reinforcements from Arkansas, was mired in northern Louisiana's mud for more than a month, endeavoring—unsuccessfully—to punch through to Vicksburg from the west. Taylor's three brigades, with the assistance of a few reinforcements from Texas, then tried—also unsuccessfully—to draw Banks away from Port Hudson by raiding the Lafourche country and threatening New Orleans. And finally Holmes's army, consisting of two small divisions and a couple of brigades, wrecked itself in a pointless and futile attempt to take Helena by storm. Concentration might have cost Smith some territory (in particular, the lower Arkansas Valley) but his failure to concentrate cost the Confederacy both Pemberton's army and its last chance to save the vital communications link across the Mississippi. Besides doing nothing to delay the fragmentation of the South, the evident aimlessness of Smith's designs, and Smith's own reluctance to assume personal responsibility for their execution, appear to have cost Smith the respect—and, in time, the loyalty—of his best lieutenant, Taylor.

When Taylor returned to Alexandria, he hoped to bring down Walker's division from the upper Red and attach it to his own army. "I was confident that, with Walker's force, Berwick's Bay could be captured, the Lafourche overrun, Banks's communication with New Orleans interrupted, and the city threatened." Taylor felt that such an operation would oblige Banks to abandon his investment of Port Hudson, and permit the Port Hudson garrison to contribute troops to the forces facing Grant. But Kirby Smith, under intense pressure from Pemberton to aid Vicksburg, vetoed Taylor's proposition. While sympathizing with Taylor's desire "to recover what you have lost in Lower Louisiana, and to push on toward New Orleans," Smith told Taylor that "the stake contended for near Vicksburg is the Valley of the Mississippi and the Trans-Mississippi Department; the defeat of General Grant is the *terminus ad quem* of all operations in the west this summer; to its attainment all minor advantages should be sacrificed."

Curiously, Smith then played for these high stakes with a short hand of cards. Instead of throwing everything available toward Vicksburg, Smith—unwilling to sacrifice the minor advantage of possession of the Teche Valley's ruins—permitted Mouton's, Green's, and Major's brigades to bivouac below Opelousas, where they were out of the game. Meanwhile, he ordered Taylor to take the field with Walker's division and General J. C. Tappan's Arkansas infantry brigade (of Price's division); Tappan had just arrived from Camden. At most, this whole force mustered some 4,500 effectives.

Staging from Monroe at the end of May, Taylor pushed through the Mississippi bottomland toward Young's Point and New Carthage,

the two river towns which bracketed the western approaches to Vicksburg. His objective was supposed to be Grant's supply line, which, according to intelligence three weeks out of date, was strung from Milliken's Bend through Young's Point and New Carthage, and on to Grand
Gulf. On June 2, Taylor reached the Mississippi. Kirby Smith rejoiced
at the news, which "exceeds our most sanguine expectation—: Gen
Taylor's position with Walker's Division opposite Vicksburg cuts off
Grant's retreat & completes the destruction of his command I hope."

Had Grant's supply line been where the Confederate high command expected it to be, Smith's hopes might have been realized. But
Grant had long since abandoned both his base at Milliken's Bend and
any thought of retreat; his army, cut loose from its communications,
was eating its way through the state of Mississippi toward the terminus
of a new supply line being opened on the Yazoo, far beyond the reach
of any Trans-Mississippi force. "As forseen," recalled Taylor, "our
movement resulted, and could result, in nothing."

Throughout this exercise in mud-marching, Taylor's teakettle temper had been simmering just below a boil. Now it boiled over. Victim-
ized by faulty intelligence and what he believed to be the stubborn stu-
pidity of his superior, he had wasted both time and men "two hundred
miles and more away from the proper theatre of action in search of an
indefinite *something*." Frustrated and angry, he asked Smith to join him
in the field and assume personal responsibility for the relief of Vicksburg. But, as if unmindful of the precepts that "the defeat of General
Grant is the *terminus ad quem* of all operations" and that "all minor advantages should be sacrificed" to this end, Smith answered that he was
too busy at Shreveport with the details of staff organization to take the
field. "The interests of the Government," said Smith, "require me to remain at H Q^s, if possible, till the Bureaus & Departments have been
organized and some general system has been introduced throughout the
Trans-Miss. Dept." In his memoirs, Taylor barely refrained from accusing Smith of cowardice: Smith, he said, remained at Shreveport, "two
hundred miles up Red River, where, remote from danger or disturbance,
he could organize his administration."

Since the maneuver opposite Vicksburg seemed to be a waste of
energy, Taylor ordered Walker's division to withdraw to the lower Red,
where it would be in position to join the three brigades below Opelou-

sas. But Smith, still under obligation to assist Pemberton, counter-manded Taylor's order, and directed Walker to remain where he was. However, Smith allowed Taylor himself the option of returning south of the Red, to take command of the forces on the Teche and to carry out —without Walker's reinforcements—his plan to invade the Lafourche country. Smith had received an urgent letter from Johnston, begging him to do something to relieve Port Hudson, and so Smith tried to sat-isfy both Pemberton and Johnston by giving each the token support of half of the West Louisiana District's tiny army. Moreover, despite the fact that Walker and Tappan would be separated from Mouton, Green, and Major by more than two hundred miles of wasteland and swamp, Smith somehow expected Taylor to exercise direct supervision over, or at least to take the responsibility for, the activities of both forces. "The commanding general," Smith's adjutant informed Taylor, "is confident you will do all in your power to relieve the garrisons at both places, and spare no efforts to throw in supplies when an opportunity offers."

In late June, two weeks after Taylor departed for New Iberia, Kirby Smith found time to come up to Monroe to confer with Walker. When Smith asked Walker what could be done to help Pemberton, Walker replied that he considered every scheme suggested to him to be "utterly impracticable." Not only was his force too weak to cut through to Vicksburg, but because of the unhealthy environment of the Missis-sippi bottomlands sickness among his men had reached epidemic pro-portions, rendering fully one-third unfit for duty. Thus Walker "and his fine division were kept idle for some weeks, until the fall of Vicksburg. The time wasted on these absurd movements cost us the garrison of Port Hudson, nearly eight thousand men; but the pressure on General Kirby Smith to *do something* for Vicksburg was too strong to be re-sisted." On July 11, seven days after Vicksburg's capitulation, Smith in-structed Walker to move his division to Alexandria and await orders from Taylor; in the early autumn, Walker reported to Taylor and was directed to bivouac north of Opelousas.[7]

While Walker's division was squatting in the mud flats opposite Vicksburg, Taylor's three brigades were running riot over the Louisiana sugar country. Upon reaching the lower Teche, Taylor conferred with Mouton, Green, and Major, and with them devised a clever but danger-ous plan for the rapid conquest of the Lafourche region. The key to the entire area was Brashear City, guarding Berwick's Bay, the mouths of the Atchafalaya and the Teche, and the western end of the New Orleans and Opelousas Railroad. Brashear, a major Federal depot, garrison town, and convalescent center, was a formidable objective, protected by extensive earthworks and a small squadron of tinclads. A direct frontal attack, across water and against the fortifications' heavy cannon, would in all probability have been suicidal. Before attacking Brashear itself, Taylor had to interdict the enemy's escape route by interposing a strong force between Brashear and New Orleans; he had to take the rail line. In addition, Brashear's garrison had to be taken by surprise, lest the assault force be wiped out.

Taylor and his brigadiers decided to split the Confederate army into two wings; to throw one wing, composed of a large cavalry contingent, far behind the Union rear; and to employ the other in a night attack upon Brashear City. In order to trap the enemy garrison, both wings had to close on Brashear simultaneously—before dawn, June 23. For the execution of this daring tactic, Taylor had at his disposal no more than 3,000 soldiers, including the men of two small cavalry regiments (Charles S. Pyron's Second Texas and Joseph Phillips' Third Arizona) which had just arrived from Niblett's Bluff. Yet the audacious design was executed exactly according to plan.

Taylor dispatched Major's Texas cavalry brigade, augmented by Phillips' and Pyron's regiments, on a wide sweep around the Union right flank. Departing Morgan's Ferry on the Atchafalaya on June 15, Major's troopers galloped eastward toward the Mississippi; en route they overran countless little Federal outposts, paroled hundreds of prisoners, scattered thousands of contrabands, burned steamboats, fired cotton, seized weapons, and destroyed supplies. Upon reaching the Mississippi they wheeled southward, circumnavigated the strong Federal post at Donaldsonville, plundered their way through Thibodeaux, and finally struck the railroad line at Terre Bonne Station, near the Lafourche Crossing. Turning westward once again, Major's yellowlegs then followed the tracks as far as Bayou Boeuf Bridge, a short distance east of Brashear City. As they approached the bridge they could hear Brashear's eleven heavy cannon booming in the distance—it was dawn, June 23. Taylor had just initiated his frontal attack, in hopes that Major would be exactly where he was.

While Major circled behind the Federals, details from Mouton's and Green's brigades had been scouring the neighborhood below New Iberia in search of small vessels—rowboats, skiffs, rafts, sugar-coolers, anything that would float. They found fifty-three, enough to ferry about three hundred men. The boats were marshaled on the west bank of the Atchafalaya, some twelve miles above Brashear City; and an assault force, composed of volunteers from the Second Louisiana Cavalry and Green's Texas cavalry brigade, was selected. Command of the amphibious element was assigned to Major Sherod Hunter of the Second Arizona Cavalry Regiment. During the night of June 22, Hunter's men drifted silently down the Atchafalaya, landing after midnight on the east bank about a mile north of Brashear City. There they were to lie in wait until Taylor's cannon announced the beginning of the battle.

As Hunter embarked, Taylor, under cover of darkness, moved the rest of his command—his field artillery, the bulk of Green's brigade and the Second Louisiana, Hunter's battalion of the Second Arizona, and Mouton's skeleton Louisiana infantry brigade—down the Teche to a point opposite Brashear City. Well before dawn, June 23, everything was in place, quiet and ready.

The battle was over before many of the Federals were aware that one had started. At first light, Taylor's batteries opened a furious bombardment of the enemy's fortifications and of the tinclads moored in Berwick's Bay. The steamers were quickly driven away; the garrison's groggy troops stumbled over to the riverside entrenchments, fired a few rounds, and ducked for safety. As Taylor's shelling drew the Federals toward the quayside, Hunter's storming party rushed the town's relatively undefended northern works, penetrated them, and swarmed into Brashear City itself, taking possession of the rearmost Union fortifications, the railroad terminal, and the telegraph office. The Federals clustered near the harbor, and those in the hospital quickly surrendered. Hunter sent his boats back across the water, to permit Mouton and Green to ferry their men to the east bank. As soon as Green landed, Hunter informed him that a single railroad train, loaded with Federal soldiers, had managed to escape the environment and was now racing toward New Orleans. A squadron of Green's troopers "mounted up" and hurried off in pursuit. They found the train stalled on the west side of Bayou Boeuf Bridge, its progress blocked by Major's deployed cavalry. After a brisk little skirmish, the encircled bluecoats displayed a white flag.

The occupation of Brashear City netted Taylor 1,700 prisoners of war (including convalescents, whom he paroled), 2,000 Negro contrabands, 2,500 stand of small arms, more than 200 wagons and tents, one railroad train (whose capture allowed Taylor to make use of the thirty miles of track between Brashear City and the Lafourche Crossing), eleven siege guns, numerous field cannon, and immense quantities of quartermaster, commissary, ordnance, and medical stores. "For the first time since I reached western Louisiana," Taylor recalled, "I had supplies, and in such abundance as to serve for the Red River campaign of 1864."

Taylor was not content with the possession of Brashear City. His objective was still the relief of Port Hudson and the interruption of Banks's communications to New Orleans. On June 24 Mouton, with two regiments of Louisiana infantry, proceeded to the Lafourche Crossing by rail and then marched on Thibodeaux, which surrendered without a fight. The cavalry were not so lucky. Green, with eight hundred troopers, drove toward the major Union depot and communications center at Donaldsonville, at the confluence of the Lafourche and the Mississippi. Arriving below Donaldsonville on the evening of June 27, he found the place defended by three gunboats and a strong earthwork, Fort Butler, manned by two hundred Negro soldiers. The Confederates stormed and breached the entrenchments at 2:00 A.M., June 28, but once inside the withering musketry and the deluge of brickbats poured upon them pinned them down in a drainage ditch until daybreak. By distracting the enemy with a flag of truce Green finally managed to extricate most of his survivors (perhaps four hundred), but a hundred of his Texans suffered the deep ignominy of being forced to capitulate to ex-slaves.

Green's failure to take Donaldsonville cost Taylor his best chance to interdict Banks's supply line, and the severe damage done to Green's command made it impossible for him to resume the attack. Green fell back to cover the roads between Donaldsonville and Thibodeaux; he rested his men and threw vedettes toward the west bank of the Mississippi. In an effort to make the best of a bad situation, Taylor forwarded Major T. A. Faries' battalion of field artillery, twelve guns, from Brashear to the Mississippi. Arriving in position late in the first week of July, Faries' cannon were emplaced in crude works dug along the levee below Donaldsonville, and were used to harass enemy shipping passing between New Orleans and Port Hudson; they managed to blockade the river for three days. Taylor also forwarded cavalry reinforcements, which began to raid the Union details that frequently came ashore on the west bank to hunt for stray cattle, to scout, to plunder, or—oddly—to drill Negro recruits.

Despite their relative success, these skirmishes were minor affairs, too insignificant to affect Banks's operation. Until July 9, the day on which the United States flag was raised over Port Hudson, Banks simply ignored the little swarm of rebel bees buzzing about his left flank. But once Port Hudson was in his hands, he was free to turn his attention to Taylor's annoying little command. On July 11, Southern scouts observing Donaldsonville reported the arrival from Port Hudson of at least ten steamboats loaded with troops; by the 12th, the Donaldsonville garrison had been reinforced by General Cuvier Grover and four infantry brigades. The following day, Grover pressed southward along the Lafourche, until, at Cox's Plantation, his foot soldiers ran into the 1,500 troopers of Green's and Major's brigades. The Confederates managed to hold their ground and drive the Federals back, but it was nevertheless obvious to all that the rebels could not stand fast for long.

Taylor, who had since learned of the fall of both Port Hudson and Vicksburg, realized that the loss of the Mississippi and the relief of Banks's army from siege duty rendered his "present position on the Lafourche extremely hazardous, and not to be justified on any military grounds." The recapture of New Orleans was now out of the question; there was no Port Hudson garrison to aid; Taylor's army was far too inadequate to defend the Lafourche country, and in addition was vulnerable to encirclement. Should a Union flotilla and expeditionary force move into Berwick's Bay and the Atchafalaya, Taylor knew that his escape route would be cut and his army exposed to annihilation. Even though Banks failed to grasp the opportunity offered to him, Taylor had no choice but to disengage his troops and to evacuate them to the security of the Teche Valley. He first stripped Brashear City's depot of everything useful to his army, burned everything else, spiked and scuttled the captured siege guns, and ran his locomotive and railway carriages into Berwick's Bay. Then, calling in his outposts, he abandoned the La-fourche and crossed his men to the west bank of the Atchafalaya; they camped along the Teche between New Iberia and Vermillionville.

In the last week of July, well after Taylor's departure, Banks's forces cautiously advanced into the sugar country and reoccupied Brashear City. They, too, displayed their usual attention to detail: "Our boys drove to the rear every pony and mule, every ox and cow and sheep. They did not leave, on an average, two chickens to a plantation. . . . A more forlorn and destitute set of people never were seen." Per-haps the most woebegone denizens of the district were the thousands of dispossessed ex-slave, ex-contraband Negroes, some of whom had been shuttled back and forth between Reb and Yank overseers a half-dozen times in the preceding four months. Large bands of them roamed aim-lessly from plantation to plantation, begging, stealing, suffering, search-ing for the freedom which their most recent liberators had promised them.[8]

A goodly number of Taylor's soldiers, weary of war and of the endless marching up and down lower Louisiana, were looking for free-dom too. Once safely west of the Atchafalaya, many of the Texas troop-ers made up their minds to continue retreating all the way to the Sa-bine, with or without official sanction. As one of them informed his family, "We will nearly all of us go home, if we have to fight our way through." Taylor appalled by the "unparalleled number of desertions" eviscerating his two cavalry brigades, implored Magruder to "picket the various frequented crossings of the Sabine River, giving instructions to your officers in charge to arrest all stragglers from this command who are making their way into Texas."

Taylor's infantry brigade was just as demoralized. Lieutenant James Delahanty, of Clack's battalion, was so depressed that he sold his effects for $214 (Confederate), gave the money to his messmates, and committed suicide. One of Mouton's officers noted that "the majority" of the "worthless" Louisiana conscripts had deserted. By mid-August, Mouton's brigade had dwindled to the size of a single thin regiment, with 300 men present for duty. Yet Mouton's infantry were still thought to be more reliable than the Texas troopers, for in late August the Louisiana foot soldiers were summoned from Vermillionville and de-

ployed around the cavalry at New Iberia, in order to help put down a
mutiny among some of Green's disgruntled companies.

Nor was this disaffection confined only to Taylor's field army.
Escapees from his ranks spread the infection throughout his District
and across the border into Texas. During August, mutinies among the
Confederate regiments stationed in distant Galveston paralyzed the
town's defenses and threw its garrison into disarray: the whole Third
Texas Infantry declined to turn out for drill and dress parade, and
troops of the Twentieth Texas Infantry and the First Texas Heavy Artillery flatly refused to force the men of the Third Texas to submit to
their own officers. Meanwhile, a disgusted enrolling officer in northern
Louisiana advised his immediate superior that it was ridiculous to continue pretending that new recruits could be raised for Taylor's army,
since the only eligible conscripts left in his entire enrollment district
were armed deserters, desperadoes, Yankee scouts, spies, and traitors.[9]

꾜 III   While Walker's division and Tappan's brigade were bogged
down in the bayou bottomlands opposite Vicksburg, and while Taylor's
three brigades were sweeping back and forth across the Lafourche country, Holmes's ragamuffin command did its best to cooperate with the
forces further south by making a bungled attack against the formidable
Federal fortifications surrounding Helena. Unlike Walker, who at least
appreciated the absurdity of his situation and thus refrained from doing
anything rash, and unlike Taylor, whose initiative and tactical genius
multiplied the effectiveness of his miniscule army, "Old Granny"
Holmes displayed neither common sense nor tactical perspicacity. During most of the spring campaign season Holmes did not even exhibit a
commander's concern for the activities of his subordinates, several of
whom mounted little campaigns of their own. Because of these diver-
sions, and perhaps because Holmes himself may have doubted the wisdom of assaulting Helena, the attempt to storm the Union stronghold
was postponed until July 4, the date of Vicksburg's capitulation. Then
the bloody repulse of Holmes's mismanaged attack simply afforded the
Federals an additional reason to celebrate the holiday.

Through the early months of 1863, the eastern portion of the District of Arkansas front remained relatively quiet. In order to reinforce Grant, the Federals evacuated Arkansas Post and reduced the garrison at Helena to 5,000 men, too few to conduct serious offensive operations in the lower Arkansas River Valley. But further upriver, in the military vacuum covering northwestern Arkansas and the northern Indian Territory, blue and gray commands were almost constantly in motion, marching and countermarching, foraging and skirmishing, burning villages, destroying crops, laying waste farms and homesteads, plundering, and devastating the land. In general, these operations did little to affect control of the disputed territory, since the country was too poor to sustain armies of occupation—the organizations committed to these glorified raids were usually obliged, after short periods of time, to retire to their bases and resupply. But one significant exception to the general rule occurred in Indian Territory, where the Federals secured permanent control of the Cherokee Nation and of the segment of the Arkansas River above Fort Smith by seizing the key position at Fort Gibson.

In January, 1863, General William Steele barely managed to salvage the disintegrating residue of Colonel Douglas Cooper's Confederate Indian brigade by concentrating the warriors along the Red River, beyond the enemy's reach. This maneuver left most of Indian Territory exposed to penetration and occupation by Union invaders. The commander of the Union Indian brigade, Colonel William Phillips, promptly took advantage of Steele's withdrawal by marching back into the Nations and pouncing upon Fort Gibson, which surrendered without a fight. Phillips and the bulk of his brigade were then obliged to return to Arkansas, to help turn back a Confederate thrust toward Fayetteville, but a strong Federal contingent was left at Fort Gibson to guard the southern approaches to the Cherokee country.

Impressed by the ease with which Phillips' column had overrun their land, depressed by the Confederacy's chronic inability to supply and provision their people, and encouraged by the protection afforded by the Northern garrison at Fort Gibson, the legislative council of the Cherokee Nation assembled at Cowskin Prairie in late February and proceeded to abrogate the Cherokee treaty with the Confederate States, to appoint commissioners to negotiate a new treaty with the United States, to emancipate the Nation's slaves, and to outlaw Colonels Stand Watie and W. P. Adair, their rebel regiments, the Cherokee delegate to the Richmond Congress, and everyone else who continued to adhere to the Southern cause.

Dismayed, General Steele tried to effect a reversal of the council's decisions with a show of force; he attempted to move cavalry north of the Arkansas River, in order to interdict and isolate Fort Gibson and to reestablish a visible Confederate presence within the limits of the Cherokee Nation. Under the joint command of Colonel Watie, the First and Second Cherokee Cavalry decamped from the Red River Vally and proceeded to the vicinity of Fort Smith, whence they sortied to harass the enemy's communications from Fayetteville and Fort Scott to Fort Gibson. Watie's return to the Cherokee country induced a few of the Nation's pro-Southern chiefs to organize a rump council at Webber's Falls, for the purpose of repealing the Cowskin Prairie council's legislation. But in mid-April, before the rump council could assemble and before Watie's raiding parties could do serious damage to Fort Gibson's supply lines, Phillips' Union Indian brigade again descended from Arkansas and swept into the Territory, routing Watie's troopers, scattering the legislators who had arrived at Webber's Falls, reinforcing the tenacious garrison at Fort Gibson, and compounding the Cherokee country's misery by bringing in a virulent epidemic of smallpox from Arkansas.

Under Phillips' aggressive direction, the Federal Indians consolidated Union authority above Fort Gibson, fought numerous successful skirmishes with Cooper's and Watie's braves, again drove the rebels well south of the Arkansas River, initiated the conquest of the Creek Nation, and began to probe toward Fort Smith itself. By the end of June, Cooper's brigade was again dissolving; Steele was trying to transfer General William Cabell's veteran brigade of conscript Arkansas cavalry into the Nations; Colonel Tandy Walker of the First Choctaw was busily conspiring with Cooper to effect Steele's removal and Cooper's elevation to command; and the Creeks, the Seminoles, and the Choctaws were all drafting petitions to Richmond, demanding supplies, provisions, overdue treaty bounties, and greater autonomy within the military command structure of the Trans-Mississippi Department.

General Steele's decision to summon Cabell's brigade into the Nations was an acknowledgment that northwestern Arkansas had been lost to the enemy, since between February and June Cabell was in command of the only regular Confederate organization deployed north and east of

Fort Smith. In February, 1863, after recovering from wounds received
at Corinth, General Cabell had been assigned to Steele's headquarters,
and had been ordered to piece together a brigade from the loose fragments of Hindman's old First Corps. By April, Cabell's "Arkansas brigade," never more than a thousand strong, was made up of neighborhood guerrilla bands, local partisan rangers, conscript Arkansans—many
of whom would have preferred to enlist in the Union army—and some
homesick Texans. With this host, Cabell was expected to defend the
western third of the state of Arkansas.

Fortunately for Cabell, Marmaduke's Springfield raid had obliged
the bulk of the Union Army of the Frontier to abandon most of the territory won at Prairie Grove and to withdraw into Missouri. Only Colonel M. La Rue Harrison's volunteer brigade of recently recruited "Arkansaw Feds," stationed at Fayetteville, posed any immediate threat to
Cabell's thin gray line. But Harrison was an audacious commander, and
the 1,500 men of his two Arkansas regiments were eager to restore
their state to the Union. As soon as the snow started to melt, Harrison's
patrols began threading through the Boston Mountains and down into
the Arkansas River Valley. By March, his squadrons had penetrated
Cabell's flimsy vedette line and were ranging to and beyond the Arkansas River itself, wrecking steamboats, demolishing bridges, cutting
wires, raiding villages, pillaging stores, collecting cotton, burning barns,
killing livestock. Ozark was reoccupied; Van Buren was twice sacked;
even the staff officers at Fort Smith could occasionally hear the tinny
cracks of some of Harrison's howitzers. Until April, Cabell's disorganized troopers could do no more than ambush a few of Harrison's straggling outriders; and even in April, Cabell could only gather some 900
troopers for a counteroffensive. But Cabell had to act; his hand was
forced by the news that Phillips' Union Indians were en route to join
Harrison. With his 900 horse soldiers and a couple of cannon Cabell
swung northward toward Fayetteville, determined to seize Harrison's
base and so precipitate the Federals' evacuation of the region.

But Cabell's plan was sabotaged by the watchful citizens of the
area, Unionists almost to a man, who kept Harrison informed of the
Confederates' every move. On April 18, as the Arkansas Rebs came
within sight of Fayetteville, they espied the Arkansas Feds drawn up in
line of battle, waiting. Colonel J. C. Monroe's Confederate First Arkan-

sas Cavalry, dismounted and in civilian dress, opened the engagement by charging Harrison's Union First Arkansas Cavalry, dismounted and in civilian dress; the ensuing melee soon dissolved into a chaotic brawl. As other units joined the fray, the Federals fell back into the town itself, where they manned the housetops, threw up barricades, and fired from windows. The pursuing Confederates were boxed in the streets, ripped apart by crossfire, and forced to retreat. They retreated all the way to Fort Smith, arriving just in time to receive Steele's summons to continue on into the Nations. Harrison remained at Fayetteville and again dispatched his patrols southward. Northwestern Arkansas was no longer Confederate.[10]

As Cabell's whipped troopers retired from Fayetteville, Marmaduke's cavalrymen broke camp and formed columns for a third raid into Missouri. After withdrawing from Springfield in late January, Marmaduke's yellowlegs had dispersed to winter quarters in the vicinity of Batesville, located on the White River about seventy-five miles north of Little Rock. During February they were frequently disturbed by General J. W. Davidson's Union cavalry, which moved into the neighborhood to harass the rebels and to push them south of the White. In March, Marmaduke, still hoping to liberate Confederate Missouri, journeyed to Little Rock to confer with Holmes and to request authority to conduct another Missouri raid. In answer to objections that such an expedition would divert forces toward a secondary objective and interfere with efforts to hold the Mississippi, Marmaduke replied that his proposal would in fact relieve pressure upon Vicksburg and eastern Arkansas by obliging the enemy to commit valuable manpower to the defense of Missouri. He also insisted that his raid would draw off the regular Federal detachments operating in northern Arkansas, thus permitting the suppression of Yankee jayhawkers and the reassertion of Confederate authority in the region; that his presence in Missouri would revitalize the citizens' Southern loyalties and encourage volunteers to flock to his standards; and that his maneuver would pave the way for a full-scale invasion of the state in the autumn. Both Kirby Smith and Holmes granted permission for the campaign. Marmaduke returned to Batesville in early April, made his plans, and ordered his brigades to prepare to move out.

According to Marmaduke's design, his regiments were to concentrate north of Batesville, to penetrate the Iron Mountains of southeastern Missouri, and to descend upon the important Union depot at Cape Girardeau, situated on the west bank of the Mississippi. En route they were to disperse Federal troops and militia and to destroy telegraph wires, bridges, forts, and anything else which might be of use to the enemy. To accomplish his intentions Marmaduke had at his disposal a division composed of two veteran and two recently conscripted horse brigades. Of the division's 5,000 soldiers, 1,200 were unarmed and 900 were without mounts, but Marmaduke, hoping to capture weapons and horses in Missouri and fearing that any left behind would desert, chose to take them all.

This decision was his first tactical mistake. Cavalry, like armor, is a mobile shock force, designed for swift maneuver. But Marmaduke's inclusion of 900 foot soldiers among his horsemen condemned the entire division to move at the speed of infantry. Marmaduke also chose to bring along a large slow train of half-empty wagons, for use should any loot come within his reach. Finally, he neglected to send more than a few scouts ahead, either to ascertain the extent of Confederate sentiment in Missouri or to gauge the Union army's ability to meet and repel his thrust. Had his reconnaissance been adequate he would surely have discovered that General Davidson knew of his plans and was making preparations to give his raiders a warm welcome.

On April 19, the day after the battle of Fayetteville, Marmaduke's regiments abandoned their camps, formed two columns, and plodded northward toward Missouri. George Carter, with his own brigade and Colton Greene's, struck the Union posts at Patterson and Bloomfield, reduced both towns to ashes, and drove the 2,600 Federals stationed in them toward Cape Girardeau. On the 24th the panicky Federals reached the security of Cape Girardeau, with the rebels still in hot pursuit. But as soon as Carter came within sight of the Mississippi he reined in his squadrons and settled down to await Marmaduke's second column. Jo Shelby, meanwhile, had taken John Q. Burbridge's brigade and his own Iron Brigade on a foray through southeastern Missouri, firing bridges, scattering militia, razing forts, and skirmishing with detachments of Davidson's cavalry. Just before dawn, April 26, Shelby joined Carter at Old Jackson, about four miles from Cape Girardeau.

The one thing that lightly armed cavalry is never equipped to do is to lay siege to a fortified town. Yet despite a torrential rainfall which was turning the countryside into a sea of mud, and despite ample evidence that the Federals had done everything to make Cape Girardeau impregnable, Marmaduke ordered a general assault against the Union earthworks. Before the charge could pick up momentum, the Confederates were bogged down in the muck and torn to shreds by the enemy's artillery and musketry. When some of his officers protested that any attempt to press the attack would produce nothing but butchery, Marmaduke directed his brigades to disengage and retire.

His change of heart came none too soon, for as he issued his order two steamboats loaded with fresh Union reinforcements were docking at Cape Girardeau, and 5,000 of Davidson's blue cavalrymen were churning down the roads leading toward the rebel left flank. At midnight, April 26, the converging Federals fell upon Marmaduke's camp and obliged the rebels to beat a hasty retreat. On the 28th, the wet and dispirited Southerners, now hiking in the opposite direction, again passed through the charred ruins of Bloomfield. On May 1, with the Federals still nipping at their rear guard, they crossed the swollen St. Francis River and demolished the bridge behind them. On the 6th, no longer exposed to hostile cavalry but desperately short of provisions and forage, they plunged into the tangled swamps below the St. Francis and followed the southerly course of Bayou Cache. By late May, most of the division's bone-weary soldiers finally managed to straggle to the vicinity of Jacksonport, Arkansas, a short distance east of Batesville. Behind them they left irreplaceable vehicles, precious weapons, mounts, 210 men, an undamaged Union depot at Cape Girardeau, and many of their illusions about Missouri's eagerness to welcome Confederate liberators; with them they brought 150 new recruits, not all of whom were volunteers. M. Jeff Thompson's guerrillas remained active in the neighborhood of New Madrid, but otherwise Marmaduke's withdrawal marked the abandonment of the region northeast of the White River to the United States army.

On February 8, 1863, at the conclusion of Marmaduke's Springfield raid, Holmes had written that Marmaduke was "the only officer I have who is fitted for a large cavalry command." By May 22, after news of the debacle before Cape Girardeau and the cavalry's subsequent flight reached Little Rock, Holmes's esteem for Marmaduke had de-

clined. He now advised Kirby Smith that he had "great, the greatest,
need of J. G. Walker, to command the division of cavalry now under
Marmaduke, who is not equal to it." Word that Carter's Texas brigade
was on the verge of mutiny probably helped sour Holmes's regard for
Marmaduke. And undoubtedly Sterling Price, who had Holmes's ear,
had done his part. Price wanted nothing so much as a chance to free his
beloved Missouri all by himself, and had—in General Orders!—blamed
the lawless, undisciplined, and un-Christian behavior of Marmaduke's
raiders for Missouri's refusal to rally to the Confederate flag. The upshot was a reorganization of most of the Arkansas District's cavalry.

The simplest solution would have been to replace Marmaduke with
another general. Holmes wanted John Walker for the position, but because Walker was about to begin his mud-march toward Vicksburg,
Kirby Smith declined to reassign him to Arkansas. Instead, Smith dispatched a spare brigadier with the same surname, L. Marsh Walker, up
to Little Rock. Unfortunately, L. M. Walker did not enjoy John Walker's solid reputation, and Holmes was not sure of his new brigadier's capacity to lead the whole of Marmaduke's cavalry. In addition, Marmaduke made it known that he intended to remain a full-fledged division
commander, no matter what Holmes or Price thought, and no matter
how many extra generals were awaiting assignments in Little Rock. To
solve his dilemma, Holmes finally decided to split his cavalry force and
to permit both Marmaduke and L. M. Walker to function as division
commanders. Though recruiting details were only able to collect enough
conscripts to man one additional regiment, Holmes created two divisions in place of Marmaduke's one. The addition of Marsh Walker's division to the District's table of organization did not change the fact that
this combined cavalry force still numbered only 5,000 men, whereas it
did much to exacerbate Marmaduke's bitter antipathy for Holmes,
Price, and Walker, the three conspirators who had robbed him of half
of his command. Marmaduke's ire was not satisfied until September,
when, on a dueling field near Little Rock, he shot Marsh Walker dead.

Virtually all of the operations conducted within the boundaries of
the District of Arkansas during the first five months of 1863 were carried out by the mounted troopers who now composed Steele's, Marmaduke's, and L. M. Walker's cavalry divisions. In May, John Walker's
Texas infantry division and J. C. Tappan's Arkansas brigade (of Price's

infantry division) had been dispatched to North Louisiana to cooperate with Taylor, but the remainder of Holmes's infantrymen spent the spring campaign season in their camps. On June 2, the day on which the cavalry reorganization was implemented, Holmes's army included two infantry divisions, commanded, respectively, by D. M. Frost and Sterling Price. Frost's division, mustering only 2,700 effectives, was little more than an augmented brigade composed of raw enlistees left behind in the vicinity of Pine Bluff after the departure of John Walker's Texans. John B. Clark's brigade was harassing enemy communications and shipping below Arkansas Post, while the rest of Frost's units were assigned to garrison and patrol duties in the interior; none of the division was available for field service. Sterling Price's disposable force consisted of the 4,500 veterans and conscripts who made up James F. Fagan's Arkansas brigade, Dandridge McRae's Arkansas brigade, and Mosby M. Parsons' Missouri brigade. On June 2, Fagan's foot soldiers were still in bivouac near Little Rock, while Price, with McRae's and Parsons' brigades, was en route from Little Rock to Jacksonport.[11]

While Holmes reshuffled his cavalry commanders and Price rearranged his infantry divisions, Grant was beginning his investment of Vicksburg and Banks was starting to pound Port Hudson. Yet, improbable as it may seem, the rebel brass in the District of Arkansas paid little attention to the deteriorating situation in the Mississippi Valley until the middle of June, barely three weeks before Vicksburg's surrender. Much of the blame belongs to Kirby Smith, who, on May 9—while Banks's Federals were still probing toward Natchitoches—had abdicated responsibility for operations in Arkansas by instructing Holmes to "act according to your own judgement. At this distance I can give no positive order. Attack the enemy, should an opportunity offer for doing so with hope of success. You can expect no assistance from this quarter." Left to his own initiative, Holmes continued to judge the liberation of Missouri to be more important than the territorial integrity of the Confederate States. He ordered Carter's brigade to cooperate with Clark's below the mouth of the Arkansas, but otherwise he persisted in dissipating his army's energies in maneuvers above Little Rock.

Holmes's disproportionate concern for his northern front became strikingly evident on May 27, when, at Price's suggestion, he authorized the transfer of McRae's and Parsons' brigades from Little Rock to

Jacksonport (that is, away from, rather than toward, Helena), and assigned Price, Missouri's self-appointed savior, to the field command of
all Confederate forces, cavalry as well as infantry, operating in upper
Arkansas and Missouri. According to the order effecting this reorganization, Price was specifically directed to "take the most active measures
to ascertain the localities, strength, and movements of the enemy in
your front, especially in Missouri." In his own General Order of June
6, in which he announced his assumption of command at Jacksonport,
Price devoted half the text to calling for the relief of loyal Missouri, but
not a word to the state of Confederate affairs along the lower Mississippi.

There seems little doubt that, even at this late date, Holmes and
Price still had visions of a grand parade to St. Louis. Had Helena been
their objective, it is unlikely that they would have concentrated the better part of three of the District's five divisions at Jacksonport, since either Little Rock or Pine Bluff would have been more convenient staging
bases for a thrust toward the east. And had the formidable fortifications
surrounding Helena been their goal, it also seems unlikely that either
Holmes or Price would have consented to a significant reduction in the
strength of Price's army; yet, on June 3, Jo Shelby's Iron Brigade was
directed to proceed westward as a reinforcement for Steele's division.
Shelby's marching orders were not countermanded until June 16, just
two days before the publication of the battle order announcing Holmes's
dispositions for an assault upon Helena.

Holmes appears to have become aware that something was amiss
in the vicinity of Vicksburg during the first week of June. On the 1st or
2d he telegraphed Kirby Smith to ask whether he should shift some of
Price's forces toward the Mississippi Valley bottomlands. Smith replied
that while an attack upon Helena might prove profitable, Holmes ought
not to make the attempt unless he were sure of success. On the 4th,
having heard nothing more from Holmes, Smith told Governor Reynolds that Holmes had evidently decided not to commit troops to a
campaign east of Little Rock. But on the 8th Holmes set out for Jacksonport to solicit advice from Price. Along the way his carriage broke
down, forcing him to return to Little Rock; but before turning back he
scribbled a note to Price, to inquire "if we could with propriety attack
Helena. Please inform me whether the condition of your troops will jus-

tify the attempt." Although the negative tone of Holmes's dispatch practically invited Price to reject the proposal, Price answered that "were a movement [against Helena] conducted with celerity and secrecy, . . . I entertain no doubt of your being able to crush the foe at that point." Price added that his troops were "fully rested and in excellent spirits," and that scouts reported the effective strength of the enemy garrison at Helena to number no more than 5,000.

But not even Price's encouraging response overcame Holmes's hesitation; perhaps the intelligence that 4,800 of Price's men were equipped with unreliable firearms, while another 1,500 were completely unarmed, caused Holmes to doubt the readiness of Price's army to storm an enemy fortress. At any rate, for the next week Holmes postponed any decision, while his District's adjutants compromised any hope of secrecy by sending numerous telegraph messages concerning a possible advance toward Helena. Finally, on June 13, Holmes made his decision: he dismissed the scheme to overrun Helena with the remark that "it would cost too much." And on the 15th he instructed Price to "have everything in readiness for a move on Missouri."

Holmes's resolution persisted less than a day. He then received from Shreveport a dispatch enclosing part of the text of a three-week-old letter from the War Department to Joseph Johnston, a letter in which Secretary Seddon expressed his unofficial opinion that the capture of Helena would "secure a great advantage to the Confederacy." The covering note added by Kirby Smith's adjutant was scrupulously noncommittal; it was, said the adjutant, "impossible for Lieutenant-General Smith, at his distance, and without any knowledge of the strength of the force at Helena (which is continually varying), to give orders in the case." Seddon's letter was therefore "submitted to Lieutenant-General Holmes to act as circumstances may justify." Now Seddon's communication was the closest thing to a strategic directive that Holmes had received in well over a month. And so, late on the 15th, after quietly shelving his inspiration to save Missouri, Holmes wired two brief sentences to Shreveport: "I believe we can take Helena. Please let me attack it." On the 16th, with a four-word telegram, Kirby Smith granted Holmes permission to do as he wished.

Considering the confusion surrounding the genesis of the Helena campaign, it is not surprising that its execution was less than brilliant.

Upon reciept of Smith's authorization to proceed, Holmes directed Shelby's brigade to remain at Jacksonport, and himself hurried up to Price's headquarters. On the 18th, Holmes assumed personal command of the forces congregated near Little Rock and Jacksonport, ordered Marsh Walker's cavalry brigade to screen and isolate the approaches to Helena, and instructed the remainder of his troops to prepare twenty days' field rations. Between the 21st and the 24th, Price's two brigades (McRae's and Parsons') and Marmaduke's two brigades (Shelby's and Greene's) decamped, formed columns, crossed the White, and converged toward a rendezvous at Cotton Point, while Fagan's brigade followed a parallel route from Little Rock to Clarendon. On the 26th, both wings of the army plunged into the murky swamps between Bayou Cache and the Mississippi, and spent the next week hacking, slogging, and swimming their way down toward Helena. The swamps consumed many animals and most of the infantry's wagons, while the soldiers were harassed by swirling swarms of gnats and flies. Not until the afternoon of July 3 did Holmes's fagged Johnnies crawl up onto the high ground of Allen Polk's plantation, some five miles west of Helena.

Holmes's six brigades mustered 7,650 effectives, half again as many as the garrison holding Helena. But considering the tactical advantages enjoyed by the defenders of fixed positions, Holmes's force was far too small to storm the Union fortress. Surrounded by steep hills bristling with field guns, protected by multiple lines of interlocking entrenchments, covered by abundant artillery mounted in four strong redoubts, and supported by the eight-inch naval cannon aboard the gunboats *Hastings* and *Tyler,* Helena was virtually invulnerable. Having surveyed Helena's defensive dispositions, Holmes should have directed his army to march back to Little Rock. Instead, he ordered his men to prepare to charge the Union breastworks.

Holmes's battle plan was a model of brutal irresponsibility. Five of the six rebel brigades were instructed to cross the five rugged and unfamiliar miles to Helena in the dark of night, to form massed columns along a single, ill-defined line of departure, and then at "daylight" to launch a simultaneous, coordinated attack all along the Union front. Marsh Walker's brigade, held in reserve, was simply directed to "act against the enemy as circumstances may justify." During the course of the engagement, Walker was to receive no further communications from

Holmes, and, left to act upon his own initiative, he was to be paralyzed by the conflicting demands for support dispatched to him by his fellow brigadiers.

The inevitable result was a catastrophic defeat for the Confederate army. En route from Polk's plantation to the line of departure, regiments strayed, companies became totally lost, and hundreds of men straggled away. Then "daylight" broke between 2:30 and 5:00 A.M., depending upon each commander's pet definition of the term, so the several rebel brigades, thrown into additional confusion by a dense morning fog, were hurled piecemeal toward the ugly rows of enemy trenches and rifle pits. Crackling musketry ripped apart the foremost Confederate ranks, while shot and shell plowed furrows through the massed assault columns. Marmaduke's cavalrymen, fighting dismounted, were stopped cold by a brigade of Indiana and Kansas horse soldiers; urgent appeals for assistance from Walker produced no response. Hundreds of Fagan's infantrymen, sickly and exhausted after their strenuous march from Little Rock, dropped away from their units and collapsed to the ground without being touched by enemy iron; 250 of them, cowering in a ditch, gladly surrendered to a small detachment of Federals. An equal number of Parsons' men and a hundred of McRae's Arkansans were trapped in a ravine and capitulated without a fight, but as they were being led to safety under guard, exasperated rebel snipers shot a number of them in the back. Except for some elements of Price's division, which did manage to overrun and occupy one of the Union artillery redoubts, none of the Confederate outfits reached their assigned objectives; and Price, exposed on open ground with both flanks in the air, was soon obliged to fall back. At 10:30 A.M., just as Grant's banners were being raised over Vicksburg, Holmes ordered his troops to disengage. As the shattered remnant of the wrecked rebel army withdrew to Polk's plantation, it left behind more than 1,600 dead, wounded, and missing, fully one-fifth of its effective strength. The encounter cost the Federals 239 casualties.

Holmes's retreat continued all the way to Little Rock, and every mile along the route he lost more men. Stragglers dropped out by squads; desertions dissolved whole companies; Jo Shelby recommended that his entire brigade be furloughed to prevent wholesale mutiny. Nor was this demoralization confined only to the enlisted ranks. Holmes ac-

cused Dandridge McRae of disobedience on the battlefield, forcing
McRae to suffer the humiliation of a court-martial (which exonerated
him). Both Holmes and Marmaduke charged Marsh Walker with dere-
liction of duty in the face of the enemy; Walker challenged Marmaduke
to a duel. Holmes intimated that Price was to blame for a failure to
reinforce Fagan; then, exhausted, he transferred command of the entire
District to Price and took to a sickbed. Price was too stunned by the
whole disaster to do more than occupy an office at headquarters and
wait numbly for Armageddon. The Arkansas legislature again packed
its archives. Prominent citizens petitioned the government for assurances that Little Rock would be held. Governor Flanagin, who had accompanied the army to Helena and back, again threatened the secession
of his state. And both Kirby Smith and Jefferson Davis, appalled by the
disintegration of morale throughout Holmes's District, wrote long,
soothing letters to the various civil and military dignitaries huddled in
Little Rock, consoling them and promising them the Confederacy's continued affection.

    Holmes, Taylor, and John Walker had all failed to impede the
Union conquest of the lower Mississippi Valley. Now, thanks to Generals Banks and Grant, the Mississippi again flowed unvexed to the sea
and the Confederacy was split in two. Within days after Vicksburg and
Port Hudson surrendered, Federal ironclads were stationed at ten- or
twelve-mile intervals between Memphis and New Orleans, while tin-
and cottonclads scoured the water between the picket stations to discourage rebels from crossing. Kirby Smith soon complained that the
"vigilance of the enemy along the Mississippi makes crossing [,] even
for individuals, extremely hazardous." One government agent, responsible for delivering a consignment of Confederate currency to Kirby
Smith's domain, spent more than a month sitting on the eastern shore,
waiting for an opportunity to row his trunkful of money across. Two
Texans and a Louisianian, who deserted from Bragg's army after the
battle of Chickamauga, discovered a regular colony of fellow absentees
awaiting transportation along the river's eastern bank. Eventually, after
paying fees of $50 apiece, they were given seats on a leaky skiff and
paddled to the other side. Perhaps the experience of First Lieutenant
L. H. Graves, of the Sixth Texas Cavalry, was more or less typical. En

route to an assignment in the Cis-Mississippi, he reached the western shore on April 15, 1864:

Could hear of no boats, or skiffs (Yankees had a gun boat anchored about every ten miles) along the Miss. but found a large canoe   Lieut. J. H. Jenkins of the 9th Tex. Infantry rather objected to crossing in this canoe & asked me, if I was willing to try it   I told him I was as it seemed to be the only show to get across the river—Some nine, or ten of us was in waiting there & the man that was to row us over said he could carry five (5) horses by this canoe at a time & would only charge us $50.00 apiece, but if he had to make three (3) trips 3 horses & men at a trip [with the horses swimming alongside] he would charge us $75.00 apiece—I told him we would pay the 75.00 in preference. So about midnight the little squad that was traveling with me made it safely over to the East side of the "Father of Waters." [12]

IV   About the only prominent Trans-Mississippian who pretended to be unconcerned about the dismemberment of the Confederacy was General Magruder, who, in a proclamation to the people of his District, extolled the defenders of Vicksburg and announced that Robert E. Lee had won the war's decisive victory at Gettysburg. But not even Magruder, for all his good cheer, was entirely immune from worry. Toward the end of his proclamation he warned: "Our barbarous foe already gloats over the prospect of your desolated homes, and your helpless women sacrificed to his unbridled licentiousness." Yet he was sure that if the Yankees came, the brave citizens of Texas would soon teach them "that the spirit of the Alamo will not suffer [Texas'] daughters to be the associates of enfranchised slaves." Governor Lubbock endorsed Magruder's manifesto, and called upon the people of Texas to "hurl back, beaten and dispirited[,] the hordes of Vandals the vile Yankee nation may throw upon our soil." Officials closer to the front lines were less prone to bombast and more susceptible to gloom. Governor Reynolds complained to a Missouri Congressman that the West had been thrown away by the bureaucrats in Richmond, and that the western population was in despair. Civil and military authorities in Arkansas trembled in expectation of the momentary arrival of an invincible army of Northern conquerors. And Senator Oldham grumbled that the Trans-Mississippi region had been "virtually and practically abandoned by the Executive and War department, and surrendered to Gen. Smith to be governed according to his discretion and to be sustained by its own resources."

Oldham's analysis was not far wrong. Ten days after Vicksburg fell, President Davis dispatched a long, detailed letter to Kirby Smith, in which he acknowledged that the interruption of regular communications across the Mississippi placed Smith's Department "in a new relation" to the rest of the Confederacy. "You now have not merely a military, but also a political problem involved in your command." Davis scrupulously refrained from suggesting that Smith was empowered, because of the extraordinary circumstances, to exercise any extraconstitutional civil authority in the states under his jurisdiction, but the President did urge Smith to confer with the four Trans-Mississippi governors, and to treat them as "valuable coadjutors without surrendering any portion of the control necessary for a commander to retain." Davis then proceeded to discuss a wide variety of topics, from the probability of a Union invasion to the productivity of western agriculture, as if he expected Smith to act as his vice-regent beyond the Mississippi.

On the same day, Secretary of War Seddon wrote Smith a letter which must have appeared less ambiguous than the President's, and which may also have appeared less scrupulous. Though the Secretary's text has been lost, subsequent references to it make clear that Seddon told Smith not only that he would have to assume complete responsibility for the conduct of military operations in the West but that he would also be obliged to "exercise powers of civil administration" as well. Later on, Seddon was to qualify this last remark by stating that it constituted no more than an unofficial personal opinion, and that in any case Smith's "powers of civil administration" could only embrace "such matters of an administrative character as were naturally promotive of or connected with military operations and appropriately pertained to the executive functions of the Confederate Executive." What Seddon had particularly in mind, he explained, "were the various administrative branches of service that minister to the supply, equipment, and furnishing of arms. . . . [These were] analogous to our [War Department] bureaus." Smith could do no more than to establish Trans-Mississippi branches of the War Department's bureaus—Subsistence, Quartermaster, Adjutant General, Ordnance, Conscription, Niter and Mining, Medical, and so forth—and to appoint qualified Trans-Mississippi officers to "discharge the duties of the corresponding bureaus" in Richmond. Smith's "powers of civil administration" did not, and could not, extend to legislative or judicial matters, or into the affairs of the Executive Departments directed by Cabinet officers other than Seddon. But Seddon did not even begin to modify his original unofficial statement until August 3, and he did not compose his definitive concordance until October 10. In the meantime, Smith had presented the Secretary's July 14 letter to an assembly of Trans-Mississippi state dignitaries, and with its help had secured promises of full cooperation from the politicians.[13]

On July 13, the day before Davis and Seddon wrote to him, Smith invited the governors and supreme court justices of the four western states to meet with him at Marshall, Texas, in the middle of August. His purpose for calling them together, he said, was to allay the public's despondency by providing convincing proof of the loyal and unanimous determination of the West's leading men to fight on to final victory, and to relieve popular fears of army despotism by arranging an exhibition of the civil government's continued supremacy over the military. But he failed to explain how a conference of state officials summoned together by a Confederate general could possibly manifest civilian supremacy. On the contrary, Smith's solicitation of the confidence, trust, and advice of the politicians, and of the aid of their states, appeared to be an assertion of his own authority over that of his civil coadjutors.

While waiting for these civilians to come together, Smith responded to an invitation from Magruder to hold a strategy conference at Rusk, Texas. The two generals met on July 20 and discussed military dispositions for the defense of Magruder's District. On the 25th, after his return to Shreveport, Smith issued a General Order directing that, because of the interruption of communications with Richmond, all army and War Department agents "on duty within the Department of Trans-Mississippi, acting under orders from Richmond, will in future receive their instructions from the department commander." This order also eliminated the evils of multiple recruiting by forbidding anyone, other than officers of General E. Greer's new Trans-Mississippi Conscript Bureau, from drafting or enlisting men of conscript age. Three days later, Smith dispatched a letter to Adjutant General Cooper, advising Cooper of his simplification of conscription procedures and of his convocation of the western governors and justices. "I hope thus to obtain the support and co-operation of the State governments in such measures as it may be necessary to take in this extraordinary condition of affairs," he explained. Then, indicating his convictions that his Department's isolation also required the national government to concede special authority to him, Smith reminded Cooper:

Communication is now extremely difficult with Richmond; in a few days it will entirely close. The department will be thrown entirely upon its own resources. Without the assumption of extraordinary powers, my usefulness as department commander will be lost. . . . Whilst my whole course as a military commander has hitherto been to keep within the limits of the laws, and to refrain from the exercise of powers not strictly granted me, I feel that I shall now be compelled to assume great responsibilities, and to exercise powers with which I am not legally invested. I trust the President will support me in any assumption of authority which may be forced upon me, and which will be used with caution and forbearance; and I entreat him to send the heads of departments west of the Mississippi, with extraordinary powers for the organization of a government, to continue until communications have been resumed with the capital.

Finally, on August 3—just as Seddon was beginning to hedge about his unofficial grant of "powers of civil administration" to the Trans-Mississippi commander, and seventeen days before Smith's letter of July 28 arrived at Cooper's office—General Smith stepped beyond "the limits of the laws" to exercise a power with which he was not legally invested. On that date, in General Orders, he announced the creation of a Cotton Bureau, to supervise "the purchase, collection, or other disposition of Government cotton" within the boundaries of his Department. More than two months later, as word of this innovation reached the War Department, Secretary Seddon was moved to dispatch a mild rebuke to Smith. The wisdom of such a step, "in view of the importance of the trade in cotton, and the necessity of regulating it, . . . is not doubted," Seddon acknowledged, but he added that "so far as practicable," such "measures should be accomplished in conformity with existing laws and through existing recognized officers." Yet Seddon refrained from ordering Smith to disband his Cotton Bureau. He merely suggested that the "aims of your Cotton Bureau, with change of name, which would probably be judicious, might also be practically as well obtained by assigning it to some quartermaster, or investing the agent selected by you with some appropriate military rank. These officers will hold, naturally, positions of proper subordination to you." [14]

On August 15, Smith's convention of state politicians met at Marshall. Arkansas was represented by Senator C. B. Mitchell, Justice W. K. Patterson, and a proxy for Governor Flanagin, Senator R. W. Johnson. From Louisiana came Governor Moore, Colonel T. C. Manning, and Justices Edwin Merrick and Albert Voorhies. Governor Reynolds, who constituted most of Missouri's rebel government, was his state's sole representative. Texas sent Governor Lubbock, Governor-Elect Pendleton Murrah, Senator Oldham, and Major Guy M. Bryan. General Smith presented Secretary Seddon's letter of July 14 and a six-point agenda which solicited advice concerning the conditions and resources of the states, the temper of the people, the currency and the cotton trade, the extent of the Department Commander's authority, the Department's foreign affairs, and the procurement of armaments. The convention's members, meeting in several subcommittees, explored each of the General's topics; and on the 18th they came together as a committee of the whole to review and vote upon each of the subcommittee reports.

Justice Merrick's subcommittee considered the touchy issue of Smith's authority, and was satisfied with a statement of principle couched in generalizations. Merrick reported, and the delegates unanimously agreed, that Smith was only at liberty to exercise those executive powers which came within the constitutional and legal purview of the Confederate Executive, and which, in addition, were "absolutely necessary" for the defense of the Department. Furthermore, in matters which came within the President's competence, but concerning which the power to establish policy had not been delegated by act of Congress to any general officer, Smith's authority was to extend only to details of administration, and was not to include the power to decide or amend policy. Referring to Seddon's July 14 letter, Merrick's report pointed out, rather forcefully, that "it could not have been the intention of the Secretary of War to advise the commanding general to exercise authority which belongs to the States, they still having officers present ready to perform their respective duties and functions." The report concluded with an affirmation that the civil authority remained superior to the military.

As a primer in government, or a manifesto of states' rights, Mer-

rick's report was quite adequate; but as a statement of the politicians'
conception of Kirby Smith's authority it was practically worthless. It
failed to specify exactly which executive functions were to be assumed
by Smith, or what powers were "absolutely necessary" for him to exercise in order to provide for the defense of his Department, or where the
line lay between matters of detail and decisions of policy. Nor, for that
matter, did the report even attempt to solve any of the basic constitutional questions regarding the legitimate extent of the Confederate Executive's power, or regarding the proper relationship between the general government and the states.

Governor Reynolds' subcommittee was directed to report upon the
conditions and resources of the states, public morale, and the procurement of arms and ordnance stores. But before exploring these issues, Reynolds' report sketched a gloomy picture of the Trans-Mississippi's isolation, and offered a far more positive and emphatic version
of Merrick's solution:

Beleaguered as we are by the enemy, the general commanding this department can neither transmit reports nor receive orders regularly from the capital. Hence the safety of our people requires that he assume at once and exercise the discretion, power, and prerogatives of the President of the
Confederate States and his subordinates in reference to all matters involving
the defense of his department. The isolated condition and imminent peril of
this department demand this policy, and will not permit delay; and we believe that all may be done without violating the spirit of the Constitution
and laws of the Confederate States, and without assuming dictatorial powers.

"As to the temper of the people," Reynolds' subcommittee was
compelled to report "some disaffection and disloyalty and more despondency in all the States of the department," but nevertheless insisted
that the "great mass of the people are loyal to the Government of their
choice," fully confident of the integrity and ability of General Smith,
and "determined that no greater calamity can befall them than subjugation by or submission to the Federal Government." These debatable
conclusions were combined with an equally debatable evaluation of the
Department's economic and military self-sufficiency. Reynolds' subcommittee felt that vigorous recruiting could easily raise 15,000 or 20,000
additional volunteers and conscripts in Texas, 8,000 to 10,000 in Arkansas, 5,000 to 6,000 in West Louisiana, and "a regiment per month"

in Missouri; that Texas had sufficient stores of foodstuffs on hand to subsist the army and its people "for at least two years," while Arkansas could furnish "immense quantities of provision and forage"; and that the Texas manufacturing complex was, in most respects, quite prepared to satisfy the Department's demands for arms, ammunition, and durable goods. However, by urging strict enforcement of the conscript laws, the mustering of the militias, and the impressment of slave teamsters to free detailed soldiers for field service, Reynolds' subcommittee hinted that it did not believe its own optimistic statements concerning the morale of the people and the abundance of manpower. Yet, despite the report's weaknesses, and despite its reformulation of Justice Merrick's advisory, the delegates adopted it without a dissenting vote.

Governor-Elect Murrah's subcommittee dealt with the question of the Department's foreign affairs. In a straightforward report, Murrah's subcommittee recommended that General Smith protect the security of the Department's vital international trade by entering into correspondence with the French and Mexican authorities south of the Rio Grande, and by dispatching competent and trustworthy commissioners to "ascertain their disposition toward our Government and people, and what we may expect from them in the way of favor or opposition." In flat contradiction to both Merrick's and Reynolds' reports, which more or less tried to reaffirm the legal limitations upon Smith's authority, Murrah's ignored the fact that no general officer had any right to operate a private State Department, and instead insisted that "the interest of the country and [the] necessities under which it labors [should] be the laws to guide [Smith's] discretion and action." Yet Murrah's report, like the first two, was unanimously endorsed by the convention.

Only Senator Oldham's report, which concerned the currency and the cotton trade, ran into trouble in the committee of the whole. Oldham's subcommittee concluded that since cotton was the Department's chief commercial asset, cotton should be used to support the economy, to stabilize the depreciating currency, and to pay for necessary imports. In order to reduce speculation in cotton, the subcommittee advised Smith to buy or impress all of the cotton within the Department, except that which he might deem advisable to exempt from government control for the welfare of private owners. For all practical purposes, in other words, Smith was being advised to nationalize the Trans-Mississippi's most important industry. To finance the wholesale purchase of cotton, and to infuse some value into government impressment vouchers, Smith was asked to raise money (under the authority of the "powers of civil administration" allegedly awarded to him by Seddon) by issuing 6 percent coupon bonds, and by recirculating the currency paid into government depositories. Before accepting Oldham's report, the convention eliminated the proviso concerning interest-bearing bonds. This amendment was probably introduced to restrict the military's ability to corner the cotton market, but it also served to eviscerate the rest of the plan by depriving the military of the degree of control over cotton needed to buy imports, suppress speculation, and shore up the currency.

Having passed on the work of the subcommittees, the assembly resolved to "infuse vigor into the patriotic efforts of the people, obtain and diffuse correct information, and discourage disloyalty," by establishing a propaganda infrastructure throughout the Department, to be composed of civilian committees of public safety and correspondence. The delegates also gave Smith a strong vote of confidence, and, after adjournment, the three governors and Senator Johnson issued for public consumption a rousing proclamation, praising Smith, lauding the Trans-Mississippi's zeal and loyalty, and promising the ultimate triumph of the Confederate cause.

The Marshall conference really decided nothing, since the meeting had no legal standing, its proceedings were at most advisory, its conclusions—especially in regard to the military's intrusion into treasury and diplomatic affairs—were sometimes contrary to law, and its recommendations exhibited some glaring contradictions. But except for Merrick's report, which was confined to philosophic abstractions, the convention's deliberations at least revealed the determination of the Southwest's leading men to persevere despite adversity, and their willingness under the circumstances to permit Kirby Smith to exercise considerable executive discretion. Even Governor-Elect Murrah, who was shortly to express states' rights scruples, encouraged the General to "act upon all civil matters pertaining" to the Department.

On September 11, Smith forwarded a transcript of the Marshall convention's proceedings to President Davis, along with an assurance that he would assume extraordinary powers "only when impelled by necessity." He promised to meet his unusual responsibilities "boldly, yet conscientiously," and trusted that his actions would be "reviewed with leniency" by his superiors. Twice he stated his readiness to resign his office at the President's request, but he affirmed that as long as the President chose to leave him in command, he would devote all of his energies to the "cause which is holy and righteous, and which, under God's providence, I believe will ultimately triumph." [15]

Before he wrote this letter—even before the Marshall conference convened—Smith had started to piece together a military administration for the Trans-Mississippi. Beginning in August, 1863, and continuing well into the following year, he gradually established semiautonomous western branches of most of the War Department's bureaus. By the summer of 1864, Smith's "War Department" included, in addition to the Cotton Bureau, sixteen executive and military agencies: Chief of Staff, Inspector General, Adjutant General, Ordnance, Quartermaster, Subsistence and Commissary, Clothing, Conscription, Medical, Paymaster, Transportation, Niter and Mining, Naval, Intelligence, Engineering, and (slave) Labor. The bureau offices were located either at Shreveport or at neighboring Marshall. Each agency consisted of a bureau head— usually a field-grade officer, but occasionally a general officer or a civilian—plus an assortment of deputies, assistants, secretaries, clerks, and field agents. Where needed, subordinate branches of these central bureaus were attached to various district and subdistrict headquarters. The manpower needed to staff these offices was customarily detailed from line regiments, much to the distress of many field commanders. All returns and reports which army regulations required to be submitted to the chief of bureaus in Richmond were, in the Trans-Mississippi, forwarded instead to the heads of the corresponding bureaus at Shreveport or Marshall. General Taylor, who beheld Smith's burgeoning bureaucracy with the jaundiced eye of a simple soldier, later complained that Smith's staff "surpassed in numbers that of Von Moltke during the war with France"; but then Von Moltke did not have to communicate with his capital through a Union blockade.

In his letter of October 10, 1863, Secretary Seddon gave Smith's western War Department his blessing, but declined to grant Smith permission to exercise a corollary authority, the power to appoint, commission, and promote officers. On September 12, Smith had asked that, in order to expedite the staffing of regiments and bureaus, the power to appoint be delegated to him. But this request threatened to infringe upon one of the Executive's most cherished prerogatives, and so, when Davis saw Smith's letter, he immediately replied that "the power to appoint cannot be delegated. The Constitution confers it upon the President only, by and with the consent of the Senate." Yet Davis and Seddon appreciated Smith's predicament, and agreed to let him make unofficial or temporary assignments to rank and duty, pending approval of his nominees by Richmond. In practice, Smith often exceeded the letter of these instructions. He refused to remove his own "officers" to make vacancies for replacements transferred from the East, he appointed men to command and rank in General and Special Orders, and he often neglected to keep the capital apprised of the names of his nominees. The later volumes of the Trans-Mississippi's *Official Records* are full of captains, majors, and colonels about whom Richmond apparently knew nothing. In early 1864, one of these uniformed civilians, John S. Ford (who held a commission in the Texas militia, but none in the Confederate army), commanded both a Confederate cavalry brigade and the Confederate Subdistrict of West Texas!

If Smith stretched his authority to assign army officers, his authority to communicate with foreign governments was nonexistent. Yet on September 2, 1863, in his first foray into foreign affairs, he sent A. Superviele to Paris with instructions to deliver a letter to the resident Confederate commissioner, John Slidell. In his letter, Smith urged Slidell to impress upon Napoleon III the desperate plight of the Trans-Mississippi Department—the Department, not the Confederate States! —and to beg the Emperor to direct the Imperial forces in Mexico to occupy the "east bank of the Rio Grande." "This succor must come speedily, or it will be too late," Smith insisted. "Without assistance from abroad or an extraordinary interposition of Providence, less than twelve months will see this fair country irretrievably lost." Smith explained that Missouri, much of Arkansas, and most of Louisiana and the Nations had already been conquered by the enemy; that the "country west of the Mississippi has been exhausted of its fighting population"; and that none but "the aged, the infirm, and the lukewarm" remained in the region still under Confederate control, to defend it, to protect France's access to cotton, and to act as a buffer between the French protectorate in Mexico and the hostile United States. It seems unlikely that Slidell, who was trying to convince the Emperor of the Confederacy's might and perseverance, ever brought General Smith's discouraging sketch of domestic disintegration to His Majesty's attention.

Even more pressing than the Department's need to attract foreign aid was the need to procure adequate funds for the payment of the Department's debts. The rapid depreciation of the Confederate currency produced an ever-increasing demand for Treasury notes; but the difficulties entailed in shipping currency from the East, and the Treasury regulations requiring the retirement of notes paid into government depositories, caused a severe shortage of currency. On June 4, 1863, Smith, upon his own authority, instructed the Treasury Department's Trans-Mississippi agents to stop canceling bills. After the Marshall conference adjourned, he directed the depositories to overstamp and reissue notes already canceled. During September he also took it upon himself to threaten anyone who refused to accept Confederate currency with confiscation and exile, to order the impressment of goods at fixed prices whether or not money was available to pay off the vouchers, to appoint tax commissioners, collectors, and assessors, to enforce the rigorous application of the Confederate tax laws, and to receive reports previously submitted to the Treasury Department. In a letter to President Davis he even threatened to raise a popular loan by issuing his own bonds, but was dissuaded from doing so by the Secretary of War. Funds were still forwarded from Richmond, but the remittances which were not waylaid en route often arrived in the form of such large drafts that Smith found it impossible to cash or disburse them.

Until July, 1864, when the Treasury Department finally established an autonomous Trans-Mississippi branch at Marshall, General Smith continued to function as if he were the Confederate West's chief Treasury official. It was not a rewarding job. After August, 1863, his military paymasters ran out of cash with which to pay his soldiers their monthly $11; some of Smith's troops never received another Confederate dollar. By the fall, pensions owed to the families of dead and disabled soldiers were far in arrears, and many army buyers had no money with which to purchase supplies for the coming campaign season. By the end of 1864, despite the funds raised by the operations of Smith's Cotton Bureau, and despite the new issues of currency circulated by the western branch of the Treasury, the Trans-Mississippi Department's accounts were sixty million dollars in the red. After that, nobody bothered to keep books.

As the date for the convocation of the fourth session of the First Confederate Congress approached, General Smith, Governor Reynolds, and countless other western dignitaries bombarded Richmond with appeals for legislation which they thought necessary to place the military and civil administration of the Trans-Mississippi Department upon a regular and legal foundation. In particular, the westerners asked for laws establishing self-sufficient War, Treasury, and Postal departments beyond the Mississippi, and for laws specifying the degree of executive discretion which General Smith might exercise. In his annual report to the President, Secretary Seddon insisted that it would be most judicious for extraordinary powers of military administration to be entrusted to Smith, including the power to act as Assistant Secretary of War for the West, and urged that legislation be provided for the creation of Trans-Mississippi branches of the Treasury and the Post Office. When Congress convened on December 7, 1863, President Davis summarized in detail the problems caused by Federal control of the Mississippi, admitted the impossibility of governing the West from Richmond, recommended the organization of autonomous western branches of the Treasury and Post Office departments, and, insofar as military affairs were concerned, asked authorization for the President and the Secretary of War to "delegate to the commanding general [of the Trans-Mississippi] so much of the discretionary power vested in them by law as the exigencies of the service shall require."

Congress proved quite ready to accept, and even to go beyond, the Executive's recommendations. On January 27, 1864, a law was enacted which empowered the President, with the consent of the Senate, to appoint a Treasury Agent for the Trans-Mississippi. For all practical purposes, the Treasury Agent was to be a Deputy Secretary, authorized to discharge for the region within his jurisdiction any duty or function that the Secretary himself was entitled to perform for the Confederacy at large. Additional bills provided for the establishment of Trans-Mississippi branches of the Auditor's and Comptroller's bureaus of the Treasury, which were empowered to receive, exchange, issue, regulate, and disburse currency, to collect taxes, to fund debts, to keep and audit accounts, and to review and file evidence of claims against the government (a function which, in the East, belonged to the Department of State).

In March, 1864, Congressman P. W. Gray of Texas was appointed Treasury Agent; in April he arrived in the Trans-Mississippi; and on July 1, having established his bureaus at Marshall and a Treasury Note Division at Monroe, Louisiana, he commenced operations. Though Gray was, by law, accountable only to the Secretary of the Treasury, it appears that until the end of the war he frequently consulted with and deferred to General Smith, with whom he maintained the most cordial relations. Although his agency eventually absorbed Smith's Cotton Bureau, for example, its disbursement of proceeds earned from the cotton trade upon receipt of requisitions or vouchers approved by Department Headquarters was almost automatic. Even the expenditures of funds derived from other sources were customarily governed by the General's office. In return for the agent's cooperation, the army detailed soldiers to conduct the agency's business, and, when necessary, assigned troops to enforce the tax laws and to protect revenue collectors.

On February 10, 1864, a law was signed which authorized the President, with the consent of the Senate, to appoint a western Post Office Agent. Although the Postal Agent's funds were to be controlled and audited by the bureaus of the Treasury Agency, the Post Office Agent in all other respects was to enjoy the same degree of autonomy and discretion as his Treasury colleague; that is, he was to be vested with the powers of a Deputy Postmaster General. Dr. James H. Starr, who had served as the Texas Republic's Treasury Secretary, was appointed Postal Agent. Establishing his office at Marshall, he imported a supply of orders, forms, and equipment from the East and, by September 1, 1864, was ready to assume supervision of all postal operations in the West. Although General Smith detailed men to staff the Postal Agency, it seems that the military had little or no occasion to become involved in the agency's everyday affairs. Starr's advent apparently had little or no beneficial effect upon the efficiency of the Trans-Mississippi's mail service, which, until the very end, remained very poor.

Congress went beyond the Executive's recommendations by instructing the Senate's Committee on Military Affairs to "inquire into the expediency of organizing and strengthening the Trans-Mississippi

Department by the appointment of an Assistant Secretary of War" for the region. But Seddon, who feared that such an appointment would unnecessarily complicate the problem of defending the West by diluting Smith's unequivocal authority, promptly voiced his opposition to the proposal. He explained that he preferred to leave General Smith in complete control of military affairs beyond the Mississippi, and reiterated that the only legislation needed was a law giving legal sanction to Smith's organization of auxiliary branches of the War Department's bureaus. The Senate abandoned its own plan—and with it, much of the principle of civilian supremacy over the military—and, on February 17, 1864, Congress passed an act which complied with Seddon's request. Specifically, the act empowered the commanding general of the Trans-Mississippi Department, under the authority of the President and Secretary of War, to create the necessary bureaus, to supervise their activities, to assign officers and clerks to duty within them, and to nominate qualified men for formal appointment to rank and office.

Thenceforth, in any legislation which touched upon the military administration of the West, Congress customarily stipulated that the commander of the Trans-Mississippi was to exercise, within the limits of his jurisdiction, powers analogous to those of the Secretary of War. For example, an act of February 15, which provided for the suspension of the writ of habeas corpus in certain cases, and an act of February 17, which set conditions for the employment or impressment of free and enslaved Negroes whose labor was required by the army, both stated that their provisions might be implemented by order of the President, of the Secretary of War, or of the commanding general of the Trans-Mississippi Department. No other general officer, not even Robert E. Lee, was allowed such broad discretion.

On April 28, 1864, after Congress adjourned, Secretary Seddon reported to the President:

The legislation of the late Congress for the Trans-Mississippi Department was both liberal and provident. Provision was made for the peculiar needs incident to its comparative isolation from the supervision of the central government, and all the agencies of a partially independent government were authorized. In the same spirit has been the action of the executive. Added rank and dignity have been bestowed on the able commander and administrator at its head, and to him have been entrusted the full measure of executive powers, which, under our constitutional system, could be exercised by others than the president.

And that same day, Davis assured Smith that "as far as the Constitution permits, full authority has been given to you to administer the wants of your department, civil as well as military." Yet although it was clear that both Congress and the Executive were prepared to treat the Trans-Mississippi as a detached province of the Confederacy, and although it was apparent that both were willing to grant extraordinary powers to the commander of the Department, some crucial questions remained unanswered—questions dealing, in particular, with the extent of Smith's civil authority. While no doubt now existed about the General's absolute control of military affairs, the legislation enacted by Congress had been silent regarding the measure of executive power he was at liberty to exercise over the two civilian agencies of his Department's "partially independent government." The laws of January 27 and February 17 stipulated, in fact, that the Treasury and Postal Agents were to be subordinate to their respective Cabinet superiors; they made no mention of the commanding general. Davis himself evaded this issue when he qualified his announcement of Smith's "full" authority, "civil as well as military," with the caution, "as far as the Constitution permits." [16]

But despite such ambiguities, it is evident that both the President and the Congress appreciated that the viability of the Trans-Mississippi's "partially independent government" depended upon close cooperation between civil and military officials, and that such cooperation could only be secured by permitting Smith, who was the one man in a position to perform the duties of an executive, to act as proconsul for the region. When, for instance, Smith took it upon himself to oversee the disbursement of Treasury funds, Congress and the Executive quietly acquiesced.

V   Neither Congress nor the President tried to delimit or define Smith's relations with the states, nor did the Marshall conference give the General much practical direction in this regard. Certain matters— conscription, impressment of labor and supplies, suspension of the writ of habeas corpus, mobilization and utilization of militia troops, the cotton trade—necessarily involved Smith in the affairs of the peoples and governments of the western states, but it was left to him and to his civilian coadjutors to discover and implement mutually satisfactory accommodations.

As a rule, the rebel governments of Missouri, Arkansas, and Louisiana, three states which were wholly or partially occupied by enemy armed forces, raised few if any serious objections to the way in which Smith conducted his Department's business. Although their citizens might be upset by incidents of alleged military usurpation, the refugee politicians who attempted or pretended to govern these three states were ordinarily shrewd enough to recognize that the survival of their administrations, if not their personal survival, depended upon the success of Confederate arms. They were therefore rarely inclined to quibble about the military's infractions of states' rights, and they seldom bothered to protest the army's interference with the liberties of citizens. Even Governor Flanagin, who at first tended to be strict about Arkansas prerogatives, seems to have lost his taste for independence after the Helena disaster and its sequel, the fall of Little Rock. But down in Texas, the one Trans-Mississippi state whose sovereignty remained more or less undisturbed by the enemy, statesmen could afford to persevere through 1863 in devotion to the abstract ideal of states' rights. Not until the spring of 1864, when Banks's second thrust up the Red River Valley threatened East Texas, would the Texas government surrender to General Smith.

The state elections of 1863, the last general elections to be held under Confederate auspices, bore witness both to the demoralized apathy of most of the western populace and to the mood of independent dissent still prevailing among those Texans who did take the trouble to vote. Everywhere, balloting was exceptionally light, while only the Texans elected to office a significant number of men who had expressed reservations about Confederate nationalism.

In Arkansas, where no gubernatorial contest enlivened the 1863 campaign, scattered balloting returned three ardently pro-Confederate incumbents and one states' rights newcomer to the House of Representatives at Richmond. Apparently, support for the three incumbents—and, by implication, for Senator Robert W. Johnson's state machine, to which two of them belonged—came from the absentee ballots cast by embittered refugees, since Rufus K. Garland, the sole states' rights advocate in the Arkansas delegation to the Second Congress, represented the state's southwestern district, the only district still wholly within the Confederate lines.

Missouri's Confederate Congressional elections were obviously complicated by the fact that the entire state was overrun by the Union army. When, in July, 1863, Governor Reynolds ordered a general registration of all qualified Missouri voters "sojourning within our lines," exactly two potential voters responded. In order to excite some interest in the campaign, Reynolds delayed the November elections until May, 1864. By then, the Governor's persistent propagandizing had induced some 8,000 Missourians—most of whom were soldiers serving in the Cis-Mississippi—to report to designated polling places established in various army camps and to cast absentee ballots.

Curiously, the chief issue in Missouri's election was not the way in which the war was being prosecuted (virtually all of the candidates expressed support for the Davis, Reynolds, and Kirby Smith administrations, and none of them complained about the erosion of Missouri's rights) but rather the "sobriety & morality" of some of the state's incumbent Confederate legislators. Inspired by the notorious misbehavior of Senator John Clark, who scandalized Richmond's staid society every time he took an alcoholic breath (he once climbed through the Secretary of War's bedroom window for a midnight chat; on another occasion he purloined Albert Pike's mistress), a number of Missouri's Representatives had likewise brought disgrace upon themselves and their state. Thomas Harris, for instance, was unable to run for reelection because he had broken a leg in a brothel.

Despite the efforts of Clark's cronies to stuff the ballot boxes, the voters threw out most of the incumbents and elected a slate of steadier men proposed by Governor Reynolds. In the absence of a functioning state legislature, Reynolds then took it upon himself to dismiss Senator Clark and to promote to the vacant Senate seat one of his own righteous politicos, Congressman George C. Vest. But then, in December, 1864, an irate lady, shouting that Senator Vest had dishonored her, stormed into the lobby of the Richmond capitol and flayed Vest with a cowhide whip. Seven months earlier, in the midst of Missouri's tumultuous election campaign, an urbane eastern Congressman, complaining as much about the Missourians' unequivocal nationalism as about their personal indiscretions, had written to his wife that he would "rather plough and feed hogs than legislate . . . with Missouri . . . to help me." [17]

In preparation for Louisiana's elections, the state's rebel legislature disqualified any citizen who was reputed to have collaborated with the Union invaders, restricted access to the polls to those eligible voters who happened to be safely within the area under Confederate control, and provided for the at-large election, on a single statewide ballot, of all six of Louisiana's Confederate Representatives. In a poll shot through with fraud and swung by the soldier vote, five incumbent Congressmen were handily returned to office (the sixth incumbent declined to stand for reelection). Four of the holdovers and the single newcomer were sturdy Southern nationalists, ready to endorse whatever drastic measures might be needed to effect Louisiana's liberation. Only John Perkins—a Yale graduate with a law degree from Harvard—continued until the very end to wave the tattered banner of states' rights.

Since Governor Moore's four-year term was about to expire, and since state law prohibited him from succeeding himself, rebel Louisiana's voters also elected a new chief executive. The leading contenders in the field of six were Colonel Leroy Stafford, of Rapides Parish, a veteran of Lee's army, and General Henry Watkins Allen, of West Baton Rouge Parish, the maimed hero of the battle of Baton Rouge. Both were more than ready to cooperate with Confederate civil and military authorities; both waged sedate campaigns, carefully avoiding personal attacks and mention of divisive issues; and both were content to run on their respective war records. Allen had a decisive advantage: whereas Stafford had been doing his fighting off in distant Virginia, Allen had had his right leg shattered while defending Louisiana's own soil. Even Stafford's home-town newspaper, the *Alexandria Louisiana Democrat,* endorsed General Allen's candidacy. Allen was swept into office by a spectacular margin, 7,401 votes to 872. In congratulating the Governor-Elect, Kirby Smith expressed the hope that the relations between Louisiana's civil government and the Department's military administration would remain "cordial and unreserved." They would; as soon as the returns were in Allen set out on a grand progress through the Confederate fragment of his state, to arouse the ardor of its dispirited people and to exhort them to greater sacrifice for the common good of the South.[18]

Because of Governor Lubbock's determination to retire from office and accept an army commission, Texas voters were also given an opportunity to pick a new executive. But unlike their neighbors in Louisiana, who chose an impassioned Confederate to lead them, Texans were not nearly so ready to acknowledge that the war might justify any subversion of the Lone Star State's sovereignty. Distressed by the army's rigorous enforcement of the conscription laws, by the military's widespread use of impressment, by the war's impact upon their economy, by the general government's wholesale consignment of Texas boys to the distant East, and by the incumbent governor's habit of excusing and endorsing the aggrandizement of Confederate power, Texans were in the mood for a change.

The extent of the Texans' malaise became evident early in 1863, when political leaders from every quadrant of the state began to voice support for the nomination of Sam Houston. The fact that Houston had been deposed from office in 1861 because of his Unionist sympathies seems not to have been regarded as a disqualification. By May, 1863, the Houston boom had reached such proportions that Guy M. Bryan reported that he was "almost certain that Houston will run for Governor. . . . should he do so he will be elected I fear. [T]he consequences would be calamitous indeed." But on May 27, having "noticed the agonizing distresses of some of the presses of Texas . . . relative to my permitting my name to go before the people for Governor of the State," the aged and mortally ill Houston was "disposed to relieve them from their painful apprehensions," and caused a letter to be published which announced that "under no circumstances, will I permit my name to be used as a candidate." A month later, the old man died.

Houston's unequivocal withdrawal left four contenders in the race, but two of them, ex-Governor (now Colonel) Edward Clark and General Henry McCulloch, both preferred service in the field, and also abandoned their candidacies. The campaign was thus reduced to a bitter fight between General Thomas J. Chambers, who had run for governor three times before and had been roundly defeated all three times, and a lawyer from Marshall, Pendleton Murrah, an enigmatic political unknown. Half the state's newspapers endorsed each candidate, and all of them proceeded to wallow in vicious diatribe. Those which backed Chambers extolled his war record and his staunch Confederate sympathies, while intimating that Murrah was a slacker, a coward, and a covert Unionist. Murrah's papers, on the contrary, emphasized Murrah's loyalty and devotion to the Lone Star State, his "republican simplicity" (for Chambers was said to be "certainly one of the wealthiest men and certainly one of the largest land and eleven league holders in Texas"), his "fine talents," his "cultivated mind," and the "noble impulses of his heart"; and while they admitted that Murrah had never fought for the Confederacy (although he had been a regimental quartermaster in 1861, before ill health forced him to retire), they maintained that Chambers' own war service had been less than distinguished.

During the first week of August, 1863, Texas voters declined for the fourth and last time to elect Chambers to the office of governor. He collected 12,455 votes, while Murrah polled 17,511. At the same time, Texas citizens discharged three of the six veteran Confederate Representatives and elected three new ones in their stead. While the three who survived generally supported whatever innovations seemed necessary to prosecute the war, the three newcomers soon proved themselves to be as enamored of their state's sovereign independence as their new governor was.

On November 5, 1863, when Governor Murrah delivered his inaugural address, he affirmed his loyalty to and respect for the Davis and Kirby Smith administrations, but took care to emphasize his profound devotion to the republican ideals of state sovereignty, personal liberty, and civilian supremacy over the military. By the time Congress convened, rumblings of Texas disaffection could be heard as far away as Richmond. Senator Williamson S. Oldham, who had been known as a defender of the Davis administration's policies and as a critic of those who undermined the Cause by harping upon states' rights, himself began to grumble that Richmond and the army seemed to regard Texas as nothing but a bountiful source of beef and common soldiers. And in December, 1863, Senator Louis T. Wigfall, whose dedication to the rights of Texas was accompanied by personal vendettas against the Confederate Executive and his subordinates, announced to a South Carolinian that he, for one, would like to hang Jeff Davis.[19]

CHAPTER FOUR

KING COTTON

On September 13, 1863, General Kirby Smith confided to General Henry McCulloch that "the Cotton business has long occupied my attention, it is the most tangled snarl that has ever come before me." The snarl was so tangled that Smith never did manage to unwind it. For cotton was king in the Confederate Southwest. It ruled the region's economy, it commanded the deployment of armies and fleets, it governed commercial intercourse, it purchased the tools of war, and it received from both its subjects and its alien tributaries the homage due a monarch.

Cotton was the only cash product of the Trans-Mississippi states capable of earning the credits necessary to sustain the wartime economy of Kirby Smith's empire. To shore up the currency, to supplement the output of the area's primitive domestic industry, and to make agriculture a remunerative occupation, the Department's bulk cotton had to be exchanged for money or, ultimately, for imported manufactures, either armaments or consumer goods. Two markets for the sale of cotton, and two sources for the procurement of useful manufactures, existed. One was the industrial and textile complex of Great Britain and Western Europe, and the other was the industrial and textile complex of the northeastern United States. And three routes for the exportation of the Southwest's cotton and the importation of finished products were available: cotton and goods could be smuggled overland through the enemy's lines, or shipped by sea through the Union blockade, or traded across the Mexican border. The progressive deterioration of the Trans-Mississippi's economy encouraged the Department's desperate authorities to foster both licit commerce with neutrals and illicit trade with the United States, by any means at their disposal.

Theoretically, until the beginning of 1864 no such thing as trade with the enemy was possible. In May, 1861, the Provisional Congress of the Confederate States outlawed such intercourse, and not until February, 1864, did the last session of the First Congress authorize the President to issue regulations to govern commerce with the North. In the interim, Congress' determination to extort recognition from foreign governments by withholding cotton from world markets, the Confederacy's need for breadstuffs, and popular patriotic aversion to commercial dealings with the enemy all conspired to restrain the flow of cotton across the lines.

Between the late spring of 1861 and the spring of 1863 Congress repeatedly passed resolutions urging the reduction of cotton cultivation and the conversion of cotton land to the production of foodstuffs, while it enacted laws designed to restrict the exportation of cotton and to enforce the destruction of any cotton in danger of capture by the Federals. Moreover, during the first year of the war the governments of most of the Confederate Trans-Mississippi states were more than ready to ratify Congress' initiatives: the Arkansas cotton industry suffered grievously under the impact of exorbitant taxation, while Louisiana's governor emphatically prohibited trade or intercourse with the enemy. In May, 1862, even the planters and citizens of Caddo and Bossier parishes, Louisiana, resolved to remove any baled cotton lying within reach of the enemy to safety in the interior, and promised to burn any cotton exposed to seizure by the Union army. Only Texas, which enjoyed access to the Confederacy's single unblockaded border, refrained from imposing any legal restrictions upon the cultivation or exchange of cotton, but even in Texas the demand for grain encouraged planters to reduce the proportion of land devoted to the production of cotton.

Yet the theoretical impossibility of trade with the enemy gave way to the actuality of extensive illegal intercourse well before the Richmond Congress saw fit to authorize and regulate commercial relations with the North. New England's textile mills desperately needed raw cotton; the South desperately needed the manufactures which cotton could buy; and producers, officials, merchants, and speculators on both sides of the military frontier were eager to satisfy these complementary demands. A certain amount of illicit trade was carried on along every sector of the Confederacy's front lines, but the accidents of geography and the fortunes of war drew the most daring entrepreneurs, the most efficient smugglers, the most corrupt officials, and the most ambitious crooks toward the lower Mississippi Valley. For there, cotton was abundant; the river systems offered convenient transportation; the bayous, swamps, and forests guaranteed clandestine traders concealment and security; the front lines were exceptionally fluid and indistinct; the rebel army was far too weak to stop every gap in the military boundary; and, as time went on, the threat of poverty and the realities of survival encouraged planters, soldiers, and citizens on the Confederate side of the frontier to wink at contraventions of the law.

The initiative for the development of trade across the lines came from the United States, which, at first, needed cotton more than the South needed manufactures. In July, 1861, when the Federal Congress officially severed commercial relations with the seceded states, it reserved to the President and the Secretary of the Treasury the right to issue licenses for such intercourse as the public good might require. As soon as Butler's army gained a foothold in lower Louisiana, a flock of duly licensed speculators descended on New Orleans and, with the general's blessing, began to exploit this legal loophole. Neighboring rebel cotton planters were invited to continue vending their staple in the city. Butler himself promised the planters safe-conduct and fair prices, assured those that were unable to transport their bales across the lines that the Union armed forces would guarantee reimbursement for cotton left exposed to confiscation, and affirmed that "the owner, were he Slidell himself, should have the pay for his cotton," if he could arrange to have it taken or shipped to New Orleans.

Initially, the planters' response was auspicious. A few somehow managed to smuggle their cotton all the way to the city, while many others, anticipating the momentary advent of Federal expeditionary forces, secreted thousands of bales along the banks of West Louisiana's navigable bayous. But then Governor Moore, determined to enforce the legal prohibitions against trade with the enemy, ordered the complete interdiction of all communication with New Orleans and directed the militias of six parishes to burn every bale within reach of the Federals. Because of Moore's intransigence, only an insignificant amount of cotton actually seeped through to New Orleans. On October 22, 1862, Butler advised the Secretary of the Treasury that he had "endeavored in every possible way to open trade in cotton through the rebel lines," but that "owing to the peculiar action of the Confederate authorities, I have not been able as yet much to succeed." [1]

By the time Butler penned this report, the Northeast's famished textile mills were starving for raw cotton. Fully 75 percent of New England's spindles lay idle. Politicians and businessmen were pouring into Washington, appealing for aid. As the result of their pleas, Butler was transferred, the army contingent stationed near New Orleans was reinforced, and Nathaniel Banks was appointed to the command of the Federal Department of the Gulf. Upon arriving in New Orleans in mid-December, Banks was shocked by the corrupt venality which pervaded the cotton trade, and was appalled by the extent to which greed had consumed soldiers and speculators alike. Banks did his best to clean out the racketeers, to discipline both the army and the speculators, to bring the cotton trade under the control of military men or honest Treasury agents, and to block the delivery of contraband and munitions to rebel cotton dealers.

Yet Banks was aware that the Northeast hungered for cotton, and that he was expected to satiate that hunger. He could not, in other words, simply prohibit commerce with the rebels; all he could do was to attempt to regulate it. Through 1863 and early 1864 he introduced a variety of rules and procedures designed to expedite the flow of cotton into New Orleans, to stop the shipment of strategic manufactures to the Confederates, and to eliminate the fraudulent practices employed by Northern middlemen. But since the very nature of this unorthodox intercourse bred opportunities for corruption, no amount of regulation could purge it of abuse. According to Banks's successor, General E. R. S. Canby, hordes of crafty and unprincipled speculators continued to attach themselves to the army, to "traffic in its blood, and [to] barter the cause for which it is fighting, with all the baseness of Judas Iscariot, but without his remorse." Even the "army of Treasury aids" appointed to supervise the cotton trade succumbed to its temptations. Referring to the way in which they competed with the speculators whom they were supposed to shepherd, Admiral Porter complained: "It is very much like setting a rat to watch the cheese to see that the mice don't get at it." Porter insisted that a "greater pack of knaves never went unhung." In 1864, virtually all of the Federals' legal and regulatory restraints upon intercourse with the rebels gradually eroded away or were subverted beyond repair, and by the end of the war something approaching free trade prevailed between the Union and Confederate segments of Louisiana.[2]

It takes two to trade, and if the Confederates' stringent sanctions against intercourse with the Federals had been enforced, the cotton commerce which flourished along the lower Mississippi after 1862 could never have reached the magnitude it did. But by the end of 1862, it was becoming evident that any hope of continuing the Confederacy's war effort virtually presupposed evasion of the trade embargo. As long as cotton was left to rot, the South's baled treasure could neither subsist its citizens nor arm its soldiers. If the Confederacy's beleaguered economy were to survive, this potential wealth had to be converted into manufactures, armaments, and foreign exchange credits. Among the Southerners most ready to accommodate to these realities were the planters and officials of the Trans-Mississippi Department, a region which, because of its isolation, its industrial poverty, its monstrous cotton surplus, and its proximity to the markets in Union New Orleans, had more occasion than most to entertain visions of the prosperity that the sale of cotton might bring.

Confederate authorities in the Trans-Mississippi West continued to discourage private commercial transactions with the enemy, but began to search for ways to convert cotton owned by the government into gold and military supplies. By late 1863, well over 105,000 bales of Treasury Department cotton were on hand in the District of West Louisiana alone, crowding wharves, warehouses, and river banks up and down the Red and Ouachita valleys. Most of this cotton had been purchased from neighboring planters with bonds issued under the provisions of the several produce loan acts of 1861, 1862, and early 1863, but once purchased it had been used for nothing but the ornamentation of waterfronts and the armor-plating of a few river gunboats. Additional cotton was already being purchased or impressed by local army officers, who, despite their inability to market their produce, seemed to share some notion that their bales could eventually be transformed into war matériel. And, as if to make the temptation to trade with the enemy intolerable, the third session of the First Congress enacted a sweeping tax-in-kind, which, when it fell due on March 1, 1864, would give the Department's Treasury Agent title to one-tenth of the region's 1863 cotton crop. It seemed absurd for the Department to hoard the one negotiable asset it possessed while its economy became more and more deranged and its army suffered from a critical shortage of supplies.

As early as March, 1863, General Smith, with Secretary Seddons' explicit permission, began to circumvent the law by authorizing civilian agents to negotiate the exchange of rebel cotton for Northern manufactures. By July, a lively trade in cotton, munitions, and contraband was blossoming along the lower Mississippi. By August, Smith found it necessary to systematize this commerce by instituting his Cotton Bureau. And by March, 1864, a Northern cotton speculator visiting Shreveport (under the protection of passes issued by both Banks and Kirby Smith) could report that the sleepy little capital of Kirby Smith's empire had been transformed by the bustle of the cotton trade into a thriving commercial metropolis.

After the first few hesitant months, there was nothing very subtle about the way in which this business was conducted. Whenever a river steamboat churned from Shreveport or Alexandria with a cargo of cotton consigned to New Orleans it was fairly obvious that responsible people were permitting trade across the lines. Rebel customs officials collected the duties due on smuggled shipments of contraband, while New York financiers openly dealt in shares of Confederate cotton. Swarms of Northern cotton buyers, bearing licenses signed by Lincoln himself, endured the rude hospitality of Shreveport, while agents dispatched by Kirby Smith and Taylor became accustomed to the amenities of New Orleans and Washington. The trade even reunited families rent apart by the passions of war. Among the more enterprising cotton dealers were two cousins, J. H. and "Major" A. W. McKee, whose disparate loyalties were overcome by their common appetite for profit. J. H. McKee, acting as General Banks's personal representative, frequently traveled up the Red River to confer with his kinsman, who happened to be one of General Smith's civilian "officers" and the ranking purchasing agent for the Shreveport branch of Smith's Cotton Bureau.

Yet a certain degree of circumspection was demanded, especially after Banks began to inhibit the sale of munitions to the rebels, and after both Congresses, in February, 1864, began to publish regulations for the control of mutual intercourse. So—on paper, at least—various evasions were introduced to obscure the more scandalous excesses engendered by the commerce. General Smith asked Colonel W. A. Broadwell, the chief of his Cotton Bureau, to issue fewer passes to Union steamboats. The Confederates agreed to accept gold, sterling, foreign exchange credits, or even United States greenbacks in place of military hardware. The Federals usually pretended that the cotton they bought came from private purveyors, and that no United States currency was ever deposited in the Confederacy's coffers; while the Confederates were generally just as ready to believe that the cotton they exported was being delivered to European consumers. The McKee clan even conspired to facilitate the wholesale "confiscation" of Confederate government cotton by the Union armed forces, in order to eliminate many of the touchy problems involved in conveying bulk cotton through the military lines. As this illicit commercial boom became progressively less inhibited, General Taylor began to protest against it; but his was the only prominent voice raised in dissent. And even Taylor's reservations were based not upon moral or legal abstractions but upon his conviction that the Department was not receiving full value for the cotton it exported.

By the summer of 1864, the Mississippi Valley cotton trade had earned at least $30,000,000 (specie) worth of supplies and credit for the Trans-Mississippi Department. But by then the Department's extant stores of government-owned cotton were practically exhausted. The exportation of cotton to the Federals and to Europe, the wholesale destruction and confiscation of cotton during the spring campaigns in Arkansas and West Louisiana, and a disappointing public response to the tax-in-kind tithe, all had served to deplete the Department's stock of baled capital. The Trans-Mississippi's economy, which had come to depend upon the proceeds of the cotton trade, was in danger of imminent collapse. Consequently, on June 1, 1864, Kirby Smith published one of the most drastic decrees of his reign. Without waiting for authorization from Richmond, he ordered the Cotton Bureau to buy or impress one-half of all the cotton within the limits of the Trans-Mississippi Confederacy. Since few planters offered to sell cotton at the artificial currency prices stipulated by the several state impressment boards, Smith's order resulted in the wholesale confiscation of cotton throughout the extent of his empire. Although not even this expedient was enough to keep the Department's books in the black, it did ensure that the cotton trade would continue to flourish without interruption until the end of the war. By early 1865, the trade in the lower Mississippi Valley had become so open that detachments of Confederate soldiers were customarily detailed to escort the wagon trains loaded with cotton down to the Federals' riverside wharves.[3]

❊ II   On May 21, 1861, eleven days after commercial intercourse with the United States was prohibited, the Confederate Congress went on to forbid the exportation of cotton and other staples except through Mexico and the South's own seaports. In April, 1862, in response to the growing effectiveness of the Union blockade, Congress restricted the list of open seaports to those actually under the control of the Confederate States, and authorized inbound blockade-runners to moor and unload anywhere along the Confederate coast. A year later, for the same reason, Congress permitted outbound vessels to take on cargo and to clear from any point along the South's extensive shoreline. Except for the mild tariff act of May 21, 1861, its even milder amendments, and an act of April 4, 1863, which allowed the Secretary of the Navy to hire civilian boats and pilots needed to run government property through the blockade, no other significant legislation concerning blockade-running was passed prior to 1864.

During the first two years of the war, most of the larger blockade-runners, including almost all of the steamers, preferred to call at the ports of the Cis-Mississippi Confederacy. The East's harbors, better developed than those of the West, were able to accept ships of almost any size, while in the Trans-Mississippi Department only Galveston offered a safe haven to vessels which drew more than six feet of water. The West's primitive domestic transportation systems also discouraged blockade-running, since the region's rude facilities made it exceptionally difficult to haul cargoes of manufactures or cotton between the seacoast and interior markets. The western ports, other than Galveston, were simply incapable of handling the same volume of traffic accommodated by Wilmington or Mobile. Finally, the distance between the Texas coast and the major neutral terminals, Havana and Nassau, encouraged most seagoing steamers to make for the more proximate eastern harbors. Since these were closer to Cuba and the Bahamas, passages consumed less time; the runners were thus less vulnerable to interception on the high seas or to the vagaries of weather, could devote more space to cargo and less to coal, and were able to make more trips and greater profit in a given time.

Yet the Texas coast had its attractions. For one thing, the Union navy was unable to concentrate many ships in the western Gulf before 1864. Little fleets of blockaders were clustered beyond the bars at Sabine City, Galveston, and a few other prominent ports, but most of the coast remained clear. Moreover, the Texas sea islands offered cover, protection, and innumerable natural moorings to vessels light enough to skim over the shallow waters between the islands and the mainland. And further, countless small entrepreneurs, who were unable to compete on even terms with the masters of steam vessels, or who were disinclined to challenge the tighter Union blockade east of the Mississippi Delta, found that sailing ships were quite adequate for running the Texas blockade. By 1863, the western Gulf was alive with sleek little sloops, schooners, and sailing brigs, carrying modest cargoes between the Texas ports and such neutral terminals as Matamoros, Tampico, Vera Cruz, and Belize. In December of that year, the United States Consul at Tampico complained to the Federal Secretary of State that "this traffic so successfully carried on impresses the people of this country [Mexico] with the belief that our navy is too impotent to enforce a blockade, and that our government has no control over any of the Southern ports."

The attitude of laissez faire that characterized blockade-running in the western Gulf during the early war years gave way to a measure of state socialism soon after Kirby Smith's arrival in the Trans-Mississippi Department. Distressed by the amount of privately owned cotton being shipped abroad without benefit to the Confederacy, and appalled by the volume of frivolous trinkets carried by inbound vessels, Smith determined to impose some order upon the blockade-running business. In the first place, Smith directed that a number of captured steam gunboats, starting with the *Harriet Lane,* be disarmed and refitted as government blockade-runners. The commanding general had no legal authority to launch his own transport fleet, but his half-dozen steamers nonetheless offered real competition to the smaller private sailing vessels. In the second place, as early as June, 1863, Smith and Magruder, endeavoring to satisfy armament contracts negotiated by army quartermasters and to fill the holds of their government steamers with cotton, began to impress consignments of privately owned cotton awaiting shipment at or near Texas port towns. The more the army impressed, the less was left for civilian supercargoes. In the third place, Smith began dispatching agents to neutral ports abroad, to ensure that cargoes shipped into the Department included a reasonable amount of war matériel and necessary consumer goods. And in the fourth place, after October, 1863, various Trans-Mississippi headquarters (again without legal sanction, but at least with the moral support of the Cis-Mississippi generals who introduced the practice) began to promulgate regulations requiring privately owned vessels to carry stipulated amounts of government cotton or munitions during every run. Magruder, for instance, insisted that anyone licensed to export a consignment of cotton had to import armaments equivalent in value to one-fourth of the cotton shipped, or to pay a stiff "tax" in lieu of impressment of the cotton.

In February, 1864, Congress finally ratified the generals' initiative by authorizing President Davis to regulate the exportation of cotton, and by prohibiting the importation of luxuries through the blockade. When the President's regulations appeared, a month later, they obliged every private blockade-runner to turn over at least half of its outbound cargo space to government cotton, plus at least another fourth to private cotton being bartered for supplies destined for consumption by the army. Yet even with these restrictions, blockade-running continued to flourish along the Texas coast until the very end of the war. More than a month after Lee surrendered his army, fleet little schooners like Dave McLusky's *Scow* and even swift oceangoing steamers like the *Phoenix* and the *Jeanette* were still slipping in and out of the port of Galveston, the last Southern harbor to remain under the Confederate flag.

It is impossible to estimate the total amount or the value of the cargo run through the Texas blockade, not only because customs, consular, and quartermasters' records are exceedingly fragmentary, but also because the records which do exist (compiled, for the most part, in Houston, the single official port of entry in Texas) seldom distinguished between freight imported overland via Mexico and freight imported through the seaports. However, from all indications it appears that the seaborne trade was far less important, in volume of goods exchanged, than either the commerce along the lower Mississippi or the intercourse across the Rio Grande. Occasionally, very large shipments did manage to pass through the blockade—one steamer ran in 12,000 stand of arms, another 10,000—but most of the craft committed to this business were incapable of carrying such loads. And since the port of Sabine City consisted of a few ramshackle wharves and a pile of rubble, and since the captain of the schooner *Rob Roy* noticed, in 1864, that grass was growing in Galveston's streets, it is unlikely that either place was excessively busy.[4]

꙳ III   Although every section of the Confederate States profited to some degree from trade with the enemy and blockade-running, only the Trans-Mississippi Department shared a common border with a neutral nation, Mexico. After Vicksburg and Port Hudson fell, therefore, only the Trans-Mississippi Department enjoyed free access to the markets of the outside world. Because West Texas was as yet so sparsely settled, because the transportation facilities below San Antonio were still very crude, because the lower Rio Grande was barely navigable, and because Mexico was convulsed by its own civil wars, trade across the Rio Grande was hardly convenient or easy. Yet this trade became the western Confederacy's chief means for the disposal of cotton and the procurement of foreign manufactures. During the last nine months of the war, in particular, this commerce was the most important single prop of the Trans-Mississippi South's economy.

In May, 1861, when the Confederate Congress prohibited trade with the United States and began to regulate the shipment of cotton through the blockade, it specifically refrained from imposing any restrictions, other than the ordinary revenue tariffs, upon commerce with or through Mexico. Not until February, 1864, did Congress authorize the President to regulate the Mexican trade; and even those regulations subsequently issued by the Executive were voided by the fiat of General

Smith. Yet by 1864 commerce across the Rio Grande was nevertheless under stringent control, for in the interim the generals and statesmen of the Trans-Mississippi West had undertaken to promulgate their own rules, and to enforce them with rigor.

As soon as the war broke out, merchants, speculators, and cotton dealers began to flock toward the lower Rio Grande country. At the same time, Davis dispatched to Mexico City a diplomatic commissioner, John T. Pickett, with instructions to cultivate amicable relations with Juarez' government and to do everything possible to encourage the development of unobstructed trade across the Rio Grande frontier. But much to the disappointment of both the Confederate government and the eager speculators, Pickett, a swashbuckling filibusterer, antagonized Juarez and raised fears in Mexico City that the Confederate Gringoes might well become more of a threat to the territorial integrity of Mexico than their more distant Yankee cousins had even been. Thomas Corwin, the United States minister to the Juarez regime, proved to be a much more accomplished diplomat, and so Corwin soon won Juarez' ear. By December, 1861, Pickett was cloistered in Vera Cruz, Corwin had the run of the Presidential Palace, and Juarez was trying to find a way to choke off the Confederates' access to the ports and markets of northern Mexico.

Fortunately for the Confederates, Juarez' influence in northern Mexico was scarcely more than nominal. Although one of his procurators sat in Matamoros and exercised control over the state of Tamaulipas, most of the other states east and north of Mexico City (including Vera Cruz, Nuevo León, Coahuila, Chihuahua, and Sonora) were governed by ambitious adventurers, men who were either indifferent or hostile to the general government. The most princely of these semi-autonomous satraps was Santiago Vidaurri, governor of both Nuevo Léon and Coahuila and unofficial overlord of the rest of the region. Although Vidaurri continued to assert his allegiance to the central government and to Juarez' Conservative Party, he seldom bothered to pay attention to orders from Mexico City. Instead, he absorbed himself with plans for the conquest of Tamaulipas, for the secession of his domains from the Republic of Mexico, and for the creation of his own independent Republic of Sierra Madre.

In May, 1861, for the purpose of negotiating an agreement to police the portion of the Rio Grande border shared by Texas and Vidaurri's states, Davis commissioned Juan A. Quintero, a citizen of Texas and a resident of Mexico, as his special representative to Monterrey, Vidaurri's capital city. Upon arriving in Monterrey, Quintero reported that Vidaurri's provinces were peaceful and prosperous, that Vidaurri himself sympathized with the Confederate cause (not only because the South appeared to be fighting for the same sort of independence which he desired, but because the prospect of trade with the South promised revenues to his treasury and profits to his states' industries), and that the governor was most eager to establish warm relations with the Confederate States. Quintero's mission was broadened to include all matters touching upon intercourse between the Confederacy and Vidaurri's empire, and Quintero himself soon struck up an intimate friendship with the governor. By 1862, Vidaurri had offered to furnish the Confederacy with all the ammunition it could use, had encouraged numerous mercantile houses to settle in Monterrey and to engage in the Confederate trade, had developed a domestic textile industry capable of supplying most of the rough cotton clothing required by the Trans-Mississippi's slaves, and had even proposed a military alliance between his states and the Confederacy (a proposal which President Davis politely rejected).

But Vidaurri's most significant contribution to the Confederate war effort was his seizure of Tamaulipas. In late 1861, a civil war exploded in Matamoros and spread rapidly throughout the vincinity; when the smoke cleared in the spring of 1862, Vidaurri was in possession of the state. His coup placed the ports of Matamoros and Tampico, plus five hundred miles of the Rio Grande border, under the jurisdiction of an administration friendly to the Confederate States. Within days, Matamoros was aswarm with cotton speculators, gunrunners, and the agents of European business firms, and trade across the lower Rio Grande was approaching the proportions of a gold rush.

Juarez ordered Vidaurri to seal the border and to proclaim martial law along the frontier. But Juarez was seven hundred miles away by mountain trail, and was, in addition, too preoccupied with a French invasion to enforce his instructions; Vidaurri could afford to ignore him. Instead of closing the border, Vidaurri reduced import tariffs, designated numerous additional ports of entry, used his troops to suppress bandits who interfered with mercantile enterprises, and did everything else within his power to encourage the commercial boom. Trade between San Antonio and Monterrey, by way of Roma, Laredo, and Eagle Pass, continued to flourish, but Matamoros, because of its proximity to Brownsville and the sea, swiftly became the undisputed commercial metropolis of northeastern Mexico. Even after the fall of 1862, when a change in fortune wrested Tamaulipas from Vidaurri's fingers, the various Juarista generals who succeeded him were most careful not to strangle Matamoros' prosperity. Occasionally, for the sake of form, one or another of them might raise a tariff or look the other way while a bandit chief ambushed a cotton train, but none of them ever allowed patriotism to stand in the way of profit.

The development of trade across the Rio Grande was not an unmixed blessing for the Confederacy. Although plenty of Confederate and Texas purchasing agents journeyed to Monterrey and Matamoros to buy military hardware and supplies, they soon found that Mexican and European vendors were reluctant to accept Confederate scrip or state treasury warrants in payment, and that private speculators, who were able to offer planters the highest prices for cotton, were rapidly cornering the stocks of cotton needed to barter for the goods. Without some sort of regulation, there was real danger that the speculators might succeed in monopolizing commerce with Mexico; if that happened, they could extort whatever prices they wished for consignments of munitions and manufactures.

The government of Texas, rather than the Confederate authorities, took the first steps to exert a measure of official influence in the Mexican trade. In order to secure funds for the purchase of weapons for the militia, the Texas legislature endeavored to float a bond issue. But since the terms of the loan were not appealing to most prospective buyers, and since even those who did buy paid for the bonds with the sort of currency that was useless in the Mexican trade, the loan failed. Next, Governor Lubbock tried to impose some restrictions upon speculation by requiring everyone engaged in hauling cotton for export to secure a license from Austin, but once his license system was instituted it so complicated legitimate transactions that it threatened to suffocate commerce across the border. Under torrents of appeals from merchants and dealers who needed cotton to fulfill their contracts, Lubbock relented, and proceeded to undermine his own licensing system by granting liberal exemptions.

Finally, in January, 1862, the legislature, meeting in secret session, enacted two laws designed to help the state compete in the cotton trade. The first established the Texas State Military Board, composed of the governor, the comptroller, and the treasurer, as the state's central office for supervising the equipment of the militia. The second authorized the military board to sell $500,000 worth of state bonds for either specie or cotton. These bonds, paying 8 percent interest and scheduled to mature in sixteen years, were to be backed by specie to be collected under the provisions of a special tax on the cotton trade; the money or cotton raised by the sale of the bonds was to be used by the military board to purchase and import arms and military stores.

In February, the board published an appeal for the patriotic cooperation of the people, divided the state into twenty-eight districts, assigned agents to each district, and began buying cotton with the bonds. However, in its instructions to its agents, the board specified that they might not pay any more than ten cents per pound for the best grade of cotton. At this price, which the speculators easily exceeded, few planters were inclined to exchange their cotton for the nonnegotiable bonds. During the two years between the beginning of 1862 and the beginning of 1864 (when the military board was reorganized), the state managed to purchase and export only 5,551 bales, barely 1 percent of the cotton raised within its boundaries between 1861 and 1863. Considering the magnitude of the cotton commerce across the Mexican frontier, this amount was insignificant.

As it became obvious that the efforts of Texas were doing little to restrain speculation, local Confederate military authorities began to interfere in the cotton trade. General Paul Hebert, then commanding the District of Texas, ruled that no cotton was to be exported without licenses from the governor and the general commanding the Western Subdistrict, Hamilton Bee, and that, in order to procure the necessary licenses, a merchant would have to agree to return a certain proportion of the value of the cotton to Texas in the form of military stores. When General Holmes assumed command of the Trans-Mississippi Department, he ratified Hebert's order. Again, Governor Lubbock was inundated by protests and appeals for exemption, but now, steadied by the army's bayonets, he proved far less receptive to the speculators' pleas. But when the protests finally reached Richmond, President Davis indignantly directed Holmes to remove the restrictions upon the cotton trade, and reminded him that only the Confederate Congress had the right to pass laws governing foreign commerce.

Within weeks after Holmes revoked Hebert's order, speculation had again reached such proportions that General Magruder, on February 22, 1863, stirred up the wrath of the speculators and his superiors alike by reinstating Hebert's licensing rules. State Senator John T. Harcourt called upon the editor of the Clarksville *Standard* to "speak out plainly against this usurpation of power by the military authorities. Let not the syren song of military convenience or millitary necessity be any pretext or justification for a palpable infraction of the Constitutional rights of the people." Austin's *Texas Almanac,* denouncing Magruder's "infamous Cotton Order," hoped "soon to see our military commanders required to confine their powers to *real military necessities alone."* Senator Oldham warned the Secretary of the Treasury that Magruder's decree amounted to a cotton embargo, in violation of the revenue laws. The Texas legislature reprimanded the general and appointed a prestigious board of inquiry to investigate and report upon Magruder's usurpation. (Some months later, to everyone's surprise, the board reported that Magruder's action, despite its patent illegality, had indeed been justified by "a military necessity paramount to every other consideration.") Finally, in April, Secretary Seddon severely rebuked the general and ordered him to cease obstructing trade forthwith. Magruder reluctantly did as he was told. The border trade was once again engulfed in speculation, and the army was once again unable to compete for supplies.[5]

Besides attempting to license speculators, various army commanders stationed in Texas—particularly Magruder and Bee—began using army funds to buy cotton needed for the purchase of military supplies. They, like the state of Texas, managed to divert a few bales from the hands of the speculators, but since planters were reluctant to accept the army's currency and the prices the army was willing to pay, the speculators easily outbid the army's purchasing agents. In fact, the army's entry into the cotton market did little more than contribute to the inflation of cotton prices, by multiplying the number of buyers bargaining for each consignment.

Matters became even more confused in the late fall of 1862, when the War Department designated its own "exclusive" purchasing agent for the Trans-Mississippi. Major Simeon Hart, a prominent San Antonio businessman with excellent connections in both Richmond and Mexico, was "intrusted with the exclusive power of purchasing cotton for the [War] Department in all the upper and western parts of Texas, and should be looked to for the supply of munitions and quartermaster's stores for the army in the Trans-Mississippi District." But Major Hart's scrip was no better than the generals' currency or Texas bonds, his schedule of official prices was no more appealing to planters, and, since the procurement of arms and stores through Hart's office was fraught with red tape and delay, neither the generals nor the Texas military board took his "exclusive power" seriously. They proceeded to bid against the War Department's representative, while the speculators continued to outbid them all.

As frustration piled upon frustration, and as the stocks of government cotton within the District of Texas began to run low, the conviction arose in official circles that the only recourse left to the army was to impress the cotton it needed to pay for its supplies. Thus far, in the absence of Confederate law authorizing impressment, no cotton had been seized; but ever since August, 1862, when the provost marshal at Dallas had taken it upon himself to fix prices and expropriate goods required by the local garrison, the movement toward impressment had been gaining momentum. That month, the War Department had acknowledged that extraordinary necessity might justify occasional impressments by field commanders. In November, the Secretary of War had instructed Major Hart to impress whatever wagons he needed to haul government cotton to the border; within two months, the impressment of transportation had become common throughout the Trans-Mississippi Department. In December, the War Department promulgated a General Order authorizing officers of the Quartermaster's and Commissary bureaus to impress private property in accordance with "army regulations," and in January, 1863, the Executive finally asked Congress for a law which would legitimatize the War Department's initiative—

which would, in other words, permit the War Department to issue the "army regulations" which it had already cited in General Orders. Senator Oldham protested that the authority to impress would give army commanders as much arbitrary power as Roman proconsuls, but Senator Wigfall, Senator Clark of Missouri, and most of the other Trans-Mississippi delegates to Congress agreed with their Cis-Mississippi colleagues that impressment seemed to be the army's only salvation.

The result of Congress' deliberations was "An Act to Regulate Impressments," signed by President Davis on March 26, 1863. The act made no explicit mention of cotton, was worded in such a way as to suggest that the only property subject to impressment was that needed for immediate consumption by troops in the field (as distinguished from that needed to barter for strategic imports), and circumscribed impressment with a number of procedural safeguards. But the act's key passage, the brief first section, was subject to broad interpretation. It read: "Whenever the exigencies of the army in the field are such as to make the impressment of forage or any other property absolutely necessary, then the impressment may be made by the officer whose duty it is to furnish such subsistence." In the months that followed, the commanders of the "army in the field" in the Trans-Mississippi Department were to decide that the "exigencies" of the service often made the impressment of "other property" like cotton "absolutely necessary." In August, when he created his Cotton Bureau, General Smith went so far as to invent an entire bureaucracy "whose duty it is to furnish such subsistence."

By the time copies of the impressment act reached West Texas, the local military cotton agents were desperate. One of Magruder's quartermasters reported that there were only seventy-five bales of government cotton left in Brownsville's warehouses, although speculators were trundling hundreds of bales through the town each day. Major Hart's Mexican and European creditors were growing so impatient that many of them threatened to withhold delivery of military stores until Hart could produce some cotton on account. Even the masters of some of the vessels standing off the mouth of the Rio Grande were beginning to refuse to offload cargoes of army supplies until they received the bales due them in payment. The military buyers needed cotton, and they needed it immediately.

On May 19, 1863, Major Hart wrote to Magruder to ask for authority to impress cotton to meet his obligations. After three weeks passed, during which Magruder failed to reply, Hart forwarded a similar request to A. C. Myers, Quartermaster General of the Confederate army. Myers sent Hart's letter on to Secretary Seddon, who, in turn, passed it on to the President. In his endorsement, Seddon acknowledged that although he appreciated the importance and even the necessity of controlling cotton speculation in West Texas, and although he recognized that the army needed cotton to barter for munitions and equipment, he was personally reluctant to see the army employ impressment. Davis then referred Hart's letter to the Secretary of the Treasury. Secretary Memminger advised that no existing law sanctioned the impressment of privately owned cotton, that the Constitution would probably prohibit the enactment of any such law, and that in the absence of legislation the "impressment of private property stands upon the naked ground of military necessity" alone. Military necessity, said Memminger, might justify the expropriation of cotton needed to build a fort or to armor-plate a gunboat, but never the seizure of cotton for the purpose of paying for other supplies. When Seddon saw Memminger's endorsement, he hastened to remind his colleague of the law of March 26, which, he said, did indeed give the army the power to "impress any property when deemed necessary for the good of the service," but Seddon's belated assertion of the army's broad discretion did not go so far as to repudiate his earlier expression of personal opposition to the widespread use of impressment. Finally, President Davis settled the argument by dismissing the entire question, saying that he had "never been willing to employ such means except as a last resort." 6

But by the time Davis put aside Hart's inquiry, Hart, Bee, Magruder, and Kirby Smith had already decided to resort to impressment. On May 20, the English steamer *Sea Queen,* carrying a large load of Enfield rifles and other valuable stores consigned to Major Hart, dropped anchor at the mouth of the Rio Grande. In return for the freight, the *Sea Queen*'s master demanded prompt payment of some 2,000 bales of cotton. Since Hart's cupboard was bare—he had no more than twenty bales at his immediate disposal—he appealed to Magruder for a written order which would permit him to impress sufficient cotton to meet his obligation. Magruder, who was still smarting from the reprimands he had received for his earlier attempt to license speculation, was in no mood to accept the responsibility for initiating cotton impressments; he passed Hart's appeal up to Kirby Smith. Smith answered by calling Magruder's attention to the impressment act of March 26, and by remarking that the act appeared to give the army the right to impress whatever was "necessary and indispensable for carrying on the operations of the Government"—an interpretation of the law which was much more liberal than any of those advanced in Richmond. But Magruder was not concerned with the meaning of the act; he just wanted Smith to tell him to execute it. So, after advising Hart to await further instructions, he asked Smith, on both June 16 and June 17, to issue an order specifically directing him to impress cotton. On the 23d, Smith replied with another evasion: "In all cases where the exigencies of the service make it necessary," Smith wired, "you will make impressments in accordance with the act, without referring the matter to these headquarters." This was too much for Magruder. In a telegram to Smith's chief of staff, Magruder warned Department headquarters that even though the Confederacy's credit in the marketplaces of northern Mexico was on the verge of evaporating, he, for one, had no intention of impressing cotton without first "referring the matter" to Shreveport; he would implement the impressment act only upon receipt of a straightforward order from Smith to do so.

On June 27, Smith finally yielded. Accepting full responsibility for the execution of the impressment act by Magruder and his subordinates, Smith ordered Magruder to impress enough cotton to meet the needs of Major Hart and the other military buyers, and to sustain the credit of the government. He even went so far as to authorize Magruder to impress whatever wagons or slave teamsters might be required to haul impressed cotton to the border. He did ask that cotton owned by the state of Texas, or privately owned cotton being exported in exchange for war goods and machinery, be exempted from impressment; and he did suggest that, because of the delicate political situation in Texas, the expropriation of privately owned cotton be conducted in a fashion as restrained and discreet as possible until after the August elections. Nonetheless he assured Magruder that Department headquarters would endorse and support any expedient Magruder might find necessary to pay the army's obligations. Upon receiving Smith's directive, Magruder ordered Bee to take whatever cotton was needed to satisfy the debts in-

curred by Major Hart and the District's quartermasters; he even went
beyond Smith's instructions to ask Governor Lubbock to allow cotton
belonging to the Texas military board to be impressed—a request
which Lubbock firmly rejected. By the beginning of August, there was
hardly a bale of privately owned cotton left south of the Nueces River.

Needless to say, the vigorous execution of the generals' cotton impressment orders met widespread disapproval. On July 30, 1863, the
editor of the *La Grange Patriot* wanted to know "by what public law so
violent a proceeding is warranted."

It is certainly not found in the law of impressment passed at the last session
of Congress. . . . When a great and fundamental principle of human liberty
[that is, the sanctity of private property] is directly assailed, while we are
all professing to guard its very portals from desecration, he who does not
raise his voice and sound a note of warning of the approaching danger is already a slave and is ready for the manacles.

The *Patriot's* appeal to principle was balanced by the Brownsville
Flag's simultaneous revelation that Kirby Smith and his cohorts were all
conspiring to conceal the effects of rampant corruption in Major Hart's
office. The *Flag* "hoped that General Smith, who has done what he had
no right to do in this instance, will stretch his assumption of authority a
little further and jayhawk Mr. Hart." The *Houston Tri-Weekly Telegraph* of the same date, rushing to the generals' defense, expressed its
dismay that "some remarks derogatory to Lieut. Gen. Smith have been
made . . . based upon the cotton impressment orders."

This attempt [to discredit the generals], when traced to the bottom motive,
will be found in a majority of instances to have its origin in disaffection and
dissatisfaction with the Confederacy. . . . Gen. Smith is no tyrant. Gen.
Magruder is no tyrant. Neither desire to injure the people of the country.
On the contrary, both have devoted their lives to our defence. Shall we
quarrel with them for taking the necessary measures to secure our safety?

But the *Telegraph's* was the minority opinion. The *Patriot,* the
Flag, and most of the other Texas newspapers were more than ready to
continue their quarrel with the generals. And so, it appears, were the
majority of Texas voters, who, the following week, elected a states'
rights lawyer to the gubernatorial chair, and three new states' righters to
the House of Representatives.

On August 3, in an effort to introduce system and sanity to the

Department's cotton trade, Smith created his Cotton Bureau and appointed Colonel Broadwell chief. But when Smith then ordered all military officers engaged in the cotton trade to report to Broadwell, Major Hart protested that his authority from the Secretary of War took precedence over Broadwell's dubious authority from General Smith. Instead of subordinating himself to Broadwell, Hart advertised that his agents alone were "empowered to make purchases, shipments or transact other business" for the Quartermaster's Bureau, and in an angry letter to Secretary Seddon he complained that General Smith was usurping the functions of that bureau. On November 9, 1863, a major on General Myers' staff advised Hart that while his authority to negotiate contracts remained unimpaired, Richmond could do nothing to relieve him from "interference on the part of Lieutenant-Colonel Broadwell. . . . It is impossible, in the existing condition of affairs, to regulate from this point details in Texas, and great discretion must of necessity be allowed the commanding general of a department so distant and inaccessible." Although Hart retained his nominal independence, in time he and the Cotton Bureau accommodated to each other's existence, and, more often than not, endeavored to cooperate.[7]

Hart's initial intractability, plus the sheer magnitude of the Texas cotton business, soon made it obvious that cotton transactions along the Rio Grande border could not be efficently supervised by Broadwell's remote Shreveport office. Consequently, a plan was devised for the creation of a branch of Broadwell's bureau at Houston. Smith induced six prominent and respected Houston businessmen to associate themselves with the enterprise, and on November 22 appointed one of them, William J. Hutchins, chief of the Texas Cotton Office. Hutchins was awarded the pay and honorary rank of a lieutenant colonel. He and his five assistants were directed to "obtain from the planters, by sale or agreement, and, if necessary, by impressment, all cotton that the government may require for the purchase of army stores of all kinds, and to meet existing liabilities heretofore accrued." All Confederate States agents, officials, and contractors within the limits of Texas who were "engaged in the purchase or removal of cotton" were to report to Hutchins' office, to submit contracts for review by Hutchins' staff, and to secure export licenses from Hutchins' agents. Local military commanders were instructed not to enter into any agreements for the purchase or exchange of cotton without Hutchins' prior approval. Hutchins himself was to report his activities to Colonel Broadwell, but otherwise, for all practical purposes, his Texas Cotton Office was to be an autonomous agency, juridically subordinate to, but actually independent of, Broadwell's central bureau.

On December 4, after conferring with Smith, Magruder, Senator Oldham, and numerous other military and civilian authorites, Hutchins published a proclamation "To the Cotton Planters of Texas," in which he outlined the details of the scheme which his office had determined to adopt. The Cotton Office proposed to purchase one-half of the bales owned by planters, merchants, dealers, or other private citizens; to give the owners, upon delivery of their cotton to designated government depots, the specie value of their bales in the form of vouchers or certificates payable in cotton bonds to be issued by Congress; and to exempt from impressment the remaining half of the bales owned by cooperative citizens, plus any wagons or teams they needed to transport cotton either to the government depots or to the Mexican frontier. But the plan also obligated the private owners to cover the cost of transporting cotton purchased by Hutchins' agents to the Cotton Office's depots, offered no guarantee that Congress would ever issue the bonds needed to honor the Cotton Office's certificates of indebtedness, and threatened anyone who refused to sell half of his bales to the Cotton Office with impressment of his entire cotton stock, his animals, and his wagons. Within weeks after the publication of Hutchins' proclamation, his agents were busily buying cotton, issuing licenses, impressing the property of uncooperative planters, disbursing certificates, and otherwise enforcing the provisions of the cotton plan.

But the citizens wanted no part of it. Typical of the public response to Hutchins' plan was an irate letter addressed to the *Houston Telegraph* by a distressed East Texas farmer:

I live a good ways from market, and last year only made a small crop of cotton—about twenty bales, out of which I set aside two bales to pay tenth [the Confederate tax-in-kind], intending to send the balance to Mexico to buy some necessaries for the use of my family, which I assure you they stood greatly in need of, and to get hard money enough to pay for my bagging and rope which I bought on credit. But just as I am looking about for wagons to haul it, I am told that I must give the Government one half be-

fore I can send the other half off my place, and worse than all, I must haul
the Government cotton to Navasota at my own expense. Now, sir, I can't
get the cotton hauled without giving the wagons half for hauling, so the wagons get half and the Government gets the other half, and I am stripped of
the fruits of a year's labor and of the only means I had or can raise to buy
shoes and clothing for my wife and children.

I cheerfully would pay the tenth lax levied by Congress, as I supposed
that was all they wanted me to, or else they would have laid a heavier tax.
Will you tell me if Congress has made a law to take all my crop, and worse
than that, involve me in debt for the bagging and rope to cover it; and what
are they going to do with all the cotton in the country after they get it?
They can't feed soldiers on it, nor their horses, but I guess the cows will get
the biggest part of it, as I am told they ate up hundreds of bales of cotton
last year, and I think I may as well let them eat up 18 bales on my farm,
and then I can save the bagging and rope.

A flood of similar complaints poured into Magruder's headquarters. Even Senator Oldham, who had helped draft Hutchins' cotton plan,
was induced by the angry voice of the people to denounce the policy as
a warrant for robbery, which "tested both the patience and patriotism of
the people of Texas." Oldham went on to warn President Davis that numerous speculators had taken advantage of the public's apprehension to
buy up, at ridiculously low prices, countless bales of cotton threatened
by impressment or purchase by the Cotton Office; that the speculators,
using fraud and bribery, had no trouble securing export licenses from
the Office; that many of the Office's own agents were themselves speculating with the cotton taken from private citizens; and that fully five
thousand troops of the line had been diverted from active service and
detailed to work as teamsters or laborers for both the Cotton Office and
the speculators. Colonel Broadwell repeated the same charges in a letter
to the Secretary of the Treasury, and then stated his conviction that the
only way to stop speculation was to enable the government to "control
all cotton, and allow none exported, except . . . to supply the military
necessities of the country and preserve our credit." [8]

꙳ IV   The metropolis of West Texas, and the city which emerged as
the northern terminus for overland trade with Mexico, was the town of
San Antonio. By June, 1864, traffic through the town had become so
dense that the City Council was forced to levy a tax on each bale car-

ried through its streets, to cover the cost of road and bridge repairs and to pay for the removal of hundreds of animal carcasses abandoned by the wagon trains. No less upsetting was the presence of a large and unruly floating population of transient wagon drivers, who rarely missed a chance to disturb the peace. San Antonio seldom passed a night without at least one lynching, a few murders, or a couple of small riots.

Upon arriving in San Antonio, southbound trains hired the teamsters and animals needed for the last leg of the pull to Mexico, repaired or replaced unserviceable vehicles, took aboard water and provisions, organized themselves into small convoys, and, when everything was ready, struck out for the Rio Grande. Each convoy consisted of ten or fifteen wagons, a few saddle horses, and twenty or thirty spare draft animals. The personnel of a typical twelve-wagon train generally included one wagon master, two section captains, twelve teamsters, a couple of armed outriders, and a "corporal" whose task it was to ride herd on the extra animals. During the six to eight weeks it took the convoys to cover the distance from San Antonio to the Mexican border, the wagons were ordinarily driven by day and parked at night. Whenever camp was made, the vehicles were drawn into defensive circles designed to protect both men and animals from marauding Indian war parties and roving outlaw bands.

But an even greater threat to the security of the trains was the wilderness country itself, "a dead level of sand, mesquite trees, and prickly pears" baked dry by a savage drought. "You cannot imagine," insisted a cavalry officer who rode through the region early in 1864, "how desolate, barren, and desert-like this country is; not a spear of grass, not a green shrub, with nothing but moving clouds of sand to be seen." Around the scattered water holes—many of which were saline, and more of which were dry—"could be seen hundreds of domestic animals, dead, their flesh seemingly dried upon their bones." To travel over this country during a drought was "a thing to be acquired by practice, and not from theory or books." Except for the single substantial house at King's Ranch, one hundred twenty-five miles north of Brownsville, the only signs of human life below the Nueces were a few miserable wooden shanties located near the major wells, and the flotsam left in the wakes of wagon trains.

Descending into the Rio Grande Valley, the cotton trains custom-

arily continued to the Mexican side of the river before stopping to resupply, refit, or offload their cargo. One reason for this precaution was
that the towns on the Texas bank were vulnerable to raids by companies
of Yankee irregulars staging from Mexican bases; another was the prevalent fear that the Federals might invade the region; and a third was the
inability of cotton dealers to secure insurance to cover the damage or
loss of bales stored along the Texas shore. Even the city of Brownsville
enjoyed relatively little of the prosperity created by the cotton trade;
throughout the war, it remained a straggling clapboard town inhabited
by no more than 3,000 civilians, hardly more than lived in it in 1860.
The other Texan settlements hugging the river up to Eagle Pass—
Edinburg, Ringgold Barracks, Rio Grande City, Roma, Carrizo, San Ignacio, Fort McIntosh, Laredo, and Fort Duncan—were nothing but dismal little frontier villages, which contrasted sharply with the thriving,
prosperous Mexican towns sprinkled down the southern shore—Piedas
Negras (opposite Eagle Pass), Nuevo Laredo, Guerrero, Mier, Car-
mago, Reynosa, and Matamoros. By 1863, the free port of Matamoros,
a mile south of Brownsville, had grown into a bustling commercial en-
trepôt populated by 9,000 souls. Its bullet-scarred walls and ramshackle
slums bore witness that its sudden growth had been painful, but the
town had high hopes for the future.

Upon reaching the Rio Grande, the wagon convoys paid the Confederate export tax of one-eighth of a cent per pound of cotton, an exorbitant ferry toll, and the Mexican import duty. Along those portions
of the frontier controlled by Governor Vidaurri, the Mexican tariff
usually ranged between one and one-half to two cents per pound, but
the greedy warlords who occasionally seized sections of the border
tended to ask for more—General Cobos charged twenty dollars per
bale, and General Cortina sometimes expropriated more than one-
fourth of a convoy's cargo. The magnitude of the intercourse across the
Rio Grande is suggested by the fact that during the better part of 1863,
even though he no longer held the city of Matamoros, Vidaurri still collected about $175,000 in import duties each month. At his usual rates,
his customhouses between Reynosa and Piedas Negras were therefore
passing the equivalent of at least 21,875 bales, and perhaps as many as
29,167 bales, into his dominions each month.

Once safely in Mexico, the cotton haulers could auction their bales immediately, could store their cotton in anticipation of a rise in price, or could continue on to Monterrey or Matamoros. One way or another, the majority of the bales eventually found their way to Matamoros, the Trans-Mississippi Confederacy's open doorway to the outside world. In January, 1865, a Union general was to complain that "Matamoros is to the rebellion west of the Mississippi what the port of New York is to the United States. It is a great commercial center, feeding and clothing the rebellion, arming and equipping, furnishing the materials of war." [9]

Matamoros was Tamaulipas' biggest incorporated city, the state's busiest official port, a bustling depot crowded with business houses, consular offices, money and commodity exchanges, and endless rows of warehouses. But a whim of nature prevented Matamoros from reaping the full benefit of its reputation and ambition. The overland distance from Matamoros to the mouth of the Rio Grande was thirty-five miles, and the distance by river was sixty-five miles—sixty-five miles of twisting shoal water, which was never more than five feet deep, and often no more than two. A steamer which was light enough to scrape its way up the channel, and short enough to negotiate the river's hairpin turns, might perform the voyage from the sea to the town in twelve hours. But usually the passage took twenty-four hours, and every time a vessel ran aground it effectively bottled up the river. Understandably, the masters of most steamers, and the captains of all sailing ships preferred to drop anchor off the coast of Tamaulipas and wait for cotton to be hauled to them.

Because of the Rio Grande's perversity, a tiny fishing village called Bagdad, located on a windblown sand dune just south of the river's outlet, was transformed between 1861 and 1863 into a gigantic sprawling slum housing 15,000 people—the largest Gulf Coast "city" between New Orleans and Vera Cruz! In April, 1863, an English visitor described Bagdad as nothing but "a miserable village" consisting of "miserable wooden shanties, which have sprung into existence since the war began." But he also remarked that "for an immense distance endless bales of cotton are to be seen." A transient Texas parson was moved to decry Bagdad as "a veritable Babel, a Babylon, a whirlpool of business, pleasure, and sin." He noted: "A common laborer could easily gain from five to six dollars per day, while a man who owned a skiff or a lighter could make from twenty to forty dollars. The saloon and hotel keepers were reaping an abundant harvest. The Gulf, for three or four miles out, was literally a forest of masts."

Before the war, Bagdad had seldom been visited by more than six seagoing vessels a year. Now the Englishman saw about seventy merchantmen standing off the Bagdad bar; a month earlier, in March, 1863, Richard Fitzpatrick, the resident Confederate States commercial agent, counted eighty; and the frustrated lookouts high atop Union blockaders on station just north of Mexican waters sometimes reported hundreds. For Bagdad was the end of the trail for the cotton trains, and the place where Texas cotton took ship to voyage to the textile mills of the world.

Profits earned from the sale of cotton were either collected in gold or reinvested in manufactures, provisions, or munitions of war carried to Bagdad by inbound ships. Most of the vessels, and most of the imports, were English or European, but it was not uncommon for ships flying the flag of the United States to bring down cargoes of contraband from Boston, New York, or Philadelphia. During one four-month period in the middle of the war, some fifty-nine merchantmen, loaded with arms, military equipment, and quartermasters' stores, sailed from New York City to Bagdad. Texas newspapers openly advertised such items as "garden seed fresh from New York via Matamoros," and were quite prepared to discuss the commerce with the North in their editorial columns:

Reader, the paper before you was bought of a citizen of Texas, who purchased it in Matamoros of a citizen in Mexico. Where he got it we don't know, but we are morally certain that it came first from New York from the fact that it is a style of paper made nowhere else. What do you say? Would [you have us] use the brown paper during the War rather than use it? But that was made in New York too. . . . Some of the shoes worn by our men were made by these Massachusetts men long after the War began. It is a curious fact, that some of the gold brought back into the State by patriotic citizens, in exchange for cotton, and which is too good to pay debts with, bears the Philadelphia mint mark.[10]

After procuring a shipment of imports, the wagon convoys turned about and plodded back to San Antonio. From there, the goods were distributed to military depots and commercial markets throughout the Trans-Mississippi Department. Because the records which survive are fragmentary, it is impossible to estimate either the total amount or the sum value of the cargoes imported; nor is it possible to determine the proportion of the imports received by either government or civilian consumers. The only thing that is certain is that neither the demands of the military nor the wants of the population at large were ever adequately met.

The various military purchasing agencies engaged in the Mexican trade were never able, for instance, to place a firearm in the hands of every one of the Department's soldiers. In the summer of 1863, one-third of the enlisted men in Arkansas were without weapons; 5,000 Arkansas militiamen could not be mustered because the state had no guns to issue to them; and the Principal Chief of the Choctaws was complaining that the Confederacy had never delivered rifles promised to his Nation. In the autumn of the same year, Department headquarters estimated that at least 10,000 veteran Trans-Mississippi soldiers were unarmed. At New Year's, after 4,200 Enfields had been forwarded from Brownsville and smaller shipments had arrived from other ports of entry, at least 4,000 soldiers were still without weapons. Losses incurred during the subsequent campaign season simply increased the number of unarmed soldiers in Kirby Smith's command.

Nor were weapons the only military necessity in perpetual short supply. In March, 1864—after the Cotton Bureau had been in operation for seven months, and the Texas Cotton Office for four—Kirby Smith complained to Colonel Hutchins that "one large battle or the loss of our army supply trains to either the [Union] Army of Arkansas or Louisiana . . . would leave us without powder and but little lead." The dread battles came soon enough, at Mansfield, Pleasant Hill, Jenkins' Ferry, and elsewhere, and the bulk of the supply train of the District of Arkansas was then lost during Price's Missouri raid. Arms and goods continued to cross the Rio Grande and find their way to army depots— between October and December, 1864, 600,000 pounds of ordnance and quartermasters' stores passed through Brownsville alone—but when it finally came time for Kirby Smith's soldiers to fight to the death or surrender, many of them still had no powder and ball and many others still had no gun to lay down.

Imports secured for the civilian market included goods of every description and variety, but the quantity was never sufficient to satisfy consumers or to restrain inflation. Occasional feasts were interrupted by prolonged periods of famine. Whenever a shipment arrived in a market town, people would gather from miles around to revel in a spree of auctioneering; when all the goods were sold, they would return to their homes and try to survive until the arrival of the next wagon convoy. In early October, 1863, the merchants of Clarksville announced the sale of the following "new goods just arrived": 4,000 yards of calico, 1,000 yards of bleached domestic, 200 yards of chambray, 100 dozen gingham handkerchiefs, 20 dozen pairs of white cotton hose, 50 yards of Irish linen, 400 fine French calfskins, 50 pounds of shoe thread, one pound of black silk sewing thread, 50,000 needles of assorted sizes, 500 pounds of soda, 76 hogsheads of sugar, 100 barrels of molasses, 40 pounds of black pepper, 12 kegs of nails, 12 dozen tin cups, and "various other articles in store which will be shown upon application." A four-day auction held in Houston in February, 1865, disposed of 200 cases of imported liquor, 67 barrels of molasses, 20 hogsheads and 25 barrels of sugar, 37 boxes of Virginia tobacco, 20 sacks of coffee, 20 sacks of rice, 5 sacks of pepper, 130 dozen cotton cards, 100 dozen cambric handkerchiefs, 100 dozen men's cashmere overshirts, 1,200 yards of prints, 100 dozen "best Mason's Blacking," 10,000 pounds of assorted iron, 1,500 pounds of sheet iron, 20,000 percussion caps, 25 dozen coarse combs, 10 gross of pantaloon buttons, 150 packages of flax thread, "sundry assorted Dry goods," "sundry household and kitchen furniture," cigars, bagging, twine, chisels, nails, shoe tacks, lead, Epsom salts, brogans, quinine, blankets, washstands, sideboards, sofas, chairs, a set of fine silverware, brooms, 30 bags of meal, nine "A No. 1 negro men" between the ages of nineteen and thirty-six, one "A No. 1 negro woman" and her six children (ranging in age from five to sixteen), and 300 slave coats.

Auctions were rarely sedate affairs. Manufactures were scarce, costly, and coveted, and the people who scrambled to the auction houses were seldom inclined to be polite. Even in San Antonio, the one city whose stores were always stocked with goods from transient trains, consumers needed a great deal of fortitude and a fair amount of muscle to carry away any prizes. A San Antonio matron once described a fairly well-policed commercial skirmish to her soldier son:

Yesterday the long talked of and looked for goods were opened at the Mutual Aid Store and all the town and all the country it seemed streamed in there. I went too, for squeeze in was the only hope, and Kate was shoeless and the darkies in rags—I went and stood wedged up and swaying about till near 12 when I actually did get to the counter and had one of the numerous clerks attention long enough to get one bolt of domestic cloth, one pr shoes and I doz candles for the $180.00. Pa went this morning and understood the crowd to be greater—he got a coffee pot and 20 pounds of coffee—for $85—most reasonable thing they had. I send you and George 5 pounds— very good it looks. Each purchaser is limited in quantity in each article so that all the numerous householders get a chance at something—I must go after more shoes and some thread—get only what is needful. I suppose all will be gone before the week is—Altho some of the directors said it was a stock cost 60,000 in specie—but the dearth of goods is so great and all the other stores are so exhorbitant.

Nor was Mrs. Maverick the only victim of scarcity and "exhorbitant" prices. Once Vicksburg and Port Hudson fell, the value of Confederate currency rapidly declined. During a single week in the fall of 1863, the price quoted in Shreveport for a hundred pounds of flour shot up from $30 to $50, the cost of shoes rose from $25 to $60, of boots from $75 to $120, and of horses and mules from $125 to more than $400. Down in San Antonio, a certain Major Gillett owed $25 for a set of coat buttons, Henry Young's new overshirt cost $20, two plugs of tobacco sold for $12, Mrs. Love bought a collar for $10, James S. Ridgeway paid $100 for a pair of silver combs, and William Leigh, upon receipt of an order to muster for militia service, offered $3,000 for a substitute.

Despite sporadic attempts to control the prices of goods sold to the public (for the schedules published by the state impressment boards applied only to merchandise bought or seized by the army), nothing stopped the wild inflation. By November, 1863, milk cost a dollar a quart in Houston. In late December, Austin's consumers spent $5 for a pound of butter, $2 for a chicken, and $60 for a hundred pounds of flour. In January, 1864, newsboys hawking the *Houston Telegraph* demanded a dollar per copy, despite the editor's repeated announcements that the price was only fifty cents. "It is entirely useless," complained the Shreveport *South-Western,* "for our brave soldiers to be shedding their precious blood and filling the country with widows and orphans, while a large portion of our citizens are doing every thing in their power to depreciate our currency." The newspaper asserted that those who failed to exercise fiscal responsibility were doing "more to injure the cause of the south than the federal army," and expressed its hope "that the extortion mania will soon cease. . . . It is the only means left to sustain our currency and our country." [11]

✄ V   Since the Rio Grande was a body of international water, the United States Navy was unable to blockade it. A small squadron of Union vessels stood off the Texas shore, waiting to pounce upon unwary merchantmen which drifted too far north, but it made relatively few captures. After 1862, Imperial French blockaders occasionally made prizes of cargo ships which entered Mexican waters, alleging that the ships were running contraband to the Juaristas, but the Frenchmen, too, did little to interrupt Confederate trade with the outside world. For all practical purposes, the mouth of the Rio Grande remained unobstructed. It became obvious to the authorities in Washington, quite early in the war, that the only sure way for the United States to interdict the Confederacy's trade through Mexico would be for the Federal army to land an expeditionary force in West Texas to seize Brownsville and the other river crossings. As early as December, 1862, the Union State and Navy Departments were already discussing plans for an invasion of the lower Rio Grande Valley.

Other voices were also raised in favor of such an expedition. New England textile manufacturers pressed the claim that Federal control of the river crossings, or of the entire state of Texas, would ensure the North a steady, reliable supply of raw cotton. Abolitionists professed the belief that the provisions of the Emancipation Proclamation could be enforced more easily and more swiftly in the poorly defended state of Texas than in any of the other rebel states. Expatriate Texas Unionists—not the least of whom was General Andrew Jackson Hamilton, Lincoln's military governor-in-exile for the state—constantly harped upon the theme that a Federal effort to liberate Texas would incite a mass uprising by the state's countless loyal citizens, and deliver a staggering propaganda blow to the Confederacy by hurrying the quick restoration of Texas to the Union.

But the event which finally precipitated the United States government's decision to act occurred in June, 1863, when a French army marched into Mexico City, declared Mexico to be a monarchy under the protection of the French emperor, set up a puppet government, outlawed Juarez, and sent him and his regime fleeing northward toward San Luis Potosí. Opening communications with the French, General Hamilton Bee found them to be far more ready to cooperate with the Confederacy than Juarez had even been. By midsummer the French, at Bee's suggestion, had even agreed to occupy Matamoros, to clean out the grafting warlords who interfered with the free flow of goods across the border, and to eliminate the many petty annoyances which complicated relations along the frontier. Washington was disturbed not only by intelligence of this Franco-Confederate rapprochement but also by rumors that the French intended, despite whatever objections their Confederate friends might raise, to continue their imperialistic adventure until Louisiana, Texas, and the territories taken from Mexico fifteen years earlier were under their protection.

On July 24, 1863, the Federal Chief of Staff, General Henry W. Halleck, advised General Banks that "every preparation should be made for an expedition into Texas." On July 29, Lincoln asked his Secretary of War "to organize a force to go to Western Texas. . . . I believe no local object is now more desirable." The following day Lincoln told Frank Blair that he had "commenced trying to get up an expedition for Texas," both to forestall France's designs and to quiet the Texas lobby at home. On August 5, the President wrote directly to Banks to say that "recent events in Mexico, I think, render early action in Texas more important than ever," and four days later he informed General Grant that "in view of recent events in Mexico, I am greatly impressed with the importance of re-establishing the national authority in Western Texas as soon as possible." On July 31, August 6, and August 10, Halleck reiterated, with a mounting sense of urgency, the administration's pressing interest in an invasion of Texas, and importuned Banks to begin the operation without delay.

That Lincoln expected Banks to focus his attention upon "Western Texas" there is no doubt. But Lincoln refrained from stipulating the strategy which Banks should adopt; on the 5th, when he directed Banks's attention to the need for early action in "Texas," he simply told

Banks that Halleck "will address you more fully upon this subject."
When Halleck did so, he gave no indication that "Western Texas" was
the President's objective. Halleck believed that the proper invasion
route into Texas was the Red River Valley, an idea which had occurred
to him the previous autumn and which had since become one of the
fixed dogmas of his military creed. His initial letters to Banks, like Lincoln's of the 5th, spoke only of an expedition to "Texas"; and in his letter of August 10 he went so far as to indulge in an expression of his
"opinion" that "if it be necessary . . . that the flag be restored to some
one point in Texas, that can be best and most safely effected by a combined military and naval movement up Red River to Alexandria,
Natchitoches, or Shreveport, and the military occupation of Northern
Texas."

Halleck's design did have some arguments in its favor. An army
moving up the Red River Valley would not depend upon a tenuous seaborne supply line, and the granary of East Texas was a far more populous and valuable prize than the West Texas desert. But other arguments could be raised in opposition: Taylor's army, reinforced by the
reserves Magruder had marshaled at Niblett's Bluff, would doubtless
contest a Union advance up the Red; an overland campaign would be
slow and tedious; and because the Red was nowhere near "Western
Texas" a Red River campaign would do practically nothing to impress
the French protectors of Mexico. Having stated his opinion for Banks's
benefit, Halleck then proceeded to abdicate responsibility for the conduct of Banks's invasion of "Texas." Banks was told that the choice of
an appropriate strategy was his, and his alone.[12]

Banks may have sensed that a march up the Red was not what
Lincoln had in mind, or he may have had his own pet plan for the liberation of the Lone Star State. Whatever the reason, he rejected Halleck's suggestion, and decided instead on an amphibious assault at Sabine City—thus neatly splitting the difference between Halleck's Red
River proposal and Lincoln's desire for an invasion of West Texas.
Banks's elaborate tactic called for a naval bombardment to reduce the
insignificant Confederate fort overlooking Sabine Pass, a landing at Sabine City, the seizure of the Texas and New Orleans railroad terminal
at Beaumont, and a lightning descent, by rail, upon the railroad hub at

Houston and the port of Galveston. Once these two cities were taken in reverse, Banks anticipated an easy conquest of the rest of the state.

Banks's plan was a clever one. It displayed a good grasp of geography, it promised to make efficient use of the Texas rail system, and it made the most of the Confederates' unpreparedness to repel an invasion staged from a beachhead at Sabine City. Virtually all of the disposable rebel forces in East Texas, plus most of the militia recently embodied by the state of Texas, had been gathered at or above Niblett's Bluff; Banks could take both the railroad and the cities before Magruder could possibly double back to block him. About the only rebels between Banks and Houston were those manning the six field cannon in the fort at Sabine Pass—one invalid captain, one healthy first lieutenant, and some forty-five enlisted members of the First Texas Heavy Artillery.

At midnight, September 6-7, a sentry strolling along the parapet of the Confederate fort noticed a busy exchange of ship signals beyond the Sabine Pass bar. Since Captain F. H. Odlum, the post commandant, was suffering from an attack of malaria, the sentry summoned Lieutenant Richard Dowling to the wall. Dowling promptly assumed command of the fort, ordered the boys of "F" Company to turn out and man their guns, and hoisted the garrison's battle flag. Dawn revealed, in addition to the half-dozen blockaders usually on station outside the Pass, an impressive array of Union might: four tinclad gunboats and twenty-two paddle-wheel transports, the latter crowded with 5,000 soldiers of General William Franklin's division of the XIX Army Corps. Dowling wired Magruder for advice; Magruder wired back a recommendation that Dowling spike his cannon and evacuate Sabine City as fast as possible. But instead of abandoning his position, Dowling carefully ranged his guns, built up his earthworks, and directed his men to eat and rest.

Finally, at 3:00 P.M., September 8, after subjecting the rebel fort to a sporadic and ineffective bombardment, the Federal fleet came about and steamed toward the mouth of the Sabine River. The rebel cannoneers held their fire until the lead gunboat was within 400 yards, and then they let loose. Forty-five minutes later, two of the gunboats were hulled, beached, and scuttled; another, disabled, had been withdrawn; the fourth had fled; the transports had been scattered and driven away; "F" Company had captured over 350 wet and dispirited Union sailors; not one rebel was scratched; and Lieutenant Dick Dowling had earned immortality in the pantheon of the Confederacy's boy-heroes. Three days later, Franklin's seasick soldiers weaved ashore at New Orleans. Four days later, the recriminations were reverberating from New Orleans to Washington. And a month later, when the news of Dowling's remarkable victory reached London, a sudden spurt of brisk buying drove the price of Confederate bonds up three points.

Magruder, hurrying down to Beaumont, was elated by Dowling's success, but he did not permit his elation to obscure the fact that the lieutenant's triumph had been a fluke. Anticipating another enemy assault further down the Texas coast, he begged Kirby Smith and Taylor for reinforcements. But Smith and Taylor were just as convinced that the Sabine Pass affair had been designed to mask the initiation of another Union offensive up the Red River Valley; they declined to forward the soldiers Magruder wanted. Smith's decision was probably influenced by Governor Moore, who was already enraged both by the recent removal of Tappan's brigade from Louisiana to Arkansas and by the evacuation of General Smith's wife and baby from Shreveport to East Texas. Smith tried to explain that Tappan's reassignment had been necessitated by a series of stunning reverses along the Arkansas front (including the capitulations of Fort Smith and Little Rock), and that his family had only fled to escape the yellow fever, but the more he explained, the more the governor complained that the army was planning to abandon Louisiana. Under the circumstances, Smith probably felt that any shift of troops from Louisiana to Texas would be an impolitic gesture. Smith not only promised to maintain the strength of Taylor's army, but he went on to intimate that Taylor, not he, was to blame for any weakness in the Red River Valley's defenses, and to suggest that Moore, not he, had the authority to call up the Louisiana militia whenever such an expedient became necessary.

Smith's explanations angered Magruder, who still wanted reinforcements; they failed to satisfy Moore, who still considered the commanding general responsible for the protection of Louisiana; and they so infuriated Taylor that he permitted his staff to leak a denunciation of Kirby Smith's performance to the press, a maneuver which earned him a fierce rebuke from his superior. The upshot of all this mutual ill will was the paralysis of the army: not one regiment was transferred from

Louisiana to Texas, or, for that matter, from Texas to Louisiana. "I have walked up & down, gone out & come back—restless, dissatisfied —everything (officially) has gone wrong," Smith confided to his wife. "I am miserable, discontented, unhappy."

While the Southerners bickered among themselves, General Banks set about devising a plan to recover the prestige lost at Sabine Pass, and to satisfy the administration's urgent desire to see a Federal flag planted in Texas. He ruled out an overland march from Brashear City to Sabine Pass as being too hazardous. He allowed Franklin's dispirited division to make a feeble thrust toward Alexandria, as if to begin another Red River offensive, but because of the poverty of the country and the demoralized state of Franklin's soldiers the division pushed only as far as Opelousas before turning back. Finally, on October 22, Banks announced his decision "to attempt a lodgement upon some point on the coast from the mouth of the Mississippi to the Rio Grande." In conformity with the President's wishes, which had since become known in New Orleans, the point chosen for the assault was Brazos Santiago, a spit of wasteland just north of the mouth of the Rio Grande.

On October 26, a fleet of escort vessels and transports carrying 6,000 fresh troops commanded by General Napoleon Dana set sail from New Orleans. On November 2, precisely at noon, the Federals stormed ashore at Brazos Santiago and hoisted the Union flag over a few acres of barren Texas sand dunes. The nearest Confederate troops were stationed more than thirty miles inland, at Brownsville, and offered no resistance to the landing. Quite the contrary, as soon as General Bee heard of Dana's arrival, he concluded that the insignificant rebel contingent at Brownsville was far too small to contest the Federals' advance, and so, on November 4—forty-eight hours before the cautious Federals came within gunshot range of Brownsville—Bee ordered all the cotton and military stores in the town to be burned, and the evacuation of the garrison inland to San Gertrudis (modern Kingsville). Richard Fitzpatrick, the Confederate commercial agent in Matamoros, considered Bee's hasty retreat to be "one of the most cowardly affairs which has happened in any country." Even though Bee protested that any attempt to hold Brownsville with his miniscule force would have been suicidal, his decision to pull back, which contrasted so sharply with Dowling's stand at Sabine Pass, eventually cost him his command.

When Dana's bluecoats swung into Brownsville they found nothing but a smoldering pile of cinders occupied by a ragtag contingent of refugees, home guards, and Mexicans. Whatever passed for command of the place had devolved upon an expatriate pro-French Mexican bandit chieftain named José Maria Cobos. Cobos surrendered the town to the Federals, gathered a motley regiment of Mexican adventurers (including Juan Cortina, the old nemesis of the Texas border country), swept across the Rio Grande, seized Matamoros, and clapped the Juarista governor of Tamaulipas, Don Manuel Ruiz, into irons. Cobos reigned supreme as overlord of Tamaulipas for two days before Cortina, proclaiming himself a Juarista, mounted a counterrevolution, shot Cobos, and took control of the state. Cortina was to retain his hold upon Matamoros as long as the Federals kept possession of Brownsville. Though he found it prudent to permit substantial amounts of Confederate cotton and goods to continue passing through his territory, his extortionate tariffs and highhanded expropriations, combined with the interdiction of trade through Brownsville, caused a temporary decline in Matamoros' prosperity.[13]

Kirby Smith learned of the fall of Brownsville on November 13. He immediately directed Magruder to order Bee to retreat up the Rio Grande Valley, to remain between the Federals and the river crossings at Laredo and Eagle Pass, and to cover the southern approaches to San Antonio with whatever cavalry he could spare. Yet Smith refused to believe that Dana's expedition was anything more than a diversionary maneuver, intended to draw the Confederates' attention away from the Red River Valley. When Magruder renewed his frantic appeals for reinforcements, Smith only relented enough to shift Thomas Green's Texas cavalry brigade from the Teche Valley to Niblett's Bluff, a curiously ineffective compromise which placed Green's veteran troopers in a position from which they could not easily be dispatched to the assistance of either Taylor or Bee.

Once Dana's beachhead was secure, his forces fanned northward from Brazos Santiago and occupied other footholds along the lower Texas Gulf Coast. Within two months after Brownsville's capitulation, Dana's soldiers had raised the Federal flag over Corpus Christi, Saluria and Fort Esperanza, Matagorda Island and the southern tip of Matagorda Peninsula, and the railheads at Indianola and Port Lavaca. By

New Year's Day, the only important coastal positions still under the Confederate flag were Forts Quintana and Velasco (at the mouth of the Brazos), Galveston City and Galveston Bay, and Sabine Pass. While Dana moved up the Texas coast, General Frederick Herron assumed over-all command of the Union army deployed in West Texas, and pushed additional troops up the Rio Grande Valley to San Gertrudis, Edinburg, Ringgold Barracks, and Rio Grande City. Here and there some of Bee's rebels stood fast long enough to fire a few rounds at the Federals, but the Confederates were too few and too scattered to do more than annoy the invaders. They were quickly brushed aside and driven into the interior.

Without reinforcements, Magruder and Bee could do nothing to check the Union offensive, so they made no serious attempt to try. Instead, they endeavored to salvage property in danger of confiscation by the enemy, they tried to raise an army from the manpower resources remaining in West Texas, and they hoped for a miracle. Property was either carried off or demolished. Thousands of bales of cotton went up in smoke. Quartermasters were directed to remove all military stores to locations well beyond the reach of enemy raiders. Coastal port facilities in and about Corpus Christi Bay, Aransas Bay, and Matagorda Bay were destroyed. The tracks of the short San Antonio and Mexican Gulf Railroad, stretching from Victoria to Indianola and Port Lavaca, were torn up and twisted around the ties. Army patrols were directed to drive all livestock herds, especially beef cattle and horses suitable for cavalry service, north of the Nueces River. And the troops were instructed to leave no Negro men within riding distance of a Union recruiting officer. If owners refused to evacuate their able-bodied male slaves, the rebels were ordered to "take forcible possession of them, or, in the last alternative, shooting them, for they will become willing or unwilling soldiers against us."

Magruder's attempts to muster an army were no less frantic. To keep the enemy worried, he circulated rumors to the effect that a host of reinforcements was en route from East Texas to San Antonio. To keep the civilian population loyal, he ordered companies of embodied Texas militia to visit the settlements below the Nueces and do what they could to inspire confidence in the Confederacy. To keep the disaffected docile, he instructed the militia to prevent potential recruits from slipping across the Mexican border or the Union lines. And to raise troops, Magruder adopted nearly every possible expedient. Men detailed as cotton teamsters were ordered to report to their regiments forthwith, lest they be advertised as deserters. Home guards and invalid reserve companies as far north as Houston were put under arms, to relieve regular garrison troops for field service. Governor Murrah was requested to call up every able-bodied white male between the ages of sixteen and seventy—a request which Murrah failed to act upon, since the militia was already embodied and the state's laws gave the governor no authority to raise additional troops. Post commanders were encouraged to enlist anyone who seemed fit enough to lift a musket. And, finally, Magruder relieved John S. Ford as chief of the Texas Conscript Bureau and dispatched him to San Antonio, with orders to enlist a brigade of men exempt from the draft, and to reconquer Brownsville. Ford reached San Antonio in the last week of December, established a recruiting station for his "Cavalry of the West," and, on the 27th, published an appeal for volunteers. But none of Magruder's expedients immediately produced the disposable force he needed to block the Union advance. Not until the middle of March, 1864, would Ford be able to initiate his counteroffensive.

What saved West Texas from conquest was a miracle. Banks, flushed with victory and eager to press his advantage, was anxious to get on with the reduction of Galveston, but General Halleck had other ideas. Halleck was still convinced that the Red River Valley route into East Texas was Banks's proper objective, and he feared that any commitment of troops to prolonged operations in West Texas would simply dissipate the forces needed to prosecute a spring campaign in lower Louisiana. Overruling Banks's protests, Halleck directed him to break off his West Texas offensive, to abandon most of the coastal and Rio Grande Valley positions occupied by Dana and Herron, to pull his regiments back to the neighborhood of Brownsville, and to return most of Herron's troops to New Orleans. Banks was told that although the need to impress the French and to interfere with Confederate trade still justified the maintenance of a Federal presence in West Texas, "this policy will be satisfied if a single point is held."

Banks had no choice but to order a general disengagement. Brownsville, Brazos Santiago, and Port Isabel (on the Texas mainland, near Brazos Santiago) were garrisoned and fortified, and a few picket posts were left scattered beyond the Brownsville perimeter, but all except 2,500 of Herron's soldiers were gradually withdrawn, most of the points recently occupied were evacuated, and no attempt was made to continue the campaign. Governor Hamilton came down to Brownsville to establish his administration on Texas soil and to publish a New Year's salutation to the citizens of Texas; recruiting officers set up shop and invited white and Negro Texas volunteers to fill the ranks of eight new regiments; a "Loyal League" established headquarters in Brownsville, won the allegiance of many local residents, held Unionist rallies, and began to smuggle propaganda leaflets through the Confederate lines. The army engineers rebuilt much of the town of Brownsville; Northern cotton speculators and cattle buyers swarmed into the Union enclave and opened a lively trade with the rebels; and, in February, President Lincoln proclaimed the end of the blockade at the port of Brownsville. Not until midsummer, when Rip Ford's Cavalry of the West came thundering down the Great River Road, would Federal possession of the southern tip of Texas be contested by the Confederates.

Because of the loss of Brownsville and its environs, the Confederate cotton traders were forced to shift their overland routes farther to the west. Laredo, 235 miles upstream from Brownsville, and Eagle Pass, another 90 miles up the Rio Grande, soon emerged as the busiest river crossings. This severe dislocation of the customary trade patterns worked hardships on everyone. Transportation costs rose at least 50 percent, and some drayage companies were soon complaining that cotton hauling had become such an expensive undertaking that it was no longer possible for firms engaged in the business to earn any profit. The West Texas countryside over which teamsters now had to drive was even more desolate than the wilderness above Brownsville, and was, in addition, more vulnerable to the incursions of marauding Indian war parties. On December 19, General Kirby Smith, having appraised the situation, wrote a gloomy letter to his wife, in which he warned her that she "must carefully keep [account] of our stock of goods, for it now really amounts to a stock, you must not be too liberal in disposing of them—the Rio Grande is in possession of the Enemy, the blockade is closed, every thing will be dearer and will increase rapidly & largely in value." [14]

ᚦ VI   For some months prior to the fall of Brownsville, the numbers of Confederate purchasing agents competing with one another for the same cotton had complicated the fulfillment of contracts with Mexican mercantile houses. In order to satisfy his own creditors, Major Charles Russell, General Bee's quartermaster at Brownsville, had gone so far as to intercept shipments of cotton en route to Major Hart's creditors in Matamoros. Russell managed to pay his own bills, but his initiative left Hart without cotton to settle War Department accounts. In a short time, the claims against Hart became so large that, as he reported, their payment would exhaust "not only what cotton the Government now has on hand in Mexico, but all it could get there within the next six months."

Hart's failure to deliver cotton created much disaffection among the Mexican suppliers who held his vouchers. Chief among these was Patricio Milmo, Governor Vidaurri's son-in-law. Milmo and Company had not only sold great quantities of stores to Hart but had gone on to underwrite sales made to him by numerous subsidiaries and associates. When the Federals occupied Brownsville, the exasperated Milmo, fearing even more delay in the settlement of Hart's outstanding debts, began to press Hart for immediate satisfaction. When none was forthcoming, he struck.

His victim was one Clarence T. Thayer, an otherwise inconspicuous field agent of the Confederate States Treasury Department. On November 6, Thayer arrived in Matamoros with seven large wooden boxes consigned to Kirby Smith. All Thayer was supposed to do was to deliver the crates to Major Russell in Brownsville, for shipment to Shreveport. But by November 6, the wrong flag was flying over the remains of Brownsville, and Major Russell had taken temporary lodgings in Matamoros. Thayer finally tracked Russell down, explained his predicament, and revealed that his seven boxes contained $16,000,000 worth of fresh Confederate treasury notes. Russell suggested that Thayer hire Milmo and Company to haul his crates through Monterrey to Piedas Negras, where they could be turned over to the quartermaster at Eagle Pass. Russell then disclosed the contents of Thayer's boxes to Milmo. Milmo took charge of the crates, Thayer went ahead to Monterrey, and then, on December 11, Milmo advised Major Hart: "In view of [your] refusal to pay a just debt so long due . . . I have sent an agent with my power of attorney to seize all Confederate cotton and goods on the road from, to, or at Piedas Negras. All property so seized, as also the contents of seven cases in charge of Mr. Thayer from Richmond, said to contain $15,000,000 [*sic*] Confederate notes and now in my possession, I will hold until you deliver the balance of cotton due."

Thayer protested to Milmo. Milmo refused to release the money. Thayer and Juan Quintero petitioned Governor Vidaurri for assistance. Vidaurri declined to interfere in his son-in-law's business affairs. Thayer, Quintero, and Major Hart then recommended to both the Confederate Secretary of State and General Kirby Smith that drastic retaliatory action be taken. In particular, they suggested that since the economic health of Vidaurri's states depended upon the cotton duties collected by his border customhouses, an embargo upon the exportation of Texas cotton might induce the governor to encourage Milmo to release Thayer's currency. Quintero did not wait for an answer from the State Department before bringing the threat of an embargo to Vidaurri's attention; he even went so far as to suggest to the governor that a spare Confederate brigade or two might be dispatched across the border to recover Thayer's crates. Nor did Kirby Smith wait for authority to act. On January 12, he published an order prohibiting the exportation of cotton and of all "property of any kind whatever belonging to Mexicans" by way of the Rio Grande, and he wrote to Vidaurri to warn that "a refusal to release the funds after [your] attention had been called to their illegal detention would seem to raise for discussion and action the unpleasant question whether or not the Mexican Government had or intended to assume a hostile attitude to the Government of the Confederate States." Yet Smith stopped well short of an overt threat of invasion. Instead, prodding Vidaurri with a carrot instead of a stick, he promised that his trade embargo would "be relaxed and, in fact, entirely repealed so soon as the present difficulty is arranged."

In order to signify his desire to negotiate a pacific settlement, Smith sent his letter to Monterrey in care of three special commissioners, Judge Thomas Devine, Colonel T. F. McKinney, and Captain Felix Ducayet. The commissioners were instructed to cooperate with Quintero's efforts to effect a swift but amicable compromise. By the time

Smith's agents reached Monterrey, Vidaurri was ready to listen to reason. "Governor Vidaurri has no other resources at present but those derived from our trade," Quintero explained to the Secretary of State. "Besides he is surrounded by many difficulties and complications," including the possibility of war with both the French and the Juaristas, "and will not endeavor to increase them by refusing an honorable and just settlement." In return for assurances that the Confederate government would pay all debts owed to Milmo, his associates, and all other Mexican creditors, Vidaurri caused Thayer's crates to be released for delivery, and brought about the resumption of normal trade relations with the Trans-Mississippi Department.

By the last day of February, the crisis had passed, and Quintero was doing his best to soothe everyone's temper. As he told the Secretary of State, "Our interests require us to forget the partial injury and to remember the favors conceded by [Vidaurri] to us." One man who could not forget was Major Russell. Cashiered from the army by order of the President himself, Bee's ex-quartermaster endured the remainder of the war in exile.[15]

⅋ VII   Neither the loss of Brownsville, nor the Milmo imbroglio, nor the internecine disputes of the army agencies competing for possession of cotton interfered with foreign trade quite as much as the efforts of the state of Texas to counteract the army's intervention into the cotton business. While the military was preoccupied by both the Federal invasion of West Texas and the Milmo affair, Governor Murrah and the Texas legislature, responding to the popular outcry against cotton impressment, temporarily nullified the army's attempts to procure cotton for export.

In December, 1863, the legislature reorganized the Texas State Military Board and floated a $2,000,000 bond issue. Instead of a part-time board composed of ex officio members, the new board consisted of Governor Murrah and two full-time military commissioners. The two commissioners had no duties assigned to them other than the procurement of supplies for the regular and militia Texas regiments. The bond issue gave the new board control of $2,000,000 worth of gilt-edged 7 percent bonds (bonds payable in Texas land warrants rather than depreciated currency) with which to buy the cotton needed to exchange for imported ordnance and quartermasters' stores.

Acting in the name of the new board, Governor Murrah promulgated a novel "State Plan" which threatened to snatch the bulk of Texas cotton from the Confederate purchasing and impressment officers. Murrah offered fair market prices, payable in the new 7 percent bonds, for bales sold to the military board's agents, and offered planters and other cotton dealers a way to protect their own cotton from seizure. The plan stipulated that if any planter, speculator, or other cotton vendor would contract to sell a consignment of cotton to the military board, the board would assume responsibility for the cotton and transport the entire shipment to the Rio Grande. Since the state would hold title to the cotton while it was in transit, the bales would be immune from impressment. But once the cotton was safely across the frontier, the military board would surrender half to the original owner, for disposal as he might see fit. The market value of the other half, less the cost of transportation, would be redeemed with the 7 percent bonds; only the half retained by the state would be used to purchase military supplies.

When Murrah subsequently announced that the military board needed 60,000 bales to pay for arms and equipment, it dawned upon his Confederate competitors that his State Plan was designed to exclude 120,000 bales from impressment—to exclude, as Colonel Broadwell complained, practically all of the baled cotton then on hand in Texas. And when the military board's agents appeared in the marketplaces, offering two or three times as much for cotton as the Confederate buyers could pay, the results left no doubt that the Texas initiative was a mortal threat to the Trans-Mississippi Department's ability to conduct foreign trade for the benefit of the army. By March, 1864, when the settlement of the Milmo affair reopened the border and permitted the resumption of trade, Confederate officials were shocked to discover that 100,000 bales had already been sold to the state, and that swarms of military board representatives were trying to corner the stocks of cotton which remained.

The implementation of Murrah's State Plan evoked heated protests from Confederate authorities throughout the Southwest. Magruder, interpreting the plan to be nothing but an act of bad faith upon the part of the governor, warned Murrah that Texas would bear the whole responsibility for any deterioration in the Department's capacity to defend itself. Colonel Hutchins advised General Smith that unless Congress soon proved willing to honor the certificates issued by the Cotton Office in return for cotton, and unless the Cotton Office were enabled to pay market prices for cotton, only indiscriminate impressment could possibly preserve the Trans-Mississippi Department's foreign credit. Hutchins even suggested that if the army did not promptly commit itself to the wholesale seizure of cotton, his Cotton Office would have to terminate operations. Colonel Broadwell insisted that Murrah's State Plan was illegal, but went on to acknowledge that the question of legality no longer made the slightest difference to Texas planters and speculators; they were, Broadwell said, already so thoroughly irritated by the military's interference in the cotton trade that they were more than eager to take advantage of every protection afforded by the State Plan. Like Hutchins, Broadwell implored Smith to impress whatever cotton the Department required, regardless of ownership. Broadwell even recommended that if Murrah should continue to obstruct Confederate attempts to engage in Mexican commerce, the Department should remove all Confederate States troops from Texas soil, leaving the state's defense to the governor and his militia.

On April 5, 1864, Kirby Smith addressed a temperate but direct appeal to Murrah, asking him to modify the State Plan or to restrain its execution. Smith granted that "the former management of the Government business on the Rio Grande was properly and severely criticised," but pointed out that Hutchins' Cotton Office had been established for the purpose of bringing order to the cotton trade, a function it could not fulfill unless Texas ceased impeding its performance. He then launched into a recitation of the ways in which the State Plan harmed the army's attempts to provide for the defense and welfare of the Trans-Mississippi, and protested that "the system inaugurated by your agents has already completely paralyzed the efforts of my officers" to procure the cotton needed to sustain the Department's military posture.[16]

Had not Banks's Federals been pushing up the Red River Valley once again, Smith, in all probability, would have journeyed to Austin to confer with Murrah in person. The best Smith could do, preoccupied as he was with the current Union invasion, was to dispatch Major Bryan to

Austin with instructions to negotiate some sort of amicable settlement with the Texas authorities. Bryan's mission was a failure. Not only did Murrah flatly deny that his State Plan interfered with the maintenance of the Department's defenses, but the Texas legislature angrily passed a joint resolution denouncing impressment, castigating the arbitrary conduct of army and Cotton Office press gangs, and demanding the payment of fair market prices for any goods sold to or taken by agents of the Confederate States.

On February 6, 1864, the Confederate Congress had enacted laws prohibiting the importation of luxuries and providing for the regulation of the export trade by the Confederate Executive. In March and April, the President and the War Department had issued uniform regulations to govern the exportation of cotton, tobacco, military and naval stores, sugar, molasses, and rice. In essence, these regulations stipulated that half of all the exports named had to be exchanged for incoming consignments of strategic goods, and that any merchant who agreed to import his allotment of war matériel would be eligible to receive a trading license from any neighborhood quartermaster.

By the end of May, when his latest attempt to come to terms with Governor Murrah went awry, Kirby Smith had reviewed the texts of Congress' trade acts, but had not yet received copies of the Executive's implementing regulations. Irritated by Murrah's intransigence, and foreseeing the imminent collapse of his command's credit, Smith decided not to wait for receipt of the official trade regulations. During the first four days of June, he promulgated his own regulations: every civilian cotton vendor was to surrender half of his cotton to the Cotton Bureau; only those merchants licensed by the bureau could engage in foreign commerce; and only those merchants who shipped nothing but government cotton, or those who agreed to import nothing but machinery, agricultural tools, ordnance, and quartermaster's stores, would be licensed by the bureau. Smith appealed to civilians to sell their cotton to the army's buyers (at prices fixed by impressment boards, and in exchange for the promissory certificates circulated by the Cotton Bureau), but minced no words when he affirmed that any cotton not presented for sale would be subject to impressment. Unlike the regulations issued in Richmond, which left room for private enterprise and speculation,

Smith's decrees promised to effect the nationalization of the Trans-Mississippi's foreign commerce, and to convert the Southwest's cotton business into a military monopoly.

Smith's regulations encountered stiff opposition from Governor Murrah and the Texas State Military Board. A flurry of excited correspondence flew between Shreveport and Austin. Murrah protested that Smith's innovations subverted Texas sovereignty and the rights of Texas citizens, while Smith replied that Murrah's State Plan threatened the interests of the Confederacy, disarmed and denuded many of the Department's soldiers, and eviscerated the Trans-Mississippi's capacity to defend itself. Impressed by the relative ease with which Union armies had recently laid waste stretches of West Louisiana and southwestern Arkansas, even some Texas newspapers rallied to General Smith's cause, and began to implore Murrah to concede the necessity of cooperation with the Cotton Bureau.

At the beginning of July, Murrah invited Smith to meet him in Hempstead, Texas, to discuss the cotton problem. No transcript of their conference survives, but the arguments Smith advanced must have had a profound impact upon Murrah, for only the conference can explain the governor's extraordinary change of heart. On July 19, shortly after the Hempstead conference ended, Murrah published an address to the people of Texas in which he capitulated, without reservation, to Smith's demands. He told the people that the survival of the army, of the Department, and of Texas itself depended upon the unobstructed importation of military supplies; that the army needed cotton to procure these supplies; that cotton could be obtained only from the people; and that it was therefore the patriotic duty of every loyal Texan to deliver his cotton to the army's agents in return for whatever compensation the army might consider just. Simultaneously, Murrah abandoned the substance of his State Plan and ceased extending state protection to shipments of privately owned cotton.

When, at the beginning of August, Smith finally received a copy of Richmond's trade regulations, the governor went so far as to urge the general to suppress the Executive's official policy and to continue the implementation of his own, not only because the latter offered surer protection against the multiplication of speculators, but also because it guaranteed more throughly military control of foreign exchange and

more adequate returns to the army. Writing to express his deep gratitude for the governor's support, the general took care to reassure Murrah that the Trans-Mississippi high command would indeed continue to
enforce its own commercial policy in preference to that promulgated by
the Confederate States government. And, in fact, Smith's regulations
continued to govern trade and impressment west of the Mississippi until
the end of the war.[17]

Ironically, the pacific settlement of the quarrel between Smith and
Murrah failed to stay the Confederate government's execution of
Smith's Cotton Bureau, for it was on August 3, 1864, only two weeks
after Murrah's sudden conversion to militant nationalism, that the Secretary of War directed Smith to surrender control of cotton transactions
to the new Trans-Mississippi Treasury Agency. Although the Hempstead conference had served to restore amicable relations between the
general and the governor, the meeting had done nothing to assuage the
widespread bitterness engendered by the army's wholesale expropriation
of cotton. During the last months of 1863 and the first half of 1864, the
ill will generated by the military's press gangs had so increased that the
Confederate government was left with little choice but to intervene.

One prevalent reason for complaint was simply the scarcity of
goods for domestic consumption created, in part, by impressment. In
April, 1864, for instance, a group of San Antonio ladies found it necessary to appeal to Major Hart for an allotment of government cotton,
since none was to be had through private suppliers:

We, the undersigned, mothers, wives, and sisters of absent soldiers in the
field would most respectfully represent to you that we have wheels and cards
and they are dull for the want of cotton, for we have been unable to purchase a pound from the merchants and speculators in the city, and we cannot furnish our husbands and sons that is now in the army with cloth[e]s
that we could manufacture at home, for the want of cotton; many of our
husbands and sons are even without socks at this time, and we are sorry that
we are under the necessity of calling on you to furnish us with this article of
prime necessity. If it be in your power to do so, as we must have it in some
way or other, we hope that you will give this request your earnest attention
without delay.

Another cause for dissatisfaction was the inadequacy of the prices
paid for impressed property. Under the provisions of the impressment
act, state boards of impressment commissioners were required to allow

for fluctuations in market prices and in the value of Confederate currency by publishing revised price schedules every two months. But, according to a protest addressed to Governor Murrah, "in scarcely a single instance does the price fixed by them [the Commissioners] reach fifty percent of the fair average market value: in many instances it is not twenty-five percent." In September, 1863, when a hundred pounds of flour fetched between $30 and $50 (Confederate) on the open market, the Texas Board of Impressment Commissioners offered $7.00; four months later, when the same barrel of flour might earn $60 or more in a private sale, the official price was pegged at $14. And in June, 1864, a horse, which might otherwise be worth anything from $1,500 to $6,000, could be seized by the army for no more than $675.

The official thievery encouraged by unrealistic price schedules was compounded by the unofficial banditry which flourished under the guise of impressment. Field officers were often driven to confiscate goods, even though they were not authorized by any quartermaster to issue legitimate vouchers for the property taken, while roving bands of robbers, passing themselves off as press gangs or itinerant troops, papered the countryside with counterfeit payment certificates or simply refused to give receipts. Countless complaints about illegal seizures of cotton, slaves, animals, produce, firearms, tools, and other property poured onto the desks of harassed civil and military authorities. In March, 1864, for example, an irate homesteader angrily informed Governor Murrah that a contingent of enlisted men stationed in his neighborhood had raided his farm, had stripped it of forage and equipment, and had ridden off with everything he owned, without leaving behind so much as an expression of gratitude. Citizens sometimes became so irritated that they took matters into their own hands. In May, 1864, Lavaca County witnessed the summary hanging of three self-appointed impressment officers, who had been going about the area devouring property and threatening the lives of uncooperative victims.[18]

When petitions, protests, and lynching bees all failed to bring relief, the people resorted to more subtle tactics. Impressment could only flourish in regions which possessed property worth impressing. Farmers in the more prosperous agricultural districts soon concluded that fallow land and empty barns offered press gangs far less reason to ravage their neighborhoods than bumper harvests did. Consequently, many farmers cut back yields or left land untilled. Cotton production continued to decline, while grain harvests were sharply reduced. In the East Texas breadbasket, less than one-third as much small grain was sown during the fall and winter of 1863–64 as had been sown during the previous fall and winter, and much of the grain that was cultivated was destroyed by a snap of exceptionally cold weather during January.

Governor Murrah implored the farmers to return to their agricultural pursuits, while editors, citing the real danger of famine, urged the farmers to sow late crops of barley and corn in every idle field. But the farmers' boycott persisted. In late January, 1864, Thomas E. Adams, a War Department inspector, was "satisfied that combinations are already forming in portions of Louisiana, Arkansas, and Texas to withhold from our armies all the aid that can possibly be withheld by declining to raise larger crops than are necessary for home consumption." And a month later, a homesteader from Dallas County took it upon himself to explain the farmers' plight to Governor Murrah:

I have no doubt that you are already apprised that there was not more than half as much wheat sown last fall as usual, and one reason for so little being sown was the illegal impressment carried on by the Confederate officers. I understand that a number who have sown say that they will not take care of their grain unless this illegal impressment is stopped, for they say that they will not have their property taken from them illegally, and then [be] insulted by an officer with twenty or thirty armed men at his heels.

Despite the extent of public disaffection, neither the legislators of Arkansas nor those of Louisiana did, or could afford to do, anything to discourage the army's abuse of impressment. Even Congress' response to the voters' complaints was surprisingly restrained. As Senator Oldham remarked, the arrest and incarceration of 750 impressment officers might reform the system, but such a reform would result in the starvation of the army. Congress was satisfied to make minor modifications in impressment procedures; it did nothing significant to provide for the overhaul, control, or elimination of the impressment system itself. Only the legislature of Texas tried to temper the press gangs' zeal. During the last five days of May, 1864, the Lone Star State's legislators passed one joint resolution and two bills designed to delimit impressment. The joint resolution demanded payment of prevailing market prices for impressed cotton and goods, the disbursement of additional allowances to help the victims of impressment cover transportation costs for which they might be liable, the restriction of impressment to articles or produce actually required by troops in the field, and the exemption from impressment of property needed to support private families, the prosecution of agriculture, or the conduct of industry. The two bills provided harsh criminal penalties for anyone, including army officers, convicted of participation in illegitimate impressment activities. Unfortunately for the beleaguered citizens of Texas, the legislators' joint resolution was not binding in law, while Governor Murrah's subsequent conversion to the military's own interpretation of its impressment authority eliminated whatever chance there might otherwise have been for strict enforcement of the penal acts.

But if the several legislatures failed to implement effective limitations upon impressment, the Confederate Executive inaugurated a sequence of events which led to major structural revisions in the Trans-Mississippi Department's impressment practices. On April 28, 1864, after remaining silent about the operations of Kirby Smith's Cotton Bureau for the better part of nine months, President Davis informed the general that "there is no authority in law for the impressment of cotton for the purpose designed by you." This thunderbolt struck General Smith at the very time that he was embroiled with Murrah in heated debate about the necessity of impressment. Davis' pronouncement forced Smith to make concessions to satisfy the letter of the law; but Smith offered only those concessions which would not, in reality, interfere with his Department's conduct of cotton impressment and trade.

In two letters to the President, dated May 12 and June 6, he urged the Executive to bear in mind the Southwest's isolation, its unique difficulties, and its need to be self-sustaining; he affirmed his own loyalty; he advised the central government to legitimize the Cotton Bureau and to provide for the redemption of its outstanding obligations; and finally he recommended that the personnel and functions of the Cotton Bureau be transferred to the jurisdiction of the Trans-Mississippi Treasury Agency. Then, during the first two weeks of June, at the same time he was issuing blanket authorizations to quartermasters and Cotton Bureau agents to impress half the cotton in the Department, Smith published orders which decried illegal impressment, which demanded prompt investigation of complaints, and which insisted that all officers charged with the authority to impress property follow appropriate procedures.

As a result of this blizzard of paperwork, the Secretary of War directed, on August 3, 1864—exactly one year since the creation of the Cotton Bureau—that the bureau be reconstituted as a branch of Judge Peter Gray's new Treasury Agency. This reorganization was gradually effected during the subsequent autumn and winter. But otherwise, nothing—except for Governor Murrah's attitude toward impressment —really changed. The Cotton Bureau continued to function; the Commanding General, with Agent Gray's hearty cooperation, continued to govern the Department's financial and commercial affairs; impressment continued to flourish; and the columns of the Trans-Mississippi's newspapers continued to run passionate denunciations of the army's usurpations.[19]

CHAPTER FIVE

SUMMER AND AUTUMN
CAMPAIGNS, 1863

When, on the morning of August 21, 1863, the sun emerged from Missouri's rolling hills to press the edge of dawn into eastern Kansas, it ascended into a clear, brisk, still sky, and appeared to herald the advent of a serene and peaceful day. An uncomfortable spell of hot, dry, dusty weather, of the sort so common in midsummer Kansas, had just passed; and the crisp, cool sparkle in this morning's calm air seemed to promise that August 21 would be a good day in which to be alive, a good day in which to till fields and mend fences, a good day in which to market or to visit friends. The war seemed far away—especially in a quiet Kansas community like Lawrence.

But the war was only as far as the first gentle rise beyond the eastern fringe of the town. For there, about 450 rebel Missourians, dressed in grimy mufti, heavily armed and well mounted, waited for their chieftain to finish surveying the approaches into Lawrence. Astride a sorrel horse near the center of the squadron, beneath the still folds of a black silk flag, sat their commander, William Quantrill—"the great general," as Kit Dalton described him, "the master mind, the human dynamo, the tender friend, the merciless enemy, and the embodiment of every principle that is grand, glorious and noble."

Once he was satisfied that Lawrence was unprepared, Quantrill spurred his mount toward the town's outskirts. The others followed in a loose, ragged column of fours. "They first made for the main street, passing up so far as the Eldridge House to see if they were going to meet with any opposition, and when they found none they scattered out all over town, killing, stealing and burning." For the next four hours, Quantrill's gang looted, sacked, and murdered. All three banks were emptied; every saloon was wrung dry; homes were indiscriminately plundered; fully one-fourth of the private residences were fired; all but two of the buildings in the business district were razed; and 183 men and boys were shot, knifed, burned, hanged, strangled, or trampled to death. Miraculously, no women or children were harmed, but far too many of them saw their fathers, husbands, and sons killed. Three days later the Leavenworth *Conservative,* in denouncing the "cowardly barbarity" of the raid, was to assert: "We have seen battle-fields and scenes of carnage and bloodshed, but have never witnessed a spectacle so horrifying as that scene among the smouldering ruins at Lawrence. No fighting, no resistance, but cold-blooded murder was there."

Shortly after 9:00 A.M., when the day's work was done, Quantrill instructed his captains to muster their companies and make preparations for a withdrawal. As the raiders straggled toward the rendezvous, they carried with them souvenirs of their victory—countless bottles of whiskey, watches and jewelry, a couple hundred fresh horses, saddles and horse equipments, bolts of calico and broadcloth, books and candlesticks, cutlery and silverware, shoes and boots, lamps, greatcoats, chairs, blankets, anything that caught their fancy. Quantrill tidied up a last-minute detail by ordering the summary execution of a handful of prisoners, and then, mounting up, he waved his hand and led his band toward the Missouri line.

After the rebels departed, Senator Jim Lane, who had managed to escape massacre only by secreting himself behind a fallen tree, enlisted a small posse, seated himself on a rickety buckboard, and set out in pursuit; and Union garrison troops from posts in the neighborhood also made feeble attempts to intercept the bushwhackers. But before the Federals had time to organize a concerted counterattack, Quantrill's nightriders melted into the countryside of southwestern Missouri. The only raider apprehended was an anonymous guerrilla left behind at Lawrence in a drunken stupor, whom the citizenry hung from a convenient tree.

The prompt lynching of Quantrill's lone straggler was but the first sign of the retaliatory spirit incited by the Lawrence raid. The current commander of the Federal Department of the Missouri, General John Schofield, himself an advocate of moderation, reported that hosts of infuriated Kansans were calling "loudly for vengeance . . . upon all the people residing in the western counties of Missouri," and added that "there was not wanting unprincipled leaders to fan the flaming of popular excitement and goad the people to madness." Among the "unprincipled leaders" Schofield had in mind was Jim Lane, who let it be known that he intended to do everything he could to transform western Missouri into a desert waste.

At a mass meeting held in Lawrence on August 26, Lane summoned all good Union men to rally at Paola two weeks later, prepared to invade and despoil Missouri. Neither Schofield nor the governor of Kansas, Thomas Carney, succeeded in muzzling Lane, although both made repeated efforts to reason with him. On the appointed day, September 8, an angry crowd descended on Paola, ready—allegedly—to carry fire and sword across the bloody border. Of all the rousing addresses heard by the mob, the one delivered by "Doc" Jennison best expressed the mood of Lane's vigilantes:

Do you suppose I will march into Missouri to ask them to take the oath? No, not by a damned sight! If they have protection papers I will hang them, for real Union men need no written proof of their loyalty. In my next proclamation I will say to every physically able-bodied man in the State of Missouri: "You must fight for your homes or be put to death. . . ." Everything disloyal from a Shanghai chicken up to a Durham cow, must be cleaned out. . . . We carry the flag, kill with the sabre, and hang with the gallows.[1]

Yet, curiously, nothing came of Lane's Paola rally. Perhaps the endless speechmaking dulled the crusaders' blood lust; perhaps their enthusiasm had never been more than rhetorical. But one reason Lane's expedition never materialized seems to have been that the Union army itself had already stolen much of Lane's thunder. For back on August 25, General Thomas Ewing, commanding the Department of the Missouri's District of the Border, had issued General Order Number 11, directing the wholesale depopulation of Missouri's Jackson, Cass, and Bates counties, and the upper half of Vernon County. Arguing that Quantrill's guerrillas had taken refuge in the homes of Southern sympathizers residing in these four counties, Ewing gave the inhabitants fifteen days in which to pack their belongings, abandon their property, and clear out. Any person found within the limits of the proscribed district after the expiration of the fifteen-day grace period was to be treated as an outlaw—that is, summarily executed.

Both Schofield and General Frank Blair denounced Ewing's order as an act of imbecility, sure to excite even more vicious retribution by the rebels. Austin A. King, once governor of Missouri and now a member of the Federal Congress, urged President Lincoln to direct Ewing to revoke his decree. But Ewing's order remained in force, and Lincoln, disclaiming any intention to intervene, appeared to add the weight of his own authority to Ewing's by instructing Schofield to use his troops to "expel guerrillas, marauders, and murderers, and all who are known to harbor, aid, or abet them" from his Department. Until he was transferred to a new command at St. Louis, Ewing continued to press the implementation of his order without mercy, inflicting gratuitous hardship upon thousands of innocent people, laying waste more fertile Missouri farmland than any Confederate army could, and creating throngs of embittered refugees from which roving companies of rebel nightriders drew a large number of fresh recruits.

Perhaps the only western Missourians not seriously inconvenienced by Ewing's order were Quantrill's bushwhackers, for by the time the decree was implemented, some 300 veterans of the Lawrence raid had already slipped back into Kansas and had begun a forced march toward the Indian Nations. On the afternoon of October 6, Quantrill's gang interrupted its flight to surround and attack the small Negro garrison at Fort Baxter, Kansas, a new stockade located about forty-five miles south of Fort Scott. While the forty-five Negroes manning the post successfully repulsed every attempt the guerrillas made to overrun them, Quantrill's rear guard spied a wagon train slowly descending the road from Fort Scott toward Fort Baxter. The wagons composed the headquarters train of General James G. Blunt, commander of the District of the Frontier, who happened to be moving his flag from Fort Scott to Fort Smith. Breaking off the siege of Fort Baxter, Quantrill doubled back to Baxter Springs, where he formed his men in line of battle astride the wagon road.

As the train wound into view, Quantrill ordered a charge. Since many of the Missouri guerrillas were dressed in Union blue, the 125

Federals escorting the train held their fire until the rebels were nearly upon them. Then, when it was too late to make much difference, the Federals "gave us a volley too high to hurt any one, and . . . fled in the wildest confusion on the prairie. We soon closed up on them, making perfect havoc on every side . . . only leaving about 40 of them alive." Those who tried to surrender were shot down. Blunt and the other survivors escaped only because their horses were fresher and faster than those of the bushwhackers.

After looting the train and burning the wagons, Quantrill's band skirted around Fort Baxter and continued its southward trek. During the six days it took the rebels to reach Douglas Cooper's lines, they "caught about 150 Federal Indians and negroes in the Nation gathering ponies. We brought none of them through."

Once Quantrill reached the Confederate Nations, he dispatched an official report of the Baxter Springs affair to Sterling Price. "At some future day," he promised, "I will send you a complete report of my summer's campaign on the Missouri River." On November 2, Price, praising Quantrill's work and asking that Quantrill's command be formally incorporated into his army, transmitted the report to Governor Reynolds. At the same time, Price's adjutant addressed a letter of congratulation to Quantrill, expressing the general's "high appreciation of the hardships you have so nobly endured." [2]

Some of Quantrill's guerrillas were only too happy to accept Price's invitation to settle down to regular soldiering. Bill Gregg and many members of his company broke away from Quantrill's band, rode over to Arkansas, and enlisted in Jo Shelby's Iron Brigade. But others had no wish to abandon bushwhacking for the relative security of line service. Bloody Bill Anderson gathered the James boys, the Younger brothers, and the rest of his clan, skirmished his way through Quantrill's and Cooper's picket lines, and slipped back into Missouri, where he spent the next year making ready for the Centralia massacre by raiding back and forth through the state's northern counties. Anderson's presence, like that of the thousands of other irregulars who continued to infest Missouri's tortured countryside, allowed the state's Unionists little time to celebrate Quantrill's departure.

As his command disintegrated about him, Quantrill himself seemed unsure of the course to adopt. Instead of returning to Missouri, where he had been proclaimed an outlaw, and instead of joining Price, under whose command he might have been exposed to capture, Quantrill, along with George Todd and the emaciated remains of his battalion, resumed his retreat into Henry McCulloch's Northern Subdistrict of Texas. But McCulloch wanted nothing to do with Quantrill. On October 22, he complained to Magruder's adjutant that Quantrill's philosophy and methods of warfare were "but little, if at all removed from that of the wildest savage; so much so that I do not for a moment believe that our Government can sanction it in one of her officers." Both Magruder and Kirby Smith—the same Kirby Smith who, just five months before, had insisted that "no good can result" from the prosecution of guerrilla warfare—rushed to Quantrill's defense. Smith assured McCulloch that Quantrill's followers were "bold, fearless men, and . . . are under very fair discipline. They are composed, I understand, in a measure of the very best class of Missourians." But McCulloch understood otherwise: "Quantrill and his men will only fight when they have all the advantage and when they can run whenever they find things too hot for them. I regard them as but one shade better than highwaymen."

In December, Quantrill thought it best to return to Indian Territory, where he stayed long enough to participate in one of Stand Watie's periodic forays through the Cherokee country. When that expedition was repulsed, Quantrill again retired to North Texas and once more encountered McCulloch's icy hostility. In January, 1864, Quantrill was instructed to report to Magruder's headquarters for reassignment. He refused to comply. On February 3, announcing that Quantrill would not obey orders, McCulloch told Magruder that "so much mischief is charged to his command that I have determined to disarm, arrest, and send his entire command to you or General Smith." But before McCulloch could act, Quantrill once again pursued his own inclinations. Decamping from McCulloch's domain, he meandered over to Arkansas, played an inconspicuous role in Price's last Missouri raid, and fled to Kentucky, where, in the waning days of the war, he met his death in a Yankee bushwhacker's ambush.[3]

⚜ II   McCulloch's antipathy toward Quantrill was based, in large part, upon the Missourian's reputation for unreliability. At the time

Quantrill's band first appeared in northern Texas, McCulloch's subdistrict was in turmoil, and the last thing the general could afford was an unreliable battalion within the boundaries of his command. McCulloch was so preoccupied by the rising despoliation of the countryside by Indian war parties, the depredations committed by roving gangs of deserters and draft dodgers, and the threat posed by the ineffectiveness of the Texas Frontier Regiment that he had no time for the work of integrating unpredictable bushwhackers into his disposable force.

Since its reorganization at the beginning of 1863, the Frontier Regiment had not proven itself able to interdict the incursions of Indian raiders into the settled portions of northwestern Texas. Deployed along a 700-mile front, and able to muster no more than two men to patrol each linear mile, Colonel J. E. McCord's regiment could not mount the defense in depth needed to suppress the marauders. During the first half of 1863, McCord's vigorous employment of search-and-destroy tactics threw the Indians off balance, but as soon as the warriors learned to avoid direct confrontations with the rangers, they once again found themselves free to roam at will behind the Frontier Regiment's picket line. Each full moon—each "Comanche moon," as Texans said—innumerable small bands of painted redskins penetrated into the frontier counties, fell upon isolated homesteads and scattered settlements, looted, burned, and killed, and slipped silently away. Lampasas County, San Saba, Williamson, Brown Cooke, Burner, Gillespie, and many others felt their deadly presence. During the war, a "tier of counties, at least three deep, was quite depopulated. The women and children had to be removed to the interior part of the state to protect them from being killed and made prisoners by cruel savages—a fate worse then death." By October, 1863, so many frontier homesteads had been stripped and abandoned that Governor Lubbock feared that the Indians would begin to raid the more heavily populated portions of the state, in search of property worth stealing.

On August 16, 1863, General Smith P. Bankhead, temporarily in command of the Northern Subdistrict of Texas, was forced to acknowledge that "the Indians are committing many outrages, and I am overwhelmed with petitions asking relief. . . . I am informed that [the Frontier] regiment is utterly inefficient, if not disaffected, and that the citizens of the border counties are petitioning for their removal." So

persistent were the complaints about the Frontier Regiment's performance that Governor Lubbock and the Texas legislature finally agreed
to permit the reassignment of the command beyond the boundaries of
Texas, thus clearing the way for the regiment's eventual incorporation
into the Confederate States army.

But this did nothing to reinforce the frontier's sense of security. If
anything, rumors of the regiment's pending departure exacerbated the
settlers' worries, since neither the local militia nor the green conscripts
who composed the bulk of Bankhead's Texas brigade could take the
Frontier Regiment's place. In September, Lubbock began to urge militiamen to volunteer for extended tours of frontier service, but the initial response was discouraging. And Bankhead was well aware that
some of his own troops were no more enthusiastic about soldiering than
were the Texas militia:

> Several companies of my command were raised in the border counties, and
> the families of several have been butchered [by the Indians]. A natural re-
> sult of this has been to render those companies exceedingly restless, and a
> disposition to desert was becoming so prevalent in one company of Harde-
> man's regiment that I disarmed the company. When I first heard of these
> [Indian] outrages ten days ago I ordered Colonel Bourland to move
> through the infested country with a squadron of cavalry. I have also deter-
> mined to send some wagons down, and move in the families of such soldiers
> of this command as have places to go and are anxious to move. I think this
> course has had a quieting influence, accompanied as it was with the solemn
> assurance that if there were any more desertions I would follow them up
> and shoot down every man I caught.

In an open letter to the Galveston *News* written three days later,
"A True Southern Woman" residing in Williamson County summed up
the dreary mood of the Texas frontier settlers:

> Permit me through the columns of your paper to make a few remarks in re-
> gard to the situation of the families living on the frontier which consist
> mostly of women and children, whose husbands, sons and brothers are in
> the army. The Indians are thick amongst us, stealing our horses and murder-
> ing our people. . . . What is to become of us is more than any of us can
> tell. The governor says we must protect ourselves. Is it becoming in the gov-
> ernor of the proud State of Texas to say that the women and children must
> take [care] of themselves? He has got a few men stationed a hundred miles
> west of us, but what good are they doing? They have never stopped the In-
> dians from coming in, for it is a certain fact that there are more Indians in

the country at this time, than there has been since the country was settled. I would like to know what kind of people Gov. Lubbock thinks we are! . . . Does he think that our husbands, sons and brothers can stay in the army and fight the battles of the country, when they hear that their wives and little ones are being murdered by the savage Indians? I answer no. . . . Men cannot fight, when they know that all that is dear to them on earth is in danger . . . I say if we are to be given up to our enemies, let us choose which will go to. If we are to be murdered, for God's sake don't let it be done by the savage Indians.[4]

Indian depredations and the problems of frontier defense were intimately related to the subdistrict's third problem, the numbers of recusant conscripts and army deserters hiding out in the "bush" beyond the limits of settlement. Not a few of these fugitives had fled from Confederate and Texas commands stationed in the neighborhood. Hundreds of others had straggled over from East Texas. Still more had escaped from the Texas brigades on duty in Louisiana and Arkansas, and some were even refugees from the armies east of the Mississippi. By the fall of 1863, when General McCulloch assumed control of the Northern Subdistrict, perhaps as many as 3,000 armed absentees were at large within the limits of his jurisdiction. They outnumbered McCord's and Bankhead's disposable forces by at least two to one.

The Trans-Mississippi Department made strenuous efforts to entice or drag these fugitives back to the colors. On August 26, with the President's approval, Kirby Smith offered a general pardon and amnesty "to all officers and soldiers now absent without leave . . . who will return to duty by the 30th day of September, prox. mo." By late September, when it was becoming obvious that the amnesty was producing little result, Smith told McCulloch that "where clemency and persuasion fail force must be resorted to." He authorized his subordinates to send cavalry dragnets through the neighborhoods known to harbor bands of deserters, and advised his district commanders to employ "the most summary punishment" against absentees. McCulloch was told that the bands within his jurisdiction had to be captured or exterminated. Smith even urged McCulloch to employ both Quantrill's bushwhackers and the absentees already apprehended to help round up or liquidate the others.

Through the fall and winter of 1863, McCulloch's regulars and McCord's rangers frequently swept through the "bush," seeking to arrest or destroy organized bodies of military fugitives. Although some absentees were apprehended or killed, the troopers dispatched on these missions were too few in number to demolish or scatter the more formidable pockets of resistance.[5]

The Confederate and Texas state troops engaged in this work were augmented by state and local militia units, companies which themselves seldom probed into the badlands, but which did provide a measure of home defense. Both Magruder and McCulloch periodically invited exempt citizens to form local "minute companies," to apprehend deserters, to arrest stragglers, to preserve public order, and to keep "a vigilant watch over traitors and all suspicious characters." And, on a few occasions, fairly large contingents of militia did execute cavalry sweeps through the "bush," resulting in the liquidation of at least one encampment of fugitives.

Perhaps the most unorthodox force to serve under McCulloch's direction was a ragtag regiment of "bushmen" raised and commanded by Congressman John R. Baylor. In November, 1863, with both Kirby Smith's and McCulloch's approval, Baylor enlisted six hundred of the very deserters who had previously submitted to the amnesty. Baylor's regiment achieved few noteworthy victories, other than the dispersal of a gang of bushwhackers in Jack County—Baylor or his superiors evidently considered his command too untrustworthy to commit it to prolonged operations—but its existence served as an inducement to other skulkers to come out of the wilderness, and its embodiment relieved steadier troops for active duty in the field.

By the end of 1863, it was obvious that the defenses of North Texas were in disarray. The Confederate regulars were ineffectual; the Frontier Regiment had fallen from grace; the performance of Baylor's bushmen left much to be desired; and the militia was too inchoate to mount anything but haphazard resistance against marauders. Since the Confederate authorities did little more than exhort McCulloch to persevere—while threatening, at the same time, to remove most of his tiny disposable force to more sensitive battle fronts—it was left to the government of Texas to solve the border country's problems.

On December 15 and 16, 1863, upon the recommendation of Governor Murrah, the Texas legislature authorized the transfer of the Frontier Regiment to Confederate States service, and overhauled the state's entire militia system, giving special consideration to the situation along the western border. One act made many additions to the list of classes and occupations exempt from military service, provided for the draft and embodiment of militiamen by lot, and enjoined the state brigadiers to encourage citizens not subject to the draft to volunteer for local defense units. A second bill empowered the governor to keep embodied militia commands in the field six months beyond the stipulated terminal dates of their service, and directed the brigadiers to furlough no more than one-third of their embodied militiamen at any given time. But the bill which brought about the most drastic modifications in the militia system, and which precipitated the most acrimonious response from Confederate authorities, was the third. In order to establish a manpower reserve from which to draw frontier troops, Texas declared all able-bodied white men of military age who resided in those counties west of a meandering line drawn from Cooke to Maverick—in all, some fifty-four counties—exempt from Confederate conscription. And in order to provide for the employment of this manpower, Texas divided these border counties into three military districts, and instructed the district commanders to keep at least one-fourth of their militia troops in the field on patrol at all times.

Both Magruder and Kirby Smith protested that no state had any right to exempt whole counties from the operation of the Confederate conscription laws, and both warned Murrah that the new militia acts would encourage regular soldiers who came from the exempt counties to desert from the Confederate army. In a curiously contradictory rejoinder, Murrah replied that the act explicitly called upon militia commanders to restore absentees to their regular units, and that, in any case, the claim of Texas upon the services of its citizens was prior to that of the Confederate States. By mid-February, 1864, Magruder protested that the Texas militia laws had induced the equivalent of at least three regiments to decamp from the army and rush home to enlist in the frontier militia, while McCulloch complained that his subdistrict was now infested with more skulking fugitives than it had ever contained before.

During the late winter and spring of 1864, Confederate forces along the Texas frontier were gradually withdrawn; Baylor's bushmen were disbanded and individually reassigned to regiments deployed along the Gulf Coast; and the Frontier Regiment, mustered into the Confederate army as the Forty-sixth Texas Cavalry, was transferred to the Eastern Subdistrict. In the meantime, the Texas militia assumed the responsibility for border protection. The organization of this new frontier defense system was substantially completed by March. Major William Quayle, of Decatur, took charge of the state's Northern Military District, containing a total enrolled force of 1,517 mounted militiamen; Major George B. Erath, of Gatesville, commanded the Middle Military District and its 1,413 men; and (Texas) Brigadier General J. D. McAdoo assumed control of the 1,334 troopers in the Southern Military District. In theory, and for the most part in practice, at least 1,091 of the 4,264 militiamen on call were thereafter constantly in the saddle, patrolling between and beyond the border forts. Except for a few minor adjustments in boundaries, troop dispositions, and command assignments—early in 1865, Brigadier General J. W. Throckmorton was given command of the Northern District, and Major John Henry Brown the Southern—this scheme for the protection of the frontier continued in force until the end of the Civil War. Unfortunately for the settlers and homesteaders whose lives depended on it, the Comanches and the neighborhood jayhawkers found the new arrangement even less intimidating than the old.[6]

※ III   If conditions along the Missouri border and in the Northern Subdistrict of Texas were deplorable, conditions in Indian Territory and Arkansas were even worse. While Quantrill cut his way back and forth across the Kansas line, William Steele's Confederate Indians lost the Creek Nation and were driven southward into the upper Red River Valley. While Texas sought a way to repulse Indian marauders, Fort Smith fell to the Union army. And while McCulloch tried to eliminate the evil of desertion from his subdistrict, desertions devoured William Cabell's Arkansas brigade, the defenses of the Arkansas River Valley disintegrated, and the Federal flag was hoisted over Little Rock. The turmoil along the Missouri border and the chaos in northern Texas were not isolated phenomena; on the contrary, they were signs of the general dissolution of the Trans-Mississippi Department's amorphous northern front.

     Ever since Colonel William Phillips' Union Indians seized Fort Gibson, General William Steele's rebels had been trying to find some way to recover the fort. Gibson was the key to the control of the Creek Nation; whoever held Fort Gibson held the bulk of Indian Territory. During May and June, 1863, Douglas Cooper's Confederate Indian brigade executed sporadic raids through the neighborhood of the fort, occasionally disrupting Phillips' communications or scattering his pastured beef herds. But none of these halfhearted forays accomplished anything noteworthy, and every one was eventually repulsed by Phillips' braves in blue.

The last and most decisive encounter was fought during the first three days of July in the vicinity of Cabin Creek, where the wagon road from Baxter Springs forded the Grand River. Having received news that a 300-wagon commissary train was en route from Fort Baxter to Fort Gibson, Stand Watie and a strong contingent of Cooper's brigade threw a battle line across the road and waited for the wagons to roll into it. But when the train lurched into view, it was covered by a thick screen of escorting cavalry and infantry. During the three-day running skirmish which ensued, the Federals punched through Watie's crowd and sent the rebels reeling southward once again.

Despite his reverses, Steele was still determined to recapture Fort Gibson. Gathering the fragments of Cooper's demoralized brigade at Honey Springs (on Elk Creek, some twenty-five miles south of the Arkansas), and summoning Cabell's Arkansas conscripts from Fort Smith, Steele set about devising a plan for the encirclement and siege of Fort Gibson. But before his brigades could rendezvous, the Federals seized the initiative. On July 11, Phillips' superior, General Blunt, arrived at Gibson with a column of cavalry reinforcements. Blunt then studied Cooper's dispositions, learned of Cabell's slow advance toward Honey Springs, and determined to disperse Cooper's horsemen before Cabell's troopers could join them.

Late on July 15, Blunt ordered the Fort Gibson garrison to begin marching; the better part of the 16th was consumed in ferrying the 3,000 bluecoats across the swollen Arkansas River; and by midmorning on the 17th, after a forced night march, the Federals were deployed in line of battle within cannon range of Cooper's encampment. After driving in the rebel pickets and engaging in a hot firefight with Cooper's main force, the Federals overran Cooper's camp and scattered his brigade. Tandy Walker's Choctaw and Chickasaw soldiers threw down their guns and fled southward in a wild panic; McIntosh's two Creek regiments bolted from the field and made for the western badlands; and many of the Texans and Cherokees ran eastward toward Fort Smith.

At 4:00 P.M., the fugitives following the Fort Smith road stumbled into the van of Cabell's little force, still plodding slowly toward the Honey Springs rendezvous. The Arkansas conscripts proved to be less a reinforcement than an addition to the panic, for they were already as demoralized as Cooper's whipped Territorials. En route from Fort Smith, Cabell's troopers had been dropping away from the line of march by squads, by platoons, by whole companies. Under the circumstances, Cabell dared do little more than make a timorous feint toward Blunt's column, wheel about, and double back to the neighborhood of Fort Smith, whose approaches he then picketed and endeavored to guard.

After frightening Cabell away from the Honey Springs battlefield, Blunt retired to Fort Gibson, rested and refitted his command, and began dispatching patrols to probe the country immediately below the Arkansas River. In the meantime, General Steele evacuated Fort Smith and removed his staff to the vicinity of the old Honey Springs encampment, where he again tried to collect a force sufficient for another thrust toward Fort Gibson. But, again, Blunt anticipated Steele's design, and again wrested the initiative from him. Descending upon Honey Springs a second time, Blunt chased Steele all the way to the banks of the Middle Boggy River, deep in Choctaw country. Once safely across the Middle Boggy, Steele garrisoned Doaksville and Boggy Depot, tried— unsuccessfully—to borrow a few reliable squadrons of horse from Texas, and fervently hoped that Blunt would retire.

Instead of pressing Steele's beaten crowd all the way to the Red River, Blunt chose to protect his base at Fort Gibson and to secure absolute control of Indian Territory and western Arkansas by occupying Fort Smith. He entrusted the reduction of Fort Smith to Colonel William Cloud, the commander of a fresh 1,500-man brigade which had just arrived from the Southwestern District of Missouri.

Cloud moved briskly toward Cabell's shaky perimeter. On August 31, at Poteau Bottom, the Federals shattered Cabell's line and drove the rebel regiments in a southeasterly direction, forcing them to cross the Arkansas boundary well below Forth Smith. On September 1, while the union infantry razed Fort Smith, Cloud's cavalry rode through Cabell's rear guard at Jenny Lind and again fell upon the rebel brigade at Backbone Mountain. After a desultory three-hour engagement, the rebel regiments broke and fled in complete disarray, abandoning their dead, wounded, cannon, rifles, and baggage.

Cabell camped at Waldron two days in order to rally as many stragglers as possible, and then, with the residue of his command—a remnant which grew smaller with each passing hour—he set out in the rough direction of Doaksville. But the troopers remaining with the colors were in no mood to return to the Nations, and so Cabell "was compelled to take roads that would keep my men from deserting, and not to take roads that . . . would have been proper under the circumstances." He was finally forced to turn eastward and aim his column toward Dardanelle and Arkadelphia, deep in the interior of southwestern Arkansas!

While Cabell nogotiated his strategy with the mutinous privates of his brigade, Cloud was treating with the hundreds of Johnnies who straggled away from Cabell's column. "My office has been constantly thronged by Mountain 'Feds,' deserters from the rebel army, who deliver themselves up," he gleefully reported to General Schofield. After spending a profitable week at Fort Smith mustering "several hundred deserters" into the service of the United States, Cloud resumed his pursuit of Cabell's dissolving brigade. En route to Dardanelle, "we were joined by six companies of Union men, about 300 all told, with the Stars and Stripes flying, and cheers for the Union." At Dardanelle, where the Second Kansas Cavalry engaged in a bloody little skirmish with Cabell's rear guard, Cloud "was assisted by three officers and about 100 men, who had fought me at Backbone, under Cabell, and it was a novel sight to see men with the regular gray uniform and Confederate State belt-plate fighting side by side with the blue of the [Union] army."

Once he was through Dardanelle, Cloud broke off the chase and permitted the fragments of Cabell's cavalry to retire peacefully toward Arkadelphia, where they eventually joined the remains of the army which Price had just evacuated from Little Rock. Cloud, meanwhile, sent his infantry back to Fort Smith and led his cavalry on a raid down the south bank of the Arkansas River. En route he enrolled even more

Arkansans in the Federal army. On September 18, Cloud's dusty horse soldiers and their volunteer auxiliaries jogged into a Federal encampment on the outskirts of Little Rock, having successfully demonstrated that the whole of the upper Arkansas River Valley was no longer part of the Southern Confederacy. Roving bands of rebel bushwhackers would continue to contest the Union army's domination of the occupied region until the very last days of the war, but the Union garrisons which were settled in the area, and the regiments of Arkansas militia which turned out to assist them, would ensure that whatever Confederate presence remained along the upper Arkansas could never be more than ephemeral.

For the remainder of 1863, almost nothing went right within the limits of Steele's old command. Squads of official inspectors reported that most of the disaffected, hungry, half-naked, sickly, unarmed warriors of the Confederate Indian brigade were worthless for field service, and that both the Creeks and the Choctaws were thinking of resuming their former relations with the United States. Because the fall of Fort Smith interdicted normal communications between Boggy Depot and Price's headquarters, Kirby Smith was obliged, on October 3, to direct the establishment of Indian Territory as a separate military district. For the next two months, Steele submitted his reports directly to Shreveport. Then, overwhelmed by the disasters that had befallen him and by the persistent failure of the Department to subsist his regiments decently, and convinced that Cooper, Tandy Walker, and many other Territorial officers were engaged in a conspiracy to disgrace him, he submitted his resignation. On December 11, much to Cooper's disappointment, Kirby Smith's headquarters announced the assignment of General Samuel B. Maxey, a fiery Lone Star politico, as commander of the District of Indian Territory.[7]

⚜ IV   If William Steele's star was eclipsed by the collapse of the Trans-Mississippi Department's upper Arkansas front, that of his bluecoat cousin Frederick was shining more brightly than ever. For back on September 10, just ten days after William Steele's rebels had been driven from Fort Smith, Frederick Steele's Federals had taken Little Rock. The Little Rock campaign was conceived about the eighth day of July, when, during the confusion attending Holmes's retreat from Helena, a Federal cavalry patrol ranging above Jacksonport happened to apprehend an anonymous Confederate lieutenant. The lieutenant soon proved to be a mine of high-echelon intelligence. According to him, the Helena operation had been nothing more than a diversion; Price, who was now in command of the District of Arkansas, planned to invade Missouri; Price's whole army, 19,000 strong, was already north of the White River and moving toward the vicinity of Bloomfield, where John W. Davidson's Union cavalry division was based. As soon as the lieutenant's revelations were forwarded to Davidson, he passed them on to Schofield. Schofield warned Grant; Grant warned Halleck; and on July 15, barely a week after the lieutenant's interrogation, Halleck ordered Schofield, Davidson, Stephen A. Hurlbut (commanding at Memphis), and Frederick Steele (who had just resumed command at Helena) to co-operate in a grand pincer movement designed to trap and crush Price's army.

Schofield was to contribute Davidson's cavalry to the campaign. Davidson's three brigades, mustering almost 6,000 troopers and three batteries of horse artillery, were to interpose themselves across Price's line of march and check his progress. Steele, meanwhile, was to proceed from Helena with two small infantry divisions, Powell Clayton's brigade of cavalry, and thirty-nine field guns, in all another 7,000 men, plus whatever reinforcements Hurlbut could spare, and close rapidly upon Price's right flank and rear. Haste was imperative, for it was obvious that Davidson's lone division could not frustrate the advance of an army three times its own size indefinitely.

It was not until the very end of July, after all preparations had been made for the commencement of the campaign, and after Davidson's troopers had already crossed into Arkansas, that it dawned upon the Union brass that their nameless rebel subaltern had embroidered the truth. Davidson's scouts reported that Marmaduke's grayback horse soldiers were still in their ramshackle camps at Jacksonport, waiting for Price to issue some orders. Steele's patrols found Marsh Walker's cavalry posted west of Clarendon, picketing the roads between Helena and the lower Arkansas River. Price's three infantry brigades—Parson's, McRae's, and Fagan's—were beginning to throw up a weak line of entrenchments just northeast of Little Rock (hardly an activity appropriate for troops about to take the offensive), while David Frost's raw con-

script recruits were still bivouacked in the camp of instruction near
Pine Bluff. Altogether, Price had no more than 8,000 effectives at his
disposal; and because of the demoralization which had set in since the
Helena fiasco, even the reliability of the men still under arms was very
much in doubt.

On July 10, two days after the Confederate lieutenant had been
captured, Kirby Smith assured Holmes that "no serious operations
against Arkansas are, I think, intended in the present position of affairs
here." Even if such operations were being contemplated by the enemy,
Smith continued, "I can give you no assistance; you must make the best
disposition you can with the troops at your disposal for the defense of
Arkansas Valley. . . . In the event of being driven from Arkansas Valley by overwhelming numbers, the concentration must be in this direction [that is, toward Shreveport]. Quietly establish depots for provisions and forage along the line of your probable march." The following
day, Smith affirmed to Governor Flanagin that "the abandonment of the
State of Arkansas has not been contemplated by the department commander, and he trusts its necessity may never arise." Yet he admitted,
rather more forthrightly than he had in his message to Holmes, that
"the valley of the Arkansas may be endangered or even temporarily occupied," and so he urged the governor "to prepare for such an emergency, either by calling out the military [militia], or organizing for its
defense a State force without the conscript limit of age."

In the ensuing weeks, as it became increasingly obvious that Steele
and Davidson were up to something, the Confederate authorities in Arkansas began to get nervous. Holmes went on sick leave, and left Price
to defend the state. Price, paralyzed by fatigue and indecision, ordered
his cavalry to picket, his infantry to dig, and his staff officers to publish
a series of patriotic proclamations. A justice of the Arkansas Supreme
Court, two congressmen, and a member of the state military board
broadcast a protest against the Confederate government's disregard for
the integrity and welfare of Arkansas, and warned that the citizenry
would probably submit to any "bogus government" installed at Little
Rock by the enemy. Governor Flanagin confessed to Senator R. W.
Johnson that Little Rock's predicament appeared hopeless, that the people were despairing, and that the loss of the Arkansas Valley seemed
inevitable.

Flanagin also authorized the enlistment in state service of all exemptees between the ages of sixteen and sixty, but, as if to confirm his gloomy appraisal of the popular mood, almost no volunteers turned out to enroll. Indeed many of the men already under arms began straying away. A "brace of female spies" who visited Little Rock and Jacksonport in late July and early August reported to Schofield that countless deserters "from Price's army, are met everywhere along the route of travel north. These men are fleeing like rats from a falling house; they give the rebellion up, and express a determination to return to their homes." [8]

Nor was the reluctance of civilians to enlist or the eagerness of soldiers to flee the only indication of disaffection. Planters all along the lower Arkansas began driving their slaves into the interior; the state legislature once again packed its archives; machinery was evacuated from Little Rock and Camden to less vulnerable locations; cotton stored along the banks of the Arkansas was burned; preparations were made to demolish railroad engines, bridges, steamboats, and the buildings of the Little Rock arsenal; and the precious copper telegraph wires recently strung from Little Rock to Fort Smith were dismantled, rolled, and shipped to the safety of Texas. On August 1, Kirby Smith made his one significant contribution to the state's defense by dispatching J. C. Tappan's infantry brigade from North Louisiana back into Arkansas. Smith then turned his attention to the establishment of his Cotton Bureau and to discussions of policy with the civil authorities gathered at Marshall, leaving the fate of Arkansas in the hands of Sterling Price.

By the first week of August, reports of Davidson's descent down the St. Francis River and the sharp acceleration of Union patrol activity east of Clarendon convinced Price that the Federals were mouting a serious thrust toward the state capital. Marmaduke's division was ordered to cover Jacksonport and delay Davidson, but to avoid a decisive engagement east of the White River at all costs (for the river might obstruct any effort to withdraw). Marsh Walker was instructed to keep his own brigade in the neighborhood of Clarendon, but to retire Archibald Dobbin's brigade to the immediate vicinity of Little Rock. Finally, Frost's conscripts, Flanagin's few state volunteers, and Tappan's foot soldiers were also summoned to Little Rock, where Frost, the ranking brigadier, assumed command of all the assembled infantry.

Most of the infantry occupied the incomplete line of field fortifications and earthworks still being dug to the north and east of the capital city—that is, on the northern bank of the Arkansas River—while only Dobbin's cavalry and Tappan's infantry were deployed on the southern shore. Little Rock was situated on the southern bank of the Arkansas, not the northern, and hence the bulk of Price's infantry and all of his entrenchments were on the wrong side of the river. Only two small brigades were in position to protect the overland approaches to the capital. And only three rickety pontoon bridges gave the rebels deployed above the river access to the city and to the escape routes leading into the interior of southwestern Arkansas.

Had the Union high command still been intent on trapping the Confederate lieutenant's imaginary army, Price's sorry tactical dispositions would have made no difference. But as it became clear to the Federals that no rebel army was invading Missouri, it occurred to them that the campaign already under way might still be turned to advantage. Almost simultaneously, every Union general involved in the operation seems to have decided that Little Rock should be the army's objective. Messages burned the wires: Hurlbut and Grant were again urged to forward as many reinforcements as they could; even John Pope, off fighting Sioux in the Dakotas since his misfortune at Second Bull Run, was asked whether he had any extra soldiers to spare; Steele and Davidson agreed to converge at Clarendon, to press westward along the rails of the Memphis and Little Rock, and to pounce on Price together. By August 5, when the point of Steele's column decamped from Helena, the Federals were no longer chasing a phantom.

Davidson's blue cavalry division swung around Jacksonport, avoided a confrontation with Marmaduke, and continued southward to Clarendon. This neat flanking maneuver deprived Jacksonport of its usefulness as a defensive position, and deprived Marsh Walker of his base. Consequently, both Marmaduke and Walker fell back to Bayou Meto, a northern tributary of the Arkansas located some twelve miles east of Little Rock. There the rebel cavalry established a forward defense line well in advance of Frost's infantry works. Price directed Walker to assume command of the combined cavalry force, an assignment which did nothing to cool Marmaduke's enduring animosity toward Walker.

Davidson occupied Clarendon on August 15. Two days later, Frederick Steele's army arrived from Helena; and so too did Colonel James M. True's 2,300-man infantry brigade, Hurlbut's contribution to the campaign. Then, on the 18th, leaving his base in the care of a thousand convalescents and a small detachment of guards, Steele led his army—14,000 officers and men, and fifty-seven guns—across the White River and into rebel country.

Little Rock was taken by maneuver, not by frontal attack or siege; and the demoralization of the Confederate army, Price's tactical ineptitude, and Steele's brilliant execution of the campaign all combined to give the city to the Federals with only the most incidental damage to themselves. During the advance from the White River to Bayou Meto, Steele encountered more high water than he had expected, which caused some delay, but otherwise his progress was almost unimpeded. Occasional snipers took pot shots at his officers, and horse patrols crossed his van and pricked his flanks, but these were brushed aside without much difficulty. By the 26th, when the Federals finally reached Bayou Meto, they were in high spirits and itching for a fight.

But Steele decided not to force his way across the bayou. On both the 26th and the 28th, elements of his army skirmished with Walker's cavalry and probed far beyond the soft rebel flanks, but no serious effort was made to punch through Walker's line. Steele just convinced everyone that he could overrun Walker any time he cared to. His resort to psychological warfare paid off on August 31, when Price, fearful that he was about to lose three irreplaceable horse brigades, ordered Walker to abandon his position, to retire to the south side of the Arkansas River, and to reinforce Dobbin and Tappan. As soon as Walker pulled back, Steele resumed his advance. By September 2, Union cannon were trained on Frost's infantry and Union troops were prepared to storm Frost's entrenchments.

Once again, Steele refrained from attacking. Instead of driving through the rebel defenses, he preferred to circumvent them. On the 3d and 4th of September, Davidson's cavalry reconnoitred both of Frost's flanks, and reported that while it would be difficult to turn the Confederate left, the right, suspended on the Arkansas River, seemed to have little beyond it but open ground and open roads to Little Rock. Leaving his infantry and most of his artillery in place to keep Frost occupied,

Steele ordered the whole of Davidson's division—almost half of his army—to cross the river, to take Little Rock, and to close on Price's rear.

Davidson was unable to find a ford, and the delay caused by the necessity to throw a pontoon bridge across the Arkansas gave Price the time he needed to extract his army from Steele's trap. The extraction was nonetheless a messy one, for almost nothing went right. The Confederates did manage to scuttle six riverboats at their moorings, but they neglected to demolish the facilities of the Little Rock arsenal, which, within days after the city changed hands, was back in production. They fired some loose bales of cotton, but most of the ordnance, quartermaster, and commissary stores housed in the capital were left for the enemy. They uprooted a few iron rails on the northern bank of the Arkansas, but forgot to decommission two locomotives parked in the Memphis and Little Rock terminal, two locomotives which soon gave the Federals the use of an operable railroad. The state's prominent civil officials were evacuated in fairly good order, but a substantial number of clerks and minor bureaucrats chose to remain behind to offer their services to the new rulers of Arkansas. And the rebel army itself suffered such demoralization that Price found it necessary, six days before the city fell, to publish a manifesto threatening both his own troops and the citizens of Pulaski County with military arrest or summary execution for desertion, unauthorized absence from places of duty or domicile, or any attempt "to pass toward the enemy under any pretext whatever, either with or without a pass." Perhaps the only rebel not impressed by the mounting evidence of confusion and disorder about Little Rock was Kirby Smith, who, on September 3, confidently advised General Taylor that the Federals had been "checked at Bayou Meto . . . and have retired to White River. . . . The enemy's force was, I believe, overestimated; his was more a reconnaissance than an advance with the purpose of permanent occupation. He will wait for winter and high water in the Arkansas." [9]

But the last thing Steele and Davidson wanted was high water. Before September 7, the river itself, and not the rebels on the southern shore, constituted their chief obstacle. In fact, the Confederates covering the overland approaches to Little Rock were virtually excused from the campaign for the better part of three days, while their two ranking generals settled a personal feud. The simmering hostility between Marsh Walker and Marmaduke, exacerbated by their current habit of hurling gratuitous insults at one another in official correspondence, finally boiled over. On the 5th, in response to rumors that a confrontation was imminent, Price directed both generals to remain in quarters, an order which hardly expedited the deployment of their troops. At dawn, September 6, Marmaduke, Walker, and their seconds defied Price's restrictions and met on a field south of Little Rock. Marmaduke satisfied his honor by shooting Walker dead. Since the laws of Arkansas prohibited dueling, Price promptly arrested Marmaduke and both squads of seconds. But on the 7th, concluding that the dismal strategic situation made Marmaduke more valuable as a cavalry general than as a prisoner, Price released him, restored him to duty, and directed him to assume control of the whole of the cavalry.

Not until the 7th, therefore, did the Confederate cavalry begin to contest Davidson's passage of the Arkansas. On the 8th and 9th, Dobbin's troopers were spread along the southern shore of the river, and rebel cannoneers did their best to slow the construction of the Federals' pontoon bridge. But on the morning of the 10th, massed Union artillery suppressed the fire of the rebel batteries, the Federal engineers finished their bridge, and Davidson's yellowlegs established a secure beachhead on the right bank of the Arkansas. Marmaduke, Dobbin, and Tappan, now reinforced by Fagan's brigade, tried to counterattack; but their efforts lacked coordination, their men lacked determination, and each was repulsed in turn.

As the southern wing of his army fell apart, Price instructed Frost to abandon the works north of the river, to evacuate his infantry via the three bridges still in Confederate hands, to burn the bridges behind him, and to withdraw toward southwestern Arkansas. At 5:00 P.M., September 10, as the last of Price's panicky stragglers fled Little Rock, the head of Davidson's blue column galloped into the city and clattered to a halt before the steps of the shabby Frontier-Greek statehouse. Two hours later, Mayor C. P. Bertrand formally surrendered Little Rock to General Steele, and then cheered lustily as the Union flag was hoisted above the capital dome.

As soon as Little Rock was taken, Steele consolidated his control of the city and its environs. Davidson assumed command of the city, ordered the construction of fortifications to cover its southern and western approaches, and detailed troops to act as a provost guard. Powell Clayton, with a large contingent of cavalry, was dispatched southward to occupy the abandoned rebel stronghold at Pine Bluff, which he seized without a fight. Other units fanned over the neighboring countryside to collect provisions and forage, to suppress guerrilla bands, and to cover Steele's communications with Devall's Bluff and Helena. A prominent "Mountain Fed," Isaac Murphy, was hastily installed as the civilian provisional governor of Union Arkansas. Steele issued oaths, amnesties, and pardons; authorized the local citizens to rearm themselves and form as a militia; and began enlisting hundreds of volunteers, Negroes, and rebel deserters into the Union army.

About the only thing which did not go well was the pursuit of Price's army, which was not pressed with enough vigor to satisfy Steele. On the morning of September 11, Colonel Lewis Merrill's horse brigade, augmented by detachments from other commands, set out in chase of the retreating rebels. But because the highway to Arkadelphia led through broken country abounding in good cover for ambuscades, and because no decent side routes paralleled the main road, Merrill made no serious effort to penetrate or flank the Confederates' rear guard. His men did, however, salvage a large amount of abandoned military gear strewn in the wake of the rebel army, and scoop up a considerable number of fagged Johnny stragglers, most of whom seemed glad to be captured. Steele was unhappy with Merrill's sluggish performance, but he was more than delighted with the evidence of the Confederate army's rot and decay accumulated by Merrill's horsemen. As Steele commented to Halleck, "With 6,000 more infantry, I think I could drive Smith and Price into Mexico."

What was left of Price's army continued down to Arkadelphia, where a slovenly barrio of shantytown camps was thrown together. Something less than 7,000 men—including the remnants of Cabell's brigade, just dragging in from Fort Smith—were still with the colors. At least 1,000 troops, and perhaps as many as 2,000, had deserted. Of those who remained, almost 2,000 were unarmed; and those who were armed were dreadfully short of ammunition. All the men were hungry; all of them were exhausted; many of them were ill; and almost none of them wanted to resume soldiering. On September 25, Holmes returned from sick leave and resumed command of the army, reducing Price to the command of his old infantry division.

The fugitive Confederate civil government of Arkansas proceeded to the village of Washington, deep in the interior of southwestern Arkansas. Washington—the only Arkansas Confederate town which still boasted its own newspaper—was to remain the rebel state capital until the end of the war. Governor Flanagin, the legislators (or, rather, what was left of them, for they never again managed to assemble a legal quorum), and the justices of the state supreme court set up shop in the Hempstead County courthouse. Shortly after the government was resettled, the justices decreed that the exigencies of war excused the rump legislature from the need to convene a quorum, and the legislators acknowledged that the state courts no longer had the use of a penitentiary by stipulating that the punishment for all felonies should be either flogging or death. Governor Flanagin received from Governor Murphy a request for the return of the state archives to Little Rock, but Flanagin demurred on the ground that he, and not Murphy, was still the duly elected chief executive of the state of Arkansas.[10]

Frederick Steele might well have continued his conquest of Arkansas had not four factors dissuaded him. One was an order from Halleck, directing him to hold, secure, and solidify his position; the second was the impending rainy season, which would soon convert every road in Arkansas into a muddy quagmire; the third was the diversion of expected reinforcements to other theaters of war; and the last was Jo Shelby's Iron Brigade.

In mid-September, Shelby stormed into Price's Arkadelphia headquarters and announced that he intended to raid Missouri. Shelby's motives were less than clear. He wanted, according to various reports, to reinvigorate the sagging morale of his troopers, to recruit another brigade of Missourians, to prevent Schofield from transferring reinforcements to the Union armies in the East, and to make way for the redemption of rebel Missouri by carrying a Confederate flag through the state. Whatever his reasons were, both Marmaduke and Price consented to the expedition and forwarded Shelby's design to Holmes. Holmes also approved, and referred the scheme to Kirby Smith. At the time, Smith was debating whether to reinforce the army in Arkansas with Taylor's two brigades of Texas cavalry, or to withdraw the troops in Ar-

kansas to the upper Red River Valley. Upon receipt of Shelby's proposal he decided to do neither, and instead gave his blessing to the
execution of a Missouri raid. Nobody, from Shelby to Smith, appears to
have weighed with any care either the purpose or the utility of such a
raid; in no sense was it a calculated military maneuver. On September
21, only six days after proposing his raid, Shelby received authorization
to ride.

The following morning, the "weather was propitious, and the glorious skies of a southern autumn flashed cheerily down upon waving
banners and glittering steel" as Shelby's horse soldiers passed in review
before Governor Reynolds and General Price. Then, with a whoop, the
troopers galloped from the parade ground and wheeled toward Missouri. From the 23d to the 27th, Shelby "traveled hard, determining to
force the line of the Arkansas River before notice could possibly be
given of my advances." On the 27th, twelve miles south of the river, he
"ran directly upon some 200 of the [Federal] First Arkansas Infantry.
. . . a simultaneous charge scattered them like chaff, and our rough rid-
ers rode them down like stubble to the lava tide." Crossing the Arkansas at Ozark on the morning of the 28th, he spent the next three days
marching at a leisurely pace through the Boston Mountains, refreshing
his horses and men, destroying the telegraph to Fayetteville, and incor-
porating into his command about six hundred irregulars belonging to
D. C. Hunter's and J. T. Coffee's partisan battalions.

On October 2, the brigade, now 1,200 strong, pressed on to Pineville, "where Missouri breezes blew and Missouri skies looked down
upon us." Two days later, the raiders descended upon Neosho and received the unconditional surrender of the three hundred Federal cavalrymen stationed there. Having pillaged Neosho, Shelby passed through
the blackened and desolated town of Sarcoxie, and on to Oregon, or Bow-
er's Mill, "a notorious pest spot for the militia, which was sacked and
then swept from the face of the earth, to pollute it no more forever."
The little forts at Greenfield and Stockton were razed on the 5th; Hu-
mansville was looted on the 6th; Warsaw was demolished on the 7th;
Camp Cole was sacked on the 8th; and on the 10th, Tipton was occupied.

While at Tipton, Shelby "sent out a cloud of scouts, ordering them
to do their worst upon both telegraph and railroad. For 30 miles either

way rails were torn up, ties burned, bridges destroyed, wire carried off, and cattle-stops and water-tanks obliterated." But the happy springtime of the raid was fast drawing to a close, for just north of Tipton Shelby's main column encountered its first serious opposition. There, the rebel troopers ran into a thousand Missouri militia, "drawn up in splendid line . . . ready and willing to dispute" the Confederates' progress. Shelby charged; the citizen soldiers broke for the rear and retreated in "dire confusion"; and the rebels chased them for ten miles, "killing and wounding a great many, for few prisoners were taken."

On the 11th, the raiders struck the Missouri River at Boonville, received the mayor's capitulation of the town, dispersed the local militia garrison, and drove away a steamboat seeking to land a contingent of bluecoat reinforcements. But, meanwhile, "a great storm was gathering." General Egbert B. Brown, commanding the Union army's District of Central Missouri, was coming up "like a black cloud from Jefferson City" with 1,600 fresh National and state troops. As Shelby's pickets "were driven in on the main body pell-mell, and the sounds of conflict came nearer and nearer," Shelby ordered his troopers to decamp and begin a slow trek westward, toward the river town of Marshall. Brown cautiously pursued, skirmishing almost continuously with Shelby's rear guard but making no effort to bag the main rebel force.

On the morning of the 13th, as the Iron Brigade's van entered Marshall, Shelby's point scouts reported that a thousand more bluecoats, under the command of General Thomas Ewing, were rapidly approaching from the west. Pinned between Brown and Ewing, Shelby had no choice but to fight his way out of the trap. Stripping all excess gear from his wagons and spiking one unserviceable cannon, he drove his troopers and his train right through the enveloping Union lines, and then, in order to confuse pursuit, he ordered his regiments to disperse.

During the next six days, the raiders, riding in several separate columns down several parallel routes, moved toward the Arkansas frontier. All along the way they continued to skirmish with various Union detachments, to burn forts and loot military property, and to sack villages. Crossing the state boundary on the 20th, the Confederates again filtered through the Boston Mountains, repulsed a cavalry brigade sent from Fayetteville to intercept them, and forded the Arkansas River at Clarksville on the 26th. Once safely on the Confederate side of the river, Shelby encountered "a very severe rain and snow storm," and so "took plenty of time" in marching the rest of the way to Washington, which was not reached until November 3. By then, his troopers were frostbitten, emaciated, and exhausted—but not too tired to boast of their achievement. "You've heard of . . . Jeb Stuart's Ride around McClellan? Hell, brother, Jo Shelby rode around MISSOURI!" [11]

For all practical purposes, Shelby's thrilling but pointless Missouri expedition was the last major operation along the Arkansas front until the following spring. In mid-October, a motley collection of rebel irregulars commanded by Colonel W. H. Brooks tried to besiege Fayetteville, but they were driven off by the small Union garrison. Two weeks later, Marmaduke, with 2,000 regulars and twelve howitzers, tried to retake Pine Bluff, but he suffered a similar humiliation. Marmaduke's failure convinced Holmes that the Arkadelphia salient was too vulnerable to hold, and he ordered the retirement of district headquarters to the town of Camden. As soon as Arkadelphia was evacuated, 4,000 Federals from Little Rock promptly occupied the place. Countless little bands of blue and gray cavalrymen raided all through the winter, but little of significance was accomplished other than the accumulation of hundreds of additional names in the death lists. In mid-October, Kirby Smith considered taking the field himself in order to lead Holmes's army back to Little Rock. But after a tour of inspection in Arkansas and some sober reflection, Smith decided instead to prepare plans, depots, and routes for the eventual evacuation of Holmes's troops to North Louisiana, and began intimating that he wanted a new lieutenant general for the District of Arkansas.

Meanwhile, most of the soldiers settled in camps, line officers drilled their men, quartermasters refitted the regiments, and staff officers shuffled paper, making various adjustments in the army's table of organization. Carter's small Texas cavalry brigade was posted to Indian Territory. Marmaduke's remaining cavalry brigades were strung across the district's northern front: Cabell's was deployed along a thin vedette line extending from the Nations toward Murfreesboro, Shelby's continued the line to Camden, and Dobbin's and Colton Greene's went into camps between Camden and Monticello. Fagan's Arkansas infantry brigade, augmented by a number of short-term state militia units, was detached from Price's division and stationed north of Camden. Price's remaining infantry regiments, including those formerly commanded by Frost, established winter quarters between Camden and Spring Hill. They were reorganized into four brigades, commanded, respectively, by Parsons, Tappan, Thomas F. Drayton (recently transferred to the Department), and Thomas Churchill (just repatriated from a Federal prison camp). General T. P. Dockery, another exchanged parolee, took charge of a new camp of instruction founded at Washington and began whipping together a sixth infantry brigade from manpower supplied by prisoner exchanges and the ubiquitous conscript press gangs. Ruthless recruiting, the even more ruthless pursuit of absentees, a gradual improvement in the army's morale, and the promise of easy living through the winter season added a fair number of men to the army's ranks, for on the last day of 1863, the monthly return of the District of Arkansas showed 11,520 effectives present for duty—out of a total enrollment of 25,623.

Exactly one year earlier, the northern front of the Trans-Mississippi Department had extended from Fort Cobb to Fort Gibson, along the Arkansas River to the vicinity of Clarksville and Lewisburg, northeastward to Batesville and Jacksonport, and down the White River Valley to the Mississippi. A tattered rebel flag still flew over Fort Cobb, which was now not only the most forlorn post in the Department but also the northernmost position west of the Mississippi still occupied by something like a regular Confederate garrison; but elsewhere the entire front had been driven far to the south.

When General Maxey assumed command in the Nations, he found that the only Nations in which any perceptible Confederate presence remained were the Chickasaw and the Choctaw; and even the northern halves of these two Nations were no-man's-lands. On paper, Maxey had an army of 8,875 troops, but in the winter camps at Boggy Depot and Doaksville he had only 2,236. The majority of his soldiers were conscript reinforcements received at the very end of the year: 1,300 members of Bankhead's Texas brigade (now commanded by Richard M. Gano) and the 138 troopers of Colonel Thomas Bass's Twentieth Texas "Regiment." Cooper's Indian brigade, allegedly the most substantial organization in the region, reported 659 present for duty and 5,585 absent!

East of the Nations, the Confederate line now straggled through

Murfreesboro, looped just north of Camden, turned abruptly southward at Monticello, and followed the Ouachita to the neighborhood of Monroe. By the end of 1863, the Stars and Stripes fluttered above Fort Gibson, Fort Smith, Van Buren, Clarksville, Lewisburg, Hot Springs, Arkadelphia, Batesville, Jacksonport, Little Rock, Pine Bluff, and scores of other Arkansas towns and villages formerly garrisoned by the rebels; the Arkansas Valley, the White River Valley, and the Mississippi Valley were lost; a Federal riverboat could proceed all the way from Memphis to the eastern frontier of the Creek Nation without once encountering a rebel patrol; and nothing remained of the Confederate State of Arkansas but a small military enclave hugging the Louisiana border.[12]

V   Down in Richard Taylor's domain, conditions were no better than in the District of Arkansas, but because General Banks was temporarily distracted from his efforts to press the conquest of West Louisiana, the area under Taylor's jurisdiction survived the latter half of 1863 and the early months of 1864 relatively unscathed. While the Federals were busy securing possession of Vicksburg and Port Hudson and consolidating their control of the lower Mississippi Valley, Taylor was free to refresh and recruit his regiments, to strengthen the fortifications being built along the Red River, and to exercise his troops in cautious maneuvers against the Federal expeditionary forces which occasionally came through the eastern marches of his district.

The beginning of August, 1863, found Taylor's little field army—Mouton's Louisiana infantry brigade and the two Texas cavalry brigades belonging to Major and Thomas Green—concentrated along the lower Teche between Vermillionville and New Iberia. The three Texas brigades of John Walker's infantry division were on the road from Monroe to Alexandria, en route to Opelousas and a rendezvous with the rest of Taylor's disposable force. Once Walker evacuated Monroe, the desolate country north and east of the Red River Valley was left to the care of Harrison's lone battalion of Louisiana cavalry, the tiny garrison of artillerists at Fort Beauregard, and some stray elements of Carter's Texas horse brigade which leaked across the Arkansas border. At Shreveport, there were feverish attempts to patch together a respectable infantry brigade out of exchanged prisoners and the dregs from the

Conscript Bureau's barrel, but the work was progressing slowly and this embryo command would not be ready for active service until the last days of autumn. General Magruder was still gathering troops at Niblett's Bluff, but his persistent appeals for the return of Major and Green to Texas suggested that the last thing he wanted was to dispatch any of his own regiments to Louisiana.

Throughout Taylor's embattled district, recruiting teams still used every means at their disposal to induce men to fill the army's thin ranks. Cavalry patrols hunted down deserters and dragged them in. The Conscript Bureau revoked the details of hundreds of soldiers and ordered them to return to their regiments. Kirby Smith called upon the citizens of the district to form local home defense or partisan companies, and urged Governor Moore "to bring out every able-bodied man in the State for the defense of his fireside." Moore tried to muster some state troops and embody some militia, but barely enough men to serve a single cannon turned out.

Perhaps the best evidence of the growing desperation was an extraordinary private letter written by Kirby Smith on September 21, 1863. In this letter, for the first time, the commanding general of a Confederate army department dared to acknowledge on paper that he would "feel no hesitation under the sanction of the acts of state legislatures upon calling out a military force from amongst the slave population, whenever arms can be obtained in sufficient quantities." Twenty months before the capitulation of his command and the collapse of his government, Kirby Smith was ready to arm slaves! [13]

The fundamental reason for this frantic recruiting was that Taylor's army, mustering no more than 10,000 effectives, was obviously far too small to hold West Louisiana. The best Taylor could expect to do, should the Federals mount a major offensive, would be to delay them long enough to permit the evacuation of stores and slaves from the Red River Valley. And even though a serious Federal invasion did not materialize, Taylor's pickets were constantly harried by enemy reconnaissance patrols, and his front was often penetrated by Union flying columns. By the end of August, for instance, bluecoat raiders had thoroughly demolished the entire railroad line from Vicksburg to Monroe, seriously impeding Taylor's attempt to subsist or maneuver the scattered troops operating in northeastern Louisiana. Then, in the first

week of September, a Union expedition staging from Natchez rolled
into the Ouachita Valley and pounced on Fort Beauregard, which was
taken without a fight. As soon as the fort was leveled, the Federals
"skedaddled and returned to Natchez where they came from."

Taylor was forever marching and countermarching his regiments
from one threatened area to another, in a desperate and usually futile
effort to plug every gap in his line. Some of his soldiers did not seem to
mind all the movement. A good-natured Texan riding with Major told
his sister that "we are living very [well] now . . . we have been marching enough to make us healthy, we have fine times eating shugar Cane,
it is very good and plenty of it." But a footsore Louisiana field officer
was less enthusiastic. In early October he complained to his diary that
"we marched 300 miles last month, and none of us can see what this
eternal movement is for. This is what is called strategy by some."

By the beginning of the fourth week of September, Kirby Smith
was convinced that "the intention of the enemy is clearly to overrun and
possess this side of the river, controlling the Mississippi." The seizure
of Fort Beauregard, the recent attack upon Sabine Pass, the occupation
of Little Rock and the lower Arkansas Valley, and the constant pressure upon Taylor's eastern front all seemed to indicate that the Federals
were getting ready to push the whole of the Trans-Mississippi army into
Texas, where it could be contained and safely ignored. The existence of
some Federal master plan for the conquest of the states bordering the
Mississippi was more or less taken for granted by the rebel brass. The
Confederate high command's only question concerned the Federals'
strategy.

Three alternatives seemed feasible. First, the Union army in Arkansas might continue to drive Holmes toward Shreveport, thus out-
flanking Taylor and forcing the evacuation of Confederate troops from
lower Louisiana and the Red River Valley. Second, Banks's army could
again advance up the Red, pressing Taylor toward Shreveport and out-
flanking Holmes. Or, finally—and this was the option most feared by
Magruder, who persisted in thinking of Texas as "virtually the Trans-
Mississippi Department"—Banks might attempt to establish another
beachhead somewhere near Sabine Pass, interdict the Texas railway system, march northward, and trap both Holmes and Taylor in the upper
Red River Valley.

Kirby Smith did not believe that Banks would try another amphibious assault right away; nor did he think that Banks would attempt an overland march from Berwick's Bay to the Sabine, since the intervening country was nearly uninhabited and devoid of forage and provisions. Smith therefore dismissed the third possibility out of hand, and, while urging Magruder to continue gathering troops in East Texas, he declined to comply with Magruder's insistent demands that the Texas regiments on duty in the other districts be returned to Texas soil.

But the remaining two alternatives appeared to be equally ominous. On the one hand, it was not yet clear that Frederick Steele's offensive in Arkansas had been terminated, since the alarms and excursions still convulsing Holmes's district made it almost impossible to evaluate the situation there. But on the other hand, rebel scouts ranging through lower Louisiana in the days immediately following the Sabine Pass fiasco began to accumulate intelligence of a sizable and rapidly concentrating Union force at Brashear City, a force estimated by Taylor to number 15,000, and by Magruder 30,000 to 40,000. Judging by Banks's past performance and the realities of Louisiana geography, both Smith and Taylor interpreted this news as proof that Banks was about to launch another campaign toward Alexandria and the Red. Only Magruder continued to believe that the Sabine was Banks's objective.

Whether the Federals descended upon Shreveport from Little Rock, or ascended toward Shreveport from Brashear City, it seemed to Smith that "a concentration [of Taylor's and Holmes's armies] in one or the other District was inevitable—the time for carrying it into execution, and the point of concentration, have alone been matters of doubt." Smith himself was inclined to consider the Arkansas front to be the more important of the two, not only because an invasion was already in progress there, but because of strong political and logistical considerations. As he wrote to Taylor on September 25:

Should the enemy advance from Little Rock, Arkansas is decidedly the place for concentration, a success there clears the Indian Territory, whilst it redeems the Ark valley. The despondency is greater in that state than elsewhere and the Indians are preparing to change their allegiance—nothing but a decisive blow struck especially in that section will prevent the loss of the whole Country east of Red River. In the event of your being ordered to reinforce Holmes what effective force can you bring?

But Smith was careful to acknowledge that he was "not posted in events and the condition of affairs" in Arkansas, and hence he directed Taylor to await further orders while he himself inspected the situation in Holmes's district. Announcing his imminent departure for Arkadelphia, Smith instructed Taylor to keep a close eye on the Federals at Brashear, to "take advantage of the least fault of his enemy," to do his best to check any attempt made by the Federals to move into Confederate Louisiana, and to avoid risking a general engagement unless there appeared to be a "reasonable chance of success." [14]

As events turned out, the two Confederate armies did not rendezvous, Steele's offensive was aborted, and Holmes's weary regiments were allowed to settle in quarters and spend a relatively quiet winter in southwestern Arkansas. The only invasion with which Magruder had to contend occurred at the wrong end of Texas (the Union occupation of Brownsville and the lower Rio Grande Valley), and Taylor was not required to deal with more than a feeble enemy demonstration up the Teche to Opelousas. All the Confederates' grand theories had been based upon a false assumption. There was no Federal master plan for the conquest of Arkansas and West Louisiana. Steele's whirlwind reduction of Little Rock had been haphazardly precipitated by the deceptions of a Confederate lieutenant; and Banks's lurch toward Opelousas appears to have been mainly an effort to employ usefully 20,000 spare soldiers attached to his command. Once, and only once, during the spring of 1864, would the Union armies in Arkansas and West Louisiana actually try to cooperate; and only once would Confederate domination of the Red River Valley be seriously endangered.

While Smith was away visiting Holmes's headquarters, Taylor probed toward Brashear City. His intention was to discover the enemy's order of battle and whatever else he could about the enemy's plans. Since Taylor lacked the strength to assault Brashear itself, he aimed at the Federals' northernmost picket, a demibrigade of 820 infantry and cavalry stationed on the east side of the Atchafalaya near Morganza. Summoning Mouton's infantry from the neighborhood of New Iberia, recalling Major's brigade from Alexandria, and reorganizing his two Texas horse brigades into a single cavalry division under Green's command, he crossed the Atchafalaya at Morgan's Ferry and plunged toward the unsuspecting Federals.

Owing, in part, to a torrential rain, the Confederates enjoyed the advantage of complete surprise. On September 29, during a brisk little engagement at Stirling's plantation, they captured two fine 10-pounder Parrotts and two stand of regimental colors, rousted 462 prisoners from Mrs. Stirling's sugarhouse and slave quarters, and drove the remainder of the picket down the road toward Morganza. Taylor was more than satisfied, for from the prisoners he began to get some sense of the composition of the army at Brashear—enough of a picture to confirm his guess that the Federals were up to something.

The disposable force at Brashear was an army as large as Holmes's and Taylor's combined. It consisted of General C. C. Washburn's detachment of the XIII Army Corps (thirty-four regiments of foot in seven brigades, plus ten batteries), General William B. Franklin's detachment of the XIX Corps (seventeen regiments in four brigades, plus six batteries), and the two understrength brigades of General Albert L. Lee's cavalry division. Franklin, the ranking officer, was in command of the whole. General Banks's reasons for concentrating these forces at Brashear City were the same as his reasons for the earlier Sabine Pass and the later Brownsville expeditions: he was still under orders to plant the flag in Texas, and was still looking for a way to do it. At the moment, Brashear City appeared to be the logical base for an overland campaign toward the Sabine (the sort of operation Magruder feared), or for an offensive through lower Louisiana and up the Red toward Shreveport (the strategy anticipated by Smith and Taylor). So Banks marshaled his hosts at Brashear, refrained from issuing any specific instructions to them, and exhorted Franklin to find some practical way to move them toward Texas.

The campaign was inaugurated on October 3, when a contingent of the XIX Corps occupied the works at New Iberia recently abandoned by Mouton. But once New Iberia was taken, Franklin seemed unable to decide how to proceed or what to do next. Instead of massing his columns for a decisive thrust toward a stipulated objective, he dissipated his forces in scattered, piecemeal, leapfrog forays aimed, roughly, at the nearest roving detachments of Taylor's little army. Since most of Taylor's men were mounted and most of the Federals were on foot, these sorties failed to do much real damage to the badly outnumbered rebels, who could ride faster than the bluecoats could walk. Each time the

Confederates were brushed aside, the Federals would make a false start
or two, creep ahead a few miles, and grind to a halt as soon as another
gray will-o'-the-wisp flickered into view.

If Franklin had not been trapped by the terrain, it seems doubtful
that his fitful push into rebel Louisiana would have enjoyed the cohesion necessary to distinguish it as a campaign. All that gave integrity to
his operation was the geography, which tended to funnel most of his
army's surges in more or less the same direction, up the Teche toward
Opelousas. Between the 4th and the 20th of October, the Federals skirmished their way from New Iberia to Opelousas, driving Taylor's main
body back upon the village of Washington. On the 21st, the Federal flag
was once again hoisted over the town of Opelousas itself.

Taylor summoned John Walker's infantry division from Alexandria to the upper Teche Valley, but even with this reinforcement he did
no more than fight a prolonged delaying action, avoiding major encoun-
ters. The Confederate regiments fell back from town to town, from
camp to camp, in a state of constant turmoil: "Horses galloping, mules
trotting, tents struck and everything in commotion." There seemed always to be "a fight or a foot-race" in progress, or a fast march from one
nameless crossroads to another "in a devil of a hurry."

Both Taylor and Kirby Smith fully expected Franklin to try to
push on from Opelousas to the Red, and then northwestward toward
Shreveport; but quite early in the campaign it became apparent that the
two generals differed on how to respond. Taylor was far less inclined
than Smith to yield ground along the Teche in hopes that a decisive
stand could be mounted farther in the interior. His only thought was to
crush the Federal offensive before it wiped Confederate Louisiana from
the map. As the enemy approached Opelousas, he began to importune
Smith's headquarters for permission to drive them back to Berwick's
Bay. Only Smith's assurances that reinforcements from Arkansas and
Texas would soon be gathered near Shreveport, combined with the commanding general's repeated insistence that Taylor continue his delaying
maneuver, kept Taylor's patience in check and prevented him from offering battle below Opelousas.

But once Opelousas fell, Taylor's unnatural prudence gave way to
angry desperation. Protesting that between Washington and the Red
there were no good defensive positions, he demanded the authority to

disperse the invaders before they could occupy the whole of lower Louisiana. Smith, however, once again replied that "difficult as you may find it, you must exercise great caution in your operations. You must restrain your own impulses as well as the desires of your men. The Fabian policy is now our true policy." Reminding Taylor of the popular demoralization pervading the District of West Louisiana, Smith explained that "a defeat of your little army would be ruinous in its effects"—but he did not say how the uncontested surrender of the Teche and Red River valleys would be any less ruinous. Yet Smith did make one concession, which was enough to change the course of the campaign. "When you strike," Smith cautioned Taylor, "you must do so only with strong hopes of success." Since Taylor's hopes of success were invariably optimistic, this was all the authorization he needed to begin his counteroffensive.

The Federal forces were disposed in a fashion which invited a counterattack. Because the route from New Iberia to Opelousas "lay over a country utterly destitute of supplies, which had been repeatedly overrun by the two armies," Franklin had spread his brigades all along the line of march, in an attempt to afford each unit a fair chance to collect forage and provisions. Opelousas and its environs were occupied by a single infantry division, Stephen Gano Burbridge's, and no reserves were within reasonable supporting distance. Nor were any en route, for Franklin was having so much difficulty subsisting his troops from the barren land that by the end of October his offensive had lost whatever forward momentum it had—Franklin himself had even begun to consider abandoning the campaign and retiring his regiments to Berwick's Bay. As far as Taylor was concerned, the isolation of Burbridge's division and the random dispersal of the remainder of the Union army offered the Confederates a superb opportunity to strike "with strong hopes of success."

Taylor left Mouton's brigade and the bulk of Walker's division at Washington to protect his communications, and with the remainder of his army he proceeded toward the Union perimeter. On November 2, the two brigades of Green's horse division, supported by three infantry regiments of John Walker's division, rushed Burbridge's pickets and drove his main force from Opelousas to the banks of Bayou Bourbeau, seven miles to the south. At eleven o'clock the next morning, before

Burbridge had time to stabilize his defenses, the rebels resumed the attack. The "whole Federal force gave way as soon as the engagement became general and close," leaving behind 250 casualties, 600 prisoners,
three cannon, and "a large quantity of improved small-arms and accouterments." The battle at Bayou Bourbeau cost Green 180 men, but, as
he later exulted, "The victory was complete."

Franklin disengaged as quickly as he could, struck his camps, skirmished only when necessary to protect his retreating columns, and withdrew at once to the vicinity of New Iberia, where he threw up works
and settled down for the winter. Taylor reoccupied the wasteland between Opelousas and New Iberia, harassed Franklin's pickets, established a hospital for the wounded at Opelousas, and herded his prisoners to Alexandria for transshipment to Shreveport and Tyler. Within
two weeks after the conflict at Bayou Bourbeau, Franklin's invasion was
terminated, all was quiet along Taylor's front, and, for all practical purposes, the campaign season in West Louisiana had been brought to a
close.[15]

But the repercussions of Franklin's expedition continued to be felt
long after his departure, for his army's meander up the Teche had
served to exhibit the Trans-Mississippi Department's incapacity to defend itself, to exacerbate antagonisms between the region's leaders, and
to intensify the disaffection and suffering of Louisiana's people. Despite
the apparent success of Taylor's counteroffensive, it was evident that he
lacked the strength to contest a well-ordered invasion of his district, for
only Franklin's bad strategy, indecision, and poor logistical arrangements had made it possible for Taylor to check the Federal advance at
Opelousas. Should the Federals launch an efficient offensive in West
Louisiana, not even Kirby Smith could conjure together the manpower
necessary to reinforce Taylor; Holmes and Steele certainly had no regiments to spare, while Magruder never stopped complaining about the
insufficiency of his own army.

Nor could the states be expected to supply an adequate number of
auxiliary troops to augment Taylor's army. During the autumn of 1863,
all three Trans-Mississippi states tried to embody militia, but the results
were disappointing. Arkansas mustered a few companies; West Louisiana enlisted almost no militiamen; and virtually none of the 10,000
Texans summoned to the colors were available for duty at the front—

many of the Texans were unarmed, most had to be detailed to frontier, coastal, or domestic police garrisons to replace or augment Confederate States units, and those who congregated at Niblett's Bluff refused to cross the border into Louisiana. Subsequent to the Opelousas operation, both Texas and Louisiana revised their militia statutes in an effort to subject more men to state drafts, and arrangements were made for the temporary attachment of Louisiana and Texas militia units to Taylor's regular army, but during the spring campaigns of 1864 the militias nonetheless made only the most meager contribution to the defense of West Louisiana.[16]

If troops were in short supply, there was no end of argument about the best way to employ those who were available. Magruder's stubborn reluctance to dispatch his Confederate and Texas regiments to Taylor's relief only worsened relations between the two district commanders. In addition, Magruder blamed the fall of Brownsville and the loss of the lower Rio Grande Valley upon Kirby Smith, who had insisted that he concentrate his disposable forces in East Texas. But the most bitter dispute was the one which arose between Smith and Taylor, who had differed about the most appropriate strategy for the defense of Taylor's district. During Franklin's advance, Smith had seemed content to concede possession of the Teche and lower Red River valleys to the enemy. He had consistently urged Taylor to avoid battle and retire, had pressed the construction of fortifications along the upper Red, had ordered the removal of heavy cannon and military stores from the neighborhood of Alexandria, and had otherwise made it clear that he did not plan to contest Franklin's progress any great distance below Shreveport. Only Franklin's bad generalship and Taylor's lucky gallantry had saved lower Louisiana from occupation. Once Franklin was checked, Taylor, whose imprudence, impetuosity, and short temper were already army legends, was not the man to forgive a superior who had shown so little initiative, daring, or concern for the people of lower Louisiana.

On November 4, the day following the crucial engagement at Bayou Bourbeau, the Alexandria *Louisiana Democrat*—the newspaper published in Taylor's headquarters town—ran a vicious editorial excoriating Kirby Smith's conduct during the Opelousas campaign and demanding Smith's immediate removal from command. Four days later Smith angrily called Taylor's "attention to these attacks, to have them controlled—being made at your H^d Quarters, they go abroad with the impression of your sanction or as being the re-echo of your views." But not for another month did Taylor feel constrained to apologize or to muzzle the assaults upon Smith, and during that month the two generals became even further alienated. Smith insisted to Taylor that "I know not why it is that the people of that section for whom I have made most sacrifices, are the only people in the Dept. who mis-appreciate my motives and falsify my acts. I have always accused myself of an undue partiality for the Dist. of La." And yet Taylor's kept newspaper continued to prefer "grave charges of imbecility" against the Departmental commander. Thereafter, the relationship between the two generals was at best no more than a shaky truce.[17]

If Kirby Smith found it hard to understand why the people of lower Louisiana mis-appreciated his partiality for them, the reason was not difficult to find. Twice since the beginning of the year an invading army had tramped through their countryside, wreaking havoc everywhere and laying waste to the land; and twice their Confederate liberators had gone on to pillage whatever the Federals had missed. In December, 1863, one of John Walker's officers lamented the utter desolation of the Teche Valley:

This section of the country might have been termed the "Paradise" of Louisiana before the war; but alas, what a change has befallen it now! The houses are all deserted; occasionally you meet with a few old, faithful negroes, left by their owners to take care of their place until their return. Here you can behold mansion after mansion, including costly sugar-houses, now going to decay.

And a month later, as the specter of famine cast its shadow across the region, one of the few remaining residents of St. Landry Parish (Opelousas) advised a refugee neighbor:

Our country I fear is destined to starve. The Yankees took all the corn. They took about 500 Barrels from me, nearly all Charley's, all from the Canal, took a good deal of sugar and molasses from me, all my horses, etc. . . . Corn will soon be all gone. All the cattle, nearly all the hogs and sheep have been destroyed.

We can do nothing next year. All the fencing is gone. Many places all the buildings.[18]

At the conclusion of the Opelousas campaign, Taylor's field force consisted of Walker's Texas infantry division (4,843 effectives organized into three brigades), Green's Texas cavalry division (Major's and Bagby's brigades, 3,229 effectives), Mouton's Louisiana infantry brigade, the fresh infantry brigade being drilled at Shreveport, the Second Louisiana Cavalry, and an odd assortment of horse companies and semi-regular bands scattered on both sides of the Red River. Walker's foot soldiers were deployed in fortified camps between Alexandria and Opelousas, where they could guard the approaches to the Red River Valley. Green's hungry horses and the men who rode them were transferred to East Texas, where hay was abundant and the living easier—at long last, when it was far too late to make any difference, Magruder was able to welcome home some of his prodigal Texans. The Second Louisiana Cavalry was retained below Alexandria and informally subordinated to General Mouton. The isolated companies north and south of the Red River were assembled into two regiments, the Third and Seventh Louisiana Cavalry, and employed as outpost pickets, patrol squadrons, convoy guards, conscript police, and scouts.

General Mouton was directed to form and take command of a new infantry division, to consist of his own brigade and the foot brigade recently organized at Shreveport. Mouton's old brigade was placed under the command of Colonel Henry Gray and transferred to northeastern Louisiana, where it was deployed in such a way as to strengthen the district's defenses along the line of the Ouachita.

The second brigade of Mouton's division was composed of conscripts, parolees, and dismounted Texas cavalrymen. During the late autumn and early winter of 1863, the four regiments of this brigade were shifted from Shreveport to the neighborhood of Harrisonburg, where they reoccupied and rebuilt Fort Beauregard, covered the lower Ouachita, and preyed upon Union shipping near the mouth of the Red. When the brigade arrived at Harrisonburg, its command was assumed by General Camille Arnaud Jules Marie, Prince de Polignac, "a French gentleman of ancient lineage" whom the soldiers promptly dubbed "Polecat." "The Texans swore that a Frenchman, whose very name they could not pronounce, should never command them, and mutiny was threatened," General Taylor later reminisced. "Order was restored, but it was up-hill work for General Polignac for some time, notwithstanding his patience and good temper." Despite the incongruity of his situation, "Polecat" eventually "gained their affection by his care and attention"; by the beginning of March, 1864, the little Frenchman and his rough-hewn frontiersmen were getting along "famously, and he made capital soldiers of them." [19]

During the winter months, strenuous recruiting augmented the ranks of Mouton's division until his muster rolls carried the names of 3,275 effectives. Walker's division and the Louisiana cavalry, however, received almost no reinforcements, and were, on the contrary, "weakened by the ordinary casualties of camp life." At the turn of the new year, by which time Green's yellowlegs were comfortably pastured in East Texas, the Confederate States troops within the District of West Louisiana numbered about 10,200 officers and men. Until the commencement of the spring campaign season, John Walker's division remained scattered along the upper Teche and the southern bank of the lower Red, Lewis Bush's Louisiana Cavalry patrolled the vacant country between the Teche and the Sabine, Vincent's Second Cavalry covered the approaches to Alexandria, Polignac's brigade was clustered near the confluence of the Red and the Ouachita, and W. H. Harrison's Louisiana Cavalry ranged eastward from Monroe.

Only Gray's (Mouton's) infantry brigade—Taylor's battered and blistered "foot cavalry"—kept on slogging through West Louisiana's "fearfully muddy" roads, while the men tried as best they could to remain insensitive to the rain, the blizzards, and the hailstorms. "Weather bitter cold, and all of our tents left behind," complained an officer (whose overcoat had just been stolen) to his pocket diary. "One blanket on frozen ground is too ridiculously thin!" By New Year's Day the brigade was "at Monroe. The ponds frozen and the boys sliding on ice. . . . The ground too cold to lie down. Pitiable at night to see them nodding around camp-fires with only one blanket. This is soldiering, this is." Between the 9th and the 11th of January the brigade moved eastward to Bayou Bartholomew ("Nothing seen but ice"), attempted—and failed—to effect the transfer of a large shipment of 26,000 stand of small arms from the Cis-Mississippi, and then started in search of a patch of ground suitable as a winter encampment. After looping toward the Arkansas border and finding nothing but frozen desolation, the brigade eventually started down the Ouachita toward the Red and Alexandria. The weather was still wicked, but by late January the diarist was apparently becoming inured to hardship: "A half dozen changes of camp. Read 'Ivanhoe' during a march of nine miles, and did not feel too tired to forget to sympathize with Rebecca, whom Ivanhoe, if he had been a decent man, would have married." Finally, in mid-February, Gray's Louisiana rebels were allowed to bivouac near Pinesville, just across the Red from Alexandria. To celebrate their delivery, the brigade's more affluent officers threw a grand fandango and dinner party, featuring "oyster soup, pickled salmon, real coffee and wine; which all got in somehow by blockade." [20]

CHAPTER SIX

THE HOME FRONT
AFTER VICKSBURG

Although the descent of winter afforded most of the soldiers of the Trans-Mississippi army a respite from campaigning, the season rescued neither the troops nor the home folk from the oppressive burden of war. The troops may have been able to sit through the winter in the relative comfort of bivouacs, interrupting their repose only now and then to picket, to scout, to drill, or to take part in occasional snowball battles; but their rations were as meager as ever, and their pay fell even further in arrears. Their mail seldom arrived, their scanty clothing and worn equipment continued to deteriorate, and their longing for home and an end to soldiering continued to intensify. Life was no easier behind the lines. Farmers watched their crops fail for want of animals, tools, and labor. Women battled for treasured scraps offered for sale in the barren markets. Children toiled at home or in dank sweatshops to fashion the implements of war. Immense gangs of slaves endured the winter building fortifications or being driven by frightened masters into the interior of Texas. The crippled, the homeless, the destitute wandered aimlessly searching for rest and charity. And desertion, crime, and despair became so prevalent that nothing could be done to control them.

In the weeks following the capitulation of Vicksburg, authorities west of the Mississippi began to press construction of trench systems designed to protect the approaches to the Department's major towns. A fortification mania soon spread throughout the Southwest. In time, no city, navigable river, or important crossroad was without its own line of parapets, revetments, or perimeter rifle pits. But the first and most ambitious digging occurred along the Red River. In September, 1863, as Union armies seemed to be converging on Shreveport from Sabine Pass, Brashear City, Little Rock, and the Nations, Kirby Smith directed his chief engineer, Major Henry Douglas, to spread rows of impregnable bastions and masked batteries down the Red from Shreveport to the Mississippi. Since Douglas lacked the time, the tools, the guns, and the material to fortify the whole valley, he was satisfied to throw up an impressive network of entrenchments in the vicinity of Shreveport, a few satellite works near the towns further downstream (particularly Grand Ecore and Alexandria), and one iron-casemated heavy battery at Fort De Russy, on the southern bank of the Red below Alexandria. Both Douglas and Taylor's chief of artillery, Major J. L. Brent, hoped that the covered "heavies" at De Russy would be able to stop any ironclad gunboat which poked into the Red, but Taylor was skeptical. "We shall see," he told the readers of his postwar memoirs, "what became of De Russy."

The laborers who built these fortifications were almost all hired or impressed Negro slaves, men, women, and children, recruited from local plantations or from the slave coffles being run into Texas. Although no existing Confederate legislation yet authorized the army to press slaves into service, the Louisiana legislature had already enacted a law providing for the impressment of male slaves between the ages of eighteen and fifty when necessary for the state's defense. Neither the Louisiana authorities nor the editorial voices of public opinion raised objections when the military began to carry off Negroes to work on entrenchments. Quite the contrary, the widespread popular resentment against the exemption of slaveowners and overseers from conscription led most columnists to rejoice, at least at first, that the Negroes "are now being impressed according to law, for such service as the government needs, and such as they are best adapted to perform." "Surely owners could not object to having their rear protected whilst they are hurrying away half frightened to death, towards the setting sun."

In September, 3,000 slaves were requisitioned from upper Louisiana and 500 from Arkansas, and these drafts were filled without protest. It was not until January, 1864, when General Magruder hinted that he might need 60,000 slaves to fortify the Texas Gulf Coast, that the newspapers began to doubt the wisdom or legality of wholesale slave impressment. Those doubts were swiftly suppressed by the Confederate Congress, when, in February, it passed a bill authorizing the President, the Secretary of War, or the commanding general of the Trans-Mississippi Department to impress up to 20,000 slaves. A year later, the last session of the South's last Congress awarded the military blanket authority to hire or impress as many Negroes as it needed.[1]

So Major Douglas had no trouble gathering manpower. If there was a surplus of anything in West Louisiana and East Texas, it was the surfeit of slaves. By August, 1863, the Shreveport papers were already imploring those "persons making preparations to leave this place with their negroes" to "give a helping hand in driving back the destroyers" of their plantations by offering "the service of their slaves to the military. . . . This is patriotism—with a vengeance." By September 2, "Movers [refugee planters] with large droves of negroes, continue to pass through our town daily, bound for Texas. Really we fear too many slaves are congregating in Texas—they may in time become very troublesome." Texas newspapers began to complain that the "country is filled with negroes, the property of refugees from other states. . . . Many think that if the refugees continue coming into our State, with their negroes, that our women and children will suffer." But still the long coffles trudged westward, choking the roads and towns with black humanity. In December, an army deserter passing through southwestern Arkansas found "the road crwuded [sic] with reffugees, bound for Texas; with hundreds, and I might truthfully say, thousands of Negroes." "The Texans complain that they have already too great an influx of this description of emigration. They also state that the slaves commit many depredations in passing through the country, by killing hogs, stealing poultry, etc. This should not be suffered." By late 1864, after the Red River and Camden campaigns generated the last great waves of Negro immigration into Texas, General Magruder estimated that since the beginning of the war the enslaved population of Texas had been swollen by the addition of 150,000 refugee bondsmen.[2]

Inevitably, the movement of such masses through Shreveport led to confusion and breakdowns in discipline. If the lost-and-found columns of the local newspapers are any indication, "the negro boy Eugene, of black complexion, about 5 feet, 5 inches high, aged about 18 years, well built," was only one of thousands who took advantage of the crowds and the turmoil to slip away from his overseer. He was last "seen in Bossier parish, opposite Fort Boggs, in company with some runaways from the public works, and it is supposed that he has gone in the direction of Minden, La." Not every fugitive ran away voluntarily. "At least thirty negroes have been 'spirited away' from this vicinity within the last ten or twelve days," announced the Shreveport *South-Western* in late September. The Austin *Gazette* and the Galveston *News* revealed that "a wholesale system of negro stealing is going on in Louisiana, in which Texans are largely concerned, and that gangs of negroes have been enticed away and brought to Texas." Many Texas slave-buyers "have been badly swindled by these operations, and we regret to learn that Texas officers and soldiers, as well as private citizens, have been engaged in these disgraceful transactions. We would caution our citizens against purchasing any negroes from Louisiana without knowing the parties offering them for sale." This outburst of slave rustling— combined with the increasing inability of existing police agencies to control the Negro population, the introduction of large-scale Negro impressment, and the public's growing uncertainty about the outcome of the war—led to a temporary, but nonetheless ominous, drop in demand for slaves. "Jim says he did not buy negroes in Houston," wrote a Texas woman to her soldier husband. He "says he would not give 75 cts for a negro now." [3]

By early September, 1863, prudence dictated "the propriety of having a regiment or battalion of soldiers" stationed near Shreveport. "A large number of unruly negroes are now, and will for some time to come, be employed about the city" to work on the fortifications, "and it is necessary that there should be an efficient force to keep them in subjection. A body of soldiers would not only protect our wives and children, but assist in guarding our property." Yet more than two months passed before the army acted, two months during which the "negroes about town [committed] many depredations and [stole] every thing that they can lay their hands upon. Our police is so limited that they cannot properly patrol the town at nights." Finally, toward the end of the year, Kirby Smith gathered a provost guard of 400 men from the nearby conscript instruction, parolee, and convalescent camps, instituted an "ironclad" passport system for the city, and asked Taylor to transfer a regular regiment to Shreveport as soon as possible (a request which does not seem to have been filled), but Shreveport's security continued to deteriorate.

Nothing the authorities tried to do could completely restore a demoralized people's faith in their crumbling peculiar institution. "If the yankees invade & overrun Texas," wrote a soldier's wife to her absent husband, "my negroes will be lost, and then, all will depend upon my exertions; and how shall I meet the emergency?" The war tended to dislocate relationships and tear households asunder; and the slaves were the first to be discarded. "If it was not for my children I would not care what became of the negroes." And when slave discipline was broken, as it was with increasing frequency as the ordinary modes of subjection became progressively less efficient, the embattled whites' terrified response could be bestial:

The Tyler Reporter says, we are informed that the negro man who, a short time ago, murdered his master, Mr. Medlin, near this place, was recently arrested at Rusk, in Cherokee county, and brought back to his home and burned at the stake by the citizens. . . . As a general thing punishment is better administered by the courts of the country, but under such circumstances as attended this case it is difficult to find a reasonable objection to the summary course pursued.[4]

As it became apparent that disciplinary sanctions alone could not stay the erosion of public morale, the Trans-Mississippi authorities began resorting to the techniques of social persuasion. Generals published proclamation after proclamation, calling upon the citizenry to support the regime with their loyalty, their enthusiasm, their treasure, and, if need be, their very lives. At the behest of civil officials, local "Confederate Associations" endeavored to unite the people in "vigorous support of the Confederate and State authorities in defence of our families and homes." The associations tried to fan the "fervid patriotism" of the people with rallies and speeches, by publishing "accurate intelligence" concerning military affairs, and through the imposition of censorship upon rumors and exaggerated reports disseminated by "unpatriotic" or "treasonable" suspects. Mass "war meetings" were frequently held, such as the San Antonio "Barbecue . . . on Saturday, the 19th day of September, 1863, at 10 o'clock A.M., to which the people of Western Texas" were all invited, or the great rally convened in the same town just eight days later, which 2,000 people attended. "Food in abundance satiated the appetites of the people, while stirring speeches were made by Gov. Lubbock, Col. J. S. Ford, and others. A spirit of hopefulness pervaded the entire meeting. When the meeting broke up, the young men and women had a dance." [5]

The incongruity between the "spirit of hopefulness" at San Antonio, where the local folk could still celebrate the war with feasts, speeches, and dancing, and the awful apprehension of the citizens of Tyler, who could find no "reasonable objection" to burning a Negro, was but another evidence of the brutality of war. People were exhausted; and, being exhausted, were apt to do irrational things.

ᔰ II   Since assuming command of the Trans-Mississippi Department, General Kirby Smith had sought to foster the establishment and growth of industries necessary to subsist his army and maintain the Department's domestic economy. Because his stated policy was "to develop and concentrate only at safe points, the means for making the Dept self sustaining," almost all of the new manufacturing enterprises initiated during his tenure were clustered in northwestern Louisiana or East Texas. (Other factors, such as the availability of transportation, the location of resources, and the concentration of the laboring force between Shreveport and Houston, also dictated where industries might be built.) One new privately owned foundry enjoyed a brief existence at Camden, Arkansas, and a number of new shops were put into production at San Antonio, but these were exceptions to the rule.

Smith was not alone in his efforts to encourage industrialization. In his inaugural address, delivered before the Louisiana legislature on January 26, 1864, Governor Allen summoned the people of his state "to follow the example that has been set us by Texas."

Encourage manufactories of all kinds. Bend all your energies to the manufacturing of every article needed at home or in the field. . . .

Call into requisition every idle man and woman in the State, who wants work. If necessary take every fifth negro woman, and put her at the loom, and take every fifth negro man and put him into the shop. . . . Ploughs and hoes, and axes, and cooking utensils, shoes and boots, and hats and clothing of every kind will be as cheap as they were before the war began. Stock the market well with these necessary articles, and then Confederate money will buy as much as gold and silver did in former days.

And four months later, Governor Murrah was able to report that, because of the attempts of Texas to foster manufacturing,

The State is now beginning to produce powder. She is perfecting the machinery and appliances necessary to make a good article. She will soon turn out, as I hope, some complete batteries from her own foundry. She is now completing carriages, caissons, ammunition chests, etc. to make available for the field some cannon of her own. . . . She is having constructed machines for spinning cotton yard, and carrying on through contract to a limited extent the manufacture of arms, pistols, etc. She is encouraging individuals and companies, and protecting them in the employment of the capital for the introduction of machinery for the manufacture of cotton and woolen goods, carding, reels, manufacture of iron, etc.

Both Texas and Louisiana initiated ambitious programs to discover and extract metallic ore. In February, 1864, the Louisiana legislature appropriated $500,000 to finance the cost of a geological survey, and offered large bounties to prospectors who struck workable ore deposits. A year of intensive prospecting, however, revealed nothing but an insignificant trace of lead and some "refractory" low-grade iron beds, none of which were worth exploitation. Allen therefore took the remainder of the appropriation—$50,000—and bought a 25 percent interest in the Sulphur Iron Works of Davis County, Texas, a new company located atop "inexhaustible beds of rich iron ore" just ninety miles west of Shreveport. "I consider this purchase very fortunate," he advised the legislature in early 1865. "Already the stock is worth double the money stipulated." [6]

East Texas possessed an abundance of good iron ore and the labor necessary to extract and process it, but machinery and the capital for developmental investment were scarce. Unlike the Louisiana legislators, the individualistic politicos in Austin were still hesitant to subsidize private enterprise. The sudden prosperity of the Sulphur Iron Works was therefore an anomaly. Far more typical of the way in which Texans exploited their untapped riches was Captain Wharton's tiny mine and mill near Houston, which, at the beginning of 1864, began to turn out a few rough iron pots per day.

Except for the armaments industry, none of those which depended on a large supply of metal experienced any substantial growth. A wire mill at Shreveport drew enough copper wire to permit the gradual incorporation of most major East Texas towns into the Department's thin telegraph net, but the wire was expensive and its production painfully slow. Facilities for the manufacture of farming tools were so inadequate that editors began to warn of the large "number of planters who will be unable to cultivate their farms to a proper advantage unless they are quickly supplied." When the river steamboat *General Hodges* was refitted and overhauled at the Shreveport yards, the fact that she was "now in every respect in complete order" was newsworthy only because dozens of her sisters had been beached for want of boilers, machinery, and parts. (So many Red River paddle-wheelers were out of commission that in November, 1863, Kirby Smith ordered two full companies of unemployed steamboatmen drafted into the service and dispatched to Taylor's army.)

But perhaps the most obvious evidence of the Trans-Mississippi iron industry's inadequacy was the continuing deterioration of the invaluable Texas railroad system. A daring adventurer who rode the Texas and New Orleans from Beaumont to Houston one day in the spring of 1864 described the ordeal:

After a long day's snail-like progress, the train stopped every few miles to take a load of wet and soggy wood, and every few minutes to get up steam, slipping, sliding, and sometimes refusing pointblank to budge until all the men get out in the mud and slush to "giv[e] her a shove," we reached Houston after midnight, tired, cold, hungry, and cross.

When, in early 1864, the single operable engine of the Houston Tap and Brazoria expired, relays of oxen were hitched to the cars. Thereafter, the fifty-mile trip from Houston to Columbia consumed three days.[7]

Most of the metal extracted in the Department found its way to the munitions factories. A number of new shops for the making of sabres, small arms, and percussion caps went into production at Austin; the homemade machinery for the manufacture of firing caps was soon making 250 each minute. The state foundry at Austin began to produce a few small smoothbore field cannon, casting the fittings from Texas iron and the tubes from Mexican brass. Related ordnance works were established at Cypress Creek, seventeen miles west of Austin, where a new state powder mill began to manufacture guncotton and gunpowder, and at Shreveport, where fifty women and adolescent girls were employed by a new cartridge shop.

The tanning and textile industries experienced some growth, but again the shortage of machinery and capital limited their development. By March, 1864, the thirty conscripts detailed to the new Confederate army tannery at San Antonio were processing 2,500 sides of leather per month, and converting a good proportion of the hides into boots, brogans, belts, and horse equipments. In January, 1864, after a two-year interval during which no new textile companies had been incorporated in Texas, a charter was granted to the Luckett Brazos Manufacturing Company, which was soon turning out a modest amount of rough clothing for the military and civilian markets. At about the same time, the Texas legislature appropriated $200,000 to subsidize the production of spinning jennies—one of the rare concessions of Texas to state socialism—and the Louisiana legislature authorized the establishment of a state factory for making cotton cards at Minden. But the Huntsville penitentiary remained the chief complex of cloth mills west of the Mississippi. During the nine months ending August 31, 1864, the prisoners wove 790,553 yards of osnaburgs, 131,209 yards of jeans, 78,693 yards of kerseys, 184 yards of plains, and 946 yards of sheep gray. Of this output, 380,791 yards of cotton cloth and 56,958 yards of woolen cloth were sold to the army, 77,513 yards were distributed to soldiers' families, 18,247 yards were retained for use by the guards and inmates at the penitentiary and the state lunatic asylum, and 635 yards were offered for purchase on the open market. The convicts' enterprise during this period earned the state of Texas $2,388,541.[8]

One enterprise greatly fostered by the war was the drug industry. Most of the Trans-Mississippi's supplies of standard formula medicines were imported by way of Mexico, but in the first two months of 1864, at the prompting of Govenor Allen, the state of Louisiana plunged into the drug business on a large scale. The legislature appropriated $500,-000 for the purchase of medicines to be distributed below cost to physicians, authorized the foundation of public dispensaries at Shreveport and Mt. Lebanon, and appropriated another $250,000 to finance the establishment of a state medicinal laboratory at Mt. Lebanon. A year later, the governor was pleased to report that $274,972 worth of drugs had been furnished to the state's citizens at one-third the prevailing market price, that another $13,790 worth had been donated to the destitute, and that the medicines in stock—some of which had been imported, but many of which had been compounded from indigenous roots, barks, and herbs—were "amply sufficient for many months to come."

The importers and the Mt. Lebanon laboratory concentrated primarily upon the provision of essential drugs (turpentine, alcohol, whiskey, castor oil, smallpox vaccine, and opiates), leaving the production of patent-medicine substitutes and home remedies to family industry. The newspapers commonly carried advertisements for such items as Dr. Porcher's popular book on medicinal herbology, often ran recipes for the concoction of guaranteed cures for every disease from cancer and epilepsy to syphilis and gout, and occasionally published editorials urging citizens to cultivate the opium poppy in their family gardens.[9]

The progressive intervention of the state governments into industrial activity required capital, and even the modest investment of state capital in manufacturing enterprises demanded that the states make some attempts to order their finances and stabilize the currency. Since the capacity of Confederate Arkansas to contribute anything of importance to the Southwest's industrialization was now negligible, Arkansas was satisfied after 1862 to maintain its existing tax and bonding schemes without significant alteration—to finance itself, in other words, on little more than hope. In December, 1863, Texas imposed a transaction tax of one-half of 1 percent on all specie, Confederate States treasury notes, state warrants, and bills of exhange; raised its merchandise, liquor, and poll taxes; and expanded its list of taxed occupations. The following month, Governor Murrah dispatched a commissioner to Richmond to wrest from the general government "full and complete settlement of all claims and demands of every kind and discription [sic] whatever due or owing to the State of Texas by the Confederate Government." However, because of lax enforcement, the new taxes produced only an insignificant amount of new revenue; and the Texas commissioner was still haggling with the Confederate Treasury when Lee surrendered at Appomattox.

Louisiana, the state most amenable to the direct subsidization of industrial enterprise, made the greatest effort to restore some semblance of order to its books, but even that state's attempts fell far short of adequacy. Louisiana's basic mistake was its failure to reinstitute the compulsory collection of taxes, which had been suspended for the previous two years. In January, 1864, in his final message to the legislature, Governor Moore appealed for an end to the tax moratorium, but on February 9 the legislators again delayed the resumption of the obligatory payment of state taxes, this time until February 1, 1865, or "until the next meeting of the Legislature thereafter." For lack of tax revenue, Louisiana continued to depend upon deficit financing; and the reforms which were made, however extensive, did little or nothing to ameliorate the fundamental flaw in the state's fiscal system.

The legislature did devise a complex plan to combat another evil, the proliferation and overabundance of inflated currencies. In both Moore's last message and Governor Allen's first, it was recommended that, in order to establish a stable and uniform currency, the state should cease issuing its own tresury notes (other than fractional change shinplasters), redeem the notes already in circulation with Confederate States bills or their equivalent, raise a fund of Confederate States bills through the sale of bonds, and prohibit outright the circulation of parish or corporate money instruments. In early 1864, each of these recommendations was implemented. The state treasurer was authorized to issue $300,000 worth of change notes, the governor was given the power to suspend the disbursement of other state notes, parishes and companies were directed to redeem and cancel their paper within ninety days, the treasurer was ordered to advertise for bids on a new $10,-000,000 issue of 6 percent bonds, and the governor was instructed to withdraw from circulation state notes equivalent in value to the bonds sold. The plan promised to remove all but Confederate bills from circulation, and to temper inflation by converting the state's indebtedness from the form of negotiable notes to the form of nonnegotiable bonds. Had there been time to implement the scheme, or had West Louisianians not been too destitute to afford the bonds, perhaps the plan could have been effective. But in January, 1865, after the bonds had been advertised for sale for more than eleven months, Governor Allen was obliged to report that only $571,940 worth had been sold, and that only an equivalent amount of state treasury notes had been redeemed and canceled. The elimination of the parish and private paper, and the suppression of a half-million dollars' worth of state notes, did serve to make Louisiana's currency somewhat more uniform, but these steps did little to stay the depreciation of the state and Confederate bills still in use.

One factor complicating every effort to stabilize the currency was, of course, the instability of the standard Confederate dollar itself. Not only the Trans-Mississippi states, but all of the Confederate States were saddled with a fiscal system tottering on the brink of collapse, and no amount of tinkering with the Texas poll tax rate or the Louisiana fifty-cent shinplaster could ever prop up the system's shaky money. By December, 1863, the Richmond Congress had concluded that only a drastic overhaul of the nation's financial arrangements could possibly save the Confederate dollar. The result was the Currency Act of February 17, 1864, which provided, in essence, for reducing the number of notes in circulation and increasing the value of the dollar by replacing the existing notes with a new issue, at the rate of two new bills for three old ones. Except for the ones and twos, the old-issue bills were to be taxed out of existence by January 1, 1865; and anyone who waited to begin exchanging his bills until April 1 or July 1, 1864 (the date depended upon the denomination), was liable to be penalized not only one-third of his paper's worth but an additional proportion measured by a sliding rate scale.

The impact of this legislation upon the finances of the Trans-Mississippi Department was drastic. For one thing, Missouri's fugitive government and its refugee citizens had nearly all their assets—$350,000,000—tied up in bundles of easily transportable currency, and the howls of protest raised by Governor Reynolds and the Missouri delegation in Congress forced amendment of the Currency Act to permit Missourians an additional grace period for the exchange of their money. This curious compromise eased some Missouri pocketbooks, but infinitely complicated money transactions west of the Mississippi, where some citizens were theoretically able to apply one value to an old-style dollar, while others were obliged to adhere to another. An even more serious problem was that the interdiction of communications across the Mississippi prohibited the shipment of any significant number of new-issue notes to the West before the April and July deadlines fell due,

leaving the people of the region stranded with no stable currency to replace that being taxed out of circulation. In order to avoid cheating his
soldiers by paying them in old-style notes, Kirby Smith simply suspended the disbursement of military pay pending the arrival of new
bills. Now the Trans-Mississippi soldiers went without their wages not
because of the inefficiency of the Treasury or of the army paymasters
but because of a policy dictated by their commanding general.

By December, 1864, the Department was $60,000,000 in debt,
only $8,000,000 worth of new-style notes had been received from the
Cis-Mississippi, the pay of most soldiers was fourteen months in arrears, no funds existed for the distribution of pensions due to war wid-
ows and orphans, and some regiments—composed of men who seemed
to consider partial pay in old-style notes preferable to no pay in the
new bills—were becoming mutinous. As Kirby Smith told the President, "It is but simple justice that the small pittance given the private in
the field should be promptly paid."

Nothing done by any of the governments stayed the depreciation of
the currency. By early 1864, the money in circulation was worth little
more than the paper it was printed on. In late January, Kirby Smith informed Magruder that in Shreveport a gold dollar was worth $25 Con-
federate; a few weeks later, in Houston, a silver dollar could be exchange for $20 in paper. On January 6, a cord of wood sold in Houston
for $50; in February, a yard of rough broadcloth sold in Shreveport for
$15; that same month, one of Polignac's soldiers at Harrisonburg pur-
chased a $12 pair of socks; in July, a pound of coffee marketed in
Houston fetched fifty-three cents in specie or $18 in new-style notes,
and a pound of cotton was worth six cents hard money or $1.50 soft. In
March, a package of twelve plain envelopes was advertised in northern
Texas for the princely sum of $4, and a single blank assessor's roll form
for $1. In January, a Texas preacher, one of the militiamen summoned
to the colors by Magruder, advised his wife—on a small blue scrap of
lined notebook paper—that "paper is so hard to get I will not write any
more. . . . I had to pay one dollar per sheet for it and hard to get at
that price." [10]

In his inaugural address, Governor Allen asserted that although
unstable and depreciated currencies were partially to blame for inflated
prices, the fundamental cause was the scarcity of goods. Allen pointed

out that land, cattle, swine, and grain were but little more expensive in early 1864 than they had been before the war, for the simple reason that these commodities were still available; but horses and slaves were now worth three times their prewar value, while nails, axes, cooking utensils, and other metalware products were "almost worth their weight in gold." Corn, said Allen, still sold for $2 per bushel, while the gallon of whiskey into which a bushel of corn could be converted was worth $100, "not because the Confederate money is so bad, but because the bad whiskey is so scarce."

Allen's analysis of the problem was correct enough, although his figures were far too optimistic. For instance, the lack of farming tools, the farmers' strike against unjust impressment, and the severe snap of cold weather had combined to reduce grain crops in many areas and to drive prices upward; so poor were the crops that some newspapers, at the very time that Allen was remarking upon the adequacy of farm output, were begging farmers to sow late barley to help "keep famine from our doors." And the slave market was already so erratic that no such things as standard prices seemed to exist any longer.

Ironically, one of the chief impediments to the efforts of state governments and private concerns to foster production and satisfy the demands of consumers was the Confederate army's resort to wholesale impressment, for impressment discouraged enterprise. In November, 1863, an Alexandria newspaper noted that while a hundred pounds of flour might bring $100 on the open market, the same flour could be impressed for $12; while a pair of shoes might sell for $40, the shoes could be impressed for $5. "Now who will make shoes," inquired the editor, "if they are liable to have them seized as soon as completed at five dollars?" In January, 1864, General Taylor himself insisted that the shortage of quartermaster and commissary stores was exacerbated by the unrealistic prices offered for impressed goods. Remarking that a $3 barrel of corn could be impressed for $1.50, Taylor pointed out that there was no incentive for farmers to grow any more corn than they needed for home use. Impressment, he contined, "alienates the affection of the people, debauches the troops, and ultimately destroys its own capacity to produce results." [11]

By early 1864 the attempts of local authorities to regulate prices and the efforts of volunteer charity organizations to subsist the destitute were far too inadequate to cope with the widespread poverty found among the common folk of the Trans-Mississippi. To some of the Department's leading politicians, it was evident that only the states could implement relief programs adequate to assuage deprivation and to succor the poor.

Louisiana, as usual, led the way. In June, 1863, during Governor Moore's administration, the Louisiana legislature sought to enable the poor to manufacture cloth in their homes by appropriating $500,000 to subsidize the importation and free distribution of cotton and wool cards. On February 9, 1864, at Governor Allen's suggestion, the legislature authorized the governor to expend $700,000 on cards to be sold, at no more than cost, to the families of soldiers and seamen and all indigent white females above the age of twelve, and empowered the executive to pay for the cards and other necessary imports by exporting state-owned cotton. Within a few weeks, Louisiana trade agents were stationed at Crockett, Navasota, San Antonio, and a dozen other Texas towns; Louisiana wagon trains were trundling cotton and some sugar from the Sabine to the Rio Grande; and Louisiana teamsters were driving loads of dry goods, medicines, tools, paper, metalware, ordnance stores, and cotton cards back from Mexico to the Red River Valley. In January, 1865, Governor Allen was able to report that, among the other benefits realized from this trade, fifteen thousand pairs of cotton cards had been sold to soldiers' kin at the prewar wholesale price of $10 per pair.

Both Arkansas and Texas tried to emulate Louisiana's example, but the destitution of Arkansas and the anarchic Texas county court system of local government undermined their attempts. In 1864, Arkansas could only appropriate $35,000 to pay for consumer imports, and the state neglected to impose a cost ceiling on the prices of goods offered to the poor. Texas did import a large supply of cotton cards, which were then tendered to the county commissioners at $10 per pair; but it was left to the county courts to decide whether to buy them, to fix their own market prices, and to devise their own distribution schemes. Some counties did market the cards at cost, but too many others either refused to become involved in the business or hawked the cards at whatever prices the traffic would bear.

Louisiana's burgeoning relief program was not limited to the distribution of cotton cards. On February 10, 1864, Louisiana introduced a state pension of $11 per month for wounded and disabled veterans, and appropriated $200,000 to pay the first quarterly installment. The following day, the legislature authorized the governor to use proceeds from the state cotton trade to purchase Confederate army commissary provisions, to be issued as rations to the families and surviving kin of soldiers and sailors. Before a year had passed, $432,882.94 worth of corn, flour, bacon, beef, and sugar had been donated to the state's military dependents. In addition to this dole, Louisiana established a "State Store" at Shreveport, "to sell cheap goods to the public, and to take payment in . . . depreciated currency." The State Store served the double purpose of removing "from circulation a large amount of State notes, thus increasing the exchangeable value of the remainder," and supplying the "citizens with articles of necessity, at prices comparatively moderate." Purveying goods purchased with state cotton and imported from Mexico, the State Store, in the first seven months of its existence, earned a clear profit amounting to $425,244.61 for the Louisiana treasury, gave away $22,159.50 worth of merchandise to the widows and orphans of soldiers, distributed $87,326.19 worth of supplies to other state agencies, and, acting as an intermediary for the Confederate government, procured and consigned $627,816.60 worth of imports to the army. Even though it sold goods at prices close to cost, Louisiana's socialized discount house was the only million-dollar business west of the Mississippi to survive the fourth year of the war with its books in the black.

The relief programs of the other two Trans-Mississippi states were in no way as ambitious as Louisiana's. Arkansas did little more than appropriate small sums of nonexistent funds from its semiextinct treasury to pay for imaginary manufactures, while the only significant concession to poverty made by Texas was to permit the sale of penitentiary cloth to the county courts. In January, 1864, the Texas legislature authorized the penitentiary to sell 150,000 yards of cloth to the counties for resale to the poor, and in November the amount of the allotment was raised to 600,000 yards. But because of the county commissioners' usual reluctance to become involved in the administration of relief, countless destitute Texans never shared in their state's cloth dole.

Despite the efforts of the states to alleviate poverty, voluntary charity remained the most important support for those reduced to destitution. As earlier in the war, the more generous merchants and farmers of the Department continued to donate provisions and firewood to their less fortunate neighbors, while subscription concerts, theatricals, and balls continued to raise funds for the benefit of the poor. In August, 1863, the ladies of Shreveport organized the Trans-Mississippi's first Soldiers' Home, a comfortable inn on Edwards Street which offered free lodgings, meals, and stable facilities to transient military personnel. Between the 13th and the 31st of August, eighty-eight soldiers were furnished with 521 free meals and 115 lodgings, at a cost to the home of $284. The ladies depended upon donations of cash and food from the local populace, but it appears that the Shreveport home managed always to raise what it needed; in January, 1865, even though 535 men were given 1,380 meals and 447 lodgings, the home still had a cash surplus of $1,713 on hand. After the Shreveport home proved to be a success at least sixty more soldiers' homes were established within the limits of the Department. Some were founded by other ladies' clubs; a good many were supported by Protestant mission and Bible societies; at least three, all in Arkansas, were subsidized by the state government; and twelve were organized "through the energy of Rev. Thos. Castleton, who has for the present devoted himself to this work." [12]

As battle casualties continued to mount, the education of disabled soldiers and the children of the deceased became a major concern. None of the Trans-Mississippi states yet maintained public school systems, and hence education fell entirely within the province of private individuals or voluntary societies. In November, 1863, the board of directors of the Texas Baptist State Convention, meeting at Independence, resolved to solicit funds for educating disabled veterans and soldiers' orphans, and asked pastors in communion with the convention to collect contributions for this purpose. In January, 1864, a philanthropist from Houston urged the prompt establishment of "soldiers' hospital schools" throughout the Department, volunteered a donation and his own services as a teacher, and recommended that crippled soldiers be hired as instructors. The following month, another citizen published a notice inviting eight or ten disabled veterans to lodge at his home in Anderson, Texas, while he taught them arithmetic and bookkeeping. If they would but "study hard and behave like gentlemen," he promised to help them secure positions as clerks or accountants in one or another government bureau.

Schools continued to offer the elementary curriculum to those children whose parents could afford the luxury of schooling. Austin College at Huntsville tutored the sons of the affluent in Latin, Greek, "Primary Mathematics," and other useful skills, while $5 specie or the equivalent in paper would still entitle a San Antonio girl to weekly piano lessons at the Clinton Female Academy. Even some children of very ordinary families somehow managed to absorb the rudiments of a formal education. In May, 1864, the young daughter of a private soldier laboriously penned a prim little progress report to her absent father:

Dear Pa

I expect you have come to the conclusion that I never intend writing. But I have been so busy during school days and for several Saturdays have been visiting with Ma so that I have never found time until now. I have finished my Third Reader and have now com[m]enced the Fourth Reader. . . . I am studying Olney[']s geography and am half through it. Bob is spelling off by heart[.] he is in the First Reader[.] he is mighty near through it.

But most children were not so fortunate. As 1864 drew to a close, the editor of the *Houston Telegraph* painted a grim picture of primary education in the Confederate Southwest:

There are 200,000 [white] children in Texas, Louisiana and Arkansas. We fear . . . that two-thirds of them are out of school. Indeed we doubt if one tenth of them are at any school worth the name. . . . if this continues, we are ruined.[13]

≋ III   Among the signs of deteriorating social cohesion in the Trans-Mississippi Department were the breakdown of law and order and the subversion of due judicial process by the military authorities. Two significant cases tried during the spring of 1864—one, *"Ex Parte Richard R. Peebles, and Others,"* in the Texas state courts; and the other, the court-martial of "Major" Andrew W. McKee, which involved both a military tribunal and the Confederate States District Court for West Louisiana—demonstrated the impotence of the civil judiciary when confronted with the might of the army.

In late October, 1863, at a time when no authority for suspending the writ of habeas corpus was on the Confederacy's statute books, General Magruder ordered the arrest of five civilians suspected of plotting treason against the Confederate States. Magruder acknowledged that he had no power to arrest civilians, but he advanced the argument of "military necessity." The five accused—Dr. Richard Peebles of Hempstead, D. J. Baldwin and A. F. Zinke of Houston, Reinhardt Hildebrand of Fayette County, and E. Seelinger of Austin County—were put in irons by provost police and shipped to the military stockade at San Antonio. While there they engaged John Hancock as their attorney, and asked him to effect their release from military custody.

In February, 1864, while the case was still pending, the Confederate Congress enacted a law allowing the President, the Secretary of War, or the commanding general of the Trans-Mississippi Department to suspend habeas corpus as necessary to combat treason, conspiracy, espionage, sabotage, servile insurrection, trading with the enemy, or desertion. Had Kirby Smith decreed a suspension of habeas corpus within his jurisdiction, the ensuing confrontation between Magruder and the Texas courts might never have occurred. But Smith did not do so, and hence Magruder was not entitled to cite the Confederate law in defense of his subsequent actions.

Peebles, Baldwin, Zinke, Hildebrand, and Seelinger remained confined under military guard at San Antonio until the beginning of March. On March 7, Hancock sued out a writ of habeas corpus in their behalf before the Supreme Court of Texas. The court ordered Lieutenant Thomas E. Sneed, commanding the provost guard at San Antonio, and General Magruder to appear before it to show cause why the prisoners should be held, and directed that the five prisoners be brought to Austin and transferred to the civil custody of the sheriff of Travis County. On March 25, Magruder's counsel, Horace Cone, presented affidavits from Major J. H. Sparks, the provost marshal at Austin, Captain E. P. Turner, of Magruder's staff, and Major Guy M. Bryan, of Kirby Smith's staff; the affidavits made no mention of any suspension of habeas corpus, but did present incontrovertible evidence of the prisoners' conspiracy to commit treason and argued that "the court should remand the prisoners to the custody of the military authorities."

Before ruling on Cone's motion, the court recessed until the following morning, and instructed the sheriff to return the prisoners to the

Travis County jail for the night. Shortly after the court adjourned, a platoon of armed soldiers commanded by Major Sparks invaded the jailhouse, overwhelmed the sheriff and his deputies, and spirited the five accused to the army stockade in Austin. The court immediately issued two writs, one directing the sheriff again to take custody of his prisoners, and the other ordering Major Sparks to show cause why he should not be held in contempt.

The following morning, Saturday, March 26, Sparks himself appeared before the court. He stated that whereas he was under orders from General Magruder to ensure the detention of the five accused, and whereas he considered the civil guard maintained at the county jail insufficient to prevent their escape, he had felt it his duty to disregard the writ of habeas corpus and to return the prisoners to military custody. The court reminded Sparks that any military order which went beyond the bounds of constitutional due process was illegal, that a soldier could execute an illegal order only "at his peril," and that, in any case, "the continued presence of the prisoners before the court, from time to time, is at least prima facie proof of the sufficiency of the [sheriff's] guard." In a strongly worded conclusion, the court argued:

Better far it would have been, for the prisoners who are in custody of the court, though doubly guilty beyond all that has been charged against them, to go unwhipped of justice than for the civil authorites of the state to be subordinated to military control, and made dependent upon the consent of the latter for the exercise of their legitimate functions. The one, though to be deprecated, would be of comparatively little importance, but the other would be a vital blow at the constitution and the principle upon which our government is organized.

Even though Major Sparks was excused on the grounds that Magruder, and not he, was primarily responsible for the illegal seizure of the prisoners, the case was hardly over. In fact, it had turned into two separate cases. On the one hand, the court, declaring General Magruder himself to be the principal offender in the Sparks imbroglio, issued a citation ordering Magruder to show cause why he should not be held in contempt for commanding the contravention of the court's writ of habeas corpus. On the other hand, the court still had to wrest Peebles *et al.* from the army, in order to complete its ruling on Attorney Hancock's original petition.

The case against Magruder was heard in April at Tyler, whither the court, traveling its customary circuit about the state, had since removed itself. Citing the Confederate law authorizing the suspension of the writ of habeas corpus, Magruder's lawyer argued that the civil courts no longer held jurisdiction in the case of Peebles and his cohorts. But the court, in a long and involved decision, found that habeas corpus had not been suspended by the commanding general of the Trans-Mississippi Department, that no inferior general had the right to take the law into his own hands, and that the court had therefore the "painful duty" of pronouncing the guilt of the "highest military authority" in the state of Texas.

As we have said in our former opinion, the order of Major General Magruder furnishes no justification for the act of Major Sparks, and the court would be fully justified in punishing him by either fine or imprisonment. But such a fine as the law authorises us to impose, would, in our opinion, be altogether inadequate to the offense of which Major General Magruder is guilty. The situation of the country . . . forbids our attempting to punish him by imprisonment. We feel that it illy comports with the dignity of the court to visit its penalties upon the subordinate offender while the principal is enabled to go unwhipped of justice. We shall, therefore, discharge the rule in this case, with a judgment against the defendants merely for costs. But as it involves questions of equal, if not greater, political than judicial importance, we will order a copy of the proceedings had in this case to be transmitted to his excellency, the Governor, that he may give them such consideration as in his judgment they may deserve, and that he may take such action in the premises as may be compatible with public policy and interest.

The court's settlement of the Peebles case was just as convoluted and just as impotent. On the evening of March 25, when Peebles and his associates were incarcerated in the Austin army stockade, Attorney Cone, Major Sparks, and Governor Murrah worked out a bargain which would permit the sheriff to resume custody of the accused while allowing the military to maintain a guard over them. On the 26th, when Sparks appeared before the court, he offered to return the prisoners if the court would authorize a provost detail to accompany them to the county jail. The court, however, refused to accept the prisoners unless they were surrendered unconditionally—but one of the justices quietly intimated to Attorney Cone that if the prisoners were surrendered, the court would release them and make no subsequent attempt to interfere should the military again seize them! The prisoners protested that the court was betraying their constitutional rights, but the court was deaf. Sparks surrendered the prisoners to the sheriff; the court discharged them; Sparks at once arrested them; and a military guard carried them off to a military stockade at Anderson. On July 20, Magruder, with no legal authority and without any attempt to stage even a drumhead court-martial, ordered the prisoners exiled forever from the territory of the Confederate States. Escorted by a troop of cavalry they were conducted to Eagle Pass, and, on August 14, driven across the Rio Grande into Mexico.

In early 1864, Andrew W. McKee was the ranking purchasing agent for the Shreveport branch of the Cotton Bureau. In cooperation with his cousin, J. H. McKee, of General Banks's staff, he arranged numerous surreptitious transfers of cotton and goods through the lines. He wore a uniform adorned with the single star and gold facings of a quartermaster major, was paid from army funds as such, and was addressed as such even by the commanding general of the Department. But neither the Senate nor the War Department had ever heard of him; he held no commission.

During the spring of 1864, it became evident that "Major" McKee was supplying the enemy with more than cotton. After an extensive investigation, he was arrested by the military authorities, tried by court-martial at Alexandria for the high crimes of treason, espionage, and aiding the enemy (in all, five charges and fifty-six specifications), and sentenced to be shot. McKee's attorneys then swore out a writ of habeas corpus before the Confederate States District Court for West Louisiana, sitting at Natchitoches; the lawyers argued that since McKee had never been commissioned, enlisted, or conscripted into the army, and since habeas corpus had not been suspended, McKee was not subject to the Articles of War or to conviction and sentence by a military tribunal. Judge Warren E. Moise agreed, and ordered McKee's immediate release. But General John Walker, who was temporarily in command of the District of West Louisiana, flatly refused to obey the writ. Walker protested that while he was willing to surrender the prisoner to civil police if trial before a civil court would be guaranteed, he could not simply let McKee go. Moise reiterated his order; Walker reiterated his refusal to obey. An angry correspondence ensued, during most of which neither the judge nor the general budged an inch. But finally an accommodation, somewhat resembling that reached in the Peebles case, was negotiated. Moise agreed to accept responsibility for the prisoner and see to it that legal charges were preferred against him, and Walker agreed to surrender him to the Confederate States district attorney. However, as soon as the exchange was effected, Moise flabbergasted Walker by releasing McKee on bail. McKee, of course, promptly jumped bail and was never seen again.[14]

The eroding status of the courts cleared the way for vigilante law and the sharp increase of crime. By 1864, frontier lawlessness and frontier justice had become normal throughout the Trans-Mississippi Department. Negro murderers were not the only victims of lynching bees. In November, 1863, a mob at Millican besieged the town jail, kidnapped five white horse thieves, hanged three, and shot the other two —and, once again, newspaper editorials found nothing wrong with the way the people had disposed of the case. In his message to the Extra Session of the Tenth Texas Legislature, Governor Murrah called attention "to the fearful demoralization and crimes prevailing throughout the State."

In some sections [said Murrah], society is almost disorganized—the voice of the Law is hushed, and its authority seldom asserted. It is a dead letter —an unhonored thing upon the unread pages of the statutes. Murder, robbery, theft, outrages of every kind against property—against human life— against everything sacred to a civilized people—are frequent and general. Whole communities are under a reign of terror; and they utter their dreadful apprehensions and their agonizing cries of distress in vain. The rule of the Mob—the bandit—of unbridled passions—rides over the solemn ordinances of the Government.

Murrah's own inclination to interfere with certain Confederate laws and policies during the first half-year of his administration did not enhance popular respect for the "solemn ordinances of the Government." Both the Texas governor's contravention of the military's efforts to control the cotton trade and his opposition to the increase of impressment served to excite popular hostility against agents of the Richmond government. But, at least initially, the cotton and impressment disputes only involved confrontations between the government of Texas and the local military command; if the conduct of the state officials was hypersensitive, part of the reason was the dubious legality of the army's initiatives. It was a third divisive issue, conscription, which led to a direct encounter between the statute laws of the Confederate States and the statute laws of Texas. Again, it was "military necessity" which determined the settlement of the argument.

By the end of 1863, recruiting officers throughout the Department —and throughout the entire South—were having a hard time finding prospects for enlistment. Recruiters in the Southwest reported the impossibility of squeezing any more draftees from the region, and a few even suggested disbanding the local branches of the Conscript Bureau. In March, 1864, Lieutenant B. J. Dye, chief of a conscript team scouring the countryside near San Antonio, reported to his immediate superior:

Well the recruiting business has played out[;] there is no use trying to get men for you cannot get them. I have not seen a man since I left camp but what he said he was in the service, and even if there were any to be had you could not get them to go. . . . I have done all I could to get men but so far to no purpose. I thought it would be a dull business before I left camp, but I was of the opinion that I could get some few at least.

On February 17, 1864, the Confederate Congress attempted to reinvigorate recruiting by enacting a new conscript law, which reduced the number of exemptions and subjected all able-bodied white males between the ages of seventeen and fifty to the Confederate draft. Those between eighteen and forty-five could be called into line regiments, while the seventeen-year-olds and those over forty-five were to be organized and drilled as a reserve corps. The new law's age limits embraced virtually every male citizen able to bear arms, and therefore eliminated the exempt manpower pools from which most states had drawn militia troops. Arkansas was not affected, inasmuch as its militia laws had not been revised since the first Confederate conscription act effectively drafted the whole of the Arkansas state forces into the Confederate army. Louisiana, on February 10, 1864—just seven days before the enactment of the new Confederate law—tried to revive its militia by extending the applicable age limits to seventeen and fifty, but as soon as the Conscript Bureau began to enroll men of the same age Louisiana gracefully yielded. The governor of Texas was, as usual, more touchy about his prerogatives; he and his legislature fought back.

During the summer and fall of 1863, some 10,000 Texas militiamen had been embodied by Governor Lubbock in compliance with a request made by General Magruder. Their six-month term of service was due to expire in February, 1864. In January, the Texas legislature, anticipating a renewal of active campaigning in the spring, extended their term by an additional six months; and Governor Murrah issued a proclamation inviting all Texans liable to military service, including those eligible for the Confederate draft, to fulfill their obligations by joining the state forces. Both Magruder and Kirby Smith were annoyed by the governor's decree, for they calculated that some 6,000 men otherwise liable to service in the regular army or the reserve corps were evading conscription by sheltering themselves in the militia.

In February, 1864, Smith, Magruder, and Murrah conferred at Houston in an effort to iron out their differences, but the meeting proved unsatisfactory. Murrah refused to acknowledge the Confederacy's right to draft men from his embodied militia, and was willing to concede only that the army might enlist militiamen after their discharge from the state forces six months hence. For the moment, Smith avoided an open break with the governor by agreeing to permit Murrah to retain the militiamen already under arms, but stipulated that all or part of the Texas militia might have to be subordinated to Confederate command in case of some future emergency. Murrah accepted the substance of this compromise, but did not promise to exclude potential Confederate conscripts from his state brigades. Militia notices, including the governor's invitation to "all persons subject to Military duty . . . to come forward forthwith," continued to be carried by the newspapers, while Confederate officers raised a chorus of complaints about whole companies of able-bodied men who were mustering themselves as militia, detailing themselves to their own farms and places of business, and furloughing themselves en masse for the period of their terms of service.

In the second week of March, as it became evident that both Banks and Frederick Steele were preparing to advance against the Department's eastern front, Kirby Smith ordered Magruder to strip manpower from Texas in order to reinforce the armies in Arkansas and West Louisiana. Magruder therewith called upon Murrah to transfer control of all state troops to Confederate field officers. In reply, Murrah refused to attach militiamen to the army unless they were per-

mitted to retain their state officers and state brigade organizations, unless the army guaranteed that the Texas militia would not be employed
beyond the limits of the state, and unless Magruder furnished conclusive
proof that a real emergency existed in fact. Murrah's letter was clearly
motivated by political considerations; as he said, he recognized that circumstances might cause him to be "driven from this position," but he
insisted that he had to have "the reasons and causes which may influence my action palpable and forcible, so as to justify me before the
country." He therefore asked Magruder to "state distinctly the number
that you desire and define the emergency which requires their presence
in the field at this time." [15]

On March 23, Magruder advised the governor that he was not authorized by Confederate law to accept organized state brigades into
Confederate service, agreed to employ the state troops within the
boundaries of Texas, and enclosed a tabulation prepared by his adjutant
which purported to show that "75,000" bluecoats were descending upon
the "30,000" regular Confederates defending the Department. A week
later, on March 31, Kirby Smith himself told Murrah that the enemy
was advancing in force through Arkansas and Louisiana, that the Department's eastern front was disintegrating, that every able-bodied man
was needed immediately, and that if Murrah's state soldiers failed to
augment or relieve regular troops needed for combat service the Federals might soon invade Texas. That same day, and again two days later,
General Magruder reiterated that "this downward course of things must
be arrested at all hazards"; he threatened to draft whomever he pleased,
to revoke all military details, to evacuate Confederate regulars from
Texas, and to leave Murrah to defend his state as best he could with
whatever militia he could gather.

The generals' insistence, reinforced by an accumulation of dismal
news regarding the progress of the Union invasions, finally produced results. On April 7—just one day before the decisive battle at Mansfield,
Louisiana, where Taylor's little army repulsed Banks's hosts and saved
both the city of Shreveport and the upper Red River Valley from
conquest—Murrah yielded. "As you have declined receiving State
troops as State troops," he wrote to Magruder, "I shall be forced, in
view of the dangers surrounding the State and country, to co-operate
with you in organizing them under the recent [conscription] law of

Congress." In a pious aside, he reminded the general that "the absence of a most cordial co-operation between the State and Confederacy and their authorities I should deprecate as the most serious of evils during this bloody struggle."

Governor Murrah's concession came too late to have any effect upon the course of the eastern campaigns, but at least it obviated any further conflict between Texas and the Confederacy regarding conscription. During the ensuing weeks, the Texas legislature brought the state's militia laws into strict conformity with the Confederate conscription act, made provision for the transfer of state troops eligible for the Confederate draft into the Confederate army, arranged for the enrollment of adolescent boys and old men in the state's local and frontier defense organizations, stiffened the penalties for draft evasion, and directed militia units to cooperate with regular detachments detailed to pursue and apprehend skulkers. By July, 1864, the ranks of the Texas militia had been stripped of able-bodied men between the ages of seventeen and fifty, some seventy-five understrength cavalry and infantry companies had been transferred from state jurisdiction to that of the Confederate States, and little remained of the right of Texas to compete with the Confederate Conscript Bureau for manpower.[16]

But if the belated capitulation of Texas removed the last official obstacle to the efficient prosecution of the draft west of the Mississippi, the weary mood of lawless apathy pervading the Southwest continued to inhibit the army's efforts to recruit and retain soldiers. Not even the abandonment by Texas of its objections to the conscription of militiamen did much to fill the army's ranks, for many of the militiamen discharged by the state subsequently failed to report for muster into the Confederate service—two of the transferred "brigades" supplied, altogether, no more than three companies of effectives to the army, while a third "brigade" produced only eighty enlistees. The manpower snared by recruiting teams and press gangs hardly compensated for the losses caused by combat, disease, and desertion. The columns of the Department's newspapers continued to be filled with lengthy death lists and even longer advertisements offering the standard $30 reward for information leading to the arrest of Private Caleb Vickers, Private John Slaughter, and thousands of other absentee Johnnies. Private W. C. Hailey, of the Third Louisiana Cavalry, was so determined to desert

that he incurred an inflated $50 price on his head by murdering a mess-
mate who tried to dissuade him from leaving.

Some blamed low pay, or excessive arrears in pay, for the lamentable number of defections. Others attributed desertion to the hardships
of camp life, the insensitivity of officers, the Westerners' typical aversion to military discipline, or the hazards of active campaigning. A "Soldier of the Line" stationed near Victoria complained to the *Houston
Telegraph* that he and most of his comrades had not been granted furloughs for more than two years, and warned that nothing but liberaliza-
tion of the army's niggardly leave policies could prevent men from furloughing themselves. The basic reason for the ordinary soldier's
disenchantment was simple homesickness—he wanted to be done with
soldiering, to quit the war, and to return to his farm and family. Men
denied permission to visit their homes periodically could "not resist the
call of wife and children" indefinitely.

Those who seldom heard from their wives worried constantly and
begged for news: a Texas militiaman embodied in the autumn of 1863
complained to his "Dear Mary" on January 2 that "up to this day and
date I have not received one line from you," and implored her to try to
keep in touch. (He conceded that because of "the uncertainty of the
mails in this confederacy letters dont get very far from home," and that
the failure to maintain correspondence might not be entirely his wife's
fault.) Those who did hear from their families, on the other hand, were
seldom reassured. On January 3, 1864, Lizzie Neblett addressed a
cheerless New Year's greeting to her husband, in which she revealed her
hearty "wish that I had no one in the world to care for but myself. . . .
I never expect you to come home alive, out of the service, for the termination of the war is remote, five or six years perhaps longer, in my estimation, and you can't live through it all." A month later, her spirits
slightly revived, Mrs. Neblett wrote of her yearning for her "Dear William," and urged him not to "give up trying to come [home], for if you
don't try you certainly will never come—When the children heard that
Uncle John had come they all wore long faces and said 'I wish Pa could
come.' 'I don't believe Pa's time to come home ever will come.' " Neblett, who appears to have been a model soldier until this time, began
"looking for a chance to get a detail," and swore that he would "continue trying until I succeed."

Those who somehow did manage to return to their families—on furlough, on detail, or as deserters—often abandoned any thought of rejoining their regiments. But countless other Rebs were never furloughed, never detailed, never able to desert, never able to overcome "the uncertainty of the mails in this confederacy," never able to assuage their loved one's grief. They disappeared, leaving their families disconsolate and desolate. "My heart is very heavy about our dear Sam," wrote a mother to another son. "We never hear from him, we never hear of him. Oh, God! can it be the silence of death between us."

As the war dragged on into its fourth year, some found a measure of peace through faith in Divine Providence. On Christmas Day, 1863, General Kirby Smith attended Episcopal services at Camden, "and at the Holy Communion table . . . I prayed for grace and assistance . . . and asked God's blessing and assistance in our efforts for spiritual improvement." Even though the "odds and chances are fearfully against us here," he informed his mother, "I have not lost my faith in the goodness of God. I know he is just—and though his way be Mysterious, he works all out right and for our good. . . . I shall struggle on hopingly fearlessly." But many others, less optimistic, less trustful, or less hopeful, could find refuge only in the darkness of despair. "Although the Almanac proclaims this day to be Christmas," Lizzie Neblett told her spouse, "yet, there is no external nor internal sign of a holiday, or rejoicing in my heart. I remember what a long weary year has already passed, and yet no sign of the war closing, and I have asked myself many times today, where and what will I be next Christmas?" "This is the last night of this unhappy year," wrote another soldier's wife a few days later. "To think of the past is terrible and how can we hope for the future [?]" [17]

CHAPTER SEVEN

THE RED RIVER AND
CAMDEN CAMPAIGNS, 1864

If the coming months seemed steeped in gloom, one reason for popular despair was the future's promise of renewed bloodshed. Winter was passing, and spring was but a few short weeks away; and with spring would come dry roads, high grass, flooded rivers, and the customary plague of invading bluecoats. As early as January, 1864, the rebel brass west of the Mississippi (except for Magruder, whose vision remained limited by the borders of Texas) not only agreed that a season of bitter, if not decisive, fighting was in the offing, but confidently expected "Louisiana to be the theatre of active operations this spring." Taylor and Kirby Smith, in particular, did not doubt that General Banks would "make the Red River Valley his great object in the coming campaign."

The Confederate generals in Arkansas occasionally imagined themselves at the head of a grand offensive into Missouri, but their fancies were invariably spoiled by the presence of Frederick Steele's Union army at Little Rock. Steele's command was poised and ready to pounce upon the Confederate bases in southwestern Arkansas and northwestern Louisiana; Steele held the initiative, and was the sort of man who would use it. Holmes and Price, like Taylor and Smith, were forced to conclude that the Red River Valley would be the Federals' main objective, that Steele would move toward the Red in cooperation with Banks, and that the paramount task of the army of Arkansas during the coming campaign would therefore be the defense of rebel Arkansas and of the northeastern approaches to Shreveport.

Of all the senior Confederate generals, only Magruder dissented. He continued to insist that twenty or thirty thousand Federals were about to mount an amphibious invasion of Texas, and so continued to fulminate against every effort made to shift regiments from his district eastward. But the rumors of impending disaster manufactured at Magruder's headquarters were given little credence elsewhere. As their conviction grew that all of the bluecoats between Little Rock and Brashear City would soon be converging toward Shreveport, Smith, Taylor, Holmes, and Price began looking to the District of Texas for reinforcements.

Numerous considerations pointed toward a concerted Union advance upon Shreveport. For one thing, it was already known that Banks was constricting the perimeter of his Brownsville enclave, evacuating his surplus troops from West Texas, and shipping these reserves back to encampments near Berwick's Bay; these activities seemed inconsistent with any serious Federal plan to press the occupation of West Texas. Second, it seemed fair to assume that the recent fiasco at Sabine Pass had tempered the Federals' enthusiasm for amphibious operations along the coast of East Texas.

Third, once it was granted that a seaborne invasion of Texas was improbable, it became evident that only the Red River Valley offered the Federals in the vicinity of Brashear City a feasible line of access into the interior of the Trans-Mississippi Department. Only this valley, squeezed between the despoiled countryside bordering the Ouachita and the desolate land west of the Teche, could subsist a substantial expeditionary force; and only the Red could carry a squadron of cooperating Union gunboats deep into the upper reaches of Taylor's district. Fourth, not only did the Red River Valley provide the only route capable of foraging and provisioning a conquering army staging from lower Louisiana, but in addition it was the only route offering such an army intermediate objectives worth conquering. The military warehouses, depots, and facilities located in the river towns at and above Alexandria, the 150,000 cotton bales scattered along or near the river's banks, the complex of shops, factories, and administrative headquarters clustered between Shreveport and Marshall, the stores and plants in the neighborhood of Tyler and Jefferson, and the vital granary of East Texas all invited the Federals at Berwick's Bay to thrust into Kirby Smith's heartland by way of the Red. Fifth, General Banks's past performance seemed to confirm Confederate suspicions regarding his future intentions. Except for his amphibious raids along the Texas shore, Banks had never aimed his periodic expeditions toward any objective other than the Red River Valley, and Taylor, for one, doubted that his perennial adversary was clever enough to invent a new strategy at this late date. Sixth, Admiral Porter's gunboats had already begun probing toward Fort De Russy in order to test the rebel defenses of the lower Red, further confirming the rebels' guesses.

Seventh, presuming that Banks would in fact push up the Red, the Union forces concentrated at other points along the northern and eastern frontiers of the Confederate Southwest would most certainly advance in conjunction with Banks's command. Frederick Steele, in particular, could not be expected to go on the defensive at Little Rock; and if Steele marched, he could only move against the rebels covering the approaches to the upper Red and Shreveport. Admittedly, Steele's army would have to campaign without the assistance of naval gunboats, since no navigable rivers paralleled the lines of march open to him; and his troops would have to depend, far more than Banks's, upon communications to and logistical support from their base depots, since they would be traversing country denuded of provision by Holmes's Confederates. But such obstacles were not likely to restrain Steele, who could overcome them with careful planning and tight campaign discipline. Though Steele might not be able to effect a rendezvous with Banks deep in the interior of northwestern Louisiana, he surely had the strength and capacity to mount a diversion sufficient to keep the Confederate army in Arkansas too preoccupied to join Taylor's command. It was also apparent that the Union troops stationed at Fort Smith and Fayetteville could easily reinforce Steele, while either Steele or Banks could draw disposable reserves from the garrisons at Memphis and Vicksburg.

And finally, the best and most conclusive evidence concerning the enemy's intentions came from Taylor's many informants behind the enemy lines. By mid-January, 1864, it was "well understood" by Taylor's agents "that the next expedition from New Orleans will move on the Red River; this as soon as there is a permanent rise in the water." By mid-February, the rebel underground had definitely "ascertained that Porter's fleet and a part of Sherman's army from Vicksburg would join

Banks's forces in the movement [up the Red], while Steele would cooperate from Little Rock, Arkansas." And on March 5, Taylor was able to predict that the invasion of his district would commence within ten days, that Banks's augmented command would number approximately 22,000 effectives, that Steele would advance toward Camden, and that the Federals would make no attempt to raid Texas. "The above information is strictly correct," Taylor affirmed to Smith. It could "be relied upon with as much confidence as if the plans had been laid here instead of New Orleans." [1]

In anticipation of the impending invasion, the Confederate hierarchy spent the first two months of the new year reorganizing itself, reassigning field officers, concentrating its forces along the most probable lines of the enemy's advance, reinforcing the Department's fixed defenses, and removing valuable property from the Federals' reach.

Since it was thought that the Nations and Texas would be the districts least threatened by the Union invaders, the disposable forces wintering in these two districts were mobilized as reserves and clustered just west of the boundaries of Louisiana and Arkansas. General Gano assumed command of all the white Texas cavalrymen stationed within the limits of the Nations, consolidated them into three horse regiments, and deployed them around Doaksville and Boggy Depot. Stand Watie took charge of the First and Second Cherokee regiments, made some token attempts to drill them as light cavalry or irregulars, and advertised his intention to raid beyond the Arkansas and to wage guerrilla warfare behind the Federal lines. Two more Indian "brigades" were composed, respectively, of McIntosh's Creeks and Seminoles and Tandy Walker's Choctaws and Chickasaws; the former were still dispersed in the western reaches of the Territory, while the latter, who were generally thought to be the most reliable heavy cavalry enlisted in the Nations, were drawn toward the Arkansas frontier. Gano henceforth reported directly to General Maxey, but the three Indian brigadiers remained more or less subordinated to Douglas Cooper, who continued to occupy an anomalous intermediate position between them and the district commander.

The disposable reserve reluctantly gathered in East Texas by Magruder consisted intially of five mounted brigades. Carter's old brigade, fagged and weary after its hard march from eastern Arkansas, had finally crossed through the Nations into Texas and was now refreshing and refitting itself near Marshall; command of this brigade had recently devolved upon its senior colonel, W. H. Parsons. In the same neighborhood, four fresh Texas regiments were being assembled into a new brigade by J. H. Hawes, an experienced field officer lately transferred from John Walker's division. Major's and Bagby's brigades of Green's division were foraging along the upper Sabine, while further to the south two fine regiments summoned from the Galveston garrison, the First and Twenty-sixth Texas Cavalry, were being brigaded under the former commander of the Texas Western Subdistrict, Hamilton Bee. As late as February 21, when Kirby Smith officially alerted Magruder to have his cavalry in readiness to "be thrown in with the utmost dispatch to any point where the enemys advance make their services necessary," it appeared that all five brigades could be committed to the coming campaign. But during the weeks immediately following, the stubborn refusal of many Texas militia organizations to assume the regulars' guard and garrison duties made it necessary to retain Parsons' and Hawes's brigades in East Texas. Only Green's veterans, augmented by Bee's raw but spirited troopers, were actually able to respond to Taylor's pleas for help.

That Taylor would need help became evident as soon as the pattern of the Federal threat began to unfold. During the winter months, death, sickness, and desertion had continued to decimate his army's ranks, until, by the beginning of March, his field command numbered no more than 6,500 effectives. In order to mount a respectable defense of the Red River Valley, Taylor was obliged to abandon Fort Beauregard and the line of the lower Ouachita, and to concentrate the bulk of his strength along the lower Red between Simmesport (near the confluence of the Red, the Atchafalaya, and the Mississippi) and Alexandria. The only appreciable force remaining north and east of the Red River Valley consisted of the Third Louisiana Cavalry, a scattering of independent irregulars, and a four-gun field battery; these troops henceforth operated under the command of General St. John R. Liddell.

The Second and Fourth Louisiana Cavalry regiments were strung along a picket arc extending from Simmesport southwestward to Opelousas; the cavalry's left flank covered the mouth of the Red, and its right the upper Teche. The three brigades of John Walker's Texas infantry division were deployed along the south bank of the Red from Simmesport westward to Marksville, while Gray's Louisiana brigade and Polignac's Texas brigade of Mouton's infantry division were camped between Marksville and Alexandria. Despite his own strong reservations about the utility of fixed fortifications, Taylor obeyed Kirby Smith's injunctions to prepare for the reception of Union gunboats by pressing the reinforcement of the works at Fort De Russy, by initiating construction of a new satellite fort (promptly dubbed "Fort Humbug" by its involuntary garrison of footloose Texans) three miles above Simmesport, by digging extensive lines of rifle pits and numerous emplacements for masked batteries along the southern shore of the lower Red, and by blockading the river channel itself with rows of driven timber piles and massive floating logjams. And despite the local civilians' vehement protests, Taylor sought to make the region below Alexandria uninviting to the enemy by decreeing that citizens, slaves, and livestock be evacuated from the area, and by ordering that his troops be prepared to burn all the property, crops, and cotton left behind.

But Taylor never believed that his dispositions could stay a serious Federal offensive. His brigadiers were given standing orders to retreat in the face of a Union advance; his staff deluged Department headquarters with requests for Magruder's cavalry reserves; and his quartermasters were directed to strip or demolish the army's warehouses, depots, and stockpiles at Alexandria. Much of the army's store of supplies was loaded aboard a fleet of transport steamers moored just above the Alexandria rapids; the vessels kept their boilers stoked and stood ready to dash upriver at a moment's notice.

To the north, in the District of Arkansas, preparations for the coming campaign were no less energetic. The important little crossroads village of Camden, which appeared to be the enemy's next logical objective, was ringed by an impressive network of earthen fortifications. Depots of commissary stores and ammunition were established along the lines of retreat from Camden toward Shreveport; district headquarters appealed for the transfer of Maxey's troopers to Arkansas; and the evacuation of the civil population and precautionary preparations for the destruction of vulnerable property were pressed with vigor.

Responsibility for the defense of the northwestern reaches of Confederate Arkansas continued to be exercised by General Fagan, whose force, with the recent addition of Dockery's fresh conscript infantry brigade and Cabell's cavalry brigade, had been raised to the status of a full division. Command of Fagan's own infantry brigade had been assumed by its ranking colonel, W. A. Crawford. Jo Shelby's and Colton Greene's brigades of Marmaduke's cavalry division were deployed in the vicinity of Camden, covering its northern and eastern approaches; while Dobbin's brigade, detached from line service and ordered to range as raiding irregulars through the occupied country above Little Rock, was busily harassing Frederick Steele's communications.

For the sake of operational flexibility, the four brigades of Price's veteran infantry division underwent a major reorganization, becoming an army corps of two divisions, General J. C. Tappan's Arkansas division and General Mosby Parsons' Missouri division. Over-all command of the infantry corps was exercised by its senior brigadier, Thomas Churchill. Churchill concentrated his forces in and below Camden, drilled and equipped his men as best he could, and made ready to march either toward Steele's invading column or toward the relative security of the upper Red River Valley.

Churchill's appointment to the command of the infantry was made necessary by Sterling Price's succession to the command of the District of Arkansas. After discovering that Kirby Smith, Senator Johnson, Governors Reynolds and Flanagin, and the Arkansas Congressional delegation were all petitioning the President for his summary discharge, General Holmes had chosen to resign. But Holmes's withdrawal solved nothing, since, for the want of another general whose commission ranked Price's, Holmes's vacated office was automatically filled by the one man whom Smith thought to be even less capable than Holmes of directing Arkansas affairs. Price took control of the district in the second week of March. Not until the critical campaign was over would he be replaced.

With his brigades organized and deployed, his fortifications and depots prepared, and his Department on the alert, Kirby Smith was ready for the advent of the enemy. "We are on the eve of active operations, threatened by superior numbers, and will probably soon have Banks', Sherman's and Steele's commands on our hands," Smith wrote to Price on March 14. "We must be prepared for a simultaneous movement from Berwick's Bay, Vicksburg and Little Rock." To meet any contingency, both Price and Taylor were ordered to do their best to hold in check the Federal columns advancing against them, while remaining prepared to rush to one another's support should rapid concentration become necessary. On March 5, Thomas Green's cavalry division was directed to break camp and march for Alexandria. On the 11th, Bee's horse brigade was ordered to follow Green, and on the 12th, Maxey was instructed to prepare for the movement of his disposable forces into Arkansas. As Taylor observed, "We shall all be put on our mettle during the spring." [2]

For once, the Federal brass actually measured up to the Confederates' anxious expectations with a coherent scheme for the conquest of the Trans-Mississippi Department. Primary responsibility for initiating the campaign rested with General Halleck. In January, Halleck informed Banks that since the Union government saw no need to press the expansion of the Brownsville enclave, Banks should once more devote himself to the occupation of the Red River Valley. Banks was instructed to work out all the details of the operation with Sherman, Steele, and Admiral Porter. Halleck then left Banks to his own devices. Banks, for his part, wanted to extend Federal political control into the interior of Louisiana, begin reconstruction there, and give the slaves of the area a chance to enlist in the Union army. He also wanted to secure absolute control of the navigation of the Mississippi and its western tributaries by pushing Kirby Smith's men into Texas, and to capture the 150,000 bales of cotton reported to be strewn along the Red.

The plan that emerged was scarcely distinguishable from the one being pieced together by the Confederate general staff. Four widely dispersed armies, based respectively at Berwick's Bay, Vicksburg, Little Rock, and Fort Smith, were to advance toward and concentrate at two separate staging points, Alexandria and Arkadelphia. Once assembled, the two wings of the Federal pincer were to converge upon Shreveport, the lesser northern wing proceeding via Camden and the larger southern wing by way of the Red River Valley. The main force, 27,000 strong, was to be commanded by Banks in person, and was to consist of 17,000 men from the Department of the Gulf plus 10,000 reinforcements from Sherman's Army of the Tennessee. Porter's flotilla, including nineteen gunboats and an immense school of transport steamers, was to accompany the detachment from Sherman's organization. Frederick Steele, commanding the northern wing, was to commit 7,000 effectives drawn from the Little Rock garrison and an additional 5,000 from General John M. Thayer's Army of the Frontier.

Banks's contingent from Berwick's Bay was expected to advance up the Teche to the Red, and then proceed to Alexandria. This force, operating under the immediate command of William Franklin, was to be composed of Robert Cameron's and William Landram's infantry divisions of McClernand's XIII Army Corps, plus Grover's and Emory's infantry divisions, Colonel William H. Dickey's Negro infantry brigade, and Albert Lee's cavalry division of Franklin's own XIX Corps.

The detachment from Vicksburg was to be conveyed by water to the mouth of the Red, to effect a juncture there with Porter's gunboats, and to establish a beachhead at Simmesport. Then the gunboats, the transports, and one infantry division were to continue upriver, while the bulk of the foot soldiers were to disembark, to take the works at Simmesport and Fort De Russy by storm, and to proceed overland to a rendezvous with Franklin at Alexandria. Originally, Sherman himself had hoped to lead his lanky veterans into West Louisiana, but since Banks's commission as major general antedated his and since Banks's reputation as a generalissimo fell short of the ideal, Sherman finally decided to allow his senior division commander, Andrew J. Smith, to march at the head of his 10,000 "bummers." A. J. Smith's element of the Army of the Tennessee was made up of Joseph Mower's and Smith's own infantry divisions of the XVI Army Corps and T. Kilby Smith's provisional infantry division of the XVII Corps. T. Kilby Smith's division was the one selected to ride Porter's steamboats.

Frederick Steele's Arkansas army, when finally assembled at Arkadelphia, would consist of Frederick Salomon's infantry division, Eugene Carr's cavalry division, and Powell Clayton's cavalry brigade of the VII Army Corps, plus Thayer's provisional frontier division.

The various Federal columns were not pieced together, nor was the invasion launched, without considerable difficulty. Porter, always apprehensive about the safety of his vessels, became uneasy when he heard that rainfall in the interior of the rebel Southwest had been light, which meant that the seasonal spring flooding of the Red would be neither as early nor as voluminous as usual. The admiral feared that his ships— especially the heavily-laden ironclads—might be grounded and trapped above the Alexandria falls. Even though he was prevailed upon to accompany Banks's expedition, he committed his fleet with the greatest reluctance.

Frederick Steele's chief problem was his isolation. Although informed in January that he was to participate in the movement, he found it almost impossible to extract precise details or explicit directions from either Banks or Halleck. It was not until the first week of March that Steele knew enough about the scheme even to give his consent. And once it was given, he had to conduct his subsequent movements in the blind, since the distance and poor communications between the two separate wings of the Federal pincer kept him from maintaining effective contact with Banks's mobile headquarters.

Some of Steele's dilemma might have been alleviated by the appointment of a single supreme commander with authority to oversee the operations in both Arkansas and West Louisiana. Halleck, indeed, wrote Sherman of his own sense "that the Departments of Arkansas and the Gulf should be under one commander." But, as Halleck acknowledged, "the difficulty is to get a suitable commander." The date on Banks's commission as major general gave him precedence over every other officer then serving in the West, but, in Halleck's blunt opinion, "General Banks is not competent, and there are so many political objections to superseding him by Steele that it would be useless to ask the President to do it." The result of this standoff was the failure to designate anybody as supreme commander. As Banks himself was later to lament, "The difficulty in regard to this expedition was that nobody assumed to give orders."

The commitment of A. J. Smith's veterans to the campaign was complicated by an understanding that they were on loan to Banks only until he took Shreveport or until April 15, whichever occurred first. The reason for this limitation was the conviction of General Grant, the newly designated General in Chief of the Northern armies, that any attempt to overrun the Trans-Mississippi Department could only be an irrelevant waste of manpower and energy. Positive that the Trans-Mississippi fragment of the Confederacy would simply decompose as soon as the Cis-Mississippi South was dismembered (a diagnosis with which Kirby Smith happened to agree), Grant saw no need to dispatch 40,000 valuable fighting men and nineteen good gunboats on a diversion toward

Texas. But by March 12, the day on which Grant assumed his new rank, the Red River campaign was already under way. On the chance that the expedition might prove to be of some value, Grant refrained from aborting it. However, he did restrict A. J. Smith's participation to a single month, on the expectation that the units composing Smith's column would then be needed to take part in the reduction of Mobile.

The final impediment to the campaign was political. The Unionist factions in both Arkansas and Louisiana were busily engaged, during the first three months of 1864, in reestablishing loyal civilian state administrations. At Little Rock, "About forty fellows, . . . most of whom are unknown to fame," came together on January 4, "and after three weeks' sitting . . . brought forth a constitution for the state." Before adjourning, the convention also confirmed Isaac Murphy's appointment as provisional governor, installed a slate of inferior executive officials in the statehouse, and provided for a popular vote to be held throughout the liberated districts on March 14 for the purpose of ratifying the new constitution. On that date, Steele should have been well along the way to Camden—originally, the campaign had been scheduled to open on March 1—but as election day approached Steele decided that his troops might be needed to police the voting. At the last moment, therefore, he postponed his army's departure from Little Rock until the week following the balloting. "If we have to modify military plans for civil elections," Sherman grumbled, "we had better go home."

The political activities were even more distracting in Louisiana. On January 11, Banks summoned the loyal voters of Louisiana to come together six weeks later to cast their ballots for a civilian state government. Between January 11 and February 22, the Federal fragment of the state was the scene of processions, rallies, parades, conventions, and windy speechifying. And on February 22, Louisiana's enfranchised inhabitants—including a large contingent of recently registered Federal soldiers—chose Banks's own candidate, Michael Hahn, for the gubernatorial office, J. Madison Welles for the lieutenant-governorship, and a group of lesser loyalists for the other executive and legislative posts. Though Sherman vigorously protested that "every hour and minute were due to the war," Banks then preoccupied himself with plans for the inauguration of the new state administration. Not until March 4, when Governor Hahn was sworn into office and only after Banks had dallied in the city another two days to lay plans for the election, on March 28, of delegates to a constitutional convention, was the general ready to lead his army northward from Berwick's Bay toward the valley of the Red.

By the time Banks reached Berwick's Bay, the forests were clothed in green, the grass was luxuriant, and the rivers seemed at last ready to flood. The Union commanders were all in the best of spirits. "I am confident of a successful result of the expedition," Banks affirmed to Halleck. Sherman promised A. J. Smith that Taylor's Confederates would either be annihilated at Shreveport or flee into Texas, and Fred Steele exclaimed that Kirby Smith's command was sure to "run without a battle" and be driven "into the Gulf." [3]

The first contingent of Federals to break camp was Albert Lee's horse division of Franklin's army. On March 7, just one week behind schedule, Lee's yellowlegs clattered away from Berwick's Bay and set out through the sugar country along the west bank of the Teche. Franklin's infantry divisions were to follow the cavalry the next day—the rendezvous with A. J. Smith at Alexandria was set for March 17—but on the 8th a torrential rainfall transformed lower Louisiana into a bottomless muddy bog, which held the foot soldiers fast for still another week. Not until the morning of the 15th did the roads dry sufficiently to permit the van of Franklin's main column to pull away from New Iberia. By that date, Lee's cavalry had already pushed aside Vincent's Louisiana troopers and, for the third time in a year, had hoisted the Federal flag over Opelousas. There they awaited the infantry, giving the rebel high command time to summon Thomas Green's horse division and Bee's mounted brigade from East Texas, and affording Taylor's scouts an adequate opportunity to espy the details of the enemy order of battle. Franklin's "Regts are all small," Taylor advised Walker, "and in bad order." It was said that the corps of cotton speculators and camp followers trailing in the wake of Franklin's army was almost as large as the army itself.

Meanwhile, the forces under Porter and A. J. Smith were reducing the rebel defenses along the lower Red. On March 3, a flying column from Natchez occupied Fort Beauregard and secured control of the lower Red's northern bank. On the 10th, Smith's corps, crowded aboard twenty-one steamers, pushed off from Vicksburg and proceeded down the Mississippi. By nightfall of the 11th, the transport flotilla had joined Porter's war squadron, and Porter's black ironclads had begun to probe into the mouth of the Red. The following morning, Mower's division of the XVI Corps sloshed ashore at Simmesport, burned one house, and seized "Fort Humbug" without a fight. During the next two days, Porter's tugs cleared a navigation channel through the log obstructions blocking access to the Red, while Smith's bummers trudged overland toward Fort De Russy. At 6:00 P.M., March 14, two of Mower's brigades, supported by naval gunfire, executed a picturebook charge against the fort. De Russy was easily overrun and its entire garrison captured; the victors then demolished the emplacement.

The fall of the Confederates' famed "Gibralter of the West" left the Federals' line of march toward Alexandria unobstructed. John Walker scrawled frantic appeals for help to Taylor and Kirby Smith, doubled rapidly back toward a rendezvous with Mouton's division above Alexandria, and dispatched scouts into the neighborhood north of Natchitoches with orders to survey the best escape routes into Texas.

The day after the capitulation of Fort De Russy, the ironclad *Eastport* and the gunboats *Ouachita* and *Lexington* dropped anchor off the Alexandria waterfront. By the time the warships arrived, the town had been evacuated by Walker's rear guard. The absence of opposition allowed Porter to call the remainder of his squadron to the city, and to begin making preparations for the reception of the first of his forty transports. On the 16th, a battalion of soldiers being conveyed aboard the lead gunboats was thrown into Alexandria to take formal possession of the town.

While Porter's fleet was probing toward Alexandria, A. J. Smith's men were tramping northward toward the same objective. All along the way, great crowds of Negroes hailed the liberators, "swinging aprons hats & Bonnets"; and even the white "wimmen generally come out to see us pass. Most of them cheer us by waving handkerchiefs." One of the houses "we passed flaunted the stars & stripes . . . and we cheered them lustily. This is something new in La when our troops are not in possession." Many other homes advertised their neutrality by displaying the French Tricolor. On the 16th, just a few hours after Porter's marines landed in Alexandria, the point of Mower's division, swung into the town. The last of T. Kilby Smith's regiments did not come up until the 19th.

As the Union soldiers crowded into Alexandria, they found Porter's sailors busily "seizing all the cotton they can get hold of." The rebels had evacuated the region in such haste that thousands of bales remained within the grasp of the invaders. "The Gun Boats are all loading themselves with cotton, and the officers are taking it without regard to the loyalty of the owners. It looks to me like a big steal." It was rather demoralizing to the soldiers "to see the navy seizing the cotton for prize on land, while they did not get any."

The spectacle became even more demoralizing after the 19th, when Banks's headquarters steamer hove into view with its staterooms bulging with cotton speculators, and Lee's division of Franklin's army arrived with even more cotton buyers in its train. By the 25th, the day on which Franklin's rear elements closed upon his column, Alexandria was crawling with contractors, all fighting with the generals, the navy, and one another for the little cotton still remaining. Banks, driven to distraction by the turmoil, did his best to suppress the cotton rush by enforcing the monopoly on cotton trading theoretically enjoyed by the purchasing agents of the Treasury. But since no one was prepared to concede the Treasury's monopoly, Banks's efforts were futile.⁴

While trying to police the confiscation of cotton, Banks arranged another election. The date previously set for the loyal people of Louisiana to choose delegates to a constitutional convention was rapidly approaching, and Banks, hoping to secure representation from as many precincts as possible, directed polls to be held in the major towns recently occupied by his troops—Harrisonburg, Marksville, Opelousas, and Alexandria. During the days prior to the balloting, hundreds of loyalty oaths were administered to civilians, and on election day itself some three hundred turned out to vote in Alexandria alone. Not a few of them, like droves of their own liberated slaves, also visited the Union army's recruiting offices.

On March 26, Banks received a message from Grant. The general in chief reminded him that A. J. Smith's command was to be returned to Sherman on April 15, "even if it leads to the abandonment of the main object of your expedition." Shreveport had to be taken, and taken quickly, if the Red River campaign was to succeed. Banks was quite aware that his army's security and his own reputation depended upon the swift reduction of rebel resistance in West Louisiana, and he had no wish to tarry in Alexandria any longer than necessary. But one obstacle, the Alexandria rapids, frustrated his progress until the beginning of April.

The campaign above Alexandria was predicated upon the cooperation of the navy, which was to parallel the army's line of march, provide heavy fire support on call, and serve as a mobile depot. But the navy's participation, in turn, was contingent upon the ability of its vessels to pass over the Alexandria rapids. When Porter arrived in Alexandria in mid-March, his worst apprehensions were confirmed: for the first time in nine years, the Red had failed to flood on schedule, and the water on the falls was still too shallow to carry his ironclads upriver. For the next two weeks, while the river made a belated and feeble effort to rise, Porter and Banks haggled over the best course to pursue. Banks insisted that Porter was under obligation to move into the upper Red if at all possible, while Porter protested that he could not accept the responsibility for the suicide of his flotilla. The admiral was especially fearful that, should the fleet make a safe passage into the upper channel, his vessels might then be trapped above the falls by a sudden drop in the water level—a fear heightened by Porter's doubts of the army's ability to retain hold of the upper Red River Valley.

However, in the last week of March, having weakened under Banks's badgering and having been encouraged by evidence that the Red was still inching upward, Porter agreed to challenge the falls. The *Eastport,* the newest and heaviest iron vessel in his command, was chosen to make the test. She promptly ran aground, effectively blocking the channel for another three days. Fortunately, the water level continued to rise, and a bevy of tugs were finally able to haul her into the upper river. The *Eastport* was followed by eight more ironclads, three tinclads, and twenty transports. The rest of the fleet remained below the falls, to guard Porter's communications and to keep Banks's lifeline from New Orleans to Alexandria open.[5]

While the Federals were consolidating their control of Alexandria, Taylor's force was encamped some thirty miles to the north, above Henderson's Hill. The rebels were left unmolested until the late evening of

March 21, when, under cover of darkness, rain, and hail, three Union brigades suddenly descended upon Vincent's Second Louisiana Cavalry and captured the entire regiment. Since this catastrophe cost Taylor the bulk of his cavalry, he immediately broke camp and raced his army another forty miles upriver to the neighborhood of Natchitoches. Along the way, he dispatched numerous appeals to Shreveport, imploring Kirby Smith to hurry along Green's division, and begging for still more reinforcements.

Additional reinforcements were already on the way. By mid-March, Kirby Smith knew only that the combined forces of Banks, Porter, and A. J. Smith were pushing Taylor's army before them and closing upon Shreveport from the southeast. The Arkansas front was still dormant. The longer Steele dallied at Little Rock, the more it appeared that Price's unoccupied forces should be used in Louisiana. Shortly after Alexandria fell, Kirby Smith concluded that the time had come to shift Churchill's infantry corps into Taylor's district. A series of forced marches brought the van of Churchill's command to the outskirts of Shreveport on March 24, the remainder of the column arrived the following day. The departure of the infantry corps from Arkansas left Price with only two divisions (Fagan's and Marmaduke's) facing Steele.

Thus the additional reinforcements Taylor so desperately wanted were well along the way—but, once they reached Shreveport, it took them another two and a half weeks to close the last eighty-mile gap between themselves and Taylor's army. Churchill was delayed at Shreveport by Kirby Smith, after Smith received intelligence that Thayer and Steele were finally on the move. The Union columns from Fort Smith and Little Rock had pulled away from their bases on March 21 and 23 respectively. Both were advancing slowly into the barren and desolate country below the Arkansas River, and were reported to be converging toward the vicinity of Arkadelphia. The receipt of this news threw the rebel high command into a fit of indecision: should Churchill's corps continue southward, to augment Taylor's thin divisions, or should it be returned to Arkansas, to reinforce Price? Indecision produced paralysis: Churchill's troops were held at Shreveport, where their muskets were of no immediate help to either Taylor or Price.

Taylor was informed of the presence of Churchill's five brigades, but he also learned, from Louisiana Congressman D. F. Kenner, that the general staff at Shreveport was persuaded that he neither needed nor wanted Churchill's divisions! Taylor, who could "scarcely conceive" how Department headquarters could imagine that he "did not want reinforcements," angrily berated Kirby Smith for displaying "so little anxiety" about the inadequacy of the army, and informed Smith that he did not intend to be "the first commander possessing ordinary sense who voluntarily declined re-enforcements while retreating before a superior force." Yet Smith continued to hold Churchill's troops in Shreveport, on the pretext that they needed time to draw ammunition from the city's ordnance stores. Smith would do no more than promise Taylor that, at an appropriate but as yet undetermined moment, the whole of the Confederate army would be ordered to converge upon and crush in detail one or another of the invading columns. Taylor, exasperated, replied that as soon as Green's Texas division reached him, he proposed to turn on Banks and "fight a battle for Louisiana"—with or without Churchill's assistance, and with or without Smith's approval. Smith answered by ordering Taylor not to risk "a general engagement . . . without hopes of success. . . . The destruction of either of the little armies at our disposal, would be fatal to the whole course, and to the Dept. Our rule must be a defensive policy."

Smith was giving much the same advice to Sterling Price. Price was directed to "use every exertion to retard" the enemy's approach, "without risking a general engagement, which you will not do, unless you have . . . some prospect of success." If the enemy columns should "resist our efforts to hold them in check," Smith continued, "the Lieut Genl Comd'g proposes to *concentrate* when they come sufficiently near upon the one *which offers the best prospect of success.*" In other words, Price also was to try to maintain his flimsy front without Churchill's help, until such time as circumstances forced Kirby Smith's headquarters to come to a decision. And, like Taylor, Price too was to avoid a decisive battle at all costs—unless he was willing to accept total responsibility for its outcome.

Needless to say, Price's feeble army was unable to stop Steele's progress. Although Marmaduke's cavalry played about Steele's flanks, the Federal column from Little Rock successfully bridged the Ouachita and pressed through to Arkadelphia, arriving, little the worse for wear, on March 29. The Southern troopers bothered Steele far less than the scarcity of forage and provisions in the devastated country paralleling his route. In order to conserve supplies, Steele found it necessary, shortly after his departure from Little Rock, to limit the consumption of the commissary stores carried in his train by putting his men on half rations. The endemic destitution of Confederate Arkansas would remain Steele's most potent adversary.

When Steele reached Arkadelphia, he discovered that Thayer's column from Fort Smith had not yet arrived. Moreover, there was no news of Thayer's whereabouts, and no way to discern when he could be expected. After waiting for the better part of three days—three days during which his men ate some 11,000 rations and fought boredom by sacking a girls' seminary—Steele decided that he could delay no longer. On the morning of April 1, his brigades broke camp and swung southwestward down an old military road leading in the general direction of Washington. The garrison troops posted at Arkadelphia to guard Steele's supply line were instructed to hurry Thayer's regiments along the same route as soon as they arrived from Fort Smith.

Steele's thrust toward Washington surprised the Confederate scouts hovering about his army. The rebels expected him to turn southward at Arkadelphia and follow the Ouachita downstream to Camden. But, as soon as the pattern of Steele's tactics began to emerge, Price ordered Shelby's brigade to harry the Federal communications, and directed the remainder of Marmaduke's and Fagan's divisions to concentrate across the enemy's line of march. The point of concentration chosen was the village of Antoine, situated about halfway between Arkadelphia and Washington. The rendezvous of a respectable field force at Antoine necessitated the evacuation of the works at Camden, which were abandoned on April 5. Meanwhile, Maxey's Territorial division was also summoned to the neighborhood of Antoine. The departure of Maxey's force from the Nations virtually stripped the Trans-Mississippi Department of its last disposable reserves.[6]

While Steele was plodding toward Antoine and his first major confrontation with Price, events along the upper Red were rapidly moving toward a climax. On March 26, Albert Lee's cavalry division decamped from Alexandria and began probing upriver toward Natchitoches. During the next three days Banks's infantry, with the exception of Grover's division of the XIX Corps, also marched from Alexandria and swung northward in the cavalry's wake. In the scorched country above Alexandria the Federals found little of the abundance they had become accustomed to farther south—here the retreating rebels had done an efficient job of burning cotton and provisions—but crowds of jubilant slaves still welcomed the invaders "with waving of handkerchiefs, bonnets and aprons and a song and a hurra for Lincoln too."

Lee's horsemen rode into Natchitoches on the evening of March 31, having encountered little resistance along the way. On April 1 and 2, A. J. Smith's and Franklin's foot soldiers came up, secured possession of both Natchitoches and the nearby waterfront village of Grand Ecore, threw up a defensive perimeter a few miles north of the two settlements, and settled down to await the arrival of Porter's gunboats. Between the evening of the 2d and the morning of the 6th, the naval contingent steamed to Grand Ecore, and Lee's patrols fought a number of sharp skirmishes with elements of Taylor's cavalry. Meanwhile the voters of Grand Ecore and Natchitoches elected delegates to Louisiana's unionist constitutional convention, Franklin's quartermasters loaded more than a thousand wagons with supplies deemed necessary to subsist the army during its eighty-mile drive to Shreveport, Banks's soldiers entertained their generals with a grand dress parade, and Banks himself reassured both his wife and General Halleck that "we hope to be in Shreveport by the 10th of April. I do not fear concentration of the enemy at that point," he continued. "My fear is that they may not be willing to meet us there; if not . . . I shall pursue the enemy into the interior of Texas, for the sole purpose of destroying or dispersing his forces."

But Banks neglected to consider a third possibility. Taylor intended neither to be trapped in the works at Shreveport nor to be driven from the soil of Louisiana. Instead, he was now making preparations to turn, stand, and fight forty miles below Shreveport, in the neighborhood of the village of Mansfield. The belated arrival of Green's division and the advantageous geographical characteristics of the country above Natchitoches induced Taylor to terminate his long retreat at Mansfield. On March 30, the evening before the approach of Lee's horse forced the Confederates to evacuate Natchitoches, the first contingent of Green's command straggled up to Taylor's picket line. During the next seven days, as the rebel infantry trudged slowly northward,

Green's and Bee's horsemen gradually drifted in. By April 6, the force under Taylor's immediate command numbered 8,800. Even though fully one-quarter of the Texas yellowlegs reported for duty without arms, Taylor was satisfied that his army's strength was now adequate to justify the risk of a decisive battle. The infantry and most of the cavalry were deployed astride the main road three miles south of Mansfield. Horse patrols were ordered to reconnoiter and report the progress of the pursuing enemy. And, in anticipation of the impending bloodbath, Taylor's medical officers set about the grim business of converting most of Mansfield's buildings into rude field hospitals.

The risk involved in offering battle without additional reinforcements was minimized by Taylor's selection of Mansfield as his point of concentration. Above Natchitoches, the main highway from Alexandria to Shreveport cut away from the bank of the Red and meandered inland, circumventing a series of large lowland swamps paralleling the river channel. By the time the road reached the hamlet of Pleasant Hill, ten miles below Mansfield, it lay roughly fifteen miles due west of the Red; and not until it passed through Keatchie, a village twenty miles above Mansfield, did the road again begin to wander back toward the river. While advancing along any segment of the highway between Pleasant Hill and Keatchie, therefore, Banks's army could depend upon neither the fire support promised by Porter's gunboats nor the infantry reinforcements carried aboard the naval transports.

In addition, the land between Natchitoches and Mansfield, unlike that farther south, was as yet generally uncultivated. Below Mansfield, the stage road passed through rolling hill country covered with a dense pine forest, a forest seldom interrupted by cleared pastures or open farmland. Such terrain would confine the Union column to the highway itself and offer the Federals little room in which to maneuver, while affording the rebels plenty of cover for the concealment of ambuscades. All things considered, Mansfield was the best defensive position in the entire Red River Valley. Taylor would make the most of it.

Wednesday, April 6, was a busy day. Porter's seamen and T. Kilby Smith's infantrymen embarked aboard their vessels, cast off from Grand Ecore, and began chugging cautiously upriver. Simultaneously, Lee's cavalry division broke camp, formed a column of fours, and, with three hundred wagons in tow, plunged into the pine forest above Natchitoches. After the departure of Lee's last wagon, Franklin's infantry, A. J. Smith's foot soldiers, and the remainder of the train were also ordered to march toward Pleasant Hill. Meanwhile, up in rebel country, Kirby Smith paid an afternoon visit to Taylor's headquarters, made a cursory inspection of the Confederate dispositions below Mansfield, informed Taylor that Churchill's infantry corps had finally been shifted from Shreveport as far as Keatchie and placed under Taylor's operational control, and, intimating that he himself was not yet certain whether Banks's army or Steele's posed the greater threat, urged Taylor not to do anything rash. Taylor emphasized that he had no desire to be besieged in Shreveport or pushed into East Texas, and solicited the commanding general's explicit authorization to give battle at Mansfield. But Smith was still unwilling to make a decision; he returned to Shreveport without giving Taylor definite instructions to hold his ground and fight.

Shortly after noon on April 7, Lee's division stumbled into the advance pickets of Major's brigade at Wilson's Farm, about three miles north of Pleasant Hill. After a vicious two-hour cavalry duel, Major's outnumbered troopers were driven from the field. But the surprising tenacity of their resistance disturbed Lee; fearful that the rebels might be preparing a warm reception in the tangled country just ahead, Lee halted his progress and asked Banks for an infantry reinforcement. Neither Banks nor Franklin were much impressed by Lee's apprehensions, but, after dickering with one another through the early evening, they finally ordered Frank Emerson's brigade of Landrum's division, XIII Corps, to bypass the cavalry train and join Lee's command. Had either of Lee's superiors taken the possibility of a Confederate ambush seriously, they might also have ordered Lee's horses and wagons to the rear: the horses were worse than useless on wooded terrain, serving only to reduce the cavalry's tactical flexibility, while the two-mile wagon train strung behind Lee effectively isolated his 4,700 bluecoats from the rest of the army. But, as Lee later complained, Banks and Franklin seemed sure "that we were not to have any fighting until we got to Shreveport."

At 9:00 P.M. the same evening, Taylor dispatched a wire to Kirby Smith to ask, once again, whether he "should hazard a general engagement" at Mansfield. He requested "an immediate answer, that I may re-

ceive it before daylight to-morrow morning." Three hours later, a courier was dispatched to Keatchie with orders summoning Churchill's
infantry to Mansfield; Churchill's corps was en route before dawn.[7]

In accordance with a decree promulgated by the Confederate
States Congress, Kirby Smith had designated Friday, April 8, "as a day
of fasting, humiliation, and prayer," a day upon which "military exer-
cises were to be "suspended" and a "strict observance" was to be "enjoined upon all troops serving in the department." Many of the people
of the Trans-Mississippi spent the morning petitioning "the Lord of
Hosts, who giveth not the battle to the strong, but upholdeth the cause
of the just." Perhaps Kirby Smith was distracted from his secular duties,
for he neglected to send "an immediate answer" to Taylor's imperative
request for explicit directions. Instead, he drafted a rambling, ambiguous, and fatherly letter suggesting that Taylor should continue to avoid
a general engagement, but urging him to "compel the enemy to develop
his intentions" while "selecting a position in rear where we can give
him battle before he can march on and occupy Shreveport. . . . Let me
know as soon as you are convinced that a general advance is being
made and I will come to the front." And, instead of telegraphing his advice to Taylor, Smith entrusted his letter to a courier, thereby guar-
anteeing that it could not possibly be delivered at Mansfield much before the evening of the 8th. Taylor did not wait. At 9:40 A.M., April 8,
Taylor—fully convinced that "a general advance" really was "being
made" by the enemy—concluded that Mansfield was "as favorable a
point . . . as any other" at which to engage the Union army. "Little
Frenchman," he shouted to the Prince de Polignac, "I am going to fight
Banks here, if he has a million of men!"

Taylor spent most of the morning supervising the arrangement of
his regiments in line of battle along the ridge of Honeycutt Hill, a
thickly wooded rise perpendicular to the stage road three miles south of
Mansfield. The rebels were deployed under the cover afforded by the
edge of a pine forest, but, since the southern slope of Honeycutt Hill
and the northern face of the opposing ridge were open pasture, they enjoyed a clear field of fire about one thousand yards deep. Bee's cavalry,
dismounted and concealed in the trees, held the Confederate right flank.
Scurry's, Waul's, and Randal's brigades of Walker's division, augmented
by cavalry and artillery, stood astride the road. Gray's, Polignac's, and

Major's brigades were buried in the forest toward the left, while the bulk of Bagby's brigade was held in reserve. Taylor's men were in the best of spirits, cheerfully and even eagerly awaiting their chance to reverse the tide of the campaign.

A short while before midday, the lead brigade of Lee's division trotted into view. Slicing their way through a thin line of Confederate cavalry skirmishers, the Union horsemen tried to charge the left wing of the main rebel line, but a withering volley delivered by Mouton's soldiers shattered their formation and sent them scurrying back toward cover. Lee emplaced his artillery along the southern fringe of the Honeycutt Hill clearing, dismounted most of his cavalry, deployed both his own troopers and Emerson's bluecoats in line of battle, and sent frantic appeals for immediate assistance to his superiors. Neither Franklin nor Banks was yet convinced that the rebels intended to make a stand so far below Shreveport, but in time they did push some additional infantry forward. By 4:00 P.M., most of the regiments of Landrum's division had moved around Lee's wagon train and were beginning to straggle up to Lee's position. At this moment, Taylor, perceiving that the enemy's forces were still in disarray, ordered Mouton to attack. Mounting his horse, drawing his saber, and calling upon his men to "charge them right in the face," Mouton led his brigades from cover and toward the Union front.

As soon as the rebels came within range, Federal cannoneers and musketeers began showering a hailstorm of canister, grape, and minie balls upon them. "The fire of the enemy was so terrible," recalled one of Gray's officers, "that almost every men in the direct attack . . . was struck with a bullet." Within the next half hour, Mouton himself, Gray's three regimental commanders, one of Polignac's colonels, seven of the Crescent Regiment's short-lived color sergeants, twelve of the eighteen members of the Eighteenth Louisiana's "O" Company, scores of field and company officers, and well over seven hundred of Mouton's 2,200 men were mowed down. And yet the tattered remnants of Mouton's regiments continued to press forward, now pausing to reload, now advancing at the double-quick, now stopping to fire or to fix bayonets, now charging with an eerie rebel yell. Lee's troopers and Landrum's foot soldiers fought, fell back, fought some more—and wavered.

Just as the first whispers of panic began flashing through the Union ranks, Major's regiments and Walker's brigades suddenly smashed into the Federals' flanks. Within minutes, the wild melee disintegrated into an utter rout as the Union line evaporated. Abandoning knapsacks, rifles, cannon, wounded, and colors, the Federals broke for the rear— only to find themselves trapped by the three hundred wagons plugging their highway to salvation. Panic boiled over into hysteria, and hysteria into madness. "Suddenly there was a rush, a shout, a crashing of trees the breaking down of rails, the rush and scamper of men," wrote a civilian traveling with the train. "We found ourselves swallowed up, as it were, in a hissing, seething, bubbly whirlpool of agitated men." Oxen milled, horses reared, mules bolted, wagons overturned, teamsters and camp followers stampeded, caissons were driven through—or over— crowds of cowering men, and everyone ran for his life.

More than two miles to the rear, this tangled jumble of racing fugitives rolled into Cameron's division of the XIII Corps, which was immediately infected, overwhelmed, and consumed by the panic. Not until the snowballing mob crashed into Emory's division of the XIX Corps, another two miles farther south, did it begin to lose momentum and regain a measure of military cohesion. Emory's steady brigades, warned in advance of the situation toward the front, were steeled for the encounter and managed to stand fast. Not only did Emory's example give the fugitives courage needed to rally, but in addition his men held off the pursuing Confederates long enough to permit Lee's officers and those of the XIII Corps to organize a respectable retreat. Fortunately for Emory, the victorious rebels were by now almost as exhausted as the whipped Federals, and so refrained from pressing their advantage. As night fell, the firing along Emory's front slowly died away. The funereal silence which ensued was interrupted only occasionally by bursts of desultory sniping or the whimpering cries of wounded men.

The battle of Mansfield cost Banks a dozen stand of colors, thousands of small arms, over twenty field cannon, 250 loaded wagons, almost 700 killed and wounded, more than 1,500 military and 1,000 noncombatant prisoners, and countless illusions. As the first dismal reports were coming in, Banks halfheartedly suggested that his bleeding army could camp in place and resume its march toward Shreveport the following morning, but a midnight council of war easily convinced him that it might be wiser to withdraw to Pleasant Hill. During the night, the remains of Franklin's corps retired to Pleasant Hill, where they rendezvoused with A. J. Smith's command. The following morning, having formed in line of battle on the crest of a low rise crossing the stage highway, the battered Federals made ready to repay Taylor's hospitality in kind.

Shortly after sunset on the 8th, Kirby Smith's messenger found Taylor and delivered the commanding general's unctuous caution against a general engagement. Taylor laughed the officer away with the exultant comment, "Too late, sir, the battle is won," and immediately turned his attention to the task of crushing Banks. For, in spite of the loss of a thousand men during the preceding afternoon, Taylor fully intended to follow up his initial success.

At 10:30 P.M., he wired Smith the news that Churchill's 4,400 muskets, now reported to be closing upon Mansfield, had "been ordered to the front before daylight to-morrow morning. I shall continue to push the enemy with utmost vigor." Through the night, he conferred with his generals and hurried his columns southward. By midmorning, Bagby's brigade, charged with the responsibility of interdicting any attempt by Porter to rush Kilby Smith's reinforcements to Pleasant Hill, was stationed squarely between the Red and Banks's encampment, while the remainder of Taylor's army, with Churchill's footsore but unbloodied corps in the lead, was fast descending upon Pleasant Hill. Taylor wasted no time in deploying his own forces: Parsons' and Tappan's divisions were positioned on the Confederate right, Walker's was posted in the center, Bee's and Major's brigades extended toward the left, and Mouton's shredded division, now under Polignac's command, was held in close reserve. Taylor awarded Churchill the honor of commencing the attack. As he told Walker, "Your men and Polignac's will have some relief as Arkansas and Missouri lead the fight. . . . They must do what Texas and Louisiana did [yester]day." But, as he had no doubt that he would need every one of his 12,000 effectives to overrun Banks's 22,000, he instructed Walker, Polignac, and Green to be prepared to advance in echelon in cooperation with Churchill's assault.

Once the orders were issued and the regiments disposed, Taylor allowed his jaded men two hours' rest. Then, at 3:00 P.M., after the Union line had been softened by an artillery bombardment, Churchill's two divisions stepped off. During the next four hours, the battle of

Pleasant Hill devoured almost every regiment on the field; hour after deadly hour, swelling waves of desperate men rolled to and fro, firing tons of lead at one another in a brutal killing match. On both sides, tired generals mismanaged their tired troops, and nobody—not even Taylor—showed the least tactical finesse. All that saved the outnumbered Confederate brigades from pounding themselves to pieces was the fact that the Federal commanders performed even more poorly than their own. As it was, Taylor's army suffered another 1,600 casualties, and Banks's just as many. Then, as nightfall snuffed out the ripples of musketry, both armies abandoned their wounded, both retired from the field, and both claimed a great victory. While his command bandaged itself, Taylor, too exhausted to worry about Banks's next move, fell asleep under a tree. Banks again announced his intention to resume his march toward Shreveport, again had his mind changed by a council of war, and again ordered a retreat—this time, to Natchitoches and Grand Ecore.[8]

By the evening of April 10, most of Banks's weary army had safely passed through Natchitoches. Twenty-four hours later, Banks ordered the abandonment of Natchitoches, the concentration of his entire force at Grand Ecore, and the fortification of a defensive perimeter surrounding the Grand Ecore enclave. During the following week, his soldiers squatted behind their breastworks and nervously eyed the grayback horse patrols hovering just beyond cannon range. Grover's division of reinforcements was transported upriver from Alexandria. Banks again toyed with—and rejected—the notion of resuming his conquest of Shreveport. Sherman formally requested the return of A. J. Smith's corps, and Banks, unwilling to lose another man, flatly rejected Sherman's summons. Meanwhile, most of the men in the trenches simply waited—either for Porter's fleet to steam to their rescue, or for Taylor's rebels to wipe them out.

When he arrived at Grand Ecore, Banks had no idea where Porter was. Since paddling upriver on the 6th, the navy had not been heard from. And perhaps it was just as well that Banks knew nothing of the fleet's adventures, for Porter's inveterate enemy, the Red River, had stalled and beaten his flotilla.

Initially, the fleet's slow progress upstream had been relatively untroubled. The water was low, too low for Porter's peace of mind, but his vessels somehow managed to creep over the sandbars. But on April 10, two hours after noon, Porter's progress was abruptly terminated. Steaming around a bend one mile above the mouth of Loggy Bayou (about one hundred miles, by water, above Grand Ecore), the flotilla encountered an impassable obstacle. The Confederates had wedged a huge cargo boat, the *New Falls City*, across the entire breadth of the Red: the scuttled steamer's prow was buried in the sands of one bank, her stern in the other, she was settling and splitting amidships, and a sandbar was making below her. "It was the smartest thing I ever knew the rebels to do," Porter later told Sherman.

With his advance impeded and the water falling, Porter could do nothing but reverse his engines and retreat. The boats paddled backwards until the river widened sufficiently to permit them to be kedged about, and then began crawling their way downstream. And then their troubles began. The *Chillicothe* was impaled on a submerged stump, closing the channel for two hours before she could be tugged off. Other vessels unshipped rudders or splintered paddles; the transport *Emerald* ran aground. And, from the shores, showers of musketry began pelting against the sides of the *Osage*, *Black Hawk*, and a number of the transports. The men-of-war responded with their eleven-inch guns, as if swatting flies with sledge hammers.

On the morning of the 12th, the *Lexington* smashed her wheelhouse in a collision with the transport *Rob Roy*, and the fleet was forced to wait while she lay in for repairs. During the delay, and later in the day, hundreds of hidden snipers continued to peck away at the flotilla; now and then, rippling volleys were delivered by large bodies of men concealed on the river's west bank. Finally, at 4:00 P.M., as the navy made ready to run past Blair's Landing (due east of Pleasant Hill, and forty-five miles, by water, above Grand Ecore), whole regiments of riflemen and four masked cannon opened fire on the boats; Taylor had dispatched the bulk of Green's division to the riverside with orders to give Porter a hot reception. The Texans did their best, delivering what one Union naval officer called "the heaviest and most concentrated fire of musketry that I have ever witnessed." Chimneys tumbled, wheelhouse walls were shot away, rudders were splintered, bulkheads were peppered, decks were awash in blood—but every vessel navigated through the gauntlet and emerged, still afloat, downstream.

The Confederates' dense fire was so deadly that many of the gunboats battened down their gun ports and made no attempt to reply, but some—the *Lexington*, in particular—tried to exchange shot for shot. Their cannonades were too haphazard to do much real damage, but one of the few rebels killed happened to be General Green: a stray grape shot disemboweled him. "We could have better lost any other man in the Department," mourned a stricken rebel officer.

The flotilla's difficulties were not yet ended. On the 13th, the transport *John Warner* ran aground, detachments of Texas cavalry continued to blast away at the leaky vessels, and the *Osage* had to fight off a battery of cannon concealed on the river's east bank by General Liddell. On the 14th, the lead vessels finally reached the security of the Grand Ecore enclave, but it was not until the following day that the last of Porter's ships—the *Fort Hindman,* with the *Warner* in tow—steamed down to the mooring. The great reunion was hardly a happy one: Banks's landsmen were appalled by the condition of Porter's floating wreckage, Porter's sailors were dismayed by the cowering army's complete demoralization, and everyone thought only of escape.

However, escape from the Grand Ecore box was interdicted by Taylor's army and a blocked river. The *Eastport* struck a rebel torpedo three miles below Grand Ecore, foundered, and bottled up the channel. Ironically, the *Eastport* was by far the more serious obstacle, for if Banks's soldiers had not been obliged to hold their works in order to defend the trapped navy, they could have punched through Taylor's army without much difficulty. Banks's 25,000 bluecoats and Porter's squadron were technically besieged at Grand Ecore, but the force besieging them, including the Texas cavalry division and the ephemeral handful of rebels on the river's eastern shore, now numbered no more than 5,000 effectives. Taylor's "army," or what remained of it, now consisted of Liddell's irregulars (who could not be shifted to the Red's west bank, since Taylor lacked pontoons and Porter still dominated the water), Polignac's decimated infantry division, and the lamented Green's three brigades of Texas horse, now under the command of an utter stranger, John A. Wharton. Fresh from the Cis-Mississippi, Wharton knew nothing of his troopers, their situation, or the terrain. Churchill's corps and John Walker's division were already more than eighty miles to the north, marching as rapidly as possible toward Arkansas.[9]

Taylor's foot soldiers had been recalled by Kirby Smith right after the battle of Pleasant Hill. At 10:00 P.M., April 9, after a hard day's gallop from Department headquarters all the way to the battlefield, Smith roused Taylor from a sound sleep and instructed him to prepare to set Churchill and Walker in motion toward Shreveport. Taylor vigorously protested that any such diminution of his strength would destroy his chance to obliterate Banks's army, but Smith insisted that the threat to Shreveport posed by Steele's column made the prompt reinforcement of Price imperative. The two generals argued bitterly over possession of the infantry, but Smith prevailed. Again on the 13th, at Mansfield, and on the 15th, at Shreveport, Taylor tried to talk Smith into returning some of the infantry, but Smith—despite intelligence from Price that Steele's army was no longer advancing, but was instead already doubling back toward Camden—adamantly refused to leave a single company behind. Nor would he permit Taylor to accompany the reinforcements into Arkansas; instead, he awarded Taylor a brevet promotion to the rank of lieutenant general, left him in charge of affairs at Shreveport, and, on the 16th, personally assumed command of the infantry column moving toward Arkansas. Taylor remained at headquarters for the next three days, signing reports and shuffling papers. On the 19th, he left the Department's business to the staff officers in Shreveport, and two days later he was back with his little army, as impatient as ever to smash Banks.

The struggle for Arkansas was virtually over by the time Smith's infantry reached Price. Between April 2 and April 4, in the vicinity of Antoine and nearby Elkin's Ferry, Price's small army interrupted Steele's advance and forced the Federal column to turn southward, in the direction of an open stretch of rolling country known as Prairie d'Ane. Once there, the two armies dug entrenchments, welcomed reinforcements—both Maxey's Territorials and Thayer's motley Frontier Division straggled in by the 9th—and stared at each other for the better part of three days. Finally, on the 10th, Steele tried to break the stalemate by ordering his artillery to pound the Confederate line; Price replied in kind. On the 11th, the two armies again spent most of the day eyeing one another, and on the 12th, at long last, they both broke the deadlock be retreating. Price, fearful that Steele might yet find a way to resume his push toward Washington, fell back to within eight miles of the state capital and began throwing up another network of field fortifications. Steele, meanwhile, turned the point of his column eastward and, after a three-day march and a skirmish with some of Marmaduke's cavalry, occupied the abandoned works at Camden.

Steele's uncharacteristic passivity was governed by the fact that his soldiers were on the verge of starvation. He had already notified the commissariat at Little Rock that he was in dire need of 225,000 rations, and he later affirmed that both the supplies in his train and those of the country through which he was marching were nearly exhausted. Not even the local water was potable; rebel irregulars had taken care to dump animal carcasses in many of the region's wells. Steele's withdrawal to Camden was designed to shorten his communications and to speed the delivery of provisions; he hoped to convert Camden into a forward base from which he could continue his conquest of Arkansas. After reaching Camden, he subsisted his men on musty rebel corn, begged the garrisons at Pine Bluff and Little Rock to hurry stores to him, and sent his wagons into the countryside to forage for food. One train managed to gather some provisions from the neighborhood without incident, but then things went awry.

On April 18, two hundred wagons, escorted by five hundred Negro and six hundred white troops, scoured the country west of Camden, collected a supply of food, and then turned back toward the town. At Poison Spring, about nine miles from Steele's fortifications, the train was swallowed up by Price's army—Price, finally convinced that he would not be besieged at Washington, was en route to Camden to lay siege to the Federals. The so-called battle of Poison Spring was a one-sided massacre: the Union escorts were cut to shreds, Tandy Walker's boys took scalps, Cabell's Arkansans deliberately drove captured wagons back and forth over the fallen Negro wounded, and execution squads went about the field shooting incapacitated prisoners. (Two days later, after visiting Poison Spring, Kirby Smith informed his wife that the enemy had lost "some 200 prisoners and left 600 reported dead on the field principally negroes who neither gave or recd quarter. . . . I saw but two negro prisoners.") One week after the battle of Poison Spring, while Marmaduke's and Maxey's troopers enveloped Camden, Fagan's division wiped out an even larger relief train at Marks's Mill, halfway between Camden and Pine Bluff. The slaughter at Marks's Mill cost the Federals' 300 wagons and 1,600 casualties; Fagan lost 150 men.

The disasters at Poison Spring and Marks's Mill, plus the belated news that Banks and Porter were in full retreat, forced Steele to conclude that his position was untenable. On the 26th, the Federals evacuated Camden, drove right through Marmaduke's lines, crossed the Ouachita, and began racing eastward toward the Saline River. Reaching the Saline on the 28th, and finding it impassable, Steele turned his column northward and started searching for a place suitable for the erection of a pontoon bridge. Such a location was found the following evening, opposite the hamlet of Jenkins' Ferry. The approaches to the bridgehead were fortified and picketed, a bridge was thrown over the river, and at dawn, April 30, Steele's artillery and his remaining wagons began to roll across it. Just then, when the Union army's back was to the river and its only escape route was blocked, Price, Churchill, and John Walker—the whole of Kirby Smith's joint command—came swinging up the road from Camden.

Smith himself had arrived at Price's headquarters eleven days earlier and had spent the intervening time trying to hurry forward his infantry. After Camden was occupied, Smith sent Maxey's braves back to the Nations and set out with the remainder of his army in pursuit of Steele. By the time the rebels reached Jenkins' Ferry, most of them were too exhausted to carry their muskets another step, but without a moment's hesitation Smith ordered each contingent of his column to storm Steele's works as soon as it reached the field.

Two miles west of Jenkins' Ferry, the road leading down to the Saline toppled over a steep bluff and plunged down a narrow defile. In the gorge, the flat land available for maneuver was no more than four hundred yards wide. The lowland itself had been drenched by a steady two-day rain, and the rain was still coming down in sheets; visibility was nil, and the gully's bottomland mire was so waterlogged that men trying to cross it would sink to their knees. At the far end of this viscous funnel, the Federals had erected formidable lines of abatis, rifle pits, and log breastworks. Smith, undaunted, threw forward his brigades piecemeal, and watched the Federals cut them to bits.

Marmaduke's division went in first, followed, at irregular random intervals, by Tappan's, Parsons', and John Walker's; Fagan's division did not come up until the battle was over, and hence escaped the bloodbath. As each sodden mass of rebels slogged within range, the Federals loosed a fusillade and chopped them down in rows. In front of the Union earthworks, everything was chaos: advancing waves of rebels had to fight their way through mobs of fleeing refugees; battered regiments and shattered brigades wandered in circles or huddled on the ground; and one crowd of Confederates was so confused that they let themselves be captured by a regiment of Negro bluecoats, whom they mistook for reinforcements!

At 12:30 P.M., after watching the slaughter for five and a half hours, Kirby Smith decided that he had seen enough. Leaving a thousand dead and wounded on the field of battle, he pulled his dispirited army back to the high ground above the bluff and permitted Steele to continue his retreat. By 3:00 P.M., Steele had crossed the river, had abandoned everything that might impede his flight (including, it seems, a wagon loaded with liberated Negro babies), had dismantled his bridge behind him, and was on his way to Little Rock. The arrival of Steele's famished and footsore column at the capital on May 3 marked the termination of the Federals' grand invasion of rebel Arkansas.

Kirby Smith gave his badly mauled command three days' rest, and then ordered Churchill's corps and Walker's division to return to Louisiana and reinforce Taylor. On the 5th, at Camden, he addressed a long letter to the President, in which he managed to claim all the credit for victories won by others and to lay all the blame for Jenkins' Ferry upon Sterling Price. "I cannot too strongly urge the necessity for better sustaining my administration," he told Davis.

A change in the command of these Districts [*sic*] is demanded by the best interests of the country. Genl Price's name and popularity would be a strong element of success in an advance on Missouri, but he is neither capable of organizing, disciplining nor operating an army, he should not be left in command of the District [or] of an Army in the field. I am greatly in want of good subordinates and of a capable chief of Staff, and with the responsibilites and multifarious duties devolving upon me and without proper support I almost despair of success—I shall however struggle on earnestly and conscientiously, begging your Excellency to bear with me and to assist me, and trusting in that Providence who orders all things for our good.

The commanding general then wrote a boastful letter to his mother, and departed for Shreveport.[10]

Meanwhile, down in the Red River Valley, Taylor was still trying to liquidate Banks's wing of the Federal pincer. On the same day that Taylor returned to Natchitoches, April 21, Porter's engineers and a sweating gang of military and contraband laborers succeeded in refloating the *Eastport*, thus clearing the way for the withdrawal of Porter's fleet and the retreat of Banks's army. Porter, already very uneasy about the depth of the Red, lost no time in raising anchor and puffing away toward Alexandria. His rapid departure left Banks with no reason to remain at Grand Ecore. On the 22d, Banks put the torch to the town, pushed aside the rebel cavalry holding Natchitoches, set a few more fires there, and hurried down the stage highway in pursuit of Porter. Along the way, his troops—in particular, A. J. Smith's bummers—looted barns, tore down houses and fences, and laid waste fields, leaving behind a swath of blackened desolation. Wharton's cavalry (now reinforced by W. H. Parsons' Texas brigade, under the command of William Steele) and Polignac's infantry worried the Federal flanks and rear, and once, at Monette's Ferry, some forty-five miles below Grand Ecore, Bee's brigade swung across Banks's line of march in an effort to stay his progress. But Bee cautiously stepped aside as soon as the Federal host came within range, allowing Banks to proceed—so cautiously, in fact, that Taylor removed Bee from command. On the 25th, the point of Banks's column reached Alexandria, and the rear came up the next day. Banks immediately set his soldiers to work improving the town's double ring of fortifications, welcomed the arrival of 6,000 reinforcements for the XIII and XVI Corps, prepared to hold off Taylor's 6,000 with his 31,000 effectives, and settled down to wait for Porter's laggard steamers.

Porter, as usual, was in trouble. On April 22, the unlucky leviathan *Eastport* ran aground. She was floated on the 23d, scraped downstream another five miles, grounded, was refloated on the 24th, slithered over two more miles of sandbars, stuck fast, was tugged another three miles on the 25th, and at last came to rest on bedrock. Efforts were made to lighten her by unshipping her guns and armor, but the *Eastport* was stuck. Finally, on the 26th, 3,000 pounds of gunpowder were stowed aboard her, and the *Eastport* was blown to pieces.

Fifteen miles farther south, near the mouth of the Cane River, Porter's flotilla encountered two hundred of Polignac's riflemen and a field battery. When the smoke cleared, the tinclads *Cricket* and *Fort Hindman* were floating hulks, the tinclad *Juliet* lay dead in the water, the transport *Champion No. 5* had been run aground and scuttled on the river's eastern shore, and the transport *Champion No. 3*, hit in the boiler by a twelve-pounder shot, had exploded, killing two hundred crew members and contraband passengers. A day later, Porter dragged the remains of his fleet down to Alexandria's wharves. On the 28th, he wrote a report in which he attributed his navy's condition to the accuracy and volume of fire delivered by the "eighteen" heavy cannon of the enemy's four-gun field battery.

Neither Porter nor Banks wanted to remain at Alexandria for very long, but once again the perverse Red obstructed their retreat. By April 27, the river had fallen so low that the channel through the Alexandria rapids was only three feet four inches deep. All of the transports and most of the tinclads were still able to negotiate the falls, but ten men-of-war, $2,000,000 worth of capital ships, needed between five and seven feet to pass down to easy water. The *Mound City, Louisville, Pittsburgh, Carondelet, Chillicothe, Osage, Neosho, Ozark, Lexington,* and *Fort Hindman*, the pride of Porter's Mississippi Squadron, were trapped. And so too was Banks's army, which could not evacuate Alexandria without abandoning the navy to the enemy.

The solution was offered by Colonel Joseph Bailey, an engineer on Franklin's staff. He proposed the construction of a temporary dam just below the falls, for the purpose of backing enough water to raise the channel to a depth of seven feet. Except for Franklin, none of the senior officers at Alexandria were much impressed by the colonel's scheme—"If *damning* would get the fleet over," swore Porter, "it would have been afloat long ago"—but for the want of a better idea, the erection of the dam was begun on April 30. Hundreds of wagons and thousands of men were pressed into service; stone was quarried, earth was excavated, and timber was felled; and much of the town of Alexandria was torn down to provide building material. For the next two weeks, the men of Banks's expeditionary force and the sailors of Porter's fleet fought a battle to the death against the Red.

Taylor took advantage of the Federals' embarrassment by tightening the noose around Alexandria. His cannon, skirmishers, and snipers kept up a steady fire against the Union works, doing little physical damage but causing great wear to the Federals' nerves. Just across the river from the Alexandria docks, Liddell's demibrigade rushed and occupied Pineville, planted a battery in the village, and began lobbing shells toward the bluecoats. To the north and west of Alexandria, William Steele's brigade interdicted the roads and prevented Banks's foragers from gathering provisions. Polignac's division, Bagby's brigade, and Bee's brigade (now commanded by George Baylor) were strung along the highway from Alexandria to Simmesport, to guard against the possible advance of a Union relief column. And on the riverbank thirty miles below Alexandria, Major's brigade and a field battery endeavored to blockade the lower Red. On May 1, Major destroyed the transport *Emma.* Three days later, the *City Belle,* bound for Alexandria with a reinforcement of seven hundred Ohio infantrymen aboard, was blown apart and sunk. And on the 5th, the transport *Warner,* carrying an Ohio regiment home on furlough, and two escorting gunboats, the *Covington* and *Signal,* were all driven ashore and captured. By the 6th, for all practical purposes, Major had closed the lower Red to the passage of Federal shipping.

But Taylor was aware that his undermanned army could not contain the Federals indefinitely. Convinced that Banks's force was "utterly demoralized and ripe for destruction," he felt that "the opportunity of striking a blow decisive of the war" lay within his grasp; but in order to take advantage of it he needed infantry, and soon. Taylor kept Kirby Smith "advised of the enemy's movements and condition," and dispatched countless pleas to the commanding general to "implore him to return and reap the fruits of Mansfield and Pleasant Hill, whose price had been paid in blood." But "not a man was sent me"—not, at least, until it was too late. "Like 'Sister Ann' from her watch tower, day after day we strained our eyes to see the dust of our approaching comrades arise from the North. . . . Not a camp follower among us but knew that the arrival of our men from the North would give us the great prize in sight. Vain, indeed, were our hopes. . . . From first to last, General Kirby Smith seemed determined to throw a protecting shield around the Federal army and fleet."

The prize slipped from Taylor's fingers on May 13, when, floating on water raised by Bailey's dam, Porter's warships rushed over the rapids and into the lower Red. During the next few days, Porter churned by Major's masked battery, rounded Fort De Russy, passed Simmesport, and made for the serene Mississippi. Meanwhile, Banks's army burned what little was left of Alexandria, drove through Taylor's vedettes, scorched its way down the stage highway, fought two desultory skirmishes with Wharton's pursuing troopers at Mansura and Yellow Bayou, and finally, on May 19—near the pile of charred debris which had once been the village of Simmesport, the place where the whole adventure had begun two months earlier—threw a pontoon bridge across the Atchafalaya and escaped. About seven days later, John Walker's division finally joined Taylor at Alexandria. Churchill's corps, however, never arrived, for on May 16 Kirby Smith had ordered Churchill to reverse course, return to Camden, and rest his command.

In the words of one of the privates in Banks's rear ranks, "The Red River campaign was over and nothing left to show for it but the great waste of men and money it had cost." It also left a valley full of wreckage, the wreckage of armies and of a state. "The destruction of this country by the enemy," Taylor reported, "exceeds anything in history." One of the Federal soldiers who retreated with Banks from Natchitoches to Simmesport acknowledged that nearly every building his regiment passed had been burned to the ground; an officer marching with John Walker saw nothing but the scarred skeletons of homes, barns, slave quarters, outhouses, cotton gins, and smokehouses; a Texas cavalryman described the land as "a perfect forrest of blackened chimneys," and exclaimed that "ruin and desolation is stamped upon the whole face of the country." After touring the length of the Red, Governor Allen could only weep:

From Mansfield to the Mississippi River, the track of the spoiler was one scene of desolation. The fine estates on Cane and Red Rivers, on bayous Rapides, Robert, and De Glaize, were all devastated. Houses, gins, mills, barns, and fences were burned; negroes all carried off, horses, cattle, hogs, every living thing, driven away or killed. You can travel for miles, in many portions of Louisiana, through a once thickly-settled country, and not see a man, nor a woman, nor a child, nor a four-footed beast. The farm houses have been burned. The plantations deserted. . . . A painful melancholy, a death-like silence, broods over the land, and desolation reigns supreme.[11]

Much of the wreckage was human. "Poor Felix Nunez," one of Gray's privates, had somehow dragged himself from the battlefield at

Pleasant Hill to the charnel houses at Mansfield. "The Doctors are cutting off one of his legs above the knee," noted one of his officers, "and he cannot survive. He was wounded in both legs and in his back besides." Four days later, "He is burried next to the grave of Lieut. Horton." Mansfield itself was described by another Johnny as "a huge hospital," and even buildings ten miles away were "all full of wounded soldiers." The usual mobs of refugees crowded all the roads; even Thomas O. Moore, late governor of Louisiana, had abandoned his plantation and was walking to Texas. Mingled with the refugees, and with the forlorn gangs of slaves being driven to safety by their overseers, were hundreds of ragged prisoners en route to stockades beyond the Sabine. On April 13, the commandant at Camp Ford, near Tyler, was ordered to prepare for the reception of 3,000 or 4,000 new charges. On the 15th, while hundreds of Negroes toiled to enlarge the Tyler compound, the first contingent of 1,000 bluecoats straggled in from Mansfield. On the 17th, 18th, and 20th, 600 more shuffled in; on May 15, more than 1,200 were brought down from Arkansas; on May 19, another 490; on the 27th, 540; on June 16, 162; and on July 6, 180. There also arrived, on June 19, "a pack of Negro dogs, which are to be kept here to catch escaped prisoners."

And some of the human wreckage wore a general's stars—in particular, General Banks. His men hooted at him, his superiors adjudged him "incompetent" or "utterly destitute of military education and military capacity," and when he returned to New Orleans, he found himself the butt of a popular new song:

> But Taylor and Smith, with ragged ranks,
> 　For Bales, for Bales;
> But Taylor and Smith, with ragged ranks,
> 　For Bales, says I;
> But Taylor and Smith, with ragged ranks,
> Burned up the cotton and whipped old Banks,
> "And we'll all drink stone blind,
> 　Johnny fill up the bowl."

By the time Banks reached New Orleans, he was no longer the Union army's southwestern generalissimo. Although he was still nominal commander of the Department of the Gulf, the departments of the Gulf, Arkansas, and Missouri had recently been absorbed by a new supercommand, the Military Division of West Mississippi; and although he was still the ranking major general west of Virginia, the new super-commander was someone else, E. R. S. Canby. Even worse, Canby made it quite clear that Banks was never again to lead so much as a regiment into battle. In September, Banks took leave, visited Washington, and petitioned the President to restore his military authority. Instead, Lincoln dismissed him and appointed Stephen A. Hurlbut to the military command of the Department of the Gulf.[12]

While Banks was trying to salvage something of his reputation, Taylor seemed to be doing his best to be charged with insubordination. Taylor's abrasive relationship with Kirby Smith flared into open hostility during the last weeks of the Red River campaign. On April 28, while eying Porter's trapped fleet and yearning for the return of his infantry, Taylor addressed a long letter to Smith, in which he castigated the commanding general for "abandoning the certain destruction of an army of 30,000 men, backed by a huge fleet, to chase after a force of 10,000 in full retreat." Asserting that Smith's strategy had been "fatally wrong," he asked to be relieved from duty. Four days later, upon receiving this letter, Smith dismissed it with the comment that it must have been written "in a moment of irritation or sickness." Taylor was indeed irritated, enough to pen an even more violent denunciation of Smith's entire administration on May 24. His troops, said Taylor, were exhausted; his brigades, dwindling to nothing; his men, unclothed, unshod, and unarmed; his cavalry and artillery, without horses—and it was all the fault of Smith's monstrous bureaucracy. "No campaign dependent on the present system of bureaucracy will succeed," he protested. "The rage for what is termed organization has proceeded so far that we are like a disproportioned garment—all ruffles and no shirt. The number of bureaus now existing in this department, and the army of employees attached to them would do honor to St. Petersburg or Paris. Instead of making the general staff a mere adjunct to promote the efficiency of the little army in the field, the very reverse is the case. . . . Requisitions for the most important articles upon which depend the fate of a campaign are lost in a mingled maze of red tape and circumlocution." And since he had no hope that the Department's administration would ever be reformed, he again asked to be relieved.

Upon receiving this harangue, Smith replied, with a deadly calm,

that Taylor's complaints were "objectionable and improper," and defended his conduct of recent operations by pointing out that "the complete success of the campaign was determined by the overthrow of
Steele at Jenkins' Ferry." When Taylor read this, he exploded. Accusing Smith of bad faith, of an inability to see facts and weigh honest crit-
icism, and of having committed "grave errors" during the bungled battle
of Jenkins' Ferry, Taylor declared that "the campaign as a whole has
been a hideous failure. The fruits of Mansfield have been turned to dust
and ashes. Louisiana, from Natchitoches to the Gulf, is a howling wilderness and her people are starving. Arkansas is probably as great a
sufferer. . . . After the desire to serve my country, I have none more ardent than to be relieved from longer serving under your command." On
June 10—the same day on which the Confederate Congress passed a
joint resolution thanking Taylor for his brilliant victories at Mansfield
and Pleasant Hill—Kirby Smith bundled copies of all this correspondence off to the President, and accepted Taylor's resignation: "Lieut.
Genl R. Taylor is relieved from Command of the District of West
Louisiana, which he will immediately turn over to Maj. Genl John G.
Walker. He will then proceed to Natchitoches, La, and there await the
pleasure of the President of the Confederate States."

By the time Smith shelved Taylor, the Red River campaign was
over, and other projects were afoot. For almost a month, in fact, Kirby
Smith had been maturing a scheme for a summer campaign, and by
June his plan was about ready. The first hint of his intentions was given
to General Churchill on May 16, when Smith directed Churchill to proceed to Camden "and there rest your command, using every possible
exertion to build up your ranks, calling in all your absentees, and making your force as strong and efficient as possible perparatory for a
movement in the direction of Missouri." [13]

CHAPTER EIGHT

THE CLOSING
CAMPAIGNS, 1864

On May 19, three days after first intimating to General Churchill that an invasion of Missouri was in the offing, Kirby Smith ordered Sterling Price to prepare for an advance northward. Now that Steele had been repulsed and Banks was in full retreat, Smith judged that the time had come to carry the war into the enemy's country. At best, a major offensive might result in the permanent reoccupation of the Trans-Mississippi Department's most populous and productive state. At least, such an expedition should afford Missouri rebels an opportunity to rally and enlist beneath the South's battle standards. And whatever the outcome, the seizure of the initiative by the Confederate forces would distract the Federals from the prosecution of their own plans of conquest.

Price was directed to draw the several detachments of his army, both infantry and cavalry, toward Camden, to press the armament and equipment of his troops, and to summon the irregular bands operating beyond the enemy lines to rendezvous with his regular divisions. He was also instructed to gather intelligence concerning Union strength and dispositions above the Arkansas River, to survey the condition of roads, bridges, railroads, and communications toward and in Missouri, and to collect reliable estimates of the availability of supplies and recruits in his home state. By the second week of July, Price was ready: his divisions were poised, his spies had informed him that thousands of Missourians were eagerly awaiting a Southern army of liberation, and his scouts had reported that Missouri's defenses were in disarray, having been weakened by the transfer of garrison troops to the eastern theaters of war. All Price needed was the order to march.

But that order was not issued. By the time Price announced his readiness to move, Kirby Smith's headquarters had been thrown into turmoil by a message from General Stephen D. Lee, temporarily commanding the neighboring Department of Alabama, Mississippi, and East Louisiana. On July 9, Lee dispatched a telegram to Shreveport informing Kirby Smith "that Canby is now moving on Mobile with twenty thousand troops." It was "vital," Lee insisted, "that a part of your troops are crossed over the Miss, or you co-operate in such a manner to divert their troops. Genl Bragg directed me to confer with you as to crossing troops." Had Lee's message been no more than a communication from one department commander to another, Kirby Smith might have replied that Price's impending expedition would provide all the diversion necessary. But by citing the authority of Braxton Bragg, who was now President Davis' personal military adviser, Lee's note intimated that the President himself gave first priority to the project of transferring Trans-Mississippi troops to the East. Any lingering doubts Smith might have had were dispelled just one week later, when, according to a second telegram from Lee, "The President instructs me to say the enemy is reported to have withdrawn his main force [from] L^a to attack Mobile and operate East of Miss river. That under such circumstances it was expected of you that you would promptly aid by sending troops to defeat the plans of the enemy, as soon as discovered." Lee's second message hinted that Davis was disappointed that the transfer had not already been effected.

Only two months earlier, Smith had notified the War Department that the Federal blockade of the Mississippi prohibited any mass redeployment of Trans-Mississippi forces to the Eastern Confederacy. Smith had also emphasized that his "30,000" soldiers were already too few to hold and garrison the remains of his department, and that any further reduction in the strength of his army would threaten the continued survival of the Western Confederacy. Until Lee's telegram of July 9 arrived, Smith had assumed that any plans Richmond might have had for the reinforcement of the eastern armies with western units had been abandoned. But in the interim, the military situation in the Cis-Mississippi Confederacy had deteriorated so rapidly that even General Robert E. Lee, who was seldom inclined to offer advice on matters of grand strategy, had urged the President to order that Joseph Johnston's army be reinforced by "a part" of Kirby Smith's command. By mid-July, 1864, Canby was moving against Mobile; Sherman had driven Johnston from the southern border of Tennessee to the outskirts of Atlanta; Grant was laying siege to Petersburg; Richmond itself was in peril. The redemption of the South's independence seemed now to hinge upon dramatic, even desperate, measures. Ironically, reports of the Trans-Mississippi army's victories at Mansfield, Pleasant Hill, Camden, and Jenkins' Ferry may have misled Bragg and the Lees into believing that Kirby Smith's Confederacy was full of spare soldiers.

During the next two weeks, telegram after urgent telegram poured into Kirby Smith's headquarters. On July 18, the War Department— which was evidently not yet aware that Taylor had been removed from command more than a month before—ordered "Lieut Gen[1] Dick Taylor, if his services can be dispensed with in the Trans Miss Dept, to this side of the Miss river." Four days later, Bragg instructed Stephen Lee to "inform Gen[1] E Kirby Smith that the President orders a prompt movement of Lieut Gen[1] Taylor and the Infantry of his Corps to cross the Mississippi, such other infantry as can be spared by Gen[1] Smith will follow as soon as possible. Gen[1] Taylor on reaching this side Mississippi will assume command of the Department" of Alabama, Mississippi, and East Louisiana. On the 23d, Lee advised Smith that "the movement of troops ordered by the President should be executed with the least possible delay."

Finally, on July 28 and 29, Smith acted. John Walker was offered the option of retaining command of the District of West Louisiana or of resuming command of his old division. Colonel H. T. Douglas, the Department's chief engineer, was dispatched to Alexandria with orders to collect pontoons and to devise a scheme for crossing the troops. Taylor was restored to duty, authorized to reassemble his staff, and placed in over-all charge of the operation. And Smith then dumped the entire responsibility for the implementation of the transfer upon Taylor: "You will proceed to Alexandria forthwith and take command of the two Infantry Divisions [Walker's and Polignac's] in the Dist of West L[a] ; with these Divisions you will cross the Mississippi River with as little delay

as possible. Upon reaching the nearest telegraph Station you will report
to Richmond for further instructions." On the 30th, Smith addressed a
letter to the President, informing him of the arrangements made, advising him of the cancellation of Price's proposed expedition, and assuring
him that it might nonetheless still be possible to mount a cavalry raid
through Missouri later in the season.[1]

Kirby Smith was far from optimistic about the chances for Taylor's
success, and was hardly enthusiastic about the prospect of losing all the
infantry in Louisiana. On August 1, he intimated to John Walker that
many of Taylor's men might mutiny when ordered to leave the Department. Two days later, he complained to Bragg that "I regret the necessity which compels the removal" of "between 9,000 and 10,000" infantrymen from the Trans-Mississippi, for with but 8,200 foot soldiers
remaining in Texas and Arkansas such a transfer "leaves me powerless
to resist any movement of the enemy made in force." On August 4,
pouring out his "miserable" discontent to his wife, he despaired that
"we are losing life, events are transpiring daily over turning all plans
and hopes [for] the future." And one week later, after telling his wife
that "our troops will cross the River (the Infantry) too late I fear for
good," he admitted that "I for the first time since the war [began] fear
for the result."

Smith was not alone in his misgivings. Taylor, whose main thought
was to remove himself from Kirby Smith's jurisdiction as soon as possible, had little faith in the project, and even less desire to become embroiled in its execution. As soon as he was restored to duty, Taylor petitioned Shreveport for permission to proceed immediately to the
Cis-Mississippi. Once he relieved Stephen Lee, he affirmed, he would
do everything in his power to prepare for the reception and rapid redeployment of Walker's and Polignac's divisions. But Smith flatly vetoed
Taylor's proposal: "You must yourself in person," he insisted, "superin-
tend the arrangement and accompany the column." If prior coordination
with Lee were required, said Smith, Taylor could easily ferry a few
staff officers across the Mississippi beforehand.

Taylor then protested that nothing but small detachments could be
slipped through the Federals' Mississippi blockade. He argued that none
of the prerequisites for an efficient troop movement—stores, provisions,
depots, transportation, intelligence—were available. He repeated his

unwillingness to accept "the responsibility either for the failure or success of the undertaking." And, circumventing the normal chain of command, he tried to secure directly from Bragg an order posting him to his new department. Such an order was delivered on August 14; without further ado, Taylor informed Kirby Smith that he was departing Alexandria for the East. "This I positively forbid," retorted Smith. "Your presence with those troops, on the eve of crossing, is of the greatest importance to the success of the movement. Should you have received instructions from higher authority . . . you will still remain in command of the troops until further orders, as I shall object to a compliance of these instructions." Taylor finally agreed to "remain with the troops . . . for the present, and . . . cross the Mississippi with them unless I receive additional news or further orders to cross at once."

John Walker was no more sanguine about the project than Taylor or Kirby Smith. When asked to choose between leading his old division across the Mississippi or remaining in the Department as a district commander, Walker chose the latter. His decision necessitated the appointment of a new commander for the Texas infantry division. As it happened, two major generals, Simon B. Buckner and John H. Forney, had recently been transferred to Shreveport from the Cis-Mississippi. Buckner, known to be a personable, popular, and talented officer, had been nominated for assignment to the Southwest by Kirby Smith himself; Smith wanted him to assume charge of a district or to supersede Boggs as chief of staff. Forney was reputed to be an erratic, despotic martinet, unpopular with superiors and subordinates alike. Given the circumstances, Smith had little trouble selecting the Texas infantry's new commander: Forney. Smith was quite aware, even before the appointment was announced, that "great opposition is being made by the prominent officers of [Walker's] division upon the rumor that [Forney is] to be assigned to its command," and that "serious difficulty will arise amongst the troops on General Forney's taking command of that division," but he insisted that "this is the only command to which he can be assigned in the department."

None of the senior officers involved in the redeployment showed much confidence in the idea, but none seemed willing to take the responsibility for declaring it impractical. And so, while the generals hedged, their subordinates set the plan in motion. Colonel Douglas first devised an elaborate proposal for bridging the Mississippi. Taylor assured Kirby Smith that Douglas' design could be executed within thirty days, but Smith, asserting that it would require at least two months to bridge the river, dismissed Douglas' grandiose proposition out of hand. Emphasizing that time was of the essence, Smith ordered Taylor to plant a few batteries above and below the point selected for the crossing, and to ferry the troops to the other side under cover of darkness. Both Smith and Taylor agreed that no more than 4,000 men could be rowed across in a single night, both doubted that the Confederates could retain control of a stretch of the Mississippi for more than one night, both appreciated that neither artillery nor wagons could be ferried to the eastern shore, and both were surely aware that the entry of a single Federal ironclad into Confederate water during the course of the transfer would spell disaster. And yet, once Smith outlined his plan, neither he nor Taylor reconsidered it. Instead, both pressed its implementation, but without much evidence of vigor.

The men of Forney's and Polignac's divisions were hardly as fatalistic as their generals. The physical and psychological wounds suffered during the Red River campaign had not yet healed; complaints about rations, furloughs, and pay—especially pay, which was now a year in arrears—were becoming louder and more numerous. The Texans were outraged by Forney's appointment to command; troop morale, already dangerously low, was reported to be deteriorating; and desertions were increasing. As early as August 1, rumors of the impending redeployment were abroad in the army; and on that day John Walker was already "quite apprehensive over the prevailing tone of discontent" in the ranks. Once marching orders were issued, demoralization worsened. "It is reported, and I believe it is true," revealed a sergeant to his diary, "that this Army is ordered over the Mississippi, and I am sorry to say that a great many will desert before they will go." As Taylor's regiments plodded from the neighborhood of Alexandria to Harrisonburg, and then struck due eastward through the miasmatic Bayou Tensas swampland, both Governor Flanagin and Senator Augustus Garland warned Richmond that "our troops here will not go; they will throw down their arms first." And as the infantry approached the western bank of the Mississippi, scores, and then hundreds, abandoned their colors. Kirby Smith found it necessary to distribute Wharton's entire cavalry division along the Red, to picket the ferries and to intercept deserters making for Texas. In mid-August, there occurred at least one "open mutinous outbreak under arms, encouraged . . . by a few officers"; a drumhead court-martial condemned a Texas captain and ten other ringleaders to death before a firing squad. By August 18, the date on which the crossing was to be attempted, Taylor feared that fully half of his command was on the verge of armed mutiny.[2]

And so, on August 18, citing as justification both the threat of an uprising and the impenetrability of the Union navy's Mississippi blockade, Taylor addressed a dispatch to the War Department "to the effect that I consider the crossing of any considerable body of troops impossible." Advising Kirby Smith that he would nevertheless "push forward the troops to the vicinity of the river and use every exertion and precaution to insure success," he expressed his hope that "the receipt of my dispatch will induce the War Department to countermand the order.' Then, at 9:00 A.M., August 19, "satisfied from personal observation and unmistakable information that it would result only in injury to the whole command," Taylor advised Smith that he had "assumed the responsibility of ordering a suspension of the movement until I could hear further from the War Department, at Richmond." By initiating direct correspondence with the War Department, Taylor in effect asserted that he would defy any further attempt by Kirby Smith to govern the redeployment of his divisions. In fact, he threatened to defy even the Chief Executive, stating that "when orders reach me from the President I shall obey them, or if in my judgment on the ground delay or suspension are necessary, I shall be governed by my discretion."

Because of his overt insubordination, Taylor might well have been prosecuted before a court-martial. But on the 19th, the same day on which his second message was telegraphed to Shreveport, another dispatch, more incredible than any of those yet exchanged during the course of this curious episode, was delivered to Kirby Smith. This dispatch, dated August 8 and signed by the President, simply negated the events of the past month. "Your telegram of 30th July 64 received. And after inquiry can find no record of a telegraph ordering you to send Gen[1] Taylor and Infantry from Trans Miss Department across the Mississippi River. No such order was ever given by me. . . . Jefferson Davis."

Evidently, Davis' message so stunned Smith that he was unable to regain his composure for three days. On the 20th, having retired to his quarters because of a fever, Smith complained at length to his wife about the "violent and bitter" attacks made against him by Taylor and Taylor's friends. On the 21st, he addressed a long justification of his entire administration to the President, and offered to serve in any capacity to which the President might see fit to assign him. And not until the 22d did Smith or his staff "send word at once to [Taylor's] Command that they are not to Cross the River also to have the men [deserters] intercepted informed to the Same effect and that if they will return at once to duty no notice will be taken of their absence." Not until the 22d, therefore, was Taylor officially authorized to "suspend the movement of the troops across the Miss. river. The two Infantry Divisions under your command will be marched without delay and take position near Monroe L^a on the Ouachita. You are yourself relieved from the Command and will proceed across the Miss river in compliance with telegram of Genl [Samuel] Cooper dated Richmond July 18, 1864, a copy of which is herewith enclosed." The scheme to cross reinforcements to the Cis-Mississippi was promptly abandoned. By September 1, Taylor's disgusted troops, suffering from malnutrition, dysentery, and fevers, were en route to Monroe. "We are certainly off for Arkansas," exclaimed one, "or perhaps to Missouri: we hope the latter, at any rate we will take Arkansas in preference to Louisiana." In the dead of night, meanwhile, Taylor, accompanied only by a guide and his manservant Tom, had paddled across the Mississippi in a leaky log canoe.

The mystery over the original redeployment order was finally resolved four months later. On Christmas Eve, President Davis addressed an ambiguous letter to Kirby Smith, in which he explained that General Bragg, "aware of my views of the importance of re-enforcements from the Trans-Mississippi Department, and authorized by me to make such arrangements as the exigency of the case might require, sent a telegram to cross the infantry designated." At the time, said Davis, Bragg was with Johnston's army in Georgia; for some unexplained reason, he had neglected to refer copies of his dispatches to Richmond. Davis' letter left the impression that "only on subsequent investigation" had Richmond become privy to the enterprise. (But, in fact, at least two messages concerning the movement had been brought to the President's attention before mid-August, and at least one ranking War Department functionary knew all about the plan on the 17th.) Nevertheless, instead of disclaiming responsibility for Bragg's initiative, Davis intimated that he "regretted" Kirby Smith's failure to forward reinforcements and expected "that you will spare no efforts to afford assistance when it is so much needed for the maintenance of the common defense."

Smith was also criticized for his announcement, on August 22, that if deserters from Taylor's ranks would "return at once to duty no notice will be taken of their absence." Buckner, protesting that "such a course, at present, would destroy the discipline of the command," urged Smith to convene courts-martial to try all intercepted fugitives; his recommendation was quietly ignored. Taylor, now safely installed as commander of his new Cis-Mississippi department, complained to Bragg that the promulgation of Smith's amnesty would so enervate discipline as to make it "useless to send further orders to cross" western troops to the East. Bragg referred Taylor's letter to Davis, who, in turn, asked Smith to "explain his conduct." Smith "respectfully returned" Taylor's complaint with the comment that it constituted "a misrepresentation. There was no order published either by myself or any subordinate commander pardoning all or any of the men who deserted when the troops were ordered across the river: prompt measures were taken to arrest and punish the deserters." He then begged the President to recall that "in acting on any communication personal to myself from Gen[l] Taylor, . . . Gen[l] Taylor's systematic misrepresentation of my motives and acts exhibit a violence and prejudice restrained neither by respect for himself nor his superiors." But, in fact, few reprisals were carried out against the absentees; in any case, the damage had already been done. As a Confederate soldier wrote in his journal on September 1, "The experiment of put[t]ing troops over the river has terminated very disastrously to the patriotism of our soldiers, for they will not go; and a considerable number DID desert."[3]

☽ II   The movement of Forney's and Polignac's infantry divisions toward Arkansas was but one element of a complex strategic redeployment affecting almost every command in the Trans-Mississippi Department. On September 12, General Boggs summed up the entire design in a brief message to General Maxey: "The mass of the army is being pushed up for active service toward the Arkansas River." Texas was practically stripped of troops; by September 30, there were only two organized brigades of cavalry remaining in the Eastern Subdistrict (James Hawes's and Paul Hebert's), one brigade in the Western Subdistrict (James Slaughter's), and one in the Northern Subdistrict (Henry McCulloch's). Bee's Texas horse brigade, transferred from lower Louisiana and placed under the command of Arthur Bagby, and a brigade from Texas led by Xavier Debray, joined Richard Gano's Texas brigade in the Nations: these three units, consolidated into a division under Maxey's personal command, were concentrated near the southwestern border of Arkansas and ordered to cooperate with the forces in that state. Tandy Walker's brigade of Cooper's Indian division continued to hold the upper Red River Valley, while Watie's Cherokee brigade, now augmented by McIntosh's Creeks, Jumper's Seminoles, and Major Broken Arm's orphan Osage battalion, ranged northward toward the Arkansas River. Major's Texas brigade, Liddell's Louisiana horse, and the Texans of Bagby's veteran "New Mexico" brigade, now under the command of William Hardeman, remained in lower Louisiana. As Magruder wryly remarked, in commenting upon the paucity of the force left to defend the lower Red, "It is . . . obvious that Louisiana is safe from invasion until the rise of Red River."

Parsons' Texas cavalry brigade, now commanded by William Steele, was led northward into Arkansas by General Wharton himself. The infantry of the District of Arkansas underwent a major reorganization. This was necessitated by the heavy casualties of the Camden campaign, by the death or transfer of many of its officers, by the requirement to incorporate large numbers of casual Texan reinforcements, elderly Reserve Corps conscripts, and recently exchanged parolees into active line units, and by the temporary induction of many veteran infantrymen into the district's cavalry. Churchill's corps was disbanded, but his own Arkansas division (lately Tappan's) was enlarged to four brigades, commanded, respectively, by John Roane, Evander McNair, James Tappan, and Alexander Hawthorne. Churchill's division, plus the two brigades of Mosby Parsons' Missouri division (Charles Mitchell's and Simon Burns's), the three brigades of Forney's division (Thomas Waul's, Richard Waterhouse's, and Robert Maclay's), and the three brigades of Polignac's division (William King's Texans, Henry Gray's Louisianians, and Allan Thomas' repatriated Louisiana war prisoners) —in all, some 14,000 foot soldiers, virtually the Department's entire disposable infantry—concentrated between Camden and Monticello.

Except for the garrison troops stationed along the Texas coast, a few scattered police detachments in the interior, some unorganized elements of the Texas Reserve Corps, the ten batteries of the reserve and siege artillery train parked at Shreveport, and some miscellaneous line and service units, this redeployment exhausted the Department's manpower resources—this, plus the 12,000 men of Sterling Price's new cavalry corps, now off on the fourth and final grand Missouri raid. The four infantry divisions had been concentrated in Arkansas to keep Frederick Steele's Federals preoccupied, the white and Indian Territorial cavalry had been directed to protect Price's probable line of retreat, and both commands were to provide for the defense of the Department's vulnerable northern perimeter during the absence of Price's horse brigades.[4]

Not even the distraction caused by the attempt to transfer Taylor's infantry to the East had completely diverted the Trans-Mississippi high command's attention from the project to invade Missouri. Price continued to believe that he could rally "tens of thousands" or "30,000" Missouri recruits to his colors, and he still insisted that an expedition into Missouri would oblige the enemy to relax the pressure against Lee's and Johnston's armies. His intelligence continued to indicate that Federal regulars were being removed from Missouri and that the loyalty of the Federal Missouri militia was at best dubious. He was still inviting guerrilla bands to rendezvous with his army. And on July 23, he reported to Shreveport that some Missouri communities, anticipating the advent of an army of liberation, had already begun to display the Confederacy's Stars and Bars.

Price's persistent advocacy of a Missouri expedition was encouraged and abetted by Governor Reynolds and Congressman Thomas Snead, Price's former adjutant. Both advised him, during the third week of July, that the President, the Secretary of War, and General Bragg were all impatiently awaiting an offensive toward Missouri (a report which, if true, merely adds to the confusion surrounding the scheme to cross infantry to the Cis-Mississippi). It was Snead's understanding that

Buckner, a Kentuckian with many friends and admirers in Missouri, had been posted to the Trans-Mississippi Department to act as Price's deputy during the advance; Reynolds volunteered to discuss the matter with Kirby Smith and to press for Price's appointment as commander of the expeditionary force. Numerous others added their voices to the chorus calling for an offensive. Most agreed that, even if infantry were not available, a "powerful diversion . . . made by cavalry alone" would serve to accomplish the purposes envisioned.

On August 4, Kirby Smith, Price, and Reynolds attended a "grand powwow" at Shreveport, at which plans for a Missouri raid were hammered out. By this time Price had been chosen to lead the expedition, although it seems that the selection had been made against Kirby Smith's better judgment. Smith had first offered the command to Buckner, but Buckner, protesting that he was an infantry officer without cavalry experience, had declined it. Smith had also tried to induce Price to accompany Walker's division to the Cis-Mississippi; only after Price made clear his fixed determination to free Missouri had command of the Texas infantry been given to Forney. Under pressure from all sides to allow Price to lead the invasion, Smith had at last reluctantly yielded —and had thus consigned the fate of 12,000 horsemen to another infantry officer without cavalry experience.

And yet, from Smith's point of view this concession did promise one advantage, for once Price departed for Missouri he could not simultaneously exercise command of the army congregated in the District of Arkansas. If nothing else, Price's proposed raid through Missouri cleared the way for the appointment of a new district commander for Arkansas. Since Price would be subordinate to his successor, some major general with a commission older than his had to fill the vacancy. The only officer eligible was Magruder, for Price ranked every other major general in the Department. And so on August 4, the same day on which the "grand powwow" at Shreveport convened, Smith's headquarters effected a major shake-up in the Trans-Mississippi's second-echelon command structure. Magruder was posted to Arkansas, John Walker was transferred to Texas, and Buckner was directed to assume command of the District of West Louisiana. Buckner promptly took charge of his new district, but Walker and Magruder were not able to shift their headquarters until September. Magruder arrived at Camden following Price's departure for Missouri, a fact which may help explain some of the subsequent lack of coordination between the operations of Magruder's infantry and those of Price's cavalry.

Price's marching orders, issued immediately after the August 4 conference, were brief, elastic, and to the point. His expeditionary force was to be composed only of cavalry; nothing was said concerning infantry support. As far as Kirby Smith was concerned, the primary purpose of the raid was to enlist recruits, collect arms, and gather supplies. Price was told to organize his cavalry into a large number of small brigades and skeleton regiments, whose ranks could be filled by volunteers gathered en route. Smith expected that the great majority of the Missouri recruits would be mounted; he advised Price to make clear to them that, because of the shortage of forage in Arkansas, they might be obliged to transfer to the infantry following the expedition's return to Confederate territory. Price was instructed to "make St. Louis the objective point" of his movement, "which, if rapidly made, will put you in possession of that place, its supplies and military stores, and will do more toward rallying Missouri to your standard than the possession of any other point." Since the raid was designed to win the minds and hearts of able-bodied Missourians, Price was cautioned to "scrupulously avoid all wanton acts of destruction and devastation, restrain your men, and impress upon them that their aim should be to secure success in a just and holy cause and not to gratify personal feeling and revenge." Should Price "be compelled to withdraw from the State" (Smith later admitted that he "had no expectation that General Price would winter in Missouri"), he was to retreat "through Kansas and the Indian Territory, sweeping that country of its mules, horses, cattle, and military supplies."

If Kirby Smith's objectives were restricted to concrete military rewards—men, arms, livestock, and matériel—Price's aspirations were more ambitious. Price was a politician, who thought in political terms. With Reynolds, he discussed his intention to seize Jefferson City; he invited Reynolds to accompany the expedition, and promised to inspire the revival of Missouri's Southern allegiance by installing Reynolds as governor in the state's legitimate capital. To others, he said he intended to interfere with the pending Northern presidential elections by depriving Lincoln of Missouri's vote; some even heard the rumor that Price would proceed on to Iowa, to disrupt the balloting there.[5]

Had Price's invasion been launched in late July as originally scheduled, and had it been mounted by an adequate joint force of infantry and cavalry, it might well have won control of much of the state. Between the end of the Camden campaign and the beginning of August, thirty-two "surplus" Union regiments were stripped from Missouri and dispatched to other theaters. On July 31, only 14,000 Federal regulars and 2,600 enrolled Missouri militia, dispersed in more than fifty scattered garrisons, remained in the state. Moreover, Price's intelligence regarding the unreliability of the militia was quite accurate. In the second week of July, General William S. Rosecrans, who had been promoted to the command of the Federal Department of Missouri following his defeat at Chickamauga, learned that many militia companies had been infiltrated by members of pro-Confederate secret societies. In mid-July, reacting with energetic determination, Rosecrans ordered the arrest and incarceration of all known ringleaders of the secret societies, including the Belgian consul at St. Louis. Rosecrans' tactics incited a premature uprising by some of the infected companies in northern Missouri: Confederate flags were hoisted over a number of militia cantonments, Confederate uniforms were donned, Platte City was occupied, Platte, Boone, and Clay counties were overrun, and the Federal garrison at Columbia was besieged. Had a large Confederate army arrived in the midst of the so-called Paw Paw Rebellion, it seems doubtful that Rosecrans could have repulsed it.

But while the Paw Paws waited for Price, and while Price waited for marching orders, Rosecrans not only put down the rebellion but also initiated the enlistment of an army both strong and reliable enough to crush anything but a full-scale invasion. General Alfred Pleasonton, in charge of the District of Central Missouri, waged a vigorous campaign within the boundaries of his jurisdiction to ensure that any militiaman suspected of treason was "transferred out of the country or otherwise disposed of." General Clinton B. Fisk, commanding the District of Northern Missouri, moved against the "treacherous Paw-Paws at Platte City" with the "hope [that] our troops will take no prisoners." Sixteen thousand troops from the Department of the Gulf were ordered to Little

Rock, within striking distance of Missouri; six thousand of these would later be committed to the pursuit of Price. A. J. Smith's veteran corps, en route from Vicksburg to the East, was held at Cairo, Illinois, and readied for redeployment to St. Louis. Pleasonton, Fisk, and Rosecrans' remaining district commanders (Thomas Ewing, John McNeil, and J. B. Sanborn) pressed the enlistment of fresh Missouri volunteers and the embodiment of loyal Missouri militia regiments with such success that, by October 1, Rosecrans' own regular force had increased to 17,500 and his dependable militia to 14,800. The July intelligence reports upon which the Confederates based their plans were true enough; in July, Missouri was in turmoil, and ripe for liberation. But by the end of September, when Price's cavalry columns finally swung into Missouri, those reports were more than two months out of date.

If the distraction caused by the attempt to transfer Taylor's infantry to the Cis-Mississippi was the sole reason for the subtraction of infantry from Price's expeditionary force, it was not the only cause for the belated departure of Price's horse soldiers. Price's marching orders were issued on August 4. Yet it was not until August 17 that he and Governor Reynolds left Shreveport, and not until August 28 that Fagan's and Marmaduke's divisions decamped from the neighborhood of Camden. It was already September 6 when the cavalry corps crossed the Arkansas River, and not until September 19 did the point element of Price's column carry the first red rebel flag into Missouri. Price's value as a political symbol did not alter the fact that he was a slow, lethargic, unaggressive infantry general, who exhibited no flair for cavalry leadership. The leisurely pace of Price's plodding campaign was to subvert its very essence as a cavalry raid, for, by failing to make use of his cavalry's mobility, Price was to throw away the chief tactical advantage he enjoyed. Not until late October, after his army had been cornered and mangled at Westport, would Price appreciate that cavalry could ride faster than infantry could walk. But by then, the remains of his command were already in full retreat.

On August 4, the bulk of the District of Arkansas regular cavalry was in bivouac near the village of Princeton, sixteen miles north of Camden. Only Shelby's Iron Brigade was absent, raiding and recruiting well behind the Union lines. On the 11th, Shelby was directed to demonstrate toward the rail line connecting Little Rock and Devall's Bluff, in order to keep Steele's troops too busy to interfere with the movement of the rest of Price's corps across the Arkansas River. During the next month, Shelby devoted himself to his mission with his customary flamboyant efficiency, accumulating some 1,100 prisoners and teaching "the secrets of rebel raiding" to the Federals. Shelby's preliminary raid served its purpose, for Steele, already badly unnerved by the outcome of the Camden campaign, did nothing to contest Price's passage across the Arkansas.

While Shelby's horsemen harassed Steele, and while Price's supply officers laboriously collected wagons, provisions, arms, and ordnance stores, the scheme to redeploy Taylor's infantry to the East ran its course and was abandoned. This made possible the belated commitment of infantry to the Missouri invasion—but no such commitment was made. Instead, Kirby Smith advised the President that he would remain content to "push a large cavalry force into Missouri and support the movement by occupying my infantry in operations against Steele." On August 22, Smith directed Buckner to move Polignac's and Forney's divisions toward Arkansas. Eight days later, Magruder wired Shreveport for explicit instructions to govern the employment of the infantry within or en route to his District of Arkansas, but Department headquarters neglected to issue any specific campaign orders. By mid-September, Magruder had concentrated about 14,000 foot soldiers in the vicinity of Monticello, and assured Price that he would operate "on the lower Arkansas to divert the enemy from you." But the maneuvers which ensued were insignificant. On September 28, one of Forney's men, still in camp at Monticello, complained to his wife that although "there are between 12,000 & 15,000 troops in this portion of the country," their most important martial exercise to date had been a grand dress parade. What Magruder "really is & what he will do remains to be tested. . . . I hope we will do something before long." [6]

Exactly one month earlier, on August 28, Fagan's division and the bulk of Marmaduke's division (less Shelby's brigade) pulled away from Princeton and started jogging toward Dardanelle, 165 miles due north. At Dardanelle, nine days later, the cavalry forded the Arkansas and swung in a northeasterly direction toward Pocahontas, another 191 miles farther on. Once the corps was across the river, its rate of progress accelerated from sixteen to nineteen miles per day, a decent pace for dismounted troops but very poor for cavalry. Price himself made no attempt to hurry his troopers; forsaking his own horse for the comforts of "a four-mule carriage driven by a black boy," he frequently stopped along the way to tell gatherings of local citizens that he was going to Missouri. On the 16th, having reached Pocahontas, a "deserted village and ruined community" just below the Missouri line, Price interrupted his march and encamped for three days, in order to allow Shelby's regulars and large numbers of irregulars to rendezvous with his army, and to reorganize his command in preparation for the final thrust into Missouri.

Three factors governed the reorganization of the cavalry. First, to prepare for the induction of thousands of Missouri recruits during the weeks ahead, it seemed advisable to designate, staff, and brigade numerous skeleton regiments beforehand. Second, the guerrilla bands and mounted infantrymen already present had to be integrated into the cavalry corps' command structure. And third, Price had been sufficiently impressed by Shelby's recent performance to want to make full use of the Missourian's talents, and the most obvious solution appeared to be the creation of a provisional division for Shelby. Between September 16 and 19, therefore, Price transformed his expeditionary force into a corps of three divisions, each of which included a high proportion of small, under-strength regiments. Fagan's Arkansas division consisted of four brigades (commanded, respectively, by Cabell, Dobbin, W. F. Slemons, and Thomas McCray), plus two additional irregular regiments, an orphan battalion, one battery, and a section of artillery. Marmaduke's Missouri division was composed of John B. Clark's brigade, Thomas R. Freeman's ill-disciplined force of domesticated guerrillas, and a spare company of Missouri cavalry. And Jo Shelby's provisional division included his own Iron Brigade, commanded initially by David Shanks and later by the Missouri Swamp Fox, M. Jeff Thompson, a brigade of veteran Missouri bushwhackers under the leadership of Sidney Jackman, another brigade of nightriders commanded by Charles Tyler, and the Forty-sixth Arkansas Mounted Infantry. Like the men of the Forty-sixth Arkansas, the soldiers of six of Fagan's regiments and one of his battalions had recently been transferred from the infantry; none had been trained in the tactical evolutions of cavalry, and some, even in the most pacific situations, found it hard to remain astride the mules issued to them by the army's quartermasters.

Aside from the mounted infantry, Price's corps boasted no more than 4,000 or 5,000 regular Confederate States soldiers. The remainder of the men were at best partisans, and at worst marauding bandits. The exact number of these irregular auxiliaries cannot be determined with any accuracy; probably neither Price nor his brigadiers ever knew, on any given day, how many troopers they had. According to Price's own campaign report, he advanced into Missouri with an army of 12,000 men, but his inspector general later testified that no more than 9,000 followed Price across the Missouri border. Once the corps passed into Missouri, the occasional estimates of its manpower fluctuated wildly. Perhaps as many as 10,000 volunteers filtered into the Confederate column during its progress through Missouri, but little more than half of these enlistees returned to Arkansas with the command. In addition, "thousands" of the veterans Price brought with him also straggled away, some when they came within hailing distance of their homes, and even more during the precipitate retreat from Westport. Some Missouri companies apparently deserted en masse, and a few even joined the Federal forces which drove Price from their state.

Whatever the total number of men under Price's command, the effective strength of the expeditionary force progressively diminished. At least 2,000, and perhaps well over 4,000 of the raiders who rendezvoused at Pocahontas came in without arms, and a smaller proportion, chiefly neighborhood bushwhackers, reported for duty on foot. Of the 1,696 men Sidney Jackman managed to muster, 1,155 had no guns and 133 were dismounted. Even the regular units were incompletely outfitted: on September 17, 278 of the Iron Brigade's 1,455 troopers were without weapons, and 48 were dismounted. During the course of the raid, some firearms and mounts were captured, but in the long run captures failed to compensate for losses. Not only were many of those who deserted veteran soldiers, but the veterans who left usually took their horses and guns with them. The green recruits who joined the column commonly reported without serviceable weapons, mounts, or experience.

Estimates of the Confederates' strength are further complicated by the fact that not all of Price's command assembled at Pocahontas. Some guerrilla captains, already operating deep within the interior of Missouri, received informal army commissions from Price and orders to prepare the way for the cavalry corps by stepping up their harassment of the state's Union garrisons. The commissions meant little to most of them, but their warrants to kill were executed with vengeance. Near Kingsville, "Colonel Yaeger's" band, "all dressed up in Federal uniform [,] . . . asked no quarter and would give none"; a detachment of bluecoats was massacred, stripped naked, and scalped. Elsewhere, "the Union men of Nort[h] Missouri are harassed and robbed by guerrillas under [John] Thrail[l]kill, Tod[d], and others further West, composed of Rebels . . . sent here for the express purpose of cooperating with Price. The day for the extermination of these wretches has arrived. . . . Now it is war to the knife. Price's friends have raised the black flag."

In the middle of September, Bloody Bill Anderson drew together a hundred guerrilla gunmen operating above the Missouri River and concentrated them in the northwestern corner of the state. He then ambushed a Union ordnance convoy at Rockport, captured thirty thousand rounds of ammunition, and started on a long, 200-mile dash toward the southeast. On the morning of September 27, Anderson's nightriders swept down the dusty streets of the sleepy village of Centralia, about fifty miles due north of Jefferson City. At 11:00 A.M., the guerrillas robbed the daily mail coach from Columbia. Thirty minutes later, they bushwhacked the North Missouri Railroad's 11:30 passenger train from St. Louis, emptied the passengers' pockets, took $3,000 in specie from the express car, and shot down twenty-four wounded Federal enlisted men going home on furlough. Two hours after Anderson's men evacuated the town, Major A. E. V. Johnson and three companies of Union cavalry arrived; the Federals dismounted, put aside their carbines, and began to help the civilians bury the dead. Just then, Anderson's gang pounded back into Centralia, slaughtered 124 of Johnson's 147 soldiers, looted the village, and again rode away. Galloping southward, the guerrillas crossed the Missouri and eventually joined Price at Boonville.[7]

Meanwhile, on September 19, Price's cavalrymen, "in fine health and spirits," evacuated Pocahontas and drove northward across the Missouri line. The following day, Shelby's troopers chased a small Federal scouting patrol from Doniphan, razed the town, and pressed on toward Fredericktown. The rest of the corps, however, continued to advance at a leisurely pace, for Marmaduke's division did not cover the intervening hundred miles until the evening of the 26th. At Fredericktown, Price learned that A. J. Smith's XVI Corps had reinforced the St. Louis garrison. Abandoning all hope of taking the city, Price decided then and there to turn the point of his column toward Jefferson City.

Even if Price had hurried his invasion, it seems unlikely that he could have taken St. Louis. Thanks to the rebels' careless security and the efficiency of the Federals' reconnaissance, none of Price's movements escaped the attention of the Union high command. Ever since August 30, two days after the Confederates' departure from Princeton, accurate intelligence regarding their progress had been accumulating on Rosecrans' desk. On September 13, Smith's corps arrived from Cairo and was put to work throwing up multiple lines of impregnable fortifications around St. Louis. During the next two weeks, McNeil, Pleasonton, and the other district commanders drew together their scattered forces and made ready to give the Southerners a hot reception. On the 25th, Rosecrans asked Governor Gamble to embody the whole of the Missouri militia. On the 26th, Thomas Ewing and 562 veteran infantrymen of the XVI Corps' Fourteenth Iowa raced southward to reinforce the 640 raw volunteers and militiamen holding the southern terminus of the St. Louis and Iron Mountain Railroad; the railhead was located at Pilot Knob, only twenty-one miles above Price's Fredericktown camp. And also on the 26th, the same day on which Price shifted his primary objective from St. Louis to Jefferson City, Rosecrans warned Samuel Curtis that Price would probably advance via Pilot Knob to Jefferson City, and then on toward Kansas. Except for the fact that Rosecrans habitually overestimated Price's effective strength, he knew almost as much about the Confederates' operations as Price did.

On September 27, as expected, Price moved against the rail terminus at Pilot Knob. Ewing's Federals occupied a formidable heptagonal earthwork, Fort Davidson, mounting seven cannon, protected by massive earthen walls, and encircled by a deep moat. However, the fort was also surrounded on all sides by a ring of commanding hills; had Price planted his twelve- and twenty-pounder rifles on the high ground, he could have lobbed shells into the basin and pounded the fort into submission without losing a man. His own chief engineer advised him that an artillery bombardment could reduce the position in twenty minutes. But a deputation of local citizens, approaching Price under the protection of a white flag, informed him that some women and children had taken refuge in Ewing's works, and asked him not to subject the fort to cannon fire. Price therefore decided to take the fort by frontal assault. His regiments, dismounted, were drawn up in four waves on a field south of the fortification. Except for a misty drizzle which dimmed the glamour of the spectacle, Price's array might have passed for an army on review. Ranks were dressed, colors were unfurled, drums rolled, and officers held their swords high. And then, with his customary lack of finesse, Price threw his brigades into the inferno piecemeal, without coordination, plan, or pattern. The Federals' cannon fire plowed through the massed Confederate battalions, while their musketry mowed down rank after rank. When a merciful darkness finally fell, bringing an end to six hours of carnage, a tattered National flag was still fluttering over the pockmarked parapet of Fort Davidson, one-fourth of Ewing's command had been incapacitated, and more than 750 dead or wounded Confederates littered the blasted ground in front of Ewing's works.

Having retired beyond the range of Ewing's cannon, Price's bruised troopers spent the night binding their wounds, making rude scaling ladders, and preparing for another assault on the morrow. But well before dawn, Ewing and his colonels, sensing that they could not maintain their position in the face of a concerted attack, saved the rebels another charge by voting to withdraw. In the dead of night, Fort Davidson's magazines, stores, and outbuildings were destroyed, the cannon were spiked and dismantled, all the wagons except those needed to carry the wounded were set afire, the fort was evacuated, and Ewing's column, having successfully slipped through a cordon of sleepy Southern vedettes, struck westward toward Rolla. The Confederates—badly battered, severely demoralized, and unfit to renew the fighting—made no attempt to pursue. [8]

For the rebel raiders, the three weeks following the battle of Pilot Knob were the "picnic period" of the expedition. Cantering north toward Jefferson City at the incredibly slow rate of ten miles per day, the Confederates entertained themselves by overrunning numerous small Federal garrisons and by demolishing bridges, telegraph wires, and miles of railroad track. They sacked occasional villages, captured 2,000 small arms and 200 serviceable wagons (the latter increased the number of wagons in Price's train to 500), and inspired panic in Union towns from St. Louis to Kansas City. They also published bombastic proclamations calling upon "Ye knights, who belong to the militia" to "buckle on your armor" and "strike with the victorious hosts under General Price and aid in the redemption of the State." There was no heavy fighting, although a number of sharp skirmishes cost the rebels some casualties. In one such engagement, Colonel David Shanks, commanding the Iron Brigade, was severely wounded, and command of the organization devolved upon M. Jeff Thompson. Finally, at twilight, October 7, the point of Price's column wound over the crest of a small rolling rise, from which could be seen the church spires, the capitol dome, and the perimeter fortifications of Jefferson City.

A cursory examination of the Union works surrounding the state capital quickly convinced Price and his brigadiers that the city could not be taken without severe loss. Scouts reported that 12,000 Federals, drawn from every Missouri military district except Ewing's, were already congregated in the town, and that A. J. Smith's corps had left St. Louis and was racing up the south bank of the Missouri toward Price's rear. Without a second thought, Price abandoned all thought of seizing Jefferson City, informed an apopletic Governor Reynolds that his formal inauguration would have to be postponed until another day, and ordered his troopers to resume their progress toward the Kansas border. On October 8, Pleasonton, the senior Federal officer at Jefferson City, formed all of the assembled cavalry—6,600 men—into three provisional brigades, appointed Sanborn their commander, and directed him to give chase. During the next two days, Sanborn's troopers fought a running skirmish with Price's rear guard (Fagan's division). On the 10th, after the rebels reached and fortified Boonville, the Federals—who had been without rations for the past thirty-six hours—broke off the pursuit and retired to the village of California, where they awaited the arrival of a commissary train from Jefferson City.

Instead of taking advantage of the reprieve granted him by Sanborn, Price chose to tarry at Boonville for the next three days. During his stay he enlisted recruits, collected arms and forage, welcomed the hundreds of sympathetic refugees who flocked into his swollen camps, and gave the enemy ample time to organize an effective pursuit. At 10:00 P.M., October 12, just as Pleasonton's cavalry (now increased to 8,100 men by the addition of a fourth brigade) and A. J. Smith's 9,000 infantry were about to swing into view, Price evacuated Boonville and, at an average pace of ten miles per day, started toward Lexington. En route, detached elements of his command overran the Union garrisons at Glasgow and Sedalia, capturing 1,200 stand of arms and six companies of infantry. On the evening of the 18th, Shelby's cavalry, riding point, swept into the village of Waverly, twenty-six miles from Lexington. Waverly happened to be Jo Shelby's home town—he had been the proprietor of the local rope factory—and no doubt he enjoyed his homecoming. But then neither he nor the rest of Price's troopers yet knew that the "picnic period" of the expedition had finally come to an end.

At dawn, October 19, Price broke camp and resumed the movement toward Lexington; Shelby's cavalry was again in the lead. For once, Price hurried his men along—scouts had reported that Pleasonton and Smith were closing rapidly on his rear—and by early afternoon Shelby's division was no more than four or five miles from Lexington. There, on a gently rolling field of prairie grass, Shelby's rebels encountered a division of 2,000 bluecoat horsemen, drawn up in line of battle and supported by eight twelve-pounder mountain howitzers. After a vicious little fire fight the Confederates drove the Federals from the field and northwestward toward Independence. The Federals continued to retreat until the following morning, when they occupied and entrenched the west bank of the Little Blue River. From prisoners taken during the battle, Shelby and Price learned that the division blocking their advance was composed of one milita and two regular cavalry brigades from the Department of Kansas, and that its commander was James Blunt. "I knew now," remarked Shelby, "there would be heavy work for us all in the future." [9]

Since mid-August, Samuel Curtis had kept abreast of Price's progress from dispatches forwarded by Rosecrans. On August 31, Curtis estimated that, because of the need to continue guarding the outlying settlements along the frontier, only 4,000 of his department's 9,000 Federal regulars could be committed to the defense of eastern Kansas. Six days later, therefore, Curtis opened negotiations with Governor

Carney for the services of the Kansas militia, a force which Curtis esteemed to be "little better than a rabble." Carney, however, "very earnestly hoped that the great expense and inconvenience of a general call of the Kansas people might be averted." Only after the arrival of news that Price was pressing westward from Jefferson City threw the civilian population of eastern Kansas into panic did Carney concede the wisdom of raising state troops.

Once the militiamen were under arms, it proved difficult to induce them to move across the state border into Missouri. Not until October 16 did Curtis extract permission from the governor to deploy the militia on Missouri's soil, and not until a recalcitrant militia brigadier, W. H. M. Fishback, was stripped of his command and placed under arrest did Curtis manage to drive his state troops over the boundary line. Even then, the militia refused to go very far into Missouri. The 6,000 men of (Kansas State) General George Deitzler's militia division would go no farther than the Big Blue River, west of Independence, while the 2,000 men of Fishback's brigade (now commanded by a regular colonel, C. W. Blair) were reluctant to ford the Little Blue.

Except for a minuscule contingent from Blair's brigade, all of the men engaged on the 19th at Lexington belonged to Curtis' two Federal brigades, led, respectively, by "Doc" Jennison and Colonel Thomas Moonlight. According to a temporary table of organization drafted by Curtis, Deitzler's militia division constituted the Left Wing of the Army of the Border, while the 6,000 troopers of Jennison's, Moonlight's, and Blair's cavalry composed the Right Wing. James G. Blunt was recalled from a raid through Indian country just in time to assume command of the Right Wing and to lead its advance element to Lexington, which he reached on October 18. Opening informal communications with Pleasonton and Sanborn, Blunt then placed his force across Price's line of march, fought Shelby below Lexington, fell back, and dug in along the Little Blue. Blunt was fighting for time—time for Peasonton's horsemen and Smith's weary foot soldiers to come up on Price's rear.

Immediately after the battle of Lexington, Price could have slipped away by cutting southward and making for the Arkansas line. But instead, for reasons that remain incomprehensible (Price's own account of the ensuing four days offers no coherent explanation for the tactics adopted), Price continued to press westward toward Independence,

Westport, and Kansas City. The two divisions of Curtis' command blocked his advance, Pleasonton's cavalry harried his rear, and Smith's infantry corps, racing forward at a killing pace (marching more quickly, in fact, than Price's cavalry ever had), swung toward the southwest and tried to interpose itself across the Confederates' most probable escape routes. After Price pushed over the Big Blue on October 22, even the terrain helped box his army: then the Missouri River lay to the north, the Kansas to the west, and the Big Blue to the south and east. The surprising thing is not that Price's corps was mangled beyond recovery but that any of the force was salvaged.

On October 20, Curtis informed Blunt that, since the bulk of the militia would not advance east of the Big Blue, the Kansas army would deploy and entrench along the line of that river. Blunt was ordered to pull back all but one brigade to the Big Blue's west bank. Moonlight's brigade, the steadiest in the division, was left to cover the fords of the Little Blue and the approaches to Independence. (When Blunt reached the Big Blue, his division was augmented by the addition of Colonel James Ford's small cavalry brigade, just back from an Indian campaign.) Meanwhile, Curtis, whose confidence in the militia had not improved, set the local citizenry to work constructing a second line of fortifications on the outskirts of Kansas City, and a third line even farther west at Wyandotte.

The following day, shortly after sunup, Marmaduke's division reached the Little Blue and attempted to force a crossing. But Moonlight's brigade held the fords, exchanging shot for shot. Marmaduke called for help; Shelby's division came up. Moonlight summoned aid; one after another, in piecemeal fashion, Blunt's three remaining brigades were hurled into the fray. Fighting on foot, and fighting hard, the Confederates eventually beat their way across the river, drove Blunt through the streets of Independence, and obliged him to retire once again to the west bank of the Big Blue.

Price's last chance to evade catastrophe was thrown away on October 22, when, instead of turning southward, he continued his march toward the Big Blue, Westport, and disaster. At 11:00 A.M., Shelby's division approached the Union line and began probing for a soft spot. Near Hickman's Mills, at the southern end of the line, Shelby discovered that Byram's Ford was only lightly defended by elements of Jennison's brigade. Pushing his way across, he drove Jennison, and then Moon-light, and finally most of the Kansas militia all the way to the state bor-der. The Federals retreated—but they retreated in good order and did not break. At the last moment, Curtis rallied his army and counterat-tacked; Shelby was stopped, doubled back, and forced to call for rein-forcements. But then, just as the van of Marmaduke's column arrived on the field, Price received word that Fagan's division, the rear guard he had left deployed along the Little Blue, had come under heavy attack by Pleasonton's horsemen. The jaws of the vise were closing tight.

Half of Marmaduke's command was ordered to remain with Shelby, while the other half, led by Marmaduke himself, was directed to turn about and rush to Fagan's support. Before Marmaduke could reach the Little Blue, he encountered a seething mass of panicky fugitives fleeing toward the west. Fagan's division had been outflanked and routed from the field. Marmaduke did his best to stabilize the front, but his own men succumbed to the hysteria and were consumed in the flight. Both Marmaduke and Cabell barely escaped capture by the for-ward elements of Pleasonton's cavalry. The day had long since passed and the night was already old before the firing on both fronts slackened sufficiently to allow Price's exhausted army to gain a few hours' rest.

"The 23d of October," reminisced Shelby, "dawned upon us clear, cold, and full of promise," but whatever promise the dawn heralded was quickly dispelled in the light of a harsh and rainy day. Leaving Marma-duke and Fagan behind to hold the line of the Big Blue against Pleason-ton, Price led Shelby's division westward against Curtis. Within the hour, Shelby's troopers encountered the whole of Curtis' army in posi-tion on an open prairie just south of the town of Westport. While Shelby flailed away at Curtis, trying to pound a gap through the Kansan front, Pleasonton smashed through Marmaduke's line, scattered Marma-duke's command, wheeled around Fagan's rear, attacked Fagan's Ar-kansans in reverse, and precipitated a wild, pell-mell rout of Price's en-tire right wing. As Marmaduke's and Fagan's divisions disintegrated, scrambling southward toward the little village of Santa Fé, Shelby's three brigades were left stranded between Curtis' host and Pleasonton's. "I knew the only salvation was to charge the nearest line, break it if possible, and then retreat rapidly, fighting the other," Shelby recalled. Ordering his brigadiers to strike southward and slash their way through

Pleasonton's command, Shelby himself resumed temporary command of Thompson's Iron Brigade and cut his own way through the enemy. The men of Jackman's and Tyler's brigades joined the general rout, but a few miles south of Westport the Iron Brigade, held together by the discipline of desperation, deployed in line of battle, maintained its integrity in the face of a furious assault by overwhelming numbers, and succeeded in covering the withdrawal of the rest of the corps.

As Shelby's troopers fell slowly back, disputing with the Federals for possession of each yard of ground, they could see on all sides the debris marking the wake of a beaten army, "dead horses, saddles, blankets, broken guns, and dead rebels." A thousand dead and wounded Confederates lay sprawled on the prairie below Westport, at least another five hundred dead had been abandoned on the fields between Lexington and the Big Blue, and two thousand prisoners remained behind in the custody of the Federals. Of the captives taken by Pleasonton's regulars, those who happened to be wearing Union blue (as many ragamuffin rebels were wont to do) were "executed instanter," some by shooting and some by hanging. The men of Curtis' ragtag regiments proved far more lenient toward the prisoners they took—perhaps because the Kansas militiamen themselves, two-thirds of Curtis' army, had gone to war in civilian clothing, with nothing to mark their military status except the scarlet sumac leaves stuck in their hats.[10]

Shortly after midafternoon, October 23, the various Federal generals participating in the campaign met together for the first time. While wolfing down cold soldiers' rations in the drafty main room of a rude farmhouse, Curtis, Pleasonton, Blunt, Deitzler, Sanborn, and Governor Carney mapped plans for the pursuit of Price's army. Had not Pleasonton made a serious miscalculation the afternoon before, no pursuit would have been necessary, for A. J. Smith's corps would have been in position to frustrate Price's retreat. But during the second battle for the Little Blue fords, Pleasonton, momentarily uncertain of his capacity to win a decisive victory without reinforcements, had summoned Smith's infantry northward. Smith's detour cleared the way for Price to make a dash for the Arkansas border. By the time the Union generals congregated for their conference, Smith's infantrymen were both in the wrong place—Independence—and far too fagged to march another step. For all practical purposes, the XVI Corps, despite its proximity, was no longer a significant factor in the campaign. Nor did Deitzler's division make any further contribution. Both Carney and Deitzler insisted that the Kansas militamen were far more valuable as voters than they were as line soldiers, and the regular generals, who tended to agree, raised no objections to the immediate discharge of Deitzler's command. (During the subsequent chase, Blair's militia, which was not included in the discharge, deserted en masse.) The disposable force remaining consisted of Pleasonton's and Blunt's cavalry divisions. The generals agreed to allow the troopers and their mounts a good night's rest, and to begin the chase at dawn the next morning.

Early on the 24th, Moonlight's brigade broke camp, cossed the state line into Kansas, and turned southward at a fast gallop. Moonlight's mission was to reach and ride herd on the right flank of the retreating Confederate column, in order to keep the rebels from swerving toward Fort Scott. He performed his task without much trouble. Meanwhile, Blunt's remaining brigades and Pleasonton's division, riding in two parallel columns, clattered away from the Westport battlefield, swept through Santa Fé, and hurried down the trail of debris left behind by the raiders.

A retreat is only successful when the force being chased runs faster than the force in pursuit. Between the early afternoon of the 23d and midnight of the 24th, Price's army marched fifty-seven miles; but between dawn on the 24th and dawn on the 25th, Pleasonton's lead brigade covered sixty miles. The reason the Federals were able to travel half again as fast as the Confederates was that neither wagons, nor refugees, nor amateur horsemen slowed them down, while the Confederates were burdened with all three. The rebel wagon train, in particular, had become a serious encumbrance; instead of melting away en route as the raiders consumed the stores it carried, the train had grown to monstrous proportions by the continual addition of captures loaded with loot and the conveyances of refugee sympathizers. Shelby's adjutant protested that the train had become the army's incubus, while Governor Reynolds bitterly complained that the army had been transformed into an "escort for a caravan." Immediately after the battle of Westport, a Confederate colonel remarked upon the "feeling of personal hostility on the part of the men to the enormous and useless wagon train," and recorded the soldiers' hope that "the column would be stripped of all superfluities

. . . and would move forty or fifty miles a day." But Price refused to abandon his wagons. The raiders were "surprised and disgusted when it became evident there was to be no decrease in the number of wagons . . . which they had to guard at the hazard of their lives"; and their disgust turned to anger when it appeared that, because of the train, the corps was retreating "at a speed that would not have been rapid for infantry." "On the morning of the 24th," recalled General Thompson, "we lost several hours in getting the train untangled . . . for in the confusion . . . men and wagons—artillery and refugees were so mixed that it was nearly impossible to unravel them."

At sunup, October 25, Pleasonton's van caught up with Price's rear guard. In an effort to cover his wagons, Price had concentrated the bulk of his combat strength toward the rear of his column. The night before, Fagan's and Marmaduke's divisions had camped on the Kansas side of the state border just above the Marais-des-Cygnes River, while the train and Shelby's division had camped eight miles due south, on the north bank of Mine Creek. Pleasonton deployed his troopers, and then, with guidons snapping and sabers drawn, they executed a classic cavalry charge, crashing through the Confederate line. Marmaduke's and Fagan's divisions dissolved. General Cabell, four colonels, 750 other rebels, and ten cannon were captured by the Federals; and Private James Dunlevy, of "D" Company, Third Iowa, earned an eight-month furlough by apprehending a dazed pedestrian dressed in faded blue jeans who turned out to be General Marmaduke. Thrown from his mount during the stampede, Marmaduke, suffering from a wrenched knee, a broken arm, and multiple abrasions, and completely disoriented on the bare Kansas prairie, was limping toward Colorado when Private Dunlevy snared him.

Hearing word of the disturbance toward the rear, Price decided to investigate. Halfway to the Marais-des-Cygnes he met the remainder of Marmaduke's men "retreating in utter and indescribable confusion, many of them having thrown away their arms. They were deaf to all entreaties or commands, and in vain were all efforts to stop them." Again the Iron Brigade rode to the rescue. Rushing north to the Little Osage, Thompson's regiments formed in line of battle and won for Price the time he needed to ford his train and the rest of his corps across Mine Creek. Then, in the face of constant assaults, and with Union yellowlegs swarming on every side, the Iron Brigade retired slowly to the south bank of the Marmaton River, nine miles below. Here, Thompson's troopers, reinforced by Jackman's brigade, made their last stand—and stood fast. At dusk Pleasonton's exhausted Federals broke off the engagement and withdrew to Fort Scott, quitting the campaign. During the night, Price burned four hundred wagons, abandoned a number of disabled cannon, destroyed a large amount of captured ammunition, crossed back into Missouri, and resumed his retreat. On the 26th, the Confederate cavalry corps rode fifty-six miles! Blunt's brigades continued the pursuit as far as Newtonia, where a brisk little skirmish was fought on the 28th. Then Blunt too disengaged, leaving the battered and demoralized remains of Price's expeditionary force free to stagger on down to Arkansas. But over 10,000 men—killed, wounded, captured, or missing—who had followed Price's flags from Princeton or who had rallied to them en route, were left behind on—or under—Missouri's inhospitable soil.[11]

❧ III   The suffering endured by the remnants of Price's decomposing army could have been relieved to some extent by concerted action on the part of the Trans-Mississippi Department's high command, but confusion and paralysis, rather than coordinated action, characterized the support given to Price by Kirby Smith. Three obvious alternatives, none of which necessarily excluded the others, were open to Smith. He could have thrown Maxey's Territorials toward Fort Scott, in order to draw off the forces pursuing Price. He could have ordered Magruder's infantry to feint toward Fayetteville or Fort Smith, in order to divert the attention of their Union garrisons long enough to assure Price an easy passage to the region below the Arkansas River. And he could, at the very least, have directed Magruder, Maxey, and Walker to concentrate supplies and establish relief depots along Price's line of retreat. The first option was implemented, but was executed prematurely by a force too small to influence events. The second was debated, and then, for no apparent reason, dropped from consideration. And the third was neglected until the penultimate moment, when it was far too late to make much difference.

At the end of June, 1864, thanks mainly to General Maxey's firm but beneficent administration of the Indian Nations, his unceasing (if often ineffectual) efforts to extort supplies of clothing and other necessities from the army quartermasters in Texas, and the relative quiet along the Territorial front, the great majority of Indian troopers, meeting in council at Limestone Prairie, had resolved to "unanimously re-enlist as soldiers for the war, be it long or short." On August 18, while writing another in a series of letters imploring Department headquarters to recognize that "shirts, drawers, socks, and pants are [as] necessary for [the] decency" of Indian soldiers as they were for whites, Maxey commented that Stand Watie, now a brigadier in the Confederate service, was anxious to raid southeastern Kansas. Watie wanted to exercise his brigade, which had not taken part in the Camden campaign, and to collect some useful loot. Seven days later, General Boggs, apologizing that Kirby Smith was "too unwell to attend to much business" himself, penned a brief note to Maxey to tell him that Smith "fully approves of the movement proposed by Brig. Gen. Stand Watie," and to recommend that Watie's raid "take place before the 1st of October, as General Price leaves immediately for a campaign into Missouri, and the two expeditions should march so as to be in their field of operations about the same time." Evidently, neither Boggs nor Kirby Smith then expected Price to spend nearly a month in Arkansas before advancing into Missouri, for by urging Watie to carry out his raid before October 1 they guaranteed that "the two expeditions" would not, in fact, be "in their field of operations about the same time." Had subsequent efforts been made to coordinate Watie's movements with those of Price, such efforts might well have contributed to the mutual advantage of both. But once Watie received his authorization to ride, no attempt was made to keep the commander of either expedition apprised of the other's progress. As a result, Watie's raid was over before Price's had fairly begun.

By the time Boggs's reply arrived at Maxey's headquarters, Watie had learned that a large Federal supply train was scheduled to travel from Fort Scott to Fort Gibson in mid-September. Since such a prize offered more loot than the whole of southeastern Kansas could, the train, rather than Kansas, was finally selected as the raid's objective. Wasting no time, Watie hurried the organization of his column as rapidly as possible. The troopers committed to the expedition consisted of Watie's own brigade (First and Second Cherokee Cavalry, 350 effectives), McIntosh's old brigade, now attached to Watie's outfit (First and Second Creek, 325 effectives, and John Jumper's Seminole Battalion, 130 effectives), and 1,200 men belonging to Richard Gano's Texas brigade. Even though Gano was Watie's senior, he waived precedence and acted with Watie "in perfect harmony and concert for the common good." According to Maxey, Gano's exemplary "patriotism," "delicacy," and sense of "justice" played an important part in allowing Watie, the only nonwhite general officer in either Civil War army, to prove that he had the capacity to conduct "one of the most brilliant and skillfully managed cavalry raids of the war."

Watie committed none of Price's mistakes. His command was lean, eager, professional, and experienced. His troopers—even though most of them were dressed in shredded rags, armed with antique firearms, and mounted on decrepit animals—were all veteran cavalrymen. His officers knew their men, and the men had learned to trust their leaders. His force was prepared to travel without baggage, to forage provisions from the land, to move rapidly, to strike hard, and to disengage quickly. And Watie's objective was both strictly defined and attainable: he had no illusions about his ability to occupy ground or to liberate territory, and he would permit no political aspirations to distract him from the task of sacking the Union wagon train. Since Watie made no errors, his campaign was the antithesis of Price's; it was, as Maxey said, a model cavalry operation.

Watie and Gano first met on September 12 to work out the tactical details of the raid. By the 13th, the expeditionary force was assembled and organized, and the very next day it splashed across the Canadian River and galloped northward into the Creek Nation. On the 15th, some distance west of Fort Gibson, the Arkansas River was forded; and on the 16th, after bearing toward the northeast, the column reached Sand Town on the Verdigris. Here the rebels found two companies of the Second Kansas Cavalry and a company of the First Kansas Infantry (Colored) cutting hay for the livestock at Fort Gibson. The Confederates stayed their progress just long enough to unlimber their cannon, spray the mowers with canister and grape, scatter the surviving whites, shoot down every Negro they could apprehend, and burn the hay already stacked. Then the raiders pressed on toward the Fort Scott road, and, on September 17, bivouacked on Wolf Creek. The following morning, Gano's reconnaissance patrols reported that the Union train, 250 vehicles, was parked exactly where Watie's intelligence had indicated it would be, near Military Crossing on Cabin Creek. Watie's division spent most of the 18th resting and preparing for battle—the Indians "made medicine," painted their faces, and waited for Greenbrier Joe, their brigade's chief shaman, to affirm that the omens were propitious —and then, well after sundown, the rebels stole quietly eastward toward Cabin Creek. At 3:00 A.M., September 19, having encircled the Federal encampment, Watie's troopers rushed the wagon park, dispersed the train's sleepy escort, mutilated and massacred a number of wounded prisoners belonging to the Second Indian Home Guards, burned half of the convoy's vehicles, and, with the remaining 130 wagons in tow, set out on the long dash back to the Choctaw Nation. Watie's fourteen-day expedition cost the Federals the wagons, 3,000 tons of hay, and $1,500,000 worth of military stores, and won the rebel Territorials enough horses, mules, weapons, and blue uniforms to remount, rearm, and clothe the entire command. But precisely because the raid was such a brilliant success, executed according to plan and exactly on schedule, it did nothing to assist Price. More than a month later, when Price's retreating corps was most in need of a supporting diversion, Watie's troopers were pasturing their fagged animals far below the Arkansas River.[12]

If the diversion mounted by Watie's cavalry was premature, Magruder's Arkansas infantry contributed even less to the safe extrication of Price's column from Missouri. At the beginning of October, in reply to a message from Magruder requesting permission to advance against Little Rock, Kirby Smith advised Magruder to hold his divisions in readiness, to resupply and drill them, and to keep "a careful watch" upon the enemy. On October 30, Magruder again asked for authority to assume the offensive, advancing the argument that the Little Rock garrison might reinforce Fort Smith and help interdict Price's line of retreat. Two days later, he asked Maxey for information concerning the condition of the roads in the neighborhood of Fort Smith. Magruder and Kirby Smith conferred at Lewisville on November 4, and Smith, conceding that Price might be "compelled to evacuate [Missouri] before the 1st of January," acknowledged that "we must provide for the most unfavorable contingency. I feel the importance of giving him support." Consequently, he and Magruder discussed possible moves against either Little Rock or Fort Smith, but reached no firm conclusions. Smith returned to Shreveport, and ten days passed, during which Smith, Magruder, and Maxey exchanged much indecisive correspondence about the advisability of an offensive toward Fort Smith. On the 14th, Magruder wired Smith to ask whether the projected advance should be initiated. Smith's reply, bearing the same date, admitted that "the expedition must start soon if it is going to help Price," but contained no specific instructions. Two days later, Magruder complained to Wharton that he had been unable to discover from Smith or any of his staff officers "if the Ft. Smith expedition should be given up; [Smith] answers in the most unsatisfactory manner, avoiding the question, and asks me what arrangements I have made with Maxey about supplies, a subject with which I had nothing to do. . . . Such is the result of the co-operation ordered by General Smith." A detachment of cavalry was detailed toward the upper Arkansas with orders to establish contact with Price, but the "idea of attacking Fort Smith with a view of relieving General Price is, of course, abandoned." In Magruder's estimation, Kirby Smith seemed to be "trusting to Providence for the relief of General Price's army." And there the matter rested.

Incredibly, at this late date, November 16, virtually no effort had yet been made to establish supply depots along Price's line of retreat. As Magruder's letter intimated, he had done nothing to provide for the subsistence of Price's corps, even though the remnants of Price's command had, by then, been south of the Missouri border for almost three weeks and had reached a point only twenty-four miles from Boggy Depot. If the token tactical support given Price's raiders by the Trans-Mississippi high command was woefully deficient, the dearth of logistical support was inexcusable.

Because of the Department's failure to respond to Price's needs, perhaps the most harrowing portion of his retreat was that which took place after his expeditionary force crossed safely into Arkansas. When Price's bedraggled squadrons straggled down from Missouri and over the state line on October 30, they were hardly in condition to keep on campaigning. At least one of Price's troopers saw himself as one "of the children of Israel marching through the Wilderness. But alas! We have no Moses to lead us. . . . A feeling of despondency pervades the army.

Low spirits and debility are playing havoc with our men. Many can scarcely go." But the raiders staggered onward for more than another month before reaching sanctuary in the interior of Kirby Smith's department.

Throwing Fagan's division and a collection of local guerrillas toward Fayetteville to keep its Federal garrison preoccupied, Price successfully skirted the Union stronghold and encamped, on November 1, at Boonsborough, near the old battlefield at Cane Hill. While there, he authorized Dobbin's, Freeman's, and McCray's brigades to disperse to their home neighborhoods, to refit, remount, and recruit. Price expected them to rendezvous with the rest of the corps at some unspecified later date, somewhere in Confederate Arkansas.

Price planned to remain at Boonsborough until Magruder could reinforce him. He then intended to cut east of Fort Smith, to cross the Arkansas, and to retire toward Camden. But on November 4, the rebel pickets were driven in by a flying column from Fayetteville, and Price's men were forced to scurry across the Cherokee border. Reforming his column the following day, Price meandered southwestward in easy stages, fording the Arkansas River on the 7th and the Canadian River on the 11th. All along the way, stragglers drifted from his regiments; and on the 10th, the Arkansans of Slemons' and Cabell's brigades flatly refused to march a step farther. Fearing a general mutiny of Fagan's division, Price furloughed the two brigades and asked their soldiers, none too hopefully, to rejoin the corps in winter quarters. Then, with only Shelby's division and Clark's brigade (now commanded by Colton Greene) still beneath his colors, Price moved into the Choctaw Nation and made for Boggy Depot.

Forage and provisions were so scarce en route that Shelby's men were obliged to scatter and subsist themselves by hunting prairie dog, wild cattle, and game birds. The men who remained with the column acquired a taste for mule- and horseflesh. Not until the 13th did Price encounter a relief train dispatched by Maxey, a train consisting of exactly three wagons. On the 17th, Maxey reported to Kirby Smith that Price's "totally demoralized" men had been drifting into Boggy Depot "for four or five days, singly, in squads, and every way. . . . Their horses are miserably poor . . . and many are being abandoned on the prairies." At Boggy Depot, Price's famished troopers were finally able to gorge themselves upon beef, corn, meal, and flour imported from Texas, but their feasting was spoiled when smallpox began to ravage the command. On November 23, having evacuated the Nations, Price's corps drifted into Bonham; and on December 2, having turned eastward, the remainder of the expeditionary force—3,500 men, only one-third of whom were armed—reached the end of the trail at Laynesport, in the southwestern corner of Arkansas. "Men are greatly demoralized," observed one of the saddlesore survivors, "and we present a pitiable, forlorn aspect. God damn Old Price." [13]

On November 16, as firm intelligence concerning the condition of Price's army accumulated in Department and district headquarters, Magruder addressed a fulsome letter of praise and congratulations to Price, and then immediately wired Kirby Smith the news that Price's "totally demoralized" corps was dissolving. Ten days later, Magruder told Smith that Price's soldiers had lost half their firearms in Missouri, that many were still throwing away their weapons, and that a number of furloughed raiders had sold their guns to civilians. The brigades already sent home, he said, might not rendezvous later on, and a considerable number of deserters from Price's ranks had already enlisted in the Union army. On December 15, after reviewing the remnants of Price's command, Magruder expressed the fear that, unless arms and men were procured, "we cannot fight in this district next spring." And on the 20th, as if acknowledging that even the cavalry corps' staff structure had collapsed, Magruder complained that "I have been unable, notwithstanding every exertion on my part [,] to get returns" from the cavalry.

If Maxey and Magruder were appalled by the disintegration of Price's corps, Kirby Smith's reaction to the situation was curiously ambivalent. He seemed incapable of admitting the truth either to others or to himself. On November 16, he wrote to tell his mother that Price's "expedition has been a success, he had no expectation of wintering in Mo, but merely made a demonstration in favor of Mobile & our army in Georgia—He started with but 4,000 men [!] and compelled a concentration of near 50,000 to drive him from Mo—. . . Price brings considerable accession to our force." Had this evaluation of the raid been addressed only to Smith's mother, it could be written off merely as an attempt to keep her spirits up. But five days later Smith repeated in greater detail the same evaluation in a report to Jefferson Davis, in which he affirmed that "I consider General Price as having effected the objects for which he was ordered into Missouri and the expedition a success." As late as March 16, 1865, Smith still insisted, in a communication to the Adjutant General, that "the movement of General Price accomplished all the objects for which it was inaugurated by me."

And yet, even as he was painting cheerful pictures for his mother and his superiors, Smith found ways to express his displeasure. The usual congratulatory order, customarily addressed to the troops by the commanding general after the conclusion of any operation, was not published. On December 9, Smith ordered a large proportion (all but two or three brigades) of the cavalry to dismount and transfer to the infantry, an order which the troopers interpreted as a humiliation, even though headquarters insisted that the move was necessary in order to conserve forage. On the 13th, Smith announced Price's demotion to the command of Mosby Parsons' Missouri infantry division (a command which Price never exercised; first he was authorized to take leave of absence until March 7, 1865, and then he was excused to attend a court convened to inquire into the conduct of his raid). And on March 2, 1865, Governor Reynolds informed Senator Waldo Johnson that, as far as General Smith was concerned, General Price was "absolutely good for nothing."

Price's own evaluation of his raid defies analysis. He reported that he had marched 1,400 miles, had fought forty engagements, and had captured and paroled more than 3,000 prisoners. He had collected great quantities of military supplies, destroyed "miles and miles of railroad" and property worth $10,000,000, had lost no more than 1,000 men, and had brought with him "at least 5,000 new recruits. . . . Recruits flocked to our flag. . . . In some counties the question was not who should go into the army, but who should stay at home. I am satisfied that could I have remained in Missouri this winter the army would have been increased 50,000 men." He gave no hint of the massive defections from his ranks, and offered no explanation why only 3,500 troopers remained with him through to the end. He failed to report that the majority of the survivors were unarmed, or that most of the captured stores had been destroyed at the Marmaton River. While boasting that eighteen pieces of artillery had been added en route to the dozen brought from Arkansas, he neglected to note that only four cannon had been salvaged during the retreat. Nor did he remark upon the legacy of hate left behind by the plundering guerrillas who rode with him, or upon the fact that Governor Reynolds, once his strongest ally, had become an embittered enemy.

In December, 1864, Reynolds published an account of the recent raid in the *Texas Republican*. In 5,000 blistering words, he denounced Price's management of the campaign, and accused him of remaining in an intoxicated torpor throughout much of the expedition. He damned the "sneaks and deadheads" who had used the raid as an excuse to pillage Missouri, and exclaimed that "if the inhabitants still in Missouri are to believe that the generalship and discipline exhibited in the late campaign are the best our Confederacy can furnish, her fate is sealed, and the next Confederate army entering [Missouri's] borders will be met even by our own friends, as a band not of brothers, but of robbers." Price responded with "A Card" published in the same paper and addressed to "one Thomas C. Reynolds, who pretends to be, and styles himself, . . . the Governor of the State of Missouri." In it, Price pronounced the "violent and malignant attack upon myself" to be nothing but "a tissue of falsehoods." The very next day, Reynolds addressed a personal letter to Price, in which he threatened to expose both Price and his son Edwin as traitors to the Confederate States, unless "you cease to be an officer in the provisional army of those States. . . . I propose that if you will at once resign your commission in that army and your position of Missouri bank commissioner . . . and abstain hereafter from any interposition, directly or indirectly, in the military or political affairs of the Confederate States or the State of Missouri, that memoir will be sent as a paper to remain in the secret archives of the Government and not be used unless necessary to meet such an interposition."

The altercation simmered until March, when Price, returning from furlough, sought a court of inquiry to clear his name. The court met at Shreveport on April 21 and sat until May 3, during which time it accumulated a mass of evidence substantiating Reynolds' charges of ill discipline and wholesale plundering during Price's raid. Price, protesting that he "stands ready to vindicate his own acts, but does not propose to vindicate the conduct of every single officer and man who accompanied him on his campaign," then called the court's attention "to the second clause of the Article of War under which all courts of inquiry are authorized and instituted, which relates to the danger of courts of inquiry being perverted and used for the destruction of military merit," and requested the court to remove itself to a less hostile locality. On May 3, the court "adjourned to meet at Washington, Ark., on Monday, the 8th instant, at 12 m., or as soon thereafter as practicable." But since the Confederate States, under whose authority the court had been assembled, shortly ceased to exist, Price was never able to offer his rebuttal.

The two raids conducted by Price and Stand Watie marked the termination of serious campaigning along the Trans-Mississippi Department's northern front. Because of the debilitation of the Confederate forces in Arkansas and the Nations, and because of the Union high command's strategic decision to concentrate upon the destruction of the Cis-Mississippi Confederacy, the last five months of the war were to be the most peaceful in the Western Confederacy's brief history. When soldiers did fight, they "fought simply to afford statesmanship an opportunity to mitigate the sorrows of inevitable defeat." But like soldiers anywhere who see the end of war approaching, Kirby Smith's men displayed no eagerness for the fray, and proved increasingly reluctant, as time went on, to expose themselves to gunfire.

Even before Price's and Maxey's troopers went into winter quarters along the upper Red, the rest of Kirby Smith's disposable force had begun to disperse in search of provisions, forage, shelter, and security. Churchill's and Parsons' infantry divisions remained in bivouac in southern Arkansas, but by the middle of January Forney's division had retired to the neighborhood of Minden, Louisiana, Polignac's division had returned to the vicinity of Alexandria, and Wharton's cavalry division was again pasturing its horses in East Texas. Although nobody yet knew it, the veteran armies of the districts of West Louisiana and Arkansas would never again come together.

Through the winter season, Kirby Smith continued to dismount cavalry regiments, in order to "save the country from being consumed by the host of mounted men in the service." The single-minded determination with which Smith brushed aside objections and ruthlessly unhorsed his troopers suggests that he himself did not expect to assume the offensive again, since the need to maintain mounted forces in the Nations and Texas (where the distances between garrisons virtually pro-

hibited the employment of infantry) left the Department with insufficient cavalry to launch another sweep into Missouri. On the last day of
1864, Smith's command included 39,700 effectives, of whom 22,800
were horsemen. By March 7, 1865, the number of mounted men had
been reduced to 17,000, and 6,000 of these were already under orders
to transfer to the infantry. Regiments were still being dismounted in
May, when the Department struck its colors.[14]

And yet, at the beginning of December, 1864, Kirby Smith's Confederacy was still a cohesive military command, possessing relatively
stable frontiers and a substantial, well-organized army. Across the Mississippi, Petersburg and Richmond were under siege, Atlanta had
fallen, Sherman was burning his way toward Savannah, Mobile was
under attack, and the Union forces in Tennessee were making ready to
smash Hood's army before Nashville. Almost inevitably, it again occurred to the South's beleaguered authorities that Kirby Smith ought to
be able to spare a few brigades for service in the Cis-Mississippi.

In the first seven days of December, 1864, both Secretary of War
Seddon and General Pierre Beauregard (commanding the new Military
Division of the West, embracing Taylor's Department of Alabama, Mississippi, and East Louisiana and Hood's Department of Tennessee and
Georgia) urged Smith to renew his efforts to cross troops to the East.
Smith referred their requests to his senior generals and solicited their
advice. Buckner was of the opinion that the "utmost" that could be
done would be "to pass men in small squads, with the disorganization
and demoralization attendant upon such a proceeding," while Wharton
exclaimed that "a bird, if dressed in Confederate gray, would find it difficult to fly across the river." On January 6, 1865, Smith, "ardently de-
siring the transfer of this army to your aid," expressed to Beauregard
his deep regret that "I am powerless to assist you."

That answer did not satisfy Beauregard, who remained convinced
"that troops can be crossed to this side of the Mississippi River, even if
it be in canoes." Nor did it satisfy President Davis, who, on January 31,
wrote Smith to tell him that "you should endeavor, as promptly as possible, to cross that river with as large a force as may be prudently
withdrawn from your present department." But on February 28, Smith
replied to Davis that "communication by individuals is uncertain, dan-
gerous, and difficult in the extreme; by bodies it is impossible." Seven

days later, having learned that both Governor Allen and Governor Murrah were adamantly opposed to any scheme to strip troops from the West, Smith reaffirmed to Davis that any movement would be "physically difficult" and its "successful execution . . . uncertain," although he did offer to make the attempt in June or July if ordered to do so by the War Department. But on March 11, in still another letter to the President, Smith simply stated that "the Mississippi [is] an impassable barrier." [15]

IV Throughout 1864, conditions along the Department's sparsely settled western frontier continued to deteriorate, as roving regiments of jayhawkers, bushwhackers, recusant conscripts, deserters, and "blanket" Indians grew increasingly bold. As renegade whites and runaway Negroes crowded into the region, in sufficient strength to seize control of half a dozen counties, the local citizenry became more than ever reluctant to cooperate with the Texas and Confederate forces assigned to police the area. The Texas State troops deployed in the border country following the transfer of the Frontier Regiment to Confederate service themselves became progressively less dependable, as numerous companies were infiltrated by the very outlaws they were supposed to apprehend. Some loyal militiamen were so distressed by the deterioration of their units that, by June, they were volunteering for duty in the Confederate States army, advancing the argument that the hazards of an occasional battle were preferable to the constant danger of a bushwhacker's bullet in the back.

By the end of 1864, Henry McCulloch's regular command had been increased to 1,330 effectives, but even these were far too few to pacify the badlands. When, in the late summer, large Indian war parties began to penetrate McCulloch's defenses and raid through the settlements, the government of Texas declared the unorganized land of West Texas to be closed until the war's end, forbade anyone to traffic with the Indians or to travel into or through the Indian country, and advised the borderland's citizens to "fort up." "Forting up"—the "get[t]ing together & building blockhouses and stockades to live in," as a state militia General Order defined the tactic—was the last resort, involving as it did the abandonment of rangeland, stock herds, farms, crops, villages, and homes to the hostiles, but it now seemed to be the only way to "insure the safety of the women & children." Thousands of West Texans spent the remainder of the war huddled in rude stockades, surviving on skimpy rations and listening, night after night, for the turkey-gobble war calls of the painted savages.

Among the forts already in existence when the advice to "fort up" was issued was Fort Murrah, about twelve miles up the Brazos from Fort Belknap. Ten or twelve families had taken refuge in the fort, including "thirty-two men and boys . . . able to shoot, all told." On October 13, 1864, Francis M. Peveler, one of the inhabitants, was "at Belknap a-gittin' up some oxen and wagons to take to Fort Murrah and go to mill with." After noon, "my brother's nigger, old Seth, and I were on the way with the wagons" when Peveler "saw smoke rising . . . and it looked like signal smoke." The two made it back to the fort without incident and were eating dinner when "Lieutenant Carson from Gainesville came running in, said he had five or six of his men killed by Indians and that the country was alive with Indians." Peveler thought at first that Carson "was a tenderfoot and just scared," but then others arrived with the same news, "and we started after our horses to the north." But they were too late. "The Indians already had all the horses belonging to the fort," and could be seen raiding and burning the neighboring homesteads. Peveler "counted three hundred and seventy-five from the Fort with my spy glass. There must have been a thousand in all," mostly Kiowas and Comanches. "As I watched, their pack horses came in so fast that I could not count them. They even had their dogs along." The Indians surrounded the fort, but Peveler and another courier managed to slip through their lines and rally a militia company and sixty "cowboys & settlers," whom they then led back toward the stockade. The Indians, warned of the approach of reinforcements, raised their siege and disappeared before dawn.

The whites retaliated for this and similar raids at Dove Creek, on January 8, 1865. A column of pacific Kickapoos, with their squaws, children, and livestock, happened to be emigrating from Indian Territory to Mexico down the eastern edge of the Texas Panhandle. The Kickapoos were not in a fighting mood; they were trying, indeed, to escape all the wars about them, to avoid the blue longknives to the north, the gray longknives to the east, and the bloodthirsty braves to the west.

They had crossed the Brazos River and were pushing slowly south-westward beyond the limits of white settlement when their presence was reported to Major G. B. Erath, commanding the Second Frontier District of Texas State Troops. Erath dispatched Captain S. S. Totten's militia battalion and Captain Henry Fossett's company of the Forty-sixth Texas in pursuit. Reaching the Indian encampment on the morning of the 8th—a camp located fifty miles from the nearest white homestead—the Texans ignored the peaceful overtures made by the Kickapoos, charged their camp, opened fire, and murdered twenty-three unarmed men and women. The rest of the terrified Kickapoos fled for their lives, abandoning their casualties and their camp equipment. The Texas troopers scalped their victims, pillaged the encampment, and, with their horses loaded with booty, turned back toward civilization.

The Dove Creek massacre (along with the far more efficient Sand Creek massacre of November 29, 1864, in which 900 Federal volunteers wiped out several hundred Cheyenne and Arapaho men, women, and children) served to quiet most of the Plains Indians, at least for a time, and the subsequent descent of a bitterly cruel winter drove even those inclined to remain on the warpath back to the security of their hogans. In February, 1865, a large contingent of Texas State Brigadier J. W. Throckmorton's mounted militia made an extended three-week sweep through the fringes of the Indian country, but, except for a single skirmish with a small war party, the Texans encountered no serious opposition. In the weeks that followed, elements of Wharton's cavalry division, since redeployed to winter quarters and pastures near the frontier, contributed to the further pacification of much of the border country by reinforcing McCulloch's command. When, in May, the Confederate States units disbanded, the Texas frontier militia continued to police the region until relieved by detachments of the United States cavalry.[16]

During the spring and summer months of 1864, while the guerrilla warfare along the western frontier of Texas intensified, the state's Rio Grande border was liberated, reoccupied, and pacified by an irregular Confederate expeditionary force assembled for the task by John S. Ford. On December 22, 1863, General Magruder excused Ford from conscript duty, ordered him to raise a command at San Antonio, and directed him to drive the Federals from Brownsville and the lower Rio

Grande Valley. "You will be very particular," cautioned Magruder, "and will not let a soul know of your intended movements. By making a sudden and rapid movement, you may be able to create a panic among the enemy; and, if so, you will follow it up and gain every advantage you can." On Christmas Day, Ford accepted the assignment, announced that he could enlist at least 1,000 men "not subject to conscription," and affirmed that "there is no doubt of success. The results from an expulsion of the Yankees from the Rio Grande would be almost equal to those following the recapture of Galveston." By New Year's Day, Ford had established his headquarters at San Antonio. He had issued a proclamation urging draft exempts to volunteer to defend their homes against the "mongrel force of Abolitionists, negroes, plundering Mexicans, and perfidious renegades" threatening to conquer Texas, and was busily enlisting anyone who reported for duty with a horse and a gun.

Ford's command, as finally organized, consisted of one Confederate States regiment, two Confederate States battalions, and a Texas State battalion, but few of the men who filled its ranks were veteran Confederate or Texas soldiers. For the most part, Ford's "Cavalry of the West" was a conglomeration of raw militiamen, a few local vigilante companies, a large proportion of neighborhood irregulars, and a strong seasoning of bandits, bushwhackers, desperadoes, outlaws, soldiers of fortune, runaway conscripts, draft dodgers, old men, adolescent boys, mixblood Indians, and army deserters. One captain reported that "fifty-seven children," ranging in age from fifteen to seventeen, had joined his company, a report which caused a Houston newspaper editor to exult that "Old Abe will find that he has undertaken an almost endless task to exterminate the seed of the rebellion. As fast as he kills one rebel, a dozen spring from his ashes."

Ford's vigorous recruiting soon produced a brigade of 1,300 effectives, a command which, if not made up of the flower of Southern chivalry, at least contained a large number of hard and wiry gunslingers. But it proved far more difficult to collect the supplies, ordnance stores, cannon, ammunition, horse equipments, and other impedimenta needed to outfit the organization, and so it was not until March 17 that Ford's cavalry broke camp and began riding southward toward the Nueces River. Reaching San Fernando, due west of Corpus Christi, on the 24th, the rebels continued along the same course as far as Los Ojuelos, and then struck west toward Laredo, forty miles away. This last maneuver, which carried the Confederates away from rather than toward their objective, was made necessary because "the country between the Nueces and the Rio Grande . . . was terribly dry, almost impossible to procure water for the men, to say nothing of the horses." It was imperative that "the march toward Brownsville . . . be made by way of the Rio Grande, where a supply of water was at all times available." Since Laredo was the first point at which the Rio Grande could be intercepted, Ford accepted the detour for the sake of his men and mounts.

Yet Ford was under imperative orders from Magruder to "press forward with all your forces" as rapidly as possible, and so, after arriving at Laredo on April 17, he immediately turned his column southeastward along the Great River Road, the highway toward Brownsville. By May 3, his brigade had reached Ringgold Barracks, an abandoned "Old Army" post situated about one hundred miles upstream from Fort Brown. Here, Ford rested and refreshed his command, culled additional recruits from both sides of the river, continued to do his best to accumulate a sufficient store of supplies, and perfected the organization of his units. Once assembled, the Cavalry of the West consisted of Lieutenant Colonel Daniel Showalter's Fourth Arizona Cavalry Regiment, Lieutenant Colonel George H. Giddings' independent Texas Cavalry Battalion, Captain Refugio Benevides' battalion of the Thirty-third Texas Cavalry, and several companies of Texas State troopers—in all, some 1,500 mounted soldiers.

While recruits and stragglers drifted into Ringgold Barracks, Ford purchased "a goodly number" of small arms in Tamaulipas, directed the manufacture of paper cartridges and leather cartridge boxes, collected provisions, assembled pack mules and a wagon train, and studied information concerning Federal dispositions near Fort Brown. Confederate spies on both banks of the lower Rio Grande supplied accurate plans of the defensive emplacements protecting Freeport and Brownsville, and somehow managed to forward occasional copies of the Union army's official morning reports. However, not all of the intelligence Ford received was correct. In the middle of June, he was erroneously led to believe that most of the enemy troops had suddenly evacuated the Rio Grande delta, "leaving only a skeleton force to defend Fort Brown and Brownsville." At the time, this "skeleton force" still numbered over

2,750 effectives, deployed along the Rio Grande from the Federal beachhead at Brazos Santiago to a picket post at Las Rucias Ranch, twenty-four miles west of Fort Brown. The Union garrison was composed of eight regiments of infantry (including two Negro regiments, the Eighty-seventh and Ninety-fifth United States), seven companies of cavalry (including a battalion of the Federal First Texas), and enough cannoneers to serve twenty-eight guns.

Toward the end of June, still supposing that Brownsville was lightly defended, Ford set out with 400 cavalrymen to reconnoiter the Union perimeter. "The drought was very severe," he later recalled. "The Palo Alto prairie was entirely nude of grass. Outside the river road the route to Fort Brown was hardly practicable for a force of any size." From a number of Mexicans apprehended along the way, Ford learned that Las Rucias Ranch was picketed by Captain Philip Temple's two companies of the First Texas Cavalry (Union). The rebel commander promptly determined to attack and scatter these "renegades." On June 25, the Confederate Texans caught the Union Texans by surprise, killed or wounded thirty of them, and took thirty-six prisoners. "A good many escaped across the laguna, many of them wounded," Ford reported. "Some of them crossed the Rio Grande and secreted themselves in the cane. . . . Those wounded in the laguna were drowned. . . . Captain Temple left early." The Confederates also captured two wagons, twenty-eight horses, and a number of "badly needed" saddles and weapons.

After the skirmish at Las Rucias Ranch, Ford's command drove to a point just five miles from Brownsville and tried to attack the enemy's main body. But finding the Union force to be larger than anticipated, the rebels disengaged, doubled back to Edinburg, and picketed the Great River Road thirty miles above Fort Brown. "It seems to be Ford's intention," observed the Federal commander at Brownsville, "to keep us in as close quarters as possible, which he can do to a certain extent owing to our want of cavalry or horses to mount infantry."

Ford waited another three weeks before initiating his final offensive. During the interim, he purchased additional ordnance and quartermasters' stores from firms at Matamoros. The Juarista general controlling Tamaulipas, Cortina, "was known to be friendly to the Union men," acknowledged Ford, "yet he was not averse to allowing his friends to earn an honest penny by supplying the Confederates." Finally, on July 19, the Cavalry of the West broke camp and again started down the Great River Road toward Fort Brown. Sharp little engagements were fought with elements of the Union garrison at Ebonal Ranch on the 22d and at Dead Man's Hollow on the 25th; in both, the Federals' vedettes were scattered and their relief columns dispersed. By July 29, the Federals concluded that Brownsville was indefensible; declaring it to be an open city, they evacuated it and pulled back to Brazos Santiago. The following day, Ford's dusty troopers swung into Brownsville, accepted the town's formal surrender from Mayor E. W. Cave, received a new silk battle flag from a delegation of local ladies, and entertained the citizenry with patriotic speeches. Colonel Ford also enjoyed a reunion with his wife, who had been waiting for him in Matamoros since March. Then, exhausted and gravely ill, Ford retired to a sickbed for the better part of August.[17]

On August 22, Ford was roused by the news that an Imperial French expeditionary force had made an amphibious landing at Bagdad and was busily fortifying the Mexican side of the Rio Grande delta. Ford, who had just won assurances from General Cortina that the Juarista Republicans would not discourage the "pleasant and mutually advantageous" commercial intercourse prevailing between Matamoros and Brownsville, now sought similar assurances from the Imperial commander at Bagdad, Captain A. Veron of the French navy. After visiting Matamoros on the evening of the 22d to confer with F. W. Latham, the senior Confederate representative in Tamaulipas State, Ford dispatched two envoys to Bagdad with a letter addressed to Captain Veron. The commissioners were instructed to conclude an agreement with the French "by which our supplies can be passed over the Rio Grande." On August 25, Veron replied: "If the exigencies of war should take me to Matamoras [and he left little doubt that they would] you may rest assured that I shall see that all persons and property covered by the flag of your nation are duly respected. With regard to the facilities I might offer you in the transportation of supplies to your camp, you may be sure that I will bestow all my care upon this matter, and that you shall not suffer in anything on account of my presence here."

Veron's gratifying attitude elated Ford, but it infuriated Cortina. The Juarista general retaliated by encouraging his soldiers to snipe at

Confederate pickets. After August 31, the Confederates posted along
the riverbank sniped back. On September 3, Cortina interdicted trade
between Tamaulipas and Texas. By the 4th, rumors were afloat that
Cortina and Colonel H. M. Day, commanding the Union forces at Bra
zos Santiago, had agreed to mount a joint attack against Brownsville
And by the 5th, batteries of Juarista artillery had been planted on the
Mexican shore of the Rio Grande, with the guns' black muzzles point
ing toward Texas. Cortina "hates Americans, particularly Texians,"
Ford reported. "He has an old and deep-seated grudge against Browns
ville. . . . If he could cut his way through our lines, plunder our peo
ple, and get within the Yankee lines, it would be a finale he would de
light in."

The volatile situation existing along the border, threatening to
plunge four armies into a common conflagration, erupted into open
conflict on September 6. Under cover of a heavy rainfall, a body of
Juarista infantry and a battery opened fire on Colonel Showalter's
Fourth Arizona Cavalry, which was on picket at Palmito Ranch, half
way between Brownsville and Brazos Santiago. Evidently, Cortina
hoped that the affair at Palmito Ranch would draw the bulk of Ford's
brigade downriver, leaving Brownsville undefended and vulnerable to
attack. But unfortunately for both Cortina's plans and the Fourth Ari
zona's morale, Colonel Showalter, who Ford insisted was "as chivalrous
a man as ever drew a sword" when "not under the influence of liquor,"
had "recourse to the bottle" during the engagement and lost control of
his regiment. The Fourth Arizona broke and retreated to Brownsville
Showalter himself "came to town in a maudlin condition," but did man
age to report that, just before his command fled from Palmito Ranch,
strong Federal column from Brazos Santiago had been seen closing on
Fort Brown from the east. "We anticipated Cortina and the Federals
would be on us early the next day."

But the Federals advanced only as far as Palmito Ranch before en
camping. Cortina gathered his Republicans opposite Brownsville and
prepared to bombard the Confederate garrison. Again Cortina seemed
to hope that the Confederates, now distracted by the Federal column
would strip troops from Fort Brown's defenses in order to push a force
toward Palmito Ranch. Instead, Ford mustered and armed the town
inhabitants, retained most of his companies in place, and addressed

biting letter to Cortina asking whether a state of "war exists between your government and that of the Confederate States." He requested Captain Veron to hasten his conquest of Tamaulipas, and threw Colonel Giddings' detachment of 370 Texas troopers toward the Union bivouac. On the 9th, Giddings' cavalry scattered the Federals' pickets and drove their main body back to the mouth of the Rio Grande. Hearing news of the Federals' defeat, Cortina made no effort to press an attack against Brownsville.

By the third week of September, no Federal soldiers remained on the Texas mainland, and the Union contingent occupying Brazos Santiago had been reduced to a token 950-man garrison. The United States government reinstituted the naval blockade of the Rio Grande, but, recognizing the futility of attempting to close an international waterway, stationed only one vessel off the mouth of the river. The Confederates emplaced a forward vedette at Port Isabel, picketed Palmito Ranch, and ignored Colonel Day's tiny army of occupation during the remaining eight months of the war. Meanwhile, on September 29, Veron's expeditionary force seized Matamoros and chased Cortina into the interior of Mexico, thereby gaining control of Tamaulipas State and ensuring the reestablishment of amicable relations along the length of the lower Rio Grande frontier. Since neither the Imperialists' control of Tamaulipas nor the Confederates' control of Texas was again challenged during the remaining months of the American Civil War, relations along the border continued to be amicable, and trade across the river flourished, until May, 1865. In fact, border patrol duty soon proved to be such a peaceable occupation that General James Slaughter, who assumed command at Fort Brown during the autumn of 1864, found it possible to transfer or furlough two-thirds of Ford's brigade. By the beginning of 1865, only Giddings' battalion and a few odd detachments of Ford's other units were still standing guard in the vicinity of Brownsville.[18]

Yet the suspension of hostilities along the Texas Rio Grande frontier gave the Confederates little reason to rejoice, for the quiet which descended upon the border country was the silence of a deathwatch. Instead of marking a revival in the South's sagging fortunes, the pacific state of coexistence near the mouth of the Rio Grande during the last few months of the Civil War was symptomatic of the Confederacy's imminent demise. In Colonel Ford's words, both the soldiers at Brazos

Santiago and those at Brownsville simply agreed "that if the contending parties met and slaughtered each other it would have no effect on the final result of the contest," and so they just stopped fighting.

As early as January 14, 1865, General Lew Wallace, commanding the Union army's Middle Department (West Virginia, Pennsylvania, and Maryland), advised General Grant of intelligence indicating that "the rebel soldiery in Western Texas, particularly those at Brownsville," were ready to abandon the Confederate cause. Wallace was so sure of the reliability of his information—it had come from a Texan schoolmate—that he requested a leave of absence in order to visit Brazos Santiago and, "upon my own authority, invite the commandant at Brownsville to an interview. . . . If the man's a soldier, I'll wager you a month's pay that I win." Grant assented, authorizing Wallace to journey to the Texas coast. On March 11, after a few days of preliminary negotiations, Wallace, Slaughter, and Ford met under a flag of truce at Port Isabel. "Very early in the interview," Wallace concluded "that both General Slaughter and Colonel Ford were not only willing but anxious to find some ground upon which they could honorably get from under what they admitted to be a failing Confederacy." Without much argument, the three officers drafted a cartel stating terms for the capitulation "of the Trans-Mississippi States and Territories" and for "the re-establishment of the authority of the United States Government over all the region above designated."

As soon as the conference adjourned, Slaughter dispatched a copy of the cartel to General John Walker, and requested Walker to forward it to Shreveport. But Walker was not yet prepared to surrender. Telling Slaughter of his "regret that you should have consented to entertain, or rather receive, the proposals . . . made," since to accede "to them would be the blackest treason to the Confederacy," Walker addressed an angry reply to Wallace. The memory of anyone who could accept such terms would be rendered "infamous for all future time. Stripped of all disguise," said Walker,

> your proposition is nothing less than that we of the Trans-Mississippi States are to lay down our arms, surrender at discretion, take an oath of allegiance to the United States Government, and in return to accept such terms of amnesty, pardon, or foreign exile as our conquerors shall graciously accord us. When the States [of the] Trans-Mississippi united their destiny with the

Confederacy of Southern States we pledged ourselves to share their good and evil fortune; and . . . it is still our unalterable purpose to share the common danger and the common fate. . . . It would be folly in me to pretend that we are not tired of a war that has sown sorrow and desolation broadcast over our land; but we will accept no other than an honorable peace. With 300,000 men yet in the field, we would be the most abject of mankind if we should now basely yield all that we have been fighting for during the last four years, namely nationality and the rights of self-government. With the blessing of God, we will yet achieve these, and extort from your own Government all that we ask.

Walker's bravado stayed the execution of the Trans-Mississippi South for an additional two months, but nothing could commute the Confederacy's impending doom. Ironically, nobody was more aware of the South's condition than Walker's superior, Kirby Smith. Had Slaughter's cartel been delivered to Shreveport, it seems possible that Smith might have responded more affirmatively than Walker. For as early as January 7—a week before Wallace wrote to Grant, and two months before the meeting at Port Isabel—Smith's façade of serene confidence had begun to crack. On that day, he admitted to his mother that "the bad news from the cis-Mississippi has cast a gloom over all, the defeat of Hood [at Nashville] and the triumphal march of Sherman [to Savannah] are events significant of greater misfortune in the coming spring campaign. . . . God in his mercy & wisdom is chastizing us with the heavy hand of misfortune." That Smith's depression was not a passing mood became evident two days later, when he granted General Polignac six months' leave, directed Polignac to sail to France, and charged him to deliver a desperate appeal to John Slidell. "Our cause has reached a crisis, which calls for foreign intervention," Smith wrote. "It cannot be too strongly emphasized upon the Emperor of the French, that the security of his Empire in Mexico, and the interests of his own government, all demand immediate interference to restore peace, and establish firmly the nationality of the Confederate States." In order to reassure Napoleon about an alliance with a republic fighting for the perpetuation of slavery, Smith went so far as to assert "that in the Great slave districts of this department, nineteen twentieths of the planters would at this time, willingly accept any system of gradual emancipation, to insure our independence as a people." [19]

Perhaps it was in composing his letter to Slidell that Smith first toyed with the notion of seeking refuge in Mexico. Or perhaps, in his state, he needed no special incentive to think of flight across the border (Even in distant Richmond, the head of the Ordnance Bureau revealed to his diary, on January 18, that he and his wife had talked "of going to Mexico to live out there the remnant of our days.") But by January 30 even the *New York Herald* had heard rumors that Kirby Smith was planning to quit the Confederacy and bolt to Mexico. According to a dispatch from the paper's correspondent at St. Louis,

Some weeks since the Provost Marshal General of this department [of Missouri] suspected, from a variety of hints, insinuations and innuendoes, that the rebel General E. Kirby Smith has been negotiating with the Emperor Maximilian for transferring nearly the whole of the rebel army west of the Mississippi river to Mexico, to fight for the French. The same story is now current among the prominent secessionists of this city, and is founded on private communications received regularly from the Trans-Mississippi Department of rebeldom. . . . The rule now adopted is this—"Every man for himself, and the devil take the hindmost." . . . The only discount on the whole story is the ability of this rebel general to control his army.

That the *Herald*'s story had some basis in fact was confirmed two days later by Edmund Kirby Smith himself. Having heard that one of Shreveport's leading citizens, Robert Rose, was planning to cross the Rio Grande on private business, Smith availed himself "of so favorable an opportunity through you of expressing to the authorites of the Imperial Government the deep interest that I take in all that concerns the prosperity & welfare of their people," and asked Rose to "assure them of my ardent desire to cultivate & extend still further, the amicable relations already existing & which I trust will continue to exist, between two coterminous nations, having like aims & pursuits, & perhaps the same great & glorious destiny." Along with this relatively innocuous note, Smith enclosed a second letter, also addressed to Rose and bearing the same date:

Whilst in the City of Mexico, I desire you, on some fitting occasion to make known to His Majesty, the Emperor, that in the case of unexampled catastrophe to our arms & the final overthrow of the Govt. which I have the honor to represent as the Military Chief of the States West of the Miss River—an event I do not now apprehend, but which may possibly occur in the future, it is my fixed purpose to leave my native land & seek asylum in Mexico. Bred to the profession of arms, having such education in my profession as the best military schools in the United States offer, with the bene-fit of foreign travel, & some experience such as is acquired by the command of armies actually engaged in the field for more than two years, it is my de-sire still to continue in the exercise of the profession of my choice—Having some knowledge of the French & Spanish languages & having been on duty at one period on the Mexican Frontier, my humble services & such influence as I could exert might be rendered available to his Majesty's Government —I therefore authorize you to tender them to him in the possibility of the contingency above alluded to.[20]

CHAPTER NINE

THE COLLAPSE OF THE
TRANS-MISSISSIPPI, 1865

As soon as the white folds of the Confederacy's national flag were again flying above Brownsville, the town's streets were churned to dust beneath the wheels of hundreds of cotton wagons. The river settlements farther upstream suffered a permanent decline, but Brownsville and Matamoros enjoyed their last and greatest wartime surge of flourishing prosperity. Visiting Matamoros toward the end of August, 1864, Colonel Ford found it to be "a city of strange denizens, a motley crowd. There were millions of dollars of merchandise in the place. Every room, every niche capable of being occupied and of holding a man was rented at a large price. Never was a place of the same size crowded with more people, and made a display of more goods." At the same time, the United States consul at Matamoros was complaining to his government that "large quantities of merchandise now cross the river daily for the interior of Texas, [the rebels] having taken advantage of the absence of our troops." During the months of October and November, more than 600,000 pounds of ordnance stores passed from Matamoros to Brownsville and on to San Antonio. By Christmas Eve, San Antonio was experiencing such a boom that specie had again become the common medium of exchange in the markets near Alamo Plaza, and the local *Herald* was able to devote seven of its fourteen columns to advertisements announcing auctions of consumer goods.

The revival of commerce across the Rio Grande happened to coin-

cide with a simultaneous sharp increase in the number and tonnage of
vessels running the Galveston blockade. Until the fourth summer of the
war, most of the seagoing steamers engaged in the intercourse with the
South had been content to run from Nassau or Havana to the Atlantic
and Cis-Mississippi Gulf ports of the Confederacy, leaving the peripheral Texas trade to the swarms of smaller sailing ships and schooners
which coasted to Galveston or Sabine City from Mexico or Honduras.
But by August, 1864, Wilmington, Charleston, Mobile, and the other
major harbors of the eastern Confederacy were tightly blockaded or
under close siege, and hence the masters of steamships staging from
Cuba and the Bahamas began looking for alternative routes and a more
inviting rebel port. At first, the steamers were hesitant to attempt the
long passage to Galveston, fearing that the coal needed for such a journey would preclude the transportation of profitable cargoes, but as the
South's other deep-water harbors were choked off, the runners were left
without another choice. In late August and early September, three
heavy steamers, the *Denbigh, Susana,* and *Francis Marion,* slipped away
from Havana and made for Galveston. When in mid-September all three
returned safely to Cuba, their masters announced that the western Confederacy was full of surplus cotton, that the western Confederates were
willing to pay ten prices for any military stores the ships could deliver,
and that the blockade of the Texas coast still amounted to little more
than the token display of a Union naval presence. Within days, six more
steamers were en route to Galveston; within weeks, the fleet of iron
steamers running from Nassau shifted its base of operations to Havana;
and by the end of 1864, scores of steamers were heading toward Galveston from Havana, Tampico, Vera Cruz, and Belize. The *Denbigh*
made the passage from Havana to Galveston so often and so regularly
that she soon earned the nickname "The Packet."

Although no comprehensive estimate of the magnitude and value
of this trade can be made, a sampling of surviving cargo manifests, bills
of lading, and other shipping documents can suggest something of the
volume, variety, and types of goods carried to Galveston by the steamers. Between November, 1864, and April, 1865, the manufactures trans-
shipped at Havana on consignment to the Trans-Mississippi Department
included, among many other items, 5,000 long Enfield rifles with bayonets, 5,000 cavalry carbines, 2,500 lots of cavalry accouterments, four

sets of horse artillery harness, 20,000 pounds of cannon gunpowder, 10,000 pounds of rifle gunpowder, 198 reams of the "Best Ammunition Paper," 120 bales of blankets, 117 uniform jackets, 148 cases of army shoes, 14 bales of gray wool shirts, 5,350 pairs of "trowsers," 100 pounds of "Blue Pills," 100 pounds of camphor, 75 pounds of potassium iodide, 25 pounds of powdered opium, seven cases of letterhead stationery, one two-foot desk ruler (worth three pence), four pairs of No. 2 pliers (at one shilling each), and one six-gun battery of rifled breech-loading cannon. Most of the imports were purchased by the Cotton Bureau, which expended £57,375.14.10 worth of cotton for the cargoes shipped aboard the ten vessels whose manifests survive, but the battery of cannon was bought by the governor of Texas and the commanding officer of the Galveston garrison, who raised the $6,000 needed by soliciting donations from the citizens of Houston.

In addition to the imports shipped through Brownsville and Galveston, Kirby Smith's Confederacy continued to procure manufactures from a variety of other sources. Some armaments still trickled through the Federals' Mississippi River blockade; in the middle of October, 1864, for example, "several thousand stand of arms were successfully landed" near the mouth of the Arkansas River and spirited safely to Monticello. Other stores were purchased from vendors beyond the Union lines; now not only the Cotton Bureau but also the State of Louisiana's Military Board was engaged in the shadowy business of exchanging cotton for consignments of contraband. And, finally, the Confederates continued to make prize of stray Federal cargo vessels which happened to run aground along the Texas coast. In the summer and autumn of 1864, Commodore Leon Smith, the head of Kirby Smith's Naval Bureau, supervised the seizure and salvage of three Northern steamers, the *Ark, Ike Davis,* and *Sonora,* which were stranded in the shallows near the mouth of the Rio Grande.[1]

But despite the increasing ease with which the Trans-Mississippi Department managed to import goods during the last year of the war, the Confederate Southwest continued to depend, in great measure, upon the output of its domestic industries to arm, equip, clothe, and sustain its armies and its people. By this time, the ordnance works at Little Rock, Arkadelphia, and Camden had either been abandoned or dismantled, but General Benjamin Huger's Ordnance Bureau still operated or supervised plants for the manufacture and repair of small arms, laboratories for the production of ammunition, foundries, powder mills, and ancillary shops at Shreveport, Marshall, Tyler, Houston, Austin, and San Antonio. The Department's military transportation system benefited from the establishment, at Jefferson, of a factory capable of manufacturing 190 wagons, six ambulances, 900 sets of harness, and 360 saddles per month, and from the foundation, in the same neighborhood, of a complex of garages for the repair of damaged vehicles. A mill for drawing copper telegraph wire was opened at Shreveport, and a plant for the manufacture of "P. Corsin's Superior Southern Matches" was placed into production at Natchitoches. Thomas G. Clemson's Niter and Mining Bureau developed and exploited numerous mines, ore refineries, and smelting furnaces in and about East Texas, and never encountered any serious impediment to the production of adequate stores of lead, niter, saltpeter, and sulphur. But, as always, iron and copper remained scarce. Not even the frequent publication of appeals for the donation of metalware, nor the cannibalization of twenty miles of the Texas and New Orleans' iron rails, did much to relieve these shortages.

After the beginning of 1864, the most successful of all the industries in Kirby Smith's Confederacy were those overseen by the Clothing Bureau, which, under the able and efficient administration of Major W. H. Haynes, actually managed to satisfy many of the army's most pressing demands. Using cloth woven at Huntsville, at a new military mill near Tyler, or at one or another of the privately owned factories in East Texas, the Clothing Bureau's many plants, at Washington, Shreveport, Jefferson, Tyler, Houston, and Austin, made thousands of hats, shirts, jeans, blankets, tents, and other textile products each month, while the bureau's shoe factories, located in the same towns, reported a monthly output of 10,000 pairs of army footwear. Haynes's various enterprises were so successful that, when it came time for the South to surrender, Kirby Smith's soldiers were probably the best-dressed troops in the Confederate army. Their uniforms were seldom uniform, but, in general, their clothing was at least sufficient to keep them decent and warm. In late September, 1864, for instance, one of the ordinary infantrymen camped near Monticello was able to tell his wife:

You need not send me any socks. I got two excellent pairs from [G. B. Lyon, a messmate]—he wanted to give them to me but I would make him take pay—I have enough clothes to last me through the winter & can always get them cheaper here than they can be bought at home.—My wardrobe consists of 3 pairs of pants a 4th not made up—1 new home made shirt 1 new calico shirt 1 new white shirt linen . . . & 1 old white shirt (the one Capt. Thompson gave me which will last a long time yet—) 2 pairs of drawers—3½ pairs of socks—4 neck ties—2 woolen over shirts—one uniform coat—my old over coat & one elastic waterproof overcoat—1 pair shoes & one pair boots—The uniform coat I wrote to you about some time ago was too small & I have bought another one from my friend D. Head , . . so you see I am well fixed.

Yet neither trade, nor smuggling, nor industry, alone or in concert, enabled the Trans-Mississippi's supply officers "to treat every soldier , . . as 'some one's absent darling.'" Despite Major Haynes's best efforts, many soldiers continued to wear rough homespun, and some companies still depended upon shipments of clothing parcels from their home districts. And despite the attempts of the Ordnance and Cotton bureaus to arm every man, thousands of soldiers continued to carry empty cartridge boxes or to drill without serviceable firearms. Weapons were so scarce and so precious that, in December, 1864, Shreveport published a schedule of exorbitant fines to be levied against soldiers who lost or damaged theirs: a private who misplaced a musket, a rifle, or a carbine was to be dunned $200, while a trooper who lost a revolver might have $500 deducted from his pay. A few weeks later, there was "an order issued from Dep't H'd Qr's, to furlough any man for 20 days at home, who shall furnish a good army gun, not now in the service." Evidently, thousands of men took advantage of the "Gun Furlough" to earn a vacation from the war; one cavalry company, mustering 120 men, granted leave to forty-eight troopers who volunteered to hunt for firearms. In time, some returned to the ranks with new rifles slung across their saddles, but others never came back.[2]

If the procurement of textile goods, manufactures, and military hardware continued to pose problems, so too did the provision of foodstuffs and animals. Some of the Department's agricultural districts were, by now, utterly destitute. In January, 1865, while reporting the results of a minor fourteen-day raid through northeastern Louisiana and southeastern Arkansas, a Union cavalry colonel remarked: "No squad of men, much less an army, can live anywhere we have been. The people have neither seed, corn, nor bread, or the mills to grind the corn in if they had it. . . . [I] cannot imagine that one company of cavalry can obtain subsistence . . . in the whole country." At almost the same time, one of Wharton's sergeants complained in his diary that even the pastureland in East Texas was just about "played out," and went on to grumble that he and the men of his company were "getting a little ravenous." Soldiers in bivouac near Alexandria referred to their camp ground as "Starvation Hollow," while the horsemen stationed in Bell County, Texas, relieved their hunger by sacking neighborhood farms and robbing the general stores in Salado and Belton. The devastation wrought by invading armies, the deserts created by the Texas drought, the common scarcity of farm laborers, and the reluctance of farmers to plant crops which might be expropriated by press gangs—all reduced the acreage under cultivation and the Southwest's crop yields.

And yet, even though the produce harvests of 1864 and 1865 were the smallest of the war years (and the cotton crop of 1865 was a complete failure), yields were sufficient to feed the army and the people of the Trans-Mississippi. Inspectors dispatched into the countryside by the commissariat affirmed that grain, garden produce, swine, and fowl were less abundant than in the past, but were nevertheless adequate to meet the demand. In August, 1864, one of the soldiers at Starvation Hollow acknowledged that fruits and melons were plentiful enough in the immediate vicinity to subsist his regiment ("and in consequence," he punned, "I was never meloncholly"), while, in December, Judge Thomas Manning wrote from Alexandria to tell ex-Governor Moore that "this country is not as bad off as I supposed. Turkeys, eggs, etc., were abundant. A few days ago I dined at a friend's house with Commodore Semmes and a large party. The table groaned with a profusion of good things, and I am ashamed to say I ate until I made myself sick."

The real problem, as in the past, was not one of production but rather one of distribution. Even though most East Texas farmers continued to enjoy relatively respectable harvests, the Trans-Mississippi's domestic transportation systems were incapable of carrying enough grain, produce, and other bulk goods from the farms of East Texas to the armies and civilian markets in Arkansas, Louisiana, West Texas, and the Nations. The Red River was the only major navigable waterway in the Southwest still under Confederate control. A few decrepit steamers plied the Texas streams, but, because of the orientation of those rivers, the boats could contribute little to the movement of cargoes from the interior to the fringes of the Department. And the Texas railroad network was on the verge of disintegration. As a newspaper correspondent reported a few months after the termination of hostilities:

There is nothing in the State of Texas so sadly out of joint, out of repair, out of time, out of efficient officers, and as we are led to believe, out of money, as our Rail-roads. A trip on one of them, is like riding in an ox-wagon over hog-wallow prairie. A discreet person never thinks of taking passage on a Texas Rail-road without first getting his life insured, saying his prayers, and then writing to some friendly freighter, to meet him half-way along the track, and transport him to the depot.

Consequently, wagon convoys remained the chief means for conveying provisions from one region to another. But by the fourth year of the war, even Kirby Smithdom's crude road transport was breaking down. Neither the wholesale impressment of wagons, nor the army's fabrication and maintenance facilities at Jefferson, produced enough military vehicles to replace those lost, destroyed, or worn beyond repair; while the army consumed so many wagons that far too few were left for the conduct of normal civilian commerce.

One significant factor in the deterioration of the Trans-Mississippi's overland transportation was the progressive debilitation of the army's draft animals. By August, 1864, many complaints regarding the way in which impressed teams were worked beyond endurance were being voiced in the newspapers, and by November even the Quartermaster Bureau's inspectors acknowledged that almost all of the Department's military train animals were in very poor condition. Too many agencies competed for the services of too few teams, and, because of the shortage of serviceable animals, the competition was ruthless. The quartermasters, the commissaries, the Ordnance and Cotton bureaus, the artillery, the engineers, and the several state military boards all consumed draft animals, and drove those which they managed to procure to death.

So, too, did the cavalry, even though saddle horses were preferred as remounts for the troopers. Despite Congress' occasional consideration of bills to authorize quartermasters to issue government-owned remounts, the Confederacy continued to oblige dismounted cavalrymen to purchase their own replacement animals. Furthermore, troopers were not reimbursed for animals which died in service unless the animals were killed in battle, and even then they were paid only the depreciated value of their mounts. The cost of a remount came from a trooper's pocket; and by 1864, because of the wild inflation of the South's currency and the rare visits of army paymasters, impecunious Johnnies often had to settle for tired dray horses or broken-down mules. After June 10, 1864, when Kirby Smith's headquarters threatened to transfer to the infantry any pedestrian cavalryman who was unable to remount himself within forty days, the troopers proved more eager than ever to beg, borrow, steal, and ride any animal which promised to be sturdy enough to bear their weight. By January, 1865, some cavalrymen needed replacement animals so desperately that they began to auction their furloughs to cannoneers or teamsters who had animals to spare. One reason for the wholesale conversion of cavalry regiments into infantry units after December, 1864, was the endemic shortage of usable draft animals which plagued the Department. The mounts abandoned by the disgruntled horse soldiers were generally reassigned to the field artillery or to one or another supply organization.

Although the Trans-Mississippi never suffered from a real scarcity of meat animals, especially after the interdiction of trade to the Cis-Mississippi closed off many of the West's best cattle markets, nonetheless the soldiers stationed on the fringes of the Department and the civilians in the outlying towns often received less than their fair ration. The loss of the military stockyard at New Iberia and the destruction of the extensive meatpacking plant at Alexandria during the spring of 1864 forced the concentration of processing and packing facilities in the secure interior of the Department. Under the supervision of Major William Thomas' Subsistence Bureau, butchering plants were established in Texas at Jefferson, Tyler, and Bonham, and in the Confederate slice of Arkansas at Fulton. But since these facilities were some distance removed from the Southwest's major markets, beeves and swine could no longer be herded directly to the consumers. Instead, processed meat now had to be freighted overland, under circumstances which permitted only the most primitive precautions to be taken to prevent spoilage or contamination. As early as January, 1864, much of the meat received by the line troops along the Department's eastern and northern fronts was barely edible, and, as time went on, the meat rations became even less palatable.

The Texas drought complicated the problem of meat supply by decimating cattle herds. During 1864, hundreds of thousands of range cattle, including many of the beeves pastured in the vicinity of the East Texas packing plants, died for want of forage and water. By November, 1864, the Texas legislature had become so apprehensive concerning the loss of stock that it passed a joint resolution calling upon the Confederate authorities to prohibit the exportation of cattle to Mexico and to limit severely the impressment of beeves by the military. One month later, the ranchers of West Texas proposed to meet in convention at San Antonio to divise means for resisting the expropriation of their herds by the army. The military commissariat responded by resorting to large-scale rustling; during the early months of 1865, detachments detailed to hunt beef cattle increasingly ignored both the spirit and the letter of the impressment laws by driving herds off to the processing pens without issuing vouchers or settling accounts with the beeves' owners. By May, 1865, newspaper editorials had begun to appeal to the state legislature to enact stringent laws against the abuse of cattle impressment. But before such laws could be passed, and before the specter of a meat famine could become a reality, the Confederacy collapsed, ending impressment, releasing the manpower needed to tend the care for the herds, and clearing the way for the revival of the commercial cattle industry.[3]

By the spring of 1864, numerous factors—the despoliation caused by enemy invaders, the activities of speculators, the demands of legitimate trade, the competition between Confederate and state supply agencies, the voluntary reduction of acreage devoted to the cultivation of commercial staples, the Texas drought, and the scarcity of transportation—had all conspired to reduce severely the stocks of cotton available to pay the Trans-Mississippi Department's debts. In late March, 1864, for the first time, the Texas Cotton Office defaulted on a major contract. Despite the personal intervention of both Kirby Smith and Judge Peter Gray, the Department's Treasury Agent, the business firm involved—Bouldin, Riggs, and Walker—was short-changed to the tune of 6,000 bales. In an exhaustive exchange of correspondence with

D. W. Bouldin, one of the company's directors, Kirby Smith often affirmed that the Cotton Bureau would "act with justice" and settle the firm's claims with "the strictest justice and impartiality," but by August 24 he was forced to admit that "the Cotton Texas Office [*sic*] has repeatedly declared and reported their inability to acquire cotton sufficient to meet the liabilities of the Govt." The imposition of strict regulations governing the cotton trade, the settlement of the dispute between the Texas and Confederate authorities concerning the expropriation of cotton by the army, the military's subsequent resort to wholesale impressment, and the gradual integration of the Cotton Bureau into the structure of Judge Gray's Treasury Agency (a process which was begun in October, but which was not completed until February, 1865)—all served to ease the crisis and to make the conduct of the cotton business considerably more efficient.

But no degree of efficiency could negate the fact that the Department's dwindling cotton reserves were inadequate to satisfy the increasing demands placed upon them. Ironically, the pacification of the Rio Grande frontier, the intensification of blockade-running, and the consequent expansion of trade occurred at the very time that the Southwest's cotton crops were most constricted. No amount of impressment could materialize bales which did not exist. Once the Cotton Bureau's accounts were in arrears, the deficit persisted and grew. On May 27, 1865, the day after the formal capitulation of the bulk of the Trans-Mississippi's military forces, King and Company, of Houston, appealed to Kirby Smith to turn his attention "to the repayment of the large advances made" by the firm to the Cotton Bureau's agents in Matamoros, advances made "without any adequate security." Two days later, in one of his last official acts, Smith scrawled the draft of a special order addressed to the quartermaster at Brownsville, authorizing him to disburse $150,000 in Confederate funds "in part payment for advances made by Messrs. King & Co." But the order was never promulgated.

During the last year of the war, the Trans-Mississippi's fiscal distress was further exacerbated by the Currency Act of February 17, 1864. The West was already short of negotiable currency, and that which was in circulation was already badly depreciated. When Kirby Smith's headquarters announced, in the third week of April, that the "old-issue" paper money then in use was shortly to be taxed out of existence, and that two "new-issue" notes would replace three of the old, the result was a financial panic. "Prices immediately 'leaped up,' " complained the Clarksville *Standard*. "Everything has an upward tendency. Yesterday [April 20], whiskey, which had been selling ten days ago for $90 per gallon, could not be bought for $120. Brown sugar $12.50 cents per pound, by the hogshead, and none offering." The *Washington Telegraph* closed its subscription lists for three weeks, and then announced that it would offer a six-month subscription in exchange for $10 worth of state treasury warrants or Confederate singles and twos; larger Confederate bills were to be discounted at least by one-third. The most ordinary transactions were thrown into turmoil. "Whenever you draw on me," wrote a citizen of San Antonio to his soldier son, "please remember to say if Confederate money, new or old issue. The old issue is twenty-five to one [specie] here now and going out of circulation. . . . Specie is asked for goods now in every store and it is rather hard times for people who haven't old clothes aplenty as we have." At least the stores in the depot town of San Antonio remained open. Elsewhere, the panic forced many merchants to suspend operations. In Clarksville, "Some dealers have absolutely shut up, and refused to do business at all, preferring to hold on to the goods, rather than to receive anything in the shape of money larger than a five dollar bill." According to the editor of the *Standard*, "All this is but the result of the sudden panic, into which the country has been thrown by the unexpected repudiation of a portion of the currency."

It was the *Standard*'s opinion that the panic was "the mere influx of the tide, and its reflux will reduce prices. . . . It seems to be generally conceded, by all parties, that prices will fall, the currency appreciate and everything get better" once new bills replaced the old. Had new-issue notes been on hand, ready for circulation, this might have happened, but the old notes began to have their value taxed away before any shipments of new paper money were received in the states west of the Mississippi. Thus instead of relieving inflation in the Trans-Mississippi, the South's monetary reform accelerated it. Remarking that "all communication between this point and Richmond is now attended with great hazard," Kirby Smith implored the Secretary of the Treasury to "make some arrangement to supply this Department regularly with the necessary funds," and, as an interim measure, asked that his Treas-

ury Agency be given authority to overstamp and reissue the old notes
withdrawn from circulation. When, in the late fall, it became apparent
that neither an adequate supply of new currency nor the requested permission would soon arrive, Smith and Judge Gray proceeded to reissue
the old bills anyway, in the hope that merchants and citizens would accept the overstamped paper as the equivalent of the Confederacy's legal
tender.

The army, in particular, was driven to all sorts of expedients in its
attempts to keep its men supplied and its books balanced. The ruthless
expropriation of cotton, cattle, transportation, and other property,
which flourished after the spring of 1864, was but one sign of the
army's financial dilemma. In the District of Texas, General Walker,
arguing that justice, equity, and necessity all demanded that his officers
and their families be supported at government expense, authorized his
officers to draw food and clothing from commissary and quartermasters'
stores. When, in October, Kirby Smith protested that commissioned officers were expected to pay for their own subsistence, Walker pointed
out that a captain's monthly salary would purchase no more than fifty
pounds of flour or three bushels of corn meal, while two-thirds of a
brigadier's income was required to rent a bedroom in a Houston board-
inghouse.

In all probability, neither Walker's hypothetical captain nor his
imaginary brigadier had received any pay for more than a year, since,
with the exception of a few regiments in West Louisiana, none of the
units in the army had been visited by a paymaster since August, 1863.
In May, 1864, in consequence of the passage of the Currency Act,
Kirby Smith, Chief Quartermaster L. W. O'Bannon, and Chief Paymaster C. E. Carr agreed to conserve funds, to reduce the circulation of un-
redeemed old-issue notes, and to excuse the troops from having to accept obsolete currency by suspending even the theoretical disbursement
of military pay. At first, the several district paymasters reported that the
men seemed convinced of "the propriety of postponing their payment"
and "well satisfied to wait for the new issue," but the ordinary soldiers'
satisfaction with the new policy did not last long. At the end of June, a
line officer, whose pay was already $700 in arrears, complained bitterly
of having to expend $20 a day for lodgings in an old icehouse; and he
was but one of thousands in similar straits.

The soldiers' frustration simmered until October, when it was rumored that the first consignment of new-issue notes, $4,000,000 in currency, had been received by the Treasury Agency at Marshall. Then the men demanded pay. On October 17, Magruder reported that many of his Arkansas infantry regiments were becoming "dangerously restive," and four days later Kirby Smith, expressing grave concern about the army's morale and emphasizing the imperative need to make some token payment to the dispirited men, urged Judge Gray to release half of the Treasury Agency's crisp new funds to the military paymasters. Gray complied, and at musters held throughout the Department toward the end of November, a fair proportion of Kirby Smith's troops were "paid off to the 31st Dec 1863." But countless other soldiers missed muster, or belonged to regiments which the paymasters overlooked. On December 13, many a rebel was still complaining that "we have not been paid off for sixteen months."

A few of the Trans-Mississippi's citizens, those fortunate enough to reside in the Southwest's pockets of affluence, were not severely discomfited by the shortage of paper money. In August, 1864, a West Texas housewife wrote: "The streets of San Antonio are always crowded, the stores full of goods, and plenty of melons and peaches for sale on the plaza. The place is actually flourishing and silver abounds." But even she knew that San Antonio was an economic anomaly. "Strangers from the east who visit here," she acknowledged, "tell us we know nothing of the war." Elsewhere, the Department's economy was falling apart. By Christmas, the army owed more than $40,000,000 to citizens from whom goods had been purchased or impressed, most producers and merchants would no longer accept the vouchers and certificates offered by press gangs, and, since the laws governing impressment required payment for the property seized, it seemed "questionable" to Kirby Smith "whether that mode of obtaining supplies will be submitted to" by the citizenry in the coming months. In fact, the impressment system had begun to collapse. On February 8, 1865, the Department's chief quartermaster reported that since the pockets of every farmer and businessman in the Southwest were already stuffed with vouchers, most people would refuse to accept any more. "We cannot use certified accounts," he asserted; " [we] cannot use the large certificates of indebtedness; cannot impress; have no currency; the army is in want; it cannot be supplied."

Kirby Smith forwarded copies of this report to the Secretary of

War, Senator Wigfall, Senator Oldham, and Judge Gray. He begged
Seddon to freight $30,000,000 or $40,000,000 in currency to Marshall,
he urged the senators to enlist all of the Trans-Mississippi congressmen
"in a common effort to secure funds at once for this department," and
he implored Gray to float a loan and to permit citizens to use their nonnegotiable impressment vouchers as if they were legal tender. Gray replied that he was "fully aware of our alarming and calamitous condition
[so] faithfully described by you," and that it "must soon overwhelm us,
unless the Government provide relief"; but the best he could do, he
said, was to recommend that Smith appeal to Richmond and to the
states for money. The Secretary of War did nothing. And Congress took
the matter under advisement. Finally, on March 13, declaring that supplies "must be had," Smith authorized his Chief of Subsistence to seize
provisions without issuing vouchers or certificates, and to employ whatever armed force might be necessary to wrest property from its owners.
Three days later, Smith explained to Senator R. W. Johnson that "if either this or some other efficient method for our relief is not resorted to,
I cannot be held responsible for the consequences." And on the 18th,
while Smith was writing a letter to the War Department to justify his initiative, the last session of the Confederacy's last Congress enacted a
law authorizing impressment officers to forgo cash payments and to
force the owners of impressed property to take promissory notes. By
then, both the law and the Congress were irrelevant.

The common folk of the Trans-Mississippi were not privy to the
ramifications of their economic distress, but they surely recognized that
consumer goods cost far too much. By July, 1864, a citizen of Houston
could buy a gold dollar for thirty-one Confederate dollars. In August,
a cheap hotel room in Shreveport, which a guest might have to share
with two or three strangers, fetched $20 per night per person. That
same month, also at Shreveport, a pound of butter cost $5, a dozen eggs
$5, a quart of beans $2.50, an apple between 25 and 50 cents, and a
melon from $1 to $5. In September, an annual subscription to the
Shreveport *News*—temporarily a weekly, because of the paper shortage
—was pegged at $4 specie or $50 currency. Two months later, at Houston, a pound of ersatz tea cost $4. In December, the State Store at
Shreveport auctioned off two silk handkerchiefs for $140, at Alexandria
a dozen secondhand cups and saucers sold for $300, and, in Texas, a

watermelon cost $5 and a pound of coffee substitute $10. At least one Texas woman paid $90 for a yard and a half of blue denim material, while the German and Mexican laborers employed at San Antonio refused to work unless paid in gold. And some commodities were virtually unobtainable. In February, 1865, a Texas soldier offered to give half his wages in return for a supply of tobacco, and in March another Texan was unable to restrain his delight when, "For once in the history of the last three years, our Commissary issues genuine RIO coffee." [4]

❧ II   On the first day of June, 1864, a "Children's Festival" was held at San Pedro Springs, Texas. "So joyous and happy an assemblage we have not seen for many a day," exclaimed the *San Antonio News.* "Mothers, fathers, kindred and strangers, old and young, were in attendance, to look upon the happy school children. . . . Dancing and waltzing wound up the day. Good cheer prevailed, and everything that could contribute to creature comforts was in abundance." Just eleven days later, the youth of San Antonio enjoyed a grand fandango. "Martha and Willie [Vance] gave a great party last night," one of the local ladies wrote; "—dancing, supper, fruits, all the young folks in town, pretty much, invited. Mary and Kate declined, but Willie [Maverick] went, and I believe had a rare time of enjoyment." In Harris County, eighty pupils, mostly boys, continued to attend Mr. Preston's school as long as the Confederacy endured, while on November 3, 1864, the daughters of Natchitoches' first families returned to their studies at the Convent School of the Sacred Heart. At the Children's Festival, at the Vances' party, at Mr. Preston's school, and behind the walls of the Natchitoches convent, perhaps some managed, momentarily, to forget the war. But not for long. Even the Sisters of the Sacred Heart, in advertising the commencement of their academic term, were careful to apprise parents "that dating from the month of January, circumstances may oblige [us] to exact the payments in gold or silver. The supply of writing paper remaining being nearly exhausted, [it] will be sold to the pupils for gold or silver."

Elsewhere than at a party or beyond the confines of the cloister, it was nearly impossible to find a place where "Good cheer prevailed." The *Washington Telegraph* celebrated "the Christmas Holidays (alas!

dull enough whilst so much sorrow surrounds us)" by issuing "a quarter-sheet for the sake of the Military Orders, and last dispatches." The three thousand Federal prisoners incarcerated in the Tyler stockade spent their holiday season plotting escapes. "They have none made their escape yet, though they have got out several times," observed one of their guards. "The dogs always find them. The Yanks think it is very hard to be hunted down by dogs, like so many run-away negroes." The prisoners recently confined at Millican were no longer behind walls, but they were no more fortunate than their comrades at Tyler. In October, after an outbreak of yellow fever ravaged the Millican compound, the survivors, under guard, were dispersed in small squads on open country near a number of Texas railroad lines. Not a few froze to death during the ensuing winter. Nonetheless, they enjoyed a measure of retribution: the yellow-fever epidemic struck the rail hub at Houston in November, and reached Galveston in December.

Among other repercussions, the epidemic forced the adjournment of the Confederate States District Court for the Eastern District of Texas, and the adjournment proved to be permanent. By this time, the legislature of Confederate Arkansas had already become a dim memory, consigned to the same limbo as the legislature of Confederate Missouri. A rump session had convened at Washington on September 22, had received the assurances of the state supreme court that it constituted a legitimate governing body despite the lack of a quorum, had debated for a week, and had then dispersed, never to reconvene. The Texas legislature, meeting in November, protested impressment and then followed the Arkansas legislature into oblivion. The Louisiana legislature, which sat in January and early February, spent most of its final session providing for the removal of mortgaged slaves to Texas, for the security of property abandoned by refugees, and for the relief of indigent citizens; then it too disbanded.

The Louisiana lawmakers' concern for refugees was prompted in part by the fact that another wave of fugitives had begun to congregate for the long trek to Texas. "It is all excitement here for the last few days, what is to be the result God only knows," a planter wrote from Alexandria on January 3. "I think I shall fix up and endeavor to remove what few negroes I have left, say 12 to 15. . . . Chambers started Friday and Mr. Wells on Sunday last, 2 inst., Ransdell I hear leaves this week, and in fact almost everyone is going. . . . we cannot live here for our own men, they will not let us live, but destroy everything we can make." A soldier who returned to Texas on furlough from the Cis-Mississippi in February, 1865, summed up the mood of the people of the western Confederacy in a letter addressed to the *Houston Telegraph*. Noting the citizens' lack of hospitality, he commented that nearly every inhabitant of the Trans-Mississippi "appeared dispirited and whipped."

And yet, not every western rebel was ready to quit. On February 25, 1865, a veteran Texas cavalry sergeant, who indeed wished that "this heartless war was over," and who willingly acknowledged his "hope [that] the day is not far off when we will again be permitted to see loved ones at home," nevertheless insisted that true peace and lasting tranquillity could only be achieved under the FREE and independent FLAG of the SO[U]THERN CONFEDERACY." Two weeks later, he actually rejoiced at the news that "all the peace rumors that have been so plentiful for the [l]ast two months are 'Gone glim[m]ering;' and I am glad of it. I say peace never, if slaveery [*sic*] is to perish with it; let's fight it out and GAIN all, or fight it out and LOSE all." In January, Governor Murrah said much the same thing in an address delivered to the people of Texas. Blaming the Confederacy's recent reverses upon popular selfishness, the absence of domestic harmony, and the lack of patriotic devotion, Murrah exhorted all Texans to dedicate their time, their wealth, and their very lives to the cause.

Some citizens continued until the very end to meet Murrah's highest expectations. In October, 1864, the Shreveport Glee Club donated the proceeds of a concert, some $5,000, to a Missouri brigade. The following month, the volunteers who staffed and funded the Houston Soldier's Home lodged and fed 492 transients. In December, the ladies of Shreveport organized a concert for the benefit of the Eighteenth Louisiana Infantry, while the faculty and students at the Mansfield Female College collected $3,517 in cash and thirty-four pairs of woolen socks for Missouri's exiled soldiers. A month later, a mass meeting at Dallas resolved to denounce the United States for waging an inhuman and barbaric war against the people of the South, and called upon the inhabitants of Texas to do all in their power to support the boys at the front and their families at home. Thereafter, public rallies, which increased greatly in both number and fervor, continued to be a feature of daily life in the Trans-Mississippi Department until the closing days of the war. During the first week of May, for example, the citizens of Fort Bend County, Texas, met to shout approval for resolutions urging the people to clothe the army, to provision the soldiers' indigent dependents, and to furnish aid to the government; while the inhabitants of Washington County convened to propose the conscription and enlistment of all able-bodied white males between the ages of thirteen and seventy.[5]

The intensity with which many citizens reasserted their dedication to the Southern cause suggests that a measure of hysteria had begun to infect the Trans-Mississippi's population. As frustration piled upon frustration, the demoralized people of the western Confederacy sought refuge in illusion. One indication of this was the proliferation of unsubstantiated rumors; after the spring of 1864, with each passing day, such rumors became more numerous, more hopeful, and more fantastic:

The Stage comes in [to Tyler] overloaded with news, and as a specimen of what RELIABLE! persons are bringing over, I will give a few samples of the latest to day; No 1 Lee and Grant has had a fight, and Lee has taken from eight to fifteen thousand prisoners. No 2, Johnston has possession of Lookout mountain, and the enemy is evacuating Chattanooga. No 3, Morgan is recruiting in Kentucky, and has eight thousand men. No 4, Forrest has taken Memphis. No 5, Genl Ross has taken Snyders Bluff and eight thousand prisoners, 5000 white and 3000 blacks. No 6, 17 thousand Negroes are now garrisoning Vicksburg, and have offered to surrender the place if they be allowed to return to their former masters. . . . No 8, Kentucky has refused to furnish any more troops to the U S Army. No 9, The Federal Congress has taken the vote direct, upon the recognition of the Confederate States, and the resolution was lost by only SEVEN votes. No 10, Lee's Army now number TWO HUNDRED AND EIGHTY THOUSAND MEN FIT FOR DUTY. Was there ever TEN as BIG LIES told in one day?

By February, 1865, rumors of an impending peace settlement pervaded the atmosphere. And in mid-May, as though to vent their repressed anger against the old man who seemed most responsible for delaying the peace, men and women throughout the Department, now the only fragment of the late Confederacy still under the rebel flag, whispered excitedly to one another that Kirby Smith had been assassinated by an enraged cotton speculator.

Not even the most optimistic rumors satisfied some individuals' craving for relief from the anguish of daily life. Only God offered them the security and peace they sought. During the summer and fall of 1864, the first waves of an enthusiastic revival of fundamentalist Protestantism rolled across the Trans-Mississippi states. A host of itinerant preachers, thousands of inspirational tracts, and at least two new religious newspapers appeared on the scene, summoning men who could no longer find hope in the world to the hope of salvation in Jesus Christ. *The Texas Christian Advocate* promised to "arouse the lukewarm, and cheer desponding hearts. It will be a missionary around the camp fire, a remembrance of other days, a link uniting [men] with home and its religion; warning the careless, and pointing all to Christ." *The Army and Navy Messenger,* which was partially subsidized by donations from Kirby Smith, Governor Allen, and the Louisiana legislature, saw "the revivals of religion in the country and in the Army" as the "first fruits of the war in its effect on national character" and "an essential part of our national revolutionary history."

They furnish a stand point amid the smoke and blood and disruption of the times from which the earnest minded Christian may look toward the future with hope. . . . There is more faith in God and Providence than there was when the war began. . . . Did not the country need this war? Did not civilization need it? Who can understand the ways of God?

As early as September 29, 1864, a regimental chaplain attached to Evander McNair's Arkansas brigade could report from Monticello that "from thirty to fifty penitents" belonging to the First Consolidated Arkansas Infantry "are nightly at the altar for prayers. . . . The coldness, deadness, and indifference which has been too characteristic of army christians are gone; and love, zeal, and devotion are manifest all around." By late February, 1865, the "very interesting revival of religion" had spread throughout the Department, and was "creating a livey [*sic*] sensation amongst the soldiers" of Wharton's cavalry division, bivouacked in East and North Texas; "there are from 80 to 100 at the Altar every night for prayer, and the good work 'Goes bravely on.'" The troopers of Charles Morgan's Texas cavalry regiment, posted near Waverly, even built an arbor in the midst of their encampment for the conduct of preaching and communion services. On March 19, after recording that "the Sacrament of the Lord's supper was administered to day out under the arbor," one of Colonel Morgan's converts exulted that "a large number of the command have professed religion and joined the Church." "This work is destined to do much good," he prophesied; "it has already had a tremendous influence upon the morals of the entire Brigade."

But neither the rumormongering nor the religious revival testified to the spread of panicky despair quite as eloquently as the Confederate government's decision, in March, 1865, to conscript, enlist, and arm slaves. The South, long haunted by the nightmare of slave insurrection, had gone to war to perpetuate its peculiar institution, and as late as March 10, 1865, a Texas horse soldier wrote that the abandonment of "slaveery" would be too great a price to pay for the restoration of peace. And yet, just three days later, in a last desperate attempt to wrest independence from defeat, the whites sitting in the Richmond Congress voted to place weapons in the hands of the Negroes whom they held in bondage. This act, more than any other event, bore witness to the Confederacy's moral collapse. With it, the Confederate government announced its abandonment of the South's basic social institution and thus of the principle justifying the Confederacy's struggle to secede.

In February, 1864, both the Confederate Congress and the Louisiana legislature had enacted bills authorizing the army to hire or impress free or enslaved Negro laborers, but no thought had then been given to the employment of Negroes as soldiers. Quite the contrary, the vast majority of Southern whites then agreed with the contention of a Texas editor that the enlistment of Negro troops would create far more problems than it could solve; white regiments, insisted the editor, would not fight next to Negro units, and no white man could contemplate with equanimity the emancipation of untold thousands of armed Negro war veterans. But by the autumn of 1864, some prominent Southerners were beginning to contemplate the unimaginable. On September 6, in a private letter to Governor Allen, Secretary of War Seddon intimated that military necessity might soon force the induction of Negro fighting men. Twenty days later, Allen replied that "the time has come for us to put into the army every able-bodied negro man as a soldier. This should be done immediately. . . . They will make much better soldiers with us than against us, and swell the now depleted ranks of our armies." On

November 7, President Davis, in his annual message to the Congress, asserted that "until our white population should prove insufficient for the armies we require. . . , to employ as a soldier the Negro who has been merely trained to labor . . . would scarcely be deemed wise or advantageous"; and yet he granted that "should the alternative ever be presented of subjugation or of the employment of the slave as a soldier, there seems no reason to doubt what should then be our decision."

Davis' ambivalence left the issue to Congress, which, during the next five months, proved no more eager than the President to resolve it. By January, 1865, many congressmen seemed privately convinced that the enlistment of slaves would be the country's only salvation, but, fearful that a black man fit to be a soldier would no longer feel fit to remain a slave, the legislators hesitated to initiate debate. But then General Lee, "whose opinions on all subjects are omnipotent," let it be known that he advocated, as a matter of military necessity, the immediate conscription and use of Negro soldiers. On February 10, Senator Oldham of Texas and Representative Ethelbert Barksdale of Mississippi introduced, in their respective Houses, similar bills providing for the induction of slave troops. After a month's heated argument, a compromise bill was narrowly passed by both Houses and signed into law on March 13. In its final form, the act authorized the President to impose new troop quotas upon the several states and to raise up to 300,000 fresh able-bodied men between the ages of eighteen and forty-five, "irrespective of color." The law explicitly refrained from offering manumission to veteran slaves. Instead, it stated that "nothing . . . shall be construed to authorize a change in the relation which the said slaves shall bear to their owners, except by consent of the owners and of the States in which they reside."

During the next ten days, the War Department issued regulations to govern the organization and discipline of Negro regiments, designated and appointed recruiting officers, and offered commissions to whites willing to command slaves in the field. Apparently, only one Trans-Mississippi white actually applied for such a commission. On April 8, 1865, Isaac Dennis, a Texas militiaman, requested Colonel Guy M. Bryan to negotiate his nomination as colonel of a Confederate Negro regiment, or, in lieu of such an appointment, to procure permission for him to raise a slave regiment. But Lee and Grant met at Appomattox the following day, and Dennis' petition was never processed.[6]

If rumors, religion, hysteria, or hope kept many of Kirby Smith's men under arms, thousands of others, more practical or more pessimistic, were detaching themselves from the army. One way for a soldier to evade field service was to secure a detail, as an agriculturist, a mechanic, an artisan, a teamster, or a clerk. By the spring of 1864, wives throughout the Department were begging their soldier husbands to try "to come home, and recruit your health, & perhaps get a detail also, so that you will not have to return soon." On July 28, 1864, 14 of the 104 cavalrymen enrolled in "I" Company, Morgan's Texas regiment, were detailed "in the various Departments in Marshall, Jefferson and Shreveport"; by May 20, 1865, 39 of the company's 120 members were absent on detail, as printers, farmers, quartermaster or commissary clerks, hospital stewards, iron miners, teamsters, or postmen. On November 11, 1864, 171 members of the Consolidated Crescent Regiment, more than half the unit's strength, were "detailed through the Department." "John Terrill has made application, for a detail to work in the pistol shop near Anderson, is now at home waiting over his time [that is, absent without leave] to hear from his application," wrote a Texas housewife to her spouse in June, 1864. "Bob Bassett has a place in some Gov department at Marshall I think. . . . Bassett is determined, to do no more field service. . . . Noah B—— is in the Gov department at Anderson doing some light work." No precise estimate of the total number of men detailed can be made, but by the end of 1864 the count approached 10,000. In February, 1865, in an effort to retain those still in the ranks, Kirby Smith's headquarters canceled furloughs and prohibited the detail of additional men, and in April Smith revoked many of the details previously granted. But by that late date, soldiers who wanted to go home were no longer applying for leaves or details; they simply deserted.

As early as the summer of 1864, some officers began to note a sharp rise in desertions. On August 10, for instance, Lieutenant R. G. Smith, commanding a battery of Louisiana "heavies" stationed in the Red River Valley, remarked upon the large number of gunners who were abandoning their posts and surrendering themselves to the enemy. Through the ensuing autumn and winter, the disaffection became even more pronounced, as the hardships of camp life, the lack of pay, the shortage of food, the insufficient clothing and shelter, the heart-rending appeals from wives and children, and the rumors of military reverses in the Cis-Mississippi all induced despondent rebels to wander away from their regiments. In November, the army began to execute recaptured absentees almost daily, but not even this draconic expedient stemmed the exodus.

By January, many regiments seemed to be melting away. Shortly after New Year's Day, both the Galveston *News* and the *San Antonio Herald* carried "a column and a half of the names of men, who are officially published as deserters." A fugitive who escaped from the garrison at Alexandria on January 25 reported to the Union provost at Morganza that, despite the summary execution of several absentees each week, "Louisiana troops are discouraged and are deserting daily, some going to Mexico, some to the Federal lines. They have not been paid for more than a year." Five days later, General Slaughter suspected that "fully one-fourth" of his command was ready to quit, and he added that he "would not be surprised if they joined the enemy." On February 28, the Union commandant at Brazos Santiago affirmed that the Confederates deployed along the lower Rio Grande were in a "demoralized state, and numbers of them are deserting." In mid-February, a foot soldier belonging to Allan Thomas' Louisiana brigade revealed that "every night as many as 6 and sometimes 12 soldiers desert from the Infantry and go home or with the Yankees. The plan of shooting still goes on—as many as 5 and 6 are sent to their long accounts every week." On March 1, the same soldier felt that "the state of things now in this Dept. approaches nearer to mutiny than anything I can say. . . . The affairs are badly managed—yes—in a horrible condition." Simultaneously, at Houston, a brace of drumhead courts-martial sentenced a dozen enlisted strays to be "shot to death with musketry," and cashiered *in absentia* eleven officers—four captains, four first lieutenants, and three second lieutenants—"for prolonged absence from duty without leave."

Two days later, General Canby, apprised of the increasing defections of war-weary Trans-Mississippi troops, did his best to hasten the decay of Kirby Smith's army by promulgating a General Order which offered good treatment, amnesty, remunerative employment, and exemption from further military service to any rebel who might seek sanctuary within the Union lines. Meanwhile, William Steele's brigade of Wharton's cavalry division had to be dispersed along the roads leading into the Northern Subdistrict of Texas, to apprehend and arrest the hundreds of absentees reported to be flocking toward the frontier bad-lands. On April 5, Texas State Brigadier J. W. Throckmorton advised Governor Murrah that neither the regulars nor his militiamen were suf-ficient to stay the tide. During the previous two weeks, he said, at least five hundred army fugitives had moved westward between the Red River and Austin, while the country east and south of Austin was satu-rated with deserters. Near Crockett, eighty-eight members of a single regiment mutinied, deserted in a body, and marched in military order down the public highways, sacking villages and plundering farms as they moved. Other large bands were robbing and jayhawking their sepa-rate ways through Wise, Denton, and Montague counties. On April 3, a Federal scout, who had spent "nearly a month" ranging "up the Rio Grande a long distance," reported to General Hurlbut that "the demor-alization in the rebel army in Texas is very extensive. In all the counties from San Antonio and Austin up to the mountains the rebel soldiers are coming home in large numbers, and in two or three places have notified the enrolling officer and provost-marshal that their services were no longer needed." It was said that the Confederate officer in charge of the border between Laredo and Ringgold Barracks, Colonel Santos Bena-vides, "has come to the conclusion not to fight against the United States Government, but . . . he will with most if not all of his command cross over into Mexico." [7]

The army's spiraling desertion rate was only one sign of the break-down of public morale. In many areas of Texas, despair so undermined social order that, during the last year of the war, normal judicial proc-esses generally gave way to vigilante law. The Weathersford County minutemen lynched at least fourteen victims; the vigilantes in both Par-ker and Gillespie counties killed numerous others, and swore to fight off any attempt by the Texas or Confederate authorities to retaliate; an armed mob of eighty men, gathered from Van Zandt, Henderson, and Kaufman counties, collected at Tyler, stormed the jailhouse, kidnapped four notorious bandits who were awaiting trial, and hanged them all from a single tree.

Along the Department's war-torn northern and eastern fronts, not even vigilantes were in control. Arkansas was a desert waste; except for the Confederate wedge in the southwestern corner of the state and the isolated Federal garrison enclaves on and above the Arkansas River, the whole state was given over to guerrillas and scavengers. In vast stretches of Louisiana, conditions were just as bad. "It is no longer the case of a few isolated desperadoes," reported an officer on picket in St. Landry Parish; the "entire community" was racked by nightriders and jayhawkers. Above St. Landry, outlaw companies, numbering from fifty to five hundred men apiece, raided and looted at will through Point Coupee, Avoyelles, Rapides, and Catahoula parishes, and through all the blackened country between the Mississippi and the Ouachita. So desperate was Louisiana's agony that on February 4, 1865, as its last official act, the Shreveport legislature authorized the state quartermaster "to deliver to each member of the General Assembly, for the use of the inhabitants of the parish he represents, to enable them to defend themselves against predatory bands and jayhawkers, ten pounds of powder and one thousand percussion caps."

As the constraints of law evaporated, crime increased. In October, 1864, a single—and not untypical—advertisement carried by the Natchitoches *Times* listed ten runaway slaves: Dinah, aged 25 years; Lewis, 35; Tucker, Daniel, and Darcus, aged between 7 and 9; Jerry, 26, Octave, 18; Cyprian, a "boy aged about 35 years"; Augustin, a "boy aged about 40 years"; and Peter, 55. A few months earlier, the *San Antonio News* was concerned that even those slaves who remained in custody were "putting on important airs" in the town's streets. In the autumn of 1864, the Bexar County court noted a sharp increase in the number of women prosecuted for keeping "a disorderly house for the purpose of public prostitution, and as a resort for prostitutes, vagabonds, free negroes, and slaves." In January, 1865, the Confederate States depositary at San Antonio, George W. Palmer, absconded to Mexico with several thousand dollars in public funds. And, also in January, Governor Murrah found that State Brigadier E. T. Nichols, the officer in charge of the Texas military board's cotton sales, had embezzled every cent earned from the state's cotton transactions during the preceding six months. When, in March, Murrah confirmed that Nichols and an accomplice, Captain John L. Williams, had secreted their gains in the safe vault of a Havana bank, he demanded an immediate accounting; but before Nichols could reply, Murrah's administration came to an end. As the La Grange *Patriot* complained in January, "These outrages are becoming so frequent, that unless they are checked, the possession of property will be an incumberance and a perpetual source of annoyance. Practically the right of private property is already nearly abolished, except in the hands of cunning thieves."

Nor was property the only thing endangered by the dissolution of law. For crimes against persons—especially crimes of passion, marked by irrational violence—also became alarmingly prevalent. A typical example occurred in San Antonio during the first week of November, 1864. Jacob Andres was lounging by the doorway of a saloon when a drunken stranger, James Freills, staggered up to him, seized him by the beard, pulled him into the barroom, and offered to buy him a drink. When Andres declined Freills's hospitality, Freills drew an army .44 and shot off the top of Andres' head.

A far more newsworthy murder was committed at 10:00 A.M., April 6, 1865, in a second-story room of Houston's fashionable Fannin House hotel. Colonel George Baylor, the commanding officer of the Second Arizona Cavalry Regiment, stormed into the hotel's lobby announcing that General Wharton owed him satisfaction for some dire insult. "Some words had taken place between the parties," hinted the Galveston *News,* "but we forbear to give particulars." General Magruder, who happened to be standing in the lobby, walked over to Baylor, took him by the arm, and led him upstairs to the then empty room occupied by Captain Edmund P. Turner, Magruder's adjutant. Magruder returned to the lobby, leaving Baylor on Turner's bed, weeping. Five minutes later, General Wharton entered the hotel and raced upstairs. After a brief interval, a single shot reverberated through the building. When Magruder, Turner, and a companion, General James Harrison, reached Turner's room, they found Baylor seated on the bed with a revolver in his hand, and Wharton dead on the floor with a bullet in his heart.[8]

❧ III   Magruder had returned to Houston only two days before, in order to resume command of the District of Texas. His reassignment was necessitated by the old problem of rank. Ever since the conclusion of the Red River campaign, during which the army suffered the loss of a large number of field and general officers, Kirby Smith had been trying to secure Presidential sanction for the interim promotions awarded by his headquarters. In April, 1864, immediately following the battle of Pleasant Hill, Smith had advanced two officers to the rank of major general and two others to brigadier; in May, he had appointed four more brigadiers, pending the approval of the President. On June 15, Secretary Seddon thought it wise to warn Smith to "be as careful and abstinent" as possible "on the delicate subject of assignments and appointments to office and command," for "these under our constitutional system are reposed in the president as a personal trust, the responsibility of which is fully realized by him, and which he cannot transfer." Seddon recommended that Smith be content to nominate men for promotion, and to delay their assumption of rank and duty until the nominations were confirmed.

Seddon also remarked that, considering the size of the Trans-Mississippi army, there already appeared to be a superfluity of general officers in the Department. In October—by which time only two nominations, to captaincies, had been approved—Smith responded by forwarding a copy of the Department's most recent table of organization to Richmond. It showed that the twenty-nine brigades stationed west of the Mississippi had been organized into eleven divisions, and the divisions into four corps (Walker's, Buckner's, and Magruder's district corps, and Price's cavalry corps), and that, of the forty-four vacancies suitable for general officers, only thirty were actually occupied by men who held either commissions or interim appointments as generals. Many of the generals, in addition, held rank inferior to that to which their offices entitled them. Only one of the four corps commanders (Buckner) was now a lieutenant general, and only eight of the eleven divisions were led by major generals (Marmaduke, Fagan, Churchill, Mosby Parsons, Wharton, Forney, Polignac, and Maxey). Three divisions were commanded by brigadiers (James Hawes, Thomas Drayton, and Douglas Cooper), and seven brigades were led by colonels. On December 23, Adjutant General Samuel Cooper insisted that, according to the Trans-Mississippi's strength returns, three of Smith's corps appeared to be little larger than divisions, and many of his divisions were nothing but brigades. Cooper recommended the consolidation of Smith's army into eight divisions, and he then advised Smith that, except for the appointment of three men to colonelcies, all of Smith's nominations would be delayed pending the reorganization of his army. "The president instructs me," Cooper added, "to say that it is improper for you to announce the promotion of general officers and assign them to duty before they are appointed by him. . . . Action here must take place before they can be promoted and assigned to duty."

Thoroughly discouraged by Cooper's reply, Smith, in March 1865, complained to Senator R. W. Johnson that "if I cannot be trusted, another commander should relieve me, with whom these powers can be safely confided." Again Smith pointed out that "communications with Richmond is [sic] growing more difficult daily—You can and must have appreciated the necessity of granting more power to the Dept. Commander. He should have the power of assigning to duty all appointments or promotions created under the law (subject to the approval of the President & confirmation by the Senate)." Because of transfers, furloughs, resignations, illness, Price's involvement in his court of inquiry, Polignac's mission to France, the redesignation of Wharton's cavalry as a corps of two divisions, and other reorganizations, now only four of the Department's twelve divisions were under major generals (Churchill, Parsons, Forney, and Maxey). Fagan and Wharton now led corps; Marmaduke was a prisoner of war; seven divisions were commanded by brigadiers (Allan Thomas, Cooper, Shelby, Clark, Hawes, Steele, and Bee), and one by a mere colonel, Arthur P. Bagby. As for the corps commanders, Walker was ranked by both Price and Forney, and Magruder was ranked by Forney; should Price be restored to duty, or should Forney's division be shifted from Louisiana, one or perhaps both of the major generals currently in command of district corps would have to be replaced. Smith felt "a delicacy in advancing these opinions as I am Dept Com^{der} , but they are necessities created by the circumstances & the times in which we live."

Prompted by these "necessities," Smith continued to appoint men to rank and to assign them to command without awaiting the President's pleasure. On at least two occasions, he went so far as to reject legitimate appointees designated by Richmond. In December, 1864, when the War Department dispatched General F. R. T. Nicholls to the Southwest to take charge of the Trans-Mississippi's Conscript Bureau, Smith protested that since the incumbent, General Greer, had performed admirably during his tenure, General Nicholls' services were neither required nor wanted. If Nicholls reported for duty, said Smith, he would be posted elsewhere.

And in August, 1864, when Richmond directed Smith to appoint Douglas Cooper commander and superintendent in the Indian Territory, Smith delayed the publication of Cooper's orders, requested the War Department to revoke them, and, insisting that General Maxey "has with skill, judgment, and success administered his duties," warned that "serious injury would result to the service were this order enforced." The Adjutant General, however, replied that Cooper's appointment was "deemed imperative and must be carried into effect"; an Indian council petitioned for Cooper's selection; Territorial Delegate Elias Boudinot lobbied in the halls of Congress to gain support for Cooper; and Cooper himself journeyed to Richmond to advance his own cause. Nevertheless, Smith managed to hold out until February, 1865, before mounting pressure from Richmond (inspired, in part, by the apprehension that the Indians were considering the abandonment of their alliance with the Confederate States) finally obliged him to elevate Cooper to the command of the Nations. "I shall give General Cooper my full support," Smith affirmed. But "the change has not the concurrence of my judgment, and I believe will not result beneficially." As soon as Cooper took charge of the district, he appointed Stand Watie to the field command of the Territorial cavalry. Maxey, relieved, was transferred to East Texas, where he eventually took charge of a provisional division composed of dismounted cavalrymen drawn from other units.[9]

Until the advent of early spring, the need to fill command vacancies was not pressing. But as Federal reconnaissance patrols began to range through the eastern and northern outskirts of the Department, and as intelligence began to show that Canby was accumulating a disposable force of 30,000 men near New Orleans, Kirby Smith was forced to turn his attention once again to his defenses. On March 7, 1865, Smith's army numbered no more than 36,000 effectives under arms, of whom 19,000 were infantry or artillery, and 17,000 were cavalry. Some 6,000 of the cavalrymen were in the process of being dismounted, which reduced their efficiency and seriously impaired their morale; for the moment they were, at best, no more reliable than green troops, and, at worst, potential deserters. (Just three weeks later, a Union brigadier in southern Missouri was to report large bodies of ex-Confederate dismounted cavalrymen passing through his jurisdiction: "These men report to their friends the breaking up of Marmaduke's [now John Clark's] command and the immediate return of most of the men to Missouri." Almost simultaneously, one of Wharton's Texas troopers was to remark that since "there are a great many who will desert rather than walk, . . . a great many of the dismounted men are deserting.") In addition to the effectives, the army's rolls carried the names of 4,000 men on furlough, 10,000 on detail, and another 10,000 belonging to the Reserve Corps, but few of these were available for line service—most of the Reserve Corps auxiliaries were unarmed. The majority of Smith's forces were concentrated in southwestern Arkansas, northwestern Louisiana, and East Texas, with a scattering of odd brigades elsewhere.

Ever since January, rumors had been trickling up to Shreveport intimating that Canby proposed to attempt a lodgment on the Texas coast, to seize Galveston, to push inland to Houston, and then, by employing the Texas rail system, to gain access to the interior of the state. As the weather improved, Smith began to prepare for the coming campaign by redistributing his forces. Wharton's corps, spread through East Texas, was alerted to concentrate at Houston; Forney's division was shifted from Minden to Shreveport; Churchill's infantry was pulled southward from Arkansas to Minden; and the white regiments attached to the Territorial division were transferred to Texas. Then, on March 7, a courier from New Orleans arrived at Walker's Houston headquarters with the news that Canby, with 40,000 troops, would set sail for Galveston within the next three days. This intelligence seemed impeccable, having been attested to by one of the Confederacy's most reliable and experienced spies, Jean Marie Odin, the Roman Catholic bishop of New Orleans. Colonel H. T. Douglas, chief of the Bureau of Engineering, was directed to press the fortification of the approaches to Houston; Churchill's infantry division was dispatched from Minden to Marshall; Parsons' and Shelby's Missouri divisions were drawn toward Shreveport (thus leaving only one division, John Clark's, to hold the District of Arkansas); and Forney's division was ordered to march from Shreveport to Huntsville, Texas.

Canby's rumored invasion was never mounted. The Federals were too preoccupied with the reduction of Petersburg and the despoliation of the rest of the eastern Confederacy to bother with the Trans-Mississippi. But the redeployment of Smith's forces precipitated a crisis, for as soon as John Forney waded across the Sabine River he became the ranking general officer on Texas soil. Smith, quite aware of Forney's unpopularity and uncertain of his capacity to command a district, decided that Forney had to be maneuvered out of the chain of command. Consequently, on April 4, Magruder arrived in Houston to resume command of the District of Texas. Fagan, the only major general remaining on active duty in Arkansas, was left in charge of that district. Walker, displaced from his district command, inherited Forney's Texas infantry, while Forney was posted to Shreveport pending further assignment. But his arrival at Shreveport created more embarrassment, since he was senior in rank to every officer in Kirby Smith's headquarters. So on April 24, William Boggs was finally eased out of the office of chief of staff and given an infantry brigade; Buckner, the only lieutenant general west of the Mississippi, became chief of staff; and Harry T. Hays, a major general recently transferred from the Cis-Mississippi, succeeded Buckner in command of the District of West Louisiana. When the Department capitulated just one month later, Forney was still a supernumerary major general waiting at Shreveport for orders.[10]

IV   Despite this eleventh-hour flurry of organizational activity, Smith had no more illusions about his capacity to defend his Department. As early as December 25, 1864, he had confided to his mother that "my stay here is . . . uncertain. My administration may cease at any moment." Even if some miracle should prevent the destruction of his command, Smith had reason to fear for his own future, for "my difficulty with Taylor has made me bitter enemies." In late August, 1864, coincident with Taylor's departure for the Cis-Mississippi, the Austin *Gazette* had opened a broadside attack on Kirby Smith's unsurpations of civil authority and contraventions of law. In October, the assault had been widened to include Smith's economic policies, in particular the impressment of cotton. That same month, because of the death in office of Congressman Benjamin Hodge, the voters of West Louisiana had an opportunity to pass judgment on Smith's administration: John L. Lewis of Claiborne Parish, a supporter of the General, was thoroughly trounced

Collapse of the Trans-Mississippi

at the polls by Colonel Henry Gray of Caddo Parish, who was known to
be Smith's bitter enemy (some months earlier, Smith had refused to promote him to the rank of brigadier general, on the grounds that "his habits . . . are not good").

Some editors tried to defend Smith, but by December the imbroglio leaked across the Mississippi and into the columns of the Richmond
Whig. The *Whig* castigated the "hesitancy and lassitude of Lieutenant
General [*sic*] Kirby Smith" and the "languid and indecisive operations
of the Lieutenant General commanding the Confederate armies in the
Trans Mississippi Department." On January 18, the *Whig* renewed the
attack, giving Taylor all the credit for the repulse of Banks's army from
the Red River Valley, and excoriating Smith's persistent failure to dispatch troops to the Cis-Mississippi. In early March, the Shreveport
News complained that the *Whig*'s editor "speaks of crossing the Mississippi, as he would of crossing a mountain stream in Virginia some fifteen steps wide and some four feet deep," and the *Washington Telegraph* tried to defend Smith with the argument that "he must see at once
the Rio Grande and the Missouri—the Indian Nation, and Balize [*sic*]
—the Mississippi and the coasts, and (sometimes weakening himself at
one point) act in all, as may best subserve the interest of the whole."
But the *Washington Telegraph*'s large view failed to convince some of
the papers, for, two weeks later, the *Houston Telegraph* continued to
note the "disposition . . . on the part of the Press . . . to find fault
with the military authorites on this side of the river." Meanwhile, the
San Antonio News had joined the opposition, with the announcement
that "Gen. Smith has been engaged in Cotton Speculation on his own
account. We know that he has been trading, openly, with the enemy,
and that in return for cotton he has not always got articles of prime necessity." The *San Antonio Herald* protested that the *News* "must be ig-
norant of the facts in the promises, or else . . . grossly imposed on,"
but the *News* asserted that "the feeling is becoming settled that Gen
Kirby Smith should be at least suspended, if not wholly relieved from
his present and almost wholly irresponsible command."

On March 9, two days after the Shreveport papers carried accounts
of the *Whig*'s assaults, Smith addressed a long apology to the President,
in which he tried to salvage something of his tattered reputation:

I have been attacked in the columns of the Richmond Whig: I know that efforts have been made through other journals East of the Mississippi to prejudice the public mind and destroy confidence in the purity of my motives and in my ability to command.

Whilst giving my energies to the maintenance and defence of the Department specially entrusted to my charge, I have ever felt the deepest interest in the struggle elsewhere; and have never failed to co-operate with the means at my disposal, in ensuring its success. I have faithfully and honestly, to the extent of my abilities, discharged the great duties confided to me. I do not know that I have given you entire satisfaction. I do know that you are often embarrassed in doing what you believe to be for the general good. I desire to aid and not embarrass you in your action, and request that this letter may be regarded an application to be relieved from the command of the Department whenever you believe that the public interests will be advanced thereby.

After two more days, he again wrote a long defense of his administration to Davis, repeating, even more emphatically, that "I earnestly desire to promote the common welfare, and would willingly sacrifice every personal consideration to that end. I will as a soldier strive honestly and faithfully to obey your instructions. If you doubt my ability or believe that another can better execute them, I request that he may be sent to relieve me of the responsible and onerous duties with which I am charged."

The *Whig* editorials, in conjunction with numerous other rumors and accusations which reached Richmond from the Trans-Mississippi, caused the government to begin an investigation into the domestic affairs of Kirby Smith's Confederacy. Twice, after listening to speeches which accused the Cotton Bureau of fraud and corruption, Congress called upon the President to provide information on the conduct of trade west of the Mississippi. Then, on March 11, in response to a proposal advanced by Representative Anthony Branch of Texas, Congress authorized the President to appoint a commission "to enquire into and examine the proceedings and transactions of the Cotton Bureau and Cotton Office in the Trans-Mississippi Department." Nine days later, Davis commissioned three prominent Westerners to carry out the Congressional resolution. Finally, on March 18, during its final sitting, the Second Congress of the Confederate States enacted a law "requiring suit to be brought against persons connected with the Cotton Bureau and

Cotton Office in the Trans-Mississippi Department" by the "attorneys of the several Confederate States district courts in the States west of the Mississippi River." The congressmen then adjourned *sine die,* after pledging themselves "during the recess to devote all our energies and influence to the maintenance of our great cause and the prosecution of the war to a successful issue." [11]

Since the beginning of 1865, the question of "reconstruction" had become a public issue throughout the Confederate Southwest, "mooted from time to time by gentlemen heretofore of high standing and character." In mid-February, the Shreveport *News* published a blistering condemnation of those who displayed "the unblushing affrontery to openly advocate the reunion of the States." In March, both McNair's Arkansas infantry brigade and Morgan's Texas cavalry regiment sought to counteract popular despair by professing their "unalterable resolution . . . to bear aloft the flag of our country, until it is recognized by the nations of the earth as the symbol of an independent people," and to "fight the incarnate fiend, so long as we have an organized force, and a kind Providence will give us the strength and power to wield a sword or aim a rifle." But even these protestations rang hollow, for, of the sixty-one troopers present for duty in Morgan's "I" Company, only thirty subscribed to the regiment's resolution. The other thirty-one "refused to sign it."

By the second week of April, reports revealed that troops throughout the Department were generally discontent, that the number of desertions was rising sharply, that large bodies of men were absconding from their regiments en masse, that gangs of stragglers and fugitives from the army (some numbering 150 men) were terrorizing whole counties, and that Clark's entire Missouri cavalry division was dissolving. Banditry and outlawry were so prevalent that Governor Murrah refused, for the first time during the war, to detail or furlough militia troops needed to help with the spring planting. Crops were abandoned, while the militia was embodied and draft-exempt volunteers were called out to police Texas.

One curious sign of the Department's desperation was a last-minute spurt of activity by Commodore Leon Smith's moribund Naval Bureau. Even though the bureau had virtually no navy—in April, 1865, there were only three usable military transports, the *Mary T., General*

Quitman, and *General Hodges,* and one small cotton-clad gunboat, the venerable *Frank Webb,* still operating on the Red River—Commodore Smith determined to break the Federals' Mississippi blockade and to reestablish water-borne communications between Shreveport and the outside world. After almost two years of inattention, work was resumed on the wooden "ironclad" *Missouri:* some hull armor was made from a supply of iron expropriated from the railroad between Shreveport and Marshall; three mismatched cannon were installed aboard her; a captain, Lieutenant Commander Jonathan Carter, was piped aboard; a crew of eleven officers and eighty seamen was enlisted; and preparations were hurried for her launching and her initial water trials under tow. It was hoped that, by midsummer, the *Missouri* would be in shape to steam downriver to New Orleans.

Meanwhile, on April 7, the spunky little gunboat *Webb,* Lieutenant Commander Charles W. Read commanding, cast away from Shreveport and chugged down to Alexandria on a fateful secret mission. At Alexandria, she took aboard a load of turpentine, rosin, and 250 cotton bales, filled her fuel bunkers with pine knots, and made ready to dash to the open sea. On the moonless and foggy evening of the 23d, disguised by darkness and displaying appropriate Federal recognition signals, the *Webb* steamed cautiously downstream to the mouth of the Red River, slipped through the small Union squadron on station below Simmesport, and safely warped into the muddy main channel of the Mississippi. Not until 9:20 o'clock the following morning, as she puffed past the Federal garrison town of Donaldsonville, was she recognized as an intruder, and not until she approached New Orleans did she encounter opposition. A short distance above New Orleans, the *Webb* hoisted a United States flag, stoked her boilers, tied down her relief valves, and opened her throttle wide. Churning past the city at twenty-five miles per hour, she succeeded in dodging all but three of the cannon balls fired at her by the waiting Union picket boats. Once New Orleans was left behind, the Gulf was but a short distance away. Soon dusk descended to envelop the *Webb* in shadow, while the air atop her decks and the water beneath her keel turned to salt. But then, just as the open sea and freedom seemed to be hers, the *Webb* ran square into the broadside battery of the Federal steam sloop *Richmond.* Commander Read spun the *Webb*'s wheel hard about, and tried to escape upstream. But a pursuing Federal gunboat, the *Hollyhock,* hove into view; the *Webb* was trapped between the two enemy vessels. As the *Richmond* loosed a barrage, the *Webb* hauled down the enemy ensign and broke out her own colors, a new national flag with a broad blood-red band at the fly. Then the *Webb,* her superstructure a shambles and her funnels shot away, made for the east bank of the river, ran aground, and was scuttled, burned, and abandoned.[12]

By the time the *Webb* pulled away from Alexandria, word had already reached the Trans-Mississippi that Richmond had fallen, and that on April 9 Robert E. Lee had surrendered his army to Ulysses S. Grant. "Through all this dark and gloomy present," a few of Kirby Smithdom's people were still able to "see a bright and glorious future," in which the enemy would "meet with tremendous [*sic*] and overwhelming reverses, and that too at a moment when least expected." But others rejoiced at the imminent demise of the Southern Confederacy; at Opelousas, the citizenry gathered to celebrate the news and cheer for the Federal flag. And the vast majority, stricken by the news, simply waited, in hopeless passivity, for the inevitable end. On April 21, in an effort to revive his army's shattered spirits, Kirby Smith issued an address to his soldiers, in which he proclaimed that "the crisis of our revolution is at hand."

Great disasters have overtaken us. The army of Northern Virginia and our Commander-in-Chief [Lee] are prisoners of war. With you rests the hopes of our nation, and upon your action depends the fate of our people. I appeal to you in the name of the cause you have so heroically maintained—in the name of your firesides and families so dear to you—in the name of your bleeding country, whose future is in your hands. Show that you are worthy of your position in history. Prove to the world that your hearts have not failed in the hour of disaster, and that at the last moment you will sustain the holy cause which has been so gloriously battled for by your brethren east of the Mississippi.

You possess the means of long-resisting invasion. You have hopes of succor from abroad—protract the struggle and you will surely receive the aid of nations who already deeply sympathize with you.

Stand by your colors—maintain your discipline. The great resources of this department, its vast extent, the numbers, the discipline, and the efficiency of the army, will secure to our country terms that a proud people can with honor accept, and may, under the Providence of God, be the means of checking the triumph of our enemy and of securing the final success of our cause.

But Smith's appeal only deepened the depression. When it was read to troops mustered at Shreveport for a dress parade, its "effect was marked in the extreme. The men instantly became dejected. Mutiny and wholesale desertion were openly talked of. This soon gave way to a general apathy and indifference, but through all could be seen by a close observer that the Army of the Trans-Mississippi was in spirit crushed." A cavalryman in East Texas, upon hearing the address, felt that if the people of the West would come together and "unite as one man; the Trans Mississippi could defy the combined power of all Yankeedom. Alas; alas, it will not be so; We as a people have not done our duty, the patriotic flash that fired the southern heart in sixty one, meteoric like, has faded away leaving darkness and gloom." A West Texas housewife moaned that she was "bowed down at the suffering and sacrifices our bleeding country is forced to endure. I do not despair, but oh, the dear lives, the precious blood that is yet to be given up for our independence appal[l]s me." And John Reagan, the Texan who served as the Confederacy's postmaster general, acknowledged that "if our people continue the contest with the spirit which animated them during the first years of the war, our independence might yet be in our reach. But I see no reason for that now."

Yet, despite the disintegration of the Cis-Mississippi South, and despite the despair spreading through the Trans-Mississippi, a measure of Confederate authority was to persist for more than another month within Kirby Smith's jurisdiction. That authority was already tenuous, but it was still sufficient to inspire a degree of hope in some hearts. On April 23, General Magruder implored his corps to prepare to resist an invasion, called upon the people of Texas to do everything in their power to provision and supply the army, and urged Kirby Smith to adopt whatever means might prove necessary to preserve domestic order. At Houston, a mass meeting resolved never to abandon the cause of Confederate independence. During the next few days, the enlisted men of the Twenty-second Arkansas Infantry Regiment, the line officers of Churchill's division, and the whole of Shelby's division reaffirmed their determination to fight on, while Governor Allen announced that Louisiana would "never—never—never" surrender. On the 27th, Governor Murrah summoned his people to "rally around the battle scarred and well known flag of the Confederacy and uphold your state government in its purity and integrity," and promised that "with God's bless-

ing, it may yet be the proud privilege of Texas, the youngest of the
Confederate Sisters, to redeem the cause of the Confederacy from its
present perils." Two days later, at a monster rally held in Shreveport,
Governors Allen and Reynolds, Generals Smith, Buckner, Price, Hays,
McNair, and Hawthorne, Judge Thomas Ochiltree of Texas, and three
colonels insisted that "a little patience and perseverence" would bring
triumph if only the people would "continue true to their colors." And in
early May, the Austin *Gazette* affirmed that the Confederacy's "revolution" could "never go back" as long as its people remained united and
committed "to fight this war to an honorable peace." Parsons' Texas
cavalry brigade and the old New Mexico brigade resolved "to stand by
our Colors, and endure any privations, and offer any sacrifices . . .
with patriotic devotion to the Standard of our country." The Galveston
News asserted that the Trans-Mississippi Department was "determined
to fight it out" until the Federals "finally let us alone. . . . To a brave,
high minded man there can be no choice. To a determined, loyal people
there can be but one course. Let us follow this course fearlessly and
unhesitatingly." [13]

But the Department lacked the men, the matériel, and the money
needed to wage war, and most of its citizens lacked the will and the
spirit to fight on. While their leaders exhorted them, the people showed
their contempt for war meetings and rallies, denounced the false bravado of the draft exempts and detailed soldiers who congregated for the
speechmaking, and blamed their own miseries on the generals and cotton speculators who seemed to be trying to prolong the conflict. Some
did more than grumble. On May 5, General Brent, commanding at Alexandria, reported that the artillerymen garrisoning the town's fortifications were demobilizing themselves; the previous evening, fifty deserters
had slipped away, and, as for the rest, "the temper of the greater part of
the troops . . . is such as to forbid the belief that they can be relied
on." A few days earlier, Magruder had remarked that the soldiers
posted about Houston were "deserting by tens and twenties a night." On
May 2, the men of "K" Company, Morgan's regiment, put down their
arms and mutinied—"as a general thing," explained one of the troopers
who helped quiet them, "they do not wish to go into active service."
"The clouds thicken around us from every quarter," wrote a resident of
Shreveport on May 8; "every countenance is filled with gloom and despondency."

The gathering storm first broke in northern Arkansas. On May 10, 1865, M. Jeff Thompson, currently commanding the Northern Subdistrict of Arkansas (that is, all of the guerrillas, irregulars, raiding parties, and recruiting patrols operating between the Arkansas River and the Iowa border), tied a white handkerchief to the tip of his saber and casually rode into the Union encampment at Chalk Bluff, Missouri. Once introduced to the senior Union officer present, Lieutenant Colonel C. W. Davis, Thompson inquired about the terms of capitulation which the Federals were prepared to offer. "He is a witty fellow," Davis wired to General Dodge, "and is continually talking about impossibilities. He has not yet decided whether to surrender or not. Shall try and convince him." Davis needed only one day to bring Thompson around, for, on the 11th, the Missouri Swamp Fox "determined to accept the terms offered, and will and hereby do surrender the forces under my command upon the terms granted to General Robert E. Lee and the Army of Northern Virginia."

A week earlier, on May 2, Kirby Smith had again asked Robert Rose to convey his regards to the Emperor of Mexico, and to bring "certain views" to His Majesty's attention. "It cannot be disguised that recent reverses of the most serious character have befallen the Confederate arms," admitted Smith. "Nor can it be denied that there is a probability of still further losses to us. It may even be that it is the inscrutable design of Him who rules the destinies of nations that the day of our ultimate redemption shall be postponed." Smith wanted the Emperor to know that "there is under my command an army of Sixty Thousand men—of these, there are nine Thousand Missourians, good soldiers, who have been driven from their homes, and would, no doubt, upon favorable inducements . . . take service with the power so favoring them." And at least ten thousand "daring and gallant spirits from other States," commanded by veteran officers, would gladly enlist as well, in order to escape "a state of vassalage to the Federal Government." Rose was to impress upon the Emperor that "the services of our troops would be of inestimable value to him." [14]

✠ **V**   During the first week of May, Lieutenant Colonel John T. Sprague, chief of staff to General John Pope, the commander of the Federal Military Division of Missouri (which now embraced everything from the northern border of Arkansas to Canada, and from the Mississippi to the Rockies), arrived at the mouth of the Red River under a flag of truce, carrying important dispatches for Kirby Smith. Two of Smith's staff officers steamed down to Alexandria to receive the dispatches, but Sprague insisted upon delivering them to the commanding general in person. On May 8, he was passed through the Confederate lines and conveyed by riverboat to Shreveport, where, in the evening, he conferred with Kirby Smith. The topic of discussion was a letter, dated April 19, from Pope to Smith. Pope announced that Lee had surrendered, that Joseph Johnston had opened negotiations with Sherman, and that Canby was in contact with Taylor (in fact, Johnston had capitulated on April 26 and Taylor on May 4; there were no longer any regular Confederate forces under arms east of the Mississippi). "In view of these results, accomplished and in the progress of speedy accomplishment," Pope explained, he had been authorized by Grant to extend to Smith the same terms as those given to Lee. He pointed out that all of the Federal armies would soon be free to concentrate against the Trans-Mississippi Department, and that should the struggle be continued, Smith would "be responsible for unnecessary bloodshed . . . devastation and misery." Under instructions from Pope, Sprague went on to say that the Federal authorities would not be too rigorous in applying the letter of the terms offered: no objections would be raised if the rebel troops in West Louisiana and Arkansas simply put down their arms, disbanded, and went home, and no obstacles would be placed in the way of military or civilian refugees who desired to flee to Mexico. And, alluding to the recent assassination of President Lincoln, he reminded Smith that continued obstinacy would invite the visitation of heavy repression "upon those who . . . resist the authority of the United States, to whom the mass of people in the North attribute, however remotely, the atrocious deed."

The following morning, May 9, Smith addressed a note to Pope in which he stated that "your proposition for the surrender of the troops under my command, are [sic] not such that my sense of duty and honor will permit me to accept." However, instead of asking Sprague to deliver this reply without delay, he invited Sprague to tarry at Shreveport for a few days while he traveled to Marshall to confer with the Trans-Mississippi governors. Because of the breakdown of communications between Shreveport and the Confederate government (the following day, in Georgia, President Davis was captured by a Union cavalry patrol), Smith, hesitant to act without some semblance of civil sanction, had invited the governors to come together "to indicate such a policy as you may deem necessary to maintain with honor and success the sacred cause in which we are engaged." In response to this invitation, Governors Reynolds, Flanagin, and Allen convened at Marshall on the 9th; because Governor Murrah was ill, Texas was represented by his agent, Guy M. Bryan. During the next three days, with General Smith in attendance, they hammered out a set of proposals whereby hostilities might cease and civil order be preserved without subjecting the Department to the humiliation of a formal surrender. Abandoning any hope of maintaining "the sacred cause in which we are engaged," the governors proposed that the army disband without parole; that officers and men be freed from all molestation and restored to full citizenship in the United States; that no prosecution be initiated in any court against any person accused of offenses committed against the United States during the war; that all persons be at liberty to remove themselves, their families, and their property beyond the jurisdiction of the United States; that the existing state governments continue to function until conventions could be called and new popular governments established; and that each state retain a number of troops under arms to act as domestic police. Immediately after the Marshall conference adjourned, Governor Flanagin returned to his capital at Washington and drafted a letter in which he offered to join with Governor Isaac Murphy in the convocation of a statewide reconstruction convention. He declared that he considered himself to be under parole, and enlisted two commissioners, Senator Augustus Garland and Judge J. J. Clendennin, to deliver his message to his Federal counterpart in Little Rock.

While Smith and the governors were meeting at Marshall, a number of prominent army officers held a round of clandestine talks at Shreveport. The officers—Generals Price, Churchill, Alexander Hawthorne, Jo Shelby, and William Preston (of Magruder's corps), Colonels George Flournoy, R. H. Musser, and L. M. Lewis, and Major O. M. Watkins—determined to "fight unto the end" or "at least until President Davis reaches this department." Should Kirby Smith "prove troublesome" and attempt to capitulate, Shelby was prepared "to hurl his splendid and massive division upon Shreveport, seize the reins of government, call upon the good and the true, march at once against the enemy and attack him for courage's sake." At Price's behest, Shelby approached Buckner, and received from him assurances that, if Smith refused to cooperate, he would take command and "fight the issue out." But Buckner, Colonel Lewis, and the secret service kept Smith fully informed of the officers' plans, and Smith let it be known, through Governor Reynolds, that while mutineers might kill him, they could not usurp his command as long as he still lived. Evidently, Smith's "calm, pure, God fearing" reaction caused the officers to reconsider, for their conspiracy came to nothing.

Returning to Shreveport on the 13th, Smith again conferred with Colonel Sprague, presented the governors' terms, and insisted that he could not "accept terms which will purchase a certain degree of immunity from devastation at the expense of the honor of [his] army." While admitting that "the Trans-Mississippi Department [could not] without assistance accomplish its independence against the whole power of the United States," and while conceding that "its people, its army, and its commander desire to avoid the unnecessary effusion of blood," he repeated that "they desire to maintain their honor, without which life would lose its attractions."

Colonel Sprague was unable to accept the arrangements advanced. While empowered a sign a military convention providing for the capitulation and parole of the Confederate armed forces, and while authorized to assure Smith that anyone who quit the war and went home quietly or who escaped to Mexico without parole would not be penalized or obstructed, he had no power to arrange a political settlement or to place his signature on a document explicitly confirming the right of Confederate soldiers to disband without the formality of a surrender. On May 15, Sprague steamed back to the Union lines, whence he reported to Pope that "the prevailing opinion" in the Southwest "was that more liberal terms should be granted to the Army of the Trans-Mississippi Department than those accepted by General Lee." A number of Federal generals thereupon urged Grant to crush the western Confederacy, and some preliminary steps were taken toward organizing an expeditionary force to invade West Texas. But General Pope counseled patience: "it is not now of consequence whether General Kirby Smith surrenders or not." On May 17, meanwhile, Smith assured Governor Murrah that "if I am supported by the troops and state authorities I do not propose to accept other terms" than those drafted by the governors.[15]

Despite Smith's intransigence and Federal impatience, General Pope's counsel proved wise. Whether Smith surrendered or not, his army was already disintegrating. The Northern Subdistrict of Arkansas no longer existed, and by now the Western Subdistrict of Texas was also evaporating. On the morning of May 13, the same day upon which Smith returned from Marshall to Shreveport, Colonel Theodore H. Barrett, currently commanding the Federal garrison at Brazos Santiago, led a force of 800 Federals onto the Texas mainland and up the north bank of the Rio Grande toward Brownsville. At Palmito Ranch, the Federals encountered 1,300 Confederates hastily gathered by Slaughter and Ford. The Federals were surprised by the rebel resistance; apparently, Barrett had expected to march into Brownsville unopposed. But the Confederates inflicted more than 100 casualties on the invaders, drove them from the field, and pushed them back to the Texas coast. Not until the battle was over, and not until Slaughter and Ford could interrogate a number of prisoners, did the West Texas rebels learn that Richmond had fallen and Lee had surrendered more than a month before!

The effect of this news upon the morale of Slaughter's troops was devastating. They abandoned their lines, raced back to Brownsville, and began to demobilize themselves. On the 19th, Slaughter had "the honor to report" to Magruder "that great dissatisfaction exists among the troops on this frontier, at least one half have already or will desert their colors." The soldiers "say, 'We are whipped, tis useless for the Trans Miss. Dept. to undertake to accomplish what the Cis Miss dept has failed to do.' War meetings have been held speeches made, but all without the desired effect, force could not be used as the rest of the troops could not as a body be depended upon."

A day or two later, six Federal officers rode into Brownsville to pay a courtesy call upon the Confederate commanders. Over a round of Havana cigars and Mrs. Ford's eggnog, the party became so convivial that the six Federals, Slaughter, Ford, and Captain John Dix decided to attend a holiday fiesta in Matamoros the following day. The next morning the Americans crossed into Mexico, watched a dress parade staged by General Tomas Mejia's Imperials, and, accompanied by General

Mejia, attended a solemn celebration of the Military Mass, "Reminiscere." "Libera nos, Deus Israel, ex omnibus angustiis nostris," chanted the choir, "ab omni . . . bellorum nequita" (Deliver us, O God of Israel, from all our afflictions, from all the wickedness of war). Incongruously, "The mass had the firing of arms as a part of the programme."

Whether or not the Americans' joint holiday was marred by a discussion of surrender terms remains unknown. At any rate, after returning to Brownsville, Slaughter and Ford decided that further resistance was useless. The post's public property was distributed to the troops; Slaughter and a few companions rode upriver toward Eagle Pass; Ford discharged the rest of the garrison; and then Ford and his wife settled in Matamoros. A few weeks later, when the Union authorities offered Ford the position of United States parole commissioner for West Texas, he accepted.

Even in the Eastern Subdistrict of Texas, the heartland of the Confederate Southwest, the symptoms of mortal corruption were already glaringly evident. "All kinds of rumors, and excitement intense," scribbled one of Steele's troopers on May 15. "The men can be seen in squads and crowds, talking and speculating over the news; some are rejoicing to think the war so near over; while others would rather see it last years upon years." General Maxey reported that his provisional division was no longer reliable; General Walker's "troops will fight no longer." And, on the night of May 14, four hundred members of the Galveston garrison mutinied and "attempted to desert the post . . . with arms in their hands." Colonel Ashbel Smith, the commandant, put down the insurrection with the help of the Eighth Texas Infantry and elements of Colonel Bernard Timmons' infantry regiment, but the mutineers remained surly. On the 16th, one of them, an anonymous private, laboriously penned a defiant declaration of independence to his commanding officer:

Col. Smith Sir it is with Pleasure that I seat myself to wright you a few lines in order to let you kno[w] that we kno[w] a thing or two as well as you[.] you and General Magruder thinks you ar[e] Both playing hell Keeping the Nuse [news] supprest[.] Col. I want you to understand very distinctly that we the soldiers on Galveston Island know that General Johnston and General Buragard is Pris[o]ners of war in the hands of the United Stat[e]s forces and we want you to distinctly understand that we know that all the troops East of the Miss River has Been surrendered on the same turms in which Lee Surrendered his[.] Yet you will threaten to hang the Editors and Put men in Irands [irons] if they Print or publish the Nuse as it is: we soldiers of galveston Island can very decentley inform you, Col, as the East side of the River is entirely whipt out and all surrendered as Prisners of war that it [is] No use for you and Mr. McGruder to try to get any fight out of these troops on the Island[.] further th[e] More we are for making the Best of a Bad thing we Can. Our Beloved country is yet unharmed By the Enemy while the country East of the Missi[ssi]ppi River is entireley Ruin[e]d, and yet you and General McGruder for the sake of get[t]ing of a few more Boat loads of cotton to havanar in order to put the money into your own Pocket you would freeley devast tat [devastate] our state and sacrafice half the men under youre command: we want you to understand that over half of the troops under youre command is men of famleys and they feel Near and dear to us[.] and we furthermore want you to understand that we are Not going into any more fights for fear that we might get Kild, and if our Country is devastated as you and General Mc[gruder] is willing for it to Be for the sake of speculation we want to Be left here in order to try to take cear [care] of our wives and little ones[.] we ar[e] ready to admit that timess will Be hard if we ar[e] subjugated[.] But it wont Bee any harder on me than it will on my wife and children with [me] kild and the country intir[e]ley Burnt out and devastated[.] so Col if you intend on fighting the Yankey any more you Need Not count me and a thousand more in for we kno[w] how things stands East of the Missipi: all tho [although] we ar[e] Not allowed to have the truth give[n] to us it is we have a way of finding it out if Mr. [Ferdinand] flak [Flake, publisher of *Flake's Tri-Weekly Bulletin*] will say he will Publish the Nuse as it is he shall have two thirds of the troops on this Island to Back him in so doing[.] so Col. you see we will have it and if you enterfear [interfere] with any one you will meat Lincoln in hell their to mingle youre voich with his[.] so I must close[.] I Been with you Nearley fore years[.] I hope we wont Bee together much longer[.] from youre friend[.]

That same day, Magruder and Walker both informed Kirby Smith that the same rebellious spirit had infected their commands. Walker affirmed that his men "consider the contest a hopeless one, and will lay down their arms at the first appearance of an enemy." And Magruder told Smith that "the officers and men" of the District of Texas "insist upon dividing the property" of the quartermasters' and commissary bureaus "before the surrender, and I think it ought to be done."

I have exerted myself [Magruder continued] more than I ever did to instill a spirit of resistance into the men, but in vain. I but make myself antagonistic to the army and an object of their displeasure. Nothing more can be done except to satisfy the soldiers, to induce them to preserve their organization, and to send them in regiments, &c., to their homes, with as little damage to the community as possible. For God's sake act or let me act.[16]

Smith acted on May 18. Leaving Buckner in immediate charge of affairs east of the Sabine River, he announced the removal of his own headquarters from Shreveport to Houston. Apparently he planned to rally the reliable remnant of Magruder's corps for a last-ditch stand in Texas, but, considering the mood of Magruder's men, any such expectation was hardly realistic. During the week it took Smith to travel to Houston—he journeyed by stage rather than by rail, and stopped en route to visit and address a number of garrisons—the army of the Trans-Mississippi Department dissolved.

Even before the 18th, "a great many of the soldiers" of Steele's cavalry had already "laid down their arms, and [had] gone home"; while "all [was already] confusion and demoralization" along the lower Red River, where "nothing like order or discipline remains." Only eighty-six men still manned the vital fortifications defending Alexandria. "All the commands of every arm of the service at or near Alexandria are destroyed." On the 18th itself, thirty troopers belonging to the Twelfth Texas Cavalry and seventy-five belonging to the Nineteenth Texas Cavalry abandoned their colors and deserted; in Louisiana, below Natchitoches, "orders and compulsory measures to make the few remaining men do their duty . . . are now at an end," and even the courier lines linking outposts and headquarters to one another were being abandoned. On the 19th, the officers of the Nineteenth and Twenty-sixth Texas cavalry regiments agreed to discharge their commands. The following day, William Parsons' Texas brigade broke up. On the 21st, Walker's entire infantry division mutinied, looted the quartermasters' and commissary stores in the neighborhood of its East Texas camps, and crumbled apart. Thomas' Louisiana infantry division threw down its arms, sacked the military and state depots at Shreveport, and disintegrated. The troops of the Galveston garrison looted the town's warehouses, commandeered a railroad train, and evacuated their post—

theirs may well have been the last troop train to operate under some semblance of Confederate auspices. General Churchill, bowing to the inevitable, published an order to his Arkansas division announcing "that furloughs will be granted all men who desire to go home to cut their wheat." By the 22d, Kirby Smith, who was then in the vicinity of Crockett, began "to meet squads of men going to their homes, taking with them different species of public property"; and on the 23d, he was "compelled to remain 36 hours in Huntsville to escape the mob of disorderly soldierly [*sic*] thronging the roads." What was left of Wharton's old cavalry corps disbanded on the 24th; and with the demobilization of the cavalry, nothing was left of Kirby Smith's army except some scattered garrison units in Texas and West Louisiana and Jo Shelby's Missouri division.

On the 25th, at Hempstead, Smith received from Magruder a telegram describing the dissolution of his forces, in which Magruder quite frankly admitted that he had "lost all control over them." Smith professed himself "astounded at this intelligence," and, like a commanding general who still had something to command, he insisted that Magruder compose and file "a full & immediate report of all the circumstances connected with this most unexpected and humiliating conduct on the part of the troops in your District." But no amount of inquiry, no investigations, no justifications could amend or reverse the fact that Kirby Smith's army was forever gone. As far as Governor Flanagin could tell, there was "not a Confederate soldier in arms in the State" of Arkansas, and not "3,000 men under arms in the department." Flanagin, for one, felt "no hesitation in acting as I would act if no such thing as a Confederate force existed."

Some veterans were crushed by the disaster. "Our bright dream is or'e [*sic*], our country is subjugated, our armies are scattered to the 'Four winds of the Heavens,' our cause is lost! *lost!!* LOST!!!" But others were more pragmatic. "I am just off a trip of about 900 miles," wrote a Texas rebel from Fort Bend County. "I am now out of the service. We had no show [no luck] at the distribution of the public property. We got nothing, and while we were gone all of my clothing was stolen, so I am without money or clothing. . . . The money that I was to get . . . was to be paid in Confederate money, so it is no use. I am flat." [17]

≈ VI   On May 26, most of the surviving fragments of the Trans-Mississippi army were formally surrendered to General Canby. But this surrender was not so tidy as those arranged in the Cis-Mississippi. One symptom of the disorder west of the Mississippi was that several Confederate leaders made at least four separate and unrelated attempts to negotiate a capitulation. And then, when a cartel was finally signed, it turned out that one rebel division had been overlooked.

Governor Flanagin's two peace commissioners, Garland and Clendennin, departed for Little Rock on May 24, but the Federal authorities declined to receive them. Instead, on the 27th, Governor Murphy and the incumbent military commandant, General J. J. Reynolds, insisted that no political accommodation could be made with the state's rebel administration. They invited Flanagin to abandon his pretensions to office and settle down as a docile and loyal citizen of the United States. Flanagin, deciding that further defiance was pointless, then visited Little Rock in person, delivered his government's archives to the Federals, and retired peacefully to his home near Arkadelphia.

Also on the 24th, Governor Murrah and General Magruder instructed W. P. Ballinger and Ashbel Smith to proceed to New Orleans and secure terms for the capitulation of the District of Texas. The Texan representatives secured clearance from the Union navy to make the trip by water, but before they embarked they learned that their district had already been surrendered by negotiators from Shreveport.

On the 23d, General Harry Hays had nominated his own agents, General Brent, Colonel Alcibiades De Blanc, and Colonel Ross E. Burke, and had sent them to Baton Rouge to surrender the District of West Louisiana. While conferring with the local Union commander, General F. J. Herron, Brent and his colleagues stated that they were authorized by Hays to "surrender" West Louisiana, and were authorized by Kirby Smith to "arrange terms for the surrender of the remaining portion of the department"—an assertion which Smith, some time later, vehemently denied. Both Herron and his superior, General Canby, were dubious as to how much authority the three Confederates possessed, and both feared that the arrangement of any "terms" with agents acting for Kirby Smith might involve something more than a simple military capitulation. Herron therefore suggested that another commission, selected by an officer superior to Hays, meet Canby in New Orleans.

And so, on the 25th, Generals Buckner, Price, and Brent steamed down to New Orleans, conferred at length with Canby, and agreed, subject to Kirby Smith's approval, to surrender the military and naval forces of the Trans-Mississippi Department. The following morning, Buckner and Canby's chief of staff, General P. J. Osterhaus, put their signatures to a "military convention" which stipulated the same terms as those given to the armies commanded by Lee, Johnston, and Taylor: officers and men of the Confederate forces were to desist from all acts of war and all resistance against the United States; officers and men were to be paroled and permitted to return to their homes without molestation; and all public or military property, other than the officers' side arms, mounts, and baggage, and the soldiers' horses, was to be turned over to agents of the United States army.

Kirby Smith reached Houston on May 27, only to discover that the army he claimed to command no longer existed. Smith's reaction to the news was a peculiar mixture of bureaucratic habit, public concern, and personal justification. On the 29th, acting as if the administrative machinery of his army was not in the least disturbed, he issued a special order convening "a court of Inquiry . . . at this place tomorrow Morning at 10 O'Clock A. M. to ascertain and report upon the causes and manner of the disbandment of the troops in the District of Texas New Mexico & Arizona." Under the presidency of General Walker, a court met briefly and reported that underlying the desertion of Magruder's corps was the disaffection and demoralization which seized the civilian population after the news of Lee's surrender reached the West. The soldiers, said the court, merely yielded to the "feeling of non resistance spread among them by the people of the state." The district's officers, in particular, were exonerated from all blame for "the acts of an armed and overwhelming mob who had become deaf alike to the dictates of duty, reason, and honor."

On the 30th, appalled by the lawlessness and disorder which accompanied the breakup of the army, Smith urged Governor Murrah to employ whatever state forces were available to protect public property and to keep the peace. That same day, in an effort to counter imputations that he had purposely delayed capitulation so that his forces might

disband without parole, Smith wrote a lengthy apology to Colonel
Sprague, affirming that his army's ill-disciplined dissolution had left
him "mortified," "powerless," and "humiliated." And, also on the 30th,
he promulgated a farewell address to his men, an address remarkable
for its bitterness: "Soldiers! I am left a Commander without an army—
a General without troops. You have made yr. choice. It was unwise &
unpatriotic, But it is final. I pray you may not live to regret it."

The following day, Smith disbursed $1,700 in secret service gold
to Generals Magruder, Forney, Walker, Hawes, and Drayton, in partial
settlement for their back pay, and directed Captain Ernest Cucullu to
deliver the $3,300 remaining in the secret service fund to General
Canby. On the 2d, while visiting Galveston in the company of General
Magruder, he scrawled a note to Canby inclosing "orders from Dept &
Dist H^d Q^{rs} under date of June 2nd/65 [which] designate the points
at which the officers & men will be paroled and the public property delivered to the U. S. Commissioners appointed to receive it—The Dist
Commanders are charged with the general superintendance of the surrender in their several dists." Smith then boarded the Federal steamer
Fort Jackson, standing off the Galveston bar, and affixed his own signature to a copy of the military convention negotiated a week earlier by
Buckner and Canby. Scribbling a postscript across the bottom of the
page, he stipulated his "understanding that by the provisions of this
convention C. S. officers observing their paroles are permitted to make
their homes either in or out of the United States." And one week later,
on June 9, the last regular Confederate States unit composed of white
men, the Consolidated Eighteenth Louisiana Infantry Regiment, paraded beneath the lacy iron façades of the balconies overlooking Natchitoches' main plaza, stacked its arms, furled its colors, and quit.[18]

But on the day the Eighteenth Louisiana disbanded, one small
rebel division was still intact, still in the field, and still at war with the
United States. In all the confusion, headquarters had neglected to inform Douglas Cooper of the Department's disintegration. Ironically, on
May 26, the very day on which Buckner capitulated to Canby, representatives of the Confederate States (General Throckmorton and Colonel
W. P. Reagan), the Five Nations, and "our brothers of the plains" had
come together in council at Camp Napoleon, in the Leased Lands, to
conclude a treaty of peace and perpetual friendship between thirteen

"blanket" tribes and the now-defunct Confederacy. "The tomahawk shall be forever buried," according to the peace terms; the "scalping knife shall be forever broken. The warpath . . . shall grow up and become as the wild wilderness. The path of peace shall be opened, and kept upon and traveled in friendship . . . and never shall it be stained with the blood of our brothers."

Not until the second week of June did the Five Nations learn that their Confederate allies had been subjugated, and not until the 15th were they able to convene, at Cleata Yamaha, Choctaw Nation, a grand council empowered to "contract anew friendly relations with the United States Government." Since the terms of capitulation arranged by Buckner embraced only the "officers and men of the Army and Navy of the Confederate States," and since the troopers of the allied Indian brigades were not, technically, either citizens or soldiers of the Southern Confederacy, the grand council recommended that the governors or principal chiefs of the several Nations, and the field commander of the Territorial division, negotiate their own separate cartels with the authorities of the United States.

By June 18, both the governor of the Chickasaws, Winchester Colbert, and the principal chief of the Choctaws, P. P. Pitchlynn, had accepted terms identical to those extended to Buckner. And on the 23d, a ragged little column of bedraggled rebel pony soldiers, with their grimy slouch hats pulled low over their eyes and their tarnished side arms rattling against their horses' lean flanks, jangled down the dusty road from Bloomdale and into the town of Doaksville. Before the day was done, their leader, Stand Watie, principal chief of the Cherokees and commanding general of the Territorial division, surrendered the remnant of his organization, his Nation, and his dreams to Lieutenant Colonel A. C. Matthews of the United States army. He agreed, in addition, to enforce the imposition of the usual terms upon the Creeks, the Seminoles, and Broken Arm's band of Osages. Five days later, after receiving from Buckner a three-week-old letter containing official notification of the Trans-Mississippi Department's capitulation, Douglas Cooper opened correspondence with the Union commandant at Shreveport, General James C. Veatch, and offered his "services . . . in restoring order among the Indians." His services were "cheerfully accepted."

Not every Trans-Mississippi soldier surrendered or went home.

According to an estimate made by Federal intelligence operatives, perhaps as many as 2,000 unreconstructed rebels fled into the vacant country west of the edge of settlement or escaped across the Rio Grande into Imperial Mexico. Most of the exiles traveled alone, or at best with a squad of companions, but toward the end of June a large column, numbering almost 500 men, crossed into Mexico at Piedas Negras. The nucleus of this column was a 300-man contingent of Jo Shelby's old Iron Brigade, which, under Shelby's personal command, evacuated the camps near Shreveport during the last week of May and set out on the long trek to the border. While passing through East Texas, the Missouri horse soldiers were joined by other refugees, including Governor Murrah, General Hawthorne, and Colonels A. W. Terrell and Flournoy. When the troopers and their guests reached San Antonio, they found it to be a town full of "fugitive generals . . . and fugitive senators and fugitive governors and fugitive desperadoes, as well." Since the desperadoes outnumbered the others, the desperadoes had "taken possession of the city and were rioting in the old royal fashion, sitting in the laps of courtesans and drinking wines fresh through the blockade from France. They had plundered a dozen stores, had sacked and burned a commissary train." At San Antonio, four ex-governors (Clark, Moore, Allen, and Reynolds), four ex-generals (Price, Magruder, Hawes, and Cadmus Wilcox), and a crowd of lesser luminaries attached themselves to Shelby's force; and one day's march south of the town, none other than Kirby Smith himself, with Colonel Douglas and a small circle of friends, caught up with the column. On the 26th, after burying the Iron Brigade's shredded battle flags under the sand of the Rio Grande's north bank, the rebels forded the river and passed into Mexico. Kirby Smith, mounted on a mule, wearing a calico shirt and a silk kerchief around his neck, with a revolver on his hip and a shotgun across his saddle, led the way. Once in Mexico, Smith and his compatriots enjoyed many wistful reunions with old comrades in arms, including Generals Bee, Slaughter, and Thomas Hindman.[19]

"Upon the disbandment of large armies," editorialized the Clarksville *Standard* on June 10, "great numbers of stragglers pass singly, or in small bodies to their homes. It would not be consistent with our knowledge of human nature, to suppose that all those individuals, or squads are governed by strict principles of honor. . . . We have *heard* of bodies of men, who *said* they intended to come in, and sack the town." Clarksville defended itself from the Department's war veterans by marshaling a citizens' vigilante battalion, the "Red River Guards," which mustered for drill every morning at 9 o'clock—all who failed to report "punctually, except in case of disability, will be considered as abandoning the organization, and not entitled to its protection." But other towns were less prepared to receive the homecoming veterans. On the night of June 11, a band of forty demobilized rebels rode into Austin, broke into the Texas State Treasury, blew open the vault, and looted the whole of the state's specie deposit, which amounted to something less than $5,000 in gold. Wisely leaving behind the bundles of Confederate currency stored in the same safe, the bandits shot their way out of town and disappeared. A sharpshooting citizen managed to chop down one of the outlaws before they escaped, but, since the sum stolen was so insignificant, the state authorities did not bother to pursue the rest of the gang.

Most of the itinerant veterans plundered only enough to subsist themselves until they arrived home. Once they reached their farms and their families, they settled down to the task of reconstructing their country and their lives. But a few, schooled too thoroughly in the brutal academy of war, found peace to be too dull and ordinary for them. In Missouri especially, scores who had spent their entire adolescence bushwhacking retired from killing only long enough to confirm that farming was not their vocation. On St. Valentine's Day, 1866, Frank and Jesse James took their first step toward a new career by holding up the bank in Liberty, Missouri. Their example was followed by dozens of others. George and Ollie Shepherd, the Younger brothers, Richard Liddil, Jack Moore, Jim White, Ed Miller, Tom and Bud McDaniels, John Jarrett, Clarence Hite, Arch Clements, Jim Cummins, and other borderland veterans all earned new reputations and prices on their heads by refining the art of banditry. Kit Dalton spent the next seventeen years robbing stagecoaches.

The timely arrival of Union occupation forces hastened the pacification of the Department's settled portions, but "the outlying districts were left to themselves for some time, and of course every man was a law to himself for the time being." With the removal of Confederate and Texas frontier troops from the western marches of the Department, the Plains Indians again resumed their raids through the border country. By August, 1865, the situation along the border seemed "to be worse than ever known before"; by September, the homesteaders in Wise County could no longer tell "where the frontier line will be after two more full moons pass." By 1866, the whole of western Texas, from the Red River to the Rio Grande, was convulsed by the depradations of the war parties, and entire counties were again being depopulated.

On June 16, 1865, a large steam transport docked at Galveston and, while a military band played "Yankee Doodle," debarked a regiment of United States Regulars. Three hundred sullen Texans watched the event, but all the newspapers found noteworthy was that the Federal soldiers appeared to be well fed, well dressed, and well armed. At about the same time, other Union columns were pushing southward from Fort Smith and Little Rock, or up the Red River Valley toward Shreveport, or inland from Brazos Santiago along the Great River Road, or eastward over the old Butterfield Stage road from New Mexico. Their dark blue uniforms were clean, their brass, buttons, sabers, and carbines bright, their horses sleek, even their accents and their alien battle hymns clipped and vivacious. None of the drabness so characteristic of the late rebel army seemed to mark these Federal forces. As the Federals spread through the Confederate Southwest, their flags were run up over town after town. Their officers came to supervise paroles, collect records, make inventories of captured military property, assist in the reestablishment of loyal reconstructed governments, and to free and police the slaves. Their enlisted men, who turned out to be not too unlike the enlisted men who had once worn butternut and gray, came to stand guard, to parade, drill, lounge, and wonder why they were there. A few curious adventurers from the distant North doubtless took leave to cross into Mexico, to see and explore the fabled wonders of Bagdad and Matamoros. But at Bagdad they found only an abandoned shantytown, and at Matamoros a quaint little Latin border village—a village which boasted an unusual number of empty warehouses and countless "For Rent" signs.

On Tuesday, July 25, General Wesley Merritt and the Eighteenth New York Cavalry escorted Governor A. J. Hamilton into Austin and installed him in his statehouse. His capital celebrated his arrival with a grand display of United States flags and a thirty-six-gun salute. Merritt and his Yorkers, having safely deposited Hamilton, then proceeded on to San Antonio, where they encamped on the outskirts of town. After the passage of a few weeks, Merritt and his volunteers were relieved by a veteran regiment of the "Old Army," the Fourth United States Cavalry, and after the Yorkers departed for home, the Regulars settled down to the dull routine of garrison and occupation duty. Except for occasional visits to town, where the troopers entertained themselves by getting drunk and kicking rats off the sidewalks, they had nothing to keep them busy. As far as Sergeant James Larson of the Fourth Cavalry was concerned, "San Antonio was without exception the dullest place" he had ever seen.[20]

꙳ **VII**   The Trans-Mississippi Department was never more than a peripheral theater of operations, and its fate hinged upon the fortunes of Confederate arms in the East. Until the end of the war, the Department continued to be affected by the decisions of the Confederate government, the convolutions of the Confederate economy, and the military successes and failures of the armies defending the Confederacy's Cis-Mississippi heartland. Indeed, certain events which occurred east of the River, such as the surrender of Robert E. Lee's army, bore directly upon the collapse of the Trans-Mississippi. Yet the Trans-Mississippi was the most extensive military department in the Confederacy; it was, at least potentially, a recruiting ground and a source of supply for the East; its very existence was a factor which the Union high command had to weigh when planning campaign strategy; it did enjoy some unique advantages and encounter some unique problems; and its history does serve to complement and refine the history of the Confederate States.

A study of the Trans-Mississippi Department leaves five major impressions. First, one fundamental flaw in Confederate grand strategy, a flaw which effectively condemned to failure the South's attempts to hold the Mississippi and to preserve the integrity of the Confederate States, was the naïve and fatal assumption that the River constituted a natural boundary to divide military departments. Unlike the Federals, who appreciated that the River itself was the proper focus for operations in the Mississippi Basin and the central terrain feature around which military jurisdictions should be constructed—and who, therefore, permitted Banks and Grant to exercise command on both sides of the water—the rebels separated responsibility for the supervision of the eastern and western banks. While Union generals easily shifted their own forces from one shore to the other as required, efforts to transfer Confederate troops prior to the capitulation of Vicksburg first required extensive coordination between distant and semiautonomous departmental headquarters, none of which were normally inclined to dispatch their own soldiers elsewhere. Ultimate responsibility for such transfers was lodged in Richmond's War Department, a situation which, considering the quality of the Confederacy's communications, was absurd. The Confederates immeasurably increased the vulnerability of the entire trans-Appalachian South by casually drawing a dotted line down the Mississippi River. Once Vicksburg fell, of course, the issue was moot.

Second, despite severe dislocations the Trans-Mississippi's economy remained viable through the end of the war. Sustained by diminishing but adequate agricultural production, access to foreign markets, and a measure of primitive industrialization, the Department generally managed to feed, clothe, and supply its people and its armies. During the last year of the conflict, while the Union forces refrained from pressing operations west of the River, some areas deep within the interior of the Department even experienced a mild economic recovery. Had it not been for the Trans-Mississippi's inadequate domestic transportation network, for the approaching exhaustion of its single cash crop, and for the army's expensive efforts to prosecute offensive campaigns, the Department's population might have endured the closing months of the war in comparative comfort.

Third, despite the Southwest's relative immunity from physical damage following the spring campaigns of 1864, the Department suffered a disintegration of morale during the last months of the conflict. The Confederate Southwest was not beaten in battle, nor was it defeated by the inadequacies of its economy. The experience of the Southwest, excused from the ravages of massive invasion or the smoke of continuous battle, serves to confirm the hypothesis that the reason for the evaporation of the Confederate war effort lies not in the objective details of political economy but in the depths of the Southern spirit. Military reverses and an erratic economy were only two of the many factors contributing to the Department's despair. Speculation, impressment, conscription, inflation, the dislocation of refugees, rumors, the rhetoric of states' rights, inept command, insensitive civil administration, the disruption of domestic discipline, poor communications, the army's interference in civil affairs for reasons of "military necessity," and a pervasive atmosphere of violence and uncertainty all contributed to the final breakdown of morale.

Fourth, the conventional thesis which states that the ideology and practice of states' rights undermined the achievement of Confederate national independence may require some modification. While it is true that localism sometimes interfered with mobilization and the conduct of the war, especially with regard to Kirby Smith's relations with the government of Texas and his various attempts to transfer troops from one district to another, nonetheless the Confederate officials west of the Mississippi usually succeeded in imposing their will upon the states and the people. Trade, commerce, communications, manufacturing, agriculture, procurement, enlistment, civil justice, and the Department's state governments and foreign relations fell under some degree of military influence or control. During the spring and summer of 1864, even the government of Texas virtually abdicated its claimed autonomy in favor of the army's authority. Insofar as the Confederacy's demise may be explained in terms of the adverse effect states' rights had upon troop recruitment and the appropriation of war matériel, the conventional thesis seems to be relatively inapplicable to the Trans-Mississippi. Indeed, insofar as defeat was the result of demoralization, the accelerating nationalization of Southwestern institutions appears to have contributed to the Department's collapse by helping to exhaust the citizens' faith in their own states' rights rhetoric.

Finally, the history of the Trans-Mississippi offers abundant evidence that the progressive demoralization of the South dated from the earliest days of the war. By 1862, conscription and impressment were deemed necessary, desertion and crime were on the rise, goods were becoming scarce, and even insurrectionary outbreaks were not unknown. Following the fall of Vicksburg, speculation spiraled beyond all reason, faith in the currency nearly evaporated, desertion and defiance redoubled, and the mood of impending defeat grew. The events of 1864, ranging from a religious revival to the implementation of an illusory scheme to liberate Missouri, merely set the stage for the Trans-Mississippi's psychological disintegration early in 1865. If any generalization may be made upon the basis of evidence taken from the history of the Confederate Southwest, it seems that the high tide of Confederate aspirations began ebbing away during the first months of the Civil War.

NOTES ❧

Chapter One: The Trans-Mississippi South, 1861–1863

1. Quoting Kirby Smith to Johnston, June 4, 1863, Letterbook; Kirby Smith to Mother, Jan. 11, 1864, Correspondence; Kirby Smith to Johnson, Jan. 15, 1864, Letterbook, Edmund Kirby Smith Papers, Southern Historical Collection, University of North Carolina. Also, *The War of the Rebellion: A Compilation of the Official Records of the Union and Confederate Armies* (Washington, D.C., 1880–1901), Ser. I, VII, 826; VIII, 734; IX, 713, 719; XIII, 829–30, 855, 860; XXII, part ii, 780, 798, 803; LIII, 819 (hereafter referred to as *O.R.*).

2. U.S. Census Office, *Eighth Census* (1860), Vol. I, *Population*, pp. iv, xiii, xv, xvii–xviii, 12–17, 19, 21, 193–95, 197, 274–98, 302–3, 484–93, 567–73, 605, 516–23; Vol. II, *Manufactures*, p. 594; Vol. IV, *Statistics*, p. 512; U.S. Census Office, *A Compendium of the Ninth Census* (1870), pp. 639, 798.

3. Quoting Richard Taylor, *Destruction and Reconstruction*, ed. Richard B. Harwell (New York, 1955), p. 183; John C. Brightman to Mother, June 14, 1863, John C. Brightman Papers, University of Texas Archives. Also, Taylor, *Destruction and Reconstruction*, pp. 121–26; *Texas Almanac, 1861* (Galveston, 1860), pp. 122–26; L. C. Gray, *History of Agriculture in the Southern United States to 1860* (Washington, D.C., 1933), II, 907; Frederick Olmstead, *A Journey Through Texas* (New York, 1857), pp. 61–62; Frederick Olmstead, *A Journey in the Seaboard Slave States* (New York, 1861), p. 639; U.S. Census Office, *Seventh Census* 1850), p. 248; *Eighth Census* (1860), *Population*, pp. 17, 194; *A Compendium of the Ninth Census* (1870), pp. 699, 701, 703; Roger W. Shugg, *Origins of Class Struggle in Louisiana* (Baton Rouge, 1939), pp. 179–80, 193; *Weekly Gazette and Comet* (Baton Rouge), March 7, 1860; *New Orleans Picayune*, April 28, Nov. 24, 861; *O.R.*, Ser. I, XV, 556–57; XXXIV, part ii, 965–66; Ser. IV, I, 625, 1020.

4. *Eighth Census* (1860), *Population*, pp. 302–3; *A Compendium of the Ninth Census* (1870), pp. 639, 691, 695, 699, 701, 703, 711; Edward C. Smith, *The Borderland in the Civil War* (New York, 1927), pp. 153, 260, 383; Lloyd Lewis, Propaganda and the Kansas-Missouri War," *Missouri Historical Review*, XXXIV Oct., 1939), 3–17; Hildegarde Herklotz, "Jayhawkers in Missouri," *Mo. Hist. Rev.*, XVII (April, July, 1923), 266–84, XVIII (Oct., 1923), 64–101; Edward R. Smith, "How Quantrill Became an Outlaw," *Kansas Historical Collections*, VII 1901–2), 214–18; Henry E. Palmer, "The Black-Flag Character of the War on he Border," *Kans. Hist. Coll.*, IX (1905–6), 459; Theodosius Botkin, "Among the overeign Squats," *Kans. Hist. Coll.*, VII (1901–2), 433; William E. Connelley, *Quantrill and the Border Wars* (Cedar Rapids, 1910), p. 281; Wiley Britton,

Memoirs of the Rebellion on the Border, 1863 (Chicago, 1882), pp. 128, 352–54; Floyd C. Shoemaker, "The Story of the Civil War in Northeast Missouri," *Mo. Hist. Rev.,* VII (April, 1913), 66 ff.; John McElroy, *The Struggle for Missouri* (Washington, D.C., 1913), p. 13; Sceva B. Laughlin, "Missouri Politics during the Civil War," *Mo. Hist. Rev.,* XXIII (1929), 583–618; Jefferson Davis, *The Rise and Fall of the Confederate Government* (New York, 1881), I, 416–17; Cyrus Peterson and Joseph Hanson, *Pilot Knob: The Thermopylae of the West* (New York, 1914), p. 18; *O.R.,* Ser. I, VII, 532; VIII, 641–42; XIII, 45; XXII, part i, 196, 200.

5. Nevin M. Fenneman, *Physiography of Eastern United States* (New York, 1938), pp. 100–21, 445, 559–630; Nevin M. Fenneman, *Physiography of Western United States* (New York, 1931), pp. 5–30, 36, 47–59, 316–17; Rupert B. Vance, *Human Geography of the South* (Chapel Hill, 1935), pp. 151, 321; *Eighth Census* (1860), *Population,* pp. 16–17, 194, 274–85, 484–93, 567, and *Agriculture,* pp. 6, 66, 92, 148; *A Compendium of the Ninth Census* (1870), pp. 691, 695, 699, 701, 711; David Y. Thomas, *Arkansas in War and Reconstruction* (Little Rock, 1926), pp. 24–25; Taylor, *Destruction and Reconstruction,* pp. 123–25; Paul I. Wellman, *Glory, God, and Gold* (Garden City, 1954), pp. 330–36; Walter P. Webb, *The Great Plains* (New York, 1931), pp. 4–8; *Texas Almanac, 1861,* p. 169; Charles W. Ramsdell, "General Robert E. Lee's Horse Supply, 1862–1865," *American Historical Review,* XXXV (July, 1930), 758–77; Stephen B. Oates, *Confederate Cavalry West of the River* (Austin, 1961), p. 74; T. R. Havins, "Texas Sheep Boom," *West Texas Historical Association Year Book,* XXVIII (Oct., 1952), 10–11; Paul Taylor, *An American-Mexican Frontier* (Chapel Hill, 1934), p. 33; Annie H. Abel, *The American Indian as Participant in the Civil War* (Cleveland, 1919), pp. 40–41; A. B. Bender, *The March of Empire: Frontier Defense in the Southwest, 1848–1860* (Lawrence, Kan., 1952), opposite p. 284; *O.R.,* Ser. IV, I, 324; William R. Peveler, "Diary," May 5–June 5, 1863, copy, University of Texas Archives; A. R. Roessler, "Military Routes of the Confederate Army in Texas," folder, Texas State Archives, Austin.

6. Robert L. Kerby, *The Confederate Invasion of New Mexico and Arizona* (Los Angeles, 1958); Ray C. Colton, *The Civil War in the Western Territories* (Norman, Okla., 1959), pp. 13–119; Martin H. Hall, *Sibley's New Mexico Campaign* (Austin, 1960); William A. Keleher, *Turmoil in New Mexico, 1846–1868* (Santa Fe, 1952), pp. 147 ff., 238 ff.; R. L. Rodgers, "The Confederate States Organized Arizona in 1862," *Southern Historical Society Papers,* XXVIII (1900), 224; F. S. Donnell, "The Confederate Territory of Arizona," *New Mexico Historical Review,* XVII (1942), 148–63; Rufus K. Wyllys, "Arizona and the Civil War," *Arizona Highways,* XXVII (1951), 34–39; Charles S. Walker, "Confederate Government in Doña Ana County," *New Mex. Hist. Rev.,* VI (July, 1931), 253–302; Edward D. Tittman, "The Exploitation of Treason," *New Mex. Hist. Rev.,* IV (April, 1929), 128–45; Robert Casey, Jr., *The Texas Border and Some Borderliners* (New York, 1950), p. 81; William C. Whitford, *Colorado Volunteers in the Civil War* (Denver, 1906), p. 42; Warner Lewis, "Massacre of Confederates by the Osages," *Osage Magazine,* I (Feb., May, 1910), 49–52, 68–70; *Houston Tri-Weekly Telegraph,* Aug. 13, 25, 1863; *San Antonio Herald,* June 7, 1862, June 6, 1863; *Rio Abajo Weekly Press,* April 21, 1863; *The Statutes at Large of the Pro-*

isional Government of the Confederate States of America, ed. James M. Mat-
hews (Richmond, 1864), pp. 242–47; *Journals of the Congress of the
Confederate States of America, 1861–1865* (Washington, D.C., 1904–5), I, 475,
51, 585, 612–20, 635, 660–61, 701; II, 59, 79; V, 80; *O.R.,* Ser. I, IX, 666; XV,
14–18; XXVI, part i, 57–58; L, part i, 1108, and part ii, 100–5; LIII, 805; Ser.
V, I, 636–46, 930; III, 76, 960–62, 1035–36.

. Quoting *The Standard* (Clarksville, Tex.), May 16, 1863. Also, J. W. Wilbar-
er, *Indian Depredations in Texas* (Austin, 1935), pp. 84–86, 320–39, 479–80,
14–17, 650–52; Charles Ramsdell, "The Frontier and Secession," *Studies in
Southern History and Politics* (New York, 1914), pp. 70–71; *Journal of the Se-
ession Convention of Texas, 1861,* ed. Ernest W. Winkler (Austin, 1912), pp.
68–74; James B. Berry, *A Texas Ranger and Frontiersman: The Days of Buck
Berry in Texas,* ed. James K. Greer (Dallas, 1932), pp. 114–16, 145; *Texas Alma-
ac, 1863* (Austin, 1863), p. 47; J. Evetts Haley, "Scouting with [Charles E.]
Goodnight," *Southwest Review,* XVII (April, 1933), 272; John S. Ford, *Rip
Ford's Texas,* ed. Stephen B. Oates (Austin, 1963), p. 349; James D. Richardson,
A Compilation of the Messages and Papers of the Confederacy (Washington,
D.C., 1905), I, 160; Francis R. Lubbock, *Six Decades in Texas* (Austin, 1900),
p. 357, 469–71, 475, 483; Joseph McConnell, *The West Texas Frontier* (Jacks-
oro, Tex., 1939), p. 62; H. P. N. Gammel, comp., *The Laws of Texas,
822–1897* (Austin, 1902), V, 452–65, 607; *Dallas Herald,* July 8, 1863; *The
Standard* (Clarksville, Tex.), Feb. 15, 1863; *Houston Tri-Weekly Telegraph,*
March 22, 1863; *Texas Almanac—Extra* (Austin), March 7, 1863; Desmond P.
Hopkins, "Diary," University of Texas Archives; "Record Book of Camp Davis,
Kerr County, Texas," copy, University of Texas Archives; Peveler, "Diary," April
, 1863; Lubbock to the Gentlemen of the Senate and House of Representatives
of Texas], Nov. 15, 1861, and Lubbock to Sayles, Nov. 21, 1862, Executive Rec-
rd Book, No. 81, Texas State Archives; Norris to Dashiell, April 23, 1862,
Hyde to Dashiell, May 2, 1862, Lane to Norris, May 8, 1862, McCord to Dash-
ell, Aug. 27, 1862, all in Records, Office of the Adjutant General of Texas,
Texas State Archives; McCord to Dashiell, May 21, 1863, Misc. Military Papers,
Texas State Archives; Lubbock to Wahrmond, April 9, 1862, and Loring to Lub-
ock, n.d., 1862, Governors' Letters (Lubbock), Texas State Archives.

. *Journal, Texas Secession Convention,* pp. 368–74; J. Fred Rippy, "Border
Troubles along the Rio Grande, 1848–1860," *Southwestern Historical Quarterly,*
XXIII (Oct., 1919), 91–111; Walter P. Webb, *The Texas Rangers* (Boston and
New York, 1935), pp. 175–93; Ford, *Rip Ford's Texas,* pp. 261–309; *Reports of
he Committee of Investigation Sent by the Mexican Government to the Frontier
f Texas* (New York, 1875), pp. 196–97; *U.S. House Exec. Docs.,* 36th Cong., 1st
ess., Vol. VII, No. 52, and Vol. XII, No. 81; *U.S. Senate Docs.,* 36th Cong., 1st
ess., Vol. XI, No. 21; Frank Owsley, *King Cotton Diplomacy* (Chicago, 1931),
p. 82–112; Claude Elliott, "Union Sentiment in Texas, 1861–1865," *Southwest-
rn Hist. Quar.,* L (April, 1947), 459–62; James Fremantle, *The Fremantle Diary,*
d. Walter Lord (Boston, 1954), pp. 7–8; *Houston Tri-Weekly Telegraph,* Dec. 5,
862, and Jan. 28, 1863; *The Southwestern* (Shreveport, La.), Jan. 6, 1864;
Brownsville *Flag,* as quoted in *San Antonio Herald,* April 4, 1863; *O.R.,* Ser. I,
V, 131–32, 137; XV, 1016–17, 1025–26, 1030–31, 1078–79, 1128–29, 1131–35;

Quintero to Browne, March 28, April 17, April 28, 1862, and Quintero to Benjamin, Aug. 30, 1862, Jan. 30, Feb. 26, March 21, April 20, 1863, all in John Pickett Papers, Library of Congress; Statement of W. W. Nelson, Jan. 17, 1860, Governors' Letters (Houston), Texas State Archives.

9. Quoting *San Antonio Herald,* Oct. 18, 1862. Also, Sam Acheson, *35,000 Day*
in Texas (New York, 1938), p. 48; Mamie Yeary, comp., *Reminiscences of the*
Boys in Gray (Dallas, 1912), p. 24; *Tri-Weekly Civilian and Gazette* (Galveston)
May 20, 1862; *Houston Tri-Weekly Telegraph,* May 23, Oct. 13, 1862; *O.R.,* Ser.
I, IV, 98; IX, 700, 710; XV, 148, 151–53, 181–83; LIII, 807; *Official Records of*
the Union and Confederate Navies (Washington, D.C., 1894–1927), XIV, 605–7,
654–55, 733–34, 825–26, 829–30, 851–55, 858; XVIII, 60, 536; XIX, 151–52,
261 (hereafter referred to as *O.R.N.*); Benjamin to Lubbock, Feb. 23, 1862, Lub-
bock to Benjamin, March 17, 1862, Tucker to Lubbock, Oct. 22, 1862, all in
Governors' Letters (Lubbock); Clark to Joseph, Sept. 10, 1861, Executive Record
Book, No. 80, Texas State Archives; Lubbock to McCulloch, Dec. 23, 1861, Lubbock to Hebert, Dec. 7, 1861, Lubbock to Joseph, Dec. 19, 1861, Lubbock to
Shepherd *et al.,* April 2, 1862, Lubbock to Dashiell, March 12, 1862, Lubbock to
Flourney, June 1, 1862, all in Executive Record Book, No. 81; Proclamation by
the Governor [Lubbock], May 24, 1862, Executive Record Book, No. 279, Texas
State Archives.

10. Quoting Lubbock to Magruder, March 15, 1863, Executive Record Book, No.
82, Texas State Archives. Also, Harry Henderson, *Texas in the Confederacy* (San
Antonio, 1955), pp. 88, 94, 108, 117, 121; Napier Bartlett, *Military Record of*
Louisiana (New Orleans, 1875), part III, p. 20; David D. Porter, *The Naval His-*
tory of the Civil War (London, 1887), pp. 269–71; E. M. Lougherty, *War and*
Reconstruction Times in Texas (Austin, 1914), p. 28; Yeary, *Reminiscences,* p.
139; Philip C. Tucker, "The United States Gunboat Harriet Lane," *Southwestern*
Hist. Quar., XXI (April, 1918), 360–80; Richardson, *Messages and Papers of the*
Confederacy, I, 337; Gammel, *Laws of Texas,* V, 650; Fremantle, *Diary,* pp.
53–56; R. F. Pray, *Dick Dowling's Battle* (San Antonio, 1936), pp. 92–98; *Hous-*
ton Tri-Weekly Telegraph, Jan. 2, 5, 7, June 9, Nov. 19, 1863; *San Antonio Her-*
ald, Jan. 10, 1863; *The Standard* (Clarksville, Tex.), Jan. 31, 1863; *O.R.,* Ser. I,
XV, 143–46, 180–81, 202–4, 237–39, 402–4, 633, 813–14, 826, 858, 931,
1096–97; XLI, part iii, 963–64; *O.R.N.,* XIX, 199–224, 227–29, 232–36, 392,
395–96, 437–81, 549, 556, 558–73, 595–96, 742, 836; XX, 105, 147–48, 157,
183–84, 371, 380; XXI, 232–34, 644, 911–12; Lubbock to Washington, Henry
and Harrison, all Dec. 9, 1862, and Lubbock to Magruder, Jan. 6, 1863, all in
Executive Record Book, No. 81; Proclamation [Lubbock], To the People and
State of Texas, Oct. 12, 1862, Executive Record Book, No. 279; "Customs Account Book, Sabine Pass," Records of the Confederate Treasury Department, War
Department Collection of Confederate Records, Record Group 109, National Archives.

11. Quoting Taylor, *Destruction and Reconstruction,* pp. 120–21; *O.R.,* Ser. I,
XV, 873. Also, Taylor, *Destruction and Reconstruction,* pp. 127, 130–131; John
Dimitry, "Louisiana," in Clement A. Evans, ed., *Confederate Military History*
(Atlanta, 1899), X, 63–64; Oates, *Cavalry,* pp. 36–37; *Shreveport Semi-Weekly*

News, May 16, Dec. 2, 9, 1862; *O.R.,* Ser. I, IV, 857; VI, 888; XIII, 813–29, 832–33; XV, 133, 736, 743–44, 753–54, 756, 767–69, 773–74, 784, 789, 791, 838, 873; LIII, 804–6, 819; Ser. III, II, 141; Ser. IV, I, 422; *O.R.N.,* XVIII, 473–76.

12. Quoting *O.R.,* Ser. I, XV, 159. Also, Taylor, *Destruction and Reconstruction,* pp. 120–27, 130, 133–34, 140–42; Bartlett, *Military Record of Louisiana,* part III, pp. 6, 38–39, 54–58, part IV, 256–57, and Hyatt, "Diary," *ibid.,* part III, p. 9; Jefferson D. Bragg, *Louisiana in the Confederacy* (Baton Rouge, 1941), pp. 127–32; Dimitry, "Louisiana," in Evans, ed., *Confederate Military History,* X, 75–79; Richard P. Weinert, "The Confederate Regular Army," *Military Affairs,* XXVI (Fall, 1962), 104; A. J. H. Duganne, *Camps and Prisons: Twenty Months in the Department of the Gulf* (New York, 1865), p. 31; *O.R.,* Ser. I, IV, 620; XV, 39–108, 129–31, 133, 158–80, 183–88, 552–53, 558, 565, 568–69, 819–20; LIII, 533–34.

13. Quoting *O.R.,* Ser. I, XV, 874; *Shreveport Semi-Weekly News,* Jan. 30, 1863. Also, *Public Laws of the Confederate States of America, First Congress, and First Session of the Second Congress,* ed. James M. Matthews (Richmond, 1862–64), pp. 29–32, 51–52, 61–62, 77–79; Albert B. Moore, *Conscription and Conflict in the Confederacy* (New York, 1924); "Proceedings of the Confederate Congress," *Southern Historical Society Papers,* XLV (1924), 26–28; *Journal of Congress,* II, 294, 310–11; Bartlett, *Military Record of Louisiana,* part IV, 257; Bragg, *Louisiana,* p. 255; *O.R.,* Ser. I, XV, 747–49, 753–54, 872, 874, 975; LIII, 836–37.

14. John R. Ficklen, *History of Reconstruction in Louisiana* (Baltimore, 1910), pp. 117–19; Shugg, *Origins of Class Struggle,* p. 193; William M. Robinson, Jr., *Justice in Grey* (Cambridge, Mass., 1941), p. 100; Taylor, *Destruction and Reconstruction,* p. 127; Fremantle, *Diary,* p. 68; *Acts Passed by the Twenty-seventh Legislature of the State of Louisiana* [since its admission to the Union; the "Sixth Legislature" since the adoption of the constitution of 1852], *Extra Session, Opelousas, Dec. 1862–Jan. 1863* (Natchitoches, 1864), pp. 5–6, 15, 18–20, 36–40; *Acts Passed by the Sixth Legislature* [since the constitution of 1852] *of the State of Louisiana, First Session, Baton Rouge, 1861–1862* (Baton Rouge, 1862), pp. 29, 79, 84–86; *Shreveport Semi-Weekly News,* Dec. 2, 9, 1862, Jan. 20, 27, Feb. 13, 1863; *O.R.,* Ser. I, XV, 526, 558, 747–49, 753–54, 838, 910–11; LIII, 836–37, 843; Ser. IV, II, 278–79.

15. Quoting Banks to Wife, Jan. 15, 1863, N. P. Banks Papers, microfilm, University of Texas Library. Also, Fred H. Harrington, *The Fighting Politician: Major General N. P. Banks* (Philadelphia, 1948); Frank M. Flinn, *Campaigning with Banks in Louisiana* (Lynn, Mass., 1887), p. 54; Hans L. Trefousse, *Ben Butler: The South Called Him Beast!* (New York, 1957), p. 133; Charles A. Peabody, "The United States Provisional Court for the State of Louisiana, 1862–1865," *Annual Report of the American Historical Association, 1892* (Washington, D.C., 1893), pp. 197–210; "Diary and Correspondence of Salmon P. Chase," *Annual Report of the American Historical Association, 1902* (Washington, D.C., 1903), II, 316, 330, 358–62; Ficklen, *History of Reconstruction in Louisiana,* pp. 119, 125; Julia Le Grand, *The Journal of Julia Le Grand, New Orleans, 1862–1863,*

ed. Kate Mason Rowland and Mrs. Morris L. Croxall (Richmond, 1911), p. 77; George H. Hepworth, *The Whip, Hoe, and Sword* (Boston, 1864), pp. 27–28; Bartlett, *Military Record of Louisiana,* part III, 39, and Hyatt, "Diary," *ibid.,* p. 9; Taylor, *Destruction and Reconstruction,* pp. 142–44; Bragg, *Louisiana,* p. 132; J. H. McLeary, "History of Green's [Sibley's] Brigade," in Dudley G. Wooten, ed., *A Comprehensive History of Texas* (Dallas, 1898), II, 695–740; *The Congressional Globe,* 37th Cong., 3d Sess., pp. 144, 164, 695, 831–36, 1030–36; *O.R.,* Ser. I, XV, 191–92, 233–37, 239–50, 395, 502–4, 581–84, 590–94, 603, 610–14, 616, 618–19, 623, 626–28, 630–34, 636, 639–41, 645–46, 652, 655–56, 662, 665, 833, 919, 954, 968–71; LIII, 462–63; Ser. IV, II, 380.

16. Quoting Taylor, *Destruction and Reconstruction,* p. 149. Also, *ibid.,* pp. 145–49; Ulysses S. Grant, *Personal Memoirs,* ed. E. B. Long (Cleveland and New York, 1952), pp. 230–37; Adam Badeau, *Military History of Ulysses S. Grant* (New York, 1868–81), I, 163–68; Edmund Newsome, *Experiences in the War* (Carbondale, Ill., 1880), entries dated Feb., 1863; William Belknap, ed., *History of the 15th Regiment Iowa Veteran Volunteer Infantry* (Keokuk, Ia., 1887), pp. 245–47; James D. Richardson, *A Compilation of the Messages and Papers of the Presidents* (Washington, D.C., 1896–99), VI, 158; Alfred T. Mahan, *The Gulf and Inland Waters* (New York, 1883), pp. 124–28; Bartlett, *Military Record of Louisiana,* part III, pp. 33, 45–53; William R. Boggs, *Military Reminiscences,* ed. William K. Boyd (Durham, N.C., 1913), pp. 53–54; David M. Strother, *A Virginia Yankee in the Civil War,* ed. Cecil D. Eby, Jr. (Chapel Hill, 1961), p. 161; *Chicago Journal,* Feb. 23, 1863; *O.R.,* Ser. I, XVII, part i, 700, 710, 719, and part ii, 551–52, 563, 570–71, 573; XXIV, part i, 4–22, 341–48, 361–71, 469–70, 473–81, 517–18, 565–70, 573–76, 684–88, and part iii, 17, 19, 32–33, 102–3, 115, 117, 131; *O.R.N.,* XIX, 665–68; XXIV, 385–96; Kirby Smith to Mother, Feb. 15, 1863, Correspondence, Kirby Smith Papers.

17. Quoting Boggs, *Reminiscences,* pp. 54–55; Kirby Smith to Wife, March 19, 1863, Correspondence, Kirby Smith Papers; *O.R.,* Ser. I, XXII, part ii, 871–73. Also, *Arkansas State Gazette* (Little Rock), Jan. 20, 1863; *O.R.,* Ser. I, XIII, 918–19; XV, 948, 972; XVII, part ii, 783–84; XXII, part ii, 798, 802–3, 830; LIII, 861–63; Reynolds to Smith, May 13, 1863, Thomas C. Reynolds Papers, Library of Congress.

18. Quoting *O.R.,* Ser. I, XIII, 830. Also, Smith, *Borderland in the Civil War,* pp. 350–56; Robinson, *Justice,* pp. 19, 91, 128; J. F. Phillips, "Hamilton Rowan Gamble and the Provisional Government of Missouri," *Mo. Hist. Rev.,* V (Oct., 1910), 1–14; H. Edward Nettles, "Sterling Price," *Dictionary of American Biography,* XV, 216; John T. Scharf, *History of St. Louis* (Kansas City, 1900), I, 514–16; Wiley Britton, *The Civil War on the Border* (New York, 1890–1904), I, 93, 143–44, 224; Lucien Carr, *Missouri: A Bone of Contention* (Boston, 1894), pp. 333–35; Eugene Ware, *The Lyon Campaign in Missouri* (Topeka, 1907), pp. 317–36; Thomas L. Snead, *The Fight for Missouri from the Election of Lincoln to the Death of Lyon* (New York, 1886), pp. 271–85; Franz Sigel, "The Military Operations in Missouri in the Summer and Autumn of 1861," *Mo. Hist. Rev.,* XXVI (July, 1932), 354–67; N. B. Pearce, "Price's Campaign of 1861," *Publications of the Arkansas Historical Association,* IV (1892), 333–51; N. B. Pearce,

Arkansas Troops in the Battle of Wilson's Creek," in Robert Johnson and Clarence Buell, eds., *Battles and Leaders of the Civil War* (New York, 1956), I,
98–303; Samuel B. Barron, *The Lone Star Defenders* (New York, 1908), pp.
4–46; James A. Mulligan, "The Siege of Lexington, Mo.," in Johnson and Buell,
eds., *Battles and Leaders*, I, 307–13; William Baxter, *Pea Ridge and Prairie
Grove* (Cincinnati, 1864), pp. 39, 102; Franz Sigel, "The Pea Ridge Campaign,"
in Johnson and Buell, eds., *Battles and Leaders*, I, 314–34; John W. Noble, "Bat-
le of Pea Ridge, or Elk Horn Tavern," *War Papers, Missouri Order of the Loyal
Legion*, I (St. Louis, 1892), 211–42; Abel, *The Indian as Participant*, pp. 31–33;
Wiley Britton, "Union and Confederate Indians in the Civil War," in Johnson
and Buell, eds., *Battles and Leaders*, I, 335–36; Samuel P. Curtis, "The Army of
the South-West," *Annals of Iowa*, VI (1868), 143–74; Harvey Ford, "Van Dorn
and the Pea Ridge Campaign," *Journal of the American Military Institute*, III
(Winter, 1939), 222–36; Frank Anderson, "Missouri's Confederate State Capitol
at Marshall, Texas," *Mo. Hist. Rev.*, XXVII (1933), 240–43; Fremantle, *Diary*, p.
6; Lewis, "Propaganda," *Mo. Hist. Rev.*, XXXIV, 3 ff.; Peterson and Hanson,
Pilot Knob, p. 41; *Report of Major General Hindman of His Operations in the
Trans-Mississippi District* (Richmond, 1864); Thomas, *Arkansas in War*, pp.
39–42; *Statutes at Large*, ed. Matthews, p. 254; *Public Laws*, ed. Matthews, pp.
, 40, 84; *Richmond Daily Enquirer*, Aug. 26, 1862; *The Standard* (Clarksville,
Tex.), June 16, 1862; *O.R.*, Ser. I, Vols. III and VIII, and Ser. IV, Vol. I, *passim*; *O.R.*, Ser. I, IX, 713, 715–16, 733–36; XXII, part ii, 127–32; XLVIII, part
, 191; LIII, 692, 828–30, 852, 870; Lubbock to Pike, June 18, 1862, Executive
Record Book, No. 81.

9. *Report of Major General Hindman*; Thomas, *Arkansas in War*, pp. 137–38,
42–48; Thomas L. Snead, "The Conquest of Arkansas," in Johnson and Buell,
eds., *Battles and Leaders*, III, 443–45, 452–53; Curtis, "Army of the South-
West," *Annals of Iowa*, VI, 158 ff.; Grant, *Memoirs*, pp. 228–29; William T.
Sherman, *The Memoirs of Gen. William T. Sherman* (New York, 1892), I,
96 ff.; William W. Heartsill, *Fourteen Hundred and 91 Days in the Confederate
Army*, ed. Bell I. Wiley (Jackson, Tenn., 1954), p. 114; *O.R.*, Ser. I, XIII, 7–10,
8, 23, 28–40, 43, 59–60, 64, 68–77, 83–89, 97, 103–19, 123–24, 126–27, 130,
133–35, 138–39, 141–51, 172–77, 192–93, 363–477, 605, 653, 666, 829, 836–37,
874–77; XVII, part ii, 546–47, 553–55, 559; XXII, part ii, 41; Maria Mann, reports to Western Sanitary Commission, Feb. 10 and April 19, 1863, Mann Papers, Library of Congress.

10. Quoting *O.R.*, Ser. I, XXII, part i, 170. Also, *Report of Major General Hindman*; Thomas, *Arkansas in War*, pp. 152–74; Snead, "Conquest of Arkansas," in
Johnson and Buell, eds., *Battles and Leaders*, III, 446–50; Oates, *Cavalry*, p. 47;
Confederate States War Department, *Regulations for the Army of the Confederate States, and for the Quartermaster's and Pay Departments, 1861* (New Orleans,
1861), pp. 103–4; *List of Field Officers, Regiments and Battalions in the Confederate Army, 1861–1865* (Washington, D.C., 1899), pp. 42–47; Fred W. Allsopp,
Albert Pike (Little Rock, 1928), p. 200; Abel, *The Indian as Participant*, pp.
179–81, 195–98, 218–19; Annie Abel, "The Indians in the Civil War," *American
Historical Review*, XV (Jan., 1910), 293; John N. Edwards, *Shelby and His Men*
(Cincinnati, 1867), pp. 77–128; Connelley, *Quantrill*, pp. 277–81; Britton, *Civil

War on the Border, I, 366–440; John F. Lee, "John Sappington Marmaduke," *Missouri Historical Society Collections,* II (July, 1906), 29; Henry E. Palmer, "An Outing in Arkansas," *Civil War Sketches, Nebraska Military Order of the Loyal Legion,* I (Omaha, 1902), 213–25; Baxter, *Pea Ridge and Prairie Grove,* pp. 179 ff.; Albert W. Bishop, *Loyalty on the Frontier* (St. Louis, 1863), pp. 69–71, 205; Noble L. Prentis, *Kansas Miscellanies* (Topeka, 1889), pp. 17–29; [James G. Blunt], "General Blunt's Account of His Civil War Experiences," *Kansas Hist. Quar.,* I (May, 1932), 232–36; Wilfred R. Hollister and Harry Norman, *Five Famous Missourians* (Kansas City, 1900), pp. 256–60; W. W. Denison, "Battle of Prairie Grove," *Kans. Hist. Coll.,* XVI (1915), 586–90; Henry C. Adams, "Battle of Prairie Grove," *War Papers, Indiana Commandery, Military Order of the Loyal Legion* (Indianapolis, 1898), pp. 451–64; William E. Connelley, *The Life of Preston B. Plumb* (Chicago, 1913), pp. 120–31; *Fort Smith New Era,* Dec. 12, 1862; *O.R.,* Ser. I, XIII, 16–28, 33, 38, 41–51, 286–307, 311, 324–37, 358, 529, 556, 601–3, 606, 609–813, 855, 860, 876–77, 881, 883–89, 898–928, 978–80; XVII, part ii, 766; XX, part ii, 424, 435–36; XXII, part i, 9–10, 36–39, 41–59, 67–158, 165, 167–73, 903–4; LIII, 458–61, 866–67; Lubbock to Wigfall, Oct. 27, 1862, Executive Record Book, No. 81.

21. S. H. Gleaves, "The Strategic Use of Cavalry," *Journal of the U.S. Cavalry Association,* XVIII (July, 1907), 9–25; Theodore H. Rodenbaugh, "Cavalry of the Civil War: Its Evolution and Influence," in *Photographic History of the Civil War* (New York, 1911), IV, 16–38; George T. Denison, *A History of Cavalry* (London, 1913), pp. 394–95; Oates, *Cavalry,* pp. 114–21; Edwards, *Shelby,* pp. 130–47; Britton, *Civil War on the Border,* I, 442–45; David O'Flaherty, *General Jo Shelby: Undefeated Rebel* (Chapel Hill, 1954), p. 168; Hollister and Norman, *Five Famous Missourians,* p. 361; Thomas, *Arkansas in War,* pp. 195–96; Farrar Newberry, "Harris Flanagin," in *Arkansas and the Civil War,* ed. John L. Ferguson (Little Rock, 1964), pp. 63–65; *Jefferson Davis, Constitutionalist: His Letters, Papers, and Speeches,* ed. Dunbar Rowland (Jackson, Miss., 1923), V, 386–88; *St. Joseph Morning Herald,* Jan. 13, 18, 22, 1863; *Arkansas True Democrat* (Little Rock), Jan. 28, 1863; *O.R.,* Ser. I, XVII, part ii, 783–84; XXII, part i, 169–73, 178–211, and part ii, 8, 24, 26, 28–38, 55–56, 67, 78, 769, 773, 780.

22. Quoting *O.R.,* Ser. I, XXII, part ii, 770, and part i, 881.

23. Quoting *O.R.,* Ser. I, XXII, part i, 28–30. Also, Annie Abel, *The American Indian as Slaveholder and Secessionist* (Cleveland, 1915); Abel, *The Indian as Participant,* pp. 13–25, 79–201, 213–20, 247–60; Abel, "Indians in the Civil War," *Amer. Hist. Rev.,* XV, 282–92; John B. Meserve, "The MacIntoshes," *Chronicles of Oklahoma,* X (Sept., 1932), 310–25; Morris Wardell, *A Political History of the Cherokee Nation* (Norman, Okla., 1938), pp. 122–41; Rachel C. Eaton, *John Ross and the Cherokee Indians* (Menasha, Wis., 1914), pp. 175 ff.; E. E. Dale and Gaston Litton, eds., *Cherokee Cavaliers* (Norman, Okla., 1940), pp. xviii, 136; E. E. Dale, "Stand Watie," *DAB,* XIX, 337–38; Mabel W. Anderson, *Life of General Stand Watie* (Pryor, Okla., 1931); Carolyn T. Foreman, *Park Hill* (Muskogee, Okla., 1948), pp. 30–31; Wiley Britton, *The Union Indian Brigade in the Civil War* (Kansas City, 1922), pp. 62–74, 204–5; Allsopp, *Pike,* pp. 131–32, 200 ff.; *Statutes at Large,* ed. Matthews, Appendix; *Journals of Congress,* I, 154,

225, 244, 263, 427, 564–65, 590–96, 601–2, 609–11, 632–35; II, 58, 324, 344, 367, 404, 432; III, 69, 530, 809; *Regulations Adopted by the War Department for Carrying into Effect the Acts of Congress Relating to Indian Affairs, &c., &c.* (Richmond, 1862); Wiley Britton, "Union and Confederate Indians in the Civil War," in Johnson and Buell, eds., *Battles and Leaders,* I, 335–36; *Report of Major General Hindman;* U.S. Indian Office, *Report of the Commissioner of Indian Affairs for the Year 1864* (Washington, D.C., 1865), pp. iii, 39, 41, 259, 304–7, 323, 326, 334, 351, 354–55, 536; Britton, *Civil War on the Border,* I, 164–68, 299–306; Angie Debo, "The Site of the Battle of Round Mountain, 1861," *Chron. of Okla.,* XXVII (Summer, 1949), 187–206; Homer Croy, *Our Will Rogers* (New York, 1953), p. 10; David M. Hodge, *Argument before the* [Senate] *Committee on Indian Affairs . . . March 10, 1880 . . . for the Payment of Awards Made to the Creek Indians Who Enlisted in the Federal Army . . .* (Washington, D.C., 1880); David M. Hodge, *Is-ha-he-char, and Co-we-Harjo, to the* [House] *Committee on Indian Affairs* [51st Congress] *. . . in the Matter of the Claims of the Loyal Creeks . . .* (Washington, D.C., 1891); U.S. Indian Office, *Report of the Commissioner of Indian Affairs for the Year 1865* (Washington, D.C., 1866), pp. 38–39, 323; Albert R. Greene, "Campaigning in the Army of the Frontier," *Kans. Hist. Coll.,* XIV (1913), 287; *Little Rock Times and Herald,* July 8, Aug. 16, 24, 1861; *Fort Smith Times and Herald,* Aug. 24, Oct. 5, 9, 1861; *The Standard* (Clarksville, Tex.), Oct. 26, Nov. 23, 1861; *Van Buren Press,* Aug. 28, Oct. 9, 16, 31, Nov. 7, 14, 21, Dec. 5, 1861, Jan. 9, 1862; *Daily Conservative* (Leavenworth, Kans.), Jan. 28, 1862; *Daily State Journal* (Little Rock), Dec. 1, 5, 12, 17, 24, 1861, Jan. 7, 1862; *Alta California* (San Francisco), Feb. 22, 1862; *Daily Missouri Republican* (St. Louis), Aug. 13, 1861; *Washington Telegraph* (Washington, Ark.), Sept. 17, 1862; *O.R.,* Ser. I, III, 390, 530, 567–625, 671–76, 690–92, 727; VIII, 5–32, 189–330, 690, 697–700, 709, 713, 732, 734, 780; XIII, 19, 40–43, 50–51, 62–63, 102, 137–38, 160–62, 181–84, 273–77, 286–307, 324–37, 463–64, 488–90, 500–5, 532, 819–26, 831, 839–54, 856–77, 885, 890–96, 899–906, 910–11, 913, 921–22, 924–27, 934–81; XXII, part i, 28–36, 43, 66–158, 172, 889, 903, 905, and part ii, 770–71, 773–79, 783, 791, 794–96, 799–802, 833; XLVIII, part i, 1237–38; LIII, 820–22; Ser.˙IV, I, 317–18, 323–24, 359–61, 379, 426–43, 445–66, 513–27, 542–54, 636–66, 669–87, 757, 775, 785–86, 792, 813, 821, 910, 927, 962.

24. Quoting Peveler, "Diary," May 13, 1863; Heartsill, *1491 Days,* p. 186. Also, Washington *et al.* to John Jumper, Dec. 15, 1861, Office of Indian Affairs, Confederate Papers, National Archives; Kirby Smith to Wife, March 19, 1863, Correspondence, Kirby Smith Papers. On March 30, 1863, Pine Bluff was the induction center and headquarters for General John G. Walker's Texas infantry division, 8,444 effectives. The three brigades of this division and the five brigades of General Thomas J. Churchill's infantry division composed the relatively inactive "Second Corps" of Holmes's Arkansas army, serving as garrison troops in the eastern half of the state. The bulk of Churchill's division surrendered at Arkansas Post. *O.R.,* Ser. I, XXII, part i, 904, and part ii, 810; Headquarters, Trans-Mississippi Department, Extract, Special Orders No. 121, Dec. 23, 1862, John G. Walker Papers, Southern Historical Collection, University of North Carolina.

25. Quoting *O.R.*, Ser. I, XIII, 33; Palmer, "Black Flag," *Kans. Hist. Coll.*, IX, 459; Kit Dalton, *Under the Black Flag* (Memphis, 1914), pp. 17, 70. Also, *O.R.*, Ser. I, XXII, part ii, 187–89.

26. Quoting *O.R.*, Ser. II, I, 270, 281; Ser. I, XIII, 451; Ser. II, V, 411; Dalton, *Black Flag*, pp. 16–17. Also, Edwards, *Shelby*, p. 399; Walter B. Stevens, *Missouri: The Center State* (Chicago, 1915), I, 353 ff.; *Jefferson Davis, Constitutionalist*, ed. Rowland, V, 408; Champ Clark, *My Quarter Century of American Politics* (New York, 1920), I, 79; *O.R.*, Ser. I, XXII, part i, 860–66. See also, for comparison, Mao Tse-tung, "On the Protracted War," *Mao Tse-tung: An Anthology of His Writings*, ed. Anne Fremantle (New York, 1962), p. 140.

27. Quoting *O.R.*, Ser. I, VIII, 615–17; Botkin, "Sovereign Squats," *Kans. Hist. Coll.*, VII, 433; *O.R.*, Ser. I, VII, 532; VIII, 641–42; XIII, 688; Ser. IV, II, 48. Also, Vo Nguyen Giap, *Guerre du Peuple, Armée du Peuple* (Hanoi, 1961); *Mao Tse-tung*, ed. Fremantle, pp. 60–142; Dalton, *Black Flag*, pp. 15–17; John N. Edwards, *Noted Guerrillas* (St. Louis, 1879), p. 17; O. S. Barton and John McCorkle, *Three Years with Quantrell* (Armstrong, Mo., 1914), pp. 29 ff.; Robertus Love, *The Rise and Fall of Jesse James* (New York, 1939), pp. 15–21, 47; Richard S. Brownlee, *Gray Ghosts of the Confederacy* (Baton Rouge, 1958), p. 53 and *passim;* John P. Burch and Harrison Trow, *Charles W. Quantrell* (Vega, Tex., 1923), pp. 77–95, 104, and *passim;* Connelley, *Quantrill*, p. 42 and *passim;* Albert E. Castel, *A Frontier State at War: Kansas* (Ithaca, N.Y., 1958), pp. 102–6; Albert E. Castel, "The Bloodiest Man in American History," *American Heritage*, XI (Oct., 1960), 22 ff.; Smith, *The Borderland*, pp. 350, 366–67; Britton, *Memoirs*, p. 373; Henry E. Palmer, "Soldiers of Kansas," *Kans. Hist. Coll.*, IX (1905–6), 432, 460; *Annual Report of the Commissioner of Patents to the Speaker of the House . . .* (Richmond, 1865), pats. no. 242, 254, 255, 256, 258, 261; Herklotz, "Jayhawkers," *Mo. Hist. Rev.*, XVII, 505 ff.; Smith, "How Quantrill Became an Outlaw," *Kans. Hist. Coll.*, VII, 215 ff.; Francis B. Heitman, *Historical Register and Dictionary of the United States Army* (Washington, D.C., 1903), I, 614; Rev. H. D. Fisher, *The Gun and the Gospel* (Chicago, 1896), p. 155; Leverett Spring, *Kansas, the Prelude to the War* (New York, 1885), pp. 275–76; E. M. Violette, *A History of Missouri* (New York, 1918), p. 381; Carr, *Missouri*, pp. 344 ff.; W. H. Stephenson, "The Political Career of General James H. Lane," *Publications of the Kansas Historical Society*, III (1930), 104–22; S. M. Fox, "The Early History of the Seventh Kansas Cavalry," *Kans. Hist. Coll.*, XI (1909–10), 240–45; [Richard J. Hinton], *The Rebel Invasion of Missouri and Kansas* (Chicago, 1865), pp. 187, 295; Palmer, "Black Flag," *Kans. Hist. Coll.*, IX, 459; S. M. Fox, "The Story of the Seventh Kansas," *Kans. Hist. Coll.*, VIII (1903–4), 23–24; *List of Field Officers and Units, C.S.A.*, pp. 42–47; *O.R.*, Ser. I, III, 482, and *passim;* VIII, 496–97, 615–17, and *passim;* XIII, 43–45, 622–23, 726–27, 835, 979, and *passim;* XXII, part i, 700–1, 904, and part ii, *passim;* XLI, part iv, 591, 873; Ser. II, I, 270; Ser. IV, I, 395, 1008, 1094–95; II, 287.

28. Quoting Smith, *The Borderland*, p. 373; *New York Herald*, June 30, 1863; Kirby Smith to Reynolds, June 4, 1863, Letterbook, Kirby Smith Papers; Love, *Jesse James*, p. 47. Also, Britton, *Memoirs*, pp. 128, 352–54; Jay Donald, *Frank and Jesse James* (Chicago, 1882), p. 71; Frank James, *Frank James* (Pine Bluff,

1926), pp. 32–33; Edwards, *Shelby,* pp. 379, 399; Stevens, *Missouri,* pp. 353 ff.; Love, *Jesse James,* pp. 17–19, 22; John C. Moore, "Missouri," in Evans, ed., *Confederate Military History,* IX, 67–68; Dalton, *Black Flag,* p. 112; Burch and Trow, *Quantrell,* p. 155; Carr, *Missouri,* p. 334; Spring, *Kansas,* p. 289; McElroy, *Struggle for Missouri,* p. 79; Connelley, *Quantrill,* pp. 42, 200–5, 259–82; Edwards, *Noted Guerrillas,* pp. 32, 51; Barton and McCorkle, *Quantrell,* p. 25; Alvin F. Harlow, "Quantrill," *DAB,* XV, 294; Castel, "Bloodiest Man," *Amer. Her.,* XI, 22 ff.; Shoemaker, "War in Northeast Missouri," *Mo. Hist. Rev.,* VII, 127; Smith, *The Borderland,* pp. 368–69; *O.R.,* Ser. I, III, 459; VIII, 57–58, 336, 346–47, 360–61, 482; XIII, 33, 45, 48, 58, 120–21, 132, 154–60, 226, 230, 237, 254–56, 314, 347, 352–53, 436–37, 471, 567–69, 622–23, 726–27, 768–71, 796, 801, 804–5; XXII, part i, 42, 572–93, 700; Ser. II, III, 468–69; M. Jeff Thompson, "Autobiography," MS, Southern Historical Collection, University of North Carolina.

Chapter Two: The Home Front, 1861–1863

1. Quoting *The Standard* (Clarksville, Tex.), Jan. 31, 1863; *Texas Republican* (Marshall), Jan. 22, 1863. Also, *Texas Almanac—Extra* (Austin), Jan. 31, 1863; *Arkansas State Gazette* (Little Rock), Jan. 20, 1863.

2. Quoting Josiah Gorgas, *The Civil War Diary of General Josiah Gorgas,* ed. Frank E. Vandiver (University, Ala., 1947), pp. 28, 39; Kirby Smith to Wife, March 19, 1863, Correspondence, Kirby Smith Papers. Also, Robert G. H. Kean, *Inside the Confederate Government,* ed. Edward Younger (New York, 1957), p. 38; Joseph Parks, *General Edmund Kirby Smith, C.S.A.* (Baton Rouge, 1954), pp. 251–52; D. S. Freeman, *Lee's Lieutenants* (New York, 1942–44), I, 610, and II, 248, 507; Stevens, *Missouri,* I, 340 ff.; Paul B. Jenkins, *The Battle of Westport* (Kansas City, 1906), pp. 172 ff.; Thomas Snead, "With Price East of the Mississippi," in Johnson and Buell, eds., *Battles and Leaders,* II, 724; *O.R.,* Ser. I, XIII, 838; XXII, part ii, 802–3, 811; XLI, part ii, 1014; LIII, 804–5, 861–63; Lubbock, Moore, Rector, and Jackson to Davis, July 28, 1862, Executive Record Book, No. 81; Reynolds to Smith, May 13, 1863, and Reynolds to Johnson, May 26, July 18, 1863, Reynolds Papers; Kirby Smith to Mother, Feb. 15, 1863, Correspondence, Kirby Smith Papers.

3. Quoting *San Antonio Semi-Weekly News,* Nov. 13, 1862; R. H. Williams, *With the Border Ruffians* (London, 1907), pp. 190, 198; *O.R.,* Ser. I, XXII, part ii, 871–73; *Shreveport Semi-Weekly News,* Feb. 13, 1863. Also, Taylor, *Destruction and Reconstruction,* p. 151; Boggs, *Reminiscences,* p. 57; *Acts, 27th Louisiana Legislature,* Extra Sess., Opelousas, pp. 18–20, 36–40; Gammel, *Laws of Texas,* V, 455–65, 498, 620–21; Ford, *Rip Ford's Texas,* pp. 354, 384n; Thomas, *Arkansas in War,* pp. 85 ff., 189–90, 197, 382–90; *Journal of Both Sessions of the* [Secession] *Convention of the State of Arkansas* (Little Rock, 1861), pp. 192–93, 234, 248; Ted R. Worley, ed., "Documents Relating to the Arkansas Peace Society," *Arkansas Historical Quarterly,* XVII (Spring, 1958), 82–111; John W. Hunter, "Heel-Fly Time in Texas," *Frontier Times,* April, 1924, pp.

35–48; *San Antonio Herald,* July 11, 1863; *The Standard* (Clarksville, Tex.), March 1, 1862; *Galveston Tri-Weekly News,* May 27, 1862; *New York Herald,* Nov. 9, 1863; *New York Times,* Dec. 4, 1863; *Houston Tri-Weekly Telegraph,* Jan. 22, 1864; *Washington Telegraph* (Ark.), March 23, 1864; *O.R.,* Ser. I, IX, 701–2, 712–13, 715–16; XV, 220, 826, 880, 887, 925–29, 931, 936, 945, 955–56, 960, 974–75, 1006, 1018, 1021, 1041; XXII, part ii, 772, 780–84, 786, 791, 793–94, 798–99, 802–3, 808, 810–11, 828, 830, 832–33, 851, 904; XXVI, part ii, 16; LIII, 454–55, 840–41, 849–50, 861–63; Ser. II, II, 1422; Ser. IV, II, 380, 398–99, 530; Alexander Pugh, "Diary," Pugh Family Papers, Archives, Louisiana State University; Reynolds to Johnson, May 26, 1863, Reynolds Papers; Lubbock to Dashiell, March 12, 1862, Lubbock to Davis, Nov. 13, 1862, and Lubbock to Washington, Dec. 9, 1862, Executive Record Book, No. 81.

4. Quoting *The Standard* (Clarksville, Tex.), Jan. 22, 1863. Also, *Acts, 27th Louisiana Legislature,* Extra Sess., Opelousas, pp. 5–6; Fremantle, *Diary,* p. 60; *Public Laws,* ed. Matthews, pp. 102–4, 192–93; *Houston Tri-Weekly Telegraph,* June 6, 9, 1862, Jan. 7, 19, 1863; *Shreveport Semi-Weekly News,* Dec. 9, 1862; *Dallas Herald,* May 6, 20, 1863; *O.R.,* Ser. I, XV, 841–42; XVII, part ii, 738, 756; XVIII, 863, 934; XXI, 1078; XXII, part ii, 907, 994–95, 1035–36; Ser. IV, I, 767, 1154; II, 26, 39, 124–25, 208, 234–35, 278–79, 469–72, 477–78, 511, 933; "Petition and Resolution from the Planters of Morehouse Parish," March, 1863, George W. Logan Papers, Southern Historical Collection, University of North Carolina.

5. Quoting *The Standard* (Clarksville, Tex.), Jan. 22, May 9, 1863; Fremantle, *Diary,* p. 61; Rebecca Smith and Marion Mullins, eds., "The Diary of H. C. Medford, Confederate Soldier," *Southwestern Hist. Quar.,* XXXIV (Jan., 1931), 220; *O.R.,* Ser. I, XIII, 980; *Dallas Herald,* Oct. 4, 1862. Also, Gammel, *Laws of Texas,* V, 614–15; Thomas, *Arkansas in War,* pp. 99–101, 319; Marquis James, *The Raven* (Indianapolis, 1929), pp. 423–33; *Acts Passed by the Seventh Legislature of the State of Louisiana, First Session, 1864* (Shreveport, 1864), pp. 16, 74; Edward Dale, "The Cherokees in the Confederacy," *Journal of Southern History,* XIII (May, 1947), 180; Britton, *Civil War on the Border,* I, 442; O'Flaherty, *Shelby,* p. 168; John M. Harrell, "Arkansas," in Evans, ed., *Confederate Military History,* X, 160; Snead, "Conquest of Arkansas," in Johnson and Buell, eds., *Battles and Leaders,* III, 450; Bartlett, *Military Record of Louisiana,* part III, pp. 17–18, 21–22, and Hyatt, "Diary," *ibid.,* p. 9; Heartsill, *1491 Days,* pp. 26–27, 37–39, 44–45, 52, 229; [Joseph Blessington], *The Campaigns of Walker's Texas Division* (New York, 1875), p. 42; Barron, *Lone Star Defenders,* pp. 17–18, 36; John Q. Anderson, *A Texas Surgeon in the C.S.A.* (Tuscaloosa, Ala., 1957), p. 26; H. A. Graves, *Andrew Jackson Potter, the Fighting Parson of the Texas Frontier* (Nashville, 1882), pp. 137–38; C. Vann Woodward, *Origins of the New South* (Baton Rouge, 1951), pp. 44, 70–72; *Washington Telegraph* (Ark.), Dec. 31, 1862; *Dallas Herald,* June 21, Sept. 13, Oct. 4, Nov. 8, 1862; *Bellville Countryman* (Tex.), Oct. 11, 1862; *Texas Almanac—Extra* (Austin), Nov. 1, 1862; *Little Rock Patriot,* Dec. 25, 1862; *The Standard* (Clarksville, Tex.), Jan. 1, 31, 1863; *San Antonio Herald,* April 18, May 2, June 6, 1863; *O.R.,* Ser. I, XV, 872–74; XXII, part i, 28–36, and part ii, 1057–58; XXVI, part i, 313–14, and part ii, 215, 241; XXXIV, part ii, 921–22; LII, part ii, 438; Ser. IV, I, 126; Reyn-

olds to Smith, May 13, 1863, Reynolds to Johnson, May 26, July 18, 1863, Reynolds Papers; "Address to the Citizens and Soldiers," July 28, 1862, Executive Record Book, No. 81.

6. Quoting *O.R.,* Ser. I, XXII, part ii, 821–22. Also, Sarah Dawson, *A Confederate Girl's Diary* (Boston, 1913), p. 233; Fremantle, *Diary,* pp. 41–42, 49; H. P. Clarke, comp., *The Confederate States Almanac and Repository of Useful Knowledge for 1862* (Vicksburg, 1862), p. 58; J. C. Schwab, *The Confederate States of America, 1861–1865: A Financial and Industrial History of the South during the Civil War* (New York, 1901), pp. 149–59, 167, 172; E. T. Miller, "The State Finances of Texas during the Civil War," *Quarterly of the Texas State Historical Association,* XIV (July, 1910), 12–13, 21–22; Thomas, *Arkansas in War,* pp. 106–7, 326; David Y. Thomas, *Arkansas and Its People* (New York, 1930), I, 128–29; *Acts, 27th Louisiana Legislature,* Extra Sess., Opelousas, pp. 20, 29–30, 35–36; Williams, *Border Ruffians,* p. 230; Leonie Weyand and Houston Wade, *An Early History of Fayette County* (La Grange, Tex., 1936), p. 252; Matthew P. Andrews, *The Women of the South in War Times* (Baltimore, 1920), pp. 416–19, 422; Lougherty, *War in Texas,* pp. 14–15; *Public Laws,* ed. Matthews, pp. 69, 193, 262; George W. Tyler, *The History of Bell County* (San Antonio, 1936), pp. 234–36; Ernest A. Smith, "The History of the Confederate Treasury," *Publications of the Southern Historical Association* (1901), V, 25–26; Robinson, *Justice,* pp. 84–88; Edmund T. Miller, *A Financial History of Texas* (Austin, 1916), pp. 134–35, 140–43; Gammel, *Laws of Texas,* V, 467–69; Edmund T. Miller, "Repudiation of the State Debt in Texas," *Southwestern Historical Quarterly,* XVI (Oct., 1912), 169–83; *Dallas Herald,* Aug. 2, 1862, Feb. 18, 25, 1863; *Washington Telegraph* (Ark.), Nov. 5, 12, 1862, Jan. 7, 21, 28, Feb. 4, 11, 18, 25, March 4, Oct. 28, Dec. 16, 1863, March 4, 1864, March 22, 1865; *Houston Tri-Weekly Telegraph,* Dec. 27, 1861, Oct. 6, Dec. 5, 1862, Feb. 4, March 4, 20, 23, 27, June 10, Dec. 6, 15, 1863, Feb. 9, Sept. 20, 1864; *The Standard* (Clarksville, Tex.), June 16, 1863; *The South-Western* (Shreveport), July 29, Nov. 18, 1863; *Shreveport Semi-Weekly News,* March 10, 1863, Feb. 2, 9, 1864; *O.R.,* Ser. I, XV, 772–73, 866, 952; Ser. II, IV, 804–5; V, 842.

7. Quoting Thomas Farrow to Son, Nov. 6, 1862, Samuel W. Farrow Papers, University of Texas Archives; Andrew Henson to Son, Nov. 14, 1862, Andrew B. Henson Papers, University of Texas Archives; Frank Moss to Sister, Oct. 28, 1862, Frank Moss Papers, University of Texas Archives. Also, Charles H. Wesley, *The Collapse of the Confederacy* (Washington, D.C., 1937), pp. 19–34; Oates, *Cavalry,* pp. 56, 60; Thomas, *Arkansas in War,* pp. 102–3; H. B. McKenzie, "Confederate Manufactures in Southwest Arkansas," *Publications of the Arkansas Historical Association,* II (Fayetteville, 1908), 204–7; Gammel, *Laws of Texas,* V, 534–37, 576–77; Taylor, *Destruction and Reconstruction,* p. 139; Charles W. Ramsdell, *Behind the Lines of the Southern Confederacy* (Baton Rouge, 1944), p. 18; E. T. Miller, "The State Finances of Texas," in *The South in the Building of the Nation* (New York, 1909), V, 538; G. P. Whittington, "Rapides Parish, Louisiana—a History," *Louisiana Historical Quarterly,* XVII (1934), 746; *Texas Almanac, 1863,* p. 31; *Houston Tri-Weekly Telegraph,* May 21, 1862; *Texas Republican* (Marshall), Jan. 22, 1863; *Daily Crescent* (New Orleans), Sept. 16, Dec. 19, 1861; *De Bow's Review,* XXX (March, 1861), 372; *Wash-*

ington Telegraph (Ark.), Dec. 31, 1862; *San Antonio Herald,* Feb. 28, April 4, 11, May 9, June 13, 1863; *O.R.,* Ser. I, XV, 986–88; Ser. IV, I, 126; Reynolds to Johnson, Aug. 27, 1863, Reynolds Papers; Clark to Carothers, Aug. 29, 1861, and Clark to Walker, Sept. 7, 1861, Executive Record Book, No. 80; Lubbock to Hood and Marshall, Feb. 18, 1862, Lubbock to Besser, Feb. 3, Oct. 7, 1862; Lubbock to Chief Justice and County Commissioners of Washington County, Aug. 25, 1862, and Lubbock to Elmore, Nov. 15, 1862, Executive Record Book, No. 81.

8. Fremantle, *Diary,* pp. 7, 16; Oates, *Cavalry,* pp. 56–57; Oran M. Roberts, "Texas," in Evans, ed., *Confederate Military History,* XI, 112–13; Andrews, *Women of the South,* pp. 416–19, 422; Lougherty, *War in Texas,* pp. 14–15; Heartsill, *1491 Days,* frontispiece, pp. 44–45; *Confederate States Army Regulations, 1862* (Richmond, 1862), Article 47; Winchester Hall, *Story of the 26th Louisiana Infantry* (n.p., n.d. [1890?]), pp. 59–60; Taylor, *Destruction and Reconstruction,* pp. 135–37; Ella Lonn, *Salt as a Factor in the Confederacy* (New York, 1933), pp. 22, 29–33, 44–46, 48, 68–71, 74–75, 109, 192–93, 207–8, 222, 238; Anderson, *A Texas Surgeon,* p. 26; *General Orders, Headquarters, Trans-Mississippi Department, from March 6, 1863, to January 1, 1865* (Houston, 1865), pp. 32–33; Whittington, "Rapides Parish," *La. Hist. Quar.,* XVII, 746; McKenzie, "Manufactures in Arkansas," *Pub. Ark. Hist. Assoc.,* II, 200–2; S. B. Buckley, *First Annual Report of the Geological and Agricultural Survey of Texas* (Houston, 1874), p. 127; Gammel, *Laws of Texas,* V, 563; *Acts, 6th Louisiana Legislature,* First Sess., Baton Rouge, pp. 27, 84; *Houston Tri-Weekly Telegraph,* Sept. 11, 18, Oct. 30, Nov. 13, 27, 1861, Jan. 22, May 14, 19, 1862; *Confederate Veteran,* XII (1904), 116; *Washington Telegraph* (Ark.), Dec. 31, 1862; *Daily Crescent* (New Orleans), Dec. 9, 1861; *The South-Western* (Shreveport), Jan. 29, 1862; *O.R.,* Ser. I, IV, 102, 105; XIII, 761, 943–45; XV, 382; Ser. IV, I, 324; Martin to Pearce, Feb. 13, 1862, Records, Texas Adjutant General; *Senate Journal of Texas,* 9th Legislature, Extra Sess., p. 305, Texas State Archives, Austin; Session Laws of Texas, 10th Legislature, 1863, Joint Resolution, chap. VIII, Texas State Archives, Austin.

9. McKenzie, "Manufactures in Arkansas," *Pub. Ark. Hist. Assoc.,* II, 199–210; Miller, *Financial History,* p. 138; Lubbock, *Six Decades,* pp. 368–69; J. W. Mallet, "Works of the [Confederate] Ordnance Bureau," *Southern Historical Society Papers,* XXXVII (Jan., 1909), 8; Gorgas, *Diary,* p. 29; Frank E. Vandiver, *Ploughshares into Swords* (Austin, 1952), pp. 191–92; Taylor, *Destruction and Reconstruction,* p. 139; Charles W. Ramsdell, "The Texas State Military Board," *Southwestern Historical Quarterly,* XXVII (April, 1924), 268, 272; Charles S. Potts, *Railroad Transportation in Texas* (Austin, 1909), p. 37; S. C. Reed, *A History of the Texas Railroads and of Transportation Conditions* (Houston, 1941), pp. 125–27; Robert Black, *Railroads of the Confederacy* (Chapel Hill, 1952), p. 299; Fremantle, *Diary,* p. 62; Thomas, *Arkansas in War,* pp. 102–3; Comte de Paris, *History of the Civil War in America* (Philadelphia, 1875–88), III, 402; Barron, *Lone Star Defenders,* pp. 17–18; Heartsill, *1491 Days,* p. 229; Wesley, *Collapse of the Confederacy,* p. 28; *Acts Passed by the Sixth Legislature of the State of Louisiana, Extra Session, 1863* (Shreveport, 1863), pp. 26–27; Eliza McHattan-Ripley, *From Flag to Flag* (New York, 1889), pp. 97–100; *Hous-*

ton Tri-Weekly Telegraph, Feb. 19, May 14, 1862, Jan. 19, April 29, 1863; *San Antonio Herald,* Aug. 24, 1861, May 31, Sept. 13, 27, Oct. 11, Nov. 1, 15, 1862, Feb. 14, 1863; *Bellville Countryman* (Tex.), Aug. 28, 1861, Aug. 22, 1863; *The Standard* (Clarksville, Tex.), Jan. 31, May 2, 1863; *The South-Western* (Shreveport), Sept. 11, 1861; *Galveston Tri-Weekly News,* Jan. 26, 1863; *Washington Telegraph* (Ark.), Dec. 31, 1862, Feb. 22, 1865; *Dallas Herald,* Feb. 11, April 29, 1863, July 2, 1864; *O.R.,* Ser. I, XV, 866, 952, 986–88; XXII, part ii, 871, 1141; Frank Brown, "Annals of Travis County and of the City of Austin," XXIII, 65, copy, University of Texas Archives; E. M. Pease and Swante Palm, "State Finances of Texas during the Civil War," report dated Oct. 30, 1865, and "Report of the Texas State Military Board, March, 1865," both in Military Board Papers, Texas State Archives; Kirby Smith to Reynolds, June 16, 1863, Letterbook, Kirby Smith Papers; Billings to Lubbock, Dec. 1, 1862, Records, Texas Adjutant General; "An Address by the Governor [Murrah] to the People of Texas," Jan. 16, 1864, Executive Record Book, No. 280, Texas State Archives.

10. Gammel, *Laws of Texas,* V, 484–85, 496, 499, 532–33; Martin Rywell, *Confederate Guns* (Harriman, Tenn., 1952), pp. 7, 22; Ramsdell, "Texas Military Board," *Southwestern Hist. Quar.,* XXVII, 253–58, 268, 272; Thomas, *Arkansas and Its People,* I, 128; Thomas, *Arkansas in War,* pp. 86, 101–4; Walter P. Lane, *The Adventures and Recollections of General Walter P. Lane* (Marshall, Tex., 1928), pp. 83, 104–5; U.S. Record and Pension Office, *Organization and Status of Missouri Troops, Union and Confederate, during the Civil War* (Washington, D.C., 1902), pp. 53, 57; *General Orders, Trans-Mississippi Department,* p. 2; Bartlett, *Military Record of Louisiana,* part III, 38n; Lubbock, *Six Decades,* pp. 368–69, 372; William Albaugh and Edward M. Simmons, *Confederate Arms* (Harrisburg, Pa., 1957); Mallet, "Works of the Ordnance Bureau," *Southern Hist. Soc. Papers,* XXXVII, 8; Taylor, *Destruction and Reconstruction,* p. 139; Kerby, *Confederate Invasion of New Mexico,* p. 73; Ralph W. Donnelly, "Rocket Batteries of the Civil War," *Military Affairs,* XXV (Summer, 1961), 85–89; Getulius Kellersberger, *Memoirs of an Engineer in the Confederate Army in Texas,* trans. Helen S. Sundstrom (Austin, 1957), pp. 33–34; Vandiver, *Ploughshares into Swords,* pp. 191–92; Richard D. Steuart, "How Johnny Got His Gun," *Confederate Veteran,* XXXII (May, 1924), 166–69; Claude Fuller and Richard D. Steuart, *Firearms of the Confederacy* (Huntington, W. Va., 1944), pp. 144–45; Richard D. Steuart, "The Confederate Colt," *Army Ordnance,* XV (Sept.–Oct., 1934), 90; H. Smythe, *Historical Sketch of Parker County and Weatherford, Texas* (St. Louis, 1877), pp. 171–72; Albert Woldert, *A History of Tyler and Smith County, Texas* (San Antonio, 1948), pp. 41–42; Hattie Roach, *A History of Cherokee County* [Texas] (Dallas, 1928), pp. 66–67; Dabney White, ed., *East Texas, Its History and Its Makers* (New York, 1940), II, 871, and III, 1248; McKenzie, "Manufactures in Arkansas," *Pub. Ark. Hist. Assoc.,* II, 207–10; Fremantle, *Diary,* pp. 18, 57; Robert S. Bevier, *History of the First and Second Missouri Confederate Brigades* (St. Louis, 1879), p. 36; Fay Hempstead, *Historical Review of Arkansas* (Chicago, 1911), I, 218; *Public Laws,* ed. Matthews, pp. 27–28, 33; Don H. Biggers, *German Pioneers in Texas* (Fredericksburg, Tex., 1925), pp. 98–99; Emmet Landers, "Some Observations Concerning Confederate Ordnance," *Southwestern Historical Quarterly,* XVII (June, 1936), 46; O. F. Allen, *The City of Houston*

from Wilderness to Wonder (Temple, Tex., 1936), pp. 41–42; Schwab, *Financial and Industrial History*, p. 271; Miller, *Financial History*, p. 138; *Daily Crescent* (New Orleans), Sept. 6, 16, 1861; *Bellville Countryman* (Tex.), Aug. 28, Sept. 11, 1861; *Daily Picayune* (New Orleans), June 16, 1861; *De Bow's Review*, XXX, 371–72; *San Antonio Herald*, Aug. 24, 1861, May 31, Sept. 13, 27, Oct. 11, Nov. 1, 15, 1862, Feb. 14, 21, 1863; *Texas Almanac—Extra* (Austin), Feb. 28, 1863; *Houston Tri-Weekly Telegraph*, May 30, 1862; *O.R.*, Ser. I, IV, 109, 422; IX, 719; XI, 734; XIII, 883, 889–90, 898, 908; XV, 986–88; XXII, part i, 153, and part ii, 1003, 1141; XXVI, part ii, 24–25; LIII, 833–34; Ser. IV, I, 422, 1096; II, 958; III, 733; Brown, "Annals of Travis County," XXIII, 3–4, 65; "Report of the Texas State Military Board, March, 1865," and Pease and Palm, "State Finances of Texas," Oct. 30, 1865, both in Military Board Papers; Merton to Bryan, March 10, 1862, and "List of Articles Needed for Use of Ordnance Department, Department Trans-Mississippi, C.S.A.," Oct., 1863, both in Guy M. Bryan Papers, University of Texas Archives; Clark to Baylor, May 13, 1861, and Clark to Shawn, Rodgers, and Felder, May 17, 1861, both in Executive Record Book, No. 80; "Address [of the four Trans-Mississippi governors] to the Citizens and Soldiers," July 28, 1862, and Lubbock to Magruder, Dec. 5, 1862, both in Executive Record Book, No. 81; Daggett to Clark, May 9, 1861, Governors' Letters (Clark), Texas State Archives.

11. Quoting "An Address by the Governor [Murrah] to the People of Texas," Jan. 16, 1864, Executive Record Book, No. 280. Also, Taylor, *Destruction and Reconstruction*, p. 137; Gammel, *Laws of Texas*, V, 594; Graves, *Andrew Jackson Potter*, pp. 137–38; Ramsdell, "Lee's Horse Supply," *Amer. Hist. Rev.*, XXXV, 758, 766; Barron, *Lone Star Defenders*, p. 20; J. K. P. Blackburn, "Reminiscences of the Terry Rangers," *Southwestern Historical Quarterly*, XXII (July, 1918), 43–45; Edwards, *Shelby*, p. 69; Heartsill, *1491 Days*, pp. 218, 228; Walter Prichard, "The Effects of the Civil War on the Louisiana Sugar Industry," *Journal of Southern History*, V (1939), 315–32; Shugg, *Origins of Class Struggle*, p. 139; *Journals of Congress*, II, 20, 57, 59, 62, 67, 69, 72, and V, 29, 76; *Public Laws*, ed. Matthews, pp. 166–67; *Department of Commerce Bulletin No. 131* (Washington, D.C., 1915), p. 82; E. Merton Coulter, "The Movement for Agricultural Reorganization in the Cotton States during the Civil War," *North Carolina Historical Review*, IV (1927), 22–36; Sarah A. Dorsey, *Recollections of Henry Watkins Allen* (New York, 1866), p. 281; Wickham Hoffman, *Camp Court and Siege* (New York, 1877), pp. 36–37; E. Merton Coulter, "Commercial Intercourse with the Confederacy in the Mississippi Valley," *Mississippi Valley Historical Review*, V (1918–19), 378–83; Thomas, *Arkansas in War*, p. 100; Fremantle, *Diary*, pp. 11, 41, 48, 50; *Historical and Biographical Record of the Cattle Industry and the Cattlemen of Texas and Adjacent Territory* (St. Louis, 1895), p. 57; *Daily State Journal* (Little Rock), March 6, 1861; *San Antonio Herald*, April 18, 1863; *The South-Western* (Shreveport), May 21, 28, 1862; *Daily Picayune* (New Orleans), July 22, 1862; *Houston Tri-Weekly Telegraph*, April 4, June 6, 9, July 7, 1862, Jan. 19, Feb. 20, April 1, 29, May 4, 1863; *Shreveport Semi-Weekly News*, Feb. 13, 1863; *Dallas Herald*, May 6, 20, 1863; *O.R.*, Ser. I, XIII, 979–80; XV, 504–10, 761; XXII, part i, 55, 157, 195, 198; XXVI, part ii, 577; XLI, part iv, 1048–49, 1057, 1061–62, 1070–72, 1077, 1104, 1110–13; LII, part ii, 438; Ser.

IV, I, 126–27; II, 468, 475–77; III, 282, 1066–67; *Senate Journal of Texas,* 9th Legis., Extra Sess., p. 267; Billings to Lubbock, Dec. 1, 1862, Records, Texas Adjutant General.

12. Rywell, *Confederate Guns,* p. 22; Lane, *Adventures and Recollections,* p. 83; Frederic L. Paxson, *History of the American Frontier* (New York, 1924), pp. 461–64; Rupert N. Richardson and Carl C. Rister, *The Greater Southwest* (Glendale, Calif., 1934), pp. 231–39; Taylor, *Destruction and Reconstruction,* pp. 119–22, 129–30, 136; William Watson, *Adventures of a Blockade-Runner* (London, 1892), pp. 19, 25–26; Rev. P. F. Parsiot, *Reminiscences of a Texas Missionary* (San Antonio, 1899), p. 56; Fremantle, *Diary,* pp. 6–7, 49–50; Black, *Railroads of the Confederacy,* pp. 5, 7, 9–10, 12, 14, 17–18, 84–85, 87, 121–22, 124–25, 299; Reed, *History of Texas Railroads,* pp. 35–36, 53–65, 73–74, 79–102, 119–20, 124–26; Potts, *Railroad Transportation in Texas,* p. 37; *Public Laws,* ed. Matthews, pp. 34–35; *Journals of Congress,* II, 335, 409; "Proceedings of Congress," *Southern Hist. Soc. Papers,* XLIX, 174–77; Charles W. Ramsdell, "The Confederate Government and the Railroads," *American Historical Review,* XXII (1917), 802; *Houston Tri-Weekly Telegraph,* Feb. 23, May 15, Aug. 3, Sept. 16, 18, 1863; *Daily Crescent* (New Orleans), Feb. 3, 1862; *Price-Current* (New Orleans), May 29, 1861; *O.R.,* Ser. I, XXXIV, part iii, 316; Ser. IV, I, 1013–14, 1073–74, 1108–9; II, 107–8; *O.R.N.,* XVII, 418–19, 446; XXVI, 94.

13. Quoting Edwin Becton to Mary Becton, Feb. 5, 1864, Becton Papers, University of Texas Archives. Also, Julius Fröbel, *Seven Years in Central America, Northern Mexico, and the Far West of the United States* (London, 1859), p. 450; Reed, *History of Texas Railroads,* p. 44; Ramsdell, "Texas State Military Board," *Southwestern Hist. Quar.,* XXVII, 265; William and George Banning, *Six Horses* (New York, 1930), pp. 110–11, 131–35, 144–51, 393–96; Fremantle, *Diary,* pp. 23–35, 45; Ford, *Rip Ford's Texas,* p. 349; August Santleben, *A Texas Pioneer: Early Staging and Overland Freighting Days on the Frontiers of Texas and Mexico* (New York, 1910), pp. 107–8; Williams, *Border Ruffians,* p. 396; Boggs, *Reminiscences,* pp. 68–69; Heartsill, *1491 Days,* pp. 214–15; *Statutes at Large,* ed. Matthews, p. 40; David Kahn, *The Codebreakers* (New York, 1967), pp. 148, 217–18; William R. Plum, *The Military Telegraph during the Civil War* (Chicago, 1882), I, 40; *Houston Tri-Weekly Telegraph,* Jan. 12, April 30, May 16, 1862, Jan. 26, 28, Feb. 16, 23, March 13, Aug. 3, 1863; *The Colorado Citizen* (Columbus, Tex.), Feb. 16, 1861; *The Standard* (Clarksville, Tex.), Jan. 31, 1863; *San Antonio Herald,* Feb. 14, May 16, 23, 1863; *The South-Western* (Shreveport), July 29, 1863, Jan. 6, 1864; *Galveston Tri-Weekly News,* Jan. 26, 1863; *O.R.,* Ser. I, XXII, part ii, 871–73; *Atlas to Accompany the Official Records of the Union and Confederate Armies* (Washington, D.C., 1891–95), plates no. 54, 153–60; John Salmon Ford, "Memoirs," VI, 1092–93, MS, University of Texas Archives; Roessler, "Military Routes in Texas"; Kirby Smith to Surget, June 3, 8, 1863, Letterbook, Kirby Smith Papers.

14. Quoting contract between D. E. Anderson and fourteen citizens of Rusk County, June 10, [1862], Henson Papers; *Houston Tri-Weekly Telegraph,* Oct. 29, 1862. Also, *San Antonio Herald,* May 2, 1863; *The Standard* (Clarksville, Tex.), June 16, 1863.

15. Quoting *Houston Tri-Weekly Telegraph*, Jan. 19, 1863. Also, Fremantle, *Diary*, p. 51; *Acts, 27th Louisiana Legislature*, Extra Sess., Opelousas, p. 26; *Acts, 6th Louisiana Legislature*, Extra Sess., Shreveport, p. 4; Andrews, *Women of the South*, pp. 422–23; Allen, *The City of Houston*, pp. 47–48; Duganne, *Camps and Prisons*, p. 243; Charles C. Nott, *Sketches in Prison Camps* (New York, 1865), pp. 92–93, 97, 100, 171–72; Chris Emmett, *Texas Camel Tales* (San Antonio, 1932), pp. 197, 204, 212; Woldert, *Tyler and Smith County*, pp. 39–40; John W. Greene, *Camp Ford Prison* (Toledo, 1893), pp. 27–32; Heartsill, *1491 Days*, pp. 198–99, 204; *Dallas Herald*, Feb. 18, 25, 1863; *The Standard* (Clarksville, Tex.), Oct. 3, 1863; *Houston Tri-Weekly Telegraph*, Nov. 25, Dec. 11, 1861, Oct. 1, Dec. 19, 1862, Jan. 19, March 4, 1863; *Shreveport Semi-Weekly News*, Jan. 20, 27, 1863; *O.R.*, Ser. I, XIII, 980; XV, 143–44, 146–47; XXII, part ii, 138, 154, 797–98, 808; Record Books of the Rock Hotel General Hospital, Little Rock, 1862–63, of the General Hospital, Shreveport, 1863–65, and of the General Hospitals, Galveston and Houston, 1862–65, Records of the Confederate Medical Bureau, War Department Collection of Confederate Records, Record Group 109, National Archives; Lubbock to Rippetoe and Fluellen, Jan. 27, 1862, Lubbock to Lane, Feb. 5, 1862, Lubbock to Bryan, July 1, 1862, Lubbock to Feris, Nov. 16, 1862, all in Executive Record Book, No. 81; Williamson S. Oldham, "Memoirs," n.d., pp. 336–37, copy, University of Texas Archives.

16. Quoting Williams, *Border Ruffians*, p. 75; *Houston Tri-Weekly Telegraph*, June 4, 1862; *The Standard* (Clarksville, Tex.), March 1, 1862; Fremantle, *Diary*, pp. 31–32. Also, Thomas, *Arkansas in War*, p. 330; Gammel, *Laws of Texas*, V, 601–2; *Acts, 6th Louisiana Legislature*, Extra Sess., Shreveport, pp. 27–28; *San Antonio Herald*, Sept. 12, 1863; Hunter to Kirby Smith, Jan. 28, 1864, Correspondence, Kirby Smith Papers; *Senate Journal of Texas*, 9th Legislature, Extra Sess.

17. Quoting *O.R.*, Ser. IV, I, 1068–69; Graham to Randolph, Nov. 17, 1862, War Department Letters Received, War Department Collection of Confederate Records, Record Group 109, National Archives; Edwin P. Becton to Mary Becton, June 7, 1864, Becton Papers. See also Moore, *Conscription and Conflict in the Confederacy*; Georgia Lee Tatum, *Disloyalty in the Confederacy* (Chapel Hill, 1934); Ella Lonn, *Desertion during the Civil War* (New York, 1928).

18. Quoting *O.R.*, Ser. I, LIII, 900–1. Also, Mary S. Estill, ed., "Diary of a Confederate Congressman, 1862–63," *Southwestern Historical Quarterly*, XXXVIII (1934–35), 283; *Ex parte Coupland*, 26 *Texas*, 386; *Ex parte Abraham Mayer*, 27 *Texas*, 715; *Public Laws*, ed. Matthews, pp. 211–15; Wesley, *Collapse*, pp. 78–82; Heartsill, *1491 Days*, pp. 137, 142, 164, 167–68, and *passim*; Elliott, "Union Sentiment in Texas," *Southwestern Hist. Quar.*, L, 459–62; Rippy, "Border Troubles," *Southwestern Hist. Quar.*, XXIII, 92; Taylor, *American-Mexican Frontier*, pp. 33, 36–39; Gammel, *Laws of Texas*, V, 484; *San Antonio Herald*, April 18, 22, 1863; *Houston Tri-Weekly Telegraph*, Nov. 25, 27, Dec. 4, 7, 9, 16, 23, 1863; *O.R.*, Ser. I, XV, 747–49, 991–98, 1006–8, 1024–25; XXII, part ii, 1057–58; XXVI, part ii, 215, 236, 241, 285, 344, 352–53, 393–94, 398, 401, 455–56, 469–71, 522–23; XXXIV, part ii, 908–11, 925–26, 945; LIII, 836–37; Ser. II, IV, 785–87; Ser. IV, III, 178–81; Lubbock to Dashiell, March 10, 1862, Lubbock to Hebert, March 7, 14, June 5, 1862, Lubbock to Burford, April 5, 1862, Lub-

bock to Davis, Nov. 13, 1862, Executive Record Book, No. 81; J. Evetts Haley, "Life of Goodnight" (University of Texas Archives, n.d.), pp. 214, 224–32; G.O. No. 16, Camp Colorado, Sept. 11, 1863, and McCord to Dashiell, Oct. 9, 1863, Records, Texas Adjutant General.

19. Worley, "Arkansas Peace Society," *Ark. Hist. Quar.*, XVII, 82–111; Wesley, *Collapse*, p. 96; Elliott, "Union Sentiment in Texas," *Southwestern Hist. Quar.*, L, 459–62; Hunter, "Heel-Fly Time in Texas," *Frontier Times*, April, 1924, pp. 35–48; Biggers, *German Pioneers in Texas*, pp. 57–61; Ella Lonn, *Foreigners in the Confederacy* (Chapel Hill, 1940), pp. 312–13; Williams, *Border Ruffians*, pp. 242–51; Fremantle, *Diary*, pp. 18, 41, 45; John W. Sansom, *Battle of the Nueces River* (San Antonio, 1905), pp. 1–15; Robert W. Shook, "The Battle of the Nueces, August 10, 1862," *Southwestern Historical Quarterly*, LXVI (July, 1962), 31–42; Wilhelm Kaufmann, *Die Deutschen amerikanischen Bürgerkriege* (Munich and Berlin, 1911), pp. 157–62; *Eduard Schmidt, 1862–1912: Festschrift zur fünfzigjahrigen erinnerungs-feier an das gefecht am Nueces, 10 August 1862* (n.p., 1912); Jacob Kuechler, "Statement of the Honorable Jacob Kuechler," in James P. Newcomb, *Address . . . Delivered at Comfort, Texas, August 10, 1887, the Twenty-fifth Anniversary of the Nueces Massacre* (n.p., 1887), pp. 2–4; H. A. Trexler, "Episode in Border History," *Southwest Review*, XVI (Jan., 1931), 237–38; Gertrude Harris, *A Tale of Men Who Knew Not Fear* (San Antonio, 1935), pp. 13–15; R. L. Biesele, *The History of the German Settlements in Texas, 1831–1861* (Austin, 1930), pp. 61–62, 163–64; "Chase Diary and Correspondence," *Report, A.H.A., 1902*, II, 101; George W. Smith, "The Banks Expedition of 1862," *Louisiana Historical Quarterly*, XXVI (1943), 342, 348–49; George B. McClellan, *McClellan's Own Story* (New York, 1887), pp. 103–4; *Eighth Census* (1860), *Population*, pp. 490, 620–23; E. F. Bates, *History and Reminiscences of Denton County* (Denton, Tex., 1918), pp. 105–7; C. D. Cates, *Pioneer History of Wise County* (Decatur, Tex., 1907), pp. 130–32; *Texas Almanac —Extra* (Austin), Dec. 18, 1862; *O.R.*, Ser. I, IV, 131–32, 137; IX, 614–16, 654–55, 701–2, 705–6, 712–13, 715–16, 735–36; XV, 220, 412, 887, 925–29, 931, 936, 945–46, 955–56, 960, 974–75, 1018; XXVI, part i, 659, 680, 682–83, 865–67; LIII, 454–55, Ser. II, II, 1399, 1402–5, 1407–8, 1422; IV, 785–87; Ser. IV, II, 39; Clark to Benavides, July 1, 1861, Executive Record Book, No. 80; Lubbock to Bee, Oct. 15, 1862, and Lubbock to Texas Congressional Delegation, Sept. 30, 1862, Executive Record Book, No. 81; Proclamation, [Lubbock] To the People of Texas, Jan. 4, 1862 [*sic;* 1863], Executive Record Book, No. 279; Haley, "Life of Goodnight," p. 214; Claude Elliott, "The Life of James W. Throckmorton" (Ph.D. dissertation, University of Texas, 1934), pp. 123–24; Thomas Barrett, "The Great Hanging at Gainesville, Cooke County, Texas," pp. 2–31, MS, dated 1885, University of Texas Archives.

20. Quoting *O.R.*, Ser. I, LIII, 900–1; XXII, part ii, 796; XXXIV, part ii, 921–22; N. B. Floyd Papers, University of Texas Archives; Mary Maverick to Lewis Maverick, March 1, 1863, Samuel Maverick Papers, University of Texas Archives. Also, Thomas, *Arkansas in War*, p. 101; Gammel, *Laws of Texas*, V, 600–1; *Acts, 7th Louisiana Legislature*, First Sess., Shreveport, p. 74; *Jefferson Davis, Constitutionalist*, ed. Rowland, V, 552; *Washington Telegraph* (Ark.), Dec. 31, 1862; *Houston Tri-Weekly Telegraph*, Jan. 22, 1864.

Chapter Three: The Loss of the Mississippi Valley

1. Quoting Theophilus Noel, *A Campaign from Santa Fe to the Mississippi: Being a History of the Old Sibley Brigade* . . . (Shreveport, 1865), p. 46. Also, *ibid.,* pp. 45–50; Fremantle, *Diary,* pp. 76–77; Thomas, *Arkansas in War,* pp. 197–99; Hepworth, *Whip, Hoe, and Sword,* pp. 272–74; Taylor, *Destruction and Reconstruction,* pp. 136, 140–42, 149–62; Bartlett, *Military Record of Louisiana,* part III, pp. 39, 54, and Hyatt, "Diary," *ibid.,* p. 9; Gorgas, *Diary,* p. 29; Weinert, "Regular Army," *Military Affairs,* XXVI, 104; *The Louisiana Democrat* (Alexandria), March 11, 1863; *O.R.,* Ser. I, XV, 251–80, 292–400, 704–5, 975, 983–84, 999, 1003, 1043; XXII, part i, 215–24, 227–33, 236–37, 239–42, 244, 246–48, and part ii, 772–73, 783, 785–94, 796–97, 800, 802–5, 808, 811–15, 817–21, 823–25; Banks to Halleck, May 4, 1863, Banks Papers.

2. Quoting Hyatt, "Diary," in Bartlett, *Military Record of Louisiana,* part III, p. 11; Noel, *History of the Sibley Brigade,* pp. 50–51. Also, Hyatt, "Diary," p. 9; Noel, *Sibley Brigade,* pp. 50–55; Taylor, *Destruction and Reconstruction,* pp. 149–50, 159–61; Gorgas, *Diary,* pp. 33–34; *O.R.,* Ser. I, XV, 292–400 *passim,* 843, 1093–95; XXVI, part ii, 241.

3. Quoting Johnson to Smith, April 18, 1863, Correspondence, Kirby Smith Papers; *O.R.,* Ser. I, XV, 1047, 1050, 387; Boggs, *Reminiscences,* pp. 57–58; Fremantle, *Diary,* pp. 64–66. Also, Taylor, *Destruction and Reconstruction,* pp. 151, 163, 166; *O.R.,* Ser. I, XV, 386–87, 1041–54; XXII, part ii, 828.

4. Quoting Flinn, *Campaigning with Banks,* p. 65; Banks to Halleck, May 4, 1863, Banks Papers; *O.R.,* Ser. I, XV, 311–13; Hyatt, "Diary," in Bartlett, *Military Record of Louisiana,* part III, p. 10; Fremantle, *Diary,* p. 68. Also, Taylor, *Destruction and Reconstruction,* p. 161; Flinn, *Campaigning with Banks,* pp. 62–65; Whittington, "Rapides Parish," *La. Hist. Quar.,* XVIII, 7–8; *O.R.,* Ser. I, XV, 298–300, 303–15, 706–20, 725–26, 1117–19.

5. Quoting *O.R.,* Ser. I, XXVI, part i, 535; Ransdell to Moore, May 31, 1863, Thomas O. Moore Papers, Louisiana State University Archives; Moore to Lubbock, May 25, 1863, and Bryan to Lubbock, May 22, 1863, both in Governors' Letters (Lubbock); Kirby Smith to Surget, June 8, 1863, Letterbook, Kirby Smith Papers. Also, Taylor, *Destruction and Reconstruction,* pp. 162–64; Bartlett, *Military Record of Louisiana,* part III, p. 36, and Hyatt, "Diary," *ibid.,* p. 10; Fremantle, *Diary,* pp. 73–74; Whittington, "Rapides Parish," *La. Hist. Quar.,* XVIII, 5–8; *Report of the Joint Committee on the Conduct of the War,* 38th Cong., 2d Sess., II, 345; *O.R.,* Ser. I, XV, 313–18, 720, 725–32, 1081–82; XXII, part ii, 835, 839–40, 855–56; XXVI, part i, 12, 35–36, 38–41, 43, 535.

6. Quoting *O.R.,* Ser. I, XXII, part ii, 965, 990; Kirby Smith to McCulloch, Sept. 13, 1863, Letterbook, Kirby Smith Papers. Also, Ficklen, *History of Reconstruction in Louisiana,* pp. 119–22; *Acts, 6th Louisiana Legislature,* Extra Sess., Shreveport, pp. 27–28; *Public Laws,* ed. Matthews, p. 2; *O.R.,* Ser. I, XV, 716–17; XXVI, part i, 688–89; Ser. II, VI, 21–22, 115; Ransdell to Moore, May 26, 1863, Moore Papers.

7. Quoting Taylor, *Destruction and Reconstruction*, pp. 162–66; *O.R.*, Ser. I, XXII, part ii, 868, 915; XXVI, part ii, 13; Kirby Smith to Reynolds, June 4, 1863, and Kirby Smith to Surget, June 3, 1863, Letterbook, Kirby Smith Papers. Also, Fremantle, *Diary*, p. 69; Taylor, *Destruction and Reconstruction*, p. 179; Grant, *Memoirs*, pp. 242 ff.; Earl Schenck Miers, *The Web of Victory: Grant at Vicksburg* (New York, 1955), pp. 138 ff.; Parks, *Kirby Smith*, pp. 266–77; Holman Hamilton, *Zachary Taylor* (Indianapolis, 1951), p. 27; *O.R.*, Ser. I, XXII, part ii, 855–57, 859, 868, 872, 885–86, 902, 904, 913–16; XXIV, part ii, 457–62, and part iii, 846, 997; XXVI, part ii, 12–13, 15, 19, 26, 28–30, 41–44, 71, 74–75, 97, 106–10, 113; Kirby Smith to Johnston, June 4, 1863, Letterbook, Kirby Smith Papers; Elgee to Walker, June 24, 1863, Walker Papers.

8. Quoting Taylor, *Destruction and Reconstruction*, pp. 170–71; *O.R.*, Ser. I, XXVI, part ii, 111; Hepworth, *Whip, Hoe, and Sword*, pp. 272–74. Also, Taylor, *Destruction and Reconstruction*, pp. 169–76; Bartlett, *Military Record of Louisiana*, part III, pp. 39, 56–57; Fremantle, *Diary*, p. 57; Gorgas, *Diary*, p. 46; Duganne, *Camps and Prisons*, pp. 125–26; Noel, *History of the Sibley Brigade*, p. 57; *Report, Committee on the Conduct of the War*, II, 313–14; *O.R.*, Ser. I, XXIV, part ii, 461–62; XXVI, part i, 13, 15–16, 55–56, 187–232, 667–68, and part ii, 43–45, 53, 66–67, 71, 74–75, 99–100, 106–7, 109–11, 113, 116–17, 209–10; Brightman to Rogers, Aug. 23, 1863, Brightman Papers.

9. Quoting Brightman to Rogers, Aug. 23, 1863, Brightman Papers; *O.R.*, Ser. I, XXVI, part ii, 241, 117–18; Hyatt, "Diary," in Bartlett, *Military Record of Louisiana*, part III, pp. 10–11. Also, Bartlett, *Military Record*, part III, pp. 39–40; *San Antonio Herald*, June 27, 1863, Feb. 13, 1864; *O.R.*, Ser. I, XXVI, part i, 241–48, and part ii, 47–48, 96–97; Lubbock to Harris, June 17, 1863, Executive Record Book, No. 82; Mayo to Logan, May 31, 1863, Logan Papers.

10. Snead, "The Conquest of Arkansas," in Johnson and Buell, eds., *Battles and Leaders*, III, 453–56; Abel, *The Indian as Participant*, pp. 243–81; Britton, *Civil War on the Border*, II, 3, 18–42, and *passim;* Eaton, *Ross*, p. 196; Frank Moore, ed., *The Rebellion Record* (New York, 1862–71), VI, 50; Harrell, "Arkansas," in Evans, ed., *Confederate Military History*, X, 161–68; Thomas, *Arkansas in War*, pp. 197–203; Anderson, *Watie*, pp. 20–22; *Report, Commissioner of Indian Affairs, 1865*, p. 36; Britton, "Indians in the Civil War," in Johnson and Buell, eds., *Battles and Leaders*, I, 336; *O.R.*, Ser. I, XXII, part i, 12–13, 28–32, 34–36, 220–24, 227–29, 242, 246, 249, 305–16, 321–22, 337–38, 341–42, 348–52, 378–82, 445, 604, and part ii, 26, 33, 56–62, 73, 85, 96–97, 100–2, 108–9, 111–15, 121–22, 126, 139–42, 147–54, 162–63, 165–66, 168–72, 181–82, 190–94, 197, 200–1, 205, 210–13, 224–25, 246–48, 256, 258, 260–62, 266, 276–77, 282–84, 297–98, 310–11, 331, 337, 355–57, 367–68, 773, 775–79, 783, 787, 791, 794–96, 799, 801–2, 804–6, 809–10, 815–23, 827–30, 833–34, 839, 842–44, 848, 883–85, 893–94, 903, 905, 909–11, 1049–53, 1116–25; LIII, 469.

11. Quoting *O.R.*, Ser. I, XXII, part i, 199, and part ii, 846. Also, Moore, "Missouri," in Evans, ed., *Confederate Military History*, IX, 131–33; Thomas, *Arkansas in War*, pp. 201–2; Oates, *Cavalry*, pp. 121–31; Moore, *Rebellion Record*, VI, 561–63; Edwards, *Shelby*, pp. 151 ff.; Bennett Young, *Confederate Wizards of the Saddle* (Boston, 1914), pp. 541–63; Charles H. Lothrop, *A History of the First Regiment Iowa Cavalry* (Lyons, Iowa, 1890), pp. 107–8; Taylor, *Destruc-*

tion and Reconstruction, p. 150; *O.R.*, Ser. I, XXII, part i, 198–99, 251–305, 525, and part ii, 781–84, 786, 788, 790–91, 793–94, 802–3, 808, 814, 818–19, 822–23, 834–36, 840–42, 844–46, 850–51, 855–56, 860–61; XXVI, part ii, 13, 42.

12. Quoting *O.R.*, Ser. I, XXII, part ii, 835, 849, 863, 866, 868, part i, 407, part ii, 903; Kirby Smith to Johnston, Sept. 11, 1863, Letterbook, Kirby Smith Papers; Graves, "Diary," April 15, 1864. Also, Thomas, *Arkansas in War*, pp. 189–93; Snead, "Conquest of Arkansas," in Johnson and Buell, eds., *Battles and Leaders*, III, 455–56, 460–61; Harrell, "Arkansas," in Evans, ed., *Confederate Military History*, X, 175–222; Parks, *Kirby Smith*, pp. 279–80; O'Flaherty, *Shelby*, pp. 177–87; Newberry, "Flanagin," in *Arkansas and the Civil War*, p. 65; Will H. Tunnard, "Running the Mississippi Blockade," *Confederate Veteran*, XXIV (Jan., 1916), 27–28; Heartsill, *1491 Days*, p. 184; *O.R.*, Ser. I, XXII, part i, 383–441, and part ii, 317, 339, 352, 853, 855–57, 860, 863–64, 866–70, 873–74, 877–79, 881–82, 886–92, 896–903, 906–9, 911–12, 916, 919–21, 923–29, 931–33, 937–39, 941–47; *O.R.N.*, XXV, 228–29; Kirby Smith to Reynolds, June 4, 1863, and Kirby Smith to Johnston, Oct. 29, 1863, Letterbook, Kirby Smith Papers; Graves, "Diary," Feb. 15, 1864, University of Texas Archives.

13. Quoting *O.R.*, Ser. I, XXVI, part ii, 114–15; Proclamation of the Governor to the People of Texas, July 24, 1863, Executive Record Book, No. 279; Oldham, "Memoirs," p. 371; *O.R.*, Ser. I, XXII, part ii, 925–27, 1039. Also, *O.R.*, Ser. I, XXII, part ii, 55–57, 854–55, 916, 952–53, 1004; Kirby Smith to Reynolds, June 4, 1863, Letterbook, Kirby Smith Papers; Reynolds to Johnson, Aug. 23, 27, 1863, Reynolds Papers.

14. Quoting *O.R.*, Ser. I, XXII, part ii, 948, 949–50, 953, 1039. Also, Florence E. Holladay, "The Powers of the Commander of the Confederate Trans-Mississippi Department, 1863–1865," *Southwestern Historical Quarterly*, XXI (1918), 279–98, 333–59; *O.R.*, Ser. I, XXII, part ii, 935–36, 1004; XXVI, part ii, 96–97; Kirby Smith to Wife, July 17, 19, 20, 1863, Correspondence, Kirby Smith Papers.

15. Quoting *O.R.*, Ser. I, XXII, part ii, 1003–10. Also, Holladay, "Powers of the Commander," *Southwestern Hist. Quar.*, XXI, 283–88; *The South-Western* (Shreveport), Sept. 2, 1863; *Shreveport Semi-Weekly News*, Sept. 4, 15, 25, 1863; *Texas Almanac—Extra* (Austin), March 17, 1863; *O.R.*, Ser. I, LIII, 892–94; Oldham, "Memoirs," pp. 369–70; Reports of the Marshall Conference, Aug. 15–18, 1863, and Proclamation of the Governors to the People of Texas, Louisiana, Arkansas, and Missouri, and the Allied Indian Nations, Aug. 18, 1863, Executive Record Book, No. 82.

16. Quoting Taylor, *Destruction and Reconstruction*, p. 183; *O.R.*, Ser. I, LIII, 895–96; XXII, part ii, 993–94; Richardson, *Messages and Papers of the Confederacy*, I, 377–78; *Journals of Congress*, III, 453; *O.R.*, Ser. IV, III, 341; Ser. I, LIII, 985–86. Also, Boggs, *Reminiscences*, pp. 59–68; Ford, *Rip Ford's Texas*, pp. 330–31, 346; *Public Laws*, ed. Matthews, pp. 140–42, 176, 184, 187–89, 202–3, 230, 235; Schwab, *Financial and Industrial History*, p. 26; Richard Todd, *Confederate Finance* (Athens, Ga., 1954), pp. 23–24, 206; *Report of the Secretary of War, November 26, 1863* (Richmond, 1864); "Report of the Treasury Agent,

Trans-Mississippi Department, December 26, 1864," *Reports of the Secretary of the Treasury of the Confederates States of America* (Washington, D.C., 1878); Ernest A. Smith, "The History of the Confederate Treasury," *Publications of the Southern Historical Association* (Harrisburg, Pa., 1901), V, 70, 93–94; Francis Bradlee, *Blockade Running during the Civil War and the Effect of Land and Water Transportation on the Confederacy* (Salem, Mass., 1925), p. 288; *Journals of Congress*, III, 728; *Galveston Tri-Weekly News*, Sept. 18, 1863, March 13, 1865; *The State Gazette* (Austin), Sept. 30, 1863; *O.R.*, Ser. I, XXII, part ii, 828, 853, 969, 990–91, 1003–4, 1028–29, 1039–40, 1060–61, 1069–70, 1128–41; XXVI, part ii, 47, 65, 212–13, 269–70, 382, 517, 580; XXXIV, part ii, 1011, and part iv, 635–36, 672; XLI, part iii, 984, and part iv, 1030, 1082, 1094, 1109, 1122; LIII, 876–77, 1016–18; Ser. IV, II, 1016–18, 1045–46; Carr to Kirby Smith, June 10, 1864, Correspondence, Kirby Smith Papers; Reynolds to Johnson, Aug. 23, 1863, Reynolds Papers.

17. Quoting Reynolds to the Missouri Congressional Delegation, Dec. 12, 1863, and Reynolds to Davis, May 10, 1864, Reynolds Papers; Turner to Wife, May 2, 1864, Josiah Turner Papers, Southern Historical Collection, University of North Carolina. Also, Newberry, "Flanagin," in *Arkansas and the Civil War*, pp. 65–67; Thomas, *Arkansas in War*, pp. 332–34; Reynolds to Johnson, Aug. 27, 1863, Jan. 7, April 13, May 12, 1864, Reynolds to Cabell, Jan. 4, 1864, Reynolds to Hagan, Jan. 9, 1864, Reynolds to Connors, Jan. 18, 1864, Reynolds to Harris, May 21, 1864, all in Reynolds Papers; Turner to Wife, Dec. 5, 1864, Turner Papers.

18. Quoting Kirby Smith to Allen, Jan. 21, 1864, Letterbook, Kirby Smith Papers. Also, *Acts, 6th Louisiana Legislature,* Extra Sess., Shreveport, pp. 9–12, 14; *Acts Passed by the Seventh Legislature of the State of Louisiana, Second Session, 1865* (Shreveport, 1865), p. 11; Robert Calhoun, "The John Perkins Family of Northeast Louisiana," *Louisiana Historical Quarterly*, XVII (1936), 82–85; *Official Journals of the House and Senate of the Seventh Legislature of Louisiana, Session of 1864* (Shreveport, 1864), pp. 14–15; Dorsey, *Recollections of Henry Watkins Allen*, pp. 233 ff.; Bartlett, *Military Record of Louisiana*, part III, pp. 1–2; *Louisiana Democrat* (Alexandria), Oct. 14, Nov. 4, 1863; *Shreveport Semi-Weekly News*, Aug. 25, Oct. 13, 20, 1863; *The South-Western* (Shreveport), Nov. 11, 1863; *O.R.*, Ser. I, XXII, part ii, 974; Ser. IV, III, 1188.

19. Quoting Bryan to Lubbock, May 22, 1863, Governors' Letters (Lubbock); *San Antonio Herald*, June 6, 27, 1863. Also, James, *The Raven*, pp. 423–33; Wooten, *Comprehensive History of Texas*, II, 142–43; T. J. Chambers, "Address to the People of Texas," in *Memorial of General T. J. Chambers to the Sixth Legislature of the State of Texas* (n.d., n.p.), copy, University of Texas Archives; James De Shields, *They Sat in High Place* (San Antonio, 1940), pp. 241–49; Mary Boykin Chesnut, *A Diary from Dixie*, ed. Ben Ames Williams (Boston, 1949), p. 329; *The Semi-Weekly News* (San Antonio), June 11, 1863; *The Texas Republican* (Marshall), March 14, May 30, 1863; *Houston Tri-Weekly Telegraph*, July 4, Aug. 1, 5, 11, 13, 25, 1863; *Bellville Countryman* (Tex.), Aug. 1, 1863; *Tri-Weekly State Gazette* (Austin), June 9, 1863; *The Standard* (Clarksville, Tex.), July 4, 18, 26, 1863; Sexton to Starr, Aug. 30, 1863, James H. Starr Papers, University of Texas Archives; "Address [by Murrah] to the Senate and

House of Representatives of Texas," Nov. 5, 1863, Executive Record Book, No
280; Oldham, "Memoirs," p. 62; Wigfall to Clay, Aug. 13, Dec. 11, 1863, Clement C. Clay Papers, Duke University Archives.

Chapter Four: King Cotton

1. Quoting Kirby Smith to McCulloch, Sept. 13, 1863, Letterbook, Kirby Smith
Papers; *Daily Picayune* (New Orleans), July 22, 1862; Benjamin F. Butler, *Private and Official Correspondence* (Norwood, Mass., 1917), II, 394–96. Also, Owsley, *King Cotton Diplomacy,* pp. 41–42; Schwab, *Financial and Industrial History,* pp. 16–17; Thomas, *Arkansas in War,* pp. 100–1; Fremantle, *Diary,* pp. 11,
41, 48, 50; *Statutes at Large,* ed. Matthews, pp. 98–99, 152–53, 170, 180; *Public
Laws,* ed. Matthews, pp. 46, 166–67, 181–82; *Journal of Congress,* I, 205–6, 251,
264, 276–77, 367, 429; II, 20, 57, 59, 62, 67, 69, 72, 325; III, 37; V, 29, 76;
Coulter, "Commercial Intercourse with the Confederacy," *Miss. Val. Hist. Rev.*
V, 378–84; Roberts, "The Federal Government and Confederate Cotton," *Amer.
Hist. Rev.,* XXXII, 262–75; James Ford Rhodes, *History of the United States*
(New York, 1906–7), V, 274–313; E. L. Erikson, ed., "Hunting for Cotton in
Dixie: From the Diary of Captain Charles E. Wilcox." *Journal of Southern History,* IV (1938), 493–513; Thomas Knox, *Camp-fire and Cotton-field* (New York,
1865), pp. 193–94, 307–9; Hoffman, *Camp Court and Siege,* pp. 36–37; Dorsey,
Recollections of Henry Watkins Allen, p. 281; *The South-Western* (Shreveport),
May 21, 1862; *Houston Tri-Weekly Telegraph,* April 4, June 6, 9, July 7, 1862,
Jan. 19, Feb. 20, April 1, 29, May 4, 1863; *De Bow's Review,* II (Rev. Ser.,
1866), 419; *O.R.,* Ser. I, XV, 504–10, 761; Ser. IV, I, 836–37; II, 468, 475–77;
III, 282, 1066–67; *O.R.N.,* XXVI, 340–52; *Senate Journal of Texas,* 9th Legis.,
Extra Sess., p. 267.

2. Quoting Canby in Coulter, "Commercial Intercourse with the Confederacy,"
Miss. Val. Hist. Rev., V, 389–90; *O.R.,* Ser. I, XXXI, part i, 780–81. Also, Edward Atkinson, *Report to the Boston Board of Trade* (Boston, 1862), pp. 2–4;
Coulter, "Commercial Intercourse," *Miss. Val. Hist. Rev.,* V, 378–90; Roberts,
"The Federal Government and Confederate Cotton," *Amer. Hist. Rev.,* XXXII,
262–75; Landers, "Wet Sand and Cotton," *La. Hist. Quar.,* XIX, 150–95; Harrington, *The Fighting Politician,* p. 135; "Chase Diary and Correspondence," *Report, A. H.A., 1902,* II, 329, 401–5; Ludwell Johnson, *Red River Campaign: Politics and Cotton in the Civil War* (Baltimore, 1958), pp. 51–57, 76–78; George
H. Gordon, *A War Diary of Events in the War of the Great Rebellion* (Boston,
1882), pp. 312–26; *New York Times,* Oct. 9, 23, 1862; *New York Weekly Herald,* Oct. 18, 1862; *O.R.,* Ser. I, XXVI, part i, 715; Weed and Butler to Banks,
Dec. 27, 1862, Banks to Wife, Jan. 16, 1863, and Jan. 15, 1864, Banks to Emory,
July 22, 1863, Banks to Halleck, Aug. 29, 1863, Banks to Dana, Oct. 15, 1863,
Banks to Lincoln, Dec. 11, 1863, Banks to Flanders, March 21, 1864, all in
Banks Papers.

3. Coulter, "Commercial Intercourse with the Confederacy," *Miss. Val. Hist.
Rev.,* V, 377–95; Roberts, "The Federal Government and Confederate Cotton,"

Amer. Hist. Rev., XXXII, 262–75; Landers, "Wet Sand and Cotton," *La. Hist. Quar.,* XIX, 150–95; Rhodes, *History of the United States,* V, 274–313; Johnson, *Red River Campaign,* pp. 51–78; Schwab, *Financial and Industrial History,* pp. 12–17, 24–27, 202–5, 266; Owsley, *King Cotton Diplomacy,* pp. 41–42; Harrington, *The Fighting Politician,* pp. 135–38; Parks, *Kirby Smith,* p. 353; Boggs, *Reminiscences,* pp. 109–11; Butler, *Private and Official Correspondence,* IV, 111; Roy P. Basler, ed., *The Collected Works of Abraham Lincoln* (New Brunswick, N.J., 1953), VII, 62–63, 114–16; Percy L. Rainwater, ed., "Excerpts from Fulkerson's Recollections of the War Between the States," *Miss. Val. Hist. Rev.,* XXIV (1937–38), 351–73; *Statutes at Large,* ed. Matthews, pp. 127–35, 177–83; *Public Laws,* ed. Matthews, pp. 69, 102–4, 122–25, 130, 181–82, 192–93, 254–55, 271–72; "Report of the Produce Loan Office, Nov. 30, 1863," *Reports of the Secretary of the Treasury,* p. 217; *Report, Committee on the Conduct of the War,* II, 34, 177, 216, 354–56; James Parton, *General Butler in New Orleans* (New York, 1864), pp. 415–16; William Diamond, "Imports of the Confederate Government from Europe and Mexico," *Journal of Southern History,* VI (1940), 497–502; *O.R.,* Ser. I, XXII, part ii, 871–73; XXVI, part i, 715, 848; XXXIV, part ii, 495, 852–53, 871, 877–78, 971–72, 977–78, 982–83, part iii, 821–22, and part iv, 638–39, 666–67; XLI, part ii, 1083, and part iii, 904; XLVIII, part i, 1316–18; LIII, 850–51, 974; Ser. IV, II, 292; III, 206–7; Banks to Emory, July 22, 1863, Banks to Stanton, Feb. 2, 1864, Banks to McKee, March 11, 1864, Banks to ——, March 16, 1864, Banks to Flanders, March 21, 1864, Dwight to Banks, Oct. 31, Dec. 10, 1863, Jan. 15, 27, 1864, Simpson to Dwight, March 11, 1864, Dwight to Howe, March 14, 1864, and many other examples in the Banks Papers; Aide-mémoire, Aug. 24, 1863, Stevenson to Broadwell, Aug. 24, 1863, Stevenson to Kirby Smith, Jan. 13, 1864, Broadwell to Davis, Jan. 15, 1864, Correspondence, Kirby Smith Papers; Kirby Smith to Broadwell, Nov. 12, 1863, Letterbook, Kirby Smith Papers.

4. Quoting Chase to Seward, Dec. 17, 1863, in Owsley, *King Cotton Diplomacy,* p. 255. Also, *Statutes at Large,* ed. Matthews, pp. 98–99, 127–35, 152–53, 170, 180; *Public Laws,* ed. Matthews, pp. 46, 50, 69, 105, 130, 154, 179–83, 254–55; Watson, *Adventures of a Blockade-Runner,* pp. 64–65, 287, and *passim;* Bradlee, *Blockade Running,* pp. 146–47; Hamilton Cochran, *Blockade Runners of the Confederacy* (Indianapolis, 1958), pp. 201–38; Owsley, *King Cotton Diplomacy,* pp. 254–55, 258–60, 278–79; Tucker, "Harriet Lane," *Southwestern Hist. Quar.,* XXI, 360–80; Frederic S. Hill, *Twenty Years at Sea* (New York, 1893), pp. 191–92; Vandiver, *Ploughshares into Swords,* p. 98; *Galveston Tri-Weekly News,* Sept. 9, 1863; *Texas Republican* (Marshall), Dec. 9, 1864; *O.R.,* Ser. I, XV, 1012–13, 1134; XVI, part ii, 118–19; XXII, part ii, 1074, 1141–42; XXXIV, part ii, 882, 941, part iii, 727–28, 798, and part iv, 666, 820–21; XLI, part iii, 962–64; LIII, 885; Ser. IV, II, 714–16, 1013–16; III, 78–82, 187–89, 569–70; Oldham, "Memoirs," p. 353; "Customs Book, Sabine Pass," Record Group 109.

5. Quoting *The Standard* (Clarksville, Tex.), May 2, 1863; *Texas Almanac— Extra* (Austin), April 7, 1863; *O.R.,* Ser. I, XXXIV, part ii, 1017–19. Also, *Statutes at Large,* ed. Matthews, pp. 127–32, 152–53, 170, 180; *Public Laws,* ed. Matthews, pp. 69, 130, 181–82, 254–55; Owsley, *King Cotton Diplomacy,* pp. 87–132; J. Fred Rippy, *The United States and Mexico* (New York, 1926), pp.

234–39; Frank C. Pierce, *A Brief History of the Lower Rio Grande Valley* (Menasha, Wisc., 1917), pp. 36–38; Fremantle, *Diary,* pp. 7–8; Ramsdell, "Texas State Military Board," *Southwestern Hist. Quar.,* XXVII, 253–63, 266–67; Miller, *Financial History of Texas,* p. 137; Gammel, *Laws of Texas,* V, 484–85, 499, 625; Ramsdell, *Behind the Lines,* p. 79; *Journal, Arkansas Secession Convention,* pp. 192–93, 234, 248; *Acts, 6th Louisiana Legislature,* First Sess., Baton Rouge, p. 29; *Texas Republican* (Marshall), Dec. 21, 1861; *Houston Tri-Weekly Telegraph,* Dec. 5, 1862; *Galveston Tri-Weekly News,* Jan. 26, 1863; *San Antonio Herald,* April 4, May 23, 1863; *Washington Telegraph* (Ark.), Jan. 7, 1863; *Shreveport Semi-Weekly News,* Feb. 2, 1864; *O.R.,* Ser. I, IV, 105, 122–23; XV, 986–88, 990; XXXIV, part ii, 1017–19, and part iii, 752–53; LIII, 873; Ser. IV, III, 78–82; *O.R.N.,* XII, 800–1; XV, 1025, 1143; XX, 289; Ser. II, III, 217, 253–55; Quintero to Hunter, Nov. 10, 1861, Quintero to Browne, Feb. 9, March 8, April 28, July 5, 1862, Quintero to Benjamin, Aug. 14, Sept. 24, Oct. 19, 1862, all in Pickett Papers; Kingsbury to Kingsbury, May 30, 1862, G. D. Kingsbury Papers, University of Texas Archives, Austin; Clark to Nichols, May 17, 1861, Clark to Bee, Aug. 15, Sept. 17, 1861, Clark to Carothers, Aug. 29, 1861, Clark to Walker, Sept. 7, 1861, "Proclamation [by Clark] to the People of Texas," Aug. 31, 1861, all in Executive Record Book, No. 80; Lubbock to Kauffman and Klainer, Dec. 24, 1861, Lubbock to Nichols & Co., Feb. 11, 1863, Executive Record Book, No. 81; "Proclamation [by Lubbock] to the People of Texas," Nov. 29, 1861, Executive Record Book, No. 279; Oldham, "Memoirs," pp. 344, 347–49.

6. Quoting *O.R.,* Ser. I, LIII, 904–5; *Public Laws,* ed. Matthews, pp. 102–4; *O.R.,* Ser. I, LIII, 869, 874. Also, Owsley, *King Cotton Diplomacy,* pp. 127–28; "Proceedings of Congress," *Southern Hist. Soc. Papers,* XLVIII, 204, 245, 259; *Dallas Herald,* Aug. 2, 1862; *O.R.,* Ser. I, XV, 866, 952; XXII, part ii, 953; XXVI, part ii, 93–94; LIII, 809–10, 867–70, 873–74, 882–83, 904–5, 1008–10; Ser. IV, II, 26, 39, 234–35, 292, 469–72, 477–78, 511; Oldham, "Memoirs," p. 357.

7. Quoting *O.R.,* Ser. I, LIII, 874; XXVI, part ii, 78; *San Antonio Herald,* Aug. 22, 1863; *O.R.,* Ser. I, LIII, 909. Also, Ford, *Rip Ford's Texas,* p. 333; U.S. Treasury Dept., *Cotton Sold to the Confederate States* (Washington, D.C., 1913), pp. 309–10; *Galveston Tri-Weekly News,* Sept. 9, 1863; *O.R.,* Ser. I, XXII, part ii, 953; XXVI, part ii, 20, 57–65, 75–78, 85–86, 89–92, 94–96, 100–1, 113–14, 122–25, 136–39, 181, 184–86, 535–38; LIII, 874, 885, 904–5, 908–9, 1039–40; Ser. IV, II, 1016; Oldham, "Memoirs," pp. 357–58. See also *Journals of Congress,* IV, 70–72; *O.R.,* Ser. IV, II, 587–90, 1071–73.

8. Quoting *O.R.,* Ser. I, XXVI, part ii, 437–38; *Houston Tri-Weekly Telegraph,* Jan. 29, 1864; *O.R.,* Ser. I, XXXIV, part ii, 820–21; XXVI, part ii, 535–38. Also, *Galveston Tri-Weekly News,* March 28, 1864; *Weekly State Gazette* (Austin), Oct. 26, 1864; *Texas Republican* (Marshall), Dec. 9, 1864; *San Antonio Herald,* Jan. 23, 1863; *O.R.,* Ser. I, XXVI, part ii, 302, 310–12, 480–82, 536; XXXIV, part ii, 830–36; Kirby Smith to Broadwell, Nov. 1, 1863, Letterbook, Kirby Smith Papers; Kirby Smith to Bryan, Nov. 1, 1863, Bryan Papers; Circular, Office of the Cotton Bureau, Headquarters, Trans-Mississippi Department, Jan. 4, 1864, Governors' Letters (Murrah).

9. Quoting Fremantle, *Diary*, p. 24; Ford, *Rip Ford's Texas*, pp. 347–48; *O.R.*, Ser. I, XLVIII, 512–13. Also, Olmstead, *Texas*, pp. 149–50; Weyand and Wade, *Fayette County*, pp. 258–60; Owsley, *King Cotton Diplomacy*, p. 120; Ford, *Rip Ford's Texas*, p. 341; Santleben, *A Texas Pioneer*, pp. 107–8; Williams, *Border Ruffians*, p. 396; Fremantle, *Diary*, pp. 10, 22, 33, 48; Watson, *Adventures of a Blockade-Runner*, pp. 25–26; Lt. W. H. Chatfield, *The Twin Cities—Brownsville, Texas, and Matamoros, Mexico* (New Orleans, 1893), p. 13; Santiago Roel, ed., *Correspondencia particular de D. Santiago Vidaurri* (Monterrey, 1946), pp. 151–52; *Houston Tri-Weekly Telegraph*, March 13, 28, Nov. 13, 1863, June 22, 1864; *The Standard* (Clarksville, Tex.), Sept. 17, 30, 1863; *Texas Almanac— Extra* (Austin), May 23, 1863; *O.R.*, Ser. I, IV, 118–19; XXII, part i, 439; XXVI, part i, 431–38, and part ii, 85–86; XXXIV, part ii, 820–21; "Journal and Minutes of the [San Antonio] City Council," Vol. C, entry dated June 20, 1864, and *passim*, City Hall, San Antonio, Texas; Ford, "Memoirs," VI, 1092–93; Quintero to Benjamin, Jan. 25, 1864, Pickett Papers.

10. Quoting Fremantle, *Diary*, p. 6; Parsiot, *A Texas Missionary*, p. 56; *Houston Tri-Weekly Telegraph*, Nov. 24, 1862, and March 23, 1863. Also, Watson, *Adventures of a Blockade-Runner*, pp. 19, 25–26; Fremantle, *Diary*, pp. 6–7; Ford, *Rip Ford's Texas*, p. 341; Comte de Paris, *The Civil War in America*, III, 402; *House Executive Documents*, 38th Cong., 2d Sess., Doc. No. 25, pp. 2–36; *Houston Tri-Weekly Telegraph*, March 13, May 15, 1863, March 7, 1865; *Texas Almanac— Extra* (Austin), May 23, 1863; *Galveston Tri-Weekly News*, March 12, 1863; *O.R.N.*, XVII, 417; XIX, 809; Fitzpatrick to Benjamin, March 12, 1863, Pickett Papers; Quintero to Lubbock, Oct. 14, Dec. 2, 11, 15, 1861, Governors' Letters (Lubbock); Kingsbury to Editor, *New York Herald*, March 1, 1864, Kingsbury Papers.

11. Quoting *O.R.*, Ser. I, XXXIV, part ii, 1019–20; *The Standard* (Clarksville, Tex.), Oct. 3, 1863; *Houston Tri-Weekly Telegraph*, Feb. 6, 1865; Mary Maverick to Lewis Maverick, Feb. 2, 1864, Maverick Papers; *The South-Western* (Shreveport), Sept. 16, 23, 1863. Also, Oates, *Cavalry*, p. 73; Parks, *Kirby Smith*, pp. 352–53; *Texas Republican* (Marshall), Dec. 9, 1864; *La Grange Patriot* (Tex.), Jan. 14, 1865; *San Antonio Herald*, June 27, 1863; *Houston Tri-Weekly Telegraph*, Oct. 9, Nov. 9, 11, Dec. 28, 1863, Jan. 1, 29, 1864; *O.R.*, Ser. I, XXII, part ii, 967, 1003, 1141–42; XXVI, 118–19, 164, 189, 304, 393, 535–38; XXXIV, part ii, 1074, and part iv, 666; XLI, part iii, 962–64; LIII, 972; Ser. IV, III, 569–70; Kingsbury to Kingsbury, Oct. 20, 1862, Kingsbury Papers; Bill "For articles Bought for account of Lt Gel E. K. Smith," Sept. 1, 1863, Correspondence, Kirby Smith Papers; Bills outstanding, Pencoast & Co., Oct., 1863, Bexar County Court Records, County Court House, San Antonio.

12. Quoting *O.R.*, Ser. I, XXVI, part i, 632, 659, 672–73; Basler, *Collected Works of Lincoln*, VI, 356, 364, 374. Also, Owsley, *King Cotton Diplomacy*, pp. 282–83; "Chase Diary and Correspondence," *Report, A.H.A., 1902*, II, 101; Smith, "Banks Expedition of 1862," *La. Hist. Quar.*, XXVI, 342, 348–49; Gorgas, *Diary*, p. 70; Rippy, *The United States and Mexico*, pp. 240–43; "Speech of Gen. A. J. Hamilton, of Texas, at the War Meeting at Faneuil Hall, April 18, 1863," and "Letter of Gen. A. J. Hamilton, of Texas, to the President of the United States, July 28, 1863," in *Documents and Speeches during the Civil War Period in Texas* (n.p., n.d.), copy, University of Texas Archives; *Senate Executive Docu-*

ments, 38th Cong., 2d Sess., Doc. No. 11, pp. 459–60, 470; *O.R.,* Ser. I, XIII, 659; XV, 412, 552, 591–92, 658, 1013–14; XXVI, part i, 659, 661, 664, 680, 682–83, 865–67, and part ii, 43, 48, 273–74, 286–87, 365, 391; Ser. III, III, 522, 738; *O.R.N.,* XVII, 418–19, 446.

13. Quoting Kirby Smith to Wife, Sept. 10, 1863, Correspondence, Kirby Smith Papers; *O.R.,* Ser. I, XXVI, part i, 292; Fitzpatrick to Benjamin, Nov. 17, 1863, Pickett Papers. Also, Porter, *Naval History of the Civil War,* pp. 346–47; Francis R. Sackett, *Dick Dowling* (Houston, 1937), pp. 16–47; O. L. Martin, "Battle of Sabine Pass," *Dallas News,* Jan. 4, 1925, part 1, p. 14; *Texas Almanac, 1864* (Austin, 1864), p. 22; Owsley, *King Cotton Diplomacy,* pp. 133–35; Pierce, *The Lower Rio Grande Valley,* pp. 42–44; Lyman L. Woodman, *Cortina: Rogue of the Rio Grande* (San Antonio, 1950), pp. 73 ff.; *Houston Tri-Weekly Telegraph,* Sept. 14, 16, 1863; *New York Herald,* Sept. 28, 1863; *London Times,* Oct. 6, 1863; *La Bandera* (Brownsville), Sept. 18, 1863; *The Standard* (Clarksville, Tex.), Nov. 28, 1863; *Louisiana Democrat* (Alexandria), Nov. 4, 1863; *O.R.,* Ser. I, XXVI, part i, 19–20, 218, 220–22, 231, 233, 286–312, 396–97, 431–38, 682–83, 695–97, 735, 776, 787, 879, and part ii, 195–96, 203–5, 403, 982; Ser. III, I, 870; III, 521–22; *O.R.N.,* XX, 514–61, 829; Banks to Wife, Sept. 22, 1863, Banks Papers; Kirby Smith to Taylor, Nov. 8, 1863, Letterbook, Kirby Smith Papers.

14. Quoting *O.R.,* Ser. I, LIII, 914–15; XXXIV, part iii, 632; Kirby Smith to Wife, Dec. 19, 1863, Correspondence, Kirby Smith Papers. Also, Harrington, *The Fighting Politician,* pp. 133–34; Potts, *Railroad Transportation in Texas,* p. 37; Clara M. Love, "History of the Cattle Industry in the Southwest," *Southwestern Historical Quarterly,* XIX (April, 1916), 378; Williams, *Border Ruffians,* pp. 373–74; Ford, *Rip Ford's Texas,* pp. 342–43, 345, 349–50; Landers, "Wet Sand and Cotton," *La. Hist. Quar.,* XIX, 159–60; Pray, *Dick Dowling's Battle,* p. 125; John H. Brown, *History of Texas* (St. Louis, 1893), II, 441–42; L. J. Wortham, *A History of Texas* (Fort Worth, 1924), IV, 360; Charles W. Ramsdell, *Reconstruction in Texas* (New York, 1910), p. 55; "Address of A. J. Hamilton, Military Governor, to the People of Texas, Jan. 1, 1864," *Documents and Speeches during the Civil War Period in Texas;* Owsley, *King Cotton Diplomacy,* p. 121; *Houston Tri-Weekly Telegraph,* Dec. 2, 4, 9, 11, 16, 18, 28, 1863, Jan. 11, 13, 20, Feb. 1, March 4, Aug. 17, 1864; *New Orleans True Delta,* Feb. 17, 1864; *The South-Western* (Shreveport), Jan. 6, 1864; *San Antonio Herald,* Jan. 16, 1864; *Galveston Tri-Weekly News,* Aug. 3, 1864; *O.R.,* Ser. I, XXVI, part i, 20–21, 410, 431–38, 785, 832, 834–35, 847, 864–65, 871–72, 876–81, 888–90, and part ii, 36, 403, 410–11, 413–14, 444, 448–49, 468, 486–87, 499, 508, 515; XXXIV, part ii, 46, 295–98, 838–39, 927; Ser. III, II, 782–83; IV, 126, 409, 474–75; Ser. IV, II, 469–71, 897–98; French to Murrah, Dec. 19, 1863, Magruder to Murrah, Jan. 13, 1864, Governors' Letters (Murrah); W. C. Cochran, "A Trip to Mexico in 1864," n.d., typed copy, University of Texas Archives, Austin.

15. Quoting *O.R.,* Ser. I, LIII, 945, 936, 951; Quintero to Benjamin, Feb. 1, 28, 1864, Pickett Papers. Also, Owsley, *King Cotton Diplomacy,* pp. 120, 125–31; Lonn, *Foreigners in the Confederacy,* pp. 83–84; *The South-Western* (Shreveport), Jan. 13, 1864; *Galveston Tri-Weekly News,* March 11, 1864; *O.R.,* Ser. I, XXXIV, part ii, 318, 536, 828; LIII, 930–51; Ser. II, III, 901–2; Fitzpatrick to

Benjamin, July 15, Oct. 23, Nov. 17, 1863, March 8, 1864, Quintero to Benjamin, Dec. 23, 1863, Jan. 25, 1864, Quintero to Hart, Dec. 28, 1863, all in Pickett Papers; Kirby Smith to Taylor, Jan. 15, 1864, Letterbook, Kirby Smith Papers.

16. Quoting *O.R.,* Ser. I, XXXIV, part iii, 734. Also, Ramsdell, "Texas State Military Board," *Southwestern Hist. Quar.,* XXVII, 269–72; Ramsdell, *Behind the Lines,* p. 79; Gammel, *Laws of Texas,* V, 663, 680, 683; *O.R.,* Ser. I, XXXIV, part iii, 730–32, 734, and part iv, 646–50; LIII, 979–80; "Message of the Governor [Murrah] to the Tenth Legislature, May 11, 1864," Executive Record Book, No. 280; Magruder to Murrah, March 28, April 4, 1864, Governors' Letters (Murrah).

17. *Public Laws,* ed. Matthews, pp. 181–82; Ramsdell, "Texas State Military Board," *Southwestern Hist. Quar.,* XXVII, 269–72; *Galveston Tri-Weekly News,* Jan. 13, 1865; *Houston Daily Telegraph,* July 6, 20, 1864; *O.R.,* Ser. I, XXXIV, part iii, 730–32, 821–22, and part iv, 638–39, 643–44, 646–50, 666–67; XLI, part ii, 1005, 1083–84; LIII, 994–95, 1010–15; Ser. IV, III, 78–82, 187–89, 206–7, 306; "Address [by Murrah] to the People of the State of Texas," July 19, 1864, Executive Record Book, No. 280.

18. Quoting Julia A. Thomas *et al.* to Hart, April 11, 1864, Bexar County Court Records, County Court House, San Antonio; Epperson to Murrah, June 14, 1864, Governors' Letters (Murrah). Also, Holladay, "Powers of the Commander," *Southwestern Hist. Quar.,* XXI, 357; Wilfred Buck Yearns, *The Confederate Congress* (Athens, Ga., 1960), pp. 136–37; *The South-Western* (Shreveport), Sept. 16, 23, Oct. 7, 1863; *Houston Tri-Weekly Telegraph,* Sept. 14, Dec. 28, 1863, May 25, 1864; *O.R.,* Ser. I, XXVI, part ii, 206; XXXIV, part ii, 811–14, 830–36, 865; LIII, 1016–18; Oldham, "Memoirs," pp. 335–36; Harcourt to Murrah, March ———, 1864, Governors' Letters (Murrah).

19. Quoting *O.R.,* Ser. I, XXXIV, part ii, 922; Daniel to Murrah, Feb. 22, 1864, Governors Letters' (Murrah); *O.R.,* Ser. I, LIII, 986. Also, Yearns, *Congress,* p. 124; Gammel, *Laws of Texas,* V, 765, 770–71; *General Orders, Trans-Mississippi Department,* p. 34; *Houston Tri-Weekly Telegraph,* Jan. 18, Feb. 3, March 7, 1864; *Houston Daily Telegraph,* Sept. 14, Oct. 19, 1864; *O.R.,* Ser. I, XXXIV, part iii, 821–22, and part iv, 639, 643–46, 666–67, 671, 683, 690; XLI, part ii, 1005, and part iv, 1059–60; LIII, 994–95, 1016–18; "An Address by the Governor [Murrah] to the People of Texas," Jan. 16, 1864, Executive Record Book, No. 280; Kirby Smith to Davis, May 5, 1864, Letterbook, Kirby Smith Papers.

Chapter Five: Summer and Autumn Campaigns, 1863

1. Quoting Dalton, *Black Flag,* p. 112; Gurden Grovenor, "Quantrill and His Guerrillas Sack Lawrence," in *The Blue and the Gray,* ed. Henry Steele Commager (Indianapolis, 1950), I, 392; *Daily Conservative* (Leavenworth), Aug. 24, 1863; *O.R.,* Ser. I, XXII, part i, 572; *Richmond Daily Enquirer,* Oct. 20, 1863. Also, Connelley, *Quantrill,* pp. 300, 314, 344, 384–85, 430, 467; Spring, *Kansas,* pp. 286–87, 290, 292, 296; Castel, "Bloodiest Man," *Amer. Her.,* XI, 24, 97–98; John C. Shea, *Reminiscences of Quantrell's Raid upon the City of Lawrence,*

Kas. (Kansas City, 1879), pp. 6, 8–9, 20–25; Henry E. Palmer, "The Lawrence Raid," *Transactions of the Kansas State Historical Society,* VI (1900), 317–18; Albert Robinson Greene, "What I Saw of the Quantrell Raid," *Kansas Historical Collections,* XIII (1912), 430–51; Fisher, *Gun and Gospel,* pp. 174–76, 185, 188–90; Edwards, *Shelby,* p. 400; Sophia L. Bissell, "See Those Men! They Have No Flag!" *American Heritage,* XI (Oct., 1960), 25; Connelley, *Life of Plumb,* pp. 154–59, 165; Daniel Geary, "War Incidents at Kansas City," *Kansas Historical Collections,* XI (1910), 284; John Speer, *Life of James H. Lane* (Garden City, Kan., 1897), p. 315; Theophilus F. Rodenbough, *From Everglade to Cañon with the Second Dragoons* (New York, 1875), p. 22; Basler, *Collected Works of Lincoln,* VI, 234; John M. Schofield, *Forty-Six Years in the Army* (New York, 1897), p. 90; *Leavenworth Bulletin,* Aug. 22, 1863; *National Intelligencer* (Washington, D.C.), Aug. 26, 28, 30, 1863; *Western Journal of Commerce* (Kansas City), Aug. 29, 1863; *Chicago Times,* June 13, 1863; *O.R.,* Ser. I, XXII, part i, 572–93, and part ii, 277, 292–93.

2. Quoting Basler, *Collected Works of Lincoln,* VI, 493; *O.R.,* Ser. I, XXII, part i, 700–1; LIII, 907–8. Also, Edwards, *Noted Guerrillas,* p. 205; Violette, *Missouri,* pp. 382–85; Carr, *Missouri,* p. 350; Herklotz, "Jayhawkers," *Mo. Hist. Rev.,* XVIII, 96; Connelley, *Quantrill,* pp. 425, 430; [Blunt], "Account," *Kans. Hist. Quar.,* I, 248; E. A. Calkins, "The Wisconsin Cavalry Regiments," *War Papers, Wisconsin Military Order of the Loyal Legion,* II (Milwaukee, 1896), 173–93; *Daily Missouri Republican* (St. Louis), Oct. 14, 1863; *Fort Smith New Era,* Oct. 8, Nov. 14, 1863; *O.R.,* Ser. I, XXII, part i, 572–74, 688–701, and part ii, 315, 473, 595–97; XLI, part ii, 727–29.

3. Quoting *O.R.,* Ser. I, XXII, part ii, 857; XXVI, part ii, 348, 382; XXXIV, part ii, 942. Also, Connelley, *Quantrill,* pp. 308, 424, 439, 445–47, 452; Frank Triplett, *The Life, Times, and Death of Jesse James* (St. Louis, 1882), pp. 33–40; William Larkin Webb, *Battles and Biographies of Missourians* (Kansas City, Mo., 1900), pp. 336–37; Castel, "Bloodiest Man," *Amer. Her.,* XI, 99; Harlow, "Quantrill," *DAB,* XV, 294; *O.R.,* Ser. I, XXII, part ii, 857, 1046; XXVI, part ii, 379; XXXIV, part ii, 853, 888–89, 902–3, 957–58; Kirby Smith to Reynolds, June 4, 1863, Letterbook, Kirby Smith Papers. See also *The South-Western* (Shreveport), Sept. 16, 1863; *San Antonio Herald,* Sept. 26, 1863.

4. Quoting Ford, *Rip Ford's Texas,* p. 349; *O.R.,* Ser. I, LIII, 890; *The South-Western* (Shreveport), Sept. 2, 1863, citing the Galveston *News.* Also, Wilbarger, *Indian Depredations,* pp. 491–92; Henderson, *Texas in the Confederacy,* pp. 123–24, 128, 131, 134–35; Gammel, *Laws of Texas,* V, 677–79; *McKinney Messenger* (Texas), Dec. 25, 1863; *Houston Tri-Weekly Telegraph,* Dec. 16, 1863; *O.R.,* Ser. I, XXII, part ii, 981; XXVI, part ii, 25, 73, 129, 188; LIII, 890; Hunter to Kirby Smith, Jan. 28, 1864, Letterbook, Kirby Smith Papers; Lubbock to McCulloch, Sept. 2, 1863, Lubbock to Ford, Sept. 18, 1863, Lubbock to Turner, Oct. 12, 1863, Executive Record Book, No. 82; Schultze to Becham, Aug. 10, 1863, and Schultze to Lubbock, Nov. 1, 1863, Records, Texas Adjutant General.

5. Quoting *The South-Western* (Shreveport), Sept. 2, 1863; Kirby Smith to McCulloch, Sept. 25, 1863, Letterbook, Kirby Smith Papers; *O.R.,* Ser. I, XXVI,

part ii, 241. Also, Heartsill, *1491 Days,* pp. 166, 168, 170–73; Williams, *Border Ruffians,* pp. 363–64; *Houston Tri-Weekly Telegraph,* Dec. 16, 1863; *O.R.,* Ser. I, XXII, part ii, 980, 997, 1030, 1081; XXVI, part ii, 129, 188, 236, 258, 285, 344, 352–56, 382–83, 393–94, 398, 401, 493–95; XXXIV, part ii, 908–11, 925–26, 945; Kirby Smith to Johnston, Sept. 14, Oct. 29, Kirby Smith to McCulloch, Nov. 21, 1863, Letterbook, Kirby Smith Papers.

6. Quoting *Houston Tri-Weekly Telegraph,* Nov. 27, 1863. Also, *Texas Almanac, 1864,* p. 22; Ford, *Rip Ford's Texas,* p. 338; Gammel, *Laws of Texas,* V, 677–79, 688–89, 698–702; Henderson, *Texas in the Confederacy,* pp. 142–43; Brown, *History of Texas,* II, 443; *The Standard* (Clarksville, Tex.), Nov. 7, 1863; *Houston Tri-Weekly Telegraph,* Nov. 25, 1863, Jan. 15, 1864; *San Antonio Herald,* Feb. 13, 1864; *O.R.,* Ser. I, XXVI, part ii, 401; XXXIV, part ii, 886–87, 908–11, 925–26, 945, 973–75; Schultze to Becham, Aug. 10, 1863, and "Memorandum" [describing the organization of the state military districts], March ———, 1864, Records, Texas Adjutant General; Kirby Smith to McCulloch, Sept. 25, Nov. 21, 1863, Letterbook, Kirby Smith Papers; "Address [by Murrah] to the Senate and House of Representatives of Texas," Nov. 5, 1863, and "Certificate" [transferring control of the Frontier Regiment], Aug. 6, 1864, Executive Record Book, No. 280; Ford, "Memoirs," IV, 1039; George B. Erath, "Memoirs," MS, pp. 106–7, University of Texas Archives, Austin.

7. Quoting *O.R.,* Ser. I, XXII, part i, 607, 599, 603–4. Also, Abel, *The Indian as Participant,* pp. 283–312; Anderson, *Watie,* p. 21; Britton, *Civil War on the Border,* II, 123; Dale and Litton, *Cherokee Cavaliers,* pp. 136, 144–45; Charles R. Freeman, "The Battle of Honey Springs," *Chronicles of Oklahoma,* XIII (June, 1935), 154–68; Thomas, *Arkansas in War,* pp. 202–6; Harrell, "Arkansas," in Evans, ed., *Confederate Military History,* X, 199–202; Dale, "Cherokees in the Confederacy," *Jour. South. Hist.,* XIII, 180–81; Mollie Ross, *Life and Times of Hon. William P. Ross* (Fort Smith, Ark., 1893), p. viii; *The Standard* (Clarksville, Tex.), Sept. 12, Oct. 10, 1863; *Daily Conservative* (Leavenworth), Jan. 3, 1864; *Chicago Tribune,* Dec. 21, 22, 27, 1863; *O.R.,* Ser. I, XXII, part i, 34–36, 337–38, 341–42, 348–52, 378–82, 439, 447–62, 597–609, 611–13, 700–1, 779, 781–83, and part ii, 246, 355–57, 367–68, 392, 398–400, 411, 437, 439–40, 445–46, 465–67, 517, 525–26, 534–35, 539–41, 595–97, 666, 727–29, 738, 742, 746, 752, 885, 893–94, 902–3, 905, 909–12, 916–17, 921–22, 925, 933, 940–41, 945, 948, 950–51, 953, 956–57, 961, 963, 965–70, 972, 975, 977, 983–84, 987, 989, 999–1000, 1012–16, 1018–27, 1030–31, 1037, 1042, 1045–46, 1049–53, 1055–56, 1063–65, 1076, 1082, 1094–95, 1097, 1100–7, 1109, 1123–24; XXVI, part ii, 378; LIII, 572.

8. Quoting *O.R.,* Ser. I, XXII, part ii, 916, 920, 492. See also below, note 10.

9. Quoting *O.R.,* Ser. I, XXII, part ii, 991–92, 989. See also below, note 10.

10. Quoting *O.R.,* Ser. I, XXII, part i, 482. Also, Thomas, *Arkansas in War,* pp. 207–19, 330; Snead, "The Conquest of Arkansas," in Johnson and Buell, eds., *Battles and Leaders,* III, 456–58, 461; Harrell, "Arkansas," in Evans, ed., *Confederate Military History,* X, 175–222; Newberry, "Flanagin," in *Arkansas and the Civil War,* pp. 65–66; Robinson, *Justice,* pp. 97–99; *Washington Telegraph*

(Ark.), Sept. 16, 1863, June 15, 1934; *O.R.*, Ser. I, XXII, part i, 468–544, and part ii, 353, 359, 361–62, 367, 374–77, 379–87, 394–95, 398, 402, 407–10, 413–16, 418, 422–27, 429–33, 435–36, 438, 440–45, 449, 452–55, 457–62, 464–65, 468–71, 475–76, 490, 496, 499–502, 505–7, 510, 512–14, 516, 518–20, 522–23, 527, 530, 533, 536–41, 911–12, 916, 918–21, 923–24, 928–48, 950–56, 958–60, 962–63, 968–69, 975–80, 982–83, 985–86, 988–92, 994–95, 997–1001, 1003, 1014–15, 1023–24, 1027–28.

11. Quoting *O.R.*, Ser. I, XXII, part i, 670–78, *passim;* Henry C. McDougal, *Recollections* (Kansas City, Mo., 1910), p. 205. Also, Thomas, *Arkansas in War,* pp. 225–29; Edwards, *Shelby,* pp. 195–97; O'Flaherty, *Shelby,* p. 191; Young, *Confederate Wizards,* pp. 204–21; Harrell, "Arkansas," in Evans, ed., *Confederate Military History,* X, 191; Moore, "Missouri," in Evans, ed., *Confederate Military History,* IX, 141–49; *O.R.*, Ser. I, XXII, part i, 621–79, and part ii, 242, 244, 988–90, 1058–60.

12. Thomas, *Arkansas in War,* pp. 227–49; Snead, "The Conquest of Arkansas," in Johnson and Buell, eds., *Battles and Leaders,* III, 458–59; *O.R.*, Ser. I, XXII, part i, 680–88, 701–78, 783–87, and part ii, 1023–24, 1027–29, 1031–36, 1043–44, 1048–72, 1080–82, 1084–95, 1100, 1102–3, 1109–15, 1125–33; XXVI, part ii, 255–56, 259, 508; XXXIV, part i, 59–68, 84–98, 101–4, 113–17, 124, 126–28, 131–35, 138–54, 161, 640–47, 649–52, 851–68, 871–77; Kirby Smith to Johnson, Oct. 2, 8, 1863, Kirby Smith to Holmes, Dec. 3, 1863, Letterbook, Kirby Smith Papers; Kirby Smith to Wife, Dec. 15, 17, 23, 1863, Correspondence, Kirby Smith Papers.

13. Quoting *O.R.*, Ser. I, XXVI, part ii, 221–22; Kirby Smith to Cushing, Sept. 21, 1863, Letterbook, Kirby Smith Papers. Also, *The South-Western* (Shreveport), Sept. 2, 1863; *Shreveport Semi-Weekly News,* Oct. 2, 1863; *O.R.*, Ser. I, XXII, part i, 25, 439, and part ii, 995–96; XXVI, part ii, 47–48, 106–10, 113, 121–22, 125–27, 133, 158–59, 173–74, 182, 186–87, 194–95, 198–99, 203–5, 209–10, 213–15, 217–18, 230–33, 241–42, 244–47, 250–52.

14. Quoting Kirby Smith to Wife, Sept. 10, 1863, Correspondence, Kirby Smith Papers; Hunter to Minor, Oct. 11, 1863, Mary J. Minor Papers, University of Texas Archives, Austin; Hyatt, "Diary," in Bartlett, *Military Record of Louisiana,* part III, p. 11; *O.R.*, Ser. I, XXII, part ii, 1023–24; XXVI, part ii, 261; Kirby Smith to Taylor, Sept. 25, 1863, Letterbook, Kirby Smith Papers. Also, Taylor, *Destruction and Reconstruction,* p. 176; Sarah L. Wadley, *A Brief Record of the Life of William M. Wadley* (New York, 1884), pp. 41–42; *O.R.*, Ser. I, XXII, part i, 439; XXVI, part i, 273–83, and part ii, 209–10, 242, 244, 250, 260–62, 323–24, 335.

15. Quoting Hyatt, "Diary," in Bartlett, *Military Record of Louisiana,* part III, p 12; *O.R.*, Ser. I, XXVI, part ii, 341–42, and part i, 20, 393–94. Also, Taylor, *Destruction and Reconstruction,* pp. 179–81; Hyatt, "Diary," in Bartlett, *Military Record,* part III, p. 11; [Blessington], *Walker's Texas Division,* p. 145; *O.R.*, Ser. I, XXII, part ii, 1049; XXVI, part i, 19–20, 320–95, and part ii, 250, 282–84, 291, 293–95, 297, 322–23, 327, 333, 335–38, 340–42, 346–51, 353–54, 356–61, 363–64, 368–70, 377–78, 382–86, 388–89, 392–93; Ser. II, VI, 367, 813, 817, 990.

16. Gammel, *Laws of Texas,* V, 677–79, 688–89, 698–702; *Acts, 7th Louisiana Legislature,* First Sess., Shreveport, pp. 24, 36–50; *Texas Almanac, 1864,* p. 22; *Shreveport Semi-Weekly News,* Jan. 29, 1864; *O.R.,* Ser. I, XXII, part i, 25; XXVI, part ii, 350–51, 354–56, 363–64, 368–70, 377–78, 383–86; XXXIV, part iii, 778.

17. Quoting Kirby Smith to Taylor, Nov. 8, 1863, Letterbook, Kirby Smith Papers; *The South-Western* (Shreveport), Nov. 25, 1863, citing the *Louisiana Democrat.* Also, Taylor, *Destruction and Reconstruction,* p. 183; Maude Hearn O'Pry, *Chronicles of Shreveport* (Shreveport, 1928), p. 167; *The South-Western,* Dec. 2, 1863; *Louisiana Democrat* (Alexandria), Nov. 4, 18, 1863; *O.R.,* Ser. I, XXVI, part ii, 356, 359–60, 368–70, 375, 393–95, 405–7, 410–12, 433–34, 439, 441, 448–49; Kirby Smith to Boggs, Oct. 5, 1863, Letterbook, Kirby Smith Papers.

18. Quoting [Blessington], *Walker's Texas Division,* p. 153; Weeks to Moore, Jan. 13, 1864, David Weeks Family Collection, Louisiana State University Archives, Baton Rouge. Also, *Official Report Relative to the Conduct of Federal Troops in Western Louisiana, during the Invasions of 1863 and 1864* (Shreveport, 1865), pp. 5–63; *O.R.,* Ser. I, XXVI, part ii, 342; XXXIV, part ii, 921–22.

19. Quoting Taylor, *Destruction and Reconstruction,* pp. 183–84; Mrs. Louise Wigfall Wright, *A Southern Girl in '61* (New York, 1905), pp. 92–93.

20. Quoting Taylor, *Destruction and Reconstruction,* pp. 183–84; Hyatt, "Diary," in Bartlett, *Military Record of Louisiana,* part III, p. 12. Also, Bartlett, *Military Record,* part III, p. 40; Henderson, *Texas in the Confederacy,* pp. 131–32; *Acts, 27th Louisiana Legislature,* Extra Sess., Opelousas, pp. 18–20; *Acts, 7th Louisiana Legislature,* First Sess., Shreveport, p. 24; *Annual Message of Governor Henry Watkins Allen to the Legislature of the State of Louisiana, January, 1865* (Shreveport, 1865); *Shreveport Semi-Weekly News,* Jan. 29, 1864; *O.R.,* Ser. I, XXII, part ii, 1092, 1110–11; XXVI, part ii, 402, 425–26, 439, 465, 476–78, 498–99, 508, 512, 518; XXXIV, part i, 155–60. On January 1, 1864, the Trans-Mississippi army's effective strength included not only the 24,000 Confederate regular and 2,000 state and embodied militia troops deployed in the Nations, Arkansas, and West Louisiana, but also some 13,000 Confederate and 11,000 state soldiers under arms in Texas. Of those in Texas, some 10,000 Confederate troops and slightly more than half of the state troops were stationed in the Eastern Subdistrict; 2,500 Confederates were on duty in the Western Subdistrict; about 500 Confederates remained in the Northern Subdistrict; and the rest of the Texas state and militia soldiers were scattered throughout the latter two subdistricts. *O.R.,* Ser. I, XXVI, part ii, 562–65; XXXIV, part ii, 814, 931–32; Ser. IV, II, 1073.

Chapter Six: The Home Front After Vicksburg

1. Quoting Taylor, *Destruction and Reconstruction,* p. 183; *The South-Western* (Shreveport), Sept. 9, 30, 1863. Also, O'Pry, *Chronicles of Shreveport,* p. 167; J. L. Brent, *Mobilizable Fortifications, and Their Controlling Influence in War* (Boston and New York, 1885), pp. 11–13; *Acts, 27th Louisiana Legislature,*

Extra Sess., Opelousas, pp. 10–11; *Acts, 6th Louisiana Legislature*, Extra Sess., Shreveport, pp. 16–17; *Journals of Congress*, VI, 507; *Report of the Secretary of War, November 26, 1863* (Richmond, 1864); *Public Laws*, ed. Matthews, pp. 235–36; *Laws and Joint Resolutions of the Last Session of the Confederate Congress (November 7, 1864–March 18, 1865) Together with the Secret Acts of Previous Congresses*, ed. Charles W. Ramsdell (Durham, N.C., 1941), pp. 61–64; *Galveston Weekly News*, Jan. 6, 1864; *Shreveport Semi-Weekly News*, Oct. 16, 1863; *O.R.*, Ser. I, XXII, part ii, 994–95; XXVI, part ii, 256, 258, 261, 293, 320, 341, 375, 412, 439, 449; XXXIV, part iii, 784–85; XLI, part ii, 1014; Kirby Smith to Cushing, Sept. 21, 1863, Kirby Smith to Johnson, Oct. 8, 1863, Letterbook, Kirby Smith Papers.

2. Quoting *Shreveport Semi-Weekly News*, Aug. 25, 1863; *The South-Western* (Shreveport), Sept. 2, 1863; *Quid Nunc* (Crockett, Tex.), Sept. 1, 1863; Heartsill, *1491 Days*, p. 186; *The South-Western*, Sept. 30, 1863. Also, *O.R.*, Ser. I, XLI, part iv, 1029–31; Kirby Smith to Johnson, Nov. 20, 1863, Letterbook, Kirby Smith Papers.

3. Quoting *The South-Western* (Shreveport), Sept. 2, 30, 1863; Lizzie Neblett to William Neblett, Feb. ———, 1864, Neblett Papers.

4. Quoting *The South-Western* (Shreveport), ˙Sept. 2, Oct. 21, 1863; Lizzie Neblett to William Neblett, Jan. 3, 1864, Neblett Papers; *The South-Western*, Jan. 27, 1864. Also, Heartsill, *1491 Days*, p. 186; Boggs to Taylor, Jan. 12, 1864, Correspondence, Kirby Smith Papers.

5. Quoting *Shreveport Semi-Weekly News*, Sept. 25, 1863; *San Antonio Weekly Herald*, Sept. 12, 1863; Mary Maverick to Lewis Maverick, Sept. 27, 1863, Maverick Papers. Also, *Shreveport Semi-Weekly News*, Sept. 15, 1863; *Houston Tri-Weekly Telegraph*, Dec. 2, 1863; *The South-Western* (Shreveport), Sept. 16, 1863; *O.R.*, Ser. I, XXVI, part ii, 581.

6. Quoting Kirby Smith to Reynolds, June 4, 1863, Letterbook, Kirby Smith Papers; *Shreveport Semi-Weekly News*, Jan. 29, 1864; *O.R.*, Ser. I, XXXIV, part iii, 748; *Annual Message of Governor Allen, January, 1865*. Also, *Acts, 7th Louisiana Legislature*, First Sess., Shreveport, pp. 32–33; *Shreveport Semi-Weekly News*, Feb. 23, 1864, Jan. 31, 1865; Mary Minor to W. B. Minor, Jan. 31, 1864, Minor Papers.

7. Quoting *The South-Western* (Shreveport), Dec. 16, Nov. 11, 1863; McHattan-Ripley, *From Flag to Flag*, p. 72. Also, Reed, *History of Texas Railroads*, p. 79; *Houston Tri-Weekly Telegraph*, Nov. 11, 25, 1863, Feb. 12, 1864; *The South-Western*, Feb. 3, 1864; *O.R.*, Ser. I, XXVI, part ii, 386, 393.

8. *Annual Message of Governor Allen, January, 1865;* "Message to the Extra Session of the Tenth Legislature, May 11, 1864," *Messages of Governor P. Murrah to the Texas Legislature* (n.p., n.d.), copy, University of Texas Library; *The South-Western* (Shreveport), July 29, 1863; *San Antonio Herald*, Aug. 22, 1863, March 19, 1864; *Houston Tri-Weekly Telegraph*, Dec. 7, 1863, Jan. 22, Dec. 30, 1864; Brown, "Annals of Travis County," XXIII, 68–69; Mary Maverick to Lewis Maverick, Feb. 7, 1864, Maverick Papers.

9. Quoting *Annual Message of Governor Allen, January, 1865.* Also, *Acts, 7th Louisiana Legislature,* First Sess., Shreveport, p. 68; *Shreveport Semi-Weekly News,* Jan. 29, 1864; *The South-Western* (Shreveport), Jan. 13, 1864; *Houston Tri-Weekly Telegraph,* Dec. 23, 1863, Jan. 15, 22, 25, Feb. 10, 1864; Mary Maverick to Lewis Maverick, March 6, 1864, Maverick Papers; William Neblett to Lizzie Neblett, Dec. 17, 1863, Neblett Papers.

10. Quoting Commission signed by Murrah, Jan. 13, 1864, Executive Record Book, No. 280; *Acts, 7th Louisiana Legislature,* First Sess., Shreveport, pp. 21–22; *O.R.,* Ser. I, XLI, part iv, 1109; W. B. Minor to Mary Minor, Jan. 24, 1864, Minor Papers. Also, Thomas, *Arkansas in War,* pp. 103–7; Gammel, *Laws of Texas,* V, 692–94; Miller, "State Finances of Texas," *Texas Hist. Assoc. Quar.,* XIV, 13; *Acts, 7th Louisiana Legislature,* First Sess., Shreveport, pp. 11–12, 72; *Annual Message of Governor Allen, January, 1865; Public Laws,* ed. Matthews, pp. 205–8, 272, 277; *Shreveport Semi-Weekly News,* Jan. 29, Feb. 2, 23, 1864, Jan. 21, 1865; *Washington Telegraph* (Ark.), Oct. 28, 1863, March 2, 1864; *The South-Western* (Shreveport), Jan. 13, 1864; *Houston Tri-Weekly Telegraph,* July 15, 1864; *The Standard* (Clarksville, Tex.), March 26, 1864; *O.R.,* Ser. I, XXII, part ii, 1060–61, 1069–70; XXXIV, part ii, 920–21; Sexton to Starr, Dec. 16, 1863, Starr Papers; Reynolds to Johnson, March 30, 1864, Reynolds Papers; Carr to Kirby Smith, June 10, 1864, Correspondence, Kirby Smith Papers; Kirby Smith to Magruder, Jan. 23, 1864, Letterbook, Kirby Smith Papers; Lizzie Neblett to William Neblett, Feb. ———, 1864, Neblett Papers; Garland to Parents, Feb. 18, 1864, J. D. Garland Papers, Louisiana State University Archives, Baton Rouge; Egan to Moore, Feb. 16, 1864, Moore Papers.

11. Quoting *Shreveport Semi-Weekly News,* Jan. 29, 1864; *The South-Western* (Shreveport), Feb. 3, 1864; *Louisiana Democrat* (Alexandria), Nov. 25, 1863; *O.R.,* Ser. I, XXXIV, part ii, 902–3. Also, Dorsey, *Recollections of Henry Watkins Allen,* p. 247; Gammel, *Laws of Texas,* V, 765, 770–71; *Acts, 7th Louisiana Legislature,* First Sess., Shreveport, pp. 8, 18, 57–58; *Houston Tri-Weekly Telegraph,* Jan. 18, Feb. 3, 12, March 7, May 25, 1864; *The South-Western* (Shreveport), Dec. 16, 1863; *Shreveport Semi-Weekly News,* Feb. 2, 1864; *Henderson Times* (Tex.), Jan. 30, 1864; *O.R.,* Ser. I, XXXIV, part ii, 865, 922; LIII, 994–95; "An Address by the Governor [Murrah] to the People of Texas," Jan. 16, 1864, Executive Record Book, No. 280; Daniel to Murrah, Feb. 22, 1864, Harcourt to Murrah, March ———, 1864, and Flewellen to Murrah, March 18, 1864, Governors' Letters (Murrah); Mary Minor to W. B. Minor, Jan. 31, 1864, Minor Papers; Oldham, "Memoirs," pp. 335–36; Kirby Smith to Wife, Feb. 1, 1864, Correspondence, Kirby Smith Papers.

12. Quoting *Annual Message of Governor Allen, January, 1865; Army and Navy Messenger* (Shreveport), Sept. 15, 1864. Also, Dorsey, *Recollections of Henry Watkins Allen,* pp. 238–41; Douglas S. Freeman, "Henry Watkins Allen," *DAB,* I, 191–93; *Acts, 6th Louisiana Legislature,* Extra Sess., Shreveport, pp. 22–23; *Acts, 7th Louisiana Legislature,* First Sess., Shreveport, pp. 22–24, 30, 70; *Acts, 7th Louisiana Legislature,* Second Sess., Shreveport, pp. 37–38; *Official Journals of the Senate and House of Representatives of the State of Louisiana, Seventh Legislature, Second Session* (Shreveport, 1865), pp. 5–7, 9–10, 36–37; Thomas,

Arkansas in War, pp. 104, 326; Gammel, *Laws of Texas,* V, 817–18; *Shreveport Semi-Weekly News,* Aug. 28, Oct. 6, 1863, Jan. 29, 1864, Jan. 5, Feb. 5, 1865; *Houston Tri-Weekly Telegraph,* Jan. 29, Sept. 16, Nov. 21, Dec. 19, 1864; *Army and Navy Messenger,* Oct. 13, 1864, Jan. 5, Feb. 5, 1865; *The South-Western* (Shreveport), Sept. 9, 1863; *Galveston Tri-Weekly News,* Aug. 19, Dec. 28, 1864.

13. Quoting *Houston Tri-Weekly Telegraph,* Feb. 3, 1864; Mary Neblett to William Neblett, May 9, 1864, Neblett Papers; *Houston Tri-Weekly Telegraph,* Dec. 29, 1864. Also, Gammel, *Laws of Texas,* V, 24; Frederick Eby, comp., *Education in Texas: Source Materials* (Austin, 1918), pp. 418–20; *Houston Tri-Weekly Telegraph,* Sept. 8, 1863, Jan. 22, 27, 1864; *San Antonio Weekly Herald,* July 4, 1863.

14. Quoting "The State *vs.* J. H. Sparks," 27 *Texas,* 627; "The State *vs.* J. H. Sparks and J. Bankhead Magruder," 27 *Texas,* 705. Also, "Ex Parte Richard R. Peebles, and Others," in C. L. Robards, *Synopses of the Decisions of the Supreme Court of the State of Texas* (Austin, 1865), pp. 17–18; *Public Laws,* ed. Matthews, pp. 187–89; *Journals of Congress,* III, 669–71, 674, 684, 693, 701–4, 708–12; IV, 22; VI, 744–46, 805–7, 822, 847, 866, 868; VII, 403, 503; Wooten, *Comprehensive History of Texas,* II, 33, 38, 45; Brown, *History of Texas,* II, 428–29; *O.R.,* Ser. II, IV, 894–97; VI, 560–61, 1095–96; VII, 4–5, 23, 41, 45, 153, 217–20, 404, 423, 434–35; Ser. IV, III, 203–5, 210–14, 225–26, 232, 256–57, 267–68, 274–75, 284; Maggie Peebles to Richard Peebles, Dec. 30, 1864, Reuben G. White Family Papers, University of Texas Archives, Austin; Andrew W. McKee File, Confederate Archives, Record Group 109, National Archives; Moise to Moore, Sept. 24, 1864, Moore Papers.

15. Quoting "Message to the Extra Session of the Tenth Legislature, May 11, 1864," Executive Record Book, No. 280; Dye to Maverick, March 4, 1864, Maverick Papers; *San Antonio Herald,* Feb. 13, 1864; *O.R.,* Ser. I, XXXIV, part ii, 1091–92. Also, Gammel, *Laws of Texas,* IV, 1280; *Acts, 7th Louisiana Legislature,* First Sess., Shreveport, pp. 36–50; *Houston Tri-Weekly Telegraph,* Nov. 13, 1863; *Shreveport Semi-Weekly News,* Jan. 29, 1864; *Louisiana Democrat* (Alexandria), March 11, 1863; *O.R.,* Ser. I, XXXIV, part iii, 778; Ser. IV, III, 178–81; Lubbock to Frederick, Oct. 9, 1863, Executive Record Book, No. 82; Duke to Logan, Oct. 29, 1863, and *passim,* Logan Papers.

16. Quoting Magruder to Murrah, March 23, 1864, and "secret" enclosure, Governors' Letters (Murrah); *O.R.,* Ser. I, XXXIV, part iii, 726–27, 747–50. Also, Gammel, *Laws of Texas,* V, 771–72, 776, 828; *Texas Almanac, 1864,* p. 22; *Houston Tri-Weekly Telegraph,* Jan. 8, March 7, 1864; *San Antonio Herald,* Jan. 28, Feb. 13, 1864; *Galveston Tri-Weekly News,* April 18, 1864; *O.R.,* Ser. I, XXXIV, part ii, 973–75, 1029, 1069, 1090–95, 1103–4, and part iii, 726–27, 739–41, 747–50, 768–69; XLI, part ii, 1002–4, 1021, and part iii, 986–87; XLVIII, part i, 1378–79; LIII, 975, 985; Kirby Smith to Murrah, March 31, 1864, and Magruder to Murrah, March 14, 23, April 2, 1864, Governors' Letters (Murrah).

17. Quoting *Houston Tri-Weekly Telegraph,* Jan. 29, 1864; W. B. Minor to Mary Minor, Jan. 2, 1864, Minor Papers; Lizzie Neblett to William Neblett, Jan. 3, Feb. 6, 1864, and William Neblett to Lizzie Neblett, Feb. 2, 1864, Neblett Pa-

pers; Mary Maverick to Lewis Maverick, Feb. 2, 1864, Maverick Papers; Kirby Smith to Wife, Dec. 25, 1863, Kirby Smith to Mother, Jan. 11, 1864, Correspondence, Kirby Smith Papers; Lizzie Neblett to William Neblett, Dec. 25, 1863, Neblett Papers; Mary Minor to W. B. Minor, Dec. 30, 1863, Minor Papers. Also, *The South-Western* (Shreveport), Jan. 13, 1864; *San Antonio Herald,* Jan. 23, 1864; *O.R.,* Ser. I, XXXIV, part ii, 1069, and part iii, 726–27, 768–69; Magruder to Murrah, April 2, 1864, Governors' Letters (Murrah); Graves, "Diary," entry dated Feb. 25, 1864.

Chapter Seven: The Red River and Camden Campaigns, 1864

1. Quoting Kirby Smith to Waul, Feb. 11, 1864, Letterbook, Kirby and Smith Papers; *O.R.,* Ser. I, XXXIV, part ii, 879; Taylor, *Destruction and Reconstruction,* p. 185; *O.R.,* Ser. I, XXXIV, part i, 572–73. Also, Johnson, *Red River Campaign,* pp. 47–49, 86; Taylor, *Destruction and Reconstruction,* pp. 184–86; Parks, *Kirby Smith,* pp. 345, 366–67; Edmund Kirby Smith, "The Defense of the Red River," in Johnson and Buell, eds., *Battles and Leaders,* IV, 369; Donald B. Sanger, "Red River—Mercantile Expedition," *Tyler's Quarterly,* XVII (Oct., 1935), 268–80; *O.R.,* Ser. I, XXVI, part ii, 41–42, 293–94, 322, 338, 341–42; XXXIV, part i, 495, 572–73, and part ii, 819, 879, 895–96, 905–6, 971, 1027–29, 1034, 1038–39, 1041, 1043–44; Kirby Smith to Davis, Jan. 20, 1864, Letterbook, Kirby Smith Papers; Kirby Smith to Price, March 14, 1864, and Cunningham to Magruder, March 12, 1864, Correspondence, Kirby Smith Papers.

2. Quoting Cunningham to Magruder, Feb. 21, 1864, and Kirby Smith to Price, March 14, 1864, Correspondence, Kirby Smith Papers; *O.R.,* Ser. I, XXXIV, part ii, 879. Also, Kirby Smith, "Defense of Red River," in Johnson and Buell, eds., *Battles and Leaders,* IV, 369; Heartsill, *1491 Days,* pp. 193–96, 198–99; Abel, *The Indian as Participant,* pp. 314–21, 326–32; Taylor, *Destruction and Reconstruction,* pp. 184–87; Bartlett, *Military Record of Louisiana,* part iii, pp. 12, 40–41; [Blessington], *Walker's Texas Division,* pp. 166–67; Thomas, *Arkansas in War,* p. 254; Parks, *Kirby Smith,* pp. 346–47, 370, and *passim*; Arthur H. Noll, *General Kirby-Smith* (Sewanee, Tenn., 1907), p. 226; Freeman, *Lee's Lieutenants,* III, 305; *O.R.,* Ser. I, XXXIV, part i, 155–60, 476–638, 779–850, and part ii, 814, 829–30, 842–43, 848, 852–54, 856–64, 868–80, 882–85, 890–98, 903–6, 917–19, 921–22, 930–35, 943, 945–46, 948, 950–61, 968, 971, 973–75, 977–78, 982–84, 987–1002, 1006–9, 1012–16, 1020–30, 1034–41, 1044, 1047–48, 1057–60; LIII, 969–70; Kirby Smith to Johnson, Jan. 15, 1864, and Kirby Smith to Davis, Jan. 20, 1864, Letterbook, Kirby Smith Papers; Reynolds to Kirby Smith, May 23, 24, 1863, Reynolds to Johnson, Dec. 24, 1863, Reynolds to Shelby, March 26, 1864, Reynolds Papers.

3. Quoting *O.R.,* Ser. I, XXXII, part iii, 289; *Report, Committee on the Conduct of the War,* II, 19; *Washington Telegraph* (Ark.), Feb. 4, 1864; *O.R.,* Ser. I, XXXIV, part ii, 448, 516; Sherman, *Memoirs,* I, 425–26; *O.R.,* Ser. I, XXXIV, part ii, 305, 546–47. Also, Johnson, *Red River Campaign,* pp. 5–27, 42–49, 78–87; Taylor, *Destruction and Reconstruction,* pp. 187–89; Parks, *Kirby Smith,*

pp. 375–77; Sanger, "Red River," *Tyler's Quarterly*, XVII, 268–80; Landers, "Wet Sand and Cotton," *La. Hist. Quar.*, XIX, 152–54; Gordon, *A War Diary*, pp. 325–26; Richard Irwin, "The Red River Campaign," in Johnson and Buell, eds., *Battles and Leaders*, IV, 345–49; Thomas Selfridge, "The Navy in the Red River," *ibid.*, 362, 366–68; Grant, *Memoirs*, pp. 357–61; M. A. De Wolfe Howe, ed., *Home Letters of General Sherman* (New York, 1909), pp. 286–87; Thomas S. Staples, *Reconstruction in Arkansas* (New York, 1923), pp. 23–47; Thomas, *Arkansas in War*, pp. 391, 395–98; Ruth Caroline Cowen, "Reorganization of Federal Arkansas," *Arkansas Historical Quarterly*, XVIII (Summer, 1959), 43–51; Bragg, *Louisiana*, pp. 284–88; Ficklen, *Reconstruction in Louisiana*, p. 62; W. M. Caskey, *Secession and Restoration in Louisiana* (Baton Rouge, 1938), pp. 80–96; Basler, *Collected Works of Lincoln*, VII, 89–90; *Report, Committee on the Conduct of the War*, II, 192; *Journal of the Convention of Delegates of the People of Arkansas* (Little Rock, 1864); *Acts, 7th Louisiana Legislature*, First Sess., Shreveport, p. 54; *True Delta* (New Orleans), Jan. 12, March 16, 1864; *O.R.*, Ser. I, XXXII, part ii, 125–28, 169, 189–90, 201–2, 224–25, 270–71, 402, and part iii, 289; XXXIV, part i, 167–76, 194 ff., 479, 494, 574, 657–59, part ii, 10, 15–16, 42, 55–56, 133–34, 144–45, 149, 179, 266–67, 293, 305, 372, 448–49, 481, 491, 494, 496–97, 512–16, 518–19, 542, 576, 616, 636, 641, 1027, and part iii, 491–92; Ser. III, IV, 22–23, 133–34, 170–72; *O.R.N.*, XXVI, 24–25, 747–48; Kirby Smith to [Johnson], March 6, 1888, Correspondence, Kirby Smith Papers.

4. Quoting Taylor to Walker, March 12, 1864, Walker Papers; William H. Stewart, "Diary," entry dated March 19, 1864, Southern Historical Collection, University of North Carolina Archives; *O.R.*, Ser. I, XXXIV, part ii, 654–55; *Report, Committee on the Conduct of the War*, II, 74. Also, Johnson, *Red River Campaign*, pp. 89–105; Bartlett, *Military Record of Louisiana*, part iii, p. 41, and Hyatt, "Diary," *ibid.*, p. 12; Irwin, "Red River Campaign," in Johnson and Buell, eds., *Battles and Leaders*, IV, 349–50; Selfridge, "Navy in Red River," *ibid.*, IV, 362; Taylor, *Destruction and Reconstruction*, pp. 186–87; *Report, Committee on the Conduct of the War*, II, 28–29; [Blessington], *Walker's Texas Division*, pp. 166–67; Newsome, *Experiences in the War*, pp. 111–16, 122; Walter C. Smith, ed., *Life and Letters of Thomas Kilby Smith* (New York, 1898), pp. 356–58; Thomas O. Selfridge, *Memoirs of Thomas O. Selfridge* (New York, 1924), pp. 96–97; *Official Report Relative to the Conduct of Federal Troops in Western Louisiana, during the Invasions of 1863 and 1864* (Shreveport, 1865), p. 84; *O.R.*, Ser. I, XXXIV, part i, 304–12, 338–39, 378, 426–27, 495, 500, 506, 561, 598–601, part ii, 426–27, 544–45, 598, 654–55, 852–53, 939–40, 971–72, 977–78, 982–83, and part iii, 4, 18–19; *O.R.N.*, XXVI, 24–26, 29–30; Kirby Smith to Taylor, March 12, 1864, Anderson to Magruder, March 5, 1864, Cunningham to Magruder, March 7, 12, 1864, Correspondence, Kirby Smith Papers; Scurry to Walker, March 12, 1864, Robertson to Walker, March 13, 1864, Walker Papers; Banks to Wife, April 2, 1864, Banks Papers.

5. Quoting *O.R.*, Ser. I, XXXIV, part ii, 610–11. Also, Johnson, *Red River Campaign*, pp. 106–10; Flinn, *Campaigning with Banks*, p. 96; Whittington, "Rapides Parish," *La. Hist. Quar.*, XVII, 549–51, XVIII, 21–22; Lawrence Van Alstyne, *Diary of an Enlisted Man* (New Haven, 1910), p. 294; Newsome, *Experiences in the War*, p. 120; *Report, Committee on the Conduct of the War*, II, 275, 280–83,

335; Selfridge, "Navy in Red River," in Johnson and Buell, eds., *Battles and Leaders*, IV, 362–63; *O.R.*, Ser. I, XXXIV, part i, 194–218; Ser. III, IV, 209; *O.R.N.*, XXVI, 39, 50; Mainor to Moore, July 7, 1864, Moore Papers.

6. Quoting *O.R.*, Ser. I, XXXIV, part i, 513, 519, 513; Kirby Smith to Taylor, March 31, 1864, Cunningham to Price, March 31, 1864, Correspondence, Kirby Smith Papers. Also, Johnson, *Red River Campaign*, pp. 96–97, 170–75; Thomas, *Arkansas in War*, pp. 255–58; Taylor, *Destruction and Reconstruction*, pp. 186–88, 191; [Blessington], *Walker's Texas Division*, p. 178; Irwin, "Red River Campaign," in Johnson and Buell, eds., *Battles and Leaders*, IV, 351; Kirby Smith, "Defense of Red River," *ibid.*, pp. 370–71; Wiley Britton, "Résumé of Military Operations in Missouri and Arkansas, 1864–65," *ibid.*, p. 375; Harrell, "Arkansas," in Evans, ed., *Confederate Military History*, X, 236–37; Abel, *The Indian as Participant*, pp. 326–27; *Report, Committee on the Conduct of the War*, II, 154–57; *O.R.*, Ser. I, XXXIV, part i, 304–12, 315–16, 323–24, 463–64, 479, 501, 505–6, 512–13, 517, 519, 521–22, 561–62, 659–850, part ii, 512–13, 576, 616, 638, 704, 707, 1056, 1062–63, 1095–96, and part iii, 77–78, 745, 761, 800; *O.R.N.*, XXVI, 41; Kirby Smith, Memorandum, "Steeles March—1864," n.d., Correspondence, Kirby Smith Papers.

7. Quoting Stewart, "Diary," entry dated April 2, 1864; *O.R.*, Ser. I, XXXIV, part i, 179–80; *Report, Committee on the Conduct of the War*, II, 64; *O.R.*, Ser. I, XXXIV, part i, 526. Also, Johnson, *Red River Campaign*, pp. 110–12, 116–27, 144–45; Taylor, *Destruction and Reconstruction*, pp. 189–94, 233–34; Newsome, *Experiences in the War*, pp. 123–24; Bartlett, *Military Record of Louisiana*, part iii, p. 41, and Hyatt, "Diary," *ibid.*, p. 13; Van Alstyne, *Diary*, pp. 299–301; Irwin, "Red River Campaign," in Johnson and Buell, eds., *Battles and Leaders*, IV, 350–51; Kirby Smith, "Defense of Red River," *ibid.*, pp. 370–71; *Report, Committee on the Conduct of the War*, II, 32, 58, 281–86, 323; [Blessington], *Walker's Texas Division*, pp. 181–83; Lubbock, *Six Decades*, pp. 534–36; Boggs, *Reminiscences*, pp. 75–76; *O.R.*, Ser. I, XXXIV, part i, 162–638 *passim*, part ii, 1029, and part iii, 35–36, 58, 72; *O.R.N.*, XXVI, 51; Banks to Wife, April 4, 1864, Banks Papers.

8. Quoting *O.R.*, Ser. I, XXXIV, part ii, 1057, and part i, 528, 526; Bartlett, *Military Record of Louisiana*, part iii, pp. 41, 42; Hyatt, "Diary," *ibid.*, p. 13; Moore, *Rebellion Record*, VIII, 548; Dorsey, *Recollections of Henry Watkins Allen*, p. 263; *O.R.*, Ser. I, XXXIV, part i, 527; Taylor to Walker, April 9, 1864, Walker Papers. Also, Johnson, *Red River Campaign*, pp. 122–69; Parks, *Kirby Smith*, pp. 382–84, 410–11; Taylor, *Destruction and Reconstruction*, pp. 193–212; Irwin, "Red River Campaign," in Johnson and Buell, eds., *Battles and Leaders*, IV, 351–56; Kirby Smith, "Defense of Red River," *ibid.*, pp. 370–72; Boggs, *Reminiscences*, pp. 75–76; Dimitry, "Louisiana," in Evans, ed., *Confederate Military History*, X, 135–43; Bartlett, *Military Record of Louisiana*, part iii, pp. 6, 8, 13, 40–43, 54–58, 61–62; Harrington, *Banks*, p. 156; [Blessington], *Walker's Texas Division*, pp. 181–200; Hoffman, *Camp Court and Siege*, pp. 89–93; Flinn, *Campaigning with Banks*, pp. 108–9; Hubert Howe Bancroft, *History of the North Mexican States and Texas* (San Francisco, 1889), II, 467; Moore, *Rebellion Record*, VIII, 549–50; Yeary, *Reminiscences*, pp. 448, 627;

Hamilton P. Bee, "Battle of Pleasant Hill—an Error Corrected," *Southern Historical Society Papers*, VIII (1880), 184–86; X. B. Debray, "A Sketch of Debray's Twenty-sixth Regiment of Texas Cavalry," *Southern Historical Society Papers*, XIII (1885), 158–59; *Report, Committee on the Conduct of the War*, II, 10, 13, 30, 32, 35, 60–62, 68, 77, 94–95, 176–79, 189, 218, 221–22, 326; *O.R.*, Ser. I, XXXIV, part i, 162–638 *passim*, and part iii, 99–100, 127–28, 759; *O.R.N.*, XXVI, 58; Banks to Wife, April 13, 1864, Banks Papers.

9. Quoting *O.R.N.*, XXVI, 60, 49; Hyatt, "Diary," in Bartlett, *Military Record of Louisiana*, part iii, p. 13. Also, Johnson, *Red River Campaign*, pp. 206–20; Taylor, *Destruction and Reconstruction*, pp. 206–9, 214–17; Irwin, "Red River Campaign," in Johnson and Buell, eds., *Battles and Leaders*, IV, 356–57; Selfridge, "Navy in Red River," *ibid.*, pp. 363–64; Kirby Smith, "Defense of Red River," *ibid.*, pp. 372–73; Bartlett, *Military Record of Louisiana*, part iii, p. 54; Newsome, *Experiences in the War*, p. 126; Hoffman, *Camp Court and Siege*, p. 97; Noel, *History of the Sibley Brigade*, pp. 91–92; Van Alstyne, *Diary*, p. 306; *Report, Committee on the Conduct of the War*, II, 35, 166, 203, 239, 275–76; *Shreveport Semi-Weekly News*, April 26, 1864; *O.R.*, Ser. I, XXXII, part iii, 242; XXXIV, part i, 162–638 *passim*, part ii, 943, and part iii, 24, 98–99, 115, 128, 153–54, 175, 265–66, 782; LIII, 592; *O.R.N.*, XXVI, 45–49, 51, 56, 59–62, 64, 68–69, 105, 778, 781, 789; Stewart, "Diary," entry dated April 10, 1864.

10. Quoting Kirby Smith to Wife, April 20, 1864, Correspondence, and Kirby Smith to Davis, May 5, 1864, Letterbook, Kirby Smith Papers. Also, Johnson, *Red River Campaign*, pp. 175–205; Parks, *Kirby Smith*, pp. 383–400, 411–13; Taylor, *Destruction and Reconstruction*, pp. 217–33; Thomas, *Arkansas in War*, pp. 256–70; Kirby Smith, "Defense of Red River," in Johnson and Buell, eds., *Battles and Leaders*, IV, 372–73; Britton, "Operations in Missouri and Arkansas," *ibid.*, p. 375; Lubbock, *Six Decades*, p. 538; Bee, "Battle of Pleasant Hill," *Southern Hist. Soc. Pap.*, VIII, 185; Edwards, *Shelby*, pp. 254–97; [Blessington], *Walker's Texas Division*, pp. 243–60; Harrell, "Arkansas," in Evans, ed., *Confederate Military History*, X, 249–65; Webb, *Battles and Biographies of Missourians*, p. 205; Abel, *The Indian as Participant*, pp. 326–27; Comte de Paris, *Civil War in America*, IV, 557; Britton, *Civil War on the Border*, II, 272, 291; *O.R.*, Ser. I, XXXIV, part i, 162–638 *passim*, 653–850 *passim*, and part iii, 77–79, 162, 267–68, 766–67, 770, 794–95, 797–98, 802; LIII, 987; Kirby Smith to Davis, April 16, 1864, Letterbook, Kirby Smith to Mother, May 5, 1864, Kirby Smith to Wife, April 12, 18, 22, May 11, 1864, Correspondence, Kirby Smith Papers.

11. Quoting James G. Wilson, "The Red River Dam," *Galaxy*, I (June, 1866), 241; Taylor, *Destruction and Reconstruction*, pp. 229–31; Van Alstyne, *Diary*, pp. 342–43; *O.R.*, Ser. I, XXXIV, part i, 580–81; Heartsill, *1491 Days*, p. 212; Dorsey, *Recollections of Henry Watkins Allen*, pp. 278–79. Also, Johnson, *Red River Campaign*, pp. 221–37, 242–49, 254–78; Taylor, *Destruction and Reconstruction*, pp. 219–35; Kirby Smith, "Defense of Red River," in Johnson and Buell, eds., *Battles and Leaders*, IV, 373; Irwin, "Red River Campaign," *ibid.*, pp. 357–62; Selfridge, "Navy in Red River," *ibid.*, pp. 363–66; Parks, *Kirby Smith*, pp. 401–2; Lubbock, *Six Decades*, pp. 539–43; Smith, *T. Kilby Smith*, p. 362; Newsome, *Experiences in the War*, pp. 134–39; Bartlett, *Military Record of Louisiana*, part III, pp. 13, 43, 54–59; Van Alstyne, *Diary*, pp. 314–28; Wilson,

"Red River Dam," *Galaxy*, I, 241–45; Flinn, *Campaigning with Banks*, p. 140; Whittington, "Rapides Parish," *La. Hist. Quar.*, XVIII, 26–38; [Blessington], *Walker's Texas Division*, pp. 266–67; *Report, Committee on the Conduct of the War*, II, 15–16, 34–35, 45, 82, 84, 132, 149, 234–35, 250, 282, 288, 335; *Official Report Relative to the Conduct of Federal Troops in Western Louisiana*, pp. 70–85; *O.R.*, Ser. I, XXXIV, part i, 11, 162–638 *passim*, 653–850 *passim*, and part iii, 190–92, 222, 244, 278–79, 294, 296, 307, 316, 333, 350, 390–91, 412–13, 429, 434, 455, 494–98, 515–17, 532, 534–35, 544, 546, 558–59, 568, 644; *O.R.N.*, XXVI, 50–54, 72, 74–76, 79, 81–84, 94, 102, 106, 108, 113–14, 117–19, 130–47, 167, 169, 176–77, 768, 781–82, 786; Surget to Walker, April 26, 1864, and Tappan to Walker, May 19, 1864, Walker Papers; Scully to Surget, May 9, 1864, Logan Papers.

12. Quoting Hyatt, "Diary," in Bartlett, *Military Record of Louisiana*, part iii, p. 13; William Tunnard, "Diary," May 2, 3, 1864, cited in Bragg, *Louisiana*, p. 172; Heartsill, *1491 Days*, p. 208; *O.R.*, Ser. I, XXXIV, part iii, 279, 332–33; Richard B. Harwell, *Songs of the Confederacy* (New York, 1951), p. 99. Also, Heartsill, *1491 Days*, pp. 200–1, 205–9; Bragg, *Louisiana*, p. 217; Johnson, *Red River Campaign*, pp. 244–48, 283; Harrington, *Banks*, pp. 159–64; Harry Williams, "General Banks and the Radical Republicans in the Civil War," *New England Quarterly*, XII (June, 1939), 270; *O.R.*, Ser. I, XXXIV, part i, 6, 312, and part iii, 331–32, 357–58, 409–10, 491; XLI, part iii, 297, and part iv, 233–34; Hyson to Moore, Jan. 3, 1865, Moore Papers.

13. Quoting *O.R.*, Ser. I, XXXIV, part i, 540–48 *passim;* Hq., Trans-Miss. Dept., Special Order No. 145, June 10, 1864, Correspondence, Kirby Smith Papers; West to Churchill, May 16, 1864, cited in Tappan to Walker, May 19, 1864, Walker Papers. Also, *O.R.*, Ser. I, XXXIV, part i, 597.

Chapter Eight: The Closing Campaigns, 1864

1. Quoting Lee to Kirby Smith, July 9, 16, 1864, Correspondence, Kirby Smith Papers; Robert E. Lee, *Unpublished Letters of General Robert E. Lee, C.S.A., to Jefferson Davis*, ed. Douglas S. Freeman (New York, 1957), p. 223; Cooper to Kirby Smith, July 18, 1864, Bragg to Lee, July 22, 1864, Lee to Kirby Smith, July 23, 1864, Boggs to Taylor, July 28, 1864, Correspondence, Kirby Smith Papers. Also, *O.R.*, Ser. I, XXXIV, part i, 482, part iii, 764–65, 828, and part iv, 642–43; XLI, part i, 90–94, and part ii, 1011, 1014, 1020, 1023–24; Boggs to Walker, July 28, 1864, Boggs to Taylor, July 29, 1864, Boggs to Douglas, July 29, 1864, Correspondence, Kirby Smith Papers.

2. Quoting Kirby Smith to Bragg, Aug. 3, 1864, Kirby Smith to Wife, Aug. 4, 10, 1864, Correspondence, Kirby Smith Papers; *O.R.*, Ser. I, XLI, part i, 92–93, 102; Kirby Smith to Taylor, Aug. 15, 1864, Correspondence, Kirby Smith Papers; *O.R.*, Ser. I, XLI, part i, 110, and part ii, 1062–63, 1035; Heartsill, *1491 Days*, p. 214; *O.R.*, Ser. I, XLI, part ii, 1048, and part i, 120. Also, Webb, *Battles and Biographies of Missourians*, p. 209; Heartsill, *1491 Days*, pp. 213–14; Edwards, *Shelby*, p. 380; Gorgas, *Diary*, p. 137; *O.R.*, Ser. I, XXXIV, part ii, 870, and part

iii, 801–8; XLI, part i, 92–124, and part ii, 1035, 1038, 1054; Hq., Trans-Miss.
Dept., Special Order No. 192, Aug. 1, 1864, Kirby Smith to Walker, Aug. 1,
1864, Correspondence, Kirby Smith Papers; Reynolds to Kirby Smith, July 25,
1864, Reynolds Papers.

3. Quoting *O.R.*, Ser. I, XLI, part i, 111–12; Davis to Kirby Smith, Aug. 8,
1864, Kirby Smith to Wife, Aug. 20, 1864, Sol Smith to Davis, Aug. 21, 1864,
Boggs to Buckner, Aug. 22, 1864, Kirby Smith to Taylor, Aug. 22, 1864, Correspondence, Kirby Smith Papers; Heartsill, *1491 Days*, p. 216; *O.R.*, Ser. I, XLI,
part i, 123–24; Boggs to Buckner, Aug. 22, 1864, Buckner to Boggs, Sept. 3,
1864, Taylor to Bragg, Oct. 4, 1864, with endorsements, Correspondence, Kirby
Smith Papers; Heartsill, *1491 Days*, p. 216. Also, Taylor, *Destruction and Reconstruction*, pp. 240–41; Gorgas, *Diary*, p. 135; *O.R.*, Ser. I, XLI, part i, 106, 108,
and part ii, 710, 884; *O.R.N.*, XXVI, 513, 517, 522, 534; Taylor to Buckner,
Aug. 18, 1864, Correspondence, Kirby Smith Papers.

4. Quoting *O.R.*, Ser. I, XLI, part iii, 927, 933. Also, *ibid.*, 854, 907, 911,
914–18, 921–23, 927–28, 930–39, 941–43, 949–50, 952, 962–71.

5. Quoting *O.R.*, Ser. I, XLI, part ii, 1011, 1041, part iv, 1068, part ii, 1040–41.
Also, Edwards, *Shelby*, pp. 378, 466–74; Stevens, *Missouri*, I, 340 ff.; Webb, *Battles and Biographies of Missourians*, pp. 208–9, 214; Jenkins, *Battle of Westport*,
pp. 172 ff.; *Texas Republican* (Marshall), Dec. 16, 17, 1864; *Hoke's Weekly Bulletin* (Galveston), Aug. 21, 1864; *Houston Telegraph*, Aug. 29, 1864; *O.R.*, Ser. I,
XXXIV, part ii, 869; XLI, part i, 104, part ii, 1023–24, 1039–41, 1068, part iii,
933, and part iv, 1007.

6. Quoting *O.R.*, Ser. I, XLI, part ii, 456, 158, part i, 649; XXXIV, part i, 482;
XLI, part iii, 926; Edwin Becton to Mary Becton, Sept. 28, 1864, Becton Papers.
Also, Edwards, *Shelby*, pp. 379, 470; Jenkins, *Battle of Westport*, pp. 24, 28–31,
34, 172 ff.; Smith, *Borderland in the Civil War*, p. 355; Peterson and Hanson,
Pilot Knob, pp. 33, 41, 107; Denison, *A History of Cavalry*, p. 445; Oates, *Cavalry*, p. 142; "Price," *DAB*, XV, 216; Webb, *Battles and Biographies of Missourians*, p. 205; *Jefferson Davis, Constitutionalist*, ed. Rowland, VI, 510; *O.R.*, Ser. I,
XLI, part i, 26, 113, 307, 320, 623, 625–26, 642–48, part ii, 234, 332, 358,
362–63, 494, 504, 526, 622, 633, 967, 974, 1085, 1091, part iii, 54, 82, 88, 157,
174, 220, 318, 473, 918, 935, and part iv, 360, 1002.

7. Quoting *O.R.*, Ser. I, XLI, part iii, 223, part i, 643; XXXIV, part i, 1001–2;
New York Tribune, Oct. 3, 1864. Also, Peterson and Hanson, *Pilot Knob*, p. 33;
Edwards, *Shelby*, pp. 434, 470; Jenkins, *Battle of Westport*, pp. 24, 34; Howard
N. Monnett, *Action Before Westport, 1864* (Kansas City, Mo., 1964), pp. 18–21;
Webb, *Battles and Biographies of Missourians*, p. 217; Ella Lonn, *Desertion dur-
ing the Civil War* (New York, 1928), p. 33; Connelley, *Quantrill*, pp. 439–54; Violette, *Missouri*, p. 388; Hollister and Norman, *Five Famous Missourians*, pp.
367, 396; Gruber, "Quantrell's Flag," *Adventure*, CII, 113; Love, *Jesse James*, pp.
22–23; James, *Jesse James*, p. 33; Triplett, *Jesse James*, pp. 33–40; Cloyd Bryner,
Bugle Echoes: The Story of the Illinois 47th (Springfield, Ill., 1905), p. 148; H.
H. Crittenden, *The Crittenden Memoirs* (New York, 1936), p. 345; *Daily Missouri Republican* (St. Louis), Nov. 5, 1864; *Western Journal of Commerce* (Kansas City), Oct. 8, 1864; *O.R.*, Ser. I, XLI, part i, 428, 625–26, 632, 641–43,
722–23, and part iii, 940.

8. Quoting *O.R.*, Ser. I, XLI, part i, 623. Also, Thomas C. Fletcher, "Battle of Pilot Knob, and the Retreat to Leasburg," *War Papers, Missouri Military Order of the Loyal Legion*, I (St. Louis, 1892), 29–53; Birdie H. Cole, "The Battle of Pilot Knob," *Confederate Veteran*, XXII (Sept., 1914), 417; *Report of General W. L. Cabell's Brigade in Price's Raid in Missouri and Kansas in 1864* (Dallas, Tex., 1900), pp. 5–6; Peterson and Hanson, *Pilot Knob*, pp. 45, 100–7, 217, 289, 316; Webb, *Battles and Biographies of Missourians*, p. 213; Moore, "Missouri," in Evans, ed., *Confederate Military History*, IX, 181–82; Monnett, *Action Before Westport*, pp. 21–25; Jenkins, *Battle of Westport*, p. 34; Edwards, *Shelby*, pp. 387, 480–86; *O.R.*, Ser. I, XLI, part i, 307, 318, 445–52, 623–32, 642–48, 655, 679–80, 709–10, 715, 721–23, part ii, 940, and part iii, 25, 49, 117, 132, 143, 164, 174, 342, 358, 365, 381, 398, 408, 960–61.

9. Quoting *O.R.*, Ser. I, XLI, part i, 656, part iii, 975–76, part i, 657. Also, Monnett, *Action Before Westport*, pp. 25–32, 50–52; Moore, "Missouri," in Evans, ed., *Confederate Military History*, IX, 182–84; Webb, *Battles and Biographies of Missourians*, pp. 214–15; Edwards, *Shelby*, pp. 395–98, 471; Stevens, *Missouri*, I, 339; Hollister and Norman, *Five Famous Missourians*, p. 365; Bryner, *Bugle Echoes*, p. 146; John B. Sanborn, "The Campaign in Missouri in September and October, 1864," *Third Series, Minnesota Commandery of the Military Order of the Loyal Legion* (New York, 1893), pp. 146–57; Peterson and Hanson, *Pilot Knob*, pp. 58–59; [Hinton], *Rebel Invasion of Missouri*, pp. 86, 113; Palmer, "Soldiers of Kansas," *Kans. Hist. Coll.*, IX, 433–37; H. Palmer, "Company A, Eleventh Kansas Regiment, in the Price Raid," *Transactions of the Kansas State Historical Society*, IX (1905–6), 435; George S. Grover, "The Price Campaign of 1864," *Missouri Historical Review*, VI (July, 1912), 171; *Daily Missouri Republican* (St. Louis), Aug. 27, 1864; *O.R.*, Ser. I, XLI, part i, 303–729 *passim*, and part iii, 61, 174, 222, 345, 416, 448, 468, 488, 521, 546, 554, 591, 646, 666, 706, 754, 783; Thompson, "Autobiography," p. 31. See also Edwards, *Shelby*, p. 389; Absalom Grimes, *Absalom Grimes, Confederate Mail Runner*, ed. Milo M. Quaife (New Haven, 1926), pp. 193–94; Scharf, *History of St. Louis*, I, 444; *O.R.*, Ser. I, XLI, part iii, 657, and part iv, 223, 236, 310, 316.

10. Quoting *O.R.*, Ser. I, XLI, part iii, 672, part i, 467, 465, 658, 659; *Western Journal of Commerce* (Kansas City), Oct. 25, 1864; *O.R.*, Ser. I, XLI, part i, 352. Also, Monnett, *Action Before Westport*, pp. 35–49, 56–124; [Hinton], *Rebel Invasion of Missouri*, pp. 30–48, 60–68, 80–182; Spring, *Kansas*, p. 298; Connelley, *Plumb*, pp. 181, 186–89; Castel, *Kansas*, pp. 180–81; Britton, *Civil War on the Border*, II, 437, 483–84, 504–5; [Blunt], "Account," *Kans. Hist. Quar.*, I, 251–59; Grover, "The Price Campaign," *Mo. Hist. Rev.*, VI, 168, 172–74; Jenkins, *Battle of Westport*, pp. 73–157; H. H. Crittenden, *The Battle of Westport* (Kansas City, 1938), pp. 35–46; Edwards, *Shelby*, pp. 345–57, 396, 435–36; Moore, "Missouri," in Evans, ed., *Confederate Military History*, IX, 184–89; Webb, *Battles and Biographies of Missourians*, pp. 230, 342; Hollister and Norman, *Five Famous Missourians*, p. 370; Samuel J. Crawford, *Kansas in the Sixties* (Chicago, 1911), pp. 148–49; Brownlee, *Gray Ghosts*, pp. 128–29; W. L. Cabell, "Capture of Cabell and Marmaduke," *Confederate Veteran*, VIII (1900), 153; Cabell, *Report*, p. 11; Sanborn, "Campaign in Missouri," *Minnesota Loyal Legion*, III, 184; John Darr, "Price's Raid into Missouri," *Confederate Veteran*, XI (1903), 361–62; Stephen H. Ragan, "The Battle of Westport," *Annals of Kan-*

sas City, I (Dec., 1923), 259–66; Palmer, "Company A, Eleventh Kansas," *Kans. Hist. Soc. Trans.,* IX, 439–40; *Leavenworth Daily Times* (Kans.), Oct. 9, 17, 18, 27, 1864; *White Cloud Chief* (Kans.), Aug. 11, Oct. 9, 13, 20, 1864; *Oskaloosa Independent* (Kans.), Oct. 15, 1864; *Western Journal of Commerce* (Kansas City), Nov. 3, Dec. 31, 1864; *Fort Smith New Era* (Ark.), Nov. 26, 1864; *O.R.,* Ser. I, XLI, part i, 303–729 *passim,* 819, part ii, 980, part iii, 279, 291, 672, 713, 724, 870, and part iv, 57, 144, 157, 164–65, 183–84, 189–90, 203–4, 1000; Thompson, "Autobiography," pp. 41–46.

11. Quoting *Texas Republican* (Marshall), Dec. 16, 1864; Moore, "Missouri," in Evans, ed., *Confederate Military History,* IX, 191; Thompson, "Autobiography," p. 46; *O.R.,* Ser. I, XLI, part i, 637. Also, Monnett, *Action Before Westport,* pp. 127–36; [Hinton], *Rebel Invasion of Missouri,* pp. 175–276, 290; Moore, "Missouri," in Evans, ed., *Confederate Military History,* IX, 191–92; Edwards, *Shelby,* pp. 440–70; Sanborn, "Campaign in Missouri," *Minnesota Loyal Legion,* III, 171, 185–200; [Blunt], "Account," *Kans. Hist. Quar.,* I, 261–63; Crawford, *Kansas,* pp. 158–202; Fletcher, "Pilot Knob," *Missouri Loyal Legion,* I, 242; Cabell, *Report,* pp. 12–13; Cabell, "Capture of Cabell and Marmaduke," *Confed. Vet.,* VIII, 153–54; Thomas, *Arkansas in War,* p. 289; *Western Journal of Commerce* (Kansas City), Nov. 3, Dec. 31, 1864; *Fort Smith New Era* (Ark.), Nov. 12, 26, 1864; *Leavenworth Conservative* (Kans.), Nov. 27, 1864; *O.R.,* Ser. I, XLI, part i, 303–729 *passim,* and part iv, 1013; Thompson, "Autobiography," pp. 45–62.

12. Quoting *O.R.,* Ser. I, XLI, part ii, 1013, 1082, part i, 780. Also, Abel, *The Indian as Participant,* p. 332; *The Standard* (Clarksville, Tex.), Sept. 3, Oct. 8, 15, 1864; *Fort Smith New Era* (Ark.), Oct. 1, 1864; *O.R.,* Ser. I, XLI, part i, 764–94, and part ii, 1072.

13. Quoting *O.R.* Ser. I, XLI, part iii, 978–79, part iv, 1028–29, 1044, 1046; Dr. J. H. P. Baker, "Diary, 1864–1865," State Historical Society of Missouri, Columbia, Missouri, entry dated Nov. 1–5, 1864; *O.R.,* Ser. I, XLI, part iv, 1058–59; William Hazen to Alex Hazen, Dec. 21, 1864, Hazen Papers, State Historical Society of Missouri, Columbia. Also, Edwards, *Shelby,* pp. 461–74; Webb, *Battles and Biographies of Missourians,* p. 243; Sanborn, "Campaign in Missouri," *Minnesota Loyal Legion,* III, 201; *O.R.,* Ser. I, XLI, part i, 303–729 *passim,* part iii, 950, and part iv, 1020, 1024, 1112, 1140.

14. Quoting *O.R.,* Ser. I, XLI, part iv, 1052, 1112, 1114; Kirby Smith to Mother, Nov. 16, 1864, Correspondence, Kirby Smith Papers; *O.R.,* Ser. I, XLI, part iv, 1068; XLVIII, part i, 1427; Reynolds to Johnson, March 2, 1865, Reynolds Papers; *O.R.,* Ser. I, XLI, part i, 625–40; *Texas Republican* (Marshall), Dec. 17, 23, 1864; *O.R.,* Ser. I, XLI, part iv, 1123, part i, 701–29; Taylor, *Destruction and Reconstruction,* p. 240; *O.R.,* Ser. I, XLVIII, part i, 1344. Also, Grant, *Memoirs,* pp. 360–61; Heartsill, *1491 Days,* pp. 224–27; Harrell, "Arkansas," in Evans, ed., *Confederate Military History,* X, 276–77; Bartlett, *Military Record of Louisiana,* part III, p. 43; *Jefferson Davis, Constitutionalist,* ed. Rowland, VIII, 525; *O.R.,* Ser. I, XLI, part i, 701–29, part ii, 719, part iv, 1053–54, 1078, 1082–83, 1103–4, 1107–11, 1124–26, 1137–46; XLVIII, part i, 1351–52, 1411, 1413, 1415, and part ii, 398–403; Ser. IV, III, 989, 1182.

15. Quoting *O.R.*, Ser. I, XLI, part ii, 764–67, and part i, 124; XLVIII, part i, 1406, 1411–12; *Jefferson Davis, Constitutionalist*, ed. Rowland, VI, 510. Also, Taylor, *Destruction and Reconstruction*, p. 233; *O.R.*, Ser. I, XLI, part i, 123.

16. Quoting General Order No. 1, 1st Frontier District, Texas State Troops, Oct. 13, 1864, Governors' Letters (Murrah); Peveler to Haley, Aug. 6, 1932, in Peveler, "Diary." Also, James K. Greer, *Bois d'Arc to Barbed Wire* (Dallas, 1936), pp. 85–249; Marilynne Howsley, "Forting Up on the Texas Frontier during the Civil War," *West Texas Historical Association Year Book*, XVII (Oct., 1941), 71–76; Heartsill, *1491 Days*, pp. 234–37; Hubert Howe Bancroft, *History of Nevada, Colorado, and Wyoming* (San Francisco, 1890), p. 466; George Bird Grinnell, *The Fighting Cheyennes* (New York, 1915), pp. 164–73; *Senate Executive Documents*, 39 Cong., 2d Sess., No. 26, pp. 1–228; *Houston Tri-Weekly Telegraph*, Dec. 21, 1864, Feb. 10, 21, 1865; *Rocky Mountain News* (Denver), Feb. 1, 1865; *O.R.*, Ser. I, XXXIV, part ii, 548–49, and part iii, 792, 794–95; XLI, part i, 948–72, part ii, 1004–5, and part iv, 1140; XLVIII, part i, 1310–11; "Proclamation by the Governor [Murrah]," May 26, 1864, Executive Record Book, No. 280; McCulloch to Murrah, March 20, 1864, Bourland to McCulloch, June 2, 1864, Earle to Culberson, June 4, 1864, Erath to Culberson, June 30, 1864, McAdoo to Burke, Feb. 20, 1865, Throckmorton to Burke, Feb. 22, 1865, Records, Texas Adjutant General; Henry Williams, "The Indian Raid in Young County, Texas, Oct. 13, 1864," typed copy, University of Texas Archives, Austin; Erath, "Memoirs," II, 107–8.

17. Quoting *O.R.*, Ser. I, XXVI, part ii, 525, 534–35; Ford, *Rip Ford's Texas*, p. 344; *Houston Daily Telegraph*, Feb. 13, 1864; Ford, *Rip Ford's Texas*, p. 358; *O.R.*, Ser. I, XXXIV, part iii, 797–98; Ford, *Rip Ford's Texas*, pp. 361, 362; *O.R.*, Ser. I, XXXIV, 1053–56; Ford, *Rip Ford's Texas*, p. 364. Also, Ford, *Rip Ford's Texas*, pp. 343–62; Rippy, *The United States and Mexico*, pp. 240–43; Owsley, *King Cotton Diplomacy*, pp. 125, 131–35; Pierce, *Lower Rio Grande Valley*, pp. 42–44; Woodman, *Cortina*, p. 73 ff.; *San Antonio Herald*, Feb. 13, March 19, 1864; *O.R.*, Ser. I, XXXIV, part iii, 738–39, 754, 775–76, 797–98, 807–8, and part iv, 610–11, 631, 635, 676, 684–85; XLI, part ii, 989–90; Quintero to Benjamin, Feb. 1, April 3, 7, June 1, Nov. 5, 1864, Pickett Papers.

18. Quoting Ford, *Rip Ford's Texas*, p. 369; *O.R.*, Ser. I, XLI, part ii, 1088–89; Ford, *Rip Ford's Texas*, pp. 365–75 passim. Also, *ibid.*, pp. 375–89; Pierce, *Lower Rio Grande Valley*, pp. 42–50; Owsley, *King Cotton Diplomacy*, p. 133; *The True Issue* (La Grange, Tex.), April 22, 1865; *O.R.*, Ser. I, XLI, part i, 185–86, 742, and part ii, 1088–89; *O.R.N.*, XXI, 607–8; Quintero to Benjamin, Sept. 5, Nov. 5, 1864.

19. Quoting Ford, *Rip Ford's Texas*, p. 388; *O.R.*, Ser. I, XLVIII, part i, 512–13, 1276–79, 1281, 1488, 1275–76; Kirby Smith to Mother, Jan. 7, 1865, Correspondence, and Kirby Smith to Slidell, Jan. 9, 1865, Letterbook, Kirby Smith Papers. Also, Rippy, *The United States and Mexico*, pp. 266–67; *Houston Tri-Weekly Telegraph*, April 4, 1865; *O.R.*, Ser. I, XLVIII, part i, 1275–82, and part ii, 457–59.

20. Quoting Gorgas, *Diary*, p. 166; *New York Herald*, Jan. 30, 1865; Kirby Smith to Rose, Feb. 1, 1865, with Enclosure, Letterbook, Kirby Smith Papers.

Chapter Nine: The Collapse of the Trans-Mississippi, 1865

1. Quoting Ford, *Rip Ford's Texas*, p. 403; *O.R.N.*, XXI, 652–53; Heartsill, *1491 Days*, p. 221. Also, Owsley, *King Cotton Diplomacy*, pp. 253–57; Watson, *Adventures of a Blockade-Runner*, pp. 286–304; Robinson, *Justice*, pp. 216–17; Dorsey, *Recollections of Henry Watkins Allen*, pp. 281–83; *Texas Republican* (Marshall), Dec. 9, 1864; *San Antonio Herald*, Dec. 24, 1864; *Houston Daily Telegraph*, May 7, 1865; *O.R.*, Ser. I, XXXIV, part ii, 1019–20; XLVIII, part i, 513, and part ii, 964, 1273–74; LIII, 1043; *O.R.N.*, XXI, 715, 737, 913; Ashbel Smith to Hutchins, Jan. 17, 1865, and Ashbel Smith to Murrah, March 1, 1865, Letterbook, Ashbel Smith Papers, University of Texas Archives; Ship Manifests for the *Adelaide, Lark, Victory, Hannah Buchman, Maria Victorina, Observador, Lochabar, Candida, Segundo Triumpho*, and two Royal Mail Steamers, in Correspondence, Kirby Smith Papers; Kirby Smith to Buckner, Feb. 15, March 5, 1865, Letterbook, Kirby Smith Papers.

2. Quoting E. P. Becton to Mary Becton, Sept. 28, 1864, Becton Papers; *The Quartermasters' Guide*, cited in Bartlett, *Military Record of Louisiana*, part III, p. 5; Heartsill, *1491 Days*, p. 227. Also, Gorgas, *Diary*, p. 91; Reed, *History of Texas Railroads*, pp. 125–27; Heartsill, *1491 Days*, pp. 227–31; *General Orders, Trans-Mississippi Department*, p. 83; *Houston Daily Telegraph*, Feb. 4, 12, Nov. 2, 1864; *Natchitoches Times*, Oct. 29, 1864; *Galveston Tri-Weekly News*, March 11, 1865; *Washington Telegraph* (Ark.), Feb. 22, 1865; *O.R.*, Ser. I, XXII, part ii, 1080, 1134–42; XXXIV, part ii, 1014; XLI, part ii, 1005–6; Ser. IV, II, 1016; John Brightman to Nancy Brightman, May 29, 1865, Brightman Papers.

3. Quoting *O.R.*, Ser. I, XLVIII, part i, 805–6; Heartsill, *1491 Days*, p. 229; Palm to Lauzin, Aug. 21, 1864, Gras-Lauzin Family Papers, Louisiana State University Archives, Baton Rouge; Manning to Moore, Dec. 27, 1864, Moore Papers; *San Antonio Tri-Weekly Herald*, Nov. 14, 1865. Also, Charles W. Ramsdell, "Texas from the Fall of the Confederacy to the Beginning of Reconstruction," *Quarterly of the Texas State Historical Association*, XI (Jan., 1908), 199–201; Parks, *Kirby Smith*, p. 350; Heartsill, *1491 Days*, pp. 203–6, 230; Gammel, *Laws of Texas*, V, 829–30; Ramsdell, "Lee's Horse Supply," *Amer. Hist. Rev.*, XXXV, 775; *Journal of Congress*, IV, 498–99, VII, 400, 419, 513, 543–44; *General Orders, Trans-Mississippi Department*, pp. 34, 66; *Houston Tri-Weekly Telegraph*, Dec. 19, 23, 1864; *Houston Daily Telegraph*, Aug. 29, 1864; *Weekly State Gazette* (Austin), May 3, 1865; *Galveston Tri-Weekly News*, April 8, 1864; *O.R.*, Ser. I, XXII, part ii, 1137–39; XXXIV, part ii, 902–3; XLI, part ii, 1005, and part iv, 1070–72; XLVIII, part i, 1422; LIII, 969; Ser. IV, I, 126–27; II, 1002–3; III, 89–90, 931–32; Magruder to Murrah, March 28, 1864, Epperson to Murrah, Jan. 20, 1865, Robertson to Murrah, March 9, 1865, Governors' Letters (Murrah).

4. Quoting Kirby Smith to Bouldin, March 27, 26, Aug. 24, 1864, Letterbook, King & Co. to Kirby Smith, May 27, 1865, and Special Order, no number, Headquarters, Trans-Mississippi Department, May 29, 1865, Correspondence, Kirby

Smith Papers; *The Standard* (Clarksville, Tex.), April 21, 1864; *Washington Tele-graph* (Ark.), June 29, 1864; Samuel Maverick to Lewis Maverick, May 25, 1864, Maverick Papers; Kirby Smith to Memminger, June 4, 1864, Letterbook, Carr to Kirby Smith, June 10, 1864, Correspondence, Kirby Smith Papers; *O.R.,* Ser. I, XLI, part iv, 1001–2; Heartsill, *1491 Days,* p. 224; John Brightman to Mary Brightman, Dec. 13, 1864, Brightman Papers; Mary Maverick to Lewis Maverick, Aug. 7, 1864, Maverick Papers; *O.R.,* Ser. I, XLI, part iv, 1129–30; XLVIII, part i, 1381–84; Gray to Kirby Smith, Feb. 24, 1865, Correspondence, Kirby Smith Papers; *O.R.,* Ser. I, XLVIII, part i, 1422; Kirby Smith to Johnson, March 16, 1865, Letterbook, Kirby Smith Papers; Heartsill, *1491 Days,* p. 232. Also, *ibid.,* p. 206; Todd, *Confederate Finance,* pp. 23–24; *Public Laws,* ed. Matthews, pp. 205–8, 272, 277; Smith, "Confederate Treasury," *Pub. Southern Hist. Assoc.,* 1901, pp. 93–94; Hyatt, "Diary," in Bartlett, *Military Record of Louisiana,* part III, p. 14; Rhodes, *History of the United States,* V, 378; *Laws of the Last Session,* ed. Ramsdell, pp. 151–53; *Acts, 7th Louisiana Legislature,* Second Sess., Shreveport, pp. 54–55; Williams, *Border Ruffians,* p. 286; McHattan-Ripley, *From Flag to Flag,* p. 102; William H. Tunnard, *A Southern Record: The History of the Third Regiment Louisiana Infantry* (Baton Rouge, 1866), p. 327; Bragg, *Louisiana,* p. 224; *The Patriot* (La Grange, Tex.), Oct. 8, 1864; *Galveston Tri-Weekly News,* Nov. 6, 23, 1864; *Texas Republican* (Marshall), May 26, 1865; *Houston Tri-Weekly Telegraph,* July 15, Nov. 3, 1864, Feb. 11, May 4, 1865; *Shreveport News,* Sept. 20, 1864; *O.R.,* Ser. I, XXXIV, part iv, 638; XLI, part iii, 994–96, and part iv, 1006, 1133; XLVIII, part i, 1401–2, 1428–29, 1435; LIII, 1016; Address by Governor Murrah "To the People of the State of Texas," July 19, 1864, Executive Record Book, No. 280; Kirby Smith to Walker, Oct. 11, 1864, Letterbook, Kirby Smith Papers; Palm to Lauzin, Aug. 21, 1864, Gras-Lauzin Papers; Manning to Moore, Dec. 27, 1864, Moore Papers.

5. Quoting *San Antonio News,* June 4, 1864; Mary Maverick to Lewis Maverick, June 12, 1864, Maverick Papers; *Natchitoches Times* (La.), Oct. 29, 1864; *Washington Telegraph* (Ark.), Dec. 28, 1864; John Brightman to Nancy Brightman, Dec. 13, 1864, Brightman Papers; Hynson to Moore, Jan. 3, 1865, Moore Papers; *Houston Tri-Weekly Telegraph,* Feb. 11, 1865; Heartsill, *1491 Days,* pp. 231–32. Also, Thomas, *Arkansas in War,* pp. 328–29; *Acts, 7th Louisiana Legislature,* Second Sess., Shreveport, pp. 12, 14–15, 21, 38–39; Gammel, *Laws of Texas,* V, 829–30; Tunnard, *Third Louisiana,* p. 329; *Houston Tri-Weekly Telegraph,* Nov. 21, 30, Dec. 12, 1864, March 8, May 3, 4, 1865; *Houston Daily Telegraph,* Feb. 7, 1865; *Shreveport News,* Dec. 13, 1864; *Dallas Herald,* Jan. 12, 1865; *O.R.,* Ser. I, XLI, part iv, 1029–31; Ser. II, VII, 994; "Address of Governor Murrah to the People of Texas," Jan. 14, 1865, Executive Record Book, No. 280.

6. Quoting Heartsill, *1491 Days,* pp. 202–3; *Texas Christian Advocate* (Austin), Dec. 12, 1864; *Army and Navy Messenger* (Shreveport), Oct. 27, 1864; Heartsill, *1491 Days,* pp. 230, 233–34; *O.R.,* Ser. I, XLI, part iii, 774; *Journals of Congress,* VII, 255; *O.R.,* Ser. I, XLVIII, part i, 1321; *Laws of the Last Session,* ed. Ramsdell, pp. 118–19. Also, Dorsey, *Recollections of Henry Watkins Allen,* p. 257; Nathaniel W. Stephenson, "The Question of Arming the Slaves," *American Historical Review,* XVIII (1912–13), 295–308; *Journals of Congress,* IV, 585, 670–71, 704, 726–27, VII, 612–13, 748; *Public Laws,* ed. Matthews, p. 235; *Acts,*

7th *Louisiana Legislature,* First Sess., Shreveport, pp. 18, 34; *Army and Navy Messenger,* Sept. 15, 1864, Feb. 16, 1865; *Houston Tri-Weekly Telegraph,* Feb. 11, 1864; *Richmond Daily Examiner,* Feb. 11, 25, March 7, 1865; *O.R.,* Ser. IV, III, 112, 207–8, 779, 1144, 1161–62, 1193–94; Oldham, "Memoirs," pp. 44–45; Dennis to Bryan, April 8, 1865, Bryan Papers.

7. Quoting Lizzie Neblett to William Neblett, June 14, 1864, Neblett Papers; Heartsill, *1491 Days,* p. 211; Hyatt, "Diary," in Bartlett, *Military Record of Louisiana,* part III, p. 14; Lizzie Neblett to William Neblett, June 19, 1864, Neblett Papers; *San Antonio Weekly Herald,* Jan. 14, 1865; *O.R.,* Ser. I, XLVIII, part i, 728, 1355, 1005; Palm to Lauzin, Feb. 12, March 1, 1865, Gras-Lauzin Papers; General Order No. 9, March 1, 1865, and General Order No. 10, March 2, 1865, Headquarters, District of Texas, "Broadside," Swante Palm Collection, University of Texas Archives, Austin; *O.R.,* Ser. I, XLVIII, part ii, 17–18. Also, Heartsill, *1491 Days,* pp. 234–35, 237, 246–48; Lougherty, *War in Texas,* p. 27; *Weekly State Gazette* (Austin), March 29, 1865; *O.R.,* Ser. I, XLI, part ii, 1005–6; XLVIII, part i, 574, 1062–63, 1385–86; LIII, 880; Oldham, "Memoirs," pp. 347–48; Smith to Gourdain, Aug. 10, 1864, Mrs. M. Owen to Husband, Nov. 27, 1864, Logan Papers; Gallegher to Murrah, April 19, 1865, Governors' Letters (Murrah); S. D. Farrow to Josephine Farrow, Jan. 15, 1865, Farrow Papers; Throckmorton to Murrah, April 5, 1865, Hill to Walsh, April 5, 1865, Records, Texas Adjutant General.

8. Quoting *O.R.,* Ser. I, XXXIV, part ii, 965–66; *Acts, 7th Louisiana Legislature,* Second Sess., Shreveport, p. 65; *Natchitoches Times* (La.), Oct. 29, 1864; *San Antonio News,* June 21, 1864; Bexar County Court Records, Fall Term, 1864, San Antonio Court House; *The Patriot* (La Grange, Tex.), Jan. 21, 1865; *Galveston Daily News* (published at Houston), April 7, 1865. Also, Heartsill, *1491 Days,* pp. 205, 237; Shugg, *Origins of Class Struggle,* pp. 179–80; Bartlett, *Military Record of Louisiana,* part III, p. 36; *San Antonio News,* Nov. 6, 1864; *O.R.,* Ser. I, XXXIV, part ii, 952–53, 962–67, 972–77; XLI, part ii, 593–94, part iii, 317, 402, 498, and part iv, 675, 901; XLVIII, part i, 775, 1385, 1398–1401, and part ii, 220, 363; Doss to Murrah, May 2, 1864, Hunter to Murrah, May 22, 1864, Ferris to Murrah, Aug. 18, 1864, Murrah to Nichols, Jan. 15, April 11, 1865, Murrah to Williams, March 21, 1865, Governors' Letters (Murrah).

9. Quoting *O.R.,* Ser. I, XXXIV, part iv, 672; XLI, part iv, 1121–22; Kirby Smith to Johnson, March 16, 1865, Letterbook, Kirby Smith Papers; *O.R.,* Ser. I, XLI, part iii, 971; XLVIII, part i, 1408–9. Also, Abel, *The Indian as Participant,* pp. 333–34; *Journal of Congress,* IV, 605; *Galveston Tri-Weekly News,* May 22, 1864; *O.R.,* Ser. I, XXII, part ii, 1103; XXXIV, part iii, 764, 768, 770, 823, 828; XLI, part ii, 1019, part iii, 965–71, and part iv, 1016–17; LIII, 895–96; Kirby Smith to Cooper, Dec. 2, 1864, Letterbook, Kirby Smith Papers.

10. Quoting *O.R.,* Ser. I, XLVIII, part i, 1287; Heartsill, *1491 Days,* pp. 234–35. Also, *ibid.,* pp. 232–37; Arndt M. Stickles, *Simon Bolivar Buckner* (Chapel Hill, 1940), pp. 256, 263–65; Boggs, *Reminiscences,* pp. 81–84; *O.R.,* Ser. I, XLVIII, part i, 68–72, 1337–40, 1351–53, 1362–63, 1366, 1387–89, 1411–12, 1416, 1428–30, 1442, part ii, 1285, 1295, 1300.

11. Quoting Kirby Smith to Mother, Dec. 25, 1864, Correspondence, Kirby Smith Papers; *O.R.,* Ser. I, XXXIV, part i, 531; *Richmond Whig,* Dec. 14, 1864, Jan. 18, 1865; *Shreveport News,* March 7, 1865; *Washington Telegraph* (Ark.), March 8, 1865; *Houston Daily Telegraph,* March 21, 1865; *San Antonio News,* March 10, 1865; *San Antonio Herald,* March 11, 1865; Kirby Smith to Davis, March 9, 1865, Letterbook, Kirby Smith Papers; *O.R.,* Ser. I, XLVIII, part i, 1418–19; *Laws of the Second Session,* ed. Ramsdell, pp. 110–11, 144–45; *Journals of Congress,* VII, 796. Also, Boggs, *Reminiscences,* p. 109; *Journals of Congress,* VII, 283, 318, 354, 367, 369, 403–4, 485, 488, 551, 669, 732, 755, 792; *Weekly State Gazette* (Austin), Aug. 24, Oct. 26, 1864; *Shreveport News,* Sept. 6, Nov. 1, 1864; *Houston Daily Telegraph,* Oct. 19, 1864; *O.R.,* Ser. I, LIII, 1309; Kirby Smith to [Johnson], March 6, 1887, Correspondence, Kirby Smith Papers.

12. Quoting *Shreveport News,* Feb. 14, 1865; "Resolution of a Mass Meeting held by McNair's Brigade, Churchill's Division, camp near Shreveport, March 28, 1865," Correspondence, Kirby Smith Papers; Heartsill, *1491 Days,* p. 233. Also, *O.R.,* Ser. I, XLVIII, part i, 203–7, and part ii, 108, 169–72, 240, 1271; Murrah to Williamson, March 17, 1865, Murrah to Robertson, March 29, 1865, Magruder to Murrah, April 5, 1865, Governors' Letters (Murrah).

13. Quoting Heartsill, *1491 Days,* pp. 238–39; *Shreveport Semi-Weekly News,* April 22, 1865; *O.R.,* Ser. I, XLVIII, part ii, 400; Heartsill, *1491 Days,* p. 239; Mary Maverick to Lewis Maverick, April 22, 1865, Maverick Papers; John H. Reagan, *Memoirs,* ed. Walter F. McCaleb (New York and Washington, 1906), p. 204; *Army and Navy Messenger* (Shreveport), May 11, 1865; "Proclamation to the People of Texas," April 27, 1865, Executive Record Book, No. 280; *Shreveport Semi-Weekly News,* May 4, 1865; *Weekly State Gazette* (Austin), May 3, 1865; Heartsill, *1491 Days,* p. 242; *Galveston Tri-Weekly News,* May 12, 1865. Also, Edwin H. Fay, *"This Infernal War"* (Austin, 1958), p. 448; Sarah Katherine Stone Holmes, *Brokenburn: The Journal of Kate Stone,* ed. John Q. Anderson (Baton Rouge, 1955), pp. 333, 340, 344–45; *Galveston Tri-Weekly News,* May 12, 1865; *Houston Tri-Weekly Telegraph,* April 24, May 10, 1865; *Texas Republican* (Marshall), May 19, 1865.

14. Quoting *O.R.,* Ser. I, XLVIII, part ii, 1294–95, 1291; Heartsill, *1491 Days,* p. 240; Wise to Moore, May 8, 1865, Moore Papers; *O.R.,* Ser. I, XLVIII, part ii, 386, and part i, 235; Kirby Smith to Rose, May 2, 1865, Letterbook, Kirby Smith Papers. Also, Ramsdell, *Reconstruction in Texas,* p. 30; *Houston Tri-Weekly Telegraph,* April 28, and all May issues, 1865; *The Patriot* (La Grange, Tex.), May 6, 1865; *O.R.,* Ser. I, XLVIII, part ii, 398–403.

15. Quoting *O.R.,* Ser. I, XLVIII, part i, 186–88; Kirby Smith to Pope, May 9, 1865, Kirby Smith to Allen *et al.,* May 9, 1865, Correspondence, Kirby Smith Papers; Edwards, *Shelby,* pp. 520–25 *passim; O.R.,* Ser. I, XLVIII, part i, 192–93, 189, and part ii, 507; Kirby Smith to Murrah, May 17, 1865, Correspondence, Kirby Smith Papers. Also, Dorsey, *Recollections of Henry Watkins Allen,* p. 288; Thomas, *Arkansas in War,* pp. 334–35; *O.R.,* Ser. I, XLVIII, part i, 186–94, and part ii, 365, 381–82, 525–26, 628–30, 647; "Secret" memorandum in Murrah's handwriting, n.d., Governors' Letters (Murrah); Kirby Smith to Governor [Reynolds], n.d., Correspondence, Kirby Smith Papers.

16. Quoting Slaughter to Magruder, May 19, 1865, Correspondence, Kirby Smith Papers; Ford, *Rip Ford's Texas*, pp. 396–97; "Missa Tempore Belli, 'Reminiscere,'" *Missalum Romanum;* Heartsill, *1491 Days,* p. 243; *O.R.,* Ser. I, XLVIII, part ii, 1308; [Anon.] to Ashbel Smith, May 16, 1865, Ashbel Smith Papers; *O.R.,* Ser. I, XLVIII, part ii, 1308. Also, Ford, *Rip Ford's Texas,* pp. 389–98, 403; Yeary, *Reminiscences,* pp. 44, 217, 642; Andrews, *Women of the South,* p. 426; Pierce, *The Lower Rio Grande Valley,* pp. 52–54; Roberts, "Texas," in Evans, ed., *Confederate Military History,* XI, 126–28; *O.R.,* Ser. I, XLVIII, part i, 266–69, and part ii, 1313–14.

17. Quoting Heartsill, *1491 Days,* p. 244; *O.R.,* Ser. I, XLVIII, part ii, 1310, 1313, 1315; Kirby Smith to Magruder, May 26, 1865, Correspondence, Kirby Smith Papers; *O.R.,* Ser. I, XLVIII, part ii, 1321; Heartsill, *1491 Days,* p. 245; John Brightman to Nancy Brightman, May 29, 1865, Brightman Papers. Also, Yeary, *Reminiscences,* p. 595; Dorsey, *Recollections of Henry Watkins Allen,* pp. 294–95; Tunnard, *Third Louisiana,* p. 337; Graves, *Andrew Jackson Potter,* pp. 174–75; Debray, "A Sketch of Debray's Twenty-sixth Regiment," *Southern Hist. Soc. Pap.,* XIII, 164; *Galveston Tri-Weekly News,* May 17, 26, 1865; *O.R.,* Ser. I, XLVIII, part ii, 1312, 1316–17; Walker to Anderson, May 24, 1865, Correspondence, Kirby Smith Papers; Oldham, "Memoirs," pp. 336–38.

18. Quoting *O.R.,* Ser. I, XLVIII, part ii, 563; Special Orders, No.————, Headquarters, Trans-Mississippi Department, May 29, 1865, with enclosed report, May 30, 1865, Kirby Smith, "Address," May [30], 1865, Kirby Smith to Canby, June 2, 1865, with enclosures, Correspondence, Kirby Smith Papers; *O.R.,* Ser. I, XLVIII, part ii, 601. Also, Newberry, "Flanagin," in *Arkansas and The Civil War,* pp. 74–77; Thomas, *Arkansas in War,* pp. 334–36; Thomas, *Arkansas and Its People,* I, 130–31; Stickles, *Buckner,* pp. 269–72; "Secret Service Funds," *Confederate Veteran,* April, 1894, p. 31; Bartlett, *Military Record of Louisiana,* part III, p. 43; *Houston Tri-Weekly Telegraph,* May 24, 31, June 2, 16, 1865; *San Antonio News,* May 30, 1865; *The Patriot* (La Grange, Tex.), June 2, 1865; *Galveston Tri-Weekly News,* June 5, 1865; *O.R.,* Ser. I, XLVIII, part i, 193–94, and part ii, 515, 562–63, 581, 591, 600–2, 626–31, 648–49, 675–76, 1319–20; *O.R.N.,* XXII, 196–97, 203; Murrah to Ashbel Smith and Ballinger, May 24, 1865, Governors' Letters (Murrah); Kirby Smith to Murrah, May 30, 1865, Kirby Smith to Sprague, May 30, 1865, Receipt signed by Walker, May 31, 1865, Kirby Smith to Grant, March 15, June 15, 1866, Cucullo to Kirby Smith, Jan. 29, 1891, Correspondence, Kirby Smith Papers.

19. Quoting *O.R.,* Ser. I, XLVIII, part ii, 1103, 1104, 601, 1107; Edwards, *Shelby,* p. 544. Also, Dale and Litton, *Cherokee Cavaliers,* p. 228; Edwards, *Shelby,* pp. 543–51; Alexander W. Terrell, *From Texas to Mexico* (Dallas, 1933), pp. 3–9; Carl C. Rister, "Carlota, a Confederate Colony in Mexico," *Journal of Southern History,* XI (Feb., 1945), 33–50; Rippy, *United States and Mexico,* pp. 250–51; *O.R.,* Ser. I, XLVIII, part ii, 1015, 1095–1107, 1266–71, 1279–80, 1307–8, 1319, 1323–24; Kirby Smith, Notebook Diary, June 14 to June 27, 1865, Kirby Smith Papers; Kirby Smith to Wife, July 4, 10, 28, undated, Aug. 21, 1865, Kirby Smith to Mother, Aug. 4, 1865, Correspondence, Kirby Smith Papers.

20. Quoting *The Standard* (Clarksville, Tex.), June 10, 1865; Williams, *Border Ruffians,* p. 386; Throckmorton to Hamilton, Aug. 20, 1865, Petition of Joseph Rey *et al.,* to Hamilton, Sept. 9, 1865, Governors' Letters (Hamilton), Texas State Archives, Austin; James Larson, *Sergeant Larson, 4th Cavalry* (San Antonio, 1935), pp. 320–21. Also, Miller, *Financial History of Texas,* pp. 115, 155; Love, *Jesse James,* pp. 70–80, 336–39; Dalton, *Black Flag,* pp. 245–47; Jim Cummins, *Jim Cummins' Book* (Denver, 1903), pp. 188–89; Ramsdell, "Texas from the Fall of the Confederacy to the Beginning of Reconstruction," *Quar. Tex. State Hist. Assoc.,* XI, 299; Ford, *Rip Ford's Texas,* p. 403; *Houston Tri-Weekly Telegraph,* June 1, 20, July 1, 1865; *Louisiana Democrat* (Alexandria), June 21, 1865; *Galveston Tri-Weekly News,* July 10, 1865; *Flake's Daily Bulletin* (Galveston), Aug. 9, 1865; *O.R.,* Ser. I, XLVIII, part ii, 866–67, 929, 957, 963–64; "Proclamation" by Hamilton, July 25, 1865, Executive Record Book, No. 280; Brown, "Annals of Travis County," XXIV, 36.

BIBLIOGRAPHY ✄

Manuscript Sources

Baker, Dr. J. H. P. Diary, 1864–65. State Historical Society of Missouri, Columbia, Missouri.

Banks, Nathaniel P. Papers, 1862–65. Microfilm, University of Texas, Austin, Texas. Originals at the Salem Institute, Salem, Mass.

Barrett, Thomas. "The Great Hanging at Gainesville, Cooke County, Texas." Memoir, dated 1885. Archives, University of Texas, Austin, Texas.

Becton, Edwin P. Papers. Archives, University of Texas, Austin, Texas.

Bexar County Court Records, 1860–65. Bexar County Court House, San Antonio de Bexar, Texas.

Brightman, Dr. John C. Letters, 1859–65. Typed copies, Archives, University of Texas, Austin, Texas.

Bringier, Louis A. Papers. Archives, Louisiana State University, Baton Rouge, Louisiana.

Brown, Frank. "Annals of Travis County and of the City of Austin." Archives, University of Texas, Austin, Texas.

Bryan, Guy, M. Papers. Archives, Texas State Library, Austin, Texas.

Clay, Clement C. Papers. Archives, Duke University, Durham, North Carolina.

Cochran, W. C. "A Trip to Mexico in 1864." Memoir, typed copy. Archives, University of Texas, Austin, Texas.

"Confederate Papers." United States Office of Indian Affairs, National Archives, Washington, D.C.

"Customs Book, Sabine Pass." War Department Collection of Confederate Records, Record Group 109, National Archives, Washington, D.C.

Erath, George B. "Memoirs." Archives, University of Texas, Austin, Texas.

Farrow, Samuel W. Papers, 1862–65. Archives, University of Texas, Austin, Texas.

Floyd, N. B. Papers. Archives, University of Texas, Austin, Texas.

Ford, John Salmon. "Memoirs." Archives, University of Texas, Austin, Texas.

Garland, J. D. Papers, 1863–70. Typed copies, Archives, Louisiana State University, Baton Rouge, Louisiana.

Gras-Lauzin Family Papers, 1783–1864. Archives, Louisiana State University, Baton Rouge, Louisiana.

Graves, L. H. Diary, 1861–64. Typed copy, Archives, University of Texas, Austin, Texas.

Haley, J. Evetts. "Life of Charles E. Goodnight." MS, n.d., Archives, University of Texas, Austin, Texas.

Hazen Family Papers. State Historical Society of Missouri, Columbia, Missouri.

Henson, Andrew B. Papers. Archives, University of Texas, Austin, Texas.

Hopkins, Desmond P. Diary, 1862–65. Typed copy, Archives, University of Texas, Austin, Texas.

Journal and Minutes of the City Council of San Antonio de Bexar, Vol. C, 1856–70. City Hall, San Antonio de Bexar, Texas.

Kingsbury, G. D. Papers, 1858–72. Archives, University of Texas, Austin, Texas.

Kirby Smith, Edmund. *See* Smith, Edmund Kirby.

Letters Received, Confederate States War Department. War Department Collection of Confederate Records, Record Group 109, National Archives, Washington, D.C.

Logan, George Washington. Papers. Southern Historical Collection, University of North Carolina, Chapel Hill, North Carolina.

McKee, Andrew W. Papers. War Department Collection of Confederate Records, Record Group 109, National Archives, Washington, D.C.

Mann, Maria. Papers. Manuscript Division, Library of Congress, Washington, D.C.

Maverick Family Papers. Archives, University of Texas, Austin, Texas.

Minor, Mary J., W. B. Minor, and W. B. Hunter. Letters, 1863–64. Typed copies, Archives, University of Texas, Austin, Texas.

Moore, Thomas O. Papers. Archives, Louisiana State University, Baton Rouge, Louisiana.

Moss, Frank. Papers. Archives, University of Texas, Austin, Texas.

Neblett Family Papers. Archives, University of Texas, Austin, Texas.

Oldham, Williamson S. "Memoirs." Archives, University of Texas, Austin, Texas.

Palfrey, W. T., and G. D. Palfrey. Papers, 1832–1918. Archives, Louisiana State University, Baton Rouge, Louisiana.

Palm, Swante. Papers. Archives, University of Texas, Austin, Texas.

Peveler, William R. Diary, 1863. Typed copy, Archives, University of Texas, Austin, Texas.

Pickett, John T. Papers. Manuscript Division, Library of Congress, Washington, D.C.

Pugh Family Papers, 1852–65. Archives, Louisiana State University, Baton Rouge, Louisiana.

Record Book of Camp Davis, Kerr County, Texas, 1862–64. Photostat copy, Archives, University of Texas, Austin, Texas.

Records, Adjutant General's Office of Texas. Archives, Texas State Library, Austin, Texas.

Records, General Hospitals, Trans-Mississippi Department. War Department Collection of Confederate Records, Record Group 109, National Archives, Washington, D.C.

Reynolds, Thomas C. Papers. Manuscript Division, Library of Congress, Washington, D.C.

Roessler, A. R. "Military Routes of the Confederate Army in Texas." Survey, Archives, Texas State Library, Austin, Texas.

Smith, Ashbel. Papers, 1863–65. Archives, University of Texas, Austin, Texas.

Smith, Edmund Kirby. Papers. Southern Historical Collection, University of North Carolina, Chapel Hill, North Carolina.

Starr, James H. Papers. Archives, University of Texas, Austin, Texas.

Stewart, William H. Diary. Southern Historical Collection, University of North Carolina, Chapel Hill, North Carolina.

Texas, State of. Executive Record Books, Nos. 80, 81, 82, 279, 280, and 281. Archives, Texas State Library, Austin, Texas.

——Governors' Letters (Governors Runnell, Houston, Clark, Lubbock, Murrah, and Hamilton). Archives, Texas State Library, Austin, Texas.

——Miscellaneous Military Papers. Archives, Texas State Library, Austin, Texas.

——Senate Journal, 9th Legislature, Extra Session. Archives, Texas State Library, Austin, Texas.

——Session Laws of Texas, 10th Legislature, 1863. Archives, Texas State Library, Austin, Texas.

Thompson, M. Jeff. "Autobiography." Southern Historical Collection, University of North Carolina, Chapel Hill, North Carolina.

Turner, Josiah. Papers. Southern Historical Collection, University of North Carolina, Chapel Hill, North Carolina.

Walker, John G. Papers. Southern Historical Collection, University of North Carolina, Chapel Hill, North Carolina.

Weeks Family Papers. Archives, Louisiana State University, Baton Rouge, Louisiana.

White, Reuben G. Papers. Archives, University of Texas, Austin, Texas.

Williams, Henry C. "The Indian Raid in Young County, Texas, Oct. 13, 1864." Typed memoir, Archives, University of Texas, Austin, Texas.

Public Documents

Acts Passed by the Sixth Legislature of the State of Louisiana, First Session, 1861–62. Baton Rouge, 1862.

Acts Passed by the Twenty-seventh [Sixth] Legislature of the State of Louisiana, Extra Session, Opelousas, December, 1862–January, 1863. Natchitoches, 1864.

Acts Passed by the Sixth Legislature of the State of Louisiana, Extra Session, 1863. Shreveport, 1863.

Acts Passed by the Seventh Legislature of the State of Louisiana, First Session, 1864. Shreveport, 1864.

Acts Passed by the Seventh Legislature of the State of Louisiana, Second Session, 1865. Shreveport, 1865.

Address of A. J. Hamilton, Military Governor, to the People of Texas, Signed January 1, 1864. New Orleans, The Era Office, 1864.

Annual Message of Governor Henry Watkins Allen to the Legislature of the State of Louisiana, January, 1865. Shreveport, 1865.

Annual Message of Governor Thomas O. Moore to the Twenty-eighth [Seventh] General Assembly, January, 1864. Shreveport, 1864.

Annual Report of the Commissioner of Patents to the Speaker of the House of Representatives. Richmond, 1865.

Buckley, S. B. First Annual Report of the Geological and Agricultural Survey of Texas. Houston, A. C. Gray, 1874.

Congressional Globe, 37th and 38th Congresses, 1861–65.

Cotton Sold to the Confederate States. United States Treasury Department Report. Washington, D.C., Government Printing Office, 1913.

Department of Commerce Bulletin No. 131. Washington, D.C., Government Printing Office, 1913.

Documents and Speeches during the Civil War Period in Texas. N.p., n.d., copy in Archives, University of Texas, Austin, Texas.

Gammel, H. P. N., comp. The Laws of Texas, 1822–1897. 10 vols. Austin, Gammel, 1902.

General Orders, Headquarters, Trans-Mississippi Department, from March 6, 1863, to January 1, 1865. Houston, E. H. Cushing, 1865.

Hodge, David M. Argument before the Committee on Indian Affairs of the U.S. Senate, March 10, 1880, in Support of Senate Bill No. 1145, Providing for the Payment of Awards Made to the Creek Indians Who Enlisted in the Federal Army, Loyal Refugees, and Freedmen. Washington, D.C., 1880.

——Is-ha-he-char, and Co-we-Harjo, to the Committee on Indian Affairs of the House of Representatives of the 51st Congress in the Matter of the Claims of the Loyal Creeks for Losses Sustained during the Late Rebellion. Washington, D.C., 1891.

House Executive Documents, 36th Congress, 1st Session, Vol. VII, No. 52; Vol. XII, No. 81.

——38th Congress, 2d Session, No. 25.

Journal of Both Sessions of the Convention of the State of Arkansas. Little Rock, 1861.

Journal of the Convention of Delegates of the People of Arkansas, January, 1864. Little Rock, 1864.

Journal of the Secession Convention of Texas, 1861. Edited by Ernest W. Winkler. Austin, Austin Print Co., 1912.

Journals of the Congress of the Confederate States of America, 1861–1865. Senate Executive Documents, 58th Congress, 2d Session, Vols. XXV–XXXI, No. 234. 7 vols. Washington, D.C., Government Printing Office, 1904–5.

Laws and Joint Resolutions of the Last Session of the Confederate Congress (November 7, 1864–March 18, 1865) Together with the Secret Acts of Previous Congresses. Edited by Charles W. Ramsdell. Durham, N.C., Duke University Press, 1941.

List of Field Officers, Regiments and Battalions in the Confederate Army, 1861–1865. United States War Department Report. Washington, D.C., Government Printing Office, 1899.

Loyal Creek Claims. United States Indian Office Report. Washington, D.C., Government Printing Office, 1916.

Official Journals of the House and Senate of the Seventh Legislature of Louisiana, Session of 1864. Shreveport, 1864.

Official Journals of the Senate and House of Representatives of the State of Louisiana, Seventh Legislature, Second Session, 1865. Shreveport, 1865.

Official Records of the Union and Confederate Navies in the War of the Rebellion. 30 vols. Washington, D.C., Government Printing Office, 1894–1927.

Official Report Relative to the Conduct of Federal Troops in Western Louisiana, during the Invasions of 1863 and 1864, Compiled from Sworn Testimony, under Direction of Governor Henry W. Allen. Shreveport, News Printing Establishment, 1865.

Organization and Status of Missouri Troops, Union and Confederate, during the Civil War. United States Record and Pension Office Report. Washington, D.C., Government Printing Office, 1902.

"Proceedings of the Confederate Congress." *Southern Historical Society Papers*, Vols. XLIV–L *passim*.

Public Laws of the Confederate States of America, Passed at the First, Second, Third, and Fourth Sessions of the First Congress, 1862–1864. Edited by James M. Matthews. Richmond, R. M. Smith, 1862–64.

Public Laws of the Confederate States of America, Passed at the First Session of the Second Congress, 1864. Edited by James M. Matthews. Richmond, R. M. Smith, 1864.

Regulations Adopted by the War Department for Carrying into Effect the Acts of Congress Relating to Indian Affairs, &c., &c. Richmond, 1862.

Regulations for the Army of the Confederate States, and for the Quartermaster's and Pay Departments, 1861. New Orleans, Bloomfield and Steel, 1861.

Regulations of the Army of the Confederate States, 1862, Containing a Complete Set of Forms. Austin, State Gazette Office, 1862.

Report of General W. L. Cabell's Brigade in Price's Raid in Missouri and Kansas in 1864. Dallas, 1900.

Report of Major General Hindman of His Operations in the Trans-Mississippi District, Published by Order of Congress. Richmond, R. M. Smith, 1864.

Report of the Joint Committee on the Conduct of the War, 38th Cong., 2d Sess., Vol. II, "Red River Expedition." Washington, D.C., 1865.

Report of the Secretary of War, November 26, 1863. Richmond, R. M. Smith, 1864.

Reports of the Commissioner of Indian Affairs for the Years 1862–1865. Washington, D.C., Government Printing Office, 1863–66.

Reports of the Committee of Investigation Sent by the Mexican Government to the Frontier of Texas. New York, 1875.

Reports of the Secretary of the Treasury of the Confederate States of America, 1861–1865. Compiled by Raphael P. Thian. Washington, D.C., 1878.

Richardson, James D. A Compilation of the Messages and Papers of the Confederacy, Including the Diplomatic Correspondence, 1861–1865. Washington, D.C., Washington Post Co., 1905.

——A Compilation of the Messages and Papers of the Presidents. 10 vols. Washington, D.C., 1896–99.

Senate Executive Documents, 36th Congress, 1st Session, Vol. XI, No. 21.

——38th Congress, 2d Session, No. 11.

——39th Congress, 2d Session, No. 26.

The Statutes at Large of the Provisional Government of the Confederate States of America, from the Institution of the Government, February 8, 1861, to Its Termination, February 18, 1862, Inclusive. Edited by James M. Matthews. Richmond, R. M. Smith, 1864.

United States Census Office. United States Eighth Census, 1860. 4 vols. Washington, D.C., Government Printing Office, 1864.

United States Census Office. A Compendium of the Ninth Census (June 1, 1870). Washington, D.C., Government Printing Office, 1872.

The War of the Rebellion: A Compilation of the Official Records of the Union and Confederate Armies. 128 vols. Washington, D.C., Government Printing Office, 1880–1901.

Books—Primary

Atkinson, Edward. Report to the Boston Board of Trade. Boston, 1862.

Badeau, Adam. Military History of Ulysses S. Grant. New York, Appleton, 1868–81.

Barron, Samuel B. The Lone Star Defenders: A Chronicle of the Third Texas Cavalry, Ross' Brigade. New York, Neale, 1908.

Barton, O. S., and John McCorkle. Three Years with Quantrell: A True Story, Told by His Scout, John McCorkle. Armstrong, Mo., Armstrong Herald, 1914.

Basler, Roy P., ed. The Collected Works of Abraham Lincoln. 9 vols. New Brunswick, Rutgers University Press, 1953.

Baxter, William. Pea Ridge and Prairie Grove; or, Scenes and Incidents of the War in Arkansas. Cincinnati, Poe and Hitchcock, 1864.

Belknap, William, ed. History of the 15th Regiment Iowa Veteran Volunteer Infantry. Keokuk, Iowa, 1887.

Berry, James B. A Texas Ranger and Frontiersman: The Days of Buck Berry in Texas, 1845–1906. Edited by James K. Greer. Dallas, Southwest Press, 1932.

Berry, Thomas F. Four Years with Morgan and Forrest. Louisville, 1880.

Bevier, Robert S. History of the First and Second Missouri Confederate Brigades, 1861–1865. St. Louis, Bryan, Brand, 1879.

Bishop, Albert W. Loyalty on the Frontier. St. Louis, Studley, 1863.

[Blessington, Joseph P.] The Campaigns of Walker's Texas Division. New York, Lange, Little, 1875.

Boggs, William R. Military Reminiscences of General William R. Boggs, C.S.A. Edited by William K. Boyd. Durham, N.C., Seeman, 1913.

Brent, Joseph L. Mobilizable Fortifications, and Their Controlling Influence in War. Boston and New York, 1885.

Britton, Wiley. The Civil War on the Border. 2 vols. New York and London, Putnam, 1890–1904.

——Memoirs of the Rebellion on the Border, 1863. Chicago, Cushing, Thomas, 1882.

——The Union Indian Brigade in the Civil War. Kansas City, Mo., Franklin Hudson, 1922.

Brown, John Henry. History of Texas from 1685 to 1892. 2 vols. St. Louis, L. E. Daniell, 1893.

Bryner, Cloyd. Bugle Echoes: The Story of the Illinois 47th. Springfield, Phillips Bros., 1905.

Burch, John P., and Harrison Trow. Charles W. Quantrell: A True History of His Guerrilla Warfare on the Missouri and Kansas Border during the Civil War of 1861–1865, as Told by Captain Trow. Vega, Texas, 1923.

Butler, Benjamin F. Private and Official Correspondence of Gen. Benjamin F.

Butler during the period of the Civil War. 5 vols. Norwood, Mass., privately printed, 1917.

Chambers, T. J. Memorial of General T. J. Chambers to the Sixth Legislature of the State of Texas. N.p., n.d., copy in University of Texas Library, Austin, Texas.

Chase, Salmon P. "Diary and Correspondence of Salmon P. Chase." Annual Report of the American Historical Association, 1902. Vol. II. Washington, D.C., 1903.

Clark, Champ. My Quarter Century of American Politics. New York, Harper, 1920.

Clarke, H. P., comp. The Confederate States Almanac and Repository of Useful Knowledge for 1862. Vicksburg, Miss., Clarke, 1862.

Crawford, Samuel J. Kansas in the Sixties. Chicago, McClurg, 1911.

Crittenden, Henry H. The Battle of Westport and National Memorial Park. Kansas City, Mo., Lowell, 1938.

——The Crittenden Memoirs. New York, Putnam, 1936.

Cummins, Jim. Jim Cummins' Book. Denver, Reed, 1903.

Dacus, Robert H. Reminiscences of Company "H," First Arkansas Mounted Rifles. Dardanelle, Ark., Post Dispatch, 1897.

Dale, Edward Everett, and Gaston Litton, eds. Cherokee Cavaliers: Forty Years of Cherokee History as Told in the Correspondence of the Ridge-Watie-Boudinot Family. Norman, University of Oklahoma Press, 1940.

Dalton, Kit. Under the Black Flag: A Guerilla Captain under Quantrill and a Border Outlaw for Seventeen Years. Memphis, Lockard, 1914.

Davis, Jefferson. Jefferson Davis, Constitutionalist: His Letters, Papers, and Speeches. Edited by Dunbar Rowland. 10 vols. Jackson, Miss., 1923.

——The Rise and Fall of the Confederate Government. 2 vols. New York, Appleton, 1881.

Dawson, Sarah Morgan. A Confederate Girl's Diary. Boston, Houghton Mifflin, 1913.

Dorsey, Sarah A. Recollections of Henry Watkins Allen. New York, Doolady, 1866.

Duganne, A. J. H. Camps and Prisons: Twenty Months in the Department of the Gulf. New York, Robens, 1865.

Eby, Frederick, comp. Education in Texas: Source Materials. Austin, University of Texas Press, 1918.

Edwards, John N. Noted Guerrillas; or, The Warfare on the Border. St. Louis, Brand, 1879.

——Shelby and His Men; or, The War in the West. Cincinnati, Miami, 1867.

——Shelby's Expedition to Mexico. Kansas City, Mo., Times Printing, 1872.

Evans, Clement A., ed. Confederate Military History. 12 vols. Atlanta, Confederate Publishing Co., 1899.

Fay, Edwin H. "This Infernal War": The Confederate Letters of Sgt. Edwin H. Fay. Edited by Bell I. Wiley and Lucy E. Fay. Austin, University of Texas Press, 1958.

Fisher, Rev. H. D. The Gun and the Gospel. Chicago, Kenwood, 1896.

Flinn, Frank M. Campaigning with Banks in Louisiana, '63 and '64, and with Sheridan in the Shenandoah Valley in '64 and '65. Lynn, Mass., Nichols, 1887.

Ford, John Salmon. Rip Ford's Texas. Edited by Stephen B. Oates. Austin, University of Texas Press, 1963.
Fremantle, James Arthur Lyon. The Fremantle Diary. Edited by Walter Lord. Boston, Little, Brown, 1954.
Fröbel, Julius. Seven Years in Central America, Northern Mexico, and the Far West of the United States. London, Bentley, 1859.
Giap, Vo Nguyen. Guerre du Peuple, Armée du Peuple. Hanoi, 1961.
Gordon, George H. A War Diary of Events in the War of the Great Rebellion, 1863–1865. Boston, Osgood, 1882.
Gorgas, Josiah. The Civil War Diary of General Josiah Gorgas. Edited by Frank E. Vandiver. University, Ala., University of Alabama Press, 1947.
Grant, Ulysses S. Personal Memoirs. Edited by E. B. Long. Cleveland and New York, World, 1952.
Greene, John W. Camp Ford Prison, and How I Escaped. Toledo, Barkdull, 1893.
Grimes, Absalom. Absalom Grimes, Confederate Mail Runner. Edited by Milo M. Quaife. New Haven, Yale University Press, 1926.
Hall, Winchester. Story of the 26th Louisiana Infantry, in the Service of the Confederate States. N.p., n.d.
Heartsill, William W. Fourteen Hundred and 91 Days in the Confederate Army. Edited by Bell I. Wiley. Jackson, Tenn., McCowat-Mercer, 1954.
Hepworth, George H. The Whip, Hoe, and Sword; or, The Gulf Department in '63. Boston, Walker, Wise, 1864.
Hill, Frederic S. Twenty Years at Sea; or, Leaves from My Old Log Books. New York, Houghton Mifflin, 1893.
[Hinton, Richard J.] The Rebel Invasion of Missouri and Kansas, and the Campaign of the Army of the Border, against General Sterling-Price in October and November, 1864. 2d ed. Chicago, Church & Goodman, 1865.
Historical and Biographical Record of the Cattle Industry and the Cattlemen of Texas and Adjacent Territory. St. Louis, Woodward and Tiernan, 1895.
Hoffman, Wickham. Camp Court and Siege: A Narrative of Personal Adventure and Observation during Two Wars: 1861–1865; 1870–1871. New York, Harper, 1877.
Holmes, Sarah Katherine Stone. Brokenburn: The Journal of Kate Stone, 1861–1868. Edited by John Q. Anderson. Baton Rouge, Louisiana State University Press, 1955.
Howe, M. A. De Wolfe, ed. Home Letters of General Sherman. New York, Scribner, 1909.
James, Frank. Frank James. Pine Bluff, Ark., Norton, 1926.
James, Jesse E. Jesse James. Cleveland, Westbrook, 1906.
Johnson, Robert U., and Clarence C. Buell, eds. Battles and Leaders of the Civil War, Being for the Most Part Contributed by Union and Confederate Officers. 4 vols. New York, Yoseloff, 1956.
Kean, Robert Garlick Hill. Inside the Confederate Government. Edited by Edward Younger. New York, Oxford, 1957.
Kellersberger, Getulius. Memoirs of an Engineer in the Confederate Army in Texas. Translated by Helen S. Sundstrom. Austin, University of Texas Press, 1957.

Knox, Thomas W. Camp-fire and Cotton-field: Southern Adventures in Time of War. New York, Bielock, 1865.

Lane, Walter P. The Adventures and Recollections of General Walter P. Lane. Marshall, Tex., News Messenger, 1928.

Larson, James. Sergeant Larson, 4th Cavalry. San Antonio, Southern Literary Institute, 1935.

Lee, Robert E. Unpublished Letters of General Robert E. Lee, C.S.A., to Jefferson Davis, and the War Department of the Confederate States of America, 1862–1865. Edited by Douglas S. Freeman. Rev. ed. New York, Putnam, 1957.

Le Grand, Julia. The Journal of Julia Le Grand, New Orleans, 1862–1863. Edited by Kate Mason Rowland and Mrs. Morris L. Croxall. Richmond, Everett Waddey, 1911.

Lothrop, Charles H. A History of the First Regiment Iowa Cavalry. Lyons, Iowa, Beers & Eaton, 1890.

Lougherty, Mrs. E. M. War and Reconstruction Times in Texas. Austin, Von Boeckmann–Jones, 1914.

Lubbock, Francis Richard. Six Decades in Texas; or, Memoirs of Francis Richard Lubbock. Austin, Ben C. Jones, 1900.

McClellan, George B. McClellan's Own Story. New York, 1887.

McConnell, Joseph C. The West Texas Frontier. Jacksboro, Tex., Gazette Printing, 1939.

McDougal, Henry Clay. Recollections, 1844–1909. Kansas City, Mo., Franklin Hudson, 1910.

McHattan-Ripley, Eliza. From Flag to Flag. New York, Appleton, 1889.

Mahan, Alfred Thayer. The Gulf and Inland Waters. New York, Scribner, 1883.

Mao Tse-Tung: An Anthology of His Writings. Edited by Anne Fremantle. New York, Mentor, 1962.

Moore, Frank, ed. The Rebellion Record: A Diary of American Events. 12 vols. New York, Van Nostrand, 1862–71.

Murrah, Pendleton. Messages of Governor P. Murrah to the Texas Legislature. N.p., n.d., copy in the University of Texas Library, Austin, Texas.

Newcomb, James P. Address of Hon. James P. Newcomb, Delivered at Comfort, Texas, August 10, 1887, the Twenty-fifth Anniversary of the Nueces Massacre. N.p., n.d., copy in the University of Texas Library, Austin, Texas.

Newsome, Edmund. Experiences in the War of the Great Rebellion. Carbondale, Ill., privately printed, 1880.

Noel, Theophilus. A Campaign from Santa Fe to the Mississippi: Being a History of the Old Sibley Brigade from Its First Organization to the Present Time; Its Campaigns in New Mexico, Arizona, Texas, Louisiana, and Arkansas, in the Years 1861–2–3–4. Shreveport, Shreveport News, 1865.

North, Thomas. Five Years in Texas; or, What You Did Not Hear during the War from January 1861 to January 1866. Cincinnati, Elm Street Printing, 1871.

Nott, Charles C. Sketches in Prison Camps: A Continuation of Sketches of the War. New York, Anson Randolph, 1865.

Olmstead, Frederick Law. A Journey in the Seaboard Slave States. New York, Dix, Edwards, 1861.

Olmstead, Frederick Law. A Journey Through Texas; or, A Saddle-Trip on the Southwestern Frontier. New York, Dix, Edwards, 1857.

Parsiot, Rev. P. F. Reminiscences of a Texas Missionary. San Antonio, Johnson Bros., 1899.

Peabody, Charles A. "The United States Provisional Court for the State of Louisiana, 1862–1865." Annual Report of the American Historical Association for the Year 1892. Washington, D.C., 1893.

Porter, David D. The Naval History of the Civil War. London, Sampson Low, 1887.

Prentis, Noble L. Kansas Miscellanies. Topeka, Kansas Publishing, 1889.

Robards, C. L. Synopses of the Decisions of the Supreme Court of the State of Texas. Austin, Brown & Foster, 1865.

Rodenbough, Theophilus F. From Everglade to Cañon with the Second Dragoons. New York, Van Nostrand, 1875.

Roel, Santiago, ed. Correspondencia particular de D. Santiago Vidaurri. Monterrey, Universidad de Nuevo León, 1946.

Sansom, John W. Battle of the Nueces River in Kinney County, Texas, August 10th, 1862. San Antonio, 1905.

Schofield, John M. Forty-Six Years in the Army. New York, Century, 1897.

Scott, Joe M. Four Years' Service in the Southern Army. Mulberry, Ark., Leader Office Print, 1897.

Selfridge, Thomas O. Memoirs of Thomas O. Selfridge. New York, Putnam, 1924.

Shea, John C. Reminiscences of Quantrell's Raid upon the City of Lawrence, Kas. Kansas City, Mo., Moore, 1879.

Sherman, William T. The Memoirs of Gen. William T. Sherman. New York, Webster, 1892.

Strother, David H. A Virginia Yankee in the Civil War. Edited by Cecil D. Eby, Jr. Chapel Hill, University of North Carolina Press, 1961.

Taylor, Richard. Destruction and Reconstruction: Personal Experiences of the Late War. Edited by Richard B. Harwell. New York, Longmans, Green, 1955.

Taylor, Thomas E. Running the Blockade: A Personal Narrative of Adventures, Risks, and Escapes during the American Civil War. London, John Murray, 1896.

Terrell, Alexander W. From Texas to Mexico and the Court of Maximilian in 1865. Dallas, Book Club of Texas, 1933.

Texas Almanac, 1861–1865. Galveston and Austin, Richardson, 1860–65.

Tunnard, William H. A Southern Record: The History of the Third Regiment Louisiana Infantry. Baton Rouge, privately printed, 1866.

Van Alstyne, Lawrence. Diary of an Enlisted Man. New Haven, Tuttle, Morehouse & Taylor, 1910.

Wadley, Sarah L. A Brief Record of the Life of William M. Wadley, Written by His Eldest Daughter. New York, Barnes, 1884.

Watson, William. The Adventures of a Blockade-Runner; or, Trade in Time of War. London, T. Fisher Unwin, 1892.

Wilbarger, J. W. Indian Depredations in Texas. Austin, Steck, 1935.

Williams, R. H. With the Border Ruffians: Memoirs of the Far West, 1852–1868. Edited by E. W. Williams. London, John Murray, 1907.

Wooten, Dudley G., ed. A Comprehensive History of Texas. 2 vols. Dallas, Scarff, 1898.

Wright, Mrs. Louise Wigfall. A Southern Girl in '61. New York, Doubleday, 1905.

Yeary, Mamie, comp. Reminiscences of the Boys in Gray, 1861–1865. Dallas, Smith and Lamar, 1912.

Books—Secondary

Abel, Annie Heloise. The Slaveholding Indians. 3 vols. Vol. I: The American Indian as Slaveholder and Secessionist; Vol. II: The American Indian as Participant in the Civil War. Cleveland, Arthur Clark, 1915–25.

Acheson, Sam. 35,000 Days in Texas: A History of the Dallas News and Its Forbears. New York, Macmillan, 1938.

Albaugh, William A., and Edward M. Simmons. Confederate Arms. Harrisburg, Pa., Stackpole, 1957.

Allen, Dr. O. F. The City of Houston from Wilderness to Wonder. Temple, Tex., privately printed, 1936.

Allsopp, Frederick W. Albert Pike: A Biography. Little Rock, Parke-Harper, 1928.

———The Life Story of Albert Pike. Little Rock, Parke-Harper, 1920.

Anderson, John Q. A Texas Surgeon in the C.S.A. Tuscaloosa, Ala., Confederate Publishing Company, 1957.

Anderson, Mabel Washbourne. Life of General Stand Watie. 2d ed. Pryor, Okla., privately printed, 1931.

Andrews, Matthew P. The Women of the South in War Times. Baltimore, Norman-Remington, 1920.

Bancroft, Hubert Howe. History of Nevada, Colorado, and Wyoming. San Francisco, The History Co., 1890.

———History of the North Mexican States and Texas. 2 vols. San Francisco, The History Co., 1889.

Banning, William, and George Banning. Six Horses. New York, Century, 1930.

Barr, Alwyn. Polignac's Texas Brigade. Houston, Texas Gulf Coast Historical Association, 1964.

Bartlett, Napier. Military Record of Louisiana. New Orleans, Graham, 1875.

Bates, E. F. History and Reminiscences of Denton County. Denton, Tex., McNitzky, 1918.

Belisle, John G. History of Sabine Parish, Louisiana. Many, La., Sabine Banner, 1912.

Bender, A. B. The March of Empire: Frontier Defense in the Southwest, 1848–1860. Lawrence, Kans., University of Kansas Press, 1952.

Biesele, R. L. The History of the German Settlements in Texas, 1831–1861. Austin, Von Boeckmann–Jones, 1930.

Biggers, Don H. German Pioneers in Texas. Fredericksburg, Tex., Fredericksburg Publishing, 1925.

Black, Robert C., III. The Railroads of the Confederacy. Chapel Hill, University of North Carolina Press, 1952.

498 Bibliography

Bradlee, Francis. Blockade Running during the Civil War and the Effect of Land and Water Transportation on the Confederacy. Salem, Mass., The Essex Institute, 1925.

Bradley, R. T. Frank and Jesse James. St. Louis, Marsh, 1880.

Bragg, Jefferson Davis. Louisiana in the Confederacy. Baton Rouge, Louisiana State University Press, 1941.

Breihan, Carl W. Quantrill and His Civil War Guerrillas. Denver, Swallow, 1959.

Brownlee, Richard S. Gray Ghosts of the Confederacy: Guerrilla Warfare in the West, 1861–1865. Baton Rouge, Louisiana State University Press, 1958.

Carr, Lucien. Missouri: A Bone of Contention. Boston and New York, Houghton Mifflin, 1894.

Casey, Robert, Jr. The Texas Border and Some Borderliners. Indianapolis, Bobbs-Merrill, 1950.

Caskey, W. M. Secession and Restoration in Louisiana. Baton Rouge, Louisiana State University Press, 1938.

Cassidy, Vincent H., and Amos E. Simpson. Henry Watkins Allen of Louisiana. Baton Rouge, Louisiana State University Press, 1964.

Castel, Albert E. A Frontier State at War: Kansas, 1861–1865. Ithaca, N.Y., Cornell University Press, 1958.

Cates, C. D. Pioneer History of Wise County. Decatur, Texas, Wise County Old Settlers' Association, 1907.

Chatfield, Lieut. W. H. The Twin Cities—Brownsville, Texas, and Matamoros, Mexico—of the Border, and the Country of the Lower Rio Grande. New Orleans, 1893.

Cochran, Hamilton. Blockade Runners of the Confederacy. Indianapolis, Bobbs-Merrill, 1958.

Colton, Ray Charles. The Civil War in the Western Territories: Arizona, Colorado, New Mexico, and Utah. Norman, University of Oklahoma Press, 1959.

Comte de Paris, Louis Philippe Albert d'Orleans. History of the Civil War in America. 4 vols. Philadelphia, Porter & Coates, 1875–88.

Connelley, William E. The Life of Preston B. Plumb. Chicago, Bowne and Howell, 1913.

——Quantrill and the Border Wars. Cedar Rapids, Iowa, Torch, 1910.

Conrad, Howard L., ed. Encyclopedia of the History of Missouri. 6 vols. New York, Southern History Co., 1901.

Croy, Homer. Our Will Rogers. New York, Duell, Sloan and Pearce, 1953.

Denison, George T. A History of Cavalry from the Earliest Times. London, Macmillan, 1913.

De Shields, James T. They Sat in High Place. San Antonio, Naylor, 1940.

Dietz, August. The Postal Service of the Confederate States of America. Richmond, Dietz, 1929.

Donald, Jay. Frank and Jesse James. Chicago, Coburn & Newman, 1882.

Eaton, Rachel Caroline. John Ross and the Cherokee Indians. Menasha, Wisc., Banta, 1914.

Eduard Schmidt, 1862–1912: Festschrift zur fünfzigjahrigen erinnerungs-feier an das gefecht am Nueces, 10 August 1962. N.p., 1912.

Elliott, Claude. "The Life of James W. Throckmorton." Unpublished Ph.D. dissertation, University of Texas, Austin, Texas, 1934.

Emmett, Chris. Texas Camel Tales. San Antonio, Naylor, 1932.

Fenneman, Nevin M. Physiography of Eastern United States. New York, McGraw-Hill, 1938.

——Physiography of Western United States. New York, McGraw-Hill, 1931.

Ficklen, John Rose. History of Reconstruction in Louisiana Through 1868. Baltimore, Johns Hopkins Press, 1910.

Foreman, Carolyn T. Park Hill. Muskogee, Okla., the author, 1948.

Freeman, Douglas S. Lee's Lieutenants: A Study in Command. 3 vols. New York, Scribner, 1942–44.

Fuller, Claude, and Richard D. Steuart. Firearms of the Confederacy. Huntington, W. Va., 1944.

Graves, H. A. Andrew Jackson Potter, the Fighting Parson of the Texas Frontier. Nashville, Southern Methodist Printing, 1882.

Gray, L. C. History of Agriculture in the Southern United States to 1860. Washington, D.C., Carnegie Institute, 1933.

Greer, James K. Bois d'Arc to Barb'd Wire: Ken Cary, Southwestern Frontier Born. Dallas, Dealy and Lowe, 1936.

Grinnell, George Bird. The Fighting Cheyennes. New York, Scribner, 1915.

Hall, Martin H. Sibley's New Mexico Campaign. Austin, University of Texas Press, 1960.

Hamilton, Holman. Zachary Taylor, Soldier in the White House. Indianapolis and New York, Bobbs-Merrill, 1951.

Harman, George D. Confederate Migration to Mexico. Bethlehem, Pa., Lehigh University, 1938.

Harrington, Fred H. The Fighting Politician: Major General N. P. Banks. Philadelphia, University of Pennsylvania Press, 1948.

Harris, Gertrude. A Tale of Men Who Knew Not Fear. San Antonio, Alamo, 1935.

Harwell, Richard B. Songs of the Confederacy. New York, Broadcast Music, 1951.

Heitman, Francis B. Historical Register and Dictionary of the United States Army from Its Organization, September 29, 1789, to March 2, 1903. Washington, D.C., Government Printing Office, 1903.

Hempstead, Fay. Historical Review of Arkansas. Chicago, Lewis, 1911.

Henderson, Harry McCorry. Texas in the Confederacy. San Antonio, Naylor, 1955.

Hollister, Wilfred R., and Harry Norman. Five Famous Missourians. Kansas City, Mo., Hudson-Kimberly, 1900.

James, Marquis. The Raven: A Biography of Sam Houston. Indianapolis, Bobbs-Merrill, 1929.

Jenkins, Paul B. The Battle of Westport. Kansas City, Mo., Hudson, 1906.

Johnson, Allen, and Dumas, Malone, eds. Dictionary of American Biography. 20 vols. New York, Scribner, 1943–58.

Johnson, Ludwell H. Red River Campaign: Politics and Cotton in the Civil War. Baltimore, Johns Hopkins Press, 1958.

Kahn, David. The Codebreakers. New York, Macmillan, 1967.

Kaufmann, Wilhelm. Die Deutschen amerikanischen Bürgerkriege, 1861–1865. Munich and Berlin, Oldenbourg, 1911.

Keleher, William A. Turmoil in New Mexico, 1846–1868. Santa Fe, Rydal, 1952.

Kerby, Robert L. The Confederate Invasion of New Mexico and Arizona. Los Angeles, Westernlore, 1958.

Lonn, Ella. Desertion during the Civil War. New York, Century, 1928.

——Foreigners in the Confederacy. Chapel Hill, University of North Carolina Press, 1940.

——Salt as a Factor in the Confederacy. New York, Neale, 1933.

Love, Robertus. The Rise and Fall of Jesse James. New York, Putnam, 1939.

McElroy, John. The Struggle for Missouri. Washington, D.C., National Tribune, 1913.

Miers, Earl Schenck. The Web of Victory: Grant at Vicksburg. New York, Knopf, 1955.

Miller, Edmund T. A Financial History of Texas. Austin, University of Texas Press, 1916.

Monnett, Howard N. Action Before Westport, 1864. Kansas City, Mo., Westport Historical Society, 1964.

Moore, Albert B. Conscription and Conflict in the Confederacy. New York, Macmillan, 1924.

Noll, Arthur Howard. General Kirby-Smith. Sewanee, Tenn., University of the South, 1907.

Oates, Stephen B. Confederate Cavalry West of the River. Austin, University of Texas Press, 1961.

O'Flaherty, David. General Jo Shelby: Undefeated Rebel. Chapel Hill, University of North Carolina Press, 1954.

O'Pry, Maude Hearn. Chronicles of Shreveport. Shreveport, Journal Printing, 1928.

Owsley, Frank L. King Cotton Diplomacy: Foreign Relations of the Confederate States of America. Chicago, University of Chicago Press, 1931.

Parks, Joseph Howard. General Edmund Kirby Smith, C.S.A. Baton Rouge, Louisiana State University Press, 1954.

Parton, James. General Butler in New Orleans. New York, Mason, 1864.

Paxson, Frederic L. History of the American Frontier, 1763–1893. New York, Houghton Mifflin, 1924.

Peterson, Cyrus A., and Joseph M. Hanson. Pilot Knob: The Thermopylae of the West. New York, Neale, 1914.

Pierce, Frank C. A Brief History of the Lower Rio Grande Valley. Menasha, Wisc., Banta, 1917.

Plum, William R. The Military Telegraph during the Civil War in the United States. Chicago, Jensen, McClurg, 1882.

Potts, Charles S. Railroad Transportation in Texas. Austin, University of Texas Press, 1909.

Pray, Mrs. R. F. Dick Dowling's Battle: An Account of the War Between the States in the Eastern Gulf Coast Region of Texas. Sun Antonio, Naylor, 1936.

Ramsdell, Charles W. Behind the Lines of the Southern Confederacy. Baton Rouge, Louisiana State University Press, 1944.

——Reconstruction in Texas. New York, Longmans, 1910.

Reed, S. C. A History of the Texas Railroads and of Transportation Conditions. Houston, St. Clair, 1941.

Rhodes, James Ford. History of the United States from the Compromise of 1850. 7 vols. New York, Macmillan, 1906–7.

Richardson, Rupert N., and Carl C. Rister. The Greater Southwest. Glendale, Calif., Arthur Clark, 1934.

Rippy, J. Fred. The United States and Mexico. New York, Knopf, 1926.

Roach, Hattie Joplin. A History of Cherokee County. Dallas, Southwest Press, 1928.

Robinson, William M., Jr. Justice in Grey: A History of the Judicial System of the Confederate States of America. Cambridge, Mass., Harvard University Press, 1941.

Ross, Mollie. Life and Times of Hon. William P. Ross. Fort Smith, Ark., Welden and Williams, 1893.

Rywell, Martin. Confederate Guns. Harriman, Tenn., Pioneer Press, 1952.

Sackett, Francis R. Dick Dowling. Houston, Gulf Publishing, 1937.

Santleben, August. A Texas Pioneer: Early Staging and Overland Freighting Days on the Frontiers of Texas and Mexico. New York, Neale, 1910.

Scharf, John Thomas. History of St. Louis City and County from the Earliest Periods to the Present Day. 2 vols. Kansas City, Mo., Hudson-Kimberly, 1900.

——History of the Confederate States Navy from Its Organization to the Surrender of Its Last Vessel. New York, Rogers and Sherwood, 1887.

Schwab, J. C. The Confederate States of America, 1861–1865: A Financial and Industrial History of the South during the Civil War. New York, Scribner, 1901.

Shugg, Roger W. Origins of Class Struggle in Louisiana. Baton Rouge, Louisiana State University Press, 1939.

Smith, Edward C. The Borderland in the Civil War. New York, Macmillan, 1927.

Smith, Walter C., ed. Life and Letters of Thomas Kilby Smith. New York, Putnam, 1898.

Smythe, H. Historical Sketch of Parker County and Weatherford, Texas. St. Louis, Lavat, 1877.

Speer, John. Life of James H. Lane, "The Liberator of Kansas." Garden City, Kans., privately printed, 1897.

Spring, Leverett W. Kansas, the Prelude to the War of the Union. New York, Houghton Mifflin, 1885.

Staples, Thomas S. Reconstruction in Arkansas. New York, Columbia University Press, 1923.

Stevens, Walter B. Missouri: The Center State. 4 vols. Chicago, Clarke, 1915.

Stickles, Arndt M. Simon Bolivar Buckner, Borderland Knight. Chapel Hill, University of North Carolina Press, 1940.

Tatum, Georgia Lee. Disloyalty in the Confederacy. Chapel Hill, University of North Carolina Press, 1934.

Taylor, Paul S. An American-Mexican Frontier. Chapel Hill, University of North Carolina Press, 1934.

Thomas, David Y. Arkansas and Its People. 2 vols. New York, American Historical Society, 1930.

——Arkansas in War and Reconstruction, 1861–1874. Little Rock, Arkansas Division United Daughters of the Confederacy, 1926.

Todd, Richard C. Confederate Finance. Athens, University of Georgia Press, 1954.

Trefousse, Hans L. Ben Butler: The South Called Him Beast! New York, Twayne, 1957.

Triplett, Frank. The Life, Times, and Death of Jesse James. St. Louis, Chambers, 1882.

Vance, Rupert B. Human Geography of the South. Chapel Hill, University of North Carolina Press, 1935.

Vandiver, Frank E. Ploughshares into Swords: Josiah Gorgas and Confederate Ordnance. Austin, University of Texas Press, 1952.

——Rebel Brass: The Confederate Command System. Baton Rouge, Louisiana State University Press, 1956.

Violette, E. M. A History of Missouri. New York, Heath, 1918.

Wardell, Morris. A Political History of the Cherokee Nation. Norman, University of Oklahoma Press, 1938.

Ware, Eugene. The Lyon Campaign in Missouri. Topeka, Crane, 1907.

Webb, Walter P. The Great Plains. New York, Ginn, 1931.

Webb, William Larkin. Battles and Biographies of Missourians; or, The Civil War Period in Our State. Kansas City, Mo., Hudson-Kimberly, 1900.

Wellman, Paul I. Glory, God, and Gold: A Narrative History. Garden City, N.Y., Doubleday, 1954.

Wesley, Charles H. The Collapse of the Confederacy. Washington, D.C., Associated Publishers, 1937.

Weyand, Leonie R., and Houston Wade. An Early History of Fayette County. La Grange, Tex., La Grange Journal, 1936.

White, Dabney, ed. East Texas, Its History and Its Makers. New York, Lewis, 1940.

Whitford, William C. Colorado Volunteers in the Civil War: The New Mexico Campaign of 1862. Denver, State Historical and Natural History Society, 1906.

Woldert, Dr. Albert. A History of Tyler and Smith County, Texas. San Antonio, Naylor, 1948.

Woodman, Lyman L. Cortina: Rogue of the Rio Grande. San Antonio, Naylor, 1950.

Woodward, C. Vann. Origins of the New South, 1877–1913. Baton Rouge, Louisiana State University Press, 1951.

Wortham, Louis J. A History of Texas from Wilderness to Commonwealth. Fort Worth, Wortham-Malyneaux, 1924.

Yearns, Wilfred Buck. The Confederate Congress. Athens, University of Georgia Press, 1960.

Young, Bennett H. Confederate Wizards of the Saddle. Boston, Chapple, 1914.

Articles

Abel, Annie Heloise. "The Indians in the Civil War," *American Historical Review,* XV (1910), 281–96.

Adams, Henry C. "Battle of Prairie Grove," *War Papers, Indiana Commandery, Military Order of the Loyal Legion* (Indianapolis, 1898), pp. 451–64.

Anderson, Frank. "Missouri's Confederate State Capitol at Marshall, Texas," *Missouri Historical Review*, XXVII (1933), 240–43.

Ashcraft, Allen C. "Confederate Beef Packing at Jefferson, Texas," *Southwestern Historical Quarterly*, LXVIII (1964), 259–70.

——"Confederate Indian Territory Conditions in 1865," *Chronicles of Oklahoma*, XLII (1964–65), 421–28.

——"Confederate Indian Troop Conditions in 1864," *Chronicles of Oklahoma*, XLI (1963–64), 442–49.

Banks, Dean. "Civil War Refugees from Indian Territory, in the North, 1861–1864," *Chronicles of Oklahoma*, XLI (1963–64), 286–98.

Barr, Alwyn. "Confederate Artillery in the Trans-Mississippi," *Military Affairs*, XXVII (1963), 77–83.

——"Confederate Artillery in Western Louisiana, 1862–1863," *Civil War History*, IX (1963), 74–85.

Bartles, W. L. "Massacre of Confederates by Osage Indians," *Transactions of the Kansas State Historical Society*, VIII (1904), 62–66.

Bearss, Edwin C. "Marmaduke Attacks Pine Bluff," *Arkansas Historical Quarterly*, XXIII (1964), 291–313.

——"The Trans-Mississippi Confederates Attempt to Relieve Vicksburg," *McNeese Review*, XV (1964), 46–76.

Bee, Hamilton P. "Battle of Pleasant Hill—an Error Corrected," *Southern Historical Society Papers*, VIII (1880), 184–86.

Bissell, Sophia L. "See Those Men! They Have No Flag!" *American Heritage*, XI (Oct., 1960), 25.

Blackburn, J. K. P. "Reminiscences of the Terry Rangers," *Southwestern Historical Quarterly*, XXII (1918), 43–45.

[Blunt, James G.] "General Blunt's Account of His Civil War Experiences," *Kansas Historical Quarterly*, I (1932), 211–65.

Borland, William P. "General Jo. O. Shelby," *Missouri Historical Review*, VII (1912), 10–19.

Botkin, Theodosius. "Among the Sovereign Squats," *Kansas Historical Collections*, VII (1901–2), 433.

Brownlee, Richard S. "The Battle of Pilot Knob, Iron County, Missouri, September 27, 1864," *Missouri Historical Review*, LIX (1964), 1–30.

Cabell, W. L. "Capture of Cabell and Marmaduke," *Confederate Veteran*, VIII (1900), 153.

Calhoun, Robert Dabney. "The John Perkins Family of Northeast Louisiana," *Louisiana Historical Quarterly*, XVII (1936), 70–88.

Calkins, E. A. "The Wisconsin Cavalry Regiments," *War Papers, Wisconsin Military Order of the Loyal Legion*, II (1896), 173–93.

Castel, Albert E. "The Bloodiest Man in American History," *American Heritage*, XI (Oct., 1960), 22 ff.

Cole, Birdie H. "The Battle of Pilot Knob," *Confederate Veteran*, XXII (1914), 417.

Coulter, E. Merton. "Commercial Intercourse with the Confederacy in the Mississippi Valley, 1861–1865," *Mississippi Valley Historical Review*, V (1918–19), 377–95.

——"The Effects of Secession upon the Commerce of the Mississippi Valley," *Mississippi Valley Historical Review*, III (1916–17), 275–300.

Coulter, E. Merton. "The Movement for Agricultural Reorganization in the Cotton States during the Civil War," *North Carolina Historical Review*, IV (1927), 22–36.

Cowen, Ruth Caroline. "Reorganization of Federal Arkansas," *Arkansas Historical Quarterly*, XVIII (1959), 32–57.

Curtis, Samuel P. "The Army of the South-West," *Annals of Iowa*, VI (1868), 143–74.

Dale, Edward Everett. "Additional Letters of General Stand Watie," *Chronicles of Oklahoma*, I (1921), 131–49.

——"The Cherokees in the Confederacy," *Journal of Southern History*, XIII (1947), 160–85.

Darr, John. "Price's Raid into Missouri," *Confederate Veteran*, XI (1903), 361–62.

Debo, Angie. "The Site of the Battle of Round Mountain, 1861," *Chronicles of Oklahoma*, XXVII (1949), 187–206.

Debray, Xavier B. "A Sketch of Debray's Twenty-sixth Regiment of Texas Cavalry," *Southern Historical Society Papers*, XIII (1885), 113–65.

Denison, W. W. "Battle of Prairie Grove," *Collections of the Kansas State Historical Society*, XVI (1915), 586–90.

Diamond, William. "Imports of the Confederate Government from Europe and Mexico," *Journal of Southern History*, VI (1940), 470–503.

Donnell, F. S. "The Confederate Territory of Arizona," *New Mexico Historical Review*, XVII (1942), 148–63.

Donnelly, Ralph W. "Rocket Batteries of the Civil War," *Military Affairs*, XXV (1961), 69–93.

Elliott, Claude. "Union Sentiment in Texas, 1861–1865," *Southwestern Historical Quarterly*, L (1947), 449–77.

Elliott, R. G. "The Quantrell Raid as Seen from the Eldridge House," *Publications of the Kansas State Historical Society*, II (1920), 179–96.

Erikson, Edgar L., ed. "Hunting for Cotton in Dixie: From the Diary of Captain Charles E. Wilcox," *Journal of Southern History*, IV (1938), 493–513.

Estill, Mary S., ed. "Diary of a Confederate Congressman [Francis B. Sexton of Texas], 1862–1863," *Southwestern Historical Quarterly*, XXXVIII (1934–35), 270–301, and XXXIX (1935–36), 33–65.

Fletcher, Thomas C. "Battle of Pilot Knob, and the Retreat to Leasburg," *War Papers, Missouri Military Order of the Loyal Legion*, I (St. Louis, 1892), 29–53.

Ford, Harvey. "Van Dorn and the Pea Ridge Campaign," *Journal of the American Military Institute*, III (1939), 222–36.

Fox, S. M. "The Early History of the Seventh Kansas Cavalry," *Kansas Historical Collections*, XI (1909–10), 240–45.

——"The Story of the Seventh Kansas," *Kansas Historical Collections*, VIII (1903–4), 23–24.

Freeman, Charles R. "The Battle of Honey Springs," *Chronicles of Oklahoma*, XIII (1935), 154–68.

Geary, Daniel. "War Incidents at Kansas City," *Kansas Historical Collections*, XI (1910), 282–91.

Gleaves, S. H. "The Strategic Use of Cavalry," *Journal of the United States Cavalry Association*, XVIII (1907), 9–25.

Greene, Albert R. "Campaigning in the Army of the Frontier," *Kansas Historical Collections*, XIV (1913), 287.

——"What I Saw of the Quantrell Raid," *Kansas Historical Collections*, XIII (1912), 430–51.

Grovenor, Gurden. "Quantrill and His Guerrillas Sack Lawrence," in *The Blue and the Gray*, I, 392–94. Edited by Henry Steele Commager. Indianapolis, Bobbs-Merrill, 1950.

Grover, George S. "The Price Campaign of 1864," *Missouri Historical Review*, VI (1912), 167–81.

——"The Shelby Raid, 1863," *Missouri Historical Review*, VI (1912), 107–26.

Gruber, Frank. "Quantrell's Flag," *Adventure*, CII (1940), 112–14.

Haley, J. Evetts. "Scouting with [Charles E.] Goodnight," *Southwest Review*, XVII (1933), 267–89.

Havins, T. R. "Texas Sheep Boom," *West Texas Historical Association Year Book*, XXVIII (1952), 3–17.

Hay, Thomas R. "The South and the Arming of the Slaves," *Mississippi Valley Historical Review*, VI (1919–20), 34–73.

Herklotz, Hildegarde. "Jayhawkers in Missouri," *Missouri Historical Review*, XVII (1922–23), 266–84, XVIII (1923–24), 64–101.

Holladay, Florence E. "The Powers of the Commander of the Confederate Trans-Mississippi Department, 1863–1865," *Southwestern Historical Quarterly*, XXI (1918), 279–98, 333–59.

Homans, John. "The Red River Expedition," *Papers of the Military Historical Society of Massachusetts*, Vol. VIII (1910).

"Hon. Thomas J. Semmes," *Southern Historical Society Papers*, XXV (1897), 317–33.

Hood, Fred. "Twilight of the Confederacy in Indian Territory," *Chronicles of Oklahoma*, XLI (1963–64), 425–41.

Howsley, Marilynne. "Forting Up on the Texas Frontier during the Civil War," *West Texas Historical Association Year Book*, XVII (1941), 71–76.

Huff, Leo E. "The Marmaduke-Walker Duel: The Last Duel in Arkansas," *Missouri Historical Review*, LVIII (1964), 452–63.

Hunter, John W. "Heel-Fly Time in Texas," *Frontier Times*, April, 1924, pp. 35–48.

Landers, Emmett M. "Some Observations Concerning Confederate Ordnance during 1861," *Southwestern Historical Quarterly*, XVII (1936), 46.

Landers, H. L. "Wet Sand and Cotton—Banks' Red River Campaign," *Louisiana Historical Quarterly*, XIX (1936), 150–95.

Langsdorf, Edgar. "Price's Raid and the Battle of Mine Creek," *Kansas Historical Quarterly*, XXX (1964), 281–306.

Laughlin, Sceva Bright. "Missouri Politics during the Civil War," *Missouri Historical Review*, XXIII (1929), 583–618.

Lee, John F. "John Sappington Marmaduke," *Missouri Historical Society Collections*, II (1906), 26–40.

Lewis, Lloyd. "Propaganda and the Kansas-Missouri War," *Missouri Historical Review*, XXXIV (1939), 3–17.

Lewis, Warner. "Massacre of Confederates by the Osages," *Osage Magazine*, I (1910), 49–52, 68–70.

Logan, Robert R. "The Battle of Prairie Grove," *Arkansas Historical Quarterly,*
    XVI (1957), 258–67.
Love, Clara M. "History of the Cattle Industry in the Southwest," *Southwestern
    Historical Quarterly,* XIX (1916), 370–99.
McKenzie, H. B. "Confederate Manufactures in Southwest Arkansas," *Publica-
    tions of the Arkansas Historical Association,* II (1908), 199–210.
McLeary, J. H. "History of Green's Brigade," in Dudley G. Wooten, ed., *A Com-
    prehensive History of Texas,* II, 695–740. Dallas, Scarff, 1898.
McNeil, Kenneth. "Confederate Treaties with the Tribes of Indian Territory,"
    Chronicles of Oklahoma, XLII (1964–65), 408–20.
Mallet, J. W. "Works of the Ordnance Bureau of the War Department of the
    Confederate States, 1861–1865," *Southern Historical Society Papers,* XXXVII
    (1909), 1–20.
Maury, Dabney H. "Sketch of General Richard Taylor," *Southern Historical So-
    ciety Papers,* VII (1879), 343–45.
Meserve, John B. "The MacIntoshes," *Chronicles of Oklahoma,* X (1932),
    310–25.
Milholland, Aline McDonald. "Early Days in Grant County [Arkansas]," *Arkan-
    sas Historical Quarterly,* VII (1948), 317–28.
Miller, Edmund T. "Repudiation of the State Debt in Texas," *Southwestern His-
    torical Quarterly,* XVI (1912), 169–83.
——"The State Finances of Texas," in *The South in the Building of the Nation,*
    Vol. V. New York, 1909.
——"The State Finances of Texas during the Civil War," *Quarterly of the Texas
    State Historical Association,* XIV (1910), 1–23.
——"The State Finances of Texas during Reconstruction," *Quarterly of the
    Texas State Historical Association,* XIV (1910), 87–112.
Mitchell, Leon, Jr. "Camp Ford Confederate Military Prison," *Southwestern His-
    torical Quarterly,* LXVI (1962), 1–16.
Muir, Andrew F. "Dick Dowling and the Battle of Sabine Pass," *Civil War His-
    tory,* IV (1958), 399–428.
Newberry, Farrar. "Harris Flanagin," in *Arkansas and the Civil War,* pp. 57–77.
    Edited by John L. Ferguson. Little Rock, Arkansas Historical Commission,
    1964.
Noble, John W. "Battle of Pea Ridge, or Elk Horn Tavern," *War Papers, Mis-
    souri Order of the Loyal Legion,* I (1892), 211–42.
Oates, Stephen B. "John S. Ford: Prudent Cavalryman, C.S.A.," *Southwestern
    Historical Quarterly,* LXIV (1961), 289–314.
——"Marmaduke's First Missouri Raid," *Missouri Historical Society Bulletin,*
    XVII (1961), 147–52.
——"Supply for the Confederate Cavalry in the Trans-Mississippi," *Military Af-
    fairs,* XXV (1961), 94–99.
Palmer, Henry E. "The Black-Flag Character of the War on the Border," *Kansas
    Historical Collections,* IX (1905–6), 459.
——"Company A, Eleventh Kansas Regiment, in the Price Raid," *Transactions
    of the Kansas State Historical Society,* IX (1905–6), 435.
——"The Lawrence Raid," *Transactions of the Kansas State Historical Society,*
    VI (1900), 317–25.

——"An Outing in Arkansas," *Civil War Sketches, Nebraska Military Order of the Loyal Legion,* I (1902), 213–25.

——"The Soldiers of Kansas," *Kansas Historical Collections,* IX (1905–6), 431–66.

Pearce, N. B. "Price's Campaign of 1861," *Publications of the Arkansas Historical Association,* IV (1892), 333–51.

Phillips, J. F. "Hamilton Rowan Gamble and the Provisional Government of Missouri," *Missouri Historical Review,* V (1910), 1–14.

Prichard, Walter. "The Effects of the Civil War on the Louisiana Sugar Industry," *Journal of Southern History,* V (1939), 315–32.

Ragan, Stephen H. "The Battle of Westport," *Annals of Kansas City,* I (1923), 259–66.

Rainwater, Percy L., ed. "Excerpts from Fulkerson's Recollections of the War Between the States," *Mississippi Valley Historical Review,* XXIV (1937–38), 351–73.

Ramsdell, Charles W. "The Confederate Government and the Railroads," *American Historical Review,* XXII (1917), 794–810.

——"The Frontier and Secession," in *Studies in Southern History and Politics,* pp. 63–79. New York, Columbia University Press, 1914.

——"General Robert E. Lee's Horse Supply, 1862–1865," *American Historical Review,* XXXV (1930), 758–77.

——"Texas from the Fall of the Confederacy to the Beginning of Reconstruction," *Quarterly of the Texas State Historical Association,* XI (1908), 199–217.

——"The Texas State Military Board, 1862–1865," *Southwestern Historical Quarterly,* XXVII (1924), 253–75.

Rippy, J. Fred. "Border Troubles along the Rio Grande, 1848–1860," *Southwestern Historical Quarterly,* XXIII (1919), 91–111.

Rister, Carl C. "Carlota, a Confederate Colony in Mexico," *Journal of Southern History,* XI (1945), 33–50.

Roberts, A. Sellew. "The Federal Government and Confederate Cotton," *American Historical Review,* XXXII (1927), 262–75.

Robinett, Paul M. "Marmaduke's Expedition into Missouri: The Battles of Springfield and Hartville, January, 1863," *Missouri Historical Review,* LVIII (1964), 151–73.

Rodenbaugh, Theodore H. "Cavalry of the Civil War: Its Evolution and Influence," in *Photographic History of the Civil War,* IV, 16–38. New York, Review of Reviews, 1911.

Rodgers, Robert L. "The Confederate State Organized Arizona in 1862," *Southern Historical Society Papers,* XXVIII (1900), 222–27.

Sanborn, John B. "The Campaign in Missouri in September and October, 1864," *Glimpses of the Nation's Struggle, Third Series, Minnesota Commandery of the Military Order of the Loyal Legion* (1893), 135–204.

Sanger, Donald B. "Red River—Mercantile Expedition," *Tyler's Quarterly Historical and Geneological Magazine,* XVII (1935), 268–80.

Scheiber, Harry N. "The Pay of Troops and Confederate Morale in the Trans-Mississippi West," *Arkansas Historical Quarterly,* XVIII (1959), 350–65.

"Secret Service Funds," *Confederate Veteran,* April, 1894, p. 31.

Shoemaker, Floyd C. "The Story of the Civil War in Northeast Missouri," *Missouri Historical Review*, VII (1913), 63–75, 113–31.

Shook, Robert W. "The Battle of the Nueces, August 10, 1862," *Southwestern Historical Quarterly*, LXVI (1962), 31–42.

Sigel, Franz. "The Military Operations in Missouri in the Summer and Autumn of 1861," *Missouri Historical Review*, XXVI (1932), 354–67.

Simpson, Amos E., and Vincent Cassidy. "The Wartime Administration of Governor Henry W. Allen," *Louisiana History*, V (1964), 257–70.

Smith, Edward R. "How Quantrill Became an Outlaw," *Kansas Historical Collections*, VII (1901–2), 214–18.

Smith, Ernest A. "The History of the Confederate Treasury," *Publications of the Southern Historical Association*, V, 1–34, 99–150, 188–227. Harrisburg, Pa., 1901.

Smith, George W. "The Banks Expedition of 1862," *Louisiana Historical Quarterly*, XXVI (1943), 3–22, 342–49.

Smith, Rebecca, and Marion Mullins, eds. "The Diary of H. C. Medford, Confederate Soldier, 1864," *Southwestern Historical Quarterly*, XXXIV (1930–31), 106–40, 203–30.

Stephenson, Nathaniel W. "The Question of Arming the Slaves," *American Historical Review*, XVIII (1912–13), 295–308.

Stephenson, W. H. "The Political Career of General James H. Lane," *Publications of the Kansas Historical Society*, III (1930), 104–22.

Steuart, Richard D. "How Johnny Got His Gun," *Confederate Veteran*, XXXII (1924), 166–69.

——"The Story of the Confederate Colt," *Army Ordnance*, XV (1934), 83–92.

Tittman, Edward D. "The Exploitation of Treason," *New Mexico Historical Review*, IV (1929), 128–45.

Trexler, H. A. "Episode in Border History," *Southwest Review*, XVI (1931), 236–50.

Tucker, Philip C. "The United States Gunboat Harriet Lane," *Southwestern Historical Quarterly*, XXI (1918), 360–80.

Tunnard, William H. "Running the Mississippi Blockade," *Confederate Veteran*, XXIV (1916), 27–28.

Walker, Charles S. "Confederate Government in Doña Ana County," *New Mexico Historical Review*, VI (1931), 253–302.

Weinert, Richard P. "The Confederate Regular Army," *Military Affairs*, XXVI (1962), 97–107.

White, Lonnie J., ed. "A Bluecoat's Account of the Camden Expedition," *Arkansas Historical Quarterly*, XXIV (1965), 82–89.

Whittington, G. P. "Rapides Parish, Louisiana—a History," *Louisiana Historical Quarterly*, Vols. XVII–XVIII (1934–35).

Williams, Harry. "General Banks and the Radical Republicans in the Civil War," *New England Quarterly*, XII (1939), 268–80.

Wilson, James G. "The Red River Dam," *Galaxy*, I (1866), 241–45.

Worley, Ted R. "The Arkansas Peace Society of 1861: A Study in Mountain Unionism," *Journal of Southern History*, XXIV (1958), 445–56.

Worley, Ted R., ed. "Documents Relating to the Arkansas Peace Society of 1861," *Arkansas Historical Quarterly*, XVII (1958), 82–111.
Wyllys, Rufus K. "Arizona and the Civil War," *Arizona Highways*, XXVII (1951), 34–39.

INDEX 🌿

Divisions (*Continued*)
349-50; Smith's (T. K.) Infantry, XVII Corps (Union), 291-311, 315-21; Tappan's Arkansas Infantry (later Churchill's), 289-321, 332; Thayer's Provisional Cavalry (Union), 291-93, 298-300, 311-15; Walker's (J.) Texas Infantry (sometime Forney's), 53, 105-6, 109, 112-15, 121, 128-29, 238-46, 248-50, 287-321, 325-31, 334, 407, 420-22, 443*n*24; Walker's (L. M.) Arkansas Cavalry, 132-34, 225-33; Wharton's Texas Cavalry (formerly Green's), 310-21, 332, 361, 365, 395-96, 399-400, 423

Dix, J., Capt., 419

Doaksville, I.T., 83-84, 222-23, 237, 286, 427

Dobbin, A., Gen., C.O., Dobbin's Brigade, 227-33, 289-93, 298-300, 311-15, 339-57

Dockery, T. P., Gen., C.O., Dockery's Brigade, 237, 289

Dodge, G., Gen. (Union), 415

Donaldsonville, La., 4, 22, 116, 118-19, 411

Douglas, H. T., Col., Chief Engineer, Trans-Mississippi Dept., 254-55, 325, 327-28, 406, 428

Dowling, R., Lt., 189-91

Drayton, T. F., Gen., C.O., Drayton's Brigade, 237, 403, 426

Drew, J., Col., C.O., 1st Cherokee, 39-41

Drought, 79, 179, 382, 385

Ducayet, F., Capt., 197

Duff, J., Col., C.O., 14th Texas Battalion, 16-17, 92-93

Dunn, B. S., 73

Dye, B. J., Lt., 276

Eagle Pass, Tex., 84, 168, 180, 192, 195-96, 274, 420; *see also* Piedas Negras

Eakins, J., 62

Eastport, U.S.S., 295, 297, 310, 315

Education, 86-87, 269-70, 391, 393

Elections: of 1863, gubernatorial and Congressional, 150-54, 174-75; of

1864 (Union), 293-94, 296, 301, 336, 350; special Congressional, of 1864, in Louisiana, 407-8

Emancipation Proclamation, 28, 186

Emory, W., Gen. (Union), C.O., Emory's Division, 25-26, 28, 98, 291-311, 314-21

Erath, G. B., Maj., 220, 365

Ewing, T., Gen. (Union), C.O., District of the Border; St. Louis garrison, 211-12, 235, 337, 342-44

Fagan, J. F., Gen., C.O., Fagan's Brigade; Fagan's Division; Fagan's Corps; District of Arkansas, 129-34, 225-33, 288-93, 298-300, 311-15, 337-57, 403, 407

Faries, T. A., Maj., C.O., Faries' Artillery Battalion, 118

Farragut, D., Adm., 20

Fayetteville, Ark., 34, 36, 47, 122-25, 234-36, 285, 352, 356

Finances: Arkansas, 60, 63-64, 262; Louisiana, 24, 63-64, 262-64; Missouri, 264; Texas, 63-64, 66, 261-62, 429; Trans-Mississippi Dept., 145-47, 161-62, 201, 263-66, 280, 328, 386-91; *see also* Currency; Inflation

Fishback, W. H. M., Gen., 346

Fisk, C. B., Gen., C.O., District of Northern Missouri, 336-37

Fitzpatrick, R., 182, 191

Five Nations, 4, 6, 10-12, 38-40, 42-43, 122-23, 220-24, 237-38, 354-55, 357, 426-27; *see also* Cooper, D.; Districts: of Indian Territory; Divisions: Indian Territorial Cavalry; Maxey, S. B.; Steele, W.; Subdistricts: Indian Territory; Watie, S.

Flake, F., 421

Flanagin, H., Governor of Arkansas, 37, 134, 136-37, 139, 150, 226-27, 233, 289, 328, 417, 423-24

Flight of officials to Mexico, 427-28

Flournoy, G., Col., 417, 428

Food supplies, 5-11, 59, 72, 77-79, 87, 141, 156, 159-61, 177-79, 205, 253,